BYZANTIUM AND THE ARABS
IN THE
FIFTH CENTURY

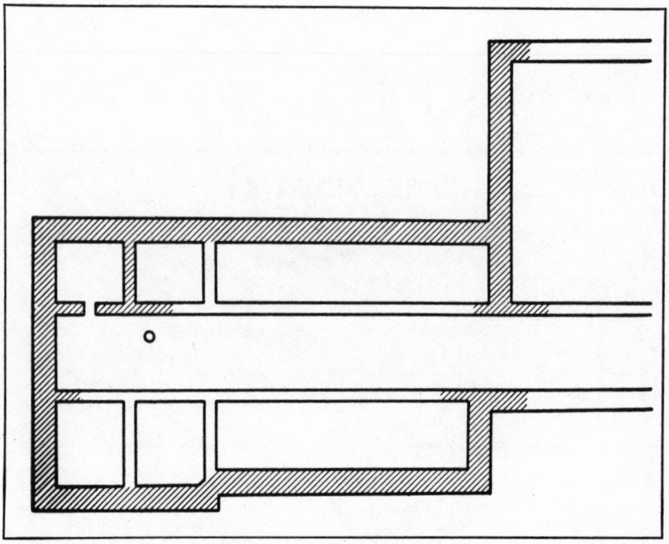

Plan of Dayr Dāwūd

The above plan of the Monastery of Dāwūd/David was drawn by A. Musil, who also discovered the monastery and identified it with al-Turkmaniyya between Isriye and Ruṣāfa in northern Syria (see below, pp. 297–300, and Musil, *Palmyrena*, 153–54).

BYZANTIUM AND THE ARABS IN THE FIFTH CENTURY

IRFAN SHAHÎD

DUMBARTON OAKS RESEARCH LIBRARY AND COLLECTION
Washington, D.C.

Library of Congress Cataloging-in-Publication Data

Shahîd, Irfan, 1926–
Byzantium and the Arabs in the fifth century / Irfan Shahîd.
p. cm.
Bibliography: p.
Includes index.
ISBN 0-88402-152-1
1. Arabs—History—To 622. 2. Byzantine Empire—History—To 527.
3. Middle East—History—To 622. I. Title.
DS62.25.S512 1989
327.495017′671—dc19 88-13098

FRANZ ROSENTHAL
PRO MAGNA ERGA ME BENEVOLENTIA
PRO MULTIS IN ME BENEFICIIS

Contents

III

The Reign of Marcian

IV

The Reign of Leo

V

The Reign of Zeno

VI

The Reign of Anastasius

VII

Three Greek Documents on Palaestina Tertia

ECCLESIASTICAL HISTORY

VIII

Theodoret of Cyrrhus

IX

Sozomen

X

Cyril of Scythopolis

XI

The Arab Episcopate in Oriens: The Conciliar Lists

Appendices

PART TWO: THE ARABIC SOURCES

XII

Oriens

Appendices

XIII

Western Arabia

Appendices

XIV

Cultural History

PART THREE: FRONTIER AND FEDERATE STUDIES

PART FOUR: SYNTHESIS AND EXPOSITION

Abbreviations

AB: *Analecta Bollandiana*

ACO: Schwartz and Straub, *Acta Conciliorum Oecumenicorum*

ActaSS: *Acta Sanctorum*

ADAJ: Annual of the Department of Antiquities of Jordan

BAFIC: Shahîd, *Byzantium and the Arabs in the Fifth Century*

BASIC: Shahîd, *Byzantium and the Arabs in the Sixth Century*

BASOR: *Bulletin of the American Schools of Oriental Research*

BGA: Bibliotheca Geographorum Arabicorum

BN: *Biblische Notizen*

BSOAS: *Bulletin of the School of Oriental and African Studies* (London)

BZ: *Byzantinische Zeitschrift*

CCSL: Corpus Christianorum, Series Latina

CH: Blockley, *Fragmentary Classicising Historians of the Later Roman Empire*

CHAL: *Cambridge History of Arabic Literature*

CHI: *Cambridge History of Islam*

CIL: *Corpus Inscriptionum Latinarum*

CSCO: Corpus Scriptorum Christianorum Orientalium

CSEL: Corpus Scriptorum Ecclesiasticorum Latinorum

DACL: *Dictionnaire d'Archéologie Chrétienne et de Liturgie*

DHGE: *Dictionnaire d'Histoire et de Géographie Ecclésiastique*

DLH: Rothstein, *Die Dynastie der Lahmiden in al-Ḥīra*

DOP: *Dumbarton Oaks Papers*

EI: *Encyclopaedia of Islam*

EO: *Echos d'Orient*

GAL: Brockelmann, *Geschichte der arabischen Literatur*

GAS: Sezgin, *Geschichte der arabischen Schrifttums*

GCAL: Graf, *Geschichte der christlichen arabischen Literatur*

GCS: Die griechischen christlichen Schriftsteller der ersten [drei] Jahrhunderte

GF: Nöldeke, *Die Ghassânischen Fürsten*

GN: Caskel, *Ǧamharat an-Nasab*

GRBS: *Greek, Roman, and Byzantine Studies*

HBE: Stein, *Histoire du bas-empire*

HE: *Historia Ecclesiastica*

HLRE: Bury, *History of the Later Roman Empire*

HMH: Rosenthal, *A History of Muslim Historiography*

HMS: Canivet and Leroy-Molinghen, *Histoire des moines de Syrie*; Theodoret's *Historia Religiosa*

IGLSYR: Jalabert-Mouterde, *Inscriptions grecques et latines de la Syrie*

JAOS: *Journal of the American Oriental Society*

JNES: *Journal of Near Eastern Studies*

JRS: *Journal of Roman Studies*

JSS: *Journal of Semitic Studies*

LRE: A. H. M. Jones, *Later Roman Empire*

MGH, *AA*: Monumenta Germaniae Historica, *Auctores Antiquissimi*

MST: Canivet, *Le monachisme syrien selon Théodoret de Cyr*

ND: *Notitia Dignitatum*

OC: *Oriens Christianus*

PA: Devreesse, *Le patriarcat d'Antioche*

PAS: Nöldeke, *Geschichte der Perser und Araber zur Zeit der Sasaniden*

PG: J. P. Migne, ed., Patrologia Graeca

PL: J. P. Migne, ed., Patrologia Latina

PLRE: A. H. M. Jones, *Prosopography of the Later Roman Empire*

PO: Patrologia Orientalis

PPUAES: *Publications of the Princeton University Archaeological Expedition to Syria*

RA: Shahîd, *Rome and the Arabs*

RB: *Revue biblique*

RE: *Paulys Realencyclopädie,* new rev. ed.

REI: *Revue des études islamiques*

RG: Ammianus Marcellinus, *Res Gestae*

RM: Grosse, *Römische Militärgeschichte*

ROC: *Revue de l'Orient chrétien*

SC: Sources chrétiennes

TE: M. Sartre, *Trois études sur l'Arabie romaine et byzantine*

TU: Texte und Untersuchungen

ZDMG: *Zeitschrift der Deutschen Morgenländischen Gesellschaft*

ZDPV: *Zeitschrift des Deutschen Palästina-Vereins*

ZPE: *Zeitschrift für Papyrologie und Epigraphik*

Preface

This is the second volume in a series of three which treats the Arab-Byzantine relationship in the proto-Byzantine period.[1] The series constitutes the middle part[2] of a trilogy whose climactic third part may be termed "Byzantium and Islam" since it deals with the century that witnessed the rise of Islam and the Arab conquests.

I

This volume discusses the Arab-Byzantine relationship in the reigns of six emperors, beginning with Arcadius (395–408) and ending with Anastasius (491–518). Although the Rhomaic Arabs are not neglected, the Arabs discussed herein are principally the *foederati*,[3] the effective shield of Byzantium against the Arabian Peninsula. The climax of these investigations is the battle of Yarmūk in 636, at which this shield finally broke. It is, therefore, important to trace its history throughout the three pre-Islamic centuries, both for its own sake and for shedding light on the outcome of that fateful battle, which cost Byzantium the loss of Oriens in its entirety and terminated the proto-Byzantine period.

Just as there was a dominant federate group in the fourth century, namely, the Tanūkhids, so there was in the fifth—the Salīḥids. This volume gives prominence to the history of this federate group, although it also discusses others in both Oriens and northwestern Arabia in Ḥijāz, that sphere of Byzantine influence and of indirect Byzantine rule. Oriens remains the chief area of investigation as it was in the previous volume, although in this century it was reduced in size, since Egypt was separated from it around A.D. 380. However, federate presence in Egypt is also discussed, since the Arabs were represented there and performed some important imperial functions.

In this study I am mainly concerned with political, military, ecclesiastical, and cultural history. The exclusion of social and economic history is dictated

[1] For this trilogy and the framework within which my research is conducted, see *Rome and the Arabs* (hereafter *RA*), ix–xii, and *Byzantium and the Arabs in the Fourth Century* (hereafter *BAFOC*), xv–xvi.

[2] The first volume of the middle part, *BAFOC*, appeared in 1984.

[3] For a fuller statement on the *foederati* as the theme of these volumes, see *BAFOC*, xvii.

by the nature of the sources and the data that can be extracted from them.[4] Hence many facets of the Arab presence in Oriens are missing. Only archeology and the discovery of new Arabic manuscripts can increase and diversify the data for Arab-Byzantine relations. When this happens, the history of these relations can be rewritten along broader lines.[5]

It follows from the nature and paucity of the sources that the subject treated herein can be written only along traditional lines. The recovery of the past is my first concern. The data, extracted and interpreted, are presented diachronically throughout the century. The first six chapters are then the mainstay of the volume as they trace federate history through the reigns of the six emperors from Arcadius to Anastasius. The sources do not furnish flashes of information continuously, but they do provide enough to permit one to present a narrative history of Arab-Byzantine relations during this period which may be described as a continuum. I have not attempted to fill in gaps when such an attempt is not justified by the sources. As a result of this diachronous treatment, it is possible to discern the genetic relationships that obtained among the various data within the century. The series as a whole should clarify the evolution of the institutional forms of federate life during this proto-Byzantine period in the three centuries before the rise of Islam.

Of all the six reigns, that of Leo receives the most illumination through a study of the role of the Arab *foederati* in the defense of the *limes orientalis* and from an analysis of a strikingly detailed fragment. However, the data on Byzantium's relation with Mecca, the future city of Islam, are the most arresting of all those provided by the Arabic sources. They document the first recorded contact between Byzantium and Mecca through an Arab federate chief in the employ of Byzantium. Equally arresting, even exciting, is a datum provided by ecclesiastical history. Theodoret writes in unequivocal terms on what many Koranic scholars have denied, namely, the existence of Ishmaelism, the concept of descent from Ishmael, among the *pre-Islamic* Arabs. Thus Muhammadan and Koranic studies receive illumination in an area of vital importance from an unexpected quarter—a fifth-century Greek source either unknown to Islamicists or not laid under contribution.

[4] Just as they dictate concentration on certain areas in Oriens; the data for the 5th century are plentiful on the two Palestines, I and III; hence the prominence given to Arab-Byzantine relations there. It should not be inferred from this that the Arab presence was strong or important in these provinces, especially the first. In fact it was not, but the extant sources give that impression. Because of the sources, more is known about the diminutive phylarchate of the Parembole than about the Salīḥids.

[5] It is very doubtful, however, that new discoveries will multiply the data to the point where rewriting the history of the *foederati* along broader lines may be possible—certainly not in the style of the *Annales* school! Even were the data to become both quantifiable and abundant, the predominance of cultural factors in the life of the *foederati* would preclude the possibility.

II

Unlike the sixth, the fifth century in Arab-Byzantine relations is practically *terra incognita* in the works of Byzantinists[6] and Byzantino-arabists[7] alike. Recently, however, Maurice Sartre treated it in a work that is a contribution to Roman provincial history.[8] Although he is not an Arabist,[9] this sober scholar gave some of his attention to the Salīḥids and raised the right questions. But knowledge of Arabic is indispensable for discussing the *foederati* of the fifth century effectively, and Arabic manuscripts are as important, or even more important, than printed works.

This, then, is the first book to appear on the Arab *foederati* of Byzantium in the fifth century and the Salīḥids in particular. In view of this and the various sets of sources used for establishing this history, the volume is divided, in the interests of clarity, into two main parts:[10]

1. A detailed analysis of the literary sources—the Byzantine and the Oriental—for extracting the relevant data. This enables the various facets of Arab-Byzantine relations to be established: (*a*) the political and military history of the *foederati* within Byzantine Oriens; (*b*) their ecclesiastical history within the Patriarchate of Antioch; (*c*) the Salīḥids and other federate tribes within the Arab tribal system in Oriens; (*d*) Byzantium's relations with Western Arabia, both in Ḥijāz and Yaman; (*e*) the cultural history of the Arab federates; and (*f*) frontier and federate studies.

2. A synthesis and exposition. The detailed, microscopic approach to the study of the sources and the variety of data that they yield make a synthesis necessary. But the whole is more than the sum of its parts, and themes that are welded from data in various parts of the book are here presented synoptically, such as the image of the Arabs in the fifth century.

September 1986 Washington, D.C.

[6] Such as J. B. Bury, *A History of the Later Roman Empire*, I (London, 1923) and E. Stein, *Histoire du bas-empire*, I (Amsterdam, 1968). Both authors deal with the 5th century, and yet the Arabs hardly figure in either work. This is understandable, since they were neither Orientalists nor Semitists and thus were unfamiliar with these aspects of Byzantine history.

[7] For the works of Nöldeke, Vasiliev, Canard, and Pigulevskaia on this pre-Islamic period, see *BAFOC*, xviii–xix. Two writers who touched on the Salīḥids were B. Moritz (see I. Shahîd, "The Last Days of Salīḥ," *Arabica* 5 [1958], 10 note 3) and R. Aigrain (see "Arabie," *DHGE* 1).

[8] See *Trois études sur l'Arabie romaine et byzantine*, Collection Latomus 178 (Brussels, 1982) (hereafter *TE*).

[9] For his knowledge of the Salīḥids he had to depend on an article in the old *Encyclopaedia of Islam*, written some fifty years ago.

[10] For the model used, see *BAFOC*, xix–xx. The first division in this volume, however, is different from the second of W. W. Tarn's work: the latter is a collection of appendices, while the first division here is not, as is clear from the description of its six parts. Appendices are used here when a detailed treatment of a topic interrupts the flow of an argument in a chapter.

Acknowledgments

I should like to express my thanks to the individuals and institutions that have contributed toward the completion of this study: first to Dumbarton Oaks where this volume was researched and written; to its Director, Robert Thomson; to the Library staff headed by Irene Vaslef; and especially to the two members of the Publications Department, Glenn Ruby and Frances Kianka, from whose conscientious care this volume has greatly benefited.

Thanks are also due to Georgetown University: to the Provost, Father Donald Freeze, S.J.; to Dr. James Alatis, Dean of the School of Languages and Linguistics, and his two associates, Dr. J. Hernandez and Mr. R. Cronin; and to Dr. Richard Schwartz, Dean of the Graduate School, and G. Mara, Associate Dean.

I owe a special debt of gratitude to Professor Albert Jamme for drawing the sketch maps of this volume and to Professor Dr. Ruth Altheim-Stiehl for permission to reproduce her photograph of the Ruwwāfa Inscription. Friends and colleagues in Jordan have been generous in their response to my requests: R. Abujaber and T. Kawar supplied me with detailed maps, while F. Zayadine and W. Kawar provided me with the photograph of ʿAyn al-Salīḥī. I am grateful to all of them.

Discussions with the following colleagues and scholars have been fruitful: Robert Browning, John Callahan, Leslie MacCoull, Nicolas Oikonomides, Jaan Puhvel, Peter Topping, and Frank Trombley. I should like to thank them all for their stimulating conversations.

In the material sense the publication of this volume has been greatly furthered by the contribution of the Diana Tamari Sabbagh Foundation, and I am very grateful to its Board of Trustees for their generous support. Last, but not least, I should like to thank my wife, Mary, for spending much time on typing and correcting a large portion of the manuscript.

The preceding volume in this trilogy, *Byzantium and the Arabs in the Fourth Century*, was dedicated to Th. Nöldeke. It is only fitting that this one should be dedicated to the scholar on whom, in a sense, Nöldeke's mantle fell and to whose writings, communications, and conversations I am much indebted.

Introduction

The introduction to the preceding volume was in four parts: a section on the sources, one on major problems and themes, one on Byzantium and the Arabs before the rise of Islam, and one on the fourth century, a synoptic view. The inclusion of the second and third sections[1] was necessary in the volume that opened the series, and the discussion there applied not only to the fourth but to all three centuries. The present Introduction consists of one section on the sources and another on the fifth century—a synoptic view. These will enable the reader to comprehend better the many and detailed analyses that follow.

I. The Sources

What was said about the souces in *BAFOC* is, generally speaking, applicable here as well. However, each of the three centuries of the proto-Byzantine period has its own sources which present problems peculiar to themselves. This section, then, builds on what was said earlier.[2]

The sources of Arab-Byzantine relations for the fifth century can be divided into two sets:[3] (1) Byzantine (Greek and Latin); and (2) Oriental (Arabic, Syriac, Sabaic, and Ethiopic).

The Byzantine Sources

Almost all the Greek and Latin sources are literary, unlike those for the previous volume which included some Greek inscriptions.[4] Only one Greek inscription, the Edict of Beersheba, is truly important. These literary sources are clearly divisible into ecclesiastical and secular[5] and illuminate only certain aspects of federate-imperial relations: the three important areas of political, military, and ecclesiastical history.

[1] For these two sections see *BAFOC*, 8–25.

[2] Hence it is important to refer to that foundation; ibid., 1–7.

[3] For a detailed enumeration of the sources, see the Bibliography.

[4] See *BAFOC*, 222–38.

[5] A distinction important to keep in mind in the study of these sources after the appearance of A. Momigliano's celebrated article, "Pagan and Christian Historiography in the Fourth Century A.D.," in *Paganism and Christianity in the Fourth Century* (Oxford, 1963), 79–99.

These sources are: (1) the Greek secular histories of Synesius, Priscus, and Malchus; the chronographies of Malalas and Theophanes; and such Latin documents and literary sources as the *Codex Theodosianus* and the panegyrics of Priscian and Procopius of Gaza; (2) the Greek ecclesiastical sources, represented by the historians Sozomen, Socrates, Theodoret, and Evagrius; Greek hagiographers such as Cyril of Scythopolis and the writer of the *Vita S. Pelagiae*; and Latin authors such as Jerome and Cassian.[6]

All these are good sources, and most of them are contemporary, such as the works of the ecclesiastical and secular historians. The data provided by these are very reliable, much of it being the result of autopsy, such as that provided by Sozomen, Theodoret, Priscus, and Malchus. Those that are not contemporary derive from earlier ones that are, such as the data of Evagrius, which derive from those of Eustathius of Epiphania. Some of these sources are documents: the *Novellae* of the *Codex Theodosianus* and the data provided by Theophanes which, because of their specificity, could only have been archival, deriving ultimately from documents, possibly preserved in some such official department as the *scrinium barbarorum*. Thus the political, military, and ecclesiastical history of the *foederati* in Oriens in the fifth century is based on excellent sources, and this has made it possible to write a continuous narrative.

The Oriental Sources

The Oriental or Near Eastern sources consist of the Arabic, Syriac, Sabaic, and Ethiopic, in descending order of importance.[7] Thus a discussion of the crucial Oriental sources amounts to a discussion of the Arabic ones.[8]

Like the Byzantine, these are mostly literary. Epigraphic sources, such as the Namāra inscription, which was so central for discussing the *foederati* in the previous volume, are non-existent or awaiting discovery.[9] These literary

[6] All these have been intensively analyzed in this volume for evaluating the data they provide on the Arabs. For these Greek and Latin authors in general, see the relevant chapters in: K. Krumbacher, *Geschichte der byzantinischen Literatur*, 2nd ed. (Munich, 1897); G. Moravcsik, *Byzantinoturcica*, 2nd ed., 2 vols. (Berlin, 1958); B. Altaner, *Patrology*, trans. H. C. Graef (New York, 1960); H. G. Beck, *Kirche und theologische Literatur in byzantinischen Reich* (Munich, 1959); J. Quasten, *Patrology*, III (Westminster, Md., 1960); and H. Hunger, *Die hochsprachliche profane Literatur der Byzantiner*, I (Munich, 1978).

[7] For the 6th century the Syriac sources assume greater importance, and they will be drawn upon extensively in *BASIC*. For the Syriac sources, see A. Baumstark, *Geschichte der syrischen Literatur* (Bonn, 1922).

[8] For an enumeration of these Oriental sources, see the relevant section in the Bibliography.

The Sabaic are the least significant of the Oriental sources in this volume and have been laid under contribution by South Arabian scholars to whom I only refer. Hence they appear in the section on the sources, represented by one inscription only.

[9] The many Arabic inscriptions, called Safaitic and Thamudic, which are spread over vast areas of northern Arabia, Jordan, and southern Syria, are not my concern, since they do not deal

sources are of two types: (1) the prose sources of later Islamic times;[10] and (2) the poetry of the pre- and early Islamic periods. The latter is important, especially the pre-Islamic poetry, which is contemporary and thus serves as a check on the prose sources of later times. In this way it almost functions as epigraphy.[11]

The prose sources consist of (1) the historians used in the preceding volume, such as Ṭabarī, Masʿūdī, Balāḏurī, Yaʿqūbī, Ibn Qutayba, Hishām, and Ibn Khaldūn; and (2) less familiar ones which provide data for this century, such as Khalīfa ibn Khayyāṭ, al-Jahshiyārī, and Ibn Saʿīd. These later Islamic sources derive from reliable earlier ones, most of them ultimately from Hishām, the foremost historian of pre-Islamic Arabia and of the Arab *foederati*. Especially rewarding has been the extraction of crucial data on the *foederati* from two of Hishām's unpublished manuscripts.[12]

These Arabic sources give flesh and blood to the skeletal structure of federate history furnished by the Greek sources, which they thus complement. While the Greek sources tell the story of the *foederati* politically, militarily, and ecclesiastically, the Arabic sources document the history of the Salīḥids, which as a dynasty was the dominant federate group, as well as that of the other federate groups that are left anonymous in the Greek sources. They are informative on inter-Arab federate matters, and above all illuminate the cultural history of the *foederati* in important areas such as Arabic literature, the rise of the Arabic script, and the appearance of an Arabic bible and liturgy in pre-Islamic times. Thus the Byzantine and the Oriental sources succeed in giving a fairly complete picture of federate life and history in the fifth century.

---

with the large and important federate groups which are treated in this book, such as the Salīḥids and the ʿUḏrites. Besides, they provide little or no historical information relevant to the themes of this series. For the 6th century a number of Arabic inscriptions found in Oriens are extremely important and relevant to the writing of *BASIC*, and they will be intensively analyzed therein.

Data from other ancillary disciplines, such as sigillography and numismatics, are entirely lacking, but papyrology is represented.

[10] There are two texts that purport to go back to pre-Islamic times; see below, Chap. 14, app. 2.

[11] The confrontation of the two sets of sources, prose and poetry, is most useful for the early history of Mecca and the Byzantine connection, involving Quṣayy, and Rizāḥ. The poetry in question is early Islamic, thus close to the pre-Islamic period.

[12] These Arabic sources have been intensively analyzed in the course of this volume. For them and their authors in general see C. Brockelmann, *Geschichte der arabischen Literatur*, I–II and supplements 1–3 (Leiden, 1943–49) (hereafter *GAL*); F. Rosenthal, *A History of Muslim Historiography* (Leiden, 1968) (hereafter *HMH*); F. Sezgin, *Geschichte der arabischen Schrifttums*, I–II (Leiden, 1967–75) (hereafter *GAS*).

The Two Sets of Sources

Although the Byzantine and Oriental sources are so different, they nevertheless share one characteristic: the fragmentary nature of the information and data that they contain. In the Greek and Latin sources this is reflected in two ways: (*a*) the secular historians of the fifth century have survived in fragments, which has thus reduced even more the little that they originally said about the Arabs;[13] and (*b*) the accounts of some of the Byzantine writers which have survived in their entirety, such as the ecclesiastical historians, consist of fragments—mere digressions and asides. This is also roughly true of the Arabic sources for this century.

This calls for some observations related to the paucity of the sources and the state of their survival as fragments:

(1) There is a special reason for this paucity, in addition to the fragmentary state of source survival. The Arabs are mentioned in the sources when they participate in the wars of Byzantium against Persia. But peace prevailed between the two powers in the fifth century, and thus the Arabs are not mentioned. When the peace was twice broken during the reign of Theodosius II, the sources start to speak of the Arabs. This is the key to understanding references to the Arabs in the Byzantine sources.

However, there are exceptions that need to be accounted for, such as the very detailed reference to the Arabs during the reign of Leo, when there was no Persian war. Yet Malchus gave an extensive and fascinating account of the adventures of an Arab chief, Amorkesos. In this case the sudden outburst of information on the Arabs during the reign of Leo can easily be considered an expression of *Kaiserkritik*.[14] The detailed information on the Arabs in the two Palestines, Prima and Tertia, is also striking. Sources of various orders record the Arab presence there: an inscription, a papyrus, an imperial *Novella*, hagiographic works (Nilus and Cyril), secular history (Malchus), chronography (Theophanes). The interest of the emperors of the fifth century in the Red Sea and western Arabia may possibly be added as explanation.

(2) Those who did mention the Arabs in their writings on the fifth century have survived in fragments. This is especially important in the case of Priscus, who was interested in Byzantine foreign relations and diplomacy,[15] and to whom we owe one fragment dealing with the Arabs in the reign of

[13] Appropriately called by their editor and translator, R. C. Blockley, *The Fragmentary Classicising Historians of the Late Roman Empire* (Liverpool, 1983), I–II (hereafter, *CH*). Blockley discusses Eunapius of Sardis, Olympiodorus of Thebes, Priscus of Panium, and Malchus of Philadelphia.

[14] For this see below, Chap. 4 on the reign of Leo.

[15] For Priscus, see Blockley, *CH*, I, 60, 65, 68, 69.

Marcian.[16] It is possible that he recorded other Arab-Byzantine military and diplomatic encounters which have not survived. The abundance of sources on the two Palestines, noted above, suggests that much was recorded but has not survived.

(3) The fragment: the *Quellenforschung* on the fifth century may be truly described as "the encounter with the fragment," an encounter which has its challenges and problems. The data appear isolated from the larger context to which they belong, and thus the task of the researcher consists in breaking the silence of the author on the context within which the fragment can recover its historical significance. This has been attempted through various confrontations, relating the fragment to events in Persia, Byzantium, or both and also to events in the Arabian Peninsula.

II. The Fifth Century: A Synoptic View

1

Unlike the fourth, the fifth century is not a tumultuous period in the history of Byzantine-Persian relations. Theodosius I bequeathed to his son and successor, Arcadius, an Orthodox state and a good-neighbor policy with both the Germans and the Persians. The policy of coexistence failed with the Germans but succeeded with the Persians. Although the former were diverted from the East, they were able to conquer the western half of the Mediterranean. Thus the Western Empire was replaced by the various Germanic kingdoms and a new Mediterranean was created. Of more immediate importance to the Eastern Empire was the long peace with Persia. This could endure because of the curious circumstance that both empires were busy with the barbarians who were hammering at their respective frontiers—the Ephthalite Huns in central Asia and the Germanic tribes in western Europe. This remarkably long peace makes of the century a genuine period in the history of Byzantium.

The six emperors of this century were "mediocrities," at least compared to those of the preceding and following centuries. Thus while it is possible to speak of the fourth as the century of Constantine and of the sixth as that of Justinian, it is not possible to speak of the fifth in such terms. But if the emperors of this century were not towering personalities, and if they did not contribute gloriously to the military annals of Byzantium, they did contribute to its cultural achievements. The *Codex Theodosianus*, which formed the basis of the legislative work of Justinian, was promulgated in this period. The reign of Theodosius also saw the founding of the University of Constantinople, which thus superseded the pagan school of Athens and became the most important cultural center in Byzantium.

[16] See below, Chap. 3, sec. I.

2

Set against this general backdrop of the fifth century, the history of the Arab *foederati* appears as a reflection of the history of Byzantium.

The empire that wanted peace and security on the eastern front in order to deal better with the Germanic peril in both East and West naturally wanted a stable front with the Arabian Peninsula. Hence the rise of a new Arab federate group, the Salīḥids, as the guardians of the Arabian frontier. Byzantium had a harmonious relationship with them throughout the century, and the emperors of both the Theodosian and Leonine dynasties made friendly gestures to the Arab tribal groups who became their *foederati*. There was almost a pro-Arab policy on the part of the emperors of this century, and this can most probably be related to their anti-Germanism. Byzantium needed *foederati* who, unlike the dangerous Germans, were safe, as the Arabs were. Furthermore, the Germans were Arians, while the Arabs were Orthodox. Their Orthodoxy made for good relations with the central government throughout the century, even though toward its end Anastasius veered toward Monophysitism. It is almost certain that after the German occupation of the western half of the Mediterranean and the multiplication of dangers and difficulties posed for navigation and trade by the Vandals, the empire looked toward the Red Sea and Indian Ocean as new outlets and spheres of influence and trade. This also explains its interest in the services of the Arab tribal groups as federates. Thus the Arab *foederati* of the fifth century emerge as guardians of the Arabian frontier for Byzantium and protectors of Byzantine commercial interests in the Red Sea and Arabian Peninsula. They participate in military operations in the west as far as Pentapolis and possibly take part in Leo's expedition against the Vandals in Africa.

Just as Byzantine imperial achievements in this century were impressive in the cultural rather than the military sphere, so it was with the Arabs in Oriens. Staunchly Orthodox, the Arabs took part in the two ecumenical councils of Ephesus and Chalcedon, and their representative bishops appear Orthodox in the subscriptions. The most articulate voice of Arab Orthodoxy was that of Petrus, the bishop of the Arab Parembole, who participated in the Council of Ephesus and contributed to the chorus of anathemas hurled against Nestorius, to whom he was also sent by the council as a negotiator. Thus the Arab *foederati* emerge as orthodox Christians, unlike those of the sixth century, the Ghassānids, who were Monophysites, a fact that ruffled their relations with the central government and had dire consequences for Arab-Byzantine relations.

But it is the contributions of the *foederati* to Arab Christianity and Arabic culture that is the more enduring part of their achievement. In this century, and partly under their inspiration and direction, some important constituents of Arabic culture were favorably affected, thus enhancing the Greek, Syriac, and Arabic triculturalism that characterized the life of Oriens in this period.[17] It is nearly certain that the Arabic script that is used in the inscriptions of the sixth century in Oriens was developed in the fifth, under the exigencies of the new political and religious life that the *foederati* were leading in Byzantium. The case is also strong for the appearance of a simple liturgy or prayerbook in Arabic and some translations from the Bible, most probably for liturgical use as a lectionary. Important Arab historical figures—for example, Dāwūd, the religious Salīḥid king; Petrus, the bishop of the Palestinian Parembole; and Elias, the Arab archbishop of Jerusalem around 500—could have inspired the appearance of these texts. Finally, Arabic literature, especially poetry, is attested, continuing the tradition of the *foederati* of the fourth century. But, in contrast, poetry of the fifth century is no longer anonymous. The name of the court poet of the Salīḥid king Dāwūd is known—ʿAbd al-ʿĀṣ—and some of the fragments pertaining to the Salīḥid supremacy have survived. Perhaps the most attractive of all is a form of love poetry that developed in Ḥijāz in the Byzantine sphere of influence among the federate tribe of ʿUḏra. It represented the confluence of Arab and Christian ideals and foreshadowed the later type of love poetry, expressing *amour courtois* which, according to one view, reached western Europe through Muslim Spain in medieval times. This federate cultural achievement is made more attractive by the solitary figure of a princess, the daughter of Dāwūd, who lamented the death of her father in an elegy of which only one verse has survived. This female royal personage naturally brings to mind the celebrated figure of the Theodosian dynasty, Empress Eudocia. And it has been argued that the Salīḥid princess who lived across the Jordan possibly owed to the Theodosian empress some inspiration in her literary endeavors, after the latter took up residence in the Holy Land.

The winds of change begin to blow toward the close of the period—in the reign of Anastasius, during which the legacy of Theodosius I comes to an inglorious end. The Orthodox state he left to his successors is now ruled by a Monophysite emperor, and the peace with Persia is shattered, possibly by the "greed" of the s̲h̲āh and the "parsimony" of the emperor. The symbiosis that obtained in imperial-federate relations throughout the century receives a jolt and is ruffled throughout the sixth, while the reign ushers in a period of continual hostilities with Persia and the supremacy of a new group of *foederati*, the Ghassānids.

[17] As explained in *RA*. Compared with the Greek and Syriac components, the Arabic is restricted but becomes more extensive in the 6th century. After the Muslim conquest of Oriens, it becomes the dominant one and gradually sweeps away the other two.

PART ONE
THE GREEK AND THE LATIN SOURCES

Political and Military History

I

The Reign of Arcadius (395–408)

Arabic sources vouch for the identity of the dominant group of Arab *foederati* in the service of Byzantium in the fourth century, the Tanūkhids, but confirming Greek and Latin sources either did not record their name or, if they did, are no longer extant. That the *foederati* mentioned by the western sources were indeed Tanūkhids had to be inferred and argued for.[1] This is not true of the Zokomids/Salīḥids, the Arab *foederati* of the empire in the fifth century, whose identity the Greek and Arabic sources explicitly record and thus mutually confirm. These sources, however, are not crystal clear about the inception of their power as the new *foederati* of Byzantium. The terminus a quo is therefore the first problem that has to be solved in the long history of Byzantine-Salīḥid relations.

The reign of Arcadius most probably witnessed the rise of the new dominant group of *foederati* in the service of Byzantium, namely, the Zokomids/Salīḥids. Even if their rise slightly antedated his reign, it must have been during this time that their power was confirmed and given new impetus. The data for the rise of the new *foederati* of Byzantium come solely[2] from Sozomen, the ecclesiastical historian who has proved so valuable for reconstructing the history of Arab-Byzantine relations during the reign of Valens. These unique and precious data deserve, therefore, a thorough examination, especially as they involve other important problems related to the reign of Arcadius.

I. Sozomen

Sozomen provides much data on the new *foederati* and the Arabs in general. What is relevant in this context is his account of a Saracen tribe and its childless chief, Zokomos, who was converted to Christianity after a monk promised that if he believed in Christ his wife would give birth to a son, as she did.

[1] See *BAFOC*, 366–72.

[2] These data have also been preserved in the late medieval Byzantine historian Nicephorus Callistus; on his value for the history of the Arab *foederati* in the 4th and 5th centuries, see *BAFOC*, 139 note 5.

Sozomen further states that after its conversion the Arab tribe prospered and multiplied, becoming formidable to both the Saracens and the Persians.[3]

(1) The most valuable item in this account is the name itself, Ζόκομος, which the ecclesiastical historian almost miraculously preserved, thus giving the historian of the Arab-Byzantine relationship a solid datum for writing the history of the Zokomids or Salīḥids. A. von Gutschmid was the first to identify the Ζόκομος of the Greek historian with the Ḍujʿum of the Arabic sources, an identification accepted by Nöldeke.[4] The name is so uncommon in Arabic that there can be no doubt that this identification is correct. Besides, the position of the Zokomids or Salīḥids in the sequence of Arab federate supremacies corroborates this, since it places them correctly in the fifth century, coming as they do in the accounts of the Arabic sources between the Tanūkhids of the fourth and the Ghassānids of the sixth.[5]

(2) This reference to Zokomos represents the point of articulation between the two federate supremacies, Tanūkh and Salīḥ, signaling the end of one and the rise of the other. Sozomen's account is not chronologically as precise as one would wish concerning the inception of the Salīḥids' power under Zokomos. It is desirable to identify at least the reign during which this happened.

Sozomen uses general adverbial phrases. In speaking of the conversion of "some of the Saracens" he says that this happened "not long before the present reign," οὐ πρὸ πολλοῦ δὲ τῆς παρούσης βασιλείας.[6] A little further on, when he gives an account of the conversion of Zokomos, he says that it, too, happened τότε, "about this period," that is, "not long before the present reign." The answer to our question then involves determining which reign Sozomen had in mind when he made this statement. Is it the reign of Valens, or is it the reign of Theodosius II, under whom, in the forties, he wrote his

[3] Sozomen, *Historia Ecclesiastica*, ed. J. Bidez, GCS 50 (Berlin, 1960) (hereafter *HE*), 299–300.

[4] See Th. Nöldeke, *Die Ghassânischen Fürsten aus dem Hause Gafna's* (Berlin, 1887) (hereafter *GF*), 8. The identification was accepted by Nöldeke after he made some valuable observations on the phonology of the name in Greek and in Arabic and the problem posed by transliterating the name from the latter to the former. In view of this, it is pertinent to note that in Nicephorus Callistus the name is spelled Ζάκομος, which is consonant with one of the two spellings of the name in Arabic. Nöldeke also drew attention to the reappearance of the name in the 6th century in Theophylactus Simocatta, spelled Ζώγομος.

The Arabic *foederati* of the 5th century are referred to in some of the Arabic sources as Ḍajāʿima (plural of Ḍujʿum), in others as Banū Salīḥ, Salīḥids. The latter is easier to pronounce and more euphonious; hence its use in this volume. On the two designations, see Chap. 12, sec. II.

For the most recent treatment of the Zokomos episode in Sozomen and of Salīḥ, see Sartre, *TE*, 144–49.

[5] See *BAFOC*, 369.

[6] Sozomen, *HE*, 299, lines 14–15.

Historia Ecclesiastica? If he meant the reign of Valens, then the Zokomids/Salīḥids would have started their career as *foederati* of Byzantium while the Tanūkhids were still in power, becoming the dominant federate power later in the century after the fall of the Tanūkhids early in the reign of Theodosius I. If he meant the reign of Theodosius II, then the Salīḥids shortly before his accession must have risen to power, either in the latter part of the reign of Theodosius I or in the reign of Arcadius.[7] Whether the Zokomid/Salīḥid alliance with Byzantium started during or before the reign of Arcadius, that reign is important to the fortunes of the Salīḥids because it either witnessed the inception of their alliance with Byzantium or their rise as the dominant federate power in Oriens. However, the chances are that Sozomen's account refers to the reign of Arcadius. In support of this the following observations may be made on the imperial mood prevailing in this period.

(*a*) In spite of the anti-barbarian sentiment that ran high in the capital, the emperor could not afford to have Oriens without a strong federate presence, especially after the fall of the Tanūkhids during his father's reign. Federate watch over the Arabs of the Peninsula[8] and over the Persians was necessary to keep the peace in the East. And the Arabs—represented by the new *foederati*, the Salīḥids—were thus welcome allies.

(*b*) Anti-barbarian sentiment in the capital was directed against the Germans, who were omnipresent there.[9] Roman patriots resented the fact that the empire was in the clutches of three German commanders—Stilicho, Alaric, and Gainas—and that the Germans were conspicuous everywhere in the capital, while one of them—Alaric—was devastating the Balkans. Synesius' Περὶ Βασιλείας was directed against one particular group of barbarians, the German Goths. The Arabs, on the other hand, were not in Constantinople, and their revolt during the early part of Theodosius I's reign broke out in faraway Oriens, when Aracadius was still a child.[10]

[7] The short account of Zokomos' conversion, in which these adverbial phrases occur, is followed immediately by a statement to the effect that his tribe became formidable to the Persians. This, as will be argued, can only refer to their participation in the Persian Wars of Theodosius II. Thus, the presumption is strengthened that the Salīḥids' conversion and subsequent rise to power took place in the preceding reign, that of Arcadius.

I have also entertained the possibility that the phrase "the present reign" refers to that of Valens; see I. Shahîd, in "The Last Days of Salīḥ," *Arabica* 5 (1958), 146–58.

[8] And also other peoples, such as the Isaurians, who in 405 made the incursion into northern Palestine noted by St. Jerome. The Salīḥids, settled in Trans-Jordan, would have participated in the defense of the province; for this incursion, see *BAFOC*, 294.

[9] Recently, Alan Cameron has cautioned against taking this anti-Germanism too seriously. He expressed this view in a paper entitled "Antigermanism in the Early Fifth Century," read at the 1985 Symposium at Dumbarton Oaks, "Byzantium and the Barbarians in Late Antiquity."

[10] Arcadius was born about 377 and was only two years old when Libanius delivered his

(*c*) The ecclesiastical policy of the reign and the official attitude of the Church were also favorable. The Germans were Arian heretics; imperial opposition to them was thus supported by the Church, which considered the defeat of the Germans and the German party in Constantinople as a victory for Orthodoxy and the Church. The Arabs were in an entirely different category. They had fought for Orthodoxy against the Arian Valens, and toward the end of the fourth century they were still staunchly Orthodox, not having been contaminated by Arianism. It was only after Chalcedon that they may have started to be touched by Monophysitism.

Thus Arcadius or his advisors could have had a pro-Arab policy. In so doing, Arcadius must have completely reversed his father's pro-German, anti-Arab policy. His departure from it was justified: in his search for new allies after his successful expulsion of the Germans, he could rest assured that in the Salīḥids he had reliable allies to watch the *limes* and who, furthermore, were Orthodox. Arcadius was only one year old when the Arab horsemen of Mavia successfully defended his capital[11] in the aftermath of the battle of Adrianople in 378. But memory of this exploit must have been fresh in the memory of many Constantinopolitans. That the Arab victory outside the walls of Constantinople was scored against the hateful Goths, the people whom Arcadius had recently expelled from the capital, only brightened the image of the Arabs in imperial circles there after it had been tarnished by their revolt during the reign of Arcadius' father.[12]

(3) In addition to the major questions of chronology and identification, the precious passage in Sozomen gives rise to the following observations:

(*a*) The first question concerns Sozomen's use of the term phylarch (φύλαρχος). Did he use it in the sense of a "tribal chief" or in the technical sense that it carries in Arab-Byzantine relations, namely, an Arab chief allied with Byzantium as *foederatus*?[13] The fact that Sozomen speaks first of his tribe (φυλή), and then of Zokomos as its phylarch could suggest that he used the term in the sense of a tribal chief. This does not necessarily imply that Zokomos was not a *foederatus*, since the Arab *foederati* kept their tribal organization even after they became allies of Byzantium; thus Sozomen may simply be pointing out that the convert was the head or chief of the tribe that was in a federate relationship to Byzantium, a fact that becomes relevant to his purpose

anti-Arab manifesto. On Libanius' Oration XXIV (dated 379) addressed to his father, Theodosius I, see *BAFOC*, 216–18.

[11] See ibid., 176–78.

[12] And if the disagreements of the Tanūkhids with Theodosius I were related to the latter's favoritism toward the Goths, this, too, would have endeared the Arabs to Arcadius and the Roman party in Constantinople; see ibid., 205–10.

[13] For the various meanings of the term *phylarchos* in the sources, see ibid., 516.

when he records the tribe's conversion as a collective act following that of its chief. And yet his conversion to Christianity is somewhat surprising; if he was a Byzantine phylarch, the chances are that he would have been a Christian, since Christianity would in this period have been a fact of his Byzantine connection. But the Salīḥids were Christian *foederati* of Byzantium, and the fact is vouched for by the Arabic sources[14] and also suggested by Sozomen's account, which speaks of the participation of the Salīḥids in the Persian Wars. It is also certain that Zokomos was the first of the Salīḥid dynasts to be a federate ally of Byzantium.[15] The problem can be solved by assuming that Zokomos and his group had crossed the *limes* only recently, were newcomers who fought their way into Roman territory, and so had not yet been Christianized.[16] Once they had been, they were accepted as allies and given the status of *foederati*.

That the Salīḥids were federate allies of Byzantium is clearly stated in the Arabic sources but only implied by Sozomen when he speaks of the Persian Wars. According to him, the Salīḥids became "formidable to Persians as well as to the other Saracens." That the Salīḥids engaged in military operations against the Saracens is not necessarily proof that they were *foederati*, since inter-tribal warfare was a fact of life in pre-Islamic Arabia. But the wars of the Salīḥids against the Persians is a clear indication that they were in the employ of Byzantium and fought these wars as *foederati*. Sozomen wrote in the 450s—after Byzantium had fought twice with the Persians in the reign of Theodosius II—and he clearly had these wars in mind when he wrote.[17] His statement regarding their wars against the Arabs and the Persians is in fact a true summary of the double function of the *foederati* in the Byzantine army in Oriens. Their "formidableness" to the Persians and the Saracens is, of course, related at least partly to their alliance with one of the two world powers, Byzantium, whence they received the sinews of war: the *annona*, their weapons, and some military training and discipline preparing them to fight in the Roman manner as a tactical unit in the Byzantine army of the Orient.

Did Zokomos, the first phylarch of the new Arab *foederati* of Byzantium, make the journey to Constantinople on the occasion of his investment with the phylarchate? Sozomen does not say, but it is possible that he did, as the

[14] See below, Chap. 12.

[15] So conceived by von Gutschmid and Nöldeke; see Nöldeke, *GF*, 8. It is noteworthy that he is referred to as phylarch, not *basileus*; on this problem, see *BAFOC*, 517.

[16] Zokomos is of course known to the Arabic sources as having crossed into Bilād al-Shām (Oriens) in the 3rd century; Bakrī, *Muʿjam*, I, 26. The Arabic sources are at their weakest when they deal with the chronology of the pre-Islamic period. And in this respect the Greek sources correct the Arabic, as they do in the case of Zokomos. For the Arabic sources on Zokomos and the Salīḥids, see below, Chap. 12.

[17] On the Persian Wars of Theodosius II's reign, see below, Chap. 1, sec. II.

first dynast of a new federate supremacy. Another phylarch made the journey to Constantinople some seventy years later and was entertained by Emperor Leo.[18]

After his encounter with the Christian monk, the first Salīḥid phylarch was blessed with the child whose birth the monk had predicted. Presumably his firstborn succeeded him when Zokomos died and, if so, this is the only reference in the Byzantine sources to the second member of the Salīḥid dynasty.[19] The Arabic sources do have a list for their kings and a genealogical table, and the son mentioned by Sozomen may be identified with a member of the dynasty. But the identification cannot be certain, and it is a pity that Sozomen did not mention his name, which must have been known in his day in the Byzantine archives that recorded the history of diplomatic relations with the barbarian allies.

(*b*) The Christianization of Zokomos and his tribe as recounted by Sozomen throws light on many aspects of Salīḥid history as it developed in the fifth century.

The Salīḥids of the Arabic sources were known for their religious zeal throughout their *floruit* as *foederati* and after their fall, well into the Muslim period. This is natural since the first phylarch, Zokomos, owed to Christianity his wife's historic pregnancy, which gave him an heir and the Salīḥids a line of descendants, and since his allegiance to Christianity clinched his Byzantine connection and made possible his emergence as the *foederatus* of the Christian Roman Empire.[20] This zeal is also inferable from the account of Sozomen. His last statement, that the tribe after Christianization prospered and became formidable to the Persians, can be seen as implying a cause and consequence. One aspect of this consequence was noted earlier—the alliance as a Christianized group with the Christian empire. Another aspect of this consequence is the religious zeal that the Salīḥids displayed for their new faith and the effect this had on their martial spirit in fighting the Persians, whom they could now view as fire-worshipers.[21]

The Christianity that the Salīḥids were introduced to was monastic Christianity. The fifth century was a period in which monasticism flourished, and so it did among the Arabs. The place of St. Simeon the Stylite in the life of the Arabs of that century is well known. Less known is the career of the

[18] See below, Chap., 4, sec. IV.

[19] The reference is as tantalizing as the one to the anonymous sons of Imru' al-Qays, the first Arab client king of Byzantium in the 4th century; see *BAFOC*, 43–45.

[20] It is natural to suppose that the son and successor whose birth the monk predicted inherited the zeal of his father for Christianity and that this became a tradition in the family.

[21] Cf. what the Arab historian Hishām al-Kalibī says on the loss of martial spirit by one of the Salīḥids, owing to his Christianity; see below, Chap. 12, sec. III.I.

Salīḥid king Dāwūd and his relation to monasticism.[22] In all probability, attachment to monastic Christianity was a tradition among the ruling family of the Salīḥids, the descendants of Zokomos, the first dynast and phylarch who had his fruitful encounter with a Christian monk.

Finally, it is important to remember the doctrinal persuasion of the new federates. The Arabs are so associated with heretical and non-Orthodox views that it is necessary to remember that not only the Tanūkhids but also the Salīḥids were strict Orthodox Christians. They remained free of the Arian heresy which plagued the Germans and of the Monophysitism which later affected the Ghassānids. Just as Zokomos' tribe converted to Christianity after he did, so it derived from him its Orthodox doctrinal persuasion, which was prevalent in Oriens in this period. The Salīḥids remained Orthodox throughout the century of their dominance and for a long time thereafter.

II. Synesius

Synesius of Cyrene[23] has a reference to Arab troops in one of his letters[24] written in 404. A thorough examination of this letter is necessary, especially as some confusion has attended one of the commentaries as far as the Arabs are concerned,[25] while the general significance of the references to the Arabs has not been noted or pointed out. Furthermore, the letter contains important references to the Arabs and the Jews, which are of special relevance to the image of the two peoples and are especially interesting, coming as they do from the Neo-Platonist of Cyrene.

1

Synesius wrote from Azarium to his brother, Euoptius, at Alexandria, in January 404 while on his way back to Cyrene.[26] He had endured the rigors

[22] On Dāwūd, see below, Chap. 12, sec. III.

[23] For the most up-to-date bibliography on Synesius see J. Bregman, *Synesius of Cyrene* (Berkeley, 1982), 185–93.

[24] One of his longest and most celebrated letters. For the text, see *Synesii Cyrenensis Epistolae*, ed. A. Garzya, Scriptores Graeci et Latini Consilio Academiae Lynceorum Editi (Rome, 1979), no. 5, pp. 11–26. For an English translation, see A. Fitzgerald, *The Letters of Synesius of Cyrene* (London, 1926), no. 4, pp. 80–91. For a discussion of Synesius' letters, see X. Simeon, *Untersuchungen der Briefe des Bischofs Synesios von Kyrene* (Paderborn, 1933). The author concluded that, in spite of following classical examples in epistolography, Synesius wrote real letters with the exception of one, no. 148; see his conclusions, pp. 82–85. Letter no. 4 is analyzed at length on pp. 62–78 but strictly in order to find classical models for the rhetorical devices employed by Synesius. There is a passing reference to the Arabs in letter no. 4 on p. 70, but the passage in which they are mentioned is not analyzed.

[25] J. C. Pando, *The Life and Times of Synesius of Cyrene as Revealed in His Works* (Washington, D.C., 1940).

[26] For the exact determination of the date of this letter as 28 January, see Fitzgerald, *Letters*, p. 80 note 4.

of a most perilous voyage on a ship whose captain was a Jew named Amarantus. The skipper, being an orthodox Jew, had abandoned the helm in the midst of a storm after sunset on the Sabbath, much to the alarm of the passengers, who tried in vain to persuade him to steer the ship. It is in this context that the reference to the Arabs occurs: "Despairing of persuasion, we finally attempted force, and one staunch soldier—for many Arabs of the cavalry were of our company—one staunch soldier, I say, drew his sword and threatened to behead the fellow on the spot if he did not resume control of the vessel. But the Maccabean in very deed was determined to persist in his observances. However, in the middle of the night he voluntarily returned to the helm."[27]

This reference to the Arabs and others implied in the letter raises a number of questions. First, who were these Arab soldiers or horsemen aboard a ship that had sailed from Egypt and was on its way to Cyrene in the Pentapolis?

One scholar who has subjected this letter to careful examination, discussing it extensively in various parts of his work has hazarded the view that they were a detachment from the Third Cyrenaica, the legion of the province of Arabia in the Diocese of Oriens.[28] This view cannot be accepted, and the following arguments may be adduced:

(1) Around 380, Theodosius I separated Egypt from the Diocese of Oriens. Thus in the reign of his son, Arcadius, Aegyptus under its *praefectus augustalis* consisted of six provinces,[29] of which Libya Superior was one. It is most unlikely that the *praefectus augustalis* of Aegyptus would have invoked the aid of the *comes Orientis* for reinforcements to be sent to Cyrene in Libya Superior.[30]

(2) Since Libya Superior was a province of the Diocese of Aegyptus it is natural to suppose that the *praefectus augustalis* moved troops from one province of the diocese to another that needed them. Indeed, in the *Notitia Dignitatum*, which goes back to the beginning of the fifth century, one finds that there were four Arab military units stationed in the Diocese of Aegyptus. It is practically certain that the Arab horsemen referred to in Synesius' letter belonged to one of these four units.[31]

[27] Ibid., p. 84. For the Greek text, see *Epistolae*, ed. Garzya, p. 16.

[28] Pando, *Life and Times*, 135 note 393. Apparently he was unaware of the Arab presence in Egypt.

[29] Libya Superior, Libya Inferior, Thebais, Aegyptus, Arcadia, and Augustamnica. Libya Superior is also known as Pentapolis and Cyrenaica.

[30] But this could happen under very special circumstances, as when the Arab troops from the oasis of Pharan in Sinai, which belonged to Oriens, fought with Athanasius, the *dux* of the Thebaid, against the Blemmyes. Proximity was no doubt one element in moving these troops from Sinai to the Thebaid; see *BAFOC*, app. 2, p. 327.

[31] Three in the *limes aegypti* and one in the Thebaid; see below.

(3) The form used by Synesius—*Arabioi* rather than *Arabes*—might suggest "Arabia in Egypt," the old Ptolemaic nome, which survived in administrative usage even after the nomes were officially abolished.[32] The Arabian nome formed part of Augustamnica (Eastern Delta) and specifically Augustamnica II, and these *Arabioi* of Synesius could have come from that nome. But the *Notitia Dignitatum* lists no Arab units there that answer to the description. The only Arab unit in Augustamnica is the *Cohors Secunda Ituraeorum*,[33] whose members were not horsemen but infantrymen and whose designation is not the generic "Arab" but the specific "Ituraeans."

(4) The *Arabioi* of Synesius must therefore be related to one of the other Arab units in the Diocese of Aegyptus. Synesius does not use the term that had become common to describe the Arabs, namely, *Saracēnoi*, probably because he heard the term *Arabioi* from the horsemen who were on the ship with him. Thus the unit from which these troops were detached must exclude the *Equites Saraceni Thamudeni*, the *Cohors Secunda Ituraeorum* already referred to, and also the *Ala Octava Palmyrenorum* stationed in the Thebaid. By elimination the unit must be the *Ala Tertia Arabum* stationed in Thenemuthi.[34] Its members are described as Arab, and they are horsemen.

It remains to discuss the technical terms that Synesius uses in this passage, both the gentilic and the military. The gentilic term used in the *Notitia* for the *Ala Tertia* is *Arabum*, the genitive of *Arabes* (Ἄραβες), not of *Arabioi* (Ἀράβιοι). One would have expected Synesius to use a gentilic related to the former, not the latter term. But Synesius was a classicizing Neo-Platonist, who followed the early authors such as Herodotus in their use of the term *Arabioi* rather than the later ones with whom the term *Arabes* became popular. Puristic reasons must also explain his employment of the Greek *tagma*[35] (τάγμα) rather than Latin *ala* to denote the unit; in so doing he is in company with many a classicizing Byzantine historian.

These troops from the *Ala Tertia Arabum* are described by Synesius as being many, συχνοί. This is of course a relative term in view of what he says on the number of the pasengers on that ship, "more than fifty." A third of them were women, and there were some thirteen sailors.[36] There could not

[32] See A. H. M. Jones, *Cities of the Eastern Roman Provinces* (Oxford, 1971), 336–37. Egeria, who traveled in Egypt toward the end of the 4th century and after the nomes were abolished, refers to "Arabia"; see *BAFOC*, 295.

[33] See above, note 31.

[34] Thenemuthi-Terenuthis lay on the western edge of the upper Delta; see *RA*, 58 note 29 and the map of Egypt in Jones, *Cities* opposite p. 295, and also p. 345.

[35] In the non-technical sense of a formation of troops. For the technical sense of τάγμα, as employed correctly by military historians, such as the author of the *Stratēgicon*, see G. Dennis, *Maurice's Strategikon* (Philadelphia, 1984), 173.

[36] Fitzgerald, *Letters*, p. 81.

have been more than ten to fifteen soldiers. But it is unlikely that only these few Arab soldiers were sent from Egypt to restore order in Pentapolis. Later on in the letter, after describing a storm that his ship encountered, Synesius says that four more ships were safely brought in to the harbor of Azarium and that other ships arrived, some of which had set sail from Alexandria the day before Synesius and his party did.[37] It is possible that Arab troops were also aboard some of these ships.

What these Arab troops were supposed to do in Cyrenaica is not hard to guess. The letters of Synesius are full of references to unrest and insecurity in Pentapolis, owing to the incursions of the barbarians surrounding the Greek cities. The year is 404, when the incompetent and corrupt Cerialis became the governor of the province[38] and when Cyrene was besieged by the surrounding barbarians, especially the Ausurians.[39]

It is noteworthy that these Arab horsemen were not, of course, *foederati*, as were those of the phylarch Zokomos mentioned in Sozomen. They were regular troops in the Byzantine army in Egypt, as recorded in the *Notitia Dignitatum*, and were presumably Roman citizens. This could perhaps be inferred also from Synesius' description of the Arab soldier that tried to force the skipper to resume control of the helm as a *stratiōtes* (στρατιώτης). Their dispatch from Aegyptus to Pentapolis might suggest that they formed part of the *exercitus comitatensis* of that province.

2

In addition to the valuable military data in Synesius' letter pertaining to the movement of troops from one province of the Diocese of Aegyptus to another, there are data pertaining to the image of the Arabs and Jews who were huddled together in a rickety ship during a perilous voyage from Alexandria to Cyrene.

The Arabs

The Arabs are referred to twice in the letter. On both occasions the reference is surprisingly complimentary, considering the dark colors with which the Graeco-Roman historians, with few exceptions, have drawn the picture of the Arabs.[40]

In the first passage, referred to above, the Arab horseman who tried

[37] Ibid., pp. 85, 86.

[38] See Fitzgerald, *Letters*, p. 40.

[39] See Pando, *Life and Times*, 136–39. The Libyans were noted horsemen who harassed the cities of Cyrenaica; thus the dispatch of Arab horsemen from Egypt to defend them becomes intelligible. On the importance of the cavalry for the defense of the region, see Pando, 133.

[40] On the image of the Arabs in Graeco-Roman historiography, see *RA*, 156–59 and *BAFOC*, 560–64.

to force the Jewish skipper to resume control of the helm is referred to as γεννάδας, which the translator of Synesius renders "staunch."[41]

The second passage comes a little further on in the letter, when Synesius admires the Arab cavalry for wanting to fall on their swords and die rather than be drowned: "As I was musing in this fashion, I noticed that all the soldiers on board[42] were standing with drawn swords. On enquiring the reason for this, I learned from them that they regarded it as more honorable to belch out their souls to the winds while still on the deck, than to gape them out to the waves. These men are by nature true descendants of Homer, thought I, and I entirely approved their view of the matter."[43]

Thus the Arabs are referred to as "staunch" or noble and are described as by nature true descendants of the heroes of the Homeric age. Set against a long history of vituperation on the part of Graeco-Roman historians, who conceived the Arabs as treacherous and unreliable, this sounds like a shrill, dissonant note, and merits investigation. The following may be adduced to explain Synesius' attitude:

(1) Perhaps Synesius was not exposed to Graeco-Roman sources that had vilified the Arabs. His readings, though extensive, may have been outside the range of these. On the other hand, he may have been influenced by Graeco-Roman writers who remembered the Arabs well, such as Strabo and Diodorus Siculus. The *Res Gestae* of Ammianus Marcellinus, with its anti-Arab sentiments, may have been unknown to Synesius, even if he could read Latin.

(2) His native city had no Arab element in it which could have caused some friction, such as existed between the Greeks and Jews of Cyrene.

(3) Perhaps he admired the courage of the Arab horsemen and certain qualities about the Arab passengers on the ship: the resolution of the horsemen who wanted to force the skipper to resume control of the helm and the determination of the other Arab horsemen to fall on their swords rather than drown. Synesius was himself a horseman and hunter, a squire who was a man of action. Furthermore, he was descended from the Heraclids and the Spartans, to whom he refers in his address to Arcadius.[44]

[41] Fitzgerald, *Letters*, p. 84. It can also be translated "noble" or "generous" and also, of horses, "highly bred." Synesius used complimentary terms for the Marcomans (ibid., 205 and *Epistolae*, ed. Garzya, 195), but these may have been facetious or sarcastic in view of the fact, noted by Pando (*Life and times*, 129), that they lost their shields to the Ausurians.

[42] As he had said earlier, many of them were Arabs.

[43] Fitzgerald, *Letters*, p. 84–85 and notes on p. 84 for quotations from Homer on drowning as a pitiable end. The Arabs, not being a seafaring people, always mistrusted the sea and must have detested, even more than the Greeks, death by drowning. For the Greek text, see *Epistolae*, ed. Garzya, 18.

[44] For his complimentary references to the Spartan king Agesilaus, see Fitzgerald, *Essay and Hymns of Synesius of Cyrene* (Oxford, 1930), I, 121, 132.

(4) Synesius was a Neo-Platonist. Many Neo-Platonists were non-Greek, and one of them, possibly two, were Arab—Porphyry and Iamblichus.[45] Synesius would have learned about these Arab Neo-Platonists during his discipleship to Hypatia in Alexandria.

(5) He was in Constantinople for some three years or so (399–402) when he addressed his Περὶ Βασιλείας to Arcadius around 400. The Arab horsemen had saved Constantinople recently (A.D. 378), and he must have heard about their encounter with the very same Goths against whom he fulminated in his address to Arcadius.[46]

The foregoing observations may explain this curiosity, namely, that the Greek squire who wrote against the Goths, Jews, and Ausurians spared the Arabs and, what is more, spoke of them in favorable terms.

The Skipper

In contrast Synesius' references to the Jews are surprisingly harsh, coming as they do from one who was apparently free from racial prejudice.[47] The Jews receive some hostile comments in the letter.[48] Of the Jews who were in the ship (some seven, mainly sailors), it is the skipper who is naturally mentioned in an extended passage, first when he drops the rudder because of the beginning of the Sabbath and later when he resumes control of it after the storm had reached perilous proportions.[49] In spite of Synesius' animadversions, the Jewish skipper comes off best of all the passengers. He appears as a courageous man, loyal to the commandments of his faith, and behaves with perfect equanimity and fortitude during the storm. In the midst of panic and confusion around him, he reads a scroll, presumably the Torah.

Synesius' references to the skipper and to the Jews are valuable inasmuch as they tell us something about Synesius himself and his knowledge of some of the books of the Old Testament. This information on Synesius can be extracted from the fact that he refers to the skipper by his name, Amarantus, and further on he refers to him as a Maccabean. Both the skipper's name and his description as a Maccabean are helpful guides:

[45] See *RA*, xxii.

[46] He was the author of Περὶ Βασιλείας whether or not he actually delivered it. See *BAFOC*, 176–78, for the Arab encounter with the Goths.

[47] These references have not been noted in "Anti-Semitismus," *RE*, Supp. 5, cols. 19–22, 38–43; "Judaïsme," *DACL* 8, cols. 95–97, 148–50; S. W. Baron, *A Social and Religious History of the Jews*, 11 vols. (New York, 1952–67); or M. Stern, *Greek and Latin Authors on Jews and Judaism: From Tacitus to Simplicius*, II (Jerusalem, 1980).

[48] For an anti-Semitic sentiment in the letter, see *Epistolae*, ed. Garzya, p. 12, line 9 and Fitzgerald, *Letters*, p. 81, line 11. For other comments, see ibid., 81–84.

[49] Ibid., 81–84.

(1) The skipper is called Amarantus, the Hellenized form of Hebrew ʿAmrām. The translator of the Hebrew Bible into Greek rendered it in two different ways, 'Αμβραμ and 'Αμραμ, both of which look and sound un-Greek.[50] If Hebrew ʿAmrām was thus translated with some latitude by the Septuagint translator, it is quite likely that Synesius wanted to complete the Hellenization of the Hebrew name by giving it a Greek-sounding and Greek-looking ending; hence the form 'Αμάραντος. If Greek 'Αμάραντος is none other than Hebrew ʿAmrām, this will explain the strict orthodoxy of the skipper in observing the Sabbath from sundown on Friday, since presumably he was given his name ʿAmrām, after the biblical figure, the father of Aaron, Moses, and Miriam, and thus could have been a Levite.

(2) More important is his description as a Maccabean.[51] This makes it practically certain that Synesius was familiar, even at this stage before he converted, with the biblical Books of Maccabees. This he must have known in various ways: (*a*) The Greek Bible was certainly known in academic circles in Alexandria, where it was translated and where Synesius sojourned as a pupil of Hypatia. (*b*) One of the Neo-Platonists, none other than Porphyry, wrote a tract "Against the Christians," and it is quite likely that he discussed there the Book of Maccabees as he did the Book of Daniel. (*c*) It was a Jew of Cyrene, Jason, who wrote a detailed history of the Hasmonean uprising, which was the source of the Second Book of Maccabees. (*d*) Finally, Synesius might have had a copy of the Septuagint from his Christian brother Euoptius or he might have acquired one after his marriage to a Christian lady in Alexandria after his return from Constantinople. This incidental reference to Amarantus as Maccabean provides one of the clues for understanding the curious fact that instead of admiring the equanimity and courage of the skipper, Synesius rather suprisingly animadverted against him.

In view of Synesius' singular lack of racial prejudice as far as the Arabs are concerned, his anti-Jewish sentiments call for an explanation:

(1) Jews lived in Cyrene, his native town, and in Alexandria where he studied, and there was friction between Greek and Jew in both these Hellenic foundations. There was recent friction in Cyrene between the two communities, and the revolts of the Jews of Cyrene during the reigns of Vespasian and Trajan were well known. Synesius' love for his city is known from his address to Arcadius. Thus he could have been ill-disposed toward any group that

[50] See Septuagint, Exod. 6:18 and Num. 26:58. In the Septuagint, ed. A. Rahlfs, 7th ed. (Stuttgart, 1962), the two versions of the name are unaccented.

[51] The normal English transliteration of Greek Μακκαβαῖος, and so transliterated by Fitzgerald, *Letters*, p. 84. As Pando transliterates "Machabean" (*Life and Times*, 146), it is not unlikely that he missed what Synesius was saying about the skipper, whom he likened, because of his fortitude and strict observance of the law, to one of the Maccabees.

seemed to him to disturb its civic life from within, as he was against the Ausurians who disturbed it from without.

(2) His anti-Jewish sentiment could not have been racist, that of a Hellene who viewed the rest of the world as barbarians, since he evinces no such sentiment against the Arabs. It must have been cultural, and his employment of the term Maccabean provides the clue. The two Books of Maccabees celebrated the struggle and triumph of Judaism against the Hellenism of the Seleucids. Synesius, the Hellene, accordingly associated the Jews with the force that had opposed Hellenism, and this was enough to range him against them. The Jews also revolted against the Romans, and thus had fought against the Graeco-Roman order to which Synesius belonged and for which he fought in word and deed.

Appendix I

Anonymous Saracens in the Sources

The Latin sources[1] contain two passages that refer to the Saracens in Byzantine territory, one to raiding Saracens in southern Palestine and one to the conversion of a large number of them by Nonnus, the bishop of Heliopolis. The period is uncertain, but a distinguished ecclesiastical historian and specialist on Arab Christianity[2] is inclined to date these incidents to the beginning of the fifth century. It is therefore appropriate to discuss them here.

John Cassian, *Collationes*, VI, 1

In his *Collationes*[3] John Cassian, the monk and ascetic of Gaul who had lived in the Orient—in Palestine and in Egypt for a few years—records a devastating raid by the Saracens in the region of Tekoa,[4] the birthplace of the Old Testament prophet Amos. The raid resulted in the massacre of many of the solitaries of the region. Their feast is commemorated in the Roman Martyrology on 28 May.

It is not clear exactly when this raid took place. The *Collationes Patrum*[5] was published after 420, while the chronology of Cassian's sojourn in Palestine and in Egypt is uncertain,[6] all of which makes the dating of this raid extremely difficult.

[1] The *Collationes* of John Cassian and *Vita S. Pelagiae*.

[2] R. Aigrain, "*Arabie*," *DHGE* 3, cols. 1193, 1196.

[3] See PL 49, cols. 643–45; *Iohannis Cassiani Conlationes* XXIIII, ed. M. Petschenig (Vienna, 1886), xiii, pars 2, p. 153.

[4] Tekoah is to the south of Bethlehem and to the west of the Dead Sea, and so it lay in Palaestina Prima.

[5] See B. Altaner, *Patrology*, 538.

[6] See *DHGE* 11, cols. 1322–23; on the chronology of Cassian's sojourn in the Orient, see O. Chadwick, *John Cassian* (Cambridge, 1968), 10, 11, 14, 15, 18.

Aigrain ("Arabie," col. 1193) draws attention to the fact that Tillemont had underlined the difficulty of identifying this raid with the invasion of 410/411 (below, Chap. 2, sec. I); this could suggest that the raid happened slightly earlier in the century, during the reign of Arcadius.

What is important is not its exact dating but the conclusion that may safely be drawn from it—that in the reign of Arcadius, Palaestina Prima was not entirely safe from Saracen raids. This constitutes another piece of evidence for the institution of an *internal* defense system in Oriens for security reasons which, *inter alia*, found expression in the employment of Arab phylarchs far from the *limes orientalis* and perhaps in the construction of what have been called transverse *limites*.[7]

Vita S. Pelagiae

In the *Vita S. Pelagiae*[8] there is a reference to the conversion of thirty thousand Saracens to Christianity near Heliopolis, in Phoenicia Libanensis or Secunda.[9] The account is haunted by a number of ghosts pertaining to the identity of the bishop who converted the Saracens, Nonnus, his episcopal see, Edessa or Heliopolis, and the number of those converted.

Nevertheless, the account has survived the scrutiny of many scholars, and an essential kernel of truth has been accepted—that early in the fifth century Phoenicia Libanensis witnessed the conversion of a large number of Saracens.[10] There remains the task of ascertaining the identity of these Saracens and their legal status, and whether a bishop—Arab or other—was assigned to them in a way analogous to that of the Saracens of the Palestinian Parembole.

Ecclesiastical history is silent on these Saracens after their notice in the *Vita*. At the end of the last century S. Vailhé proposed the first fruitful datum that could be relevant to the discussion of their fortunes. He suggested that Eustathius, the bishop who participated in the Council of Chalcedon in 451, could have been the bishop of the descendants of these Saracens.[11] He is described as "the bishop of the Saracens," and he signed with the bishops of Phoenicia Libanensis. So the account of the *Vita* and the description of Eustathius in the episcopal list of Chalcedon seemed for Vailhé to interlock.

In his review of Vailhé's conclusions, H. Charles noted that the former did not take into account the conclusions of the Bollandist savant Cornelius Byeus, who argued that Nonnus was never in his ecclesiastical career the bishop of Heliopolis in Phoenicia Libanensis. On the other hand, Charles said that Byeus did not discuss whether Nonnus did in fact convert the thirty thousand Saracens and the city of Heliopolis. Charles then drew his conclusions, namely, that one could accept conver-

[7] See *BAFOC*, 479–83.

[8] The notorious courtesan and actress of Antioch, surnamed Peccatrix, after her conversion. The *Vita* is said to have been written by Jacobus, the deacon of Heliopolis, an eyewitness of her conversion.

[9] See *ActaSS*, t. IV, Oct. *Vita S. Pelagiae*, no. 16, p. 265. It is on the Latin version in *ActaSS* that the discussion of the conversion of the thirty thousand Saracens has been based; see below, notes 10–12. Very recently the various versions of the *Vita* in seven languages—Greek, Latin, Syriac, Arabic, Armenian, Georgian, and Slavonic—have been studied and published by P. Petitmengin and a group of distinguished scholars; see *Pélagie la Pénitente. Métamorphoses d'une légende*. Tome I: *Les textes et leur histoire*, Études augustiniennes (Paris, 1981).

[10] Aigrain, "Arabie," col. 1196.

[11] See S. Vailhé, "Notes de géographie ecclésiastique," *EO* 4 (1900–1901), 15.

sion in this region, that it was effected by a local bishop, and that these Saracens were finally amalgamated with the sedentary population of the region.[12] Eustathius is left out of these conclusions, and thus what Vailhé brought together, Charles separated. Charles was unaware of the strong Arab federate presence in Oriens in the fifth century and of the two Saracen units, listed in the *Notitia Dignitatum*, that were stationed in Phoenicia Libanensis.[13] These two facts may now be added to that of the episcopate of Eustathius over a group of Saracens in Phoenicia for a discussion of the fortunes of the thirty thousand Saracens said to have been converted by Nonnus. No certainty can be attained, in spite of the accumulation of relevant data, but it places the discussion on a firmer basis. New possibilities may be explored and left for future analysis when more data are uncovered.

The conversion of the thirty thousand Saracens is a matter of considerable importance in the history of Arab-Byzantine relations.[14] The question arises as to their tribal affiliation, whether they were Salīḥids or belonged to some other tribal group. They could not have been Salīḥids because it is known from Sozomen that they were converted by a monk, not by a bishop. Therefore, they must have belonged to another tribal group in Oriens—perhaps Saracen newcomers who arrived there in the fifth century.[15] It is also possible that they belonged to Arab tribal groups that had settled in Oriens in the preceding century,[16] but it is doubtful that these would have remained unconverted for so long. On the other hand, pockets of paganism persisted even in Asia Minor, the Byzantine heartland, until the sixth century when John of Ephesus wiped them out.

It is possible that, as Charles suggested, the case of the thirty thousand Saracens was an instance of transhumance in this region where the desert met the sown; that they were a group of Arabian Saracens who were driven by a Peninsular drought to seek pasture within the *limes* and were thus stranded in the vicinity of Heliopolis. If so, they were probably allowed to settle within the *limes* on condition that they be christianized and pay the tribute.[17]

It is also possible that a bishop was given to them, but there is no clue as to who he was or who his successors were.[18] The same obscurity shrouds their status. They could have had federate status,[19] or they may have merged with the local Rhomaic

[12] H. Charles, *Le christianisme des arabes nomades sur le limes* (Paris, 1936), 46–48, esp. 47 note 5 on the controversy surrounding Cornelius Byeus' position.

[13] On these two units, see *BAFOC*, 486 note 81 and below, Part 3, sec. 1.

[14] The number is repeated in the various versions of the *Vita* (see below, note 21).

[15] Such as Iyād; see below, Chap. 2, app. 2.

[16] Or centuries; see *BAFOC*, 284–93.

[17] For a group of Saracens who wandered into Oriens because of a drought, see Marcellinus Comes, MGH, *Chronica Minora*, II, 105.

[18] It is not altogether impossible that Eustathius was their bishop or one of their bishops, but it is a very remote possibility; see below, Chap. 11, sec. I.

[19] Especially if it could be shown that they were related to the two Saracen units stationed in Phoenicia Secunda and mentioned in the *Notitia Dignitatum*; see above, note 13.

population which, in Phoenicia Libanensis, was strongly Arab in complexion.[20] Whatever the exact number of the Saracens baptized,[21] their conversion reflects the progress that Christianity was making among the Arabs in the fifth century and, what is more, attests a strong Arab presence in Phoenicia Libanensis.

Appendix II

Synesius: Περὶ Βασιλείας

The address that Synesius delivered before Arcadius during his stay in Constantinople for the triennium 399–402 has been referred to earlier in this chapter in connection with the rise of the Salīḥids to power. This "anti-German manifesto," Περὶ Βασιλείας, has some material relevant to our concerns here.

1. The titulature of the Byzantine ruler and his *official* assumption of the title *basileus* after it had been *autokrator* is an important problem which has been much discussed, and it is related to the titulature of the rulers of the Arab *foederati* of Byzantium in this pre-Islamic period.[1] The material in Section 13 of Περὶ Βασιλείας supports the view that *autokrator*, not *basileus*, was the official title of the Byzantine ruler, and it may be added to what John Lydus says on the problem in *De magistratibus*. Both Synesius and Lydus have been referred to in the course of my discussion of the official assumption of the *basileia* in 629, but the reference was consigned to a footnote.[2] However, the following passages may be quoted here with profit. From Περὶ Βασιλείας, Section 13:[3]

I

> For it is from this source that while we call you kings, while we deem you worthy of the title, and write you down as such, you whether you know it or not, yielding to established customs, seem to evade the dignity of the title. And so, when you write to a city, or to an individual, to a viceroy or to a foreign

[20] A century later Imru' al-Qays the Kindite, the foremost poet of pre-Islamic Arabia, passed through Heliopolis/Baalbek, and it could be inferred from one of his poems that there was an Arab element in the ethnic makeup of the city. See W. Ahlwardt, *The Divans of the Six Ancient Arabic Poets* (London, 1870; rpr. Osnabrück, 1972), p. 131, line 2.

[21] The number thirty thousand, which seems exaggerated, is found in four versions of the *Vita*—the Greek, Latin, Syriac, and Armenian. In the Georgian, the reference is to thirty thousand camels(?), while in the Arabic version the number of Saracens is three thousand; see *Pélagie la Pénitente*, p. 157, sec. 32 and note 16; p. 344, sec. 32.

It is noteworthy that in the *Vita* the account of the conversion of these Saracens is part of the speech of one who is not noted for his veracity, namely, the Devil himself. Yet the account has the strong ring of authenticity and consequently has been rightly accepted as belonging to the factual, not the fictitious, portions of the *Vita*.

[1] See my articles "The Iranian Factor in Byzantium during the Reign of Heraclius," *DOP* 26 (1972), 293–320 and Πιστὸς ἐν Χριστῷ Βασιλεύς, *DOP* 34–35 (1982), 225–37; for more literature on the problem, see *BAFOC*, 520 note 1.

[2] See "The Iranian Factor," 301 note 31.

[3] Trans. Fitzgerald, *The Essays and Hymns of Synesius of Cyrene* (Philadelphia, 1930), I, 130–31.

> ruler, you have never shown pride in the title of king, but rather you make yourself absolute rulers.[4]
>
> II
>
> It is true that in Athens there was a certain individual called king who occupied a petty post, and was accountable for his administration; the people, I suppose, having given him this name in jest, for they were an uncompromisingly free people. Their absolute ruler, however, was not a monarch, and both the title and the office were respected. Is not this, then, clear evidence of a wise policy in the Roman constitution, that although it has manifestly developed into a monarchy, it is cautious in so asserting itself by reason of its hatred of the evils of tyranny, and employs the title of king sparingly?

From *De magistratibus*, part 1, chapter 4:[5]

> As for the cognomen *Caesares*, or rather supreme commanders,[6] it is not indicative of kingship, nor even, however, of tyranny, but rather of absolute rule and absolute authority for better controlling the disturbances that arise against the republic and for commanding the army how it is to fight with adversaries; for "to command" is rendered by the Italians *imperare*, from which *imperator* is derived. That the name "supreme commander" or "Caesar" cannot be indicative of kingship is perfectly clear by the fact that both the consuls and the *Caesares* after them received the cognominal title of *imperatores*, so-called.

2. The legal status of the *foederati* of the fourth and following centuries is an important question, especially whether or not *civitas* was extended to them. The question has been raised about the Germans and the Arabs.[7] Unlike Jordanes, who wrote about the Goths of the fourth century much later[8] and derived his material from Cassiodorus, Synesius was a contemporary, lived in Constantinople itself for a time (399–402), and was close to the imperial establishment. Thus he was well informed about the status of the Goths. The following passage from Περὶ Βασιλείας Section 15 on Theodosius I and the Goths is especially important.

> He raised them up from their prostrate position, made allies of them, and accounted them worthy of citizenship. Moreover, he threw open public offices to them, and made over some part of Roman territory to their bloodstained hands, expending the magnanimity and nobility of his nature upon a work of clemency.[9]

[4] Greek αὐτοκράτωρ.

[5] Trans. A. C. Bandy (Philadelphia, 1983), 13.

[6] Greek αὐτοκράτωρ.

[7] See *BAFOC*, 507–9.

[8] In A.D. 511 according to one Jordanes scholar; see C. C. Mierow, *The Gothic History of Jordanes* (rpr. Cambridge, 1960), 13.

[9] Fitzgerald, *Essays*, 138. For the Greek text see N. Terzaghi, *Synesii Cyrenensis Hymni et Opuscula*, Scriptores Graeci et Latini Consilio Academiae Lynceorum Editi (Rome, 1944), 50.

The important phrase is "made allies of them and accounted them worthy of citizenship": καὶ συμμάχους ἐποίει καὶ πολιτείας ἠξίου," with its two technical terms, σύμμαχοι and πολιτεία. The crucial one is πολιτεία, but it has been variously interpreted. One translates it "citizenship," while another "political rights."[10]

[10] A. A. Vasiliev, *History of the Byzantine Empire* (Madison, 1952), 93, line 13.

II

The Reign of Theodosius II (408–450)

Arab-Byzantine relations are well documented for the reign of Theodosius. The sources provide valuable data throughout the long reign: (1) references in St. Jerome; (2) accounts of the Persian Wars; (3) data on the phylarchs of the Palestinian Parembole; (4) references in the Codex Theodosianus; and (5) a reference for A.D. 447 in one of the classicizing fragmentary historians, Priscus. These isolated references will be analyzed in an attempt to discover the historical contexts for the events recorded.

I. The Arabian Front

In a letter[1] written in the year 410, Jerome refers to a general invasion of Oriens by the barbarians. It was directed against the limitrophe provinces from the Euphrates to the Nile, and included the provinces of Egypt, Palestine, Phoenicia, and Syria. The invasion is described as "a torrent that carried everything with it"; its impact was deeply felt in Oriens, so much so that it affected Bethlehem in Palaestina Prima (not a limitrophe province) where Jerome had settled in 385.

> Ezechielis uolumen olim adgredi uolui et sponsionem creberrimam studiosis lectoribus reddere, sed in ipso dictandi exordio ita animus meus occidentalium prouinciarum et maxime urbis Romae uastatione confusus est, ut iuxta uulgare prouerbium quoque ignorarem uocabulum, diuque tacui sciens tempus esse lacrimarum, hoc autem anno, cum tres explicassem libros, subitus impetus barbarorum, de quibus tuus dicit Uergilius: lateque uagantes Barcaei et sancta scriptura de Ismahel: contra faciem omnium fratrum suorum habitabit, sic Ægypti limitem, Palaestinae, Phoenices, Syriae percucurrit ad instar torrentis cuncta secum trahens, ut uix manus eorum misericordia Christi potuerimus euadere.

[1] Letter no. CXXVI, for which see PL 22, col. 1086, and CSEL 56, ed. I. Hilberg (Vienna, 1918), p. 144. For Jerome's *Letters* see B. Altaner, *Patrology*, 470–73.

This irruption by those whom Jerome describes as *barbari* is further confirmed by a passage[2] in the preface to Book III of his commentary on Ezekiel, in which he laments the invasion of the Orient by these barbarians and their occupation of his beloved Bethlehem itself.

> Quis crederet ut totius orbis extructa victoriis Roma corrueret, ut ipsa suis populis et mater fieret et sepulcrum: ut tota Orientis, Ægypti, Africae littora olim dominatricis urbis, servorum et ancillarum numero complerentur: ut quotidie sancta Bethleem, nobiles quondam utriusque sexus, atque omnibus divitiis affluentes, susciperet mendicantes?

In these two passages Jerome speaks in general terms of *barbari* and does not indicate their identity, but it is practically certain that they were Arabs or Saracens. This is amply clear from the facts of geography. A group of *barbari* who invaded the provinces of Oriens and Egypt[3] could only have been Arabs or Saracens. Furthermore, the biblical reference in the first quotation to Ishmael and in the second to "servorum et ancillarum numero" can only be to the Arabs, who were identified by ecclesiastical historians with the sons of Ishmael, and who were often referred to as Ishmaelitae or Hagarenoi.[4]

Thus the reign of Theodosius II opens with a major disturbance along the oriental *limes*. The cause of this invasion of Oriens by the Arabs is shrouded in obscurity, as is the identity of the group or groups who mounted it. One can only suggest the following:

1. It is not altogether impossible that there was a severe drought in northern Arabia at this time which drove its tribes to seek pasture in the Byzantine half of the Fertile Crescent. In the following century or so such a drought drove an Arab group to cross the Byzantine *limes*.[5]

2. This invasion may have been mounted by one of the groups that were seeking military and political self-expression in northern Arabia at this time, such as the Ghassānids or the Kindites. It is not altogether unlikely that the

[2] See PL 25, col. 75. For Jerome's biblical commentaries, see Altaner, *Patrology*, 470.

[3] Egypt was separated from the Diocese of Oriens by Theodosius I around 380. The reference to Egypt may have been an exaggeration, but on the other hand Queen Mavia included Egypt in her offensive against Byzantium some forty years before. For Mavia, see *BAFOC*, 138–238 and on Egypt, 144–47.

[4] For this image of the Arabs, see *BAFOC*, 560–64, and *RA*, 95–112. The reference to Ishmael is decisive in identifying these *barbari* as Saracens because it distinguishes them from other *barbari* who had overrun the Oriens shortly before, namely, the Huns in 402 and the Isaurians in 405. The reference to the Arabs in the second quotation is not as clear as that in the first; what is involved in the phrase "servorum et ancillarum numero" is a reference to the Arabs as the descendants of the handmaid, Hagar, Ishmael's mother and Sarah's ancilla.

[5] On this, see Marcellinus Comes, MGH, *Chronica Minora* (Berlin, 1894), II, 105.

two groups may have concerted their actions as they were to do some ninety years later.[6]

3. The Arab invaders may have belonged to the tribe of Kalb. This powerful tribal group was settled over a vast territory extending from Palmyra to Tabūk in Northern Ḥijāz. This could explain the remarkably wide range of the Arab invasion—which extended from Syria to Egypt—a fact that could plausibly point to Kalb. Furthermore, the invasion may have been related to the fall of the Tanūkhids and the rise of the Salīḥids. Kalb, it has been argued, may have been related to the Tanūkhids through Mavia, the fourth-century Arab federate queen.[7] It is noteworthy that the theater of war during Mavia's revolt extended from Phoenicia to Egypt, almost coterminous with that of the Arab invasion in 410. If this invasion was indeed conducted by Kalb, it could have been a repetition of Mavia's, which she may have mounted from the territory of Kalb, and it would have been directly related to the rise of the new Arab federate supremacy, the Salīḥids.

4. These are the three principal tribal groups in northern Arabia who were sufficiently powerful to launch major assaults. The Lakhmids cannot be entirely ruled out and must remain a remote possibility. In spite of the peace with Persia that technically obtained in the fifth century (with the exception of the two wars of Theodosius' reign), the Lakhmids could have been involved in these attacks. As semi-independent clients, they could act separately and independently, or the Persians could have used them to express their displeasure with Byzantium, for example, over the annual subsidies.

There are echoes in the sources that could support this conclusion. The year 410 falls within the reign of the Persian king Yazdgard I (399–420) and that of Nuʿmān, his Lakhmid client-king.[8] It is explicitly stated in the *Chronicle* of Ṭabarī that al-Nuʿmān raided far and wide in Oriens (in Ṭabarī called al-Shām), and this statement agrees with the range of the invasion in 410, which reached Palestine.[9] What is more, his Persian overlord is said to have

[6] Theophanes, *Chronographia*, ed. de Boor, I, 141. I have discussed this invasion of 500 in "Ghassān and Byzantium: A New *terminus a quo*," *Der Islam* 33 (1959), 232–55. That the Ghassānids were already in northern Arabia and in Ḥīra in the 4th century has been argued in *BAFOC*, 121–23; Kinda was certainly a power in central Arabia even before the 5th century.

[7] On this, see *BAFOC*, 196–97; a close examination of the sources, however, reveals that the mater eponymus of the Kalbite group, Banū Māwiya, belonged to the tribe of Bahrāʾ.

[8] On the duration of his reign and how much of it overlapped with that of Yazdgard, see Nöldeke, *Geschichte der Perser und Araber zur Zeit der Sasaniden* (Leiden, 1979), 85 (hereafter *PAS*); and G. Rothstein, *Die Dynastie der Laḫmiden in al-Ḥīra* (Berlin, 1899), 62 (hereafter *DLH*).

[9] A century later Mundir, the Lakhmid, raided as far as Palestine; see Rothstein, *DLH*, 146. According to Procopius, he also reached the confines of Egypt; see Procopius, *De bellis libri*, ed. J. Haury and G. Wirth, Bibliotheca Teubneriana (1962), I.xvii,41 (hereafter Procopius, *Wars*).

put at his disposal two cavalry regiments, called al-Shahbā' and Dawsar, with which he conducted his compaigns in both Arabia and Oriens.[10] Finally, this Lakhmid king is known to have reached Oriens, where he met St. Simeon the Stylite before renouncing the world and becoming a wanderer, sometime between 413 and 420. So Oriens was known to Nuʿmān as a seeker of the Christian saint and probably earlier as a raider of the Roman *limes*.

What part the Salīḥids played during this invasion is not recorded in the sources. But it is quite possible that they shouldered most of the responsibility for repelling it. Sozomen (or his source) probably had this and similar engagements in mind when he wrote that the Salīḥids proved formidable not only to the Persians but to the Saracens as well.[11]

II. The Persian Front

The two Persian Wars of this reign were of short duration (420–422 and 440–442), and no detailed account of them has survived.[12] Consequently, they have been treated rather unceremoniously[13] along with the Arab partici-

[10] Nöldeke, *PAS*, 83 note 3, in which Nöldeke says that his raids against Oriens can be entertained as a possibility, although he is also inclined to believe that they are confused with those of his namesake of a later date. Furthermore, this was a period of peace between Persia and Byzantium, and, according to the well-known accounts in Procopius and Agathias, Yazdgard had accepted the guardianship over Theodosius II on the death of Arcadius in 408; see Averil Cameron, "Agathias on the Sassanians," *DOP* 23–24 (1969–70), 149. But doubts have been cast on the accounts of the two Byzantine historians (ibid.); Yazdgard may have been engaged in some duplicitous diplomatic behavior or conduct, and, more likely, Nuʿmān may have acted independently on ideas of his own without respecting his overlord's peace with Byzantium and guardianship over its autokrator. Furthermore, Nöldeke seems not to have noticed the account of Jerome on the raid of 410. If he had, he might have been more inclined to believe that Nuʿmān's campaign against Oriens was more than a possibility. For Nuʿmān and his reign, see Rothstein, *DLH*, 65–68. Rothstein entertains Nöldeke's doubts about Nuʿmān's campaign against Shām, and consequently denies the ascription of the two divisions to him, but thinks (p. 67) that the title "Qā'id al-Furs" suggests he was commander of the two divisions.

[11] Sozomen wrote about the middle of the 5th century, and thus his statement applies to encounters with the Peninsular Arabs that took place in the first half of that century—such as this one in 410 and possibly one referred to in Priscus for the year 447 (see below, Chap. 3, sec. I). Such encounters must also include those that involved the Salīḥids with the Lakhmid Arabs in the course of the two Persian Wars that broke out in the reign of Theodosius, especially the first Persian War (see below, sec. II).

[12] Priscus of Panium would have included in his work a detailed account of the second Persian War, since his primary interest was the East, while Olympiodorus of Thebes, who dedicated his history to Theodosius II, wrote only on the West. On these historians, see Blockley, *CH*.

[13] A tradition that seems to go as far back as Gibbon, who may have influenced subsequent historiography on these two wars. For Gibbon's description of the events of the first war ("such events may be disbelieved or disregarded") see his *Decline and Fall of the Roman Empire*, ed. J. B. Bury (London, 1897), III, 391.

pation in them.[14] The first and more important of these wars was only recently subjected to thorough and fruitful reexamination.[15] The Arab role in them must receive similar treatment, especially as it was substantial and as it throws light on the general course of the wars as well as on the various facets of the Arab-Byzantine relationship. The discussion involves the Arab allies of both Persia and Byzantium, the Lakhmids and the Salīḥids respectively.

The First Persian War

The first of the two wars was by far the more important,[16] and the Arabs were heavily engaged in its inception, in its course, and in the terms of the peace treaty that concluded it.

A

1. Among the causes that led to the outbreak of this war was the flight of Persian Christians to Roman territory. The Persian embassy failed to retrieve these Christian fugitives from the Byzantines.[17]

[14] The Arabs in these two wars hardly figure in modern works on the reign of Theodosius II or on the history of this period. Nöldeke was the first to discuss the role of the Arabs seriously and professionally in the notes to his masterly work on Ṭabarī (*PAS*, p. 108 note 2, p. 116 note 2); Rothstein does not go further than Nöldeke on the subject (*DLH* 68–69). The standard histories of Byzantium for this period, Bury, (*HLRE*) and Stein (*HBE*) simply repeat what Socrates says on the Lakhmid king, and what Malchus says on the Lakhmids and the clause in the treaty of 422. Even a specialized work on the Sasanids, A. Christensen's *L'Iran sous les Sassanides* (Copenhagen, 1944), has only one paragraph on the first war, without any reference to the Arabs (p. 281), and a sentence on the second (p. 283); in the most recent work on Iran, the first Persian War is dismissed in a paragraph, while the second is dismissed in one sentence; see *The Cambridge History of Iran* (Cambridge, 1983), 3 (1), pp. 145, 146.

[15] See K. G. Holum, "Pulcheria's Crusade, A.D. 421–422, and Ideology of Imperial Victory," *GRBS* 18 (1977), 153–72. Elements from this article were incorporated in the same author's book *Theodosian Empresses* (Berkeley, 1982), 109–11, but the article remains the main source for the new interpretation of the first Persian War of Theodosius' reign. Among other things, this article is remarkable for the use of the numismatic evidence for unlocking some of the secrets of the war and neutralizing the tendentious tone of the literary-ecclesiastical historians. Most recently the two Persian Wars have been treated by B. Croke in an article, "Dating Theodoret's *Church History* and *Commentary on the Psalms*," *Byzantion* 54 (1984), 59–74. Although primarily a contribution to the dating of Theodoret (which he argues belongs to the mid/late 440s rather than the early 440s, p. 73), this article has a valuable discussion of the two wars and is a welcome addition to the little-studied Persian Wars of Theodosius' reign.

[16] It is referred to as the "Greatest War" by Malchus. For an interpretation of this phrase in Malchus, see Holum, "Pulcheria's Crusade," 171. On the other hand, Malchus may simply have wanted to distinguish it from the other war in the reign (and indeed it was the much more important of the two) in order to make clear that the clause in the peace treaty he was discussing related to the first war and not the second. Since the first was the much more important of the two wars, Malchus found it convenient to describe it as the "greatest war." But it is noteworthy that Socrates describes it as δεινός; see *Socratis Scholastici Ecclesiastica Historia*, ed. R. Hussey (Oxford, 1853), II, p. 767, line 16.

[17] See ibid., 766–67.

Their identity is not indicated in the sources, but it is possible, even likely, that many of the fugitives were Christian Arabs. The Arabs were the most important ethnic group living in this limitrophe region between the two empires. Their mobility is well known; their frequent crossing of the frontier from the territory of one empire to the other testifies to it, and Christianity was widespread among them. The Lakhmid capital, Ḥīra, was the great center for Christianity even at this early period, although the royal house itself had not been Christianized.[18] Furthermore, they were unruly and often rebellious when their religious feelings were ruffled. The history of Arab-Persian relations in the fourth century evidences all this, and indeed the Arab *foederati* of Byzantium in that century, the Tanūkhids, were Christian fugitives from Persian religious persecution.[19] The tribal affiliation of the Christian Arabs who fled is difficult to pin down, but the chances are that they were the Iyād group.[20]

In addition to the account of the ecclesiastical historian Socrates, Malchus, the fragmentary classical historian of the fifth century, refers to one of the terms of the peace treaty that terminated this war, namely, that neither power should receive the Arab allies of the other.[21] The clear implication of this clause is that some of Persia's Arab allies had defected to Byzantium just prior to the outbreak of the war. Malchus' language makes clear that this was another category of fugitives from Persia, different from those that fled because of religious persecution. While the identification of the tribal affiliation of the first group is hypothetical, hagiography helps to pin down the group of Arab allies. In a well-known chapter Cyril of Scythopolis recounts the fortunes of Aspebetos, an Arab commander in the service of Persia who fled with his own Arab subjects to Roman territory and who answers to the description.[22] Aspebetos was clearly not Christian when he fled because he was baptized only later by St. Euthymius. Whether the clause in the treaty referred only to Aspebetos and his group is not entirely clear. It could have been so, since he must have been an important figure on the Persian military scene judging from his name, which is a Persian title of a high-ranking military office. On the other hand, other groups of allies may have defected; this seems the more plausible view since it would justify inserting in the peace treaty the stipulation against the recurrence of such defections. If so, the

[18] As early as 410 it had a bishop, and slightly before the war, its Lakhmid ruler, Nuʿmān, had met St. Simeon and renounced the world; on this see below, Chap. 8, app. 2.

[19] For the fortunes of the Tanūkhids as Christian fugitives from Persia, see *BAFOC*, 418–19.

[20] For this, see below, App. 2.

[21] See Blockley, *CH*, II, p. 404, 11. 4–7.

[22] On Aspebetos, see below, Sec. IV.

stipulation could include the Iyād group,[23] who could have been, like the Lakhmids, allies or clients of Persia (although their status vis-à-vis the Persians is not as clear as that of the Lakhmids).

Thus there was a flight of Christian Arabs from Persia and a defection of Arab allies, who found their way to Roman territory. Both were important contributory factors to the outbreak of the first Persian War.

2. The Lakhmid Mundir, a client-king of Persia, cuts a large figure in this war, as is clear from Socrates. According to him, Bahram or Vahranes, the Persian king, called on his Arab ally Mundir for help in his attempt to relieve Nisibis, which was being besieged by the Roman army. Mundir responded with a large reinforcement of Arab warriors, promising to defeat the Romans and deliver Antioch in Syria into Bahram's hands. But his plan failed: thinking that the Roman army was falling upon them, the Arabs were seized with a panic and threw themselves into the Euphrates, where a hundred thousand of them were drowned.

This is a precious passage on Arab participation in the war, coming as it does from a reliable, contemporary historian. With the exception of the number of Arabs drowned in the Euphrates, which is an obvious exaggeration, the account must be accepted as a true report of what happened to the Lakhmid expeditionary force. But it needs to be analyzed carefully in the light of incontestable evidence from the Greek and Arabic sources in order to help explain the Arab role in the siege of Nisibis.

a. The first gift of Socrates is the name of the Lakhmid king, which is important for establishing the chronology of the dynasty in the fifth century[24] and enables us to confront the Greek and Arabic sources to good result. It leads to the *locus classicus* on the reign of Mundir, a chapter in Ṭabarī, the best of Arabic sources, on both Mundir and his overlord, Bahram. Ṭabarī's long chapter is full of significant details for a better understanding of the Arab role in this war.[25]

It is clear from Ṭabarī that Mundir was important in the history of the Lakhmids and of Lakhmid-Sasanid relations. In addition to being host to Bahram in Ḥīra when the latter was still a prince, Mundir secured Bahram's election to the throne when it was contested. Consequently the Lakhmid king was very influential with the "king of kings," and it is practically certain that

[23] According to this reasoning, Iyād would have been implied both by the statement in Socrates on the Christian fugitives and in Malchus on the Arab defectors among the allies of Persia.

[24] And it reminds the student of this period of another onomastic gift of his for the 4th century, namely, the name of the Roman officer to whom Mavia's daughter was married, Victor; see *BAFOC*, 159, note 80.

[25] The chapter in Ṭabarī is translated and commented on by Nöldeke, *PAS*, 85–112.

his role in the war was even more extensive than Socrates' account would have us believe. Furthermore, according to Socrates, he was an ἀνὴρ γενναῖος καὶ πολεμικός who had at his disposal, in addition to other troops, the two celebrated regiments, al-Shahbā' and al-Dawsar.[26] In short, he was ready for military adventures, and since he was a pagan and most likely also anti-Christian, he could very well have been instrumental in driving Bahram to go to war with Byzantium, or to embrace the prospect of war when it arose. In so doing he was foreshadowing the role of some of his illustrious successors among the Lakhmids, namely, the warmonger Nuʿmān II toward the end of the century[27] and Mundir III in the first half of the sixth century.

b. The campaign against Antioch: the laconic statement in Socrates on Mundir's intentions and the sequel involving both Antioch and the Euphrates clearly reveal the military plan of the campaign and the intentions of Mundir. The strategic thinking behind Mundir's plan may be inferred from a comparison with an analogous situation that occurred a century or so later, when another Mundir planned the strategy of the Persian campaign that culminated in the battle of Callinicum. The account of Procopius makes clear that Mundir recommended a direct attack on Antioch in Syria because Roman Mesopotamia was well fortified and garrisoned, while Syria was not. His forebear Mundir, of the war of 421, recommended a similar course on similar grounds. This offensive was probably a diversionary movement[28] designed to relieve pressure on the main Persian Imperial army engaged in the north at Nisibis by Ardabur. The course of the Arab contingent's march along the Euphrates and the spot where they tried to cross the river into the Roman province of Syria must of course remain conjectural.[29]

[26] For which, see Nöldeke, *PAS*, 83. These are associated with the name of his father, Nuʿmān, but Mundir inherited them from his father. One might add the following to what Nöldeke has said on the two regiments. The first could have been a regiment of *cataphractarii* because of the name. The second, according to him, carried a Persian name although composed of Arabs from Tanūkh, presumably those who stayed on in the Land of the Two Rivers after the emigration of their relatives to Roman territory in the 4th century; but the name could be related to the Arab tribe, Dawsar, to be found in the name, Wādī al-Dawāsir, or to the grammatical pattern *fawʿal*, from the root related to *dusur*, iron pegs, etc. On these two regiments, see also Christensen, *L'Iran*, 270 and M. J. Kister, *Studies in Jāhiliyya and Early Islam*, (London, 1980), III, 165–67, which has important new material on Ḥīra. For the phrase in Socrates describing Mundir, see *HE*, 770, line 8.

[27] Rothstein, *DLH*, 73–74.

[28] Cf. what the two Roman dukes, Recithancus and Theoctistus, say to Belisarius during the Assyrian campaign in 541, namely, that their presence in Assyria is only exposing Lebanon and Syria to Mundir's raids; Procopius, *Wars*, II, xix, pp. 33–34.

[29] Some light may be thrown on it by the march of Mundir in 531, which culminated in the battle of Callinicum. According to Procopius, Mundir crossed the Euphrates in Assyria, marched through a desert and uninhabited country, and fell upon Commagene, (*Wars*, I, xviii, 2). The toponyms associated with the campaigns are Chalcis, Gabboulon, Sura, and Callinicum

c. The Lakhmid disaster on the Euphrates: Socrates' account must be accepted after expurgating the one incredible element, the number drowned. The miraculous, it is true, dominates Socrates' account of the war,[30] but this does not impugn the general veracity of the author or the credibility of the account, which is true in general but inaccurate in details. Extracting the facts from Socrates' account, then, entails rejecting the miraculous as the cause of the defeat and the number of those who were drowned in the Euphrates.

The causes behind the Lakhmid panic and subsequent drowning can only be conjectured. It should be remembered that Mun<u>d</u>ir's army was a composite one, reflecting the composite nature of Ḥīra[31] and its environs: (1) There were Christian Arabs living in Ḥīra, Babylonia, and Mesopotamia. It is quite possible that the Christian element in Mun<u>d</u>ir's army revolted against the idea of fighting a war that was brought on partly by the late king Yazdgard's persecution of Christians, especially as the campaign was directed against one of the great religious centers in the Christian Orient—Antioch itself, the seat of the patriarchate. Thus the Christian element may have revolted after it became aware that it was being marched against Antioch, and this could have caused general confusion.[32] (2) Mun<u>d</u>ir inherited from his father, Nuʿmān, the two famous regiments al-Shahbā' and Dawsar. According to the Arabic tradition, the latter was formed of Arabs whose tribal affiliation was Tanūkhid.[33] But the Tanūkhids were also employed by Byzantium and were in the fourth century its dominant Arab federate group. After their fall in the reign of Theodosius they stayed on in the service of Byzantium as *foederati* to fight its war.[34] The Dawsar regiment may thus have revolted at the idea of fighting its kinsmen on the Byzantine side. One of these two causes, or both of them, seem the more plausible explanation for what happened to the Lakhmid host; the revolts led to confusion and contributed to the defeat.[35]

(*Wars*, I, xviii, 8, 13, 14). Since the facts of military history and of physical geography were the same for the 5th and 6th centuries, the chances are that the two Mun<u>d</u>irs followed roughly the same road to Antioch. The φόβος referred to by Socrates as over-taking the Saracens in 421 may be paralleled with that of Mun<u>d</u>ir and the Persian commander Azarethes, κατορρωδήσαντες when after crossing the Euphrates they heard that a Roman army was encamped at Gabboulon ready to meet them; *Wars*, I, xviii, 9.

30 As when he speaks of angels appearing to people in Bithynia, assuring them that the Romans would be victorious; see Socrates, *HE*, 769.

31 See Rothstein, *DLH*, 18– 20.

32 An instructive parallel may be drawn for the year 503 when the Christian Arab chief in Ḥīra tries to dissuade Nuʿmān, the Lakhmid descendant of Mun<u>d</u>ir, from attacking another city holy to the Christians of the Orient, namely, Edessa; see *The Chronicle of Joshua the Stylite*, ed. W. Wright (Cambridge, 1882), 46–47. There are also instances of Christian insubordination in the army of the famous Mun<u>d</u>ir, his son, in the 6th century.

33 See above, note 26.

34 See *BAFOC*, 455.

35 For more on the defeat, see the following section on the Salīḥid participation in the war.

Socrates' reference to the Euphrates makes it possible to reconstruct what happened in this compaign (which is recorded only in Socrates among the ecclesiastical historians).[36] It is clear that the Lakhmid army had crossed the Byzantine frontier and was operating in one of the two provinces, Osroene and Euphratensis, which the Euphrates divides, and in that part of the two provinces which was closest to Antioch, Mundir's destination. Hardy and seasoned desert warriors, familiar with desert terrain, would not have thrown themselves into the Euphrates out of fear. They must have been forced to do so, and this can be explained only by the supposition that they were sandwiched between an opposing Roman army and the river behind them. With revolts in the ranks of the Lakhmid contingent, Mundir could not withstand the advancing Roman army that opposed him and so he retreated, only to find the Euphrates behind him. His heavily armed troops probably tried to swim to the safety of the other bank, but they were drowned in the process.[37]

Reference to the Euphrates raises the question whether the Lakhmid army fought near it in Osroene or whether it crossed the river and fought in Euphratensis. Much light would have been cast on this problem if the final section in Chapter XVIII in Socrates, which mentions the Byzantine commander, Vitianus, had been more detailed and explicit.[38] Socrates there recounts how the survivors of the catastrophe at the Euphrates were given short shrift by Vitianus, whom he describes simply as *stratēgos*. Had he been more specific about the province Vitianus was in charge of, one would be able to answer the geographical question of where in Oriens the Lakhmid host was vanquished.[39] As the narrative stands, it is not clear whether the Lakhmid

[36] Socrates is the principal contemporary source; the other sources are late, derivative, and not very informative; Theophanes, *Chronographia*, ed. de Boor, 85-86; Bar-Hebraeus, *The Chronography of Gregory Abū'l Faraj*, trans. E. A. W. Budge (London, 1932), I, 67; and Michael Syrus, *Chronique de Michel le Syrien*, ed. and trans. J. B. Chabot (Paris, 1899–1924), II, 22.

[37] Socrates speaks of those who drowned as ἔνοπλοι. This would be especially true of the two divisions, al-Shahbā' and al-Dawsar, which, as was observed earlier, were heavily armed, accoutered in the Persian manner, as *cataphractarii*. But these apparently survived the disaster, since they are attested in the reign of the last Lakhmid. On the two regiments, references to them in Arabic poetry, and whether their first appearance should be associated with Nuʿmān I or Nuʿmān II, see Rothstein, *DLH*, 134– 36; see also above, note 26.

[38] He was clearly informed, since he says that he will not describe in what manner Vitianus finished the Saracens off.

[39] In the entry on Vitianus in *PLRE*, it is stated that "he is unlikely to have been another *magister militum* or the *dux* of one of the local military areas, since the supreme commander was evidently Aradabur 3 while Vitianus himself presumably operated across military boundaries to defeat the Saracens; he will have been a military *comes* under the authority of Ardabur"; see *PLRE*, II, 1178. This is possible, but that he was a *dux* of a Euphratesian province such as Osroene or Euphratensis can be entertained. The reasoning in the entry does not take into account that Vitianus may not have crossed provincial boundaries to defeat the Saracens, who may have crossed the Euphrates in order to reach Antioch. That Vitianus may thus have beaten them in Euphratensis is only one possibility. Since no *dux* for either Osroene or Euphratensis is

army was beaten in Osroene or in Euphratensis, or whether the second phase of the defeat associated with Vitianus was enacted on the same side of the Euphrates that witnessed the first phase—before the Lakhmids tried to cross the Euphrates and drowned.

Finally, the number of troops involved in Mundir's campaign against Antioch, as noted earlier, must be drastically reduced. But it should be remembered that Ṭabarī, an independent and excellent source on Mundir, mentions that he was able to muster ten thousand cavalry in support of Bahram's claim to the throne.[40] Thus the expeditionary force must have been a fairly considerable one and, what is more, it must have included the al-Shahbā' and al-Dawsar regiments.[41] Thus the Arabic sources supplement what the Byzantine sources have to offer with many significant details on this campaign and on the Persian War in general.

In a war with Persia and her Arab allies, it is practically certain that Byzantium also employed her allies. For it was specifically for this purpose—meeting the Perso-Arab menace on the eastern front—that the Arab federate alliance in the Orient was called into being in the fourth century and was revived for the fifth after the fall of the Tanūkhids. It may, therefore, be safely assumed that the *foederati* of Byzantium, and not only the predominant group, the Salīḥids, participated in the war and, what is more, took an active part in it and distinguished themselves. A strong Arab federate presence associated with the first Persian War is clearly reflected in the terms of the peace treaty that concluded it, with its clear reference to ὑπόσπονδοι on both sides[42] and in the important role they played in the operations of the war. Sozomen was thinking of this role when he wrote that the Zokomids—the group descended from the baptized Arab chief—proved themselves formidable to the Saracens and to the Persians,[43] since this was the first war that broke out between the two world powers and the most important one during the reign of Theodosius and indeed in the entire fifth century.

---

attested for this period, Vitianus' ducate over either of these two provinces cannot be entirely ruled out; on the *duces* of Osroene, and Euphratensis, see ibid., "Fasti," 1299.

[40] Nöldeke, *PAS*, 92. On p. 94 Ṭabbarī speaks of thirty thousand cavalry at the disposal of Mundir. These figures, too, may not be accurate but they argue that Mundir could muster from the Arab tribes a great number of troops. Northeastern Arabia, where restless and turbulent tribes roamed, was a vast recruiting ground for the Lakhmids. What Dīnawarī says on Mundir is relevant: that Bahram gave him authority over all the Arabs; Dīnawarī, *Al-Akhbār al-Tiwāl*, ed. A ʿĀmir and J. Shayyāl (Cairo, 1960), 69.

[41] Assuming that Ṭabarī is right in associating them with Nuʿmān I; Nöldeke, *PAS*, 83. See Nöldeke's doubts and the possibility that Nuʿmān I is confused with Nuʿmān II, ibid., 83, note 3. See also above, note 10.

[42] See below, Sec. II.C on the terms of the treaty and the reference to the Arab allies.

[43] See above, Chap. 1, sec. I.(3).

With the exception of this solitary reference to the Zokomids/Salīḥids, the sources are silent on them; at least there is no explicit reference to their role in the Persian War. This is not a serious argument against their participation, since these sources are sporadic and unsatisfactory, coming mainly from those historians who were more interested in the *ecclesia* than in the *imperium*.[44] The bits and pieces of evidence for their role can now be reassembled.

1. There are three junctures at which the Salīḥids, the Arab *foederati* of Byzantium, are likely to have participated:

a. The first and obvious one is the campaign of the Lakhmid Mundir against Antioch. The previous section has analyzed this campaign and suggested that of Callinicum in 531 as a parallel. In a campaign in which the Lakhmids were so dominant, it is impossible to believe that they were not opposed by their counterparts, the Salīḥids. In the last section, the miraculous element was discounted and other causes were suggested for the Lakhmids' defeat.[45] It is practically certain that one of these causes must have been the presence of the Salīḥids, Byzantium's Arab allies, who were fighting in terrain familiar to them and employing appropriate desert tactics.[46] They must have soundly trounced the Lakhmids, as the Ghassānids did the famous Mundir in 554 near Chalcis, when they succeeded in killing him.[47] Thus Mundir miscalculated when he counseled Bahram about invading and capturing Antioch. Contrary to what he thought, the city was most probably heavily guarded, if not by regular Roman soldiers, by Arab *foederati* stationed there to protect Syria against such an attack while the *magister militum*, Ardabur, was busy in the north, first fighting in Arzanene and then besieging Nisibis.

b. The Arab allies of Byzantium are likely to have fought in the battle between Aerobindus on the Byzantine side and Ardazanes on the Persian.[48] This belongs to a phase of the war later than the campaign of Mundir, when Theodosius decided to give the patrician Procopius a command independent of that of Ardabur and sent him against Bahram. At the suggestion of Bahram

[44] But see above, note 12 on Priscus of Panium.

[45] It may be mentioned in this connection that B. Croke draws attention to and revives an old view that the Lakhmid disaster on the Euphrates referred to by Socrates is the same incident that Theodoret reports in *HE*, 37, namely, the retardation of the Persian advance through twenty days of hail and rain; Croke, "Dating," 69, note 44.

[46] Thus the φόβος referred to by Socrates as the miraculous element that helped vanquish the Lakhmids can be related to the prowess of the Salīḥids who induced it in their adversaries. It is noteworthy that Sozomen, who extols this prowess, uses the term φοβερόν when he speaks of the Salīḥids. It is equally noteworthy that at the battle of Callinicum (531), the Arab *foederati* of Byzantium, the Ghassānids, were stationed on the right wing, facing the Arab *foederati* of Persia, the Lakhmids, stationed on the left wing; Procopius, *Wars*, I, xviii, 26, 30.

[47] See Nöldeke, *GF*, 18–19.

[48] Malalas, *Chronographia*, ed. Dindorf (Bonn, 1831), 364: Cedrenus, *Historiarum compendium*, ed. I. Bekker (Bonn, 1838–39), 599.

both parties agreed to have the war decided by single combat, and it was decided in favor of Byzantium when its protagonist, the Goth Areobindus,[49] vanquished his adversary, Ardazanes. In the account of this duel occurs the precious phrase *comes foederatorum* as a description of Areobindus, who was in Procopius' army. This immediately suggests the Arab allies of Byzantium who were *foederati*. Although Areobindus' *foederati* may have included others, such as the Goths,[50] it is practically certain that the Arabs formed a major part of the troops fighting under him. They were *foederati* of Oriens par excellence.

c. The last reference to the Arabs in the sources for this war is related to the defeat of the remnants of the Lakhmid host by Vitianus. In Socrates' narrative it comes as one among other operations which took place in a later phase and after the disaster that befell the Lakhmids on the Euphrates. If the Arab *foederati* of Byzantium participated in defeating the Lakhmids so disastrously at the Euphrates, the chances are they also participated in the sequel that involved defeating the survivors. That the Byzantine victory is associated with the name of a Roman general, Vitianus, does not preclude Arab participation, because on the second occasion of their participation the Arabs (as has been argued), fought as *foederati* under another Roman general, Areobindus. There must also have been a second group of *foederati*, different from the one that fought under Areobindus.

Since this Persian War was of short duration and the sources are scanty and not very informative, one cannot easily describe its various phases. But a temporal sequence is clearly indicated in Socrates. The Arabs fought in more than one sector of the Persian front: they first fought near the Euphrates, either in Osroene or Euphratensis, when they contributed to the defeat of the Lakhmid Mund̲ir and also when they fought under Vitianus and completed the annihilation of the Lakhmid survivors. They also fought to the northeast under Areobindus in military operations associated with the Persian siege of Theodosiopolis, recently built for the defense of Roman Armenia.[51] On the first occasion they confronted their counterparts, the Arab allies of Persia, and on the second they fought away from their bases in Oriens, against the Persian imperial army in Armenia presumably led by Bahram himself.

2. The above analysis of the participation and the contribution of the Arab *foederati* of Byzantium in the first Persian War leaves a number of questions unanswered.

[49] On Areobindus see *PLRE*, II, 145–46.

[50] See below, App. 2.

[51] Malalas' account of the *monomachia* between Ardazanes and Areobindus has to be accepted, since it is confirmed in its essential features by Socrates in his account of this first Persian War. What cannot be accepted from Malalas' account is that this phase of the war consisted only of the *monomachia*. Other unacceptable elements in Malalas' account have been perceptively pointed out by Croke in "Dating," 70, note 47.

a. As is clear from a study of the structure of the Arab federate presence in the fourth century, the Arab federates consisted of more than one tribal group. It was argued that even after their fall as the dominant federate group, the Tanūkhids stayed on in the service of Byzantium. So the tribal structure of the federate presence in the fifth century was also complex.[52] As far as this Persian War is concerned, only the Salīḥids (Zokomids) are specifically mentioned in Sozomen. But it has been argued here that a Tanūkhid as well as an Iyādid participation may have taken place.[53]

b. As to the secret of the Byzantine victory over the Lakhmid Arabs, it may be sought partly in the two important features of Arab federate life. The first is their Christianity; the Salīḥids were (like the Tanūkhids before them and the Ghassānids after them) converts to Christianity who were aware of their special relationship to that religion after the conversion of their chief, Zokomos, in the fourth century. They fought the war as crusaders fighting against the fire-worshipers and pagan Arabs. The second feature may be related to their presumed provenance from the Land of the Two Rivers. The Salīḥids according to some of the Arabic sources, came from Mesopotamia themselves, and so of course did the others such as the Tanūkhids and the Iyādids, (if indeed the latter did emigrate in this period).[54] These tribal groups knew the land of their adversaries and still had relatives, connections, and tribal affiliations in that country. All this must have helped in winning the war against the Lakhmid Arabs and their other Arab allies.

c. Finally, the question of federate leadership must arise. In the fourth century the federates were led by their kings and phylarchs. But in this first encounter with the Persians, the sources are silent on their commanders. Who led them in the operation that caused the Lakhmid catastrophe on the Euphrates is not clear; in this case they may have been led by their phylarchs or kings, but the description of the later phase of this operation which makes mention of Vitianus, suggests that they were under his leadership. The reference to Areobindus as *comes foederatorum* is more explicit. It has been argued that the federates involved here were principally Arab. They could easily have been led by Areobindus in much the same way that another Arab federate force was led in 503 by another Areobindus, his grandson.[55] It must have been an indirect command in the sense that the *foederati*, although led by their own chiefs, were ultimately responsible to him.

[52] On the tribal structure of Arab presence in Oriens in the fifth century see below, Chap. 12, sec. IV.

[53] On Tanūkhid participation, see the discussion of the Dawsar regiment, above, note 26; on the Iyādid, see above, note 23 and App. 1.

[54] See below, App. 2, and the section on Iyād in Part III, sec. IV.

[55] On Areobindus and the Arab *foederati*, see below, App. 1. On the Areobindus of the year 503, see Theophanes, *Chronographia*, 146.

C

The peace treaty that concluded this first Persian War has been skillfully reconstructed and perceptively reinterpreted.[56] As mentioned earlier, one of the treaty's clauses stipulated that neither of the two powers should receive the Arab allies of the other when they revolted. Its inclusion is noteworthy and requires further analysis here.

It has been noted that "since Anatolius had so received Aspebetos in 420, this provision was directed against Roman encroachment upon the *status quo* and was a Roman concession."[57] To this true assessment of which of the two powers was the beneficiary of this clause may be added the following observation. The changing of sides involving Persia and Byzantium, as far as their Arab allies was concerned, was in one direction, namely, from Persia to Byzantium. This was true of the period before and after the peace treaty, and was the story of defectors from the days of Imru' al-Qays of the Namāra inscription in the reign of Constantine. Thus the case of Aspebetos was not an isolated one. Persia was the beneficiary of this clause, since no Arab ally of Byzantium desired to leave Roman territory and join the Persians except in extreme cases.[58]

The question arises as to why Persia insisted on the non-acceptance by Byzantium of her own Arab allies. One may argue that this defection was hurting the Persian cause in many ways. It was suggested earlier that the powerful tribal group Iyād migrated or defected at this time and that their new allegiance to Byzantium was one of the causes for the Lakhmid disaster on the Euphrates. The defection of Iyād and other tribal groups would have been injurious to Persian interests because they were well informed about routes leading to Persia and about its military posture; what is more, they had relatives and friends among the Arabs of Persia. None of this would have helped the war effort against Byzantium. When the defector happened to be someone of the stature and influence of Aspebetos, Persian sensitivity becomes even more understandable. As a high-ranking officer in the Persian army, he presumably knew military secrets which Persia would not want him to share with the *magisterium* of the Orient in Byzantium.[59] As to the question of what value rebellious allies were to Persia, it is not clear from the clause whether Byzantium was to return them to the Persians. But there is no doubt that it

[56] See Holum, "Pulcheria's Crusade," 170–71.

[57] Ibid., 170.

[58] As when some of the Lakhmids returned to Persia in the 4th century, for which see *BAFOC*, 214; and as when some of the Ghassānids went over to Persia after the decentralization of the Ghassānid phylarchate in the reign of Maurice; see Nöldeke, *GF*, 31.

[59] On Aspebetos, see below, Sec. IV.

was meant to discourage prospective defectors, who otherwise would have been welcomed with open arms by the secular enemy, Byzantium.

The final question about this clause must be that of enforcement. There is no doubt that because of the special condition that obtained in the fifth century—with both powers wanting peace between them—the clause was observed. Yet there was an apparent violation in the reign of Leo with the defection of the adventurer Amorkesos and his acceptance by Leo,[60] and of course after the outbreak of the war in the reigns of Anastasius and Kawad it ceased to be binding.

In addition to the clause that pertained to the Arab allies of the two empires, there was a clause concerning religious toleration. When the Persians agreed that they would end the persecution of the Christians in their territory, this certainly affected the Arabs in those parts. Christianity had spread quickly among the Arabs of the Land of the Two Rivers, both in the north and in the south. The Magian persecution of the Christians initiated in the reigns of Yazdgard and Bahram must have affected them. The policy of toleration would have relieved them and especially affected Ḥīra, the great center of Christianity among the Arabs and on the Lower Euphrates. As recently as 410 it had become the seat of a bishop.[61] The Lakhmid rulers would not adopt Christianity because of fear of their Sasanid overlords, and one of their kings—Nuʿmān—may have become a wanderer after adopting Christianity because of this.[62] The relaxation of religious animosity toward the Christians in this period must have had some effect on the progress of Christianity among the Arabs and in Ḥīra in the Land of the Two Rivers.

The Second Persian War (440–442)

The second Persian War of the reign was shorter, and the sources for it are scantier than those of the first. The evidence that the Arabs were involved in it comes from Marcellinus, who states that in 441 the Persians, Saracens, Tzani, Isaurians, and Huns attacked Roman territory and laid it waste, but that they were defeated by Anatolius and Aspar, the *magistri militiae*, who concluded peace with the Persians.[63] The role of the Arabs in this war can be

[60] On Amorkesos, see below, Chap. 4, sec. I.3.

[61] On Christianity in Persia, its spread among the Arabs, the rise of Ḥīra as a Christian center, and the Lakhmid policy towards Christianity, see J. Labourt, *Le Christianisme dans l'empire perse sous la dynastie sassanide* (Paris, 1904); Rothstein, *DLH*, 139–43.

[62] On Nuʿmān, who was suspected earlier in this book of mounting the offensive of 410 against Byzantium, see above, Sec. I.3–4.

[63] Comes Marcellinus, MGH, *Chronica Minora*, ed. Th. Mommsen (Berlin, 1894), II, 80. Stein allies the Arab attack to that of the Persians and separates both from those of the Tzani and the Isaurians; and surely he is right, Stein, *HBE*, I, 291.

assessed after determining who these Saracens were that Marcellinus mentions and after discussing other problems related to their identity.

Greek ecclesiastical sources are silent on the role of the Arabs in this war, but some light on the Arab participation comes from a Syriac source, Isaac of Antioch. According to him the Persian Arabs attacked and laid waste the Roman city of Beth Hur in the vicinity of Nisibis.[64] Since this is the only explicit reference in the sources to a Saracen attack in this period and, what is more, to an attack that can be located geographically in the northern sector of the Persian-Byzantine front, it must be taken into account in assessing the Arab role. But it is impossible to believe that the Lakhmids of the southern sector on the Lower Euphrates remained inactive in this war. Although the Persians, like the Byzantines, had Arab allies all along the front, the Lakhmid Arabs in Ḥīra were their allies par excellence, and one of their most important assignments was to participate in the wars against Byzantium. What is more, the Persians often used them, because of their semi-independent position, on such occasions; the Lakhmids could pick a quarrel with the Romans in order to reflect Persian displeasure without the Persians' putting themselves diplomatically in the wrong.[65] In view of the peace treaty that had concluded the first Persian War of twenty years before, it is practically certain that the Lakhmids, too, were employed by the Persians to reflect their displeasure, and that they may have acted either simultaneously or in concert with the group mentioned by Isaac that attacked in the north. Furthermore, it must be remembered that the Lakhmid king whom Socrates described in the first Persian War as πολεμικός was still alive. He must have been still smarting under the defeat inflicted on him and so was probably anxious for a resumption of the war to restore his reputation.[66] All this could lead to the conclusion that the Arabs again may have been at least partially responsible for the outbreak of the second Persian War.[67]

[64] Nöldeke's important contribution to the study of this war gives some precision and definiteness to what is left general and vague in Comes Marcellinus; see his long and learned footnote on this war in *PAS*, 116 note 2. Cf. the Persian Arabs' raid on Roman territory in the same region in 484, which created tension between the two empires; see *Synodicon Orientale*, ed. J. B. Chabot (Paris, 1902), 532.

[65] The strata dispute of the year 539 affords a good parallel; see Procopius, *Wars*, II, i, and also Shahîd, "The Arabs in the Peace Treaty of A.D. 561," *Arabica* 3 (1956), 181–213.

[66] He reigned from 418 to 462. The other loser, Mihr-Narseh, who commanded the imperial Persian army, may also have been anxious to retrieve his military reputation, tarnished in the first Persian War.

[67] The Arab clients of Persia were aggressive, constituted an element of instability in the region, and created tensions between the two empires. On the other hand, the new Persian king, Yazdgard II (438–457), may have been anxious to project the image of a warrior-king at the beginning of his reign, after the death of his father, Bahram. Although the peace treaty was to last for a hundred years, it may technically have been dissolved on the death of Bahram and had to be renewed.

As the war was of very short duration,[68] the Arab participation was also short. This perhaps explains why the Syriac source gives prominence to the non-Lakhmid participation in the north. The boundaries of the two empires were contiguous there, and while it would have taken the Lakhmids some time to arrive from the Lower Euphrates in the south, it was easy for those Arab allies of Persia in the north to make a sally against Roman territory, as apparently they did.

Even less is known about the clauses of the peace treaty that concluded this Persian War than the earlier one. That the Arabs were also involved is practically certain, since it has been plausibly assumed that *inter alia* the clauses confirmed those of the previous treaty.[69] Specifically, the clause calling on each of the two parties not to accept the rebellious Saracen allies of the other must have been reaffirmed. This reaffirmation may even be implied in Malchus' fragment on Imru' al-Qays, who seceded from his alliance with Persia and defected to the Romans in the reign of Leo. If the stipulating clause had been in abeyance since 440–441, Malchus would not have referred to it as a violation during the reign of Leo (457–474).

According to Malalas, Emperor Theodosius divided the province of Syria into Prima and Secunda, and it is tempting to think that it was partly owing to the danger which the Lakhmid Arab raids had posed to that province in their attempt to capture Antioch in the first Persian War.[70]

III. The Invasion of 447

One of the fragments that have survived from the history of Priscus,[71] describes the plight of the Romans in their negotiations with Attila. The year is 447, that is, after the Huns appeared south of the Danube and before the treaty of 448. Priscus enumerates the peoples who were either taking up arms or threatening the empire. In addition to the Vandals, Isaurians, and Ethiopians, there is mention of the Arabs and a guarded reference to the Persians. The first are described as "ravaging the Eastern parts of their dominions," while the Persians, referred to as Parthians, are described as "preparing for hostilities."

[68] Apparently it was again the Hunnic threat to the Persians that made the latter desire to seal the Byzantine front and attend to the Hunnic peril: see Bury, *HLRE,* II, 6.

[69] Ibid.

[70] Cf. the creation of Palaestina Secunda and Phoenicia Libanensis in the reign of Theodosius I, possibly related to the Mavian revolt of the 4th century; see *BAFOC*, 215; also the division of the Thebaid by Theodosius II into Inferior and Superior for the better protection of the province against the attacks of the Blemmyes and the Nobadae; see Stein, *HBE*, I, 291. On the division of Syria into Prima and Secunda by Theodosius II, see Malalas, *Chronographia*, 365.

[71] Fragment no. 10, Blockley's edition; see R. C. Blockley, *CH*, II, 242.

The phrase that describes the Persians is carefully worded. Yazdgard II (438–457) had abided by the treaty of 442 and transferred his seat from Ctesiphon to Nishāpūr in northeastern Iran in order to prosecute better the war against his own Huns, the Hephthalite Huns.[72] Priscus may have had this in mind, namely, that the Persians were in a state of preparation for war against the Huns. But there may have been some friction with Byzantium concerning the annual subsidies which Byzantium may have been lax in paying, owing to the exorbitant demands of Attila for Byzantine gold, which caused a great drain on the imperial treasury.

As the Persians are mentioned in the same passage that refers to the Saracen raids into Byzantine territory, it is not impossible that these were conducted by the Lakhmid Arabs of Persia, who were still ruled by the man described by Socrates as γενναῖος καὶ πολεμικός, Mundir I (418–462), who had been defeated in 421 and recently cheated of retrieving his reputation by the quick conclusion of the peace of 442. Mundir could have taken advantage of the preoccupation of his overlord in central Asia and of Byzantium with Attila to invade the Roman frontier. But without the reference to the Persians, one would be inclined to think of Arab groups other than the Lakhmids, probably the Kindites, whose adventurous king Ḥujr was active in North Arabia toward the middle of the fifth century.[73] The lack of geographical precision as to which sector of the imperial frontier felt these Arab raids makes the task of identifying the raiders rather difficult.[74]

IV. The Phylarchs of the Parembole: Aspebetos–Terebon

Closely related to the outbreak of the first Persian War and its causes is the curious and fascinating episode of Aspebetos and his house. He had originally been in the service of Persia, but changed allegiance after the persecution of the Christians there in 420. The *magister militum per Orientem*, Anatolius, received him well and endowed him with the phylarchate of the province of Arabia. The fame of St. Euthymius in the Jordan Valley attracted Aspebetos' attention, and the saint succeeded in curing his son, Terebon. As a result he and his followers were baptized. At a later date he was deemed worthy of the episcopate and was consecrated by Juvenal of Jerusalem around 427. Aspebetos started a line of phylarchs, who are attested as late as the middle of the sixth century in Palestine.

[72] Who exactly these adversaries in Central Asia were is not entirely clear; but probably the Hephthalites; see the *Cambridge History of Iran*, ed. E. Yarshater (Cambridge, 1983), 3.1, p. 146.

[73] The Ghassānids cannot be excluded altogether.

[74] On Priscus' vague topography and geography, see Blockley, *CH*, I, p. 69.

The fortunes of the house of Aspebetos have been largely in the hands of ecclesiastical historians,[75] who have limited themselves to piecing together into consecutive narrative the various references to it scattered in the work of the hagiographer Cyril of Scythopolis, the only source for its history.[76] But the importance of the house of Aspebetos, which might also be termed the Phylarchs of the Parembole, is also part of the larger theme, Byzantium and the Arabs. The secular aspect of the history has not been seriously studied except very recently, in spite of the light it throws on important aspects of this theme,[77] and it is time that the history of these phylarchs is related to the larger theme of the "Phylarchate of Oriens." It is therefore to Aspebetos as a Roman phylarch rather than as a Christian bishop that this section is devoted.[78]

1. Most writers on these phylarchs have accepted the Arab origin of Aspebetos and that of his descendants and successors.[79] But two scholars, Nöldeke,[80] a specialist on the history of the Arabs before the rise of Islam, and Christensen,[81] a specialist on Sasanid Persia, expressed doubts based on the description of the first of these phylarchs as Aspebetos. Nöldeke thought he was not an Arab, presumably because the high Persian title of Sipahbādh was applied only to the Persians. Christensen added that he might also have been a member of the Iranian family of Aspahbadh. These views cannot be accepted for the following reasons:

a. The account in Cyril points to him as the chief of a Saracen group in Persia, and this clearly indicates that he was an Arab.[82] His association with

[75] R. Génier, *Vie de Saint Euthyme le Grand* (Paris, 1909), passim, especially the chapter devoted exclusively to the Parembole, pp. 94–117. This work contains the most extensive treatment of Aspebetos from the point of view of ecclesiastical history and its more enduring portions are those written by Father Féderlin, summing up the results of his inspection and excavation of the site associated with Aspebetos; see pp. 104–11. Génier has unfortunately depended on de Percival for Arab history, and wrote before Schwartz's edition of Cyril appeared. R. Aigrain, "Arabie," *DHGE* 3, col. 1193–96; H. Charles, *La christianisme*, 40–49. Charles unfairly accuses Génier of writing *con amore*, and speaks of Aspebetos as Génier's "hero" (p. 42). Génier may have written *con amore*, but he also wrote *sine studio*.

[76] See *Kyrillos von Skythopolis*, ed. E. Schwartz (Leipzig, 1939) (hereafter *Kyrillos*), passim.

[77] The first to subject their secular history to a serious treatment and raise the pertinent questions was Sartre in *TE*, 149–53. His chapter concentrates on the fortunes of Aspebetos and Terebon within the framework of the history of the Provincia Arabia. Françoise Thelamon subjected the history of Aspebetos to a treatment from the point of view of ecclesiastical history, in *Païens et chrétiens au IV siècle*, Études augustiniennes (Paris, 1981), 139–40.

[78] For the history of Aspebetos and his house of bishops, see below, Chap. 10, sec. I.

[79] See for instance Aigrain, "Arabie," col. 1193.

[80] See *GF*, 12 note 1.

[81] See *L'Iran*, 280 note 3. On Aspahbadh, the Persian family, and Aspahbadh, the title, see the index to this work, pp. 530 and 550 respectively.

[82] He is referred to as phylarch, a distinctively Arabic title, and was later put in command of the Arabs in the province of Arabia; see *Kyrillos*, p. 18, line 25, p. 19, lines 8–9.

the Saracens continues throughout the account, when he changes allegiance. The term "phylarch"[83] applied to him while he was in Persia, and in association with "Saracens" when he came over to the Romans, points in the same direction. This can only be an Arab in charge of an Arab group. Furthermore, the name of his son, Terebon, obscured in its Greek form and presenting some difficulty, can only be an Arab name,[84] and he, too, is described as a Saracen. Aspebetos' defection to the Romans is far from being an isolated episode in the history of Sasanid-Byzantine relations, and can be paralleled many times before and after him with instances of Arab chiefs changing their allegiance from the Sasanids to the Byzantines.[85]

b. Although it is rather startling to find the title Sipahbādh applied to an Arab chief, it is not impossible that this is one of those rare cases when it was applied. This is all the more probable since in this century the Arab clients of Persia assumed an important role in the history of the Sasanid Empire, and examples are not lacking for the application of many high Persian titles to Arab military figures.[86] On the other hand, the title may have applied loosely to this Arab chief as a nickname, possibly by his followers, to indicate both his high military rank and his Persian connection.

2. Aspebetos' title, far from being an argument against his Arab origin, may even solve the problem of his tribal affiliation. The Arab king of Ḥīra, the client of the Great King, was in control of all the Arab groups allied to Persia, as Procopius testifies in the sixth century,[87] and the Lakhmid was a centralized phylarchate and kingdom. One of the most powerful tribal groups under the Lakhmids were the Tamīm,[88] who were their *ardāf*,[89] and it is

[83] Although a Byzantine administrative dimension was imparted to it, it continued to signify an Arab chief in charge of Saracens.

[84] On this name and its possible Arabic forms, see Nöldeke, *GF*, 12 note 1. The name could also be related to the root, *t-r-b*.

[85] Such as the Imru' al-Qays of the reign of Constantine and Amorkesos of the reign of Leo.

[86] Ammianus Marcellinus, *RG*, XXIV, ii, 4: "et Malechus Podosacis nomine, phylarchus Saracenorum Assanitarum"; "Podosacis," which has exercized the ingenuity of commentators, could be the Persian title *bidakhsh* in its Latinized form; see *BAFOC*, 119–23. The quotation is relevant also because, like Aspebetos, this Arab chief is called phylarchus in addition to his Persian title; for *bidakhsh*, see Christensen, *L'Iran*, 22, 102, 137; the Lakhmid king Mundir I of the 5th century is said to have been honored with the titles Ramavzudh-Yazdgard and Mahisht, while Nuʿmān is also said to have been called *qāʾid al-furs*, "the leader of the Persians" obviously a military title, which may be the Arabic translation of Sipahbādh; see Rothstein *DLH*, 67–69; Christensen, op.cit., 274.

[87] See Procopius, *Wars*, I, xvii, 45. Also Ṭabarī states that the Persian king made Nuʿmān, the Lakhmid contemporary of Aspebetos, king of the Arabs, Nöldeke, *PAS*, 86.

[88] For Tamīm, and its Ḥīran Lakhmid connections, see J. S. Trimingham, *Christianity among the Arabs in Pre-Islamic Times* (1979), 278, and the fundamental article of M. J. Kister "al-Ḥīra," in *Studies in Jāhiliyya and Early Islam* (London, 1980), 149 ff.

[89] For this office among the Lakhmids, see Rothstein, *DLH*, 133. It was the equivalent of *wazīr*, minister. Also Kister, *Studies*, 149.

quite possible that this Aspebetos was a Tamīmī. This may be supported by the fact that this particular tribe was one of the few that was influenced by Zoroastrianism (*majūsiyya*), as the Arabic sources testify,[90] and, more important, many of its members had the title Sipahbādh, transliterated al-Ṣabahbad or al-Asbaḏiyyūn, although the correct etymology of the term was lost on some classical Arab authors.[91]

3. The Byzantine officer who received Aspebetos, Anatolius, has been the subject of a controversy. It has been maintained that there is confusion in the sources between the first Persian War and the second; that Anatolius, a well-known figure in Oriens, could not have been the officer who received Aspebetos because his administrative and military *floruit* belongs to the fourth and fifth decades of the century.[92]

The identity of the officer who received Aspebetos cannot affect the facts about the latter's career and chronology after he defected. There is no doubt that he went to the Romans just before the outbreak of the first Persian War, since his career in the twenties and his participation in the Council of Ephesus in 431 point to this. Arguments have been advanced recently, however, supporting the essential accuracy of the narrative of Cyril of Scythopolis, namely, that the Roman officer who negotiated the settlement with Aspebetos was Anatolius[93] and that he was indeed *magister militum per Orientem*, exactly as the hagiographer says.[94]

[90] See Ibn Ḥazm, *Jamharat Ansāb al-ʿArab*, ed. ʿA. Hārūn (Cairo, 1962), 491. Also, some association with the religion of the Magians is clearly expressed in Terebon's speech before St. Euthymius when he came to him to be healed; for which see *Kyrillos*, p. 19.

[91] See Yāqūt, *Muʿjam al-Buldān* (Beirut, 1956) I, s.v. "Asbaḏ". The term appears in the *Dīwān* of the Umayyad Tamīmī poet, Jarīr, as Ṣabahbad, and he clearly understood the term. It is also noteworthy in this context of the Persian connection of Tamīm that some members of the tribe had resoundingly Persian names such as Bisṭām and Zibriqān (Zabergan).

The Arabic form "al-Ṣabahbad" could also argue that "Aspebetos" is an Arabicized form of Spahbad. The *alpha* which appears initially in "Aspebetos" suggests this. That the title in Persian does not have it can be accounted for by assuming it is the *aliph* of the definite article in Arabic prefixed to the Persian title; so it appears in Arabic with the definite article, al-Ṣabahbad.

If Aspebetos and his group turn out to be Tamīmī Arabs, this means that the phylarchs of the Parembole introduced into the tribal structure of the phylarchate of the Orient a new element different from those already there or those who were to join later in the 6th century. It is a group that is related to Muḍar, one of the two main branches of the north Arabs subsumed under ʿAdnan; see *EI*, s.v.

[92] See *PLRE*, II, s.vv. Anatolius (p. 85) and Aspebetos (p. 169).

[93] See Holum, "Pulcheria's Crusade," 169 note 66.

[94] See Croke, "Dating," 68 note 38, and 70 note 45, where he argues crisply that Anatolius apparently succeeded Maximinus as *magister militum per Orientem* after the latter had been killed in some insurrection in 420. Some support for the view that a *magister militum* was involved may come from the fact that Aspebetos was put in charge of all the Saracens in Arabia, an extraordinary measure which suggests that the one who recommended it was a high-ranking officer in Oriens such as the *magister militum*. M. Sartre, too, accepts the fact that it was Anatolius as *magister militum* who dealt with Aspebetos; see *TE*, 149.

Whether or not the Roman official who received Aspebetos was the *dux* of Arabia or Anatolius, the *magister militum per Orientem* is relatively unimportant. But the arrangements that he made for Aspebetos and the light these throw on the Phylarchate of Oriens are significant.[95]

a. The first question that arises is why Aspebetos was installed as phylarch in the Provincia Arabia.[96] One would have thought a province closer to the Persian frontier whence he had come would have been more natural, such as Euphratensis or Syria or Phoenicia Libanensis. Perhaps in his flight from Persia, Aspebetos took the route that finally brought him to Dūmat at the southern entrance of Wādī Sirḥān, through which he would have arrived in Azraq in the Provincia Arabia, where he was naturally installed. This is where Imru' al-Qays of the Namāra inscription, also a fugitive from Persia, was installed in the fourth century. Even further to the south, in Palaestina Tertia, another fugitive, Amorkesos, was installed in the reign of Leo.[97]

b. What induced the Byzantine official to endow a fugitive with the phylarchate of Arabia and, what is more, a phylarchate that put him in charge of Arabs that belonged to tribal groups other than his own? Surely this was an extraordinary arrangement. The only explanation must be the personality and background of the incumbent. His title, Aspebetos, and its significance were not lost on the Byzantine official, who must have appreciated its value in the event of a war with Persia. Perhaps even more important must have been his personality. There is no explicit statement in the sources on this aspect of the problem, but it is easily inferable from the speed with which his promotion in the new setting was effected. It must have been his impressive personality that induced St. Euthymius to recommend him for the episcopate and Juvenal of Jerusalem to take him to the Council of Ephesus, where he distinguished himself even more by being one of the party that negotiated with Nestorius.[98] These are the three personalities whom Aspebetos did not fail to impress —Anatolius, Euthymius, and Juvenal—and it is impossible to believe that all of them were fooled by him, the three being so different from one another: a *magister*, a saint, and a bishop.

c. Aspebetos was put in charge of the Saracen allies of Byzantium in the Provincia, and these belonged to tribal groups other than his own. They could have been *all*[99] the Arab allies in the Provincia. This was an extraordinary arrangement, since these Arab allies were usually commanded by their own

[95] Some of the following points have been raised very perceptively by M. Sartre: see ibid., 150.

[96] As Sartre has indicated, this could only be the Provincia and not the Peninsula; ibid.

[97] See Chapter 4 on the reign of Leo.

[98] On this, see below, Chap. 10, sec. I.A, and Chap. 11, sec. I.A.

[99] As Sartre (*TE*, 150), has argued. See also his important historical commentary on the significance of this (ibid.). Whether Aspebetos' phylarchate was the first instance or the first

phylarchs. Surely the Byzantine authorities recognized the outstanding personality of Aspebetos, which could give cohesion and leadership to the Arab allies in the Provincia: and since the phylarchate was a Byzantine administrative function, the authorities could appoint him to that office. As to his acceptance by the tribal groups themselves, it is easy to see that his fame and prestige among the Arabs would have induced them to do so, especially with official support. His fame as a warrior must have reached the Arabs in Oriens. And if Aspebetos turns out to be not a Tamīmī but a Lakhmid king, his phylarchate over the Arab allies in Arabia would be even more intelligible, because the Provincia had many Lakhmid Arabs among the *foederati* since the days of Imru' al-Qays, the Lakhmid king who defected to Byzantium in the reign of Constantine and was installed in the same province.[100]

d. A major question arises regarding the Arab allies over whom Aspebetos was made phylarch. The Salīḥids were the dominant federate group in Oriens in the fifth century,[101] and it is doubtful that Aspebetos' phylarchate would have encompassed them. So the presumption is that he would have been in charge of groups in the Provincia other than the Salīḥids. While Aspebetos remained phylarch of Arabia the symbiosis with other tribal groups apparently worked. After his death there occurred an episode in which his son Terebon, while making the trip from Palestine, where he was phylarch, to Arabia, was, through the intrigues of a fellow phylarch, put in jail in Bostra. This might argue that the phylarchate of Aspebetos over these tribes was resented and led to some friction and tension, which found expression after his death in this intrigue involving Terebon, now the phylarch of Palestine.[102]

e. The last aspect of Aspebetos' connection with the Byzantine official who received him is that the former was "Romanized" before he was Christianized. His baptism came later when his son was cured by St. Euthymius. His Christianization is thus an instance of the pattern of conversion prevalent in this period; it follows the exercise of the miraculous power of healing on the part of a Christian monk or saint.[103] What is relevant here is the light this throws on important aspects of the extraordinary career of Aspebetos.

---

recorded instance of the installation of an Arab phylarch over tribal groups not his own remains to be shown. I am also inclined to think that Zokomos, in Sozomen, became a phylarch in the new sense of the term—as an administrative Roman title—but that the ecclesiastical writer did not know the fact or care to expatiate on it. In the case of the Arethas the Ghassānid, his phylarchate was much more comprehensive and encompassing, since it went beyond the frontiers of the Provincia Arabia; it was diocesan and not only provincial.

[100] See *BAFOC*, 31–53.

[101] On this see below, Chap. 12, sec. II.

[102] See below, Chap. 4, app. 2.

[103] Cf. the conversion of Zokomos after the Christian hermit cured his wife of her sterility; above, Chap. 1, sec. I.

That Aspebetos was accepted within the Roman system and honored with the phylarchate of an important province without first converting to the religion of the Christian Roman Empire is unusual in this period, when conversion before permission to settle in Roman territory was practically the norm. That it did happen in the case of Aspebetos points only in one direction—that he presented to the Roman authorities such a rare catch that it was unnecessary to insist on conversion. This transaction also throws light on his personality. He had defected from Persia, where he was held in high esteem, for purely altruistic reasons, namely, his outrage at the sufferings of the Christians, of whom he was not one. This implies that the Arab chief was endowed with a sense of justice and compassion. These are the personality traits that can be recovered with confidence from an examination of his background while still in Persia. They illuminate somewhat the personality of this extraordinary Arab chief, left opaque in the sources. These traits make intelligible his rapid promotion to bishop and active participation in the Council of Ephesus as a champion of Orthodoxy. Perhaps they also explain why the Roman official did not find it necessary to insist on conversion before endowing him with the phylarchate. He knew that one possessed of such qualities would soon come to the fold without coercion or persuasion, as in fact he did.

4. Aspebetos became the phylarch of the Provincia Arabia and held this position for some time. His extraordinary career after his conversion presents many problems:

a. Deeply moved by the miraculous healing of his son by St. Euthymius in Palaestina Prima, Aspebetos was converted, adopted the name Petrus,[104] and became a zealous missionary who brought pagan Saracens from Arabia, as well as his own, across the Jordan to be baptized by the saint. This is valuable evidence for the contribution of the phylarchs of Oriens toward the process of Christianization and Byzantinization among their own people, assumed or implied in the case of other phylarchs but stated explicitly in the case of Aspebetos.[105] It is also possible to see in the process of bringing his Saracens to Palestine and of finally settling there an attempt on the part of Aspebetos to avoid friction with Saracen groups not affiliated with him tribally but over which he was made phylarch by the Roman administration. This view might find confirmation in the quarrel of Terebon[106] with his fellow phylarch in Arabia around 460.

[104] It is tempting to think that his Arabic name or one of them was Ṣakhr or Jandala, of which Petrus is a translation.

[105] The implication is that there were still Saracens in the 5th century within the boundaries of the Christian Roman Empire who had not been converted. Such pagan pockets survived even in the 6th century and in the Byzantine heartland, Anatolia, and it was left to John of Ephesus to convert them.

[106] On Terebon and his imprisonment in Bostra, see below, Chap. 4, app. 2.

b. A few years after Aspebetos' conversion,[107] St. Euthymius decided to make a bishopric of the little Saracen colony in the Jordan Valley. Euthymius brought Aspebetos to the attention of Juvenal of Jerusalem, who consecrated him the first bishop of the Parembole in Palestine.[108] This consecration poses a relevant question, which has been raised by Françoise Thelamon, namely, whether the consecration was inspired by Aspebetos himself in an attempt to maintain his religious as well as political authority over the Saracens of the Parembole.[109] This is possible. On the other hand, it is more likely that the consecration was simply the expression of Euthymius' confidence in this extraordinary Saracen, whose personality impressed him and the bishop of the Holy City, both of whom thought that the genuinely pious phylarch had in him also the making of a bishop and, what is more, that he would be able to shepherd the ecclesiastical fortunes of his flock smoothly and efficiently since he was their respected chief and also spoke their language. The consecration simply reflected sound ecclesiastical administration and was quite unlike that of Moses during Queen Mavia's reign in the fourth century when doctrinal matters were in question.[110] The subsequent career of Aspebetos and his active participation in the Council of Ephesus, only four years after his consecration, could support this view.

c. Finally, there is the question of Aspebetos' provincial jurisdiction after his consecration as bishop of the Parembole in Palestine around 427. He was then also the phylarch of Arabia, but did he continue as such, and if so, how long? According to one view, his son Terebon succeeded him as the phylarch of Arabia as soon as Aspebetos became bishop; the trip of the son to Bostra around 459–460, during which he was put in jail by the governor of Arabia, could give this some support.[111] This is possible, but it is more likely that the family of Aspebetos ceased to be associated with Arabia after his consecration, and instead became associated with Palestine. Terebon is attested as phylarch, but he died late in the century.[112] It is difficult to believe that he would have served as phylarch since 427. He was still a small child ca. 420 when St. Euthymius cured him, and it is doubtful whether he was ready to assume the phylarchate only seven years later.[113] The chances are that As-

[107] In 427 according to Aigrain, "Arabie," col. 1194.

[108] Undoubtedly Palaestina Prima, and not Secunda as Le Quien had thought; ibid.

[109] See *Païens et chrétiens*, 140.

[110] On Moses, see *BAFOC*, 152–58.

[111] Sartre, *TE*, 151.

[112] In 483, when he was succeeded by his son, Petrus II, see Aigrain, "Arabie," col. 1195.

[113] Aigrain thinks he probably succeeded his father immediately as phylarch after the latter was consecrated bishop in 427; but it is not clear whether he has in mind the phylarchate of Arabia or the Parembole; ibid. Further on in the same column (1195) he seems to suggest that he was the phylarch of Palestine.

pebetos continued to exercise his functions as both bishop and phylarch for some time after his consecration. The Saracen community that settled near Jericho in the Jordan Valley was very small, and it became mostly a peaceful Christian community rather than a group of warrior Arabs. Aspebetos, the bishop of the Parembole and the former phylarch of Arabia, could easily have continued to administer both their secular and ecclesiastical affairs.[114] As long as the extraordinary Aspebetos was alive he could combine the two functions, but on his death Terebon assumed the phylarchate of the Parembole, while a bishop named Auxolaus assumed the episcopate.[115]

The year of Aspebetos' death is not known, but as he did not participate in the second Council of Ephesus in 449 the presumption is that he was dead by then. He must have died sometime in the period between the first and second Councils of Ephesus, possibly in the forties when Terebon and Auxelaus succeeded him in his two offices.

5. It has been argued that the association of the house of Aspebetos with the province of Arabia came to an end with the consecration of Aspebetos as bishop of the Parembole in 427 and that Terebon I, his son, became the first phylarch of the Parembole, in Palaestina Prima, possibly sometime in the forties. In support of this, two observations may be adduced:

a. The episode related by Cyril of Scythopolis gives a clue. The hagiographer relates that Terebon (ca. 459–460) went to Bostra driven by a certain necessity and that the intrigues of a fellow-phylarch landed him in jail there.[116] Perhaps the more natural interpretation of this passage is that Terebon was the phylarch of the Parembole in Palaestina Prima and only necessity—ἀνάγκη—drove him to cross provincial boundaries to Arabia. Thus the use of the term ἀνάγκη[117] in the passage supports the view that he was not the phylarch of Arabia, as does the treatment he suffered there, which suggests that he was not in his own province.

b. Something has been said above about Terebon's age when his father was consecrated bishop around 427. It is quite unlikely that one so young would have been put in charge of an important assignment such as the command of the Arab federates in the Provincia *Arabia* especially as these belonged to groups other than his own. It was only the extraordinary personality of Aspebetos that induced the Byzantine authorities to adopt such an unusual

[114] On becoming ecclesiastics, Byzantine administrators naturally relinquished their secular duties as Ephraim, the *Comes Orientis* of the reign of Justinian, did when he became Patriarch of Antioch. But in the case of Aspebetos this could have happened in view of the diminutive ecclesiastical jurisdiction of the Parembole in Palaestina Prima.

[115] On Auxolaus, see below, Chap. 11, sec. I.A.

[116] See *Kyrillos*, 52, lines 19–25. Sartre has quite rightly dated this episode to the reign of Leo, around 459–460.

[117] Ibid., line 20.

measure, and still the arrangement does not seem to have worked smoothly. In fact, it is possible to interpret the transference of the community from Arabia to the Jordan Valley as a reflection of the difficulties that Aspebetos was encountering in that province, while the intrigues of the symphylarch[118] which landed Terebon in jail seem also to be a reflection of resentment on the part of Arab groups who were subjected to the control of a leader not their own.[119]

V. *Novella* XXIV

In 443 Theodosius and Valentinian addressed to Nomus, *magister officiorum*, a *novella*[120] entitled: *De ambitu et locis limitaneis inibi redhibendis*. It deals with the military administration of the imperial frontiers and their upkeep. It utters warnings against illegal solicitation and strongly enjoins fairness to the *limitanei* and *foederati* in matters pertaining to the *annona*.

In the second paragraph of this novel, the limital *duces* are instructed not to extort or embezzle anything from the subsistence allowance of the Saracen *foederati* or those of other *gentes*: "De Saracenorum vero foederatorum aliarumque gentium annonariis alimentis nullam penitus eos decerpendi aliquid vel auferendi licentiam habere concedimus."[121]

1. The Saracens are singled out for special attention by the limital *duces*. Since ducal malpractice seems to have been general and prevalent along all the various *limites* and with respect to other *gentes*, there must have been a reason for this explicit reference to the Saracen *foederati*. This can only have been their place in keeping the peace along the *limes orientalis*[122] via-à-vis both the Arabian Peninsula and the Persian Empire. Their role in the two Persian Wars of the reign of Theodosius makes this reference intelligible. In a sense it is almost a commentary on their military performance, an acknowledgment by the central government of the importance of keeping them satisfied[123] and thus efficient and alert to their duties, especially in view of the delicate inter-

[118] The hagiographer might have solved many an important problem for Byzantinoarabica in the 5th century if he had given the name of his phylarch, just as Sozomen did when he recorded the conversion of Zokomos.

[119] Even the redoubtable Arethas, the Ghassānid, encountered difficulties in leading tribal groups other than his own in the 6th century as will be discussed in *BASIC*.

[120] See *Theodosiani libri XVI cum constitutionibus Sirmondianis et leges novellae ad Theodosianum pertinentes*, ed. Th. Mommsen and P. M. Meyer (Berlin, 1954), 61–64.

[121] Ibid., 62, lines 13–16.

[122] The term "limes orientalis" appears in the genitive form in paragraph 5 of this *novella*, ibid., 63, line 20, and is distinguished from that of Pontus and of Egypt.

[123] The warning expressed in this *novella* against such malpractice was apparently forgotten in the 7th century just before the Muslim Arab invasion of Palestine; see Theophanes, *Chronographia*, 335–36.

national situation involving the Germans in the West and, even more so, the Huns in the Balkans.[124]

2. Who are these Saracen *foederati* mentioned in the novel? It has been argued in the preceding section that this unique reference to them argues for their importance as *foederati*, and since they were stationed along the *limes orientalis* facing Persia they must have been *foederati* that distinguished themselves in the Persian Wars. In view of what Sozomen says on the effectiveness of the Zokomids/Salīḥids against the Persians in the wars, the Saracens referred to in the novel were almost certainly the Salīḥids. The paucity of references to them makes this mention welcome. It documents their federate presence and their place in Byzantium's scheme of things after a long silence in the sources; the explicit reference to them in the pages of Sozomen, relating to the inception of their supremacy, may be dated almost a half century before.

3. In addition to informing us on the importance of the Arab *foederati* of Byzantium in the fifth century and on their presence toward mid-century along the *limes orientalis*, this reference documents three important facts about these Arab allies of Byzantium: (*a*) they were indeed technically called *foederati*; (*b*) they did receive the *annona*; and (*c*) judging from the use of the term *gens* for them and other *foederati*,[125] it is practically certain that they were still non-citizens and were not considered *Rhōmaioi*.

Appendix I

Areobindus: *Comes Foederatorum*

The most important passage concerning Arab participation in Byzantium's war against Persia in 421 is in Malalas. The chronographer gives an account of the duel betweeen the Persian Ardazanes and the Byzantine general Areobindus whom Malalas describes as κόμητα φοιδεράτων.[1] There is no doubt that the account rests on historical facts, since Socrates, a contemporary historian, briefly mentions the exploit of Areobindus.[2] Malalas supplies the details of the combat that Socrates knew but would not digress on, and there is no reason to doubt the historicity of the details. He obviously used a source that is not extant. What one may reject is that Bahram decided there was no need for the two armies to engage each other and that combat between two individuals, representing the two empires, would suffice to determine

[124] It was in this fifth decade of the century that Attila was ravaging the Balkans and it was in the same year as this novel was issued that Anatolius negotiated for Byzantium the humiliating peace with Attila.

[125] See *Novella* XXIV (above, note 120), p. 62, line 23.

[1] Malalas, *Chronographia*, 364 and also Cedrenus, *Historiarum Compendium* (Bonn), 599. Only the first volume of *The Chronicle of John Malalas* has so far appeared, a translation by E. Jeffreys, M. Jeffreys, and Roger Scott, Byzantina Australiensia 4 (Melbourne, 1986).

[2] Socrates, *HE*, 771, lines 5–7.

the issue of the war. This is quite incredible and, furthermore, is not vouched for by Socrates, who speaks of other military operations and sets the combat within this general context.

The phrase that Malalas uses to describe Areobindus is extremely important for the history of the Arab allies of Byzantium in the fifth century, but is riddled with difficulties concerning the two terms *comes* and *foederati*. These must be disposed of before the phrase can contribute to a better understanding of Arab federate history.[3]

A

The more important of the two terms here is the second, φοιδερᾶτοι. It poses two problems: (*a*) in what sense is the term used in Malalas? and (*b*) what ethnic group or groups did these φοιδερᾶτοι represent?

(*a*) In the sixth century the term came to be used in the sense of regular troops serving in τάγματα, regiments in which they were enrolled. But Areobindus commanded in 421, when the term still meant what it had in the fourth century—barbarian troops and *foederati* of Byzantium.[4] In its clearest acceptation the term belongs to the reign of Justinian, and its earlier association with Vitalianus and his father Patriciolus in the reign of Anastasius is still controversial.[5] Malalas must have used it in the old sense it had in the fourth and fifth centuries.

(*b*) If the φοιδερᾶτοι of Malalas designated the earlier fifth-century *foederati*, which ethnic group did they belong to? In spite of his Gothic origin, Areobindus was a Roman officer who became *magister militum* and consul, and so his ethnic origin does not necessarily argue that he was commanding his own people. What is involved is a military group in Oriens who were the *foederati* of Byzantium, and the question becomes simply the determination of which ethnic groups they consisted of.

An ethnic group of this description operating in Oriens, and against the Persians, was almost certainly Arab. This was the principal ethnic group among the so-called barbarians in Oriens; they were native to the area and had been in the service of Byzantium since the reign of Constantine early in the fourth century. One of their most important assignments was participation in the campaign of the Byzantine army of Oriens against the Persians. Sozomen clearly states how formidable they were to the Persians, and their role in the first Persian War has been examined and elucidated. Consequently, when a reference to the *foederati* appears in the sources associating them with war against the Persians, it is natural to assume that they were Arab. Indeed the Arabs would have been conspicuous by their absence if they had *not* been included in this term used by Malalas. The examination of the course of the first Persian War even suggests that after the victory scored against the Lakhmid Arabs on the Euph-

[3] This phrase has never been analyzed, in spite of its crucial relevance to the whole problem of the new meaning that the term *foederati* acquired in the 6th century and the fact that military historians have much to say on it. It was only noted in passing by Grosse, *RM*, 280 note 2 and by Jones *LRE*, 665.

[4] For a discussion of the *foederati* in this 6th-century sense, see Grosse, *RM*, 280–83; and more recently, Jones, *LRE*, 663–65.

[5] On Vitalianus and his father Patriciolus, see *PLRE*, II, s.vv.

rates, the emperor or the *magisterium* of Oriens decided to use the Arab *foederati* again for a possible repeat of their performance and dispatched them to fight in Mesopotamia and Armenia, in the engagements that centered around Theodosiopolis.[6]

The *foederati* in Malalas, then, were most probably Arab. It cannot be ruled out that there were other ethnic strains in the composition of this group, but if there were, they could not have been prominent. Since Areobindus was a Goth, it might be thought that he also commanded some of his own people. This is possible, but the Gothic element in Oriens in this period was certainly not strong, as the course of Roman-Gothic relations can easily demonstrate. (i) It is known from Ammianus that after the battle of Adrianople Julius, *magister militiae trans Taurum*, massacred the Goths of Asia. This is especially important for examining this passage in Malalas, since it deals with operations in a neighboring region, Armenia; Asia was rid of its Goths.[7] (ii) Theodosius initiated a pro-German policy, but his son Arcadius reversed it. Theodosius had settled some Goths as *coloni* in Phrygia, and they contributed a squadron of cavalry to the Roman army. The Goths in Phrygia revolted under Tribigildus, who finally took them to Lampsacus and thence crossed to Thrace, after which he died.[8] The Goths of Gaïnas in the capital, as is well known, were massacred by the citizenry. Thus the army of East Rome was rid of the Goths around 400.[9] (iii) Only in the second half of the fifth century was there a revival of German influence in Constantinople. After the dissolution of the Hunnic empire many Germans offered their services as recruits. The revival of their influence was due to the Alan Aspar, who may have represented the German interest through his wife, possibly an Ostrogoth.[10] The German party was crushed in 471 when Emperor Leo, with the help of the Isaurians disposed of both Aspar and his family.[11]

It is clear from this quick survey of Roman-Gothic relations in the East in the fifth century that there was no strong Gothic presence in Constantinople or Oriens when the first Persian War erupted in 421. This makes it practically certain that most or all of the *foederati* mentioned by Malalas as fighting under Areobindus were Arabs.[12]

B

It remains to examine the other term used by Malalas to describe the commander of these *foederati*, Areobindus.

[6] Cf. The dispatch of the Arab *foederati* of the 6th-century, the Ghassānids, to fight in Armenia in the operations which finally centered around Martyropolis in Amida in 531: see Shahîd, "Procopius and Arethas," *BZ* 50 (1957), 48.

[7] Ammianus Marcellinus, *RG*, XXXI, 16.8.

[8] On Tribigidus, see *PLRE*, II, s.v.

[9] See *Grosse, RM*, 264, where he speaks of the annihilation of 35,000 Goths.

[10] See Bury, *LRE*, I, 316–17.

[11] The reference in the sources to the Goths of this period in the reign of Leo are likely to be mostly to Goths as free retainers and bodyguards, kept or employed by wealthy or influential people: see Bury, *LRE*, I, 321, and Jones, *LRE*, 666. For such references, see *Chronicon Paschale*, 594, 596, 597.

[12] Cf. the situation in the last war Byzantium fought with Persia, that is, in the reign of Julian, when the *foederati* were Arab; see *BAFOC*, 108, B and note 8.

It has been argued that the φοιδερᾶτοι whom Areobindus commanded were fifth-century *foederati* and not sixth-century troops. It is, then, completely out of the question that the term κόμης is used in the sense that it acquired later in the sixth century to designate the commander of these regular troops, who also had been called ἄρχων.[13] This is a specialized, technical term that was reserved in the sixth century for a commander of such troops. This view derives much support from the realization that Malalas was not a careful author. Although some unique data, such as the reference to the Strata Diocletiana, is owed to him, he did indulge at times in anachronisms, of which this phrase may be an example.[14]

The term κόμης as used in this phrase could not, therefore, have been used with the technical accuracy it acquired later, but simply to describe the commander of this group of *foederati*. Since Malalas used this particular term rather than a more general one such as *archōn* or *hēgemōn*, it is possible that the officer in question was a *comes rei militaris*, a military official who crossed provincial boundaries and could have commanded the Arab *foederati* on this occasion.[15]

The most plausible explanation, however, remains that Malalas indulged in an anachronism. As a sixth-century writer, familiar with the term as it emerged in his time he anachronistically applied it to Areobindus to describe the Roman imperial officer who commanded the *foederati*. But he has also informed the reader that the *foederati* of the first Persian War were commanded by an imperial officer of Gothic origin, Areobindus. This enables a related question to be raised: who commanded these autonomous ethnic units in the Roman army, their own officers or imperial Roman officers? The phrase seems to indicate that they were commanded by a non-Arab imperial officer. Although possible, this does not seem likely. The better explanation is that Areobindus had general supervision of the strategy of the campaign, conducted mainly by the *foederati*, while their own phylarch commanded them as tactical units, in much the same way that Areobindus' namesake of the reign of Anastasius directed military operations and had under him Arab *foederati* commanded by their phylarch, al-Aswad.[16] In the case of the latter operation, Theophanes mentioned the name of the Arab phylarch, while in the case of the former, of 422, Malalas did not, and so gave the impression that the Arab *foederati* were directly commanded by an imperial officer.

Appendix II

Iyād

The well-known Arab tribal group Iyād played an important role in the history of the Arabs before the rise of Islam in both halves of the Fertile Crescent.[1] In its emigration

[13] See Grosse, *RM*, 281. It is as late as 548/9 that the first firm attestation of the term *comes foederatorum* occurs, applied by Justinian to Artabanus, who was concurrently appointed *magister militum in praesenti*. Jones, *LRE*, 665.

[14] The phrase the "limes of Chalcis" is one; see *BAFOC*, 470–76.

[15] Such as Vitianus is suspected to have been; see *PLRE*, s.v.

[16] Theophanes, *Chronographia*, 146.

[1] For a succinct account of this tribe, see J. Fück's article in *EI*², IV, 289 and Caskel, *GN*, II, Register, 359–60.

from the eastern half of the Crescent away from the Persians to the western half and Roman territory, it is representative of a trend prevalent in this period. The Arabic sources contain many accounts of the migration of Iyād at various junctures in the Sasanid period.[2] The following explores the view expressed above, that one of these defections or emigrations could have taken place in the fifth century, possibly ca. 420.

(*a*) Iyād was a Christian tribe,[3] and so it is likely to have renounced its allegiance to the Persians and decided to leave Persian territory because of the great persecution instituted by Yazdgard I, in much the same way that Aspebetos and his group, who, though not Christian at the time, found the persecution of the Christians revolting and decided to desert to the Romans.

(*b*) Another defection is dated to the reign of another Persian king, Chosroes, but the sources are divided on which Chosroes is meant. Some say it is Anushravan, son of Kawād, others say it is Parviz, son of Hormuz.[4] It is also possible to suggest a third Chosroes, who reigned around 420, when the first Persian War broke out. He was the first choice of the Magian priesthood to ascend to the throne after the death of Yazdgard and, according to Ṭabarī, ruled for a short time before Mundir secured the throne for Bahram.[5] The Arabic sources could have confused this Chosroes with the more famous one in the sixth century, with whom they were better acquainted.[6]

(*c*) An echo of an Iyādid presence in Oriens in the fifth century has been preserved in the person of ʿAbd al-ʿĀṣ, the poet of Dāwūd al-Lathiq,[7] one of the kings of Salīḥ. It is difficult to imagine that the poet was the single Iyādi in Oriens who defected from the Land of the Two Rivers. The chances are that an Iyādi group emigrated in the same century, which is consonant with a defection ca. 420. Thus it was one of these that later became the court poet of the Salīḥid king.

The clause of the treaty of 422 on the defection of the Arab allies of the two powers, and the implication that an Arab group allied to Persia had defected ca. 420, can thus be connected with what the Arabic sources say on the emigration of Iyād from Persian to Roman territory.

[2] One emigration is dated to the 4th century and to the reign of Shāpūr II; see Masʿūdī, *Murūj al-Ḍahab*, ed. Ch. Pellat (Beirut, 1966), I, 295–96, 302. Another is dated to the reign of Chosroes Anushravan in the 6th century, for which see Balādurī, *Ansāb al-Ashrāf*, ed. M. Ḥamīduddin (Cairo, 1959), II, 27. For Nöldeke's views, see below, Chap. 12, sec. IV.

[3] On the four monasteries of Iyād in Ḥīra and its vicinity, see Balādurī, *Ansāb al-Ashrāf*, 26.

[4] See Bakrī, *Muʿjam*, ed. M. al-Saqqā (Cairo, 1945), I, 70–71.

[5] For this Chosroes, see Nöldeke, *PAS*, 91–97.

[6] There is a detail in one account of the Arabic sources which could support the view that an emigration did take place in the 5th century. In this account Iyād, fleeing from Mesopotamia, are drowned in the Euphrates. This brings to mind the fate of the Lakhmid host of Mundir, the twenty thousand who were drowned in 421. This significant detail could reflect a confusion in the Arabic sources for this distant past (not unusual), which made their authors think those who drowned were the Iyād who fled Persian territory rather than the Lakhmids who invaded Byzantine Osroene or Euphratensis. For Iyād's drowning in the Euphrates, see Bakrī, *Muʿjam*, I, 75.

[7] See below, Chap. 12, sec. III.I.B.6.

III

The Reign of Marcian (450–457)

Two military operations involving the Arabs are recorded for the reign of Marcian. Unlike those of 410 and 447 of the reign of Theodosius, there are at least some geographical indications as to where they were fought or conducted. They are recorded respectively by Priscus of Panium and the ecclesiastical historian Nicephorus Callistus for the year 453.

I. Priscus

In one of his fragments for the reign of Marcian, Priscus records an encounter with the Arabs near Damascus in Phoenicia Libanensis:[1] "Ardabur,[2] the son of Aspar, was fighting the Saracens in the region of Damascus. When Maximinus[3] the *stratēgos*, and Priscus, the historian, arrived there, they found him conducting peace negotiations with the envoys of the Saracens."

Coming from a historian who was singularly lacking in precision regarding matters of geography and topography,[4] the fragment is welcome for the great precision that informs it in many respects. The following data can be extracted:

1. That Ardabur was fighting the Arabs and negotiating with them suggests that the encounter was important enough to be worthy of the personal attention of the *magister militum per Orientem* himself, and that the Arabs involved were worth the time he was spending on the negotiations. His negotiating with them also suggests that they were not a band of marauding Saracens who were beaten off the *limes* and presented no further problem for the military adminstration of Oriens, but that they were sufficiently important to induce the *magister* to engage in peaceful negotiations that entailed their sending ambassadors for that purpose.[5]

[1] For the Greek text, see Blockley, *CH*, II, 322.

[2] This is Ardabur Junior, *magister militum per Orientem*, 453–466; see *PLRE*, II, 135–37.

[3] For Maximinus, possible *comes rei militaris*, see ibid., 743, no. 11.

[4] See Blockley, *CH*, I, 69. On Priscus in general see ibid., 48–70.

[5] Cf. R. Devreese, *Le patriarcat d'Antioche, depuis la paix d'église jusqu'à la conquête arabe* (Paris, 1945), 248, note 4.

2. This tantalizing reference to what must have been a major Saracen thrust into Phoenicia Libanensis may be added to the data relating to Saracens in this province of Oriens: the reference in the *Vita S. Pelagiae*[6] to the conversion of thirty thousand Saracens and that in the *Notitia Dignitatum* to the existence of two Saracen units stationed there.[7] How these various data can be brought to bear on one another is not clear, but they are assembled here for a future investigation when more data are recovered.[8]

3. Unfortunately, Priscus does not identify the Arabs involved in this encounter or, if he did, the identification has not survived in the fragment. It is unlikely that they were the Lakhmids. Their overlord, Yazdgard, had only recently returned from Nishāpūr after the conclusion of the first Hunnic War in his reign (451) and was at the time warring with the Armenians. Al-Mundir was getting old and would die in 462, after a long reign which began in 418. By elimination the Arabs referred to are more likely to have been one of the two groups who were restless and in motion in this period in north Arabia—the Kindites or the Ghassānids, probably the former.

II. Nicephorus Callistus

In the same year the ecclesiastical historian Nicephorus Callistus records a military operation against the Arabs,[9] during the disturbances that broke out in Palestine when the Monophysites chased its patriarch, Juvenal, out of the Holy City. Dorotheus, the commander who was conducting the operation, was forced to recross the Jordan and hurry back to Jerusalem.

Nicephorus is precise in giving the name of the commander who battled the Arabs and the location of the military operation—Moabitis. The short but precise account may be supplemented by the following observations:

1. Dorotheus was *comes (et dux Palaestinae)*, which meant that he was in charge of military operations in the three Palestines.[10] This particular operation against the Saracens must have been in Palaestina Tertia or Salutaris, since Moabitis was within this division of tripartite Palestine, lying to the southeast of the Dead Sea. Whether the *dux* of the adjacent province of Arabia was also involved is not clear, but he could have been. One of the cities of Moabitis, Areopolis, is listed in the *Notitia Dignitatum* as belonging not to

[6] See above, Chap. 1, app. 1.

[7] See below, 1176–1178.

[8] For a tentative attempt to involve the two Saracen units in the operation against the Saracens, see below, Sec. III.

[9] For the Greek text, see *Historia Ecclesiastica*, PG 147, Chap. ix, col. 32C, where the Arabs are referred to as barbarians: περί που τὴν Μωαβῖτιν πρὸς βαρβάρους ἐνασχολούμενος.

[10] For Dorotheus, see *PLRE*, II, 377, no. 7. For the military organization of the three Palestines, see F. M. Abel, *Géographie de la Palestine*, II (Paris, 1938), 178–84.

Palestine but to the province of Arabia.[11] So the operations against the Saracens in Moabitis may have involved the dukes of the two provinces, Palestine and Arabia, and Dorotheus may have found it possible to rush back to Jerusalem because he could depend on his fellow *dux* of Arabia to continue the conduct of the military operation against the Saracens.[12]

2. Who were these Arabs with whom Dorotheus battled? They could have belonged to the same tribal groups that Ardabur was fighting to the north in the region of Damascus in Phoenicia Libanensis. The chronological and geographical closeness[13] of the two operations is such that there is something to be said for this view of a synchronized offensive by one group against two different sectors of the *limes*. If so, they could have been Kindites, but also, perhaps, two independent groups who allied themselves against the Romans and attacked synchronously in much the same way as the Kindites and Ghassānids who attacked the *limes* ca. 500 in the reign of Anastasius.[14]

III. The Two Operations

The two operations of the reign of Marcian were conducted along the Arabian frontier. The question naturally arises concerning the whereabouts of the Arab *foederati* of Byzantium in this century, especially the Salīḥids.

The *foederati* must have taken part in these operations, since one of their most important assignments was to guard the Arabian front. Byzantine historians do not refer normally to them, but only to the regular imperial army to which the *foederati* were attached. Only rarely do they mention Arab federate participation, for instance, when the historian is writing a detailed account of a military operation, as Procopius did when he wrote the annals of the Persian Wars of Justinian's reign. Had it not been for this account and an incidental reference in a chronographer who was particularly interested in Oriens, Malalas, no one would have suspected that the Arab allies of Byzantium, the Ghassānids, constituted the right wing of Belisarius' army at Callinicum and contributed five thousand horse. Thus it is more than likely that the two Saracen units stationed in Phoenicia Libanensis and listed in the *Notitia Dignitatum* bore the brunt of the war with the Saracens with whom Ardabur battled and that other units listed in the same document for Palestine and Arabia did the same, fighting the Saracens under Dorotheus in Moabitis.

[11] For the third Palestine and for Areopolis, see ibid., 177–78. For Moabitis, see the various maps of Abel at the end of vol. II.

[12] For a military operation against the Saracens that involved the cooperation of two Byzantine commanders in the 4th century, see *BAFOC*, 150–52.

[13] The operation in Moabitis is dated 452 in *PLRE*, II, s.v. Dorotheus 7.

[14] See below, Chap. 6, sec. IV.

Furthermore, it is stated by Priscus that Ardabur conducted negotiations with the envoy whom the Saracens dispatched. As an Alan and a Roman, he knew no Arabic. Thus the negotiations must have been conducted by the most natural dragomans in this segment of Oriens, namely, the Arab *foederati* of Byzantium, since it is out of the question that the interpreters came from the staff of the *magister officiorum* in Constantinople, who normally supplied interpreters to Roman diplomats engaged in negotiations with foreign states and peoples.

IV

The Reign of Leo (457–474)

Arab-Byzantine relations for the relatively long reign of Leo are documented by a single account involving the adventurous and incredibly successful career of the Arab chief Amorkesos.[1] But this single account is a mine of information: it is related with such significant details that it floods with light many obscure aspects of Arab-Byzantine relations in the entire fifth century. It is, therefore, imperative to subject it to an intensive analysis in order to extract from it the precious data it can provide. This is especially called for since this fragment has never been analyzed in a way that would reveal the entire range of problems it raises concerning the Lakhmids, the Ghassānids, Byzantine-Persian relations, and Arab-Byzantine relations.[2] Such an analysis will also throw light on the historian who wrote of Amorkesos, Malchus of Philadelphia, in whom there is renewed interest.[3]

In view of the complexity and importance of this "fascinating"[4] frag-

[1] The only other episode pertains to inter-Arab—or rather inter-phylarchal—relations involving some strife between the phylarch of Arabia and the phylarch of Palaestina Prima around 459–460; see below, App. 2.

[2] The fragment has attracted the attention of Byzantino-arabists since the days of Nöldeke; see *GF*, 13 note 3 and App. 1, below. There are inaccurate references to it in histories that deal with the 5th century, as in Bury, *LRE*, II, 8; Stein, *HBE*, I, 357–58; Vasiliev noted it in *Justin the First* (Cambridge, Mass., 1950), 365–66; see also A. Musil, *The Northern Heǧāz* (New York, 1926), 306–9. These and others who have written general histories merely summarize the account of Malchus and do not address themselves to unlocking the secrets of this fragment. More serious treatment may be found in Aigrain, "Arabie," cols. 1197–98 and in F.M. Abel, "L'île de Jotabè," *RB* 47 (1938), 510–38, which will be discussed in the course of this chapter. The most recent treatment of the fragment is that of M. Sartre, which has some perceptive observations in spite of its brevity; see his *Trois études*, 154–55, and his commentary on the Bostra Edict of Anastasius involving the island of Iotabe, *IGLS*, XIII, no. 9046, 107–19.

[3] See B. Baldwin, "Malchus of Philadelphia," *DOP* 31 (1977), 91–107; and more recently, R. C. Blockley, who made a study of the historian in *CH*, I, 71–85, and who translated and commented on the fragments in II, 402–62. Before him, C. D. Gorden included a translation and commentary on Malchus in *The Age of Attila* (Ann Arbor, 1960). For the latest edition and study of Malchus, see Lia Raffaella Cresci, *Malco di Filadelfia: Frammenti*, Byzantina et Neo-Hellenica Neapolitana 9 (Naples, 1982).

[4] So understood and described by Baldwin, "Malchus," 101.

ment, it will be summarized below[5] and discussed in eight parts: (I) the Persian background of Amorkesos; (II) the military operations; (III) negotiations with Leo; (IV) Amorkesos in Constantinople; (V) the phylarchate of Amorkesos; (VI) the Vandal War; (VII) Leo's Arab policy; and (VIII) historiographical observations.

Summary

Sometime during the reign of Leo, an Arab chief named Amorkesos, who was allied to the Persians, decided for some unknown reason to sever his relations with them and seek a Roman connection; in so doing he violated a treaty between the two powers. He began by emigrating to a part of Arabia that was adjacent to Persia, whence he warred not against the Romans but against the Arabs. After establishing himself, he attacked Roman territory, seized the island of Iotabe, from which he drove the Roman customs officers, and amassed great wealth by collecting the taxes himself. He then desired to be allied with the Romans and to become a phylarch of the Saracens in Arabia Petraea. He therefore sent Petrus, the bishop of his tribe, to Constantinople to arrange this with Emperor Leo. The bishop was successful, and Leo asked Amorkesos to come to the capital. This took place in the seventeenth year of Leo's reign, 473.

Amorkesos traveled by land to Constantinople. He was treated royally by the emperor, who invited him to his table, had him attend the meetings of the Senate, and even gave him a seat among the first patricians. The two also exchanged gifts. The Arab chief gave the emperor a golden image of himself, inlaid with precious stones, while the emperor gave him money from the public treasury and also ordered the senators to give him gifts. Finally, Leo made him phylarch, confirming his possession of Iotabe and, what is more, adding a number of villages to be placed under his control.

In addition to these valuable data on the career of this adventurous Arab chief, Malchus expresses some animadversions on Leo's conduct of the negotiations: (1) disapproving of Leo's invitation to visit the capital, he says that imperial interests would have been better served if Amorkesos' endowment with the phylarchate had taken place in Arabic Petraea and not in Constantinople; (2) the emperor insulted all the Romans when he had the Arab chief sit among the first patricians, especially after he circulated a rumor that the chief had become a Christian; and (3) finally, by making him a phylarch he strengthened the position of one who was not going to work for the greater glory of Rome.

[5] For the Greek text of the fragment, see below, App. 3. It has been appended to this chapter for the convenience of the reader and it should be consulted whenever the Greek text becomes important. For translations of this fragment, see above, note 3.

I. The Persian Background of Amorkesos

This is a much more complex aspect of the career of Amorkesos than the short statement in Malchus would suggest. It presents the following problems: his name and tribal affiliation; his motives for leaving the service of the Persians; and the legal problem involved in his seeking a Byzantine connection.

1. The traditional view is that Greek Amorkesos is Arabic Imru' al-Qays, a well-known pre-Islamic personal name.[6] Accordingly, the Amorkesos of Malchus could have been one of various personages of that name during this period.[7] It is out of the question that he was Imru' al-Qays, the father of the famous Lakhmid king Mundir of Procopian fame,[8] and rather unlikely that he was a prince of the tribal group Kinda.[9] By elimination the chances are that he was the Ghassānid chief of that name whom the sources mention in the genealogy of that tribe: (*a*) a Ghassānid Imru' al-Qays is mentioned in the sources for roughly this period and region;[10] (*b*) he is referred to in the sources as *biṭrīq*, (*patricius*), an epithet that brings to mind the passage in Malchus that associates him with the first patricians;[11] (*c*) his Persian background points in the same direction. Recent research has shown that the Ghassānids had lingered in Ḥīra and in Lakhmid-Persian territory before they crossed over to the Romans;[12] (*d*) the sources for the Lakhmids do mention for this period a civil war or strife involving the Lakhmids and the Ghassānids in the camp of the Persian Arabs, which ended in a Lakhmid victory. This could make Imru' al-Qays' change of masters intelligible.[13]

On the other hand, Greek Amorkesos could be an Arabic name other

[6] See T. Fahd, *Le panthéon de l'Arabie centrale à la veille de l'Hégire* (Paris, 1968), 136–38.

[7] For this, see W. Caskel, *GN*, II, 355 and a host of names s.v. Imra'alqais," 354–7.

[8] For the difficulties are many. They involve the correct patronymic of Mundir and the course of events associated with his immediate predecessors, Nuʿmān and Abū Jaʿfur, for which see Rothstein, *DLH*, 73–79.

[9] As suspected by Nöldeke (*GF*, 13 note 3). That Kindite princes had this name is undoubted. For a Kindite with this name, see Ibn Ḥazm, *Jamharat*, ed. ʿA. Hārūn (Cairo, 1962), 428, where he mentions that the famous Kindite king, Al-Ḥārith, surnamed Ākil al-Murār, had a brother by the name of Imru' al-Qays. But other Arab royal houses also had this name. The very strong probability that the Amorkesos of Malchus was a Ghassānid, as will be argued in this section, precludes the possibility that he was a Kindite.

[10] See Ḥamza, *Tārīkh* (Beirut, 1961), 99 and other sources cited in App. 1. On the Ghassānids who had the name of Imru' al-Qays in Ibn Ḥazm, see *Jamharat*, 372, 374, 375.

[11] For this, see below, App. 1, where the question of his patriciate is discussed.

[12] See the discussion in *BAFOC* involving Podosacis, 119–23.

[13] For this struggle between the Lakhmid king al-Aswad and the Ghassānids, see Rothstein, *DLH*, 73. When Rothstein wrote his excellent monograph on the Lakhmids in 1899, the Ghassānid presence in Ḥīra was unknown to him, as it was also to Nöldeke. So he thought the Ghassānids of Ḥīra were not the Ghassānids who became *foederati* of Byzantium in the 6th century. The Arabic sources, however, agree on the identity of the two Ghassānid groups, and recent research has confirmed this identity. On other motives for Amorkesos' change of masters, see below, Sec. II.

than Imru' al-Qays.[14] Its Greek form and the vocalic sequence in it could answer to another Arabic name and its patronymic. In the sources for the history of Ḥīra there is reference to a certain ʿAbd al-Masīḥ, who is described as "son of ʿAmr, son of Kays." The segment of this genealogical line ʿAmr, son of Kays could have been transliterated from Arabic into Greek as Amorkesos.[15] Supporting this view is the fact that this historical personage is a Ghassānid, who thus could have left the service of the Persians after a quarrel with the Lakhmids, the dominant Arab group in Ḥīra in the service of Persia. Against this view is the fact that this personage is the father of ʿAbd al-Masīḥ according to the genealogists, and since ʿAbd al-Masīḥ was alive in the thirties of the seventh century, ʿAmr would have been a sixth-, not a fifth-century figure. However, ʿAbd al-Masīḥ, according to the Arab historians, was one of the *Muʿammarūn*, *macrobiotes*, who lived inordinately long lives. If he lived well over a hundred years,[16] ʿAmr son of Kays, his father, could have been active in the second half of the fifth century.

There is a further consideration which argues in favor of Greek Amorkesos' being ʿAmr, son of Kays. In a rare mood, the Greek source mentions not only the name of the Arab chief but also his clan affiliation, Nokalios.[17] This has been identified with Nukhayla, but Nukhayla is a toponym, not a clan name.[18] ʿAbd al-Masīḥ is referred to in the Arabic sources as belonging to the clan or tribe of Bukayla or Bukaila/Buqayla, a clan within the larger

[14] The fundamental article on the problem of transliterating Imru' al-Qays and related names into other classical languages is that of A. Fischer, in two parts, "Imra'alqais," *Islamica* 1.1 (1924), 1–9; 1.2 (1925), 365–89. The *schluss* to this long study of Imru' al-Qays' name, announced as the third part on p. 389, does not seem to have seen the light of day.

[15] In Greek "Amr, son of Qays" or "Amro ibn Kais" would have appeared as 'Αμϱ ὁ Κέσου with the use of "the genitive of the patronymic." The Greek copyist of the document or the historian himself could have thought it one word in the genitive and thus restored it to the nominative case as 'Αμοϱκέσος. The first omicron in Greek 'Αμοϱκέσος and the non-existence of Arabic *al* (the definite article which appears in the other name, Imru' al-Qays) could suggest that Greek 'Αμοϱκέσος is a transliteration of Amr(ʿo) Kais rather than Imru' al-Qays. The metathesis involving οϱ in Greek is common, and leads to the transliteration into Greek 'Αμοϱκέσος of either Imru' al-Qays or ʿAmr, son of Qays. For a similar confusion in the transliteration of Arabic names into Greek, see below, note 17.

[16] On this figure and his Ghassānid group, see Rothstein, *DLH*, 114, and L. Cheikho, *Shuʿarā' al-Naṣrāniyya baʿd al-Islam* (Beirut, 1967), 14–20. For hostile relations between the Ghassānid clan of this ʿAbd al-Masīḥ and that of Tamīm, to which the poet ʿAdi ibn Zayd belonged, see Rothstein, *DLH*, 114 note 2, and Nöldeke, *PAS*, 322.

[17] Greek Νοκαΐλου experienced metathesis involving the lambda; the word should read Νοκαΐλου. Blockley translates this as "tribe," but *genos* (γένος) is here distinguished from *phylē* (φυλή), which appears later in the text, where it surely means tribe. Sartre correctly understood that what is involved here is the narrow clan to which he belonged and not the larger tribal group; see *TE*, 154.

[18] See O. Blau, "Arabien im sechsten Jahrhundert," *ZDMG* 23 (1869), 578. One would expect Arabic "*kh*" in Nu*kh*ayla to appear as Greek chi not kappa, as it appears in Νοκαλίου.

Ghassānid tribal group. It is notorious that diacritical marks in the Arabic script change one letter into another by their position in relation to it. In the case of this particular word, "Bukaila" can easily become "Nukaila" if the diacritical mark attaching to the first letter is transposed from beneath the line to the space above it.[19] It is quite possible that this happened in the process of transcribing the name. It is also possible that the diacritical was omitted during transliteration.[20]

It is difficult to tell which of the two Arabic names stands behind Greek Amorkesos. But the investigation of the only two possibilities has made practically certain that the Arab chief involved was a Ghassānid who belonged to the clan Bukaila/Buqayla in Ḥīra.[21] His name may have been ʿAmr ibn-Kays or Imru' al-Qays; hence the Greek version of his name, Amorkesos, in its transliterated form, has been used in this chapter rather than one of the two possible Arabic names.

The Ghassānid affiliation of Amorkesos receives considerable support from the events of some twenty years later, when a recognizably Ghassānid name and figure, Jabala, is mentioned in the sources. He is occupying the same island, Iotabe, that had been occupied by Amorkesos, but Romanus, the *dux* of Palestine, dislodges him in 498 and restores it to Roman rule.[22] The natural interpretation of the sequence of events is that the Ghassānid Jabala is

[19] That this particular word is susceptible to corrupt readings is evidenced by the fact that it sometimes appears as Nufayla as a result of the misplacement of one diacritical mark above the second consonant instead of two.

[20] Aigrain's gallant attempt ("Arabie," col. 1197) to relate the clan of Amorkesos to that of the Kindite Ākil al-Murār cannot be said to have been successful. On phonetic grounds it is so distant that it has to be ruled out completely. Besides, the personage in question is a refugee from Persia, and no Kindite prince is known to have fled from Persia before the famous Arethas in the reign of Justinian; see Rothstein, *DLH*, 87 ff and Shahîd, "Ghassān and Byzantium" *Der Islam* 33 (1958), 251–52 and "Byzantium and Kinda," *BZ* 53 (1960), 60.

Blockley followed de Boor's text in his edition of Malchus, which restored the important sentence in the passage involving the exchange of gifts between the phylarch and the emperor, but he also followed him in accepting the reading Νομαλίου, for Νοκαλίου. The former has no support in Arabic genealogies and appears very rarely, as a toponym and not a clan name, in such faraway places as Yamāma and Najd in eastern Arabia; for Numayla, see Yāqūt, *Nuʿjam al-Buldān* (Beirut, 1957), V, 306. With the exception of de Boor all the other editors have rightly accepted Νοκαλίου; see Niebuhr in the Bonn edition, (14), p. 232 as early as 1829; C. Müller in *FHG*, IV, p. 113 in 1851; and L. Dindorf in the Teubner edition, *Historici Graeci Minores*, I, p. 385 in 1870; see also Dindorf in the *praefatio*, p. lxiv, for his palaeographical note on Νοκαλίου.

[21] It is not entirely ruled out that behind the term Buqayla may stand the name Banū-Qayla, that is, "the sons of Qayla," the mother of the two famous Azd tribes of Medina, al-Aws and al-Khazraj, who were related as Azdites to the Ghassānids. But these resided in Medina, not in Ḥīra whence Amorkesos came. That they had wandered to Ḥīra in the 5th century is possible, but is nowhere attested in the sources. On Qayla, see Ibn Ḥazm, *Jamharat*, 332.

[22] For a discussion of these events narrated by Theophanes, see below, Chap. 6.

in line with Amorkesos from whom he derived sovereignty over the island either directly or indirectly through his father. There is no mention in the sources that Jabala had occupied the island anew, and the presumption is that rule over it had devolved from one Ghassānid, Amorkesos, of the reign of Leo, to another, Jabala, of reign of Anastasius.[23]

2. What actually motivated Amorkesos to change sides and opt for the Romans is not clear. Malchus gives two possible explanations: either because he had not attained an honorable position in the service of the Persians or because he thought that life with the Romans was better than with the Persians and, consequently, that he would do better in Roman territory. Neither explanation is convincing; the first seems hardly credible considering his exceptional talents, which would have been usefully employed among the Persians. The second explanation is too vague and general to be informative. But knowledge of the history of the Persian Arabs in this period, especially of the Lakhmids and Ḥīra and the relations of the Persian Arabs to their overlords, could throw much light on the motives of Amorkesos in changing sides. The most plausible explanation must be one of two, and the two may possibly be related.

a. Ḥīra, the capital of the Lakhmids, was tribally a composite city inhabited by many groups of Arabs, although the Lakhmids, who ruled the city, were dominant.[24] It is possible that there was friction between the group of Amorkesos, the Ghassānids, and the Lakhmids or one of the other tribal groups in Ḥīra. Indeed, the sources speak of the strife between the Lakhmid king, al-Aswad, and the Ghassānids and their massacre by him. The sources also speak of friction between the Ghassānids, especially the tribe of Banū Buqayla, and that of the powerful Tamīm group of ʿAdī ibn Zayd.[25] Such bitter internal strife in Ḥīra could easily have induced the Ghassānid chief to leave in search of greener pastures.

b. The Persians were intolerant of Christianity, a proselytizing religion, and they frowned on attempts of their Arab clients—the Lakhmids—to convert. This must also have been their attitude toward other Arab groups in

[23] The correct identification of this historical figure, whose history has been miraculously preserved in this fragment of Malchus and who has tantalized all who have tried to unlock his secret, may be added to other correct identifications in the history of Byzantino-arabica, such as, Podosacis, Nonnosus, Iob, and Aggaios, for whom see *BAFOC*, 119–23; Shahîd, "The Conference of Ramla," *JNES* 23 (1964), 116–19.

This confrontation of the Greek with the Arabic sources for the pre-Islamic period contributes to the justification of the essential soundness of the Arabic tradition relating to that period. On how to use these sources for pre-Islamic times and what to expect from them, see Shahîd, "Last Days," 154–56.

[24] See Rothstein, *DLH*, 19–20.

[25] For friction and enmity between the Ghassānids on the one hand and Lakhm and Tamīm on the other, see ibid., 73, 114.

Ḥīra and elsewhere in their territory who might have envisaged the adoption of Christianity. But some of these groups did convert, and this led to friction, which more often than not resulted in the emigration of a Christianized group to the territory of the Christian Roman Empire. In spite of what Malchus says about the Christianity of Imru' al-Qays, it is practically certain that Amorkesos already was a Christian when he sent his bishop to negotiate a settlement with Leo, and the chances are that he had been Christian while he was still in Persian territory. If so, his religion could have been the cause of friction with the authorities that led to strife and emigration.[26]

The emigration of Amorkesos, first to Arabia and then to Roman territory, becomes intelligible in the light of these two explanations. In so doing he treaded the path of many an Arab chief in the service of Persia, his best-known predecessor being Aspebetos.

3. Finally, there is the question of his defection from Persia and his violation of the treaty that prohibited the reception of Arab fugitives on the part of either empire. The stipulation goes back to the treaty[27] concluded some fifty years before the irruption of Amorkesos into Palaestina Tertia, but even so it became an element in his story and is important not only theoretically for Persian-Byzantine relations but also because it throws light on some aspects of the pre-Roman phase of his career.

Ten years before, the Persian king Pērōz (459–484) complained to Emperor Leo about his reception of certain refugees from Persia.[28] It is possible that Pērōz may have had Amorkesos and his followers in mind: the Persian king would not have complained about an ordinary defector, but he would have about Amorkesos, a potentially dangerous foe. His defection would have been reported to the king and would have attracted his attention, especially as most of his reign was spent in fighting the Ephthalite Huns and he did not want to be distracted by Arab attacks against his southwestern frontier. If so, this would set the date when Amorkesos defected from Persia in the early sixties. Even if the Persian king was inquiring about some other fugitive Amorkesos must still have defected about this time or shortly after. This gives rise to the following observations:

(1) For Amorkesos to have built his power in Arabia and to have become a threat to Rome in the region of Palaestina Tertia, he must have been wan-

[26] The Ghassānids of Ḥīra were considered *ʿIbād* by Arab writers, that is, Christians, "servants of Christ." On this and on their church in Ḥīra called "Biʿat Bani Zimmān," see Ibn Ḥazm, *Jamharat*, 374; also *BAFOC*, 121 note 59.

[27] On this, see above, 36–37.

[28] On Bury, *LRE*, II, 7. In 464 Leo had not yet received Amorkesos, but Pērōz would not have known the fate of the refugees or whether or not they were in fact received by Leo. All he knew was the defection, and he assumed that the Romans would receive them or had in fact done so.

dering and adventuring in Arabia for some time before feeling strong enough to attack the Romans. He may have spent as much as ten years in Arabia, making many connections there. This must have entered into Leo's thinking when he decided to court him.

(2) Amorkesos may also have decided to spend some time in Arabia before joining the Romans because he knew that if he went over to them directly, there would be a crisis in Persian-Byzantine relations. The persumption is that he wanted some time to elapse between his defection from Persia and his acceptance by the Romans so that his entry into the Roman orbit would be a smooth one.

(3) This could also explain the statement in Malchus that after his defection he did not escape to the Arabia that was adjacent to the Romans but to the one that was adjacent to the Persians. This surely was deliberate, since it would have given the Persians the impression that he was fleeing neither to Roman territory nor to territory adjacent to them whence he could appeal for asylum.

(4) The final stage in his Arabian journey confirms this supposition. Before he approached the Romans, he had reached northern Ḥijāz, that is, the farthest region from the Persian border that he could reach. From that base he could comfortably approach the Romans. After years of wandering in the Arabian Peninsula, and after finally settling in northern Ḥijāz, Amorkesos could join the Romans not as a fugitive from Persian territory but as a newcomer from Arabia. That he first attacked them before sending overtures of peace only confirms the suspicion that he was hostile to them—as were the Persians and the Arab vassals of Persia, one of whom he had been. In the meantime, he had made himself a power in North Arabia and in northern Ḥijāz, and thus was in a very strong bargaining position vis-à-vis the Romans—as a valuable ally whose overtures they could not resist.

II. The Military Operations

The military adventures of this exceptional Arab chief fall into two stages, the Arabian and the Roman.

1. Malchus mentions that the part of Arabia to which he moved was that adjacent to Persia, not the Roman Empire. This must have been the case since on leaving Ḥīra, on the Lower Euphrates, he would have moved into a part of Arabia close to Persia—near the Persian Gulf or Najd.

But this could have been only the first phase in his victorious march to Roman territory. It is practically certain from Malchus' description of his operations against Roman territory that the second phase of his Arabian adventure unfolded in northern Ḥijāz. Dūmat al-Jandal[29] most probably was a station on his journey from eastern to western Arabia, but it is clear that he must have settled in northern Ḥijāz before he finally entered the second stage of his military adventure, the assault on Roman territory. The Azd tribal group, to which the Ghassānids belonged, had moved northward from South Arabia along the Sharāt range that goes through western Arabia, and two of their important tribes, al-Aws and the Khazraj, had settled in Yathrib/Medina.[30] It is quite likely that they had already been settled there in the second half of the fifth century. If so, the Ghassānid adventurer would have had a power base in northern Ḥijāz from which to operate against Roman territory in Palaestina Tertia.

Amorkesos' adventures in northern Arabia reveal an exceptionally skillful warrior who wanted to build his military strength and become a political power there before challenging the Romans in Palaestina Tertia.[31]

2. The second phase represents his operations against Roman territory. Two are mentioned by the historian:

a. He seized the island of the Iotabe, at the mouth of the Gulf of Eilat. This was a bold stroke for an Arab chief who was a land warrior. This was an amphibious operation and implies that the chief had at his disposal some ships or rafts to convey his troops to the island. It is not entirely clear whether he sailed from an adjacent port on the Red Sea or was already in possession of a strip of land on the eastern coast of the Gulf of Eilat. Whatever his route was, it was a remarkable operation for an Arab chief who had operated with horses and camels and not with ships.[32]

[29] Dūmat was the obvious port of call for those who wandered from Ḥīra on their way to Ḥijāz in western Arabia or to Byzantine Oriens since it controlled Wādī Sirḥān—the gateway to the Provincia Arabia. A more famous march in the 7th century brought Khalid ibn al-Walid from Ḥīra to Dūmat before he entered Oriens and fought the battle on the Hieromax in 636. It should also be noted that this important oasis was possessed in the 6th century by Kalb and Ghassān. Thus Ghassānid influence at Dūmat may be traced back to Amorkesos, who could have established some Ghassānid presence there already in the 5th century.

[30] For this important tribal group, see *EI*^{2}, s.v.

[31] And he must have written an important chapter in the history of Ḥijāz in the second half of the 5th century—a period of turmoil and restlessness owing to important tribal migrations from South Arabia to Ḥijāz involving the important Azd tribal group. The Ghassānids were related as Azd to the two Arab tribes in Yathrib/Medina, and so it is quite likely that Amorkesos may have helped them settle there in so doing involved himself in hostilities against the Jewish inhabitants of Yathrib. He was to repeat this when he occupied Iotabe, which also had a Jewish community living there—from time immemorial according to Procopius (*Wars*, I, xix, 4). So Amorkesos would have crossed the paths of the Jews twice, both in Ḥijāz and in Iotabe.

[32] This was a most unusual military operation on the part of an Arab and Ghassānid chief, the only instance when the Ghassānids are known to have engaged in an amphibious operation or possessed an island, and is another indication of the versatility of this exceptionally

His military or strategic plan was also remarkable in that it affected the empire adversely in an area that was vital for imperial trade in the Red Sea area and which was also a source of revenue, owing to the customs dues that the Roman official collected from ships that put in.[33] So the Arab chief must have had a very clear conception of the importance of Iotabe for the eastern trade of Rome. Malchus states that he not only inconvenienced the Romans by occupying the strategically located island, but also amassed great wealth by collecting the taxes himself.[34]

b. After seizing the island of Iotabe, Amorkesos attacked the neighboring villages, and it was only then that he "expressed a wish to become an ally of the Romans and a phylarch of the Saracens under Roman rule in Arabia Petraea."[35] This part of the account presents problems and calls for several observations.

The historian does not specify, as he did when he referred to Iotabe, where these villages lay. But it may be assumed that they were not far from Iotabe and hence on the two coasts of the Gulf of Eilat, most probably the eastern coast (close to ancient Midian and the Ḥismā regions in northern Ḥijāz) rather than the western, which would have placed him in Sinai, far from his base of operations in northern Ḥijāz. However, Malchus is specific when he speaks of the area over which Amorkesos desired to be phylarch, namely, Arabia Petraea. Since Palaestina Tertia was a large, curiously shaped province, comprising Sinai, the Negev, and the region to the east of the valley of Wādī ʿAraba, running from the southern tip of the Dead Sea to Eilat, it may be assumed that he wanted to be phylarch over the third and last-mentioned part of Palaestina Tertia. Malchus, a classicizing historian, did not wish to use the administrative term Palaestina Tertia, a recent coinage of the

---

gifted Ghassānid phylarch. But his background in Ḥīra might explain his ability to undertake amphibious operations. Ḥīra was not far from the Euphrates, and the Arabs of that region were familiar with the sea and sea-faring in the Euphrates and the Persian Gulf.

[33] The best study on Iotabe is by F.-M. Abel, "L'île de Jotabè" (op. cit.), 510–38. The article also contains a discussion of the eastern trade of Byzantium, but the discussion of Amorkesos (526–27) has no great value, as the writer merely summarizes Malchus and repeats his prejudices; he also makes Amorkesos a possible descendant of Imru' al-Qays of the Namāra inscription. The writer of the entry "Amorcesos" in *PLRE*, II, 73 may have followed Abel when he included at the end a reference to P. K. Hitti's *History of the Arabs* (London, 1937), 82, which mentions Imru' al-Qays of the Namāra inscription. On Iotabe, see also M. Sartre, in *IGLS*, xiii, 9046.

[34] To have not only attacked the island but also to have kept it under his control suggests considerable self-confidence on the part of Amorkesos, and an ability to defend himself even when isolated on an island such as Iotabe and fighting in an element with which he was not familiar.

[35] Textual critics have argued whether Πετραίαν should be preceded by ἐπί, as suggested by Valesius, or κατά, as suggested by Bekker. For the Greek text, see below, App. 3.

fourth century, but instead chose to express himself through the geographical idiom of Strabo, who conceived of this region as Arabia Petraea. The reference is specific enough, since it indicates that Amorkesos was made phylarch not over Palaestina Tertia in its entirely but over the Trans-ʿAraban part of it, which Malchus referred to as Arabia Petraea. This could indicate that the villages he attacked were also in that region, since they were also closer to his base in Ḥijāz than villages in Sinai.[36]

The foregoing may solve the problem of the phrase in Malchus ὑπὸ/ἐπὶ/κατὰ Πετραίαν. The facts should guide the textual scholar in the choice of the correct preposition and in the interpretation of the phrase. (1) Petra is out of the question[37] since its orthography is different, and Malchus employed the classical term used by Strabo and hallowed after him by usage. He himself came from Philadelphia and was very familiar with the terms he was using; consequently Petraea has to be understood to mean Arabia Petraea. It is also unlikely that Amorkesos would have attacked the region of the city of Petra, since this would have brought him perilously near the *limes Arabicus* and its fortifications, while the region east of the Gulf of Eilat would have been open to his raids. So it is practically certain that Amorkesos attacked villages not around Petra but in "Rocky" Arabia, east of the Gulf of Eilat, and this is primarily where he wanted his phylarchate to be. From the Roman point of view, this, rather than the region near Petra, would have been the more appropriate one, since it was more exposed to hostile Saracen raids from northern Ḥijāz. (2) It is also almost certain that Amorkesos' phylarchate was within Roman territory or at least the Roman sphere of influence in Palaestina Tertia. The southern boundaries of this province cannot be ascertained, but Amorkesos' desire to be the phylarch of the Saracens "subject to the Romans" makes it certain that he operated within the boundaries of Palaestina Tertia. Even without this phase, his occupation of Iotabe establishes that he was within the territorial boundaries of the empire. Thus he operated within the confines of Palaestina Tertia, desired to be recognized as a phylarch over the Arabs within that province, and was in fact later confirmed by Leo as phylarch there.[38]

3. Finally, how was it possible for an Arab chief in the reign of Leo to effect deep penetrations within Roman territory and, what is more, to occupy one of the Roman islands, especially one that had such strategic importance

[36] The port of Maqnā would have been the closest of these localities to Amorkesos on Iotabe. If he occupied it, he would also have had an encounter with Jews of this port, and possibly also those of Medina, if he included that town in his activities in Ḥijāz.

[37] It, rather than Arabia Petraea, appears in the entry on Amorkesos in *PLRE*, II, 73.

[38] Thus the most appropriate of the three prepositions listed above, note 35, is the one which refers to an area *within* the province.

for Roman interests in the Red Sea, lying as it did between the southern mouths of the Gulf of Eilat and that of Clysma? Furthermore, the Arab chief's occupation of the island entailed the eviction of its Roman tax collectors, and this would have dealt a blow not only to Roman material interests but also to its pride and prestige in the whole Red Sea area and western Arabia. The military dispositions of Byzantium make this all the more surprising. Palaestina Tertia, which witnessed the brunt of Amorkesos' thrusts, was well defended. The *Notitia Dignitatum* is informative on the units that were deployed there in the fifth century. Ayla, at the head of the Gulf of Eilat, was the station of *Legio Fretensis*, transferred there from Jerusalem in the reign of Diocletian, and its transfer was inspired by some such potential danger from Arabia and the Arabs. There were also military units and forces in the neighboring provincia Arabia.[39] All or any of these forces in Palaestina Tertia and in the Provincia Arabia could have come to the rescue of the beleaguered province under attack from Amorkesos, in much the same way as, toward the end of the century, Romanus, the energetic *dux* of Palestine, was able to disperse a coalition of tribes that had posed a serious threat to the same region and, furthermore, to evict the Arabs from the same island.[40] Not only regular Roman troops but also Arab *foederati* of Byzantium, especially deployed for meeting such a threat, could have dealt with this situation. Federate presence is attested in the fifth century in Palaestina Tertia and in the Provincia Arabia. In view of this overwhelming evidence for regular Roman and federate Arab presence in the region, the successes of Amorkesos pose a real problem for which there must be an answer. Surely these forces, both imperial and federate, must have been on an overridingly important assignment elsewhere and were too far from the field of operations to be able to come to the rescue of Palaestina Tertia and the island of Iotabe, both assaulted by an exceptionally resourceful and powerful warrior such as Amorkesos. The question thus arises as to where these forces could have been deployed.

The last years of the reign of Leo provide the answer. In 468 and 470 Leo dispatched a huge armada from the East against the Vandals of Gaeseric in Africa. The estimates sometimes provide fantastic figures but historians agree on the magnitude of the expedition in terms of ships, men, and centenaria of gold spent on it. According to modest estimates, the fleet consisted of 1,113 ships, which carried 100,000 soldiers; the cost was 100,000 pounds of gold. This was a huge expedition; the mustering of an expeditionary force of this size must have entailed mobilizing many contingents from the *limes orientalis*. This was possible because of the peace that reigned between the two

[39] For the units stationed in Palestine and Arabia, see below, 467–69.

[40] For this, see Theophanes, *Chronographia*, I, 141.

world powers in the fifth century. The last war fought with Persia was in the reign of Theodosius II; no doubt this, and the fact that the Persians were busy with the Ephthalite Huns, facilitated even more the transfer of troops from a front that was non-operational. There were precedents for the transfer of legions and *limitanei* from one front to another, as there were for the transfer of federate troops.[41] Thus a situation obtained in which the southern part of the *limes orientalis*, as well as Egypt, was stripped of its troops, both federate and imperials. This temporary military vacuum occasioned by Leo's expedition against the Vandals created suitable conditions for the military exploits of Amorkesos by land and sea, which would otherwise have been completely incomprehensible.

In addition to explaining these military successes, Leo's Vandal expedition solves another problem which the fragment from Malchus raises, namely, the chronology of Amorkesos' military activity and movements after he left Persia.[42] The first military expedition against the Vandals took place in 468 and the second in 470. Whether Amorkesos attacked Palaestina Tertia during the first or second expedition is a matter of detail. The chances are that he attacked in 468 and that he continued to attack after the end of the first ill-starred expedition, while Byzantium was preparing for the second. It is, therefore, possible that the military operations of Amorkesos in Palaestina Tertia began in 468 and ended with his visit to Constantinople in 473. This chronology also makes it certain that the Arabian phase of his career—after he left Persia—extended from some unknown year in the reign of Leo until 468. That year thus separates the Arabian from the Byzantine phase of his career.

III. Negotiations with Leo

After his successes on land and sea, the Arab chief sent Petrus, the bishop of his tribe, to Constantinople to negotiate with Leo the question of his phylarchate in Palaestina Tertia. The emperor was receptive and asked Amorkesos to come to the capital. This extraordinary diplomatic triumph calls for a number of comments.

Amorkesos' diplomacy was the climax of his successes in war and signaled also a desire to win the peace. In this case diplomacy was the continuation of war by other means. The Arab chief had demonstrated his military worth by his successes and now wanted to reap the harvest by a triumph in another area—by becoming a phylarch of the Romans. This desire reflects how this office, modestly called the phylarchate, was much coveted by Arab chiefs, even as successful as Amorkesos. What mattered to these chiefs in the

[41] See below, 94.

[42] Further on Leo's African expedition against the Vandals, see below, Sec. vi.

end was not only military successes in Arabia but the Roman connection, which carried with it the title phylarch.

To achieve his goal, Amorkesos sent no ordinary emissary, but the bishop Petrus.[43] His dispatch of Petrus reflects his astuteness and understanding of the importance of ecclesiastical diplomacy in the Christian Roman Empire.[44] Petrus' mission and its success raise a number of important problems concerning him, Amorkesos, and the latter's overtures to Constantinople:

1. *Petrus*. The first question is that of his ecclesiastical jurisdiction. Aigrain, and after him Abel,[45] argued that he was the bishop of Iotabe, and cited bishops for this island who took part in ecclesiastical councils: Markianos at Chalcedon in 453 and Anastasius at Constantinople in 536. But it is quite unlikely that Petrus was the bishop of Iotabe. If he had been, Malchus would have said so, since he wrote an account of Amorkesos that is so specific and detailed, devoting special attention to Iotabe and Amorkesos' occupation of it. On the other hand, Malchus refers to the bishop twice, and on both occasions leaves no doubt about the jurisdiction of Petrus' episcopate. He refers to him not as the bishop of Iotabe but "the bishop of his tribe," and in the opening sentence of the fragment he describes him as "the priest of the Christians among the tented Arabs." The two descriptions leave no doubt that Petrus was not the bishop of Iotabe but of the Arabs of Amorkesos.

Was he an Arab? Abel thinks so,[46] and the chances are good that he was: (1) Malchus' description of him indicates this. (2) In the fourth century the ethnic identity of bishops over the Arab *foederati* was an issue,[47] and Queen Mavia insisted on having an Arab as bishop of her *foederati*. (3) It was easier for an Arab bishop to serve a community of Arab believers, especially if they were *foederati* living in the limitrophe. (4) Christianity had spread extensively in the fifth century among the Arabs in Oriens, in Ḥijāz, and in northern

[43] The journey of a bishop from Arabia Petraea to Constantinople must have been made with the knowledge and approval of the local Roman authorities in Oriens. The *agens in rebus* at this time, Modestus (*PLRE*, II, 764), active in Leo's service 472, must have sent approving reports. Petrus would have traveled through the state post, the *cursus publicus*, open since the days of Constantine to bishops who attended synods and, presumably, still open in the 5th century for bishops who traveled on state business such as this mission: see F. Dvornik, *Origins of Intelligence Services* (New Brunswick, N.J., 1974), 123.

[44] The mission of this ecclesiastic in the history of Arab-Byzantine relations recalls that of Moses (*BAFOC*, 152–58) and Abraham/Abramius in the sixth (*PLRE*, II, 3).

[45] Aigrain, "Arabie," 1197–98; Abel, "Jotabè", 534; see also his section on the bishopric of Iotabe, 533–53. Le Quien thought it belonged to the Palestinian Parembole, while Duchesne thought it belonged to Sinaitic Pharan both of which, Aigrain decided quite rightly, are out of the question.

[46] Ibid., 534, where he speaks of him as *d'origine arabe*.

[47] On Moses see *BAFOC*, 152–58.

Arabia; Eusebius testifies to the number of churches of the Saracens in the desert near Petra,[48] and Sozomen to the number of bishops among the Arabs in their villages.[49] It is therefore natural to suppose that the community within which Christianity was widely spread did not fail to produce most of its own clergy,[50] and the Arab origin of some of these bishops is attested.[51] The chances, then, are that Petrus was an Arab who came from the region of Arabia Petraea.[52]

More important is his doctrinal persuasion and his ecclesiastical affiliation:

a. Petrus made the journey to Constantinople in 473, that is, some twenty years after the Council of Chalcedon. The question thus arises whether he was a Diophysite or a Monophysite. Leo was staunchly Orthodox and Chalcedonian. Petrus would not have made the journey to Constantinople and would not have expected any success with the very Orthodox emperor if he had come to him as a representative of the Monophysite heresy. The chances, then, are that he was a Diophysite, especially since Palestine and those regions had not yet been touched by the Monophysite movement. This was to come later, with the Ghassānids of the reign of Anastasius in the sixth century.

b. After Amorkesos concluded a *foedus* with Leo, Petrus became technically the bishop of the *foederati*. These belonged administratively to Palaestina Tertia, and so their bishop, too, must have belonged ecclesiastically to the church of Palaestina Tertia which, after Chalcedon, was under the newly created patriarchate of Jerusalem. Palaestina Tertia had four bishops, those of Petra, Ayla, Zoara, and Elusa. Thus Petrus joined the rank of these four bishops, but naturally had a special position as the bishop of the *foederati*. How he was affiliated before the conclusion of the *foedus*, when his phylarch, Amorkesos, was still warring with the Romans, is not clear. But the *ecclesia* often acted independently of the *imperium*, and it is possible that in the years preceding his own journey to Constantinople, he became bishop over the

[48] That is not far from the area where Amorkesos was operating; for the reference in Eusebius, see G. Bowersock, *Roman Arabia* (Cambridge, Mass., 1983), 141 note 13.

[49] Sozomen, *HE*, VII, 19, p. 330.

[50] The Arabs of the Provincia Arabia produced sophists, historians, and rhetoricians as part of Arab Hellenism (see below, p. 104). It would thus be unnatural to suppose that when their Hellenism was Christianized they did not provide the Church with Arab clergy.

[51] It is practically certain that many or even most the bishops of the *cities* of the Provincia Arabia and of Palaestina Tertia were Arabs ethnically, in spite of their assumption of Greek and biblical names. Although called ἱερεύς in the fragment, Petrus was a bishop; on the indifferent employment of Roman and Christian terminology in Malchus, including ἱερεύς for ἐπίσκοπος, see Baldwin, "Malchus," 106.

[52] He could also have come with Amorkesos from Ḥīra, but this is a difficult question, depending on the Christianity of Amorkesos—whether it was recent, related to his moving in the Roman orbit, or old, going back to the time when he was still in Persian territory.

Arabs of Amorkesos through the missionary efforts of the episcopal sees close by, such as Ayla, Petra, or Iotabe itself. The *ecclesia* may have carried on missionary activity among the Arabs of Amorkesos, possibly in response to his overtures; he may have realized the value of conversion to the faith of the empire as a step toward his acceptance and assimilation in the Byzantine system. If so, this resulted in the assignment of a bishop for his Arabs such as those Sozomen speaks of.[53]

2. *Amorkesos*. A relevant question in this context is whether or not he was a Christian when he dispatched Petrus to Leo. The question was raised by Malchus, who denied that he became a Christian in Constantinople and said that Leo only pretended that he had in order to justify seating him among the first patricians.

An Arab chief who became a *foederatus* with the blessings of the Orthodox Cristian emperor Leo in the fifth century and came to Constantinople itself for investiture could only have been Christian, or have become Christian in the capital. His conversion may have taken place during one of three phases: the pre-Roman one, while in Persian territory; when he reached the Roman frontier and spent some years at the limitrophe of the Christian Roman emperor; or while in Constantinople. It is impossible to tell in which phase he became a Christian, and so the only course open is to explore all three possibilities:[54] (*a*) Before he wandered into Arabia, Amorkesos had been in a region that had witnessed the propagation of Christianity, and he probably lived in Ḥīra, the great Arab urban center in Persian territory and center of Christianity on the Lower Euphrates. The Ghassānids to whom he almost certainly belonged had embraced Christianity, and the church of Banū Zimmān was associated with their name.[55] It is even possible that his defection from Persia was motivated by his being Christian or sympathetic to Christianity. (*b*) In the second phase he lived in northern Ḥijāz and in biblical Midian,[56] penetrated by missionaries from nearby Palaestina Tertia, from such advanced posts as the bishoprics

[53] Sozomen, 462–65. The background of Petrus is difficult to penetrate and two questions remain unanswerable: (1) whether he was a member of the tribe of Amorkesos or simply a bishop appointed over that tribe from the outside; (2) whether he could have come with Amorkesos from Persia, in view of the fact that Christianity was not unknown among the Ghassānids of Ḥīra. This could be supported by the possibility that Amorkesos left Persia because his religion was an issue. These pertinent questions can be posed but cannot be answered. The chances, however, are that Petrus was not a bishop who came with Amorkesos from Persia but became his bishop while Amorkesos was within the Roman orbit, even though he was warring with the Romans. This is more consonant with what is known of this resourceful phylarch, whose diplomacy was as impressive as his military prowess. A bishop approved of by the Byzantine Church had better chances of success as an emissary to Leo than one who was not.

[54] The third possibility will be discussed in its context in the following section.

[55] See above, note 26.

[56] On Christianity in these regions, see *BAFOC*, 383 note 124, and below, Chap. 14.

of Ayla and Petra.[57] It is equally important that his tribe, or most of it, was Christian or had been converted to Christianity, since Malchus speaks of Petrus as its bishop. The presumption is that if his tribe was Christian, so was he, since otherwise one has to assume that the tribe adopted Christianity and received a bishop while the chief chose to remain pagan, which is most unlikely. The converse was more likely to be true, namely, the ruler adopted Christianity, and his people followed him. It does not seem likely that an Arab chief of a Christian tribe which had a bishop over it would send this bishop to the Christian Roman emperor while he himself remained pagan.

As to his doctrinal persuasion, what has been said of his bishop may with equal truth be said of the phylarch, that is, assuming that he was Christian at this time.[58] Palestine, or what was now the Patriarchate of Jersualem, comprising the three Palestines, was solidly Chalcedonian, Diophysite, and remained untouched by Monophysitism. If Amorkesos received his Christianity from the bishops and missionaries of Palaestina Tertia, his Christianity would have been Diophysite. This is a fact of some importance in the history of the Ghassānids, who in the sixth century appear as strongly Monophysitic and indeed, are the champions of the Monophysite movement, a fact which had far-reaching effects on the course of their history. Thus the doctrinal persuasion of Amorkesos, the first Ghassānid chief in the employ of Byzantium in the fifth century, becomes important, as it suggests that the Ghassānids of the sixth century must have been converted to Monophysitism sometime after the reign of Leo, most probably in the reign of Anastasius.

3. *The overtures.* These, according to Malchus, reflected the wishes of Amorkesos to become an ally of the Romans and phylarch of the Roman Arabs in Arabia Petraea. The historian adds that Petrus' mission was successful, and Leo accepted these proposals, asking that Amorkesos appear personally in Constantinople.

Surely, the account in Malchus must be highly elliptical. It is difficult to believe that the Roman *autokrator* would have accepted such humiliating proposals from an Arab chief who had harassed the Roman frontier and occupied a strategic island and neighboring Roman villages. The emperor must have heard from the ecclesiastic an account of Amorkesos that projected an image different from that presented by the historian. Otherwise Amorkesos' proposals would simply have added insult to injury. Petrus must have ex-

[57] The propagation of Christianity in northern Ḥijāz must have been facilitated by the consanguinity between the proselytizers and the proselytized. The Provincia Arabia and Palaestina Tertia were ethnically Arab regions, and their ecclesiastical hierarchy must have been predominantly Arab. Hence their success among their congeners in this region.

[58] Whether he was touched by Nestorianism while he was in Ḥīra remains an open question.

plained to Leo that imperial interests would be well served by this doughty warrior who appeared so dramatically on the Byzantine limitrophe and had proved himself by scoring such signal successes. These imperial interests, and others related to them, are as follows:

a. Southern Oriens, bordering on Ḥijāz and the northern Red Sea, needed a strong federate presence to protect it against inroads by the Saracens, and the successes of Amorkesos seemed to confirm this fact. Since this was an important area strategically it was deemed prudent to accept the fait accompli presented by these successes and treat Amorkesos as an ally and Roman phylarch to defend the frontier and Roman interests in the region, especially as he took the initiative in asking for the friendship of the Roman people. This was the century of the Germanic invasions that dismembered the western half of the empire; this may have induced in the emperors (and Leo in particular after the failure of his Vandal expedition) a willingness to be accommodating and to accept the fait accompli. Rather than fight a redoubtable desert chief in difficult terrain, the emperor found it more convenient to win over the phylarch as a friend and convert him from a raider of the *limes* to a sentinel on the imperial frontier.

b. Closely related to the military defense of the region was the question of trade in that vital area, through which passed the northern termini of the spice route, the *via odorifera*, which ran through western Arabia. Control of the northern sector and insuring the safety of caravans through it would have been part of the newly appointed phylarch's duties. There was also the route through the Red Sea, connecting the world of the Mediterranean with that of the Indian Ocean. Clearly, Amorkesos was involved in this, since he was in occupation of a strategic island and was energetic in administering it. Finally, through his tribal affiliation with the Azd group, one of the most important tribal groups in western Arabia, he could insure some measure of security for Byzantine trade interests. There was an Azd colony, the Aws and the Khazraj, in Medina, one of the stations on the trade route. There was another, Khuzāʿa, in Mecca, including the descendants of Quṣayy, whom Byzantium had helped establish in Mecca. In Najrān, too, there was an Azd component among the population. These were all Arab communities, and two of them were Arab cities, situated in the middle sector of western Arabia, between the Jewish oases of Ḥijāz and the Ḥimyarites, traditionally hostile to Rome and Byzantium. Thus it is possible that Amorkesos suggested to Leo through Petrus that his appointment as phylarch would result in a resuscitation of the tradition of Roman trade in western Arabia and the Red Sea through his friendly contacts with the Arab communities of this middle sector.[59]

[59] For the Byzantine presence in the cities of the middle sector, especially Najrān and Mecca, see below, Chap. 13, secs. II and III.

c. Finally, as a convert to Christianity who chose an ecclesiastic as his mouthpiece, Amorkesos may have suggested to the Christian emperor Leo that his phylarchate would entail the assertion of a Christian presence among the Arabs, especially in Ḥijāz and western Arabia. Christianity had established a foothold in Najrān early in the century, and the chief, Ḥayyān,[60] who introduced Christianity to his city, had a Byzantine connection. Mecca, whose chief, Quṣayy, had the same connection, conceivably had a faint Christian presence, and the same may have been true of Medina. The members of the *ecclesia* in the Near East were in touch with one another,[61] and thus it is possible that this aspect of Amorkesos' functions was first suggested to him by Petrus, who most probably was aware of what was going on in the various Christian centers of western Arabia.[62] This, too, must have carried weight with the Christian emperor, who was *fidei defensor.*[63] The fact that Judaism was making headway in this region and in the south may have won over Ḥimyar itself,[64] could have inclined Leo to accommodate Amorkesos, especially as conversion to Judaism, in the alignments of the period, was politically significant; it entailed the spread of anti-Byzantine sentiments and an increase of anti-Byzantine pockets in western Arabia.

IV. Amorkesos in Constantinople

Amorkesos' visit to the capital was the occasion for a number of friendly encounters with the emperor. The two dined together, Leo asked the phylarch to attend Senate meetings, and the two exchanged gifts. The visit[65] and these

[60] For Ḥayyān/Ḥannān, see below, Chap. 13, sec. iii. It is tantalizing to think that Amorkesos and Ḥayyān/Ḥannān were related. It was argued earlier in this chapter that the Amorkesos of the Greek text may be ʿAmr, son of Qays, of the Buqayla clan in Ḥīra. According to his genealogy, ʿAmr had a grandfather by the name of Ḥannān/Ḥayyān. Since Ḥayyān's *floruit* was in the first half of the 5th century and that of Amorkesos was in the second, the former could have been the grandfather of the latter; for the genealogy of ʿAmr, son of Qays, see Cheikho, *Al-Naṣrāniyya.*

[61] The most outstanding example of this was Simeon of Bēth-Arshām, who energetically informed members of his Monophysite communion in the Fertile Crescent of the persecution of Christians in South Arabia, around 520.

[62] It was also in the reign of Leo that the martyrdom of ʿAzqīr in Najrān took place. This was most probably known to Petrus; if so, it would have drawn his attention to the plight of Christians in Najrān. He could very well have seen in the energetic phylarch a protector of Christianity in western Arabia. On ʿAzqīr and the problems involved in the Ethiopic account of his martyrdom, see A. F. L. Beeston, in *L'Arabie du Sud*, ed. J. Chelhod (Paris, 1984), I, 272; idem, "The Martyrdom of ʿAzqīr," *Proceedings of the Seminar for Arabian Studies* 15 (London, 1985), 5–10.

[63] Leo may have felt about the Christians of South Arabia as Theodosius II had felt about the persecution of Christians in Persia around 420.

[64] See the cautionary remarks of Beeston, in *L'Arabie*, 277–78.

[65] There is no record of how phylarchs were entertained in Constantinople when they visited. On how the ambassadors of the Persian king in pre-Islamic times and those of the Arab

extraordinary familiarities present problems and call for the following comments:

1. Amorkesos made his journey to Constantinople by land.[66] This is implied by Malchus' saying that on his way to Constantinople he was able to see the Roman cities of the Orient, defenseless and luxuriant. His journey can easily be reconstructed: from Palaestina Tertia through Oriens to Derebe and thence through Anatolia to Constantinople. His namesake of the sixth century, the Kindite poet-prince Imru' al-Qays, who also journeyed to Constantinople,[67] mentions passing through the Ḥawran, Baʿlabakk, Ḥamā, Shayzar, and Emesa before he reached Derebe.

2. The journey to Constantinople could have significant meaning for the office of the phylarchate in this period. That he was made phylarch there and not in some city of Palaestina Tertia in Oriens—for instance Alya or Petra—could mean that it was customary for Arab chiefs to be installed in the office in the capital, which indicates its importance. On the other hand, it could be argued that the emperor endowed him with the phylarchate in Constantinople because of the special circumstances that attended his appearance on the Roman scene, as described by Malchus.[68]

3. It is clear from the attention given to Amorkesos by the emperor while he was in Constantinople that the Arab chief fulfilled Leo's expectations. The list of honors gives a glimpse of what barbarian princes were treated to when they visited the capital: private audience with the emperor, dinner at his table, attending the sessions of the Senate, and the exchange of gifts. One of the two striking items in this list is Amorkesos' sitting among the protopatricians in the Senate, which, according to Malchus, outraged Constantinople. This led Nöldeke to think that Amorkesos was actually made *patricius*. It has been argued in detail by the present writer that this was not

caliphs in Islamic times were treated, see the two chapters in Constantine Porphyrogenitus, *De Ceremoniis*. The phylarchs of pre-Islamic times were not as important as these ambassadors, but the two chapters in *De Ceremoniis* could give an idea how lesser personages were treated.

[66] For the *cursus publicus* he used see L. Bréhier, *Le monde byzantin* (Paris, 1948), II, 325–33, and F. Dvornik, *Intelligence Service*, 122–219.

[67] He apparently never reached it, but died on his way. His ode, which might be termed "the Caesar Ode" will be analyzed in *BASIC*. He, too, used the *cursus publicus* and refers to the *veredi* in his poetry, a word which was imported into Arabic in pre-Islamic times as *barīd*.

[68] The journies of other Arab figures to Constantinople in this pre-Islamic period, especially the Kindite and the Ghassānid princes of the 6th century, such as the Ghassānid Arethas and the Kindite Qays, are attested and will be treated in *BASIC*. Sometimes the emblems of office were sent to allied chiefs wherever they happened to be rather than given them in Constantinople; for an instance of this, see what Procopius says of the Lazi of Colchis, *Wars*, II, xv, 2.

the case.[69] The association of Amorkesos with the title *patricius* in the Arabic sources is, however, noteworthy. The legend of his patriciate may have arisen among the Arabs in the following manner: (1) He himself circulated it after his return from Constantinople to enhance his prestige, or he may have simply recounted his mingling with the patricians, which was wrongly interpreted by his followers as tantamount to the conferment of that honor. (2) The title may have been applied to him by his followers not in a technical manner but merely to reflect the Roman connection which he had recently contracted, since the patriciate was a distinctly Byzantine title and often appears in the Arabic sources to designate a *Rhōmaios*, especially an important one.

4. The purple patch in this "fascinating fragment" of Malchus, however, is the passage in which the historian describes the exchange of gifts between the emperor and the phylarch. The first problem which this passage raises is a textual one. In its complete and fullest form it appears in de Boor's edition:

> καὶ τέλος ἀπέπεμψεν αὐτόν, ἰδίαν μὲν παρ' αὐτοῦ εἰκόνα τινὰ χρυσῆν καὶ κατάλιθον λαβὼν σφόδρα τε οὖσαν πολυτελῆ, χρήματα δὲ καὶ αὐτὸς ἐκείνῳ ἐκ τοῦ δημοσίου ἀντιδοὺς καὶ τῶν ἄλλων κελεύσας ἕκαστον εἰσενεγκεῖν, ὅσοι ἐτέλουν εἰς τὴν βουλήν.
>
> . . . and finally, he (the emperor) dismissed him (the phylarch), after receiving from him a very valuable portrait of him in gold, set with precious stones, and after giving him in return money from the public treasury and ordering all the senators to give him gifts.

In his standard edition of the text,[70] de Boor restored the passage as it appears above and was rightly followed by the latest editor of Malchus, R. C. Blockley.[71] Previous editors of Malchus had toyed with Niebuhr's emendation[72] of λαβών to λαβόντα, which would have made the emperor the donor rather than the recipient of the *eikōn*, the picture or portrait. But de Boor's reading is the sound one, since it recognizes that there was an *exchange* of gifts between the emperor and the phylarch. This is confirmed by ἀντιδούς, "giving him in return," spoken of the emperor. Niebuhr may have been inclined to read λαβόντα because he thought it incredible that the phylarch, a "no-

[69] See below, App. 1. A few more relevant bibliographical items may be added to those in the article that appears as App. 1. The outrage of Malchus concerning barbarians mingling with the senators and the magistrates had been voiced earlier by Synesius; see Stein *HBE*, II, 788, Excursus C.

[70] For the fragment in its entirey, with its apparatus criticus, see below, App. 3.

[71] See Blockley, *CH*, II, 406, lines 36–40.

[72] Such as L. Dindorf in *Historici Graeci Minores* (Teubner, 1870), I, 386, lines 14–15, where he entertains it in the text as a possibility.

mad," would have given the emperor an *eikōn*. But this is a mistaken view of Amorkesos, as will be seen presently. It is the result of Malchus' description of him as the chief of "the tented Saracens," and of the legacy of Ammianus, who equated Arab with Saracen and nomad.

In addition to restoring λαβών, de Boor restored the vulgate reading ἰδίαν, rejecting ἰδία, which is to be found only in manuscript B. This restoration changes the interpretation of *eikōn*. Instead of interpreting it as a picture given to Leo privately or as a personal gift, the term ἰδίαν should be translated so as to make the *eikōn* a *personal* portrait of the phylarch. This is the correct reading of the text and its correct translation.[73] The case for the *eikōn*'s being a personal portrait of the phylarch may be presented as follows. Something, it must be conceded, may be said for ἰδία, mainly because it contrasts with ἐκ τοῦ δημοσίου, spoken of Leo. The contrast would be in consonance with Malchus' antipathies, since it tells against the emperor's greed and unscrupulousness. But ἰδία is not the vulgate's reading; it is only in B, and it is otiose. After all, a present from a visiting phylarch in the form of an *eikōn* would naturally be a private present and does not need to be advertised as such. Furthermore, if it had been just another picture, and not the phylarch's own portrait, it would have lost its interest, since Constantinople was full of pictures and images. But it was not full of images that depicted the phylarch. The chances are then that ἰδίαν here means an image of the phylarch who, being exceptionally clever and talented, wanted to impress the emperor and leave with him a memento of his visit that would permanently commemorate it.[74]

It remains to show that Amorkesos could easily have had an image of himself made somewhere in North Arabia and brought it with him to Constantinople.

a. Amorkesos was not a nomad, in spite of the fact that he may have commanded troops, some of whom were nomads or semi-nomads. The view that Amorkesos was a nomad may have been held by scholars who were influenced by the opening statement in Malchus, which was a reflection of the picture that Ammianus had drawn of the Arabs. Amorkesos had most probably lived in an Arab urban center—Ḥīra, on the Lower Euphrates—before his defection, and so he was a city-dweller and remained so in spite of his wanderings in northern Arabia and Palaestina Tertia, amidst peoples who may have been nomads or semi-nomads. In Ḥīra he would have seen churches,

[73] Both Profs. C. Mango and N. Oikonomides, with whom I discussed this passage, share this view.

[74] This is what a Roman emperor of the 6th century, Justin I, did when he received Tzath the King of the Lazi. He gave him, among other things, a picture of himself as a memento; see Malalas, *Chronographia*, 413 for this very colorful description of the Lazic king.

monasteries, and palaces with many pictures, images, and even icons, which became numerous in the East from the fifth century on. Ḥīra was the great Christian Arab center in pre-Islamic times, and Sasanid as well as Christian influences on its art and architecture need no elaboration.[75]

b. The last phase of his wanderings after he left the Persians brought him to northern Ḥijāz, whence he attacked Roman territory in Palaestina Tertia. Ḥijāz had many urban centers, especially the various oasis-cities. The Jewish settlers of these oases were well known in Arabia as workers in iron, silver, and gold.[76] Thus Amorkesos was living not far from urban centers where painting, metal work, and goldwork were not unknown.

c. After wandering in a region that had craftsmen of the minor arts, it is not unnatural to assume that he conceived the idea of carrying with him to Constantinople a gift, a portrait of himself carved in gold and set in precious stones, which a local craftsman from one of the nearby urban centers could have made for him. Perhaps the sight of the Byzantine *solidus* with its effigy of the emperor suggested the idea to him. He could not strike coins with his image, but he could have a portrait of himself made. It did not have to be a great work of art and probably did not reflect a faithful likeness of the phylarch, but it was adequate.[77] It conveyed what the phylarch looked like, and in so doing it fulfilled his expectations.

5. The emperor's gift consisted of money—no doubt splendid Byzantine

[75] On Ḥīra, see the present writer in *EI*^{2}, s.v.

[76] Such as Wā'il ibn-ʿAtiyya, the 6th-century goldsmith of Fadak, who belonged to a Jewish community long established in northern Ḥijāz; see A. Ḥillī, *al-Manāqib al-Mazyadiyya*, ed. S. Daradika and M. Khuraysāt (Amman, 1984), I, 287. M. J. Kister had drawn attention to this important source, *al-Manāqib*, while still in manuscript form.

There are also references in the sources to the fact that paintings were not unknown in Ḥijāz: (1) According to Iṣbahānī, the Jews of Medina painted the picture of Mālik ibn al-ʿAjlān in their synagogues; see *Aghānī* (Beirut, 1960), XXII, 105. (2) According to Masʿūdī, portraits of the chiefs of Mecca, including Quṣayy, were to be seen on the wall of the Kaʿba; see below, Chap. 13, sec. II.

The Roman military painter of legionary shields was also known in Ḥijāz, as is clear from a Greek inscription left by one such military painter in Madā' in Ṣāliḥ (Hijr), deep in the heart of Ḥijāz. The Arabic term for ornamentation "zukhruf" is a loanword from Greek ζωγραφία and entered Arabic in this pre-Islamic period; see below, 477 note 74. This is witness to the fact that representational art was known in Ḥijāz. All these data leave no doubt whatsoever that Amorkesos could very well have had a portrait of himself made in Ḥijāz and taken it with him to Constantinople.

[77] The modesty of the artistic endeavor may be reflected in the idiom of the historian, who speaks of an ἑικόνα τινά. The τινά after ἑικόνα sounds an echo of the fact that it was artistically indifferent, and may be translated as "some kind of portrait." Also, τινά would not have been used by the historian if the εἰκών had been given the phylarch by the emperor. The emperor would have given him a picture that reflected an excellent likeness of himself and not one which would have been described by the historian in a manner that expressed some aesthetic reservation.

solidi, such as were struck in the reign of Leo, bearing the effigy of the emperor himself. It was an appropriate return gift; the Byzantine coinage projected the imperial image in much the same way that the icon did for saints.[78] And, of course, it reciprocated the portrait given Leo by Amorkesos. It is not unlikely that Leo may also have given Leo a medallion of himself.[79] The senators, too, gave Amorkesos gold *solidi* to affirm that the phylarch had the support of that venerable body, and not only that of the *autokrator*.

The reference to the public treasury raises the question whether this was an advance of the *annona foederatica*[80] that Amorkesos was entitled to as phylarch and the further question whether this was paid him in the future in money or in kind.

V. The Phylarchate of Amorkesos

At the end of his stay in Constantinople, Leo formally endowed Amorkesos with the phylarchate. He confirmed him in his possession of the island of Iotabe and even gave him authority over a large number of villages. This was an unusual arrangement.

1. This is the only instance recorded in the extant sources of an Arab phylarch being given charge of an island and, what is more, one that was so strategically located: at the meeting of the two gulfs of Clysma and Eilat, clearly of great importance for controlling trade in the Red Sea, between the Mediterranean and the Indian Ocean. That the Arab phylarchs in Oriens were assigned functions other than their purely military ones is practically certain, but is rarely stated in the sources. This fragment from Malchus is consequently valuable, since it indicates, at least by implication, one non-military function of the phylarch, namely, securing the trade routes that led from South Arabia and the world of the Indian Ocean to that of the Mediterranean.

The island of Iotabe was only a part of Amorkesos' territorial jurisdiction. His principal phylarchate must have been over the *foederati* on the mainland in Midian to the east of the Gulf of Eilat. That Leo added to his responsibilities by entrusting him with a number of villages can only reflect the confi-

[78] See A. Bellinger, "The Coins and Byzantine Imperial Policy," *Speculum* 31 (1956), 70. How the effigy of the Byzantine emperor on the *nomisma* furbished up the imperial image in Ceylon is recounted by Cosmas Indicopleustes in a well-known passage involving the merchant Sopatrus. On the icon, see the recent study, "The Role of the Icon in Byzantine Piety" by L. Rydén, in *Scripta Instituti Donneriani Aboensis* 10 (Stockholm, 1987), 41–52.

[79] What the phylarch received in Constantinople may still be seen in coins of Leo that have survived.

[80] This was the point that was raised by Malchus as part of his *Kaiserkritik*, for which see below, 100–101.

dence that the phylarch inspired in the emperor. The villages are not named in the fragment, but may have included some Jewish settlements known from Muhammadan times, such as Maqnā, along the coast of the Gulf of Eilat.

2. Malchus mentions Arabia Petraea as the area within which Amorkesos coveted his phylarchate. This phrase, which Malchus resuscitated from Ptolemy, suggests that Amorkesos' phylarchate extended over that area which lay east of Wādī ʿAraba (the valley of ʿAraba) and which possibly comprised the Sharāt range, Midian, and Ḥismā in northern Ḥijāz.

3. An important question raised by the fragment is how a phylarch was installed in his office: whether this was done on the spot in Oriens, roughly where the phylarch was going to operate, or whether he had to come to Constantinople. The sources are silent on the point, but the fragment has hints and some vague indications.

The first reference to a journey to the capital comes in connection with the sending of Bishop Petrus to the emperor in Constantinople. The tenor of the sentence suggests that phylarchs were normally installed there. However, a closer look suggests that Constantinople was involved in the account because of the unusual circumstances that attended Amorkesos' career, especially that his employment by Byzantium would have violated one of the clauses of the treaty between the two world powers, to the effect that the one should not accept the rebellious Saracens of the other. This is also supported by the opening sentence, in which Petrus' visit is explained ἐξ αἰτίας ταύτης. This refers to the sentence immediately following, which describes the Persian-Byzantine treaty on the non-acceptance of rebellious Saracens. Presumably such an important clause in the treaty could not be violated without the express approval of the emperor, who had to be consulted on such matters. Although the dispatch of Bishop Petrus related to other important matters involving Amorkesos, this was certainly one of the most important.

On the other hand, the passage in which Malchus expresses disapproval of Leo's inviting Amorkesos to Constantinople strongly suggests that the installation of an Arab chief in the office of phylarch was normally done not in Constantinople but in the relevant province of the diocese. He says that the emperor should have done this from afar, πόρρωθεν, by means of imperial officials in the province, and that this would have made a better impression on the prospective phylarch, who would have respected the emperor more from afar than after seeing him and becoming familiar with him. The passage is valuable, in spite of the prejudice against Leo which it exudes, since it gives a glimpse of where and how the ceremony was perhaps normally conducted—in the limitrophe.

Between the prejudice of Malchus, which emerges from his *Kaiserkritik* and other statements, the truth seems to be that important phylarchs had to come to Constantinople for installment,[81] while minor phylarchs could be installed locally in whatever province they happened to be assigned to.

The extant sources are silent on the ceremonies that attended the investiture of the Arab phylarchs and kings as *foederati*, whether in Constantinople or in the provinces and the limitrophe.[82] But evidence has survived on some of the chiefs and kings of other peoples who were in the same federate relationship to Byzantium as the Arabs, such as the Lazi and the Armenians of the Caucasus and the Mauri of Africa. Amorkesos must have been ceremonially invested with the phylarchate in Constantinople. Although Malchus chose not to describe it, this is implied in the elaborate description of Amorkesos' visit.[83] Perhaps the most colorful part of the ceremony was the emperor's handing the phylarch the symbols of office.

An investiture ceremony that took place a half century later is described by Malalas. Tzath, the king of the Lazi, was received by Justin I and was given elaborate royal robes and a diadem.[84] As Tzath was a king and not a phylarch, the passage in Procopius that describes the emblems of the *archontes* of the Mauri is perhaps a more appropriate reference:[85] "A staff of silver covered with gold, and a silver cap—not covering the whole head, but like a crown and held in place on all sides by bands of silver—a kind of white cloak gathered by a golden brooch on the right shoulder in the form of a Thessalian cape, and a white tunic with embroidery, and a gilded boot."[86]

It is unlikely that Byzantium devised very different emblems or "tokens of rule" for the Arabs. Those described by Procopius for the Armenians and the Mauri are likely to have been much the same for all the peoples whom the Romans considerd barbarian allies, including the Arabs. Amorkesos, then, must have returned to Palaestina Tertia as its phylarch carrying with him

[81] As was the case with the Ghassānid phylarchs of the 6th century, who were also kings.

[82] Except for some echoes involving the Ghassānid phylarch/kings in the 6th century. These will be examined in *BASIC*.

[83] And possibly in the employment of the term, χειροτονῆσαι, which sounds more formal than the less technical terms which he sometimes uses, such as ποιεῖν; for which, see Blockley, *CH*, frag. 5, line 5 (p. 410) and frag. 9 (4), line 7 (p. 416).

[84] Malalas, *Chronographia*, 412–13. The royal gifts involved pictures of the emperor which were embroidered on these robes. This may have been in the mind of Niebuhr when he thought that Leo gave his own portrait to Amorkesos and conseqently emended λαβών into λαβόντα. This passage in Malalas will be analyzed in *BASIC* in the course of discussing the *basileia* of Arethas, the Ghassānid phylarch king.

[85] In *BAFOC*, 511 note 188 these were referred to briefly, but they are precious and rare documents, and are worth quoting in full, especially as the sources on such matters pertaining to the Arabs are so arid. These descriptions for the Mauri bring to life the ceremonies of investiture of the Arab kings and phylarchs in Constantinople.

[86] Procopius describes these emblems in the course of his chapter on Belisarius' campaign in Africa against the Vandals; see *Wars*, III, xxv, 7. The English version quoted above is that of H. B. Dewing in the Loeb Classical Library.

these emblems or ones very similar: a silver staff, silver cap, white cloak, white tunic, and gilded boot.

4. The fragment from Malchus is especially important for our understanding of some technical terms that express Amorkesos' legal status or the legal relations that obtained between him and the empire after he was confirmed in his phylarchate.

a. The term ὑπόσπονδος is applied to Amorkesos even while he was allied to Persia. Later in the text the same term is used to reflect his Roman connection, or his position in wishing to become allied with the Romans. Another term, *phylarchos* (φύλαρχος), is also used, and the two terms applied to him within the same legal context are thus related. *Phylarchos* expressed his function in the Roman military system, while ὑπόσπονδος reflected the legal status of his relationship to Rome. Uniting the two terms in one fragment, Malchus anticipates the formal definition of this new important barbarian office in the proto-Byzantine period which Procopius established in the sixth century, namely, that a phylarch is an Arab chief in a treaty relationship to Rome. Thus Amorkesos emerges from this transaction as a phylarch in the technical sense and an ally of Rome, that is, a *foederatus*. That the term ὑπόσπονδος, used by these fragmentary classicizing historians, is identical with that used for the other *foederati* of the empire in the fifth century, including the Germans, is clearly indicated in another fragment of Malchus, where he uses the term *foederati* only to explain it as a Latinism.[87] The Arabs of the fifth century, as those of the fourth, were *foederati* of the empire in the same way that the Germans were, and one and the same idiom is used in the sources to describe the two groups. In this connection, another term may be added to these two, namely, the Greek σύμμαχοι. All these Arab *foederati* were also σύμμαχοι, and in this century the two terms are identical, the only difference being that *foederati* expressed the legal relationship that obtained between the two parties, while σύμμαχοι expressed more the functional aspect of the relationship, namely, that these *foederati* were "fighters with" Rome, making war their principal function.[88]

b. The use of the term *phylarchos* rather than *rex* (βασιλεύς) is striking. The fourth-century sources tend to use the term βασιλεύς (king) of the Arab chiefs allied to Rome rather than *phylarchos*. In the fifth century this does not seem to be the case. Even the first of the Salīḥids, the dominant federate Arab

[87] See Blockley, *CH*, 420, frag. (1), lines 2–3.

[88] The term σύμμαχοι is used in a passage in Procopius in the technical sense of allies. It is also used there as verb συμμαχεῖν (to fight with), thus betraying etymologically the principal function of these *symmachoi*; Procopius, *Wars*, III, xxv, 2-3. In the 6 century σύμμαχοι superseded Latin *foederati* as a description of the Arab allies of Byzantium, the Ghassānids, and *foederati* now written in Greek characters, assumed a new meaning; see above, Chap. 2, app. 1.

group, is referred to in the Greek source Sozomen as phylarch.[89] Although hardly anything is said about them in the Greek sources after that reference, the Arabic sources describe them as kings (*mulūk*). Thus the chances are that this barbarian office developed in the fifth century as a term more convenient than βασιλεία for expressing the relationship between the Arab client and his Byzantine overlord.[90] The presumption, then, is that Amorkesos was confirmed as phylarch and not as king. It has been noted that the term *rex* in its Greek form ῥήξ is absent in Malchus, while *phylarchos* is not. But it is not clear whether he was following Olympiodorus in using *phylarchos* as the commander of a confederacy (which Amorkesos may well have been) or simply the leader of a tribe, since there is reference to his tribe (φυλή) when Malchus describes Bishop Petrus.[91]

c. Amorkesos went back to Palaestina Tertia after he and Leo had struck a *foedus*, the well-known legal instrument that regulated and regularized the relations between the barbarian chief and Rome. Amorkesos' occupation of Iotabe and his military exploits in Palaestina Tertia put him on a very small, almost Lilliputian scale, in the same camp as the German chiefs who seized Roman territory in the Occident and carved from them the various Germanic *regna*. The *foedus*, too, although on a much smaller scale, must have been the same as was struck with these Germanic chiefs, who also were endowed with "the symbols of office." The *foedus* recognized the fait accompli that Amorkesos had confronted the Romans with. This was unlike the other *foedera* that Rome might have struck with the Salīḥids, for instance, when the circumstances were completely different and the Arab party was not negotiating as victor in a military[92] context. Amorkesos, rather, like many a Germanic chief in the West, was in occupation of Roman territory which he had forcibly seized; the emperor simply confirmed him in this and made him an ally in much the same way that he had done with the Germanic chiefs.

The terms of the treaty have not been prserved in detail; Malchus mentions only what suits his *Kaiserkritik* of Leo. But one may assume that they were the usual ones of settling his followers on Roman territory and of extending the *annona* to him in return for military service and the protection of Roman interests—military, commercial, and other—in that strategic area. But both the spirit and the letter of this *foedus* may be discernible in the events of some twenty-five years later when, during the reign of Emperor Anastasius, in 498, the *dux* of Palestine, Romanus, reoccupied the island of

[89] As has been noted of Zokomos, the first of them; see above, 6.

[90] See *BAFOC*, 510–18 esp. 517.

[91] See Baldwin, "Malchus," 106.

[92] On the rise of the Salīḥids and the conversion of their first phylarch, Zokomos, see above, Chap. 1, sec. I.

Iotabe, restored it to direct Roman rule, and evicted Jabala, the Ghassānid chief. The presumption is that Jabala was in direct line of succession to Amorkesos and that he or one of his predecessors had acquired rule over the island from him. One of the terms of the treaty, then, was that it was renewable on the death of either of the two parties. In this case Zeno would have renewed it with Amorkesos in the following year, since Leo died in 474, and Anastasius would have renewed it with the Arab lord of Iotabe in 491. On the Arab side, Jabala would have renewed it with Anastasius or with Zeno, depending on how long Amorkesos lived after 473 and on whether his successor was his direct descendant or collaterally related to him.[93]

The *foedus*, then, was struck in Constantinople in 473. A Greek or Latin copy of it must have been preserved in the bureau of the *magister officiorum*, and there must have been a copy of it in the bureau of barbarian affairs, the *scrinium barbarorum*. Malchus derived his detailed and precise information on the *foedus* from some such source or at least partly from it.[94]

A *foedus* struck between the emperor and a barbarian chief was certainly written in Latin or Greek or both, since these were the two languages of the empire which were used by the administration. It was not until the reign of Heraclius that Greek was substituted for Latin in writing such documents and issuing imperial legislation. But the barbarian chief, on his return home, must have carried with him a document which he understood, and which explained clearly to him the terms of the *foedus*. Surely this must have been in Arabic. The *scrinium barbarorum* had its corps of interpreters and translators for accommodating such visitors and for redacting just such documents. Arabic had been used by the *foederati* since the days of Imru' al-Qays, the "king of all the Arabs," who was buried in Namā in 328. The presumption is that Arabic was used, if not very extensively, at least for such transactions, and for such vital documents in the history of Arab-Byzantine relations as the *foedus*, for it was on the observance of the terms of the *foedus* that the smooth working of these relations depended.[95]

5. The geographical precision of the historian when he speaks of Amorkesos' phylarchate is rare and therefore welcome—Iotabe and Arabia Patraea, that is, Palaestina Tertia east of Wādi ʿAraba, the Valley of ʿAraba; it is Trans-ʿAraban. This precision enables one to raise the question of the phylarchal structure in Palaestina Tertia and the provincial boundaries of this curiously shaped province in the reign of Leo.

a. It is practically certain that Palaestina Tertia, because of its size and

[93] On these events involving Romanus and Jabala, see below, Chap. 6, sec. II.

[94] On this see below, 105–6.

[95] This Arab-Byzantine *foedus* is an element in the difficult and complex history of *written* Arabic in the 5th century. See below, Chap. 14, sec. II.III.B.

curious shape, presented the imperial government with some administrative and organizational problems. Its size and shape are the key to realizing that there must have been more than one phylarch in this province. The physical geography of the province is dominated by the great rift, the Wādī ʿAraba and the Gulf of Eilat. Thus it is possible to speak of Cis-ʿAraban and Trans-ʿAraban Palaestina Tertia. Cis-ʿAraban Palaestina Tertia had two clearly defined parts—Sinai and the Negev. The Trans-ʿAraban may be divided into the Sharāt Range, Midian, and Ḥisma. It follows from this that Palaestina Tertia must have had more than one phylarch, perhaps several. The phylarch of the Negev could not possibly supervise Sinai, let alone the Trans-ʿAraban region.[96]

The last Arab known to the sources who had controlled the Arabs of the Trans-ʿAraban region was Imru' al-Qays in the fourth century. Amorkesos of the reign of Leo is the first attested Arab phylarch since the days of that king. Malchus does not mention the presence or opposition of any Arab phylarch to Amorkesos when he penetrated the Roman frontier and carved for himself a phylarchate in Palaestina Tertia.[97] It is possible that Malchus simply omitted mention of such a phylarch; or perhaps the fact was unknown to him, or the region, after its separation from the Provincia Arabia toward the middle of the fourth century, did not have a phylarch. If so, Amorkesos would not only have been the first *attested* phylarch of this region but actually its first phylarch.[98]

b. The employment of Amorkesos as a Roman phylarch represented the reassertion of Roman power in northern Ḥijāz, in that fluctuating border of Palaestina Tertia adjacent to the Arabian Peninsula. The *limes Arabicus* was manned by regular Roman soldiers in the zone extending from Ayla northward along the Via Traiana,[99] but the regions enumerated above—Ḥisma,

[96] On the κοινόν of phylarchs in the Negev see below, Chap. 7, sec. II.

[97] This could suggest that the power of Salīḥ was on the wane or that it did not extend so far to the south. The question of Salīḥ's non-participation in the defense of Palaestina Tertia against Amorkesos was raised by Sartre, *TE*, 155. But, as will be argued below, the most plausible explanation is their withdrawal from Oriens to participate in Leo's Vandal expedition; see Sec. VI.

[98] The second attested phylarch of Palaestina Tertia was the Ghassānid Abū-Karib, of the 6th century.

[99] The successful military operations of Amorkesos before his appointment as phylarch could throw light on the administrative reorganization of Palestine and Arabia in the reign of Diocletian, which resulted in the separation of what later become Palaestina Tertia from Arabia and its incorporation in Palestine. It could explain why Trans-ʿAraba was incorporated in Palestine, because the legion of Palestine, Ferrata, now at Ayla, had more work to do in Trans-ʿAraba than in Sinai. If Trans-ʿAraba had not been incorporated in Palestine, the legion of Ayla would have had little work to do in Sinai. The situation in southern Ḥijāz and Trans-ʿAraba also explains why the legion, transferred from Jersusalem, was stationed in Ayla. It may be safely assumed that insecurity in those regions, reflected in the military operations of Amorke-

Midian and Sharāt—were probably left to Amorkesos to defend. Thus a strong Roman presence was revived and maintained in this area through the convenient device of employing Arab phylarchs. It is not possible to determine precisely how deeply Roman influence reached in Ḥijāz in the second half of the fifth century. In the sixth century contemporary Arabic poetry allows one to identify the area of indirect Roman rule through the power of their clients, the Ghassānids.[100]

6. Finally, the endowment of Amorkesos with the phylarchate of Palaestina Tertia may now be related to the conclusion drawn earlier on his Ghassānid affiliation. This affiliation throws much needed light on the early history of the Ghassānid-Byzantine relationship. Some aspects of this early history have already been touched upon, and more will be said later, but a summary is useful here.

a. The first Ghassānid-Byzantine encounter has been assigned to either the reign of Anastasius (491–518) or to that of Zeno (474–491).[101] But the intensive examination of the fragment of Malchus and of the career of Amorkesos has placed this first encounter in the reign of Leo, which witnessed, after some years of hostile relations, a *foedus* between Byzantium and the Ghassānids represented by their chief, Amorkesos. Thus they were already part of the phylarchate of Oriens as early as 473.

b. Amorkesos' career makes it practically certain that the Ghassānids, or some of them, did come from Ḥīra and the Persian sphere of influence before they became vassals of the Romans. A Ghassānid affiliation has been argued for the fourth-century figure Malechus Podosacis,[102] and this new figure, coming from the same area, confirms that Ḥīra did have its Ghassānids. Furthermore, this episode of Amorkesos throws light on and makes intelligible the careers of two other Ghassānids in the service of Byzantium: (1) Jabala of ca. 498, whose occupation of the island of Iotabe is unintelligible without this background information which goes back to the reign of Leo and to his Ghassānid relative; and (2) Abū Karib, the Ghassānid phylarch whom Justinian made the phylarch of Palaestina Tertia ca. 530. The career of Amorkesos shows that the Ghassānids were phylarchs in this province as early as 473. The extraordinary arrangements made in the interests of the Ghassānid house and the two brothers, Ḥārith and Abū Karib, around 530 suggest that Abū Karib was given not only what Amorkesos had had, that is, a portion of Palaestina

---

sos had also obtained in the reign of Diocletian, when the two provinces were reorganized; see *BAFOC*, 48–51.

[100] This will be treated in *BASIC*.

[101] Or roughly around 490. See Shahîd, "Last Days," 145–50.

[102] See *BAFOC*, 119–23.

Tertia, east of Wādī ʿAraba, but possibly the whole province, including Sinai, the Negev, and the Trans-ʿAraban region.[103]

c. The accounts of the Greek sources are in apparent conflict with the Arabic sources as far as the first encounters between the Ghassānids and the Byzantines are concerned. The Arabic sources definitely involve the Salīḥids, but these are conspicuous by their absence in the Greek sources that deal with these first encounters, as related by Malchus and Theophanes, concerning Amorkesos and Jabala.[104] The Greek sources have to be followed here, but a reconciliation with the Arabic sources is not difficult. There are various ways of interpreting the discrepancies: (*a*) The Ghassānids were divided into many royal clans, all of whom were biding for supremacy and military ascendancy; the Byzantines may, and indeed must have dealt with more than one of these clans. The intensive analysis of the fragment of Malchus has revealed that the first of the Ghassānid figures to appear on the stage of Byzantine history was a phylarch or a *sayyid* by the name of Amorkesos, who most probably belonged to the Buqayla clan of the Ghassānids in Ḥīra, and a Ghassānid clan or house of Imru' al-Qays is attested in the Arabic sources.[105] Previous research on the Ghassānids shows that there was a Ghassānid clan or house of Banū Thaʿlaba[106] and another of the Jafnids, Banū Jafna.[107] Various clans or houses of the Ghassānids started to gravitate toward the Roman *limes* after the initial successes of Amorkesos. Some of these belonged to clans other than his, and possibly came from the south (from Ḥijāz) rather than from the east (from Ḥīra). The Greek sources relate the encounters of some of these with the Byzantines, while the Arabic relate the encounters of others.[108] (*b*) According to the Arabic sources, the Salīḥids encountered the Ghassānids when their paths crossed near Damascus, that is, in Phoenicia Libanensis. This, rather than Palaestina Tertia, may have been the jurisdiction of the Salīḥids.[109]

[103] This important phylarch, Abū-Karib, will receive a detailed treatment in *BASIC*.

[104] For the non-participation of the Salīḥids in the operations against Amorkesos, see above, note 97.

[105] See Ibn Ḥazm, *Jamharat*, 472 on "Banū-Imru' al-Qays" and also a verse by al-Nābigha al-Jaʿdi, which could be construed as a reference to the Ghassānid house of Imru' al-Qays; *Dīwān*, published by al-Maktab al-Islāmī (Damascus, 1964), 61, line 11. The verse reads, *ladā malikin min āli Jafnata khāluhū wajaddāhu min āli Imri'i al-Qaysi azharā*.

[106] See Shahīd, "Ghassān and Byzantium," 242–47; 251–55.

[107] The Banū-Jafna after whom Nöldeke named his monograph.

[108] See "Last Days," 145–59.

[109] See below, App. 2, for a conflict between the phylarch of Palaestina Prima and that of Arabia when the former crossed into Arabia. Phylarchal jurisdiction was apparently clearly and severely defined, and if the Salīḥids were not the phylarchs of Palaestina Tertia they would not have crossed the path of the Ghassānid Amorkesos there. But even if a phylarch's jurisdiction did not extend beyond his own province, it is doubtful that the Salīḥids would not have been rushed from wherever they were in Oriens to deal with Amorkesos in Palaestina Tertia, since this was a serious breach of the Roman frontier.

Furthermore, the site of the encounter in the Damascus area, and later at the unknown al-Muḥaffaf, suggests that these Ghassānids had entered Oriens not from Palaestina Tertia, as the group of Amorkesos had done, but from some other path, probably Wādī Sirḥān, which brought them from Dūmat to Azraq in the Provincia Arabia. This makes it almost certain that they are not the same group as the Ghassānids of Amorkesos, and goes a long way toward reconciling the Arabic and Greek sources.

d. Finally, the question of the Christian faith of the Ghassānids arises in connection with Amorkesos. Their doctrinal persuasion is a most significant fact in the course of their history in the sixth century and is the key to understanding its checkered career. In that century they were staunch Monophysites—indeed the iron fist of the Monophysite movement. But from the accounts of Malchus it is almost certain that Amorkesos was a Diophysite, or became one. This would mean that the first encounter of the Ghassānids with Christianity was with its Diophysite version, and that Monophysitism was a later stage in their relations with Byzantium, when Zeno and Anastasius veered to that position. An alternative explanation is that those who adopted Chalcedonian Christianity were a group of Ghassānids different from those of later times, and that when the latter group first dealt with Byzantium, the emperor was either Zeno or Anastasius, both of whom were inclined toward Monophysitism. Thus the Ghassānid newcomers simply adopted the religious complexion of the reigning *basileus*.

VI. The Vandal War

The intensive examination of the fragment from Malchus can now throw light on another federate Arab group in Oriens and on the contribution of Oriens to the war effort against the Vandals.

1. As has been pointed out, Amorkesos' military successes can be explained only by supposing that the imperial and federate forces that had protected the *limes* were engaged elsewhere, namely, fighting the Vandals in the West as part of Leo's expeditionary force of 468, 470, or both. The participation of troops from Oriens in the campaign against Gaeseric raises many problems.

a. The case for their participation can be based on the extraordinary figures that describe the expeditionary force. These have been exaggerated by such later historians as John Lydus, but the conservative estimate of a sober historian such as Procopius may be accepted as roughly true.[110] According to the latter, Leo spent 130,000 pounds of gold on the expedition and had over

[110] For the figures involving the number of ships, soldiers, and pounds of gold that were spent, see Ch. Courtois, *Les Vandales et l'Afrique* (Paris, 1955), 201 and notes.

100,000 soldiers in a fleet which, according to Cedrenus, came to 1,113 ships. Surely in this period, when Roman armies were relatively small, these are staggering figures, even if Procopius exaggerated. Since they came from the Pars Orientalis, such numbers of soldiers and ships could have been reached only if most or part of the army of the Diocese of the Orient had been sent to fight in the West. Legions and troops were often withdrawn from the front where they were normally stationed to fight in another.[111]

In addition to these general observations, there are specific circumstances which make it certain that troops from the Diocese of Oriens fought in the Vandal War.[112] The first expedition consisted of a huge armada of over a thousand ships and an army of a hundred thousand. Theophanes, following the contemporary historian Priscus,[113] stated that the fleet was mustered or collected ἐκ πάσης τῆς ἀνατολικῆς θαλάσσης, and this must be true of the army too. Reference to all the Orient, or the Pars Orientalis, must include the Diocese of Oriens, especially because of the peace that prevailed between Persia and Byzantium. The last war had been fought in the reign of Theodosius II, and the two empires desired peace with each other because of their external problems. Pērōz, Leo's contemporary,[114] was only too anxious to preserve the peace in view of his continual wars with the Ephthalites. Thus it was possible to withdraw troops from the East for duty in the West. It is safe to assume that, together with what was withdrawn from Oriens, the *Legio Fretensis* was also withdrawn from Eilat in Palaestina Tertia,[115] and whatever Byzantine shipping there was in the Red Sea, which could have protected Iotabe from Amorkesos, was requisitioned.

The second expedition was commanded by Count Heraclius and Masus the Isaurian and drew troops from Egypt, the Thebaid, and the desert.[116]

[111] For instance, the *Equites Nona Dalmatiae*, which was building a *burgus* near Umm al-Jimāl in Arabia in 371, but around 400 is attested in the *Notitia Dignitatum* as part of the eastern *comitatus*, probably transferred there after the disaster of Adrianople in 378; see S. T. Parker, *Romans and Saracens: A History of the Arabian Frontier* (Philadelphia, 1986), 26.

[112] For Leo's Vandal War, I have followed Ch. Courtois. His masterly analysis of the sources has invalidated previous accounts of the war and the theory of a three-pronged attack for the encirclement of Carthage in 468, which had been accepted by many scholars, including L. Schmidt, in *Geschichte der Wandalen* (Munich, 1942), 90. For Courtois's critique of the sources and his resetting of the course of Leo's Vandal War, see *Les Vandales*, 200–204. For his evaluation of Schmidt's work, see ibid., 363.

[113] Theophanes, *Chronographia*, 115, echoed by Procopius *Wars*, III, vi, 1.

[114] Reigned 459–483.

[115] *Fretensis* had also been withdrawn in 359 by Constantius for the defense of Amida, in the north of Oriens, against the Persians. At least a vexillation of it was sent; see *BAFOC*, 74. It is attested again in Eilat several decades later in the *Notitia Dignitatum*.

[116] Theophanes, *Chronographia*, 117: καὶ στρατὸν ἐξ Αἰγύπτου καὶ Θηβαΐδος καὶ τῆς ἐρήμου. Frank Clover drew my attention to the *Life of Daniel the Stylite*, which mentions a troop of *buccellarii* Leo recruited from Gaul.

Heraclius picked up the expeditionary force in Egypt and then sailed to Tripolitania where he disembarked, fought and beat the Vandals, took the coastal towns, and marched by land against Carthage. It is likely that a contingent from Oriens joined the expedition, perhaps from neighboring provinces in Oriens such as Palaestina Tertia, since troops from this province occasionally fought in Egypt.[117] The "desert" could, among other deserts, refer to Sinai, which was part of Palaestina Tertia.[118] The indifferent performance of the fleet under Basiliscus in 468 may have convinced Leo that a land operation was safer and more assured of success against the Vandals.

b. The participation of troops from Oriens and Egypt in the Vandal War certainly involved Arab troops stationed in these eastern provinces, both Rhomaic and federate, although their numbers must remain conjectural.

i. An examination of the units in the *Notitia Dignitatum* has yielded the conclusion that there were many that were ethnically Arab, in Oriens as well as in Egypt and the Thebaid.

In addition to the *cuneus equitum secundorum clibanariorum Palmirenorum*, under the command of the *magister militum per Orientem*, there were the following units in the Thebaid and Egypt: three units in the *limes Aegypti* under the command of the *comes rei militaris*, namely, the *equites Saraceni Thamudeni*, *ala tertium Arabum*, and *cohors secunda Ituraeorum*; in the Thebaid was the *ala octava Palmyrenorum*, to which may be added five units of *equites sagittarii indigenae*, one unit of *equites promoti indigenae*, and three units (*alae*) of *dromedarii*.

In the provinces of Oriens were the following units: (1) in Phoenicia, two recognizably Arab units, the *equites Saraceni indigenae* and the *equites Saraceni*; other possibly Arab units were the seven units of *equites sagittarii indigenae*; (2) in Syria, five units of *equites sagittarii indigenae*, who were possibly Arab; (3) in Euphratensis, the *equites promoti indigenae*, possibly Arab; (4) in Palestine, the *equites indigenae*, one unit called *equites primi felices sagittarii indigenae Palaestini*, and one unit of *ala Antana dromedariorum*; (5) in Osroene, two units of *equites promoti indigenae* and three units of *equites sagittarii indigenae*, all possibly Arab; (6) in Mesopotamia, the *cohors quinquagenaria Arabum* and, possibly Arab, one unit of *equites promoti indigenae* and three units of *equites sagittarii indigenae*; (7) in Arabia, the *cohors tertia felix Arabum* and possibly four units of *equites promoti indigenae*.[119]

How many of these units were withdrawn to fight in the Vandal War cannot be determined, but it is safe to assume that some or even many of

[117] For Arab troops from Pharan in Sinai fighting under the *dux* of the Thebaid in the 6th century see *BAFOC*, 327.

[118] Or, more properly, to the desert between the Nile and the Red Sea with its Arabian Mountains, for which see ibid., 146, 156 note 68.

[119] For an analysis of the Arab units in the *Notitia Dignitatum*, see below, Part 3, sec. I.

them were because of the peace with Persia.[120] With the possible exception of the two units of *equites Saraceni indigenae* stationed in Phoenicia, these units were composed of regular soldiers in the Roman army who were *cives*, and may be described as Rhomaic Arabs to distinguish them from the Arab *foederati* who were not. The withdrawal of these units from the two provinces of Palestine and Arabia is especially relevant to the discussion of the military successes of Amorkesos in Palaestina Tertia.

ii. Not only Rhomaic Arabs were withdrawn for the Vandal War, but also Arab *foederati* in Oriens. Federate presence is attested in the various provinces,[121] and some of these *foederati* must have been drafted for service in the Vandal War, especially as they were a mobile force and formed part of the imperial *comitatus*.

There were precedents for such movement of Arab *foederati* in this Byzantine period. A century or so before, the *foederati* of Queen Mavia were transferred from service along the oriental *limes* to fight the Goths in Thrace, Adrianople, and Constantinople.[122] Even closer to the events of Leo's reign was the movement of some Arab troops from Egypt to fight in Pentapolis[123] in the reign of Arcadius ca. 404. These were probably withdrawn from a regular unit in the Roman army stationed in Egypt. The sea voyage of these Arabs in the reign of Arcadius suggests that it was easier to reach Pentapolis by sea than by land across the desert. The participation of Arab troops in the Vandal War in Africa may represent the most westerly point that the Arab troops reached in the service of Byzantium.

c. The establishment of this new connection between the Vandal Wars and the Byzantine military posture in Oriens is fruitful in many ways. It shows that the units were employed in a major imperial adventure in the West. But it also represents a military dislocation in Oriens, both imperial and federate: if the Oriental troops were lost in the disaster of the battle of Cape Bon, this would have required a major reorganization of the military establishment in Oriens in the second half of the fifth century. Also, as the dominant federate power, it is practically certain that the services of the Salīḥids were needed in the Vandal War and that they embarked from the ports of Oriens together with the other troops who joined the army of Basil-

[120] Justinian's conquest of Vandal Africa began in 533 and of Gothic Italy in 535, that is, during the peace between the two Persian Wars.

[121] For these references to phylarchal and federate presence, especially in the reign of Theodosius, see above, Chap. 2, secs. IV and V. For phylarchal presence in the Negev, involving the *koinon* of phylarchs, see below, Chap. 7, sec. II. Around 459–460 two phylarchs of Palestine and Arabia are attested in the hagiographic work of Cyril of Scythopolis; for which see below, App. 2.

[122] See *BAFOC*, 169–83.

[123] See above, 9–12.

iscus against the Vandals. Thus a new field of operation in the West is discovered for them.[124]

Their employment in the Vandal War throws light on some problems of Salīḥid history in this period and adequately explains the military successes of Amorkesos.[125] Although it is not clear exactly where their power was in Oriens, there is no doubt that they were not far from the scene of operations and would have been called upon to take part in the defense of Palaestina Tertia against him.[126] The Vandal War also explains the apparent decline of the Salīḥids toward the end of the fifth century, beginning with the reign of Zeno (474–491). What happened to the Tanūkhids after Adrianople,[127] most probably happened to the Salīḥids after Cape Bon in Africa. The general disaster that befell the fleet must have affected them, and they must have lost heavily. Those who returned to Oriens must have been a pitiable remnant and their power was reduced, at least numerically. This may explain their defeats at the hands of the Ghassānids, who first appeared while the Salīḥids were away in Africa. The Ghassānids could thus establish a bridgehead in Oriens which enable them to gain the upper hand in their later encounters with the Salīḥids during the reigns of Zeno and Anastasius. Thus the Vandal War most probably spelt disaster for Salīḥ, and was the beginning of the end of their supremacy.

d. The participation of troops from Oriens, and especially Arab troops, in Leo's expedition against the Vandals raises the general question of whether such participation in western campaigns took place during the reigns of other emperors of the fifth century. Marcian and Zeno did not intervene in the affairs of the West militarily, but Theodosius II did. He sent many expeditions to help his western colleagues against the Germans: (1) an *arithmos* of 4,000 soldiers to aid his uncle Honorius against Alaric in 410; (2) Ardabur

[124] Troops from Egypt (and possibly Oriens) thus fought in both expeditions against the Vandals, in 468 and in 470. In the first they fought as part of the general armament, which included troops from the whole of the Pars Orientalis; in the second, they bore the main brunt of the fighting since the troops were almost entirely from the valley of the Nile—from Egypt and Thebaid and the nearby desert. Since the Arabs were also represented in Egypt and the Thebaid, it is possible that they too fought twice. For the second expedition, troops from the neighboring provinces of Oriens may have been enlisted too, as was suggested earlier in this section.

[125] If large numbers of troops were withdrawn from the Oriental *limes* to fight in Africa, the fact would have become known locally and Amorkesos would have sensed it and timed his military operations against Palaestina Tertia accordingly. In so doing, he did what Chosroes was to do in 539, when he chose to open the second war against Byzantium while Justinian was fighting the Goths in Italy. On the speech of the envoys of Vittigis, the Goth, to Chosroes, see Procopius, *Wars*, II, ii, 4–11.

[126] The question about the whereabouts of Salīḥ at this time was perceptively raised by Sartre, in *TE*, 154.

[127] See *BAFOC*, 75–183, 203–16.

and Aspar to help restore the throne to Valentinian III on the death of Honorius in 423 (successful in 425); (3) in 431–433 Aspar with a "large army" comprising troops from Rome and Constantinople against Gaeseric; and (4) for the fourth time, a large fleet in 441 against the Vandals.[128]

Thus Theodosius sent four expeditions to the West, but whether the Arabs participated in them remains problematical. The reign witnessed the outbreak of two Persian Wars, but these were quickly contained, and only the fourth expedition of Theodosius coincided with a Persian War in the East, the second in 440–442. So if there was any Arab participation, it would have been associated with the three other expeditions.

VII. Leo's Arab Policy

The welcome that Leo accorded Amorkesos was extraordinary. Why was the emperor so receptive to the Arab phylarch?

1. The previous section examined Leo's ill-starred expedition against the Vandals in Africa. The empire was both financially and morally exhausted by the severe blow that the disaster had dealt to Roman prestige, especially vis-à-vis the barbarians. The Vandals had beaten the empire that had made every effort to conquer them.[129]

Against this bleak background, Leo's receptiveness toward Amorkesos in 473 becomes perfectly intelligible. The empire was militarily depleted: troops that had embarked from Oriens, both imperial and federate, were badly mauled, and some probably never returned to man the *limes orientalis*. For the emperor, the prudent course was to come to terms with the powerful chief who then appeared with an olive branch, asking to become his ally.

The terms of their agreement were examined in a previous section when the *foedus* was discussed. It remains to say that Leo was no fool, although he may have negotiated under duress. What the compact amounted to was not a *cessio* of territory to a hostile barbarian but changing the status of the barbarian from a raider of the imperial *limes* into an ally to defend it. Amorkesos was no longer an Arab *sayyid* or *shaykh*, although he may have remained so to his people. He was now a Roman officer put in charge of Roman interests. In the fifth century the empire had ceded territory to barbarians under the guise of legal fictions and charged them with defending the Roman frontier as allies, *foederati*. On a much smaller scale this was the case with Amorkesos. This is the framework within which the extraordinary *foedus* has to be understood. Leo employed the concept of the phylarchate with considerable latitude. He

[128] For a lucid account of Byzantine intervention in the affairs of the West against the Germans, see W. Kaegi, *Byzantium and the Decline of Rome* (Princeton, 1968), 3–58.

[129] For the disastrous consequences of the expedition against the Vandals, see Bury, *LRE*, 337.

made it include administrative duties with which the Arab phylarch was normally not saddled, namely, supervision of shipping and the collection of custom duties in Iotabe.[130]

2. Another circumstance that must have weighed with Leo in his accommodation of Amorkesos was the massacre of the two Alan chiefs Aspar and Ardabur, and the elimination of the German element in the East. Leo wanted to counterbalance the German preponderance in the East by "recruiting regiments from native subjects no less valiant and robust." He thus relied on some hardy mountaineers, including the future emperor Zeno, and initiated what historians have called the Isaurian policy.[131]

Leo's dealings with Amorkesos may then be set against this background. He too belonged to a people that the empire had dealt with as *foederati* and *phylarchi* since the days of Constantine. They had fought the hated Goths in the fourth century at Adrianople in Thrace, and had even saved Constantinople from them in the time of Queen Mavia.[132] More recently they had performed creditably in the two Persian Wars during the reign of Theodosius II, and they had taken part in Leo's expedition against the Vandals in 468 and possibly in 470. In this context the appearance of the Arab chief Amorkesos and the hearty welcome accorded him by Leo becomes even more intelligible. For Leo, Amorkesos must have looked like Tarasicodissa (Zeno), the efficient chieftain who represented a race on whom he could rely. What is more, the Arabs belonged to the East, had long been settled in it, and had had normal relations with the empire since the reign of Constantine.[133] Also, they were acceptable to Orthodox Leo, unlike the Germans, who were Arians.

[130] This extraordinary arrangement, whereby the Arab phylarch was put in charge of an island, lasted for twenty-five years. It was terminated by Romanus, the *dux* of Palestine, in 498 in the reign of Anastasius; see Theophanes, *Chronographia*, I, 141.

The relevant passage in Theophanes confirms what Malchus had said. According to the former, Romanus' victory over the Arabs enabled the Roman merchants to lead again an autonomous existence on the island, control the cargoes coming from India, and return customs dues to the imperial treasury. Malchus had spoken of Amorkesos as "having possessed himself of the island, ejected its Roman tax collectors, and enriched himself considerably through collecting its taxes himself." The passage in Theophanes has been controversial. Stein called into question Abel's translation of τοῖς Ρωμαίοις πραγματευταῖς as "aux agents commerciaux de l'Empire," suggested "aux marchands romains," and argued that the same is true of the δεκατηλόγοι in Malchus; see Stein, *HBE*, II, 91 note 5.

Whatever the precise rendering of Theophanes and Malchus turns out to be, it is quite clear that the arrangement whereby the Arab phylarch was allowed to function in Iotabe was striking. The only explanation must be that he was performing a very important function for the empire in the Red Sea area and in western Arabia, as has been argued in this section.

[131] See Bury, *LRE*, I, 317.

[132] See *BAFOC*, 169–83.

[133] This too may have "implications for the study of regionalism within the fifth-century Roman Empire and for the growth of a distinctive 'byzantine' society in the East"; see Kaegi, *Byzantium and the Decline of Rome*, 15.

The Isaurians helped Leo rid the East of the two dangerous Alan chiefs and of the powerful German element there, but the Arabs of Amorkesos, unlike the Isaurians, lay astride some of the main arteries of trade in the Red Sea and western Arabia. The possibilities that thus opened before the emperor, who had suffered grievous losses in the West, were a compelling attraction. He was casting about in search of new allies for eliminating the Germans, and Amorkesos provided him with the opportunity for rercuiting reliable allies and, through them, retrieving his losses in the Vandal War. The Mediterranean had witnessed his defeats; the Germans who roamed its basin had proved too strong for him, practically excising the Pars Occidentalis. Thus the Red Sea and Arabian Peninsula opened new prospects for the emperor who was groping for a field of operation that offered fairer chances of success than the Mediterranean.

3. What were these prospects in the new Orient? As mentioned earlier, there were three areas in which Byzantine interests could be advanced in the Red Sea area, especially in western Arabia: commercial, political, and religious. The first of these was by far the most important at this point; the other two were related, but subordinate, goals.

Toward the end of the third century trade had slipped from the hands of Roman traders into those of intermediaries: the Ḥimyarites, Ethiopians, and Persians. In the fourth century the aggressive Byzantine policy of Constantius (and possibly his father) had led to some gains among the southern Semites, Ḥimyarites and Ethiopians. But the situation changed, and these gains must have been lost after the death of Constantius and the beginning of a new orientation for Byzantine policy.[134] In the fifth century Byzantium was busy with the Germanic invasions in the West; thus the Red Sea and Arabian Peninsula slipped even further into the background. Trade with the Orient remained in the hands of the Persians, who were, in spite of the prevailing peace, an age-old enemy. So it is possible that after his disappointments, reverses, and losses in the Mediterranean, Leo wanted a new field of operation, and thus established direct contact with the world of the Indian Ocean and Far Orient without Persian mediation.

4. Leo died a year after his compact with Amorkesos. If he had truly initiated an Arab policy and looked east and south to the Red Sea and Indian Ocean, Zeno would have continued it, since he disregarded the West and wanted no part of the involvement that had soured Leo. Is there any evidence for the continuation of Leo's Arab policy in these regions?

The sources on such matters are notoriously meagre and uninformative, but two might suggest that the Arab policy of Leo was a reality that bore

[134] In the reigns of Julian and Theodosius II, for whom see *BAFOC*, 135, 208–9.

fruit. (1) The first concerns Sopatros, the Roman merchant of the reign of Zeno or Anastasius who had an audience with the king of Ceylon and won the contest with his Persian adversaries concerning who the greater sovereign was—the Byzantine or the Persian ruler—by citing the splendor of the golden *nomisma*;[135] (2) The second was the dispatch of a bishop named Silvanus from Byzantium to Ḥimyar in the reign of Anastasius.[136] Both could reflect a Byzantine presence, secular and ecclesiastic, and it is possible that they were the remote consequences of Leo's brisk diplomacy with the Arab phylarch.

It is agreeable to think that these two data can be related as links in the chain of events that Leo's Arab policy had prepared in the Orient. Whatever the truth may be, analysis of the precious fragment from Malchus has repaid the effort, since it adds a new dimension to Leo's reign, which is otherwise blank with regard to his relations with this area. Except for this one fragment, there is no record that the *imperator* of the Pars Orientalis had any interest in the Orient. Thus Malchus, most probably inspired by *Kaiserkritik*, provides us with the only document that suggests that "the butcher" had an enlightened Arab policy.

5. Finally, Leo's Arab policy touches on one of the most important historical questions, the Pirenne Thesis.[137] According to Pirenne, the unity of the Mediterranean was not broken by the Germanic invasions in the fifth and sixth centuries, but by the Arabs and Islam in the seventh and the eighth. The thesis was attacked and, on the whole, rejected. Norman H. Baynes was one of its earliest critics: ". . . the unity of the Mediterranean world was broken by the pirate fleet of Vandal Carthage and . . . the shattered unity was never restored."[138] Thus the Vandals of the reign of Leo are involved in this large historical problem, and the evidence from secular and hagiographic sources seems to support Baynes' view;[139] so what the British scholar said in the twentieth century may have been felt by Leo himself in the fifth. The latter's Arab policy as a reaction to his disappointments in the Occident could be viewed as a contemporary perception of the historical significance of the Vandal conquest of Africa and its implication for Mediterranean history.

[135] See Cosmas Indicopleustes, *Topographie chrétienne*, ed. W. Wolska-Conus, SC (Paris, 1968–73), III, 349–51.

[136] On this, see below, Chap. 13, sec. IV.

[137] For the latest on the Pirenne thesis with bibliography, see R. Hodges and D. Whitehouse, *Mohammed, Charlemagne, and the Origins of Europe* (Ithaca, N.Y., 1983).

[138] See N. H. Baynes, *Byzantine Studies and Other Essays* (London, 1960), 315 (repr. from *JRS* 19 [1929]). In this, Baynes was followed by H. St. L. B. Moss, "Economic Consequences of the Barbarian Invasions," *Economic History Review* (May 1937), 209–16.

[139] On Vandal depredations of Illyricum, most of the Peloponnesus, Greece, and the islands that lie near it, see Procopius, *Wars*, III, v, 23. On their vandalism in Alexandria, there is evidence from the *Life of Daniel the Sylite*, quoted by L. Schmidt, *Wandelen*, 88 note 4.

VIII. Historiographical Observations

In addition to illuminating the course of Arab-Byzantine relations in the fifth century, the fragment from Malchus raises some important questions of Byzantine historiography pertaining to this fragmentary classicizing historian.

A

The most striking features of this fragment on Amorkesos are the hostile comments about Leo—a severe form of *Kaiserkritik*. (1) The note of disapproval is sounded in the very first sentence, which describes the emperor as μακέλλης, a butcher, and notes the utter confusion that prevailed during the seventeenth year of his reign. (2) There follows an implied criticism that Leo, contrary to the Byzantine-Persian treaty of the reign of Theodosius II, received the rebellious Saracen ally of Persia. (3) Another implied criticism regards the emperor's willingness to receive a chief who had harassed the Roman frontier and had possessed himself of a Roman island, Iotabe, after driving out its Roman tax collectors. (4) The emperor compounded his error of judgment by receiving the offender in Constantinople instead of leaving it to his provincial subordinates to negotiate with him and install him as a phylarch on the spot in Palaestina Tertia. (5) The journey of the Arab chief to Constantinople could not have induced in him a sense of obedience and loyalty but rather the contrary, since it enabled him to see the cities of the empire, rich, luxurious, and undefended. (6) The emperor also showed poor judgment in heaping honors on the phylarch while he was in the capital; the most revolting was seating him among the first patricians in the Senate. (7) Leo was also disingenuous in justifying his decision to let Amorkesos sit in the Senate by pretending that he had been persuaded to become a Christian. (8) He demonstrated his greed when, in reciprocating the phylarch's gift, he gave money not from his own private purse but from public funds. (9) Finally, the terms of Amorkesos' appointment were too generous for a phylarch who was not likely to serve the best interests of the empire.

Thus the antipathy of the historian toward Leo is sustained, explicit, and striking, coming as it does in a fragment. The historical situation toward the end of Leo's reign and the imperial interests that were at stake have been discussed. Consequently one may conclude that Malchus was prejudiced[140] and was writing from a certain viewpoint. But a few more observations in defense of the emperor may be made:

a. Leo may have been a butcher, but a butcher is not necessarily a fool. If

[140] Cf. Blockley, *CH*, 79. There is something to be said for the view that in dwelling on the phylarch's occupation of the island of Iotabe Malchus was trying to contrast Leo with Anastasius, under whose rule the island was restored to Roman rule; ibid., 80.

he had appointed Amorkesos phylarch without seeing and talking to him but only on the recommendation of Petrus, Malchus' criticism might have been justified. But this was not the case. While in Constantinople the Arab must have impressed the emperor considerably, thus providing the grounds for the unusual honor which he received.

b. The animadversion on the phylarch's journey to Constantinople, which makes the emperor look like a fool, is certainly unjustified. The historian may have unconsciously betrayed himself when he used the term χειροτονῆσαι for the installment of the phylarch. This rather technical word suggests that it may have been normal for the investiture to take place in Constantinople rather than locally in Oriens as he suggested. At least this was the case for important chiefs, such as Amorkesos, whom the administration deemed worthy of being invited to the capital.

c. The whole point in inviting Amorkesos is obscured by the historian. Barbarian visitors to the city were awed by its splendor, which induced in them a sense of obedience and a desire to be faithful allies to the empire. In the case of German chiefs who led large armies or migrating tribes, this may have been dangerous, since it could whet their appetite to conquer and pillage. In the case of the Arab chief such a possibility never existed.[141]

d. Finally, the sight of Roman cities on his way to Constantinople could not have aroused in him the sentiments that Malchus mentions.[142] Before passing through the prosperous cities of Oriens, Amorkesos would have crossed the rather forbidding *limes Arabicus*, which he had avoided attacking while he was engaged in his military operations in Palaestina Tertia. A phylarch, however resourceful and clever he may have been, could not have mounted an offensive against Oriens or the empire.[143] All that these phylarchs wanted was the opposite—the Roman connection, the *annona*, and permission for themselves and their followers to settle on Roman territory.

B

The phylarch also comes in for criticism by Malchus, and with him the Arabs in general. This is clearly implied in the fragment: (1) in the opening

[141] Malchus may have had in mind Alaric and Gaeseric in Rome in 410 and 456 respectively. If so, this was an erroneous and false analogy.

[142] Cf. Baldwin, "Malchus," 103.

[143] Even the Ghassānids of the 6th century, at the peak of their power, could not do much of anything in Oriens against Byzantium, when Byzantium drove them to rebel late in that century. No Arab tribal group or confederacy in this proto-Byzantine period could do more than scratch the surface of the Byzantine defense system in Oriens, and it was only with the extraordinary events of the first half of the 7th century—with the rise of Islam which united the Arabs in the Peninsula under its banner—that the Arabs were able to effect the serious and deep penetrations in Oriens that finally resulted in their permanent occupation of that diocese.

sentence, where Malchus presents Petrus as a bishop of "tented Arabs"; (2) in the statement that, true to his nomadic instincts, Amorkesos acted as a rapacious hawk against Roman territory and interests; (3) in the description of his journey to Constantinople, in which Malchus presents him as a greedy, prospective raider after seeing the cities full of luxuries and empty of weaponry; and finally (4) in the last sentence, where the Arab chief appears as one whose loyalty to the empire was far from certain, even after the emperor's folly heaped on him all the extraordinary honors enumerated by the historian earlier in the fragment.

That these criticisms were unjustified should be clear from the detailed commentary and analysis undertaken earlier. This raises some important questions about Malchus' historiography, namely, whether his antipathy to the emperor derived from his feelings toward the Arabs or vice versa, or whether Malchus was ill-disposed to both Leo and the Arab chief, who was the representative of an undesirable barbarian group. Malchus' prejudice against the emperor and the phylarch may now be set against what is known of the historian, who wrote as a concerned Roman about Roman decline.[144]

Malchus loathed Leo, but on what grounds? Leo was an Orthodox Chalcedonian emperor, but whether this was the cause is not certain, since Malchus' doctrinal persuasion is controversial.[145] Perhaps his prejudice is related to his alienation from the central government in view of its failure to deal with the barbarians.[146] In the case of Leo it was the failure of the campaign against Gaeseric and the Vandals in 471, and possibly his dependence on the Isaurians as a counterbalance to his Alan *magister militum*, Aspar, and his Germans.[147]

Malchus' antipathy to Amorkesos derives from his dislike of the barbarians.[148] Like all historians who were analysts of Roman decline, he saw them as the cause of imperial decay. But he also realized that the empire must come to terms with the powerful Ostrogoths, who were now settled on Roman territory and were there to stay.[149] To him, the Arabs were barbarians, and *scenitae* at that, and so they were included in his general stricture on barbarians. However, unlike the powerful Ostrogoths, they did not need to be courted.

[144] On Malchus, see the article in *RE*, 14, 851, 856, s.v.; and more recently Baldwin, "Malchus" and Blockley, CH; for *Kaiserkritik*, see H. Tinnefeld, *Kategorien der Kaiserkritik in der byzantinischen Historiographie von Prokop bis Niketas Chroniates* (Munich, 1971) and the more recent article by P. Magdalino, "Byzantine Kaiserkritik," *Speculum* 58 (1983), 326–46.

[145] See Baldwin, "Malchus," 94; Blockley, *CH*, 77.

[146] Blockley, *CH*, 91.

[147] Ibid., 80. His dislike of Leo could not have been motivated by racial prejudice against Leo as a Thracian or a Dacian; Malchus himself did not belong to the Graeco-Roman establishment which viewed the rest of the world as barbarians.

[148] On his attitude to the barbarians, see Baldwin, "Malchus," 102.

[149] Blockley, *CH*, 93.

Whatever the real explanation for Malchus' dislike of Leo, the fact is clear, and perhaps accounts for the precious fragment on the career of Amorkesos. Malchus used the occasion of his visit to bring his two antipathies together, berating the inefficiency of imperial power as well as the influence of the barbarians. Perhaps the historian was more interested in *Kaiserkritik* than in the Saracens; he may have used the latter only to indulge in the former. Nevertheless, he provides precious information on the Arabs and Arabia, which, in a sense, is the more permanent value of his *Kaiserkritik.*[150]

C

Malchus' criticisms are especially curious in view of his ethnic background. Like other fifth-century historians, such as Candidus the Isaurian and Olympiodorus of Thebes, Malchus did not belong to the Graeco-Roman establishment. What is more, the little that is known about him suggests that he could have belonged to the same people toward whom he was so unsympathetic in the fragment. If so, his antipathies become a little paradoxical, but make him even more interesting. It is therefore of some importance to begin this probe with an investigation of his ethnic origin.

According to the few notices of him,[151] Malchus came from Philadelphia. In view of his Semitic name, this could not have been the Lydian or the Egyptian Philadelphia, but the Arabian city of the Decapolis in the Provincia Arabia. The name Malchus is a common Semitic one. However, at this period the chances are that he belonged to one of two peoples—the Arabic or the Aramaic-speaking peoples of Oriens. But Malchus was born in the strictly Arab portion of Syria, in the Provincia Arabia, and not in a province that is more closely associated with non-Arab ethnic groups. This province had such a distinct Arab character that the Romans called what was, before its annexation, Nabataea by that name.[152] The chances that he was of Arab origin are enhanced by the fact that "Malchus" is a proper noun, and most probably transliterates not *malik* but Mālik, a well-known Arab name. This makes it practically certain that Malchus was an Arab from the Provincia Arabia.

The scanty account of his life[153] and internal indications in his work suggest that he spent time as a sophist in Constantinople and wrote his *History* there, probably during the reign of Anastasius (491–518). This could partly explain his attitude toward the Arabs—he was an assimilated *Rhōmaios* who

[150] The case of Procopius and Arethas in the 6th century is a parallel, not unlike this one involving Malchus and Amorkesos; see Shahîd, "Procopius and Arethas," *BZ* 50 (1957), 39–67; 362–82.

[151] See the Testimonia in Blockley, *CH*, II, 402–4.

[152] To Justinian, even as late as the 6th century and after some five centuries of Romanization, the Provincia Arabia was still τὴν 'Αράβων χώραν; see *RA*, 15.

[153] See Baldwin, "Malchus," 91, 92 and Blockley, *CH*, 72.

severed his connections with his city and country of birth and lived in the Byzantine metropolis. Thus his assimilation was complete. He identified himself with the empire of which he was a citizen and became one of its historians, writing not its ancient but its contemporary history. Consequently his interest in the *imperium* was not that of a detached analyst of Roman decline but of a concerned Roman who was witness to the great events that changed the course of Roman history, including the fall of Rome (twice) and the West to the Germanic tribes. Thus for him it was the barbarians[154] who brought about the downfall of the empire in the Occident; hence his dislike of Leo, the butcher, and Amorkesos, the Saracen.[155]

Malchus and three other fragmentary historians of the fifth century have been described as classicizing historians by their most recent editor:[156] "they all clearly and continually emphasized their links with classical antiquity." In the case of Malchus it is possible within the context of this discussion to detect traces of continuity with the more recent past of the fourth century, and with the work of Ammianus Marcellinus, himself a secular and classicizing historian. His statement on the Arabs, the "*scenitae* Arabs whom they call Saracens" (τὶς τῶν Σκηνιτῶν Ἀράβων οὓς καλοῦσι Σαρακηνούς), recalls Ammianus: "et scenitas praetenditur Arabas, quos Sarracenos nunc appellamus."[157] The last statement on Amorkesos' loyalty after his endowment with the phylarchate, καὶ ὅσοι οὐκ ἔμελλε τοῖς δεξαμένοις λυσιτελεῖν, is reminiscent of Ammianus' well-known dictum: "Saraceni tamen nec amici nobis umquam nec hostes optandi."[158]

Malchus of Philadelphia thus could join the group of Arabs from the Provincia who had represented Arab Hellenism in Roman times, such as Callinicus of Petra, a sophist who practiced rhetoric in Athens, and Genethlius, his compatriot, who also taught rhetoric there in the third century. Callincus also wrote a history of Alexandria which he presented to Queen Zenobia.[159] Unlike them, the sophist of Philadelphia did not change his Arabic Semitic name to a Greek one.

[154] And thrice if he was born before 410.

[155] And this is how the assimilationist Malchus viewed his own people, namely, as nomads and raiders of the Roman *limes*. That some of them in the Peninsula were nomads cannot be denied, but he seems to have fallen victim to Ammianus' preaching on the equation of all Arabs with tented nomads, the *Scenitae* (*BAFOC*, 239–68). Sedentary Arabs themselves were antipathetic to the nomadic Arabs, and the Koran itself speaks of them in pejorative terms.

[156] See Blockley, *CH*, 90.

[157] *RG*, XXII, 15.2. It has not been noted that this is taken out of Ammianus; cf. Baldwin, "Malchus," 106.

[158] *RG*, XIV. 41.1.

[159] On these representatives of Arab Hellenism in the Roman period, see Bowersock, *Roman Arabia*, 135.

The extremely detailed information that this fragment from Malchus yields must inevitably raise the question of his sources. Since he was writing contemporary history, these can be divided into two. (1) Personal observation: In all probability Malchus wrote under Anastasius (491–518); he was not far removed from the events described in the fragment, which took place in 473. He may even have been in Constantinople when the Arab phylarch visited the city. The statement in the fragment that it offended the Romans that the phylarch sat among the first patricians could not have come from a written source, but must have been a rumor which he heard then or shortly after from those who witnessed the extraordinary transaction. (2) A written source: No doubt most of the fragment came from such a source, especially the information on the phylarch's tribal affiliation, all of which suggests that Malchus had before him a document.[160] This must be the case in spite of his prejudice against Leo, which does not invalidate the reliability of his account, since his prejudice can be ignored and neutralized, as it has been earlier in this section.[161] What kind of document did he have and what was its provenance?

Earlier in this section it was argued that the text of the *foedus* was available to Malchus and that a copy of it must have rested at the *scrinium barbarorum*. This is the department that must have had the responsibility of looking after the Arab visitor while he was in Constantinople and making all the arrangements while he was in the capital. It is almost certain that not only the text of the *foedus* rested in this *scrinium* but also background information on Amorkesos and his doings before he came to Constantinople. This, including his tribal affiliation, was probably supplied by Petrus who, too, must have been the ward of the *scrinium* during his visit; this information was preserved in a document in Amorkesos' dossier. Malchus must have used such a document when he wrote his account of the Arab chief.

This document raises the same question that was raised when the *foedus* was discussed, namely, whether an Arabic version existed at the *scrinium barbarorum*. The important version of this document was no doubt the Greek and Latin one. But it is possible that there was also an Arabic version at the *scrinium barbarorum*, considering the statement in the fragment on Amorkesos' tribal affiliation. It was suggested earlier that the Greek form of this affiliation could have been an error or a corrupt reading of the Arabic original, which read Buqayla and not Nuqayla. This sort of mistake could have been

[160] Theophanes gives the precise tribal affiliation of the Arab chief Arethas, with whom Byzantium had to deal around 500; see *Chronographia*, I, 141. It is practically certain that Theophanes or his source extracted this information from a document which probably was of the same provenance as the one which Malchus used, the *scrinium barbarorum*.

[161] On Malchus' lack of objectivity and the extent of his reliability, see Baldwin, "Malchus," 105.

made if the Greek document was translated from an Arabic one which the copyist or the translator had before him and which he misread. Alternatively, it could have been wrongly heard by the interpreter[162] and the Greek recorder of this background information, since conceivably Petrus supplied it to the authorities in Constantinople. For phonetic reasons the former is the more likely interpretation. Thus a good case can be made for the existence in Constantinople of an Arabic version of a document on Amorkesos and his background. But the stronger case must rest on the *foedus*, for, as was argued earlier, it is impossible to believe that the Arab phylarch left Constantinople without a document in his own language that clearly explained its terms to him. That an Arabic, and not only a Greek copy, also existed at the *scrinium* cannot be completely ruled out.

Appendix I

The Patriciate of Amorkesos

This appendix deals with the problem posed by Nöldeke when he suggested that the dignity of *patricius* was conferred on Amorkesos by Leo while he was in Constantinople. It is based on an article that I wrote in 1959 and published in the *Festschrift* for Philip K. Hitti, *The World of Islam* (London, 1959), 74–82.

In the course of discussing the titles and ranks with which the Ghassānids were endowed by the Romans, Nöldeke stated that the dignity of *patricius* with which the Romans honored Arethas, son of Jabala, in the sixth century had already been conferred on Amorkesos in the fifth.[1] If Nöldeke's view is correct, then some important conclusions inevitably follow. In the pre-Islamic history of the Arabs, the "patriciate" of Amorkesos in 473 would contest the view that the first Arab to have attained such a high honor in the Byzantine hierarchy of ranks and titles was Arethas, and would consequently entail antedating the first certain instance of a patriciate conferred on an Arab by seventy years.[2] Nöldeke's view would also necessitate adding the name of an Arab chief to the succession of German princes in the West who were endowed with the patriciate, a matter of some importance, since the dignity was conferred sparingly before the sixth century. It will be argued here that Nöldeke's view on the "patriciate" of Amorkesos is mistaken and that the conclusions which inevitably follow from such a view, whether expressed or implied, cannot be true.

[162] The presence of interpreters, ἑρμηνευταί, for Arabic in the 6th century is attested, but it is practically certain that this was also the case in the 5th. Whether there were not only interpreters but also translators of written documents is not clear.

[1] Nöldeke, *GF*, 13 note 3, referring to the edition of Malchus' fragment by L. Dindorf, *Historici Graeci Minores* (Leipzig, 1870–71), i, 386. This corresponds to Müller's edition of the same fragment, loc. cit., which will be the one referred to in this discussion.

[2] See my article, "The Patriciate of Arethas," *BZ* 52 (1959), 321–43.

I

An examination of the text of Malchus discloses no explicit reference to a patriciate conferred on Amorkesos.[3] The honors accorded him during his stay in Constantinople consisted of: (1) sharing the imperial table with Leo, (2) admission to the meetings of the Senate, (3) receiving a valuable picture from the emperor, and (4) other gifts from the senators. Before his departure, Leo also (5) transferred to him possession of the island of Iotabe, and (6) made him phylarch of Palaestina Tertia. Considering Malchus' detailed account of these honors, he certainly would have mentioned the conferment of the patriciate as well; therefore his silence on the matter cannot be satisfactorily explained away as an error of omission.

Also, Malchus' attitude toward Leo would have induced him to refer to the patriciate if it had been conferred. Malchus was not a great admirer of Leo, and his account of the reign is full of strictures and innuendos. In the same fragment that deals with Amorkesos, he severely criticizes the emperor for inviting him to the capital.[4] It is clear from all this that Malchus was not burdened with any inhibitions that would have restrained him from saying what he thought of the emperor. Consequently the conferment of the patriciate would not have been left unmentioned, but rather would have been unequivocally stated, especially as that dignity was bestowed in a splendid ceremony.[5] Malchus, with his penchant for the picturesque, could not, in his attempt to vilify Leo, have afforded to neglect it; rather, he would have expatiated on it as the most eloquent testimony for the folly and misplaced generosity of the emperor whom he was so busily engaged in denigrating.

Finally, the history of the patriciate in the fifth century makes it clear that such a high honor could not possibly have been conferred on a chief of the stature of Amorkesos. The *patriciatus dignitas* was introduced by Constantine. It was not attached to any office, and was conferred only when exceptional services had been rendered to the state.[6] It was a very high honor, only sparingly conferred in the fourth and fifth centuries. Two emperors, Theodosius II (408–450) and Zeno (474–491), enacted restrictions on its conferment,[7] and it was not until 537 that the reigning emperor, Justinian, relaxed them and opened the patriciate to all those who had the rank of *illustris*.[8] Amorkesos certainly was not *illustris* and, moreover, needed to be more than that in the fifth century in order to have had the dignity conferred on him, since the illustrate did not automatically ensure for its holder the patriciate. He probably became *clarissimus*, the lowest rank in the sequence *clarissimus-spectabilis-illustris*. Nor had he, by the time he visited Constantinople, performed any service to the empire, small

[3] For the original, see Müller, loc. cit.

[4] Ibid. For the severe *Kaiserkritik* expressed in the fragment, see above, 100.

[5] For the ceremony of a later age, see *De Ceremoniis*, ed. A. Vogt (Paris, 1935–39), II, pt. 1, 51–60.

[6] See W. Ensslin, "Aus Theodorichs Kanzlei," *Wüzburger Jahrbücher für die Altertumswissenschaft*, 2.1 (1947), 75–82.

[7] *Codex Justinianus*, xii, 3,3.

[8] *Nov. Just.*, lxii, 5.

or great, that could be compared to those of the barbarian princes who were warding off invasions in the West. Therefore, the conferment of the dignity was uncalled for, and would have placed Amorkesos on the same level as Aetius or Theodoric, compared to whom his services were slight and, at the time of his visit, not yet rendered.

II

It remains now to explore the reasons that must have led Nöldeke to state that the patriciate was conferred on Amorkesos.

First, the fragment from Malchus contains a statement that Nöldeke undoubtedly had in mind. It is couched in terms that lend themselves to being misunderstood, and might suggest that the historian did have in mind the conferment of a patriciate: καὶ τό γε δὴ αἴσχιστον ὄνειδος τῶν Ῥωμαίων, ὅτι καθέδραν αυτῷ τὴν πρωτοπατρικίων ἀποδοθῆναι ἐκέλευσε σχηματισάμενος ὁ βασιλεύς, ὅτι δὴ χριστιανὸς ἀνεπείσθη γενέσθαι.[9] In particular, the words καθέδραν and πρωτοπατρικίων must have convinced Nöldeke that the patriciate was actually conferred. But it was not. What the statement means is something quite different: that the emperor, in full conformity with his previous record of extravagant hospitality to the Arab chief, allowed him to take a seat in the Senate, which gave him precedence over the patricians.[10] This cannot be construed as a reflection of Amorkesos' position in the hierarchy of ranks and titles, but merely as an indication of his place in the seating arrangement in the Senate at that particular session. Thus it cannot support Nöldeke's view. The Arab chief was touring the capital and being entertained by Leo; no measure of hospitality could have been greater than the privilege of taking a seat in the Senate. The invalid reasoning involved in Nöldeke's view is further illustrated by applying it to two other statements in the fragment. Amorkesos had shared the imperial table before he was privileged to attend the Senate's meetings; if the latter implied the conferment of a patriciate, then, according to the same reasoning, Amorkesos would also have been considered a member of the imperial household on

[9] "And the most disgraceful thing for the Romans was that the emperor ordered a seat belonging to first patricians to be granted to him [Amorkesos], alleging that he had been persuaded to become a Christian," Müller, loc cit.

[10] In this connection reference may be made to the *prima sedes* of the Urban Prefect in the Senate, for which see *Novella* lxii, 2.

Synesius has some pertinent remarks on barbarian chiefs who were accorded extraordinary welcome in Constantinople and were invited to enter the Senate in the reign of Arcadius. But it is clear from the account that this did not mean they were endowed with the patriciate. This passage from Περὶ Βασιλείας is worth quoting; see *The Essays and Hymns of Synesius of Cyrene*, trans. A. Fitzgerald (Oxford, 1930), I, 135–36. "But first let all be excluded from magistracies and kept away from the privileges of the council who are ashamed of all that has been sacred to the Romans from olden times, and has been so esteemed. Of a truth both Themis, herself sacred to the Senate, and the god of our battle-line must, I think, cover their faces when the man with leathern jerkin marches in command of those that wear the general's cloak, and whenever such an one divests himself of the sheepskin in which he was clad to assume the toga, and enters the council-chamber to deliberate on matters of State with the Roman magistrates, having a prominent seat perhaps next the consul, while the lawful men sit behind him."

the strength of his having dined with the emperor. Again, Amorkesos was given precedence over the patricians in the Senate, and consequently he would have become not only a *patricius* but also a πρωτοπατρίκιος,[11] since this is the exact term used in the fragment, a conclusion that demonstrates the fallaciousness of such reasoning by *reductio ad absurdum*. Another fragment that survives from Malchus' *History* also argues against Nöldeke by affording an instance of how he would have expressed himself on the conferment of the patriciate *if* the honor had actually been bestowed. While he was recording the events of the reign of Zeno, Malchus referred to the promotion of Severus[12] to the patriciate in language that leaves the reader in no doubt that the honor was conferred: καὶ πατρίκιον αὐτὸν ποιήσας . . . , with no circumlocutions.[13] It is, however, possible that Malchus was being deliberately vague in his account and indulging in a *suggestio falsi*. Without doing harm to his reputation for veracity by actually saying that the emperor conferred the patriciate, he described the visit of Amorkesos to the Senate—a visit that undoubtedly did take place—in such terms as to make it possible for the reader to conclude that the dignity was also bestowed, thus embarrassing Leo.

Second, Nöldeke might have been influenced by references in the Arabic sources to an Amorkesos described as *biṭrīq* (*patricius*).[14] If so, these sources need to be examined, since they have also contributed to the genesis of an erroneous view. In solving a problem like the one under consideration, the Arabic sources cannot be taken seriously. They are all secondary sources written in the Muslim era, long after the events described had taken place, and thus cannot compete with a historian like Malchus, who was writing under Anastasius. Furthermore, a close examination of these references can easily explain *biṭrīq* away: (1) The sources make this *biṭrīq* a Ghassānid chief, which immediately creates difficulties for Nöldeke's view since, according to him, Amorkesos belonged to the tribe of Kinda.[15] (2) These references to a *biṭrīq* probably record a faint echo of the patriciate which was conferred on the more illustrious Ghassānid chief Arethas in the reign of Justinian, whom the Arabic sources might have confused with Amorkesos. (3) The sources may have confused Amorkesos with Imru' al-Qays, the Kindite prince and poet who, according to the Arabic sources, was supposed to have visited Constantinople and to have been highly honored by Justinian.[16] (4) The term *biṭrīq* might be a corruption of *ghiṭrīf*, which appears in the sources in close proximity to *biṭrīq*. Diacritical marks in the Arabic script, when misplaced, can easily cause such confusion.[17] (5) Finally, the term *biṭrīq*, used as an epithet, may have nothing to do with the Roman dignity *patricius*. It may simply be

[11] On this term, see the Postscript to this Appendix.

[12] Zeno's envoy to Gaeseric.

[13] Müller, op. cit., 114.

[14] See Ibn Durayd, *al-Ishtiqā*, ed. F. Wüstenfeld (Göttingen, 1854), 258. Ḥamza al-Iṣfahānī, *Annales*, ed. Joseph Gottwald (Leipzig, 1844), 116; al-Nuwayri, *Nihāyat al-Arab (Cairo, 1924)*, 314.

[15] Nöldeke, *GF*, 13 note 3.

[16] Abū al-Faraj al-Iṣbahānī, *Kitāb al-Aghānī* (Būlāq, 1868–88), viii, 73.

[17] The word means "chief," "lord," etc. See E. W. Lane, *Arabic-English Lexicon*, Bk. I, pt. 6 (New York, 1956), 2270.

the indigenous word which, according to the lexicographers, means "proud," "self-conceited," and thus a mere homograph or homophone of the Latin term *patricius* naturalized in Arabic as *biṭrīq*.[18]

Perhaps the foregoing has sufficiently demonstrated that Nöldeke's view is untenable. Consequently it follows that Amorkesos cannot be added to the list of the great *magistri militum*, the German commanders of the fifth century who, for their importance or exceptional services to the state, were endowed with the patriciate, namely, Ricimer, Odovacar, and Theoderic. It also follows that the peak in the history of Arab assimilation to Byzantium's administrative system, and of the promotion of Arab chiefs in the imperial hierarchy, had not yet been reached in the fifth century. No Arab phylarch of the fourth or fifth century had attained sufficient importance in Byzantium's scheme of things to merit the patriciate, and it was not until the sixth century, when the structure of the Arab phylarchate had been fundamentally changed in response to the exigencies of the Persian Wars, that the high dignity was deservedly earned by a Ghassānid prince and was conferred by Justinian on Arethas, son of Jabala.

Postscript

The term πρωτοπατρίκιος poses an interesting and important problem. Cantoclarus seems to have considered it suspect, and to have suggested instead τῶν πατρικίων. The proposed emendation was rejected by Valesius, who drew attention to the designation of Aspar in the sources as *primus patriciorum*. In defense of the *vulgata lectio* he wrote: "nam πρωτοπατρίκιος erat primus Patriciorum, is videlicet, qui ante alios omnes Patriciatus dignitatem a Imperatore acceperat. Sic Aspar primus Patriciorum dicitur in Chronico Marcellini, Leone IV et Probiano Coss" (Malchus, Corpus Scriptorum Historiae Byzantinae, 540). The importance of the term πρωτοπατρίκιος in Malchus depends on whether it was used with technical accuracy or merely as a literary locution. If it is simply a literary locution, meaning the most eminent or important patricians, then its occurrence in Malchus loses much of its interest. It is possible to argue that it may have been so used. Within the ranks of the various grades and dignities, precedence was determined by office; for instance, a praetorian prefect was superior to a *magister militum*, although each was *illustris*. The same rule applied to the patricians, among whom consuls were given precedence over other patricians (*Nov. Just.*, lxiii, 2). If, on the other hand, the term πρωτοπατρίκιος was used with technical accuracy, then its use by Malchus might be of some significance in the history of ranks and dignities in the Byzantine hierarchy. In the course of a discussion on the πατρίκιοι Bury recorded a use of the term πρωτοπατρίκιος in 711 and its application to Barisbakurios, the count of the Opsikion theme. According to him, the term "appears to mean that he was the senior or doyen of the ἱερὰ τάξις τῶν ἐντίμων πατρικίων (J. B. Bury, *The Imperial Administrative System* [London, 1911], 28). But the occurrence of the term in Malchus argues that it had been in use as early as the fifth century, and its plural form suggests more than one "senior" or "doyen." The

[18] Lane, *Lexicon*, Bk. I, pt. 1 (New York, 1955), 217.

Arabic sources contain expressions that seem to be literal translations of the term πρωτοπατρίκιος: *al-biṭrīq al-kabīr*, "the great patrician," *biṭrīq al-baṭāriqa*, "the patrician of the patricians," and *akbar al-baṭāriqa*, "the greatest of the patricians." All these expressions refer to conditions that obtained later than the fifth century, and consequently do not throw much light on the use of the term by Malchus. But they are relevant for the subsequent history of πρωτοπατρίκιος, and can argue that the term was technically significant and sufficiently well known to be current among the Arab authors. See al-Tanūkhi, *Al-Faraj baʿd al-Shiddah* (Cairo, 1955), 153; al-Ṭabarī, *Annales*, ed. M. J. de Goeje, III (1880), 2103; ibn-Khurdadhbih, *Bibliotheca Geographorum Arabicorum*, VI, 112; for the application of the term *biṭrīq al-baṭāriqa* to the Armenians, see M. Canard, "Sayf al Daula," *Bibliotheca Arabica* (Algiers, 1934), 77 note 1.

Appendix II

Inter-Phylarchal Relations

Although the fragment from Malchus is the only detailed and extensive document for Arab-Byzantine relations in the reign of Leo, there is an account in the *Life of Euthymius* by Cyril of Scythopolis that is informative on inter-Arab or inter-phylarchal relations, and through these on Arab-Byzantine relations in the same reign.[1]

The account involves Terebon I, the son of Aspebetos, who ca. 459–460, went from Palaestina Prima to the province of Arabia and through the machinations of a co-phylarch[2] in Arabia was put in jail in Bostra by the governor of Arabia. It was only through the intervention of St. Euthymius with the bishop of Bostra, Antipatrus, that Terebon was freed and sent home to Palaestina Prima with a *viaticum* from the bishop.

The account raises some important problems of inter-phylarchal relations and the relationship that obtained between the provincial Arab phylarch and the provincial Roman governor:

1. It clearly indicates that the phylarchal sphere of operation was severely circumscribed and limited by provincial boundaries. Once Terebon crossed from the province to which he was assigned, Palaestina Prima, into Arabia he was not entirely secure, in spite of the fact that he was in the employ of the Romans and still on Roman territory. He could be put in jail for charges brought against him rather than returned to his own province for trial.

2. The co-phylarch in Arabia had no authority over the phylarch of Palaestina Prima in the former province; it was the Roman governor of the province who could put the phylarch in jail and not his fellow phylarch. This makes it clear that the

[1] The account was discussed from a different point of view in the chapter on Theodosius II; see above, 48.

[2] Among other things, the episode attests phylarchal presence in the Provincia Arabia and in Palaestina Prima simultaneously. The Greek term for co-phylarch, συμφύλαρχος, is a welcome addition to the sparse terminology of the Arab phylarchate of the Orient.

phylarch was actually under the jurisdiction of the *dux* or the moderator of the province. It is not clear who the governor of Arabia[3] was around 460.

3. The language of the hagiographer is cryptic when it comes to what lay behind the incarceration of Terebon I. He speaks of the machinations of the co-phylarch, but it must have been something that carried conviction for the governor, who actually put him in jail. The tribal friction between the group of the Arabian phylarch and that of Terebon was mentioned earlier.[4] Apparently the charges were finally deemed not important enough to justify a prolonged incarceration, since the bishop of Bostra freed him and sent him home. Perhaps he crossed provincial boundaries without the knowledge or permission of the *dux* of Palestine or Arabia.

4. Finally, the episode proves that the phylarchate of the Orient was not unified, as it was to be around 530 under the Ghassānid Arethas. Each phylarch was assigned to his own province. A phylarch could come to grief if he crossed provincial boundaries, and he was clearly under the authority not of a supreme phylarch in Oriens who would have investigated the complaint of one phylarch against another, but under the jurisdiction of the Roman governor of the province in which he happened to be.

Appendix III

Malchus: Fragment I

The text of this fragment is that of C. de Boor in *Excerpta Historica iussu imp. Constantini Porphyrogeniti Confecta: Excerpta de Legationibus* (Berlin, 1903), Volume I, pars I, pp. 568–69. As noted above, de Boor has the important passage on the exchange of gifts between the emperor and the phylarch correct. In his text only Νομαλίου in line 8 is incorrect, and I have changed it to Νοκαλίου.

Ὅτι ἐν τῷ ἑπτακαιδεκάτῳ ἔτει τῆς βασιλείας Λέοντος τοῦ Μακέλλη, πάντων πανταχόθεν τεταράχθαι δοκούντων, ἀφικνεῖταί τις τῶν Σκηνιτῶν Ἀράβων, οὓς καλοῦσι Σαρακηνούς, ἱερεὺς τῶν παρ' ἐκείνοις Χριστιανῶν, ἐξ αἰτίας τοιαύτης. Πέρσαι καὶ Ῥωμαῖοι σπονδὰς ἐποιήσαντο, ὅτε ὁ μέγιστος πρὸς αὐτοὺς ἐπὶ Θεοδοσίου συνερράγη πόλεμος, μὴ προσδέχεσθαι τοὺς ὑποσπόνδους Σαρακηνούς, εἴ τις ἐς ἀπόστασιν νεωτερίσαι προέλοιτο. ἐν δὲ τοῖς Πέρσαις ἦν ὁ Ἀμόρκεσος τοῦ Νοκαλίου γένους· καὶ εἴτε τιμῆς οὐ τυγχάνων ἐν τῇ Περσίδι γῇ ἢ ἄλλως τὴν Ῥωμαίων χώραν βελτίω νενομικώς, ἐκλιπὼν τὴν Περσίδα εἰς τὴν γείτονα Πέρσαις Ἀραβίαν ἐλαύνει, κἀντεῦθεν ὁρμώμενος προνομὰς ἐποιεῖτο καὶ πολέμους Ῥωμαίων μὲν οὐδενί, τοῖς δὲ ἀεὶ ἐν ποσὶν εὑρισκομένοις Σαρακηνοῖς ἀφ' ὧν καὶ τὴν δύναμιν αὔξων προήει κατὰ μικρόν. μίαν δὲ τῶν Ῥωμαίων παρεσπάσατο νῆσον Ἰωτάβην ὄνομα, καὶ τοὺς δεκατηλόγους ἐκβαλὼν τῶν Ῥωμαίων αὐτὸς ἔσχε τὴν νῆσον, καὶ τὰ τέλη ταύτης λαμβάνων χρημάτων εὐπόρησεν οὐκ ὀλίγων ἐντεῦθεν. καὶ ἄλλας δὲ ὁ αὐτὸς Ἀμόρκεσος τῶν πλησίον ἀφελόμενος κωμῶν ἐπεθύμει Ῥωμαίοις

[3] The governor of Arabia is not attested for this period; see M. Sartre, *TE*, 77–120 and Bowersock, *Roman Arabia*, 160–61.

[4] See above, note 1.

ὑπόσπονδος γενέσθαι καὶ φύλαρχος τῶν κατὰ Πετραίαν ὑπὸ Ῥωμαίοις ὄντων Σαρακηνῶν. πέμπει οὖν πρὸς Λέοντα τὸν βασιλέα Ῥωμαίων Πέτρον ἐπίσκοπον τῆς φυλῆς τῆς ἑαυτοῦ, εἴ πως δύναιτο ταῦτα πείσας ποτὲ διαπράξασθαι. ὡς δ' ἀφίκετο καὶ διελέχθη τῷ βασιλεῖ, δέχεται τοὺς λόγους ὁ βασιλεὺς καὶ μετάπεμπτον εὐθὺς ποιεῖται τὸν Ἀμόρκεσον ἐλθεῖν πρὸς αὐτόν, ἀβουλότατα τοῦτο διανοησάμενος καὶ ποιήσας. εἰ γὰρ δὴ καὶ φύλαρχον χειροτονῆσαι προῄρητο, ἔδει πόρρωθεν ὄντι τῷ Ἀμορκέσῳ τοῦτο προστάξαι, ἕως καὶ τὰ Ῥωμαίων ἐνόμιζε φοβερὰ καὶ τοῖς ἄρχουσιν ἀεὶ τοῖς τυχοῦσι Ῥωμαίων ἔμελλεν ἥκειν πεπτηχὼς καὶ τήν γε προσηγορίαν βασιλέως ἀκούων αὐτήν· καὶ γὰρ διὰ πολλοῦ κρεῖττόν τι τῶν ἀνθρώπων εἶναι τῶν ἄλλων ἐνόμιζεν. νῦν δὲ πρῶτον μὲν αὐτὸν διὰ πόλεων ἦγεν, ἃς ἔμελλεν ὄψεσθαι τρυφῆς μόνον γεμούσας, ὅπλοις δὲ οὐ χρωμένας· ἔπειτα δέ, ὡς ἀνῆλθεν ἐς Βυζάντιον, δέχεται παρὰ τοῦ βασιλέως ἀσμένως, καὶ τραπέζης κοινωνὸν βασιλικῆς ἐποιήσατο καὶ βουλῆς προκειμένης μετὰ τῆς γερουσίας συμπαρεῖναι ἐποίει· καὶ τό γε δὴ αἴσχιστον ὄνειδος τῶν Ῥωμαίων, ὅτι καθέδραν αὐτῷ τὴν πρωτοπατρικίων ἀποδοθῆναι ἐκέλευσε σχηματισάμενος ὁ βασιλεύς, ὅτι δὴ Χριστιανὸς ἀνεπείσθη γενέσθαι· καὶ τέλος ἀπέπεμψεν αὐτόν, ἰδίαν μὲν παρ' αὐτοῦ εἰκόνα τινὰ χρυσῆν καὶ κατάλιθον λαβὼν σφόδρα τε οὖσαν πολυτελῆ, χρήματα δὲ καὶ αὐτὸς ἐκείνῳ ἐκ τοῦ δημοσίου ἀντιδοὺς καὶ τῶν ἄλλων κελεύσας ἕκαστον εἰσενεγκεῖν, ὅσοι ἐτέλουν εἰς τὴν βουλήν. τὴν δὲ νῆσον ἐκείνην, ἧς ἐμνήσθημεν πρόσθεν, οὐ μόνον κατέλιπεν αὐτῷ ἔχειν βεβαίως, ἀλλὰ καὶ ἄλλας αὐτῷ κώμας προσέθηκε πλείονας. ταῦτα παρασχὼν Ἀμορκέσῳ ὁ Λέων καὶ τῶν φυλῶν ἄρχοντα, ὧν ἤθελε, ποιήσας ἀπέπεμψεν ὑψηλόν, καὶ ὅσος οὐκ ἔμελλε τοῖς δεξαμένοις λυσιτελεῖν.

V

The Reign of Zeno (474–491)

Arab-Byzantine relations during the reign of Zeno are documented in accounts of two episodes, which took place in 474 and 485.

I. The Offensive of 474

In his account of the reign, Evagrius relates that the empire was assaulted simultaneously in the East by the Arabs and in the West by the Huns. He is precise on the geographical sector into which the Huns irrupted, Thrace, but is vague on the Arabs.[1] Theophanes pins the Arab invasion down to Mesopotamia,[2] and so, if precision is attainable here, it is reducible to a discussion of Theophanes' accuracy.[3] (1) It is possible that Theophanes was confusing this invasion with that recorded for the year 484, when the Persian Arabs did indeed invade Roman Mesopotamia.[4] (2) On the other hand, Theophanes has preserved some of the most valuable data on Byzantino-arabica, and leaves Evagrius far behind him in precision and detail.[5] It is likely that Theophanes used an independent source that provided this precise datum, namely, the sector of the *limes orientalis* which the Arabs attacked. (3) The term Mesopotamia is rather vague, since it could apply to the whole northern part of the

[1] Speaking of the East molested by the Arabs, he refers to them as "tented barbarians," ἔνθεν μὲν τῶν σκηνιτῶν βαρβάρων πάντα ληϊζομένων. See his *Ecclesiastical History*, ed. J. Bidez and L. Parmentier (London, 1898), 100. Evagrius' excessive dislike of Zeno (ibid., III, chaps. 1 and 2) may have made him exaggerate the disasters of the reign.

[2] Theophanes, *Chronographia*, 120, who identifies them as Saracens.

[3] Nicephorus Callistus confirms Theophanes on Mesopotamia, and as a Church historian calls the Saracens of Theophanes "descendants of Hagar." See his *Ecclesiastical History*, PG 147 (3), col. 118. It is noteworthy that in his reference to Mesopotamia he did not follow Evagrius but Theophanes or some other independent source. His variants have been described by the editors of Evagrius as having "no value save frequently happy conjectures" but this is an instance where the departure from Evagrius is not merely an instance of happy conjecturing; see the introduction to Evagrius' *History*, p. ix (above, note 1). On the value of Nicephorus Callistus for Arab history, see *BAFOC*, 139 note 5.

[4] See below, Sec. II.

[5] An instance of this is their two accounts of the Kindite and Ghassānid offensive against the Roman *limes*, ca. 500. See Evagrius, *Ecclesiastical History*, III, 36, p. 135 and Theophanes, *Chronographia*, 141. These have been treated by me in two publications, "The Last Days of Salīḥ," 152, and "Ghassān and Byzantium," 235–38.

Land of the Two Rivers (contrasting with the southern part, Babylonia), thus comprising two Byzantine provinces of Oriens, namely, Osroene and Mesopotamia; or it could refer only to the smaller Byzantine province with that name, adjacent to Osroene and to its northeast. If the Mesopotamia of Theophanes is the former, the attacking Arabs must have come from northern Arabia, from the angle where the Byzantine and Persian frontiers met. If the latter, the attacking Arabs could only have come from Persian territory, since it is impossible to reach Mesopotamia from northern Arabia without first crossing Osroene.

It is difficult to tell who these Arabs were since there are no onomastic or other indications in the text which could help solve this problem,[6] and it is possible that the offensive may have been Persian-inspired, reflecting the displeasure of the Persian king[7] at the reception accorded to Amorkesos, the Arab chief who defected from Persia and was received by Emperor Leo in the preceding year, 473.

II. The Operation of 485

In the second of six letters addressed by Bar-Ṣauma, the Nestorian metropolitan of Nisibis, to his superior, Acacius, the Nestorian catholicus of Nisibis,[8] an account is given of raids undertaken by the Arabs of the two empires in 485. The Persian Arabs of Mesopotamia made an incursion into Roman territory, and this elicited a response from the Romans, who assembled at the frontier with their own Arabs. The Persian satrap of the area, Qardag Nakōragan, arranged for talks that ended with an agreement that each side, the Persian and the Roman Arabs, would give up what it had captured and pillaged from the territory of the other, and the frontier would be delimited by a treaty. To this end the King of Kings[9] ordered the king of the Arabs and the satrap of Bēth-Aramāyē to go to Nisibis, whither the Roman commander was also persuaded by Bar-Ṣauma to come. During the amicable encounter at

[6] As in the case of the account in Theophanes of the Arab offensive of 500 (above, note 5), where such names as Jabala clearly establish the Ghassānid provenance of the Saracen invaders.

[7] The Persian king during whose reign the incident took place was Pērōz (459–484). The reigning Lakhmid king was al-Aswad, who according to the Arabic sources reigned for twenty years after the death of his father Mundir in 462; see Rothstein, *DLH*, 53.

It is not altogether impossible that this assault on Roman territory may have been made by the Persian Arabs, in view of the location of Mesopotamia. And it could possibly have coincided with the death of Leo and the accession of a new emperor, a suitable occasion for renewing demands for the annual subsidies and sending raiding parties in case they were denied.

[8] See *Synodicon Orientale*, ed. J. B. Chabot, 526–27. The French translation of the Syriac text is on pp. 532–34. For the chronology of the letters, see p. 537 note 4.

[9] Balāš (484–488). Pērōz (459–484) had died early in 484; see Nöldeke, *PAS*, Anhang A. opposite p. 434.

Nisibis, the Persian Arabs again went on a raiding expedition against the villages in Roman territory; this incensed the Roman commander, who thought he had been cheated or lured to come to Nisibis so that the Persian Arabs might lay waste Roman territory with impunity. However, nothing serious seems to have resulted from the action of the unruly Arabs of the Persians, and the Byzantine-Persian peace was not ruffled for the remainder of the reign of Zeno.

Bar-Ṣauma's account contains elements that are important to the history of Byzantine-Persian relations:

(1) It is possible that the background of this episode was Zeno's having recently (483) stopped the annual subsidy that Byzantium paid the Persians for the upkeep of the Caspian Gates, and his demanding the return of Nisibis to the Romans as a condition for the resumption of these payments.[10] The Persians could conveniently use their Arabs to express their displeasure against Persia without committing themselves to a technical violation of the treaty and the peace that had reigned between them and the Romans since 442. On the other hand, it is possible that the drought that had afflicted Persian Mesopotamia, and about which Bar-Ṣauma speaks in the opening part of his letter, may have driven the Saracens, who lived in the southern part of the province,[11] to raid Roman Mesopotamia.[12] However, the two explanations are not mutually exclusive, and it is possible that both climatic and political considerations were behind the Saracen raid into Roman Mesopotamia.[13]

(2) The letter is fortunately precise and informative on the group of Persian Arabs who conducted the raid; this is rare in the sources, which normally refer to them in vague, general terms.

a. In addition to the fact that their geographical location is indicated—Persian Mesopotamia, or rather the southern part of it—the letter gives an estimate of their fighting force when it describes their second raid into Roman Mesopotamia, while the representatives of the two empires were conferring with each other in Nisibis. They could put some four hundred

[10] See Stein *HBE*, II, 64 note 4. For a recent treatment of legal relations between the two empires, see E. Chrysos, "Some Aspects of Roman-Persian Legal Relations," *Kleronomia* 8 (1976), 1–56.

[11] *Synodicon Orientale*, 532 note 2.

[12] On drought as a possible cause for Arab raids into Roman territory, see above, Chap. 1, app. 1.

[13] It should be remembered that the metropolitan Bar-Ṣauma would not have been acquainted with the designs of the Persian king. The latter or his counselors would have been careful to keep this a state secret, especially from a Christian ecclesiastic such as Bar-Ṣauma because of suspected loyalty to the Christian Roman Empire. So it is possible that in Bar-Ṣauma's account the Saracen invasion of Roman Mesopotamia appears as possibly motivated by climatic and material causes such as the drought that had prevailed in Mesopotamia.

horsemen into the raiding expedition.[14] If one Arab tribe could provide this number of cavalry—and it is not necessarily the maximum that they could provide—then the Arabs in the service of Persia (and also those in the service of Byzantium) could muster for their overlords a large army of mounted auxiliaries.[15]

b. The letter specifically calls this group of Arabs Ṭouʿāyē[16]—the most precious datum that it provides. This is probably the well-known pre-Islamic Arab tribe of Ṭayy, the tribe whose name became the generic name for the Arabs among Syriac authors, namely, Ṭayāyē. It has been argued that the two different but close orthographies were used by Syriac authors to distinguish the generic term for the Arabs from the specific term for the tribe of Ṭayy.[17] Apparently this portion of the tribe was still pagan in the fifth century, but in the sixth it was converted to Christianity and appears to be zealous for the faith it had adopted. Some of its priests, such as Abraham and Daniel, are known.[18]

c. Their legal status under the Persians is not clear from the idiom of the Syriac writer. Chabot translates the Syriac term as "*sujets*"[19] which raises the question whether they were technically a subject people who paid the tribute as *vectigales*, or whether they were allies, *foederati*. Their relations with the Lakhmids and their king presents further difficulties. In the letter, the Persian king calls on the "king of the Arabs" (undoubtedly the Lakhmid king of Ḥīra) to come up to the north and deal with the situation created by the raid of these Persian Arabs into Roman territory. The natural presumption is that this group of Arabs in Persian Mesopotamia was independent of the Lakhmids and free to do what it wanted, without regard to the latter. But when the "King of Kings" so desired, he could ask the Lakhmids to control other Arabs in Persian territory. At the beginning of the letter Bar-Ṣauma also complains of their ravages of Persian Mesopotamia itself before they crossed over to Roman Mesopotamia. This does not seem like the conduct of Arab allies of Persia, and so they are likely to have been a tribal group allowed to settle in Persian Mesopotamia[20] as ὑπήκοοι, a category of peoples recognized in the

[14] *Synodicon Orientale*, 533.

[15] The Ghassānid ally of Byzantium, Arethas, had under him 5,000 Arab horsemen at the battle of Callinicum in 531.

[16] Thus transliterated by Chabot in *Synodicon Orientale*.

[17] See *BAFOC*, 421 note 17.

[18] For Abraham, see ibid., and for Daniel see W. Wright, *Catalogue of Syriac Manuscripts of the British Museum* (London, 1871), II, 988.

[19] *Synodicon Orientale*, 532. For the Syriac phrase, equivalent of "sujets des perses," see ibid., 526, line 26.

[20] Perhaps not unlike the pocket of 30,000 Saracens in Phoenicia Libanensis, for which see above, 17–19.

Persian-Byzantine treaty[21] of 561. This is confirmed by a contrast with Persian Arabs in Mesopotamia some two decades later; these were evidently *foederati* or allies of the Persians and in their employ. They, too, crossed into Roman territory, but it is clear from the idiom of Joshua the Stylite and the fact that they did not molest Persian, but Roman territory that they were allies (*foederati*, σύμμαχοι), not ὑπήκοοι.[22]

(3) Most interesting and important is the reference to "the king of the Arabs." He rushes to the north with the Marzban of Bēth-Aramāyē to deal with the emergency created by the restive Arabs of Mesopotamia. It is practically certain that "the king of the Arabs" is the Lakhmid king of Ḥīra in the south, the Arab client-king of Persia. He is likely to be Mund̲ir II,[23] the son of Mund̲ir I, the contemporary of Theodosius II. The drive to the north is evidence that the Lakhmid king was responsible for disturbances in the dominion of Persia that the Arabs of the north caused by their raid into Roman territory. This confirms what the Arabic sources say on the powers vested in his father, Mund̲ir I, by the Persian king Bahram.[24]

(4) Finally, there is the reference to the Roman Arabs, who hurried with the Roman army to the frontier after news of the Saracen raid became known. The problem arises as to their legal status and whether they were in the same category as the Persian Arabs.

Bar-Ṣauma describes them with a term that is similar to that which he applies to the Persian Arabs, deriving from the same root but with a different nuance. Chabot translates the two terms identically as "subjects."[25] But it is clear from the context that these Roman Arabs were not in the same category

[21] For this category, see the seventh provision of the Treaty, in *The History of Menander the Guardsman*, ed. and trans. R. C. Blockley (Liverpool, 1985), 77.

[22] On these, see *The Chronicle of Joshua the Stylite*, ed. and trans. W. Wright (Cambridge, 1882), 69.

[23] Chabot thinks he was probably al-Aswad, the son of Mund̲ir I and the brother of Mund̲ir II, see *Synodicon Orientale*, 533 note 2. This is possible, but it was more likely Mund̲ir II, his brother. Al-Aswad is said to have reigned for twenty years after the death of his father Mund̲ir I in 462. Thus al-Aswad would have died in 482, when he was succeeded by his brother Mund̲ir II, who reigned for seven years until 489. See Rothstein, *DLH*, 52–53 and 72–73. Hardly anything is known about Mund̲ir II (ibid., 73) and if he was indeed the king of Ḥīra at this time, then this drive to the north would be a welcome addition to data on his reign. It is a sharp disappointment to the historian of the Lakhmid dynasty that Bar-Ṣauma does not mention the king by name. If he had, he would have solved the question of the chronology of the Lakhmids in this second half of the fifth century and settled once and for all whether al-Aswad was still alive in 485.

[24] See Dīnawarī, *Al-Akhbār al-Ṭiwāl*, 69. This does not contradict what Ṭabarī says on Mund̲ir III—that Chosroes gave him (possibly around 530) command over many Arabs, since this was an extension of the authority of Mund̲ir from within Persian territory to the Arabs in the Arabian Peninsula. See Nöldeke, *PAS*, 238.

[25] The Roman Arabs are described as "leurs sujets," the Persian Arabs as "sujets des perses"; for the Syriac version, see *Synodicon Orientale*, 526, lines 25, 26.

as the Persian Arabs. The Roman Arabs came with the Roman army, which suggests that they came as auxiliary troops who were *foederati*, in much the same way that the Lakhmid king came with the Marzban of Bēth-Aramāyē to the north.[26] Thus the *dux* of Mesopotamis came with his Arab *foederati*. Surely Byzantium had Arab *foederati* in this key province where the two frontiers met and which for long had been a bone of contention between the two empires. This is confirmed testimonially by reference to such *foederati* in this province some two decades later in the *Chronicle* of Joshua the Stylite.[27]

Whether the *foederati* mentioned in Joshua were the same as those who accompanied the *dux* of Mesopotamia to Nisibis in 485 is relatively unimportant. What matters is the reality of federate presence in this province of Oriens in the penultimate decade of the fifth century—in a province where federate presence is not as well documented as in others in Oriens. However, the tribal identity of these *foederati* remains obscure.

The reign of Zeno thus does not seem to have been eventful for Arab-Byzantine relations. It is possible that the sources are silent on these or, if they did record them, they are not extant. So Arab participation in military operations must be inferred or only suspected. One example is the first Samaritan revolt of 484, which broke out in Palestine. It is quite likely that the Arab *foederati* of Byzantium, whether the Salīḥids in Arabia or those of the Parembole in Palaestina Prima, took part in quelling it, as they did the second revolt, which broke out in 529 and in which the Ghassānid Arabs definitely participated.[28]

[26] The Romans come "avec les Ṭayyayē leurs sujets" (*Synodicon Orientale*, 532); again "le Roi des rois a ordonné au roi des Ṭayyayē et au marzban du Beit Aramayē de venir ici et le chef des Romains, avec tours leurs soldats et leurs Ṭayyayē sont fixés sur les frontière"; ibid., 533.

[27] See *The Chronicle of Joshua the Stylite*, 70, where the normal term for Arabs allied with Rome is used, namely, "the Arabs of the Romans."

[28] On the Arab participation in the second Samaritan revolt, see Shahîd, "Arethas, Son of Jabalah," *JAOS* 75 (1955), 207–9. A fresh interpretation of the consequence of Samaritan revolts has been offered by K. Holum in his communication to the Byzantine studies Conference, Dumbarton Oaks, 1977; see "Caesearea and the Samaritans," *Abstracts*, 41.

VI

The Reign of Anastasius (491–518)

Anastasius reigned for almost three decades. However, only the first of these belonged to the fifth century, which is the chronological scope of this volume. It is, therefore, to the events of this first decade of his reign that this chapter is devoted.[1]

Arab-Byzantine relations in this decade are documented in the sources by references to events assigned to 491–492 and 498.

a. In 491–492 the Arabs or the Saracens made an inroad into Phoenicia Libanensis and penetrated as far as Emesa, molesting one of the nearby monasteries. This is not mentioned by the chronographers, but by the hagiographer Cyril of Scythopolis in the *Vita Abramii*.[2] It could have been a local raid, but considering that the Arabs reached Emesa, deep in the heart of the province, it may have been of more than local importance. It is noteworthy that it coincided with the beginning of Anastasius' reign. The Persian king pressed his claims for the payment of the subsidies related to the Caspian Gates, but the new emperor, following in the footsteps of Zeno after 483, refused to pay in spite of Kawad's demands and threats.[3] Accordingly, this Arab invasion may have been Persian-inspired and undertaken by the Arab allies of Persia, the Lakhmids,[4] who had obliged on similar occasions in the past when the king wanted to express his displeasure without seeming to violate the peace that was supposed to prevail between the two empires.

[1] For the reign of Anastasius, the most lucid accounts are those of Bury, *LRE*, I, 429–52 and Stein, *HBE*, 77–111, 157–217; Stein has refined on Bury's chapter. As far as Arab-Byzantine relations during the reign are concerned, the best and the most recent account is that of Sartre in *TE*, 155–62. I have dealt with these relations in two articles that appeared in the fifties: "The Last Days of Salīḥ," 145–58 and "Ghassān and Byzantium," 232–55.

It is not only for chronological reasons that the last two decades of the reign are left out. The *foedus* between Byzantium and the Ghassānids was struck in 502, and the *foedus* signaled the initiation of a new federate supremacy, that of the Ghassānids of the 6th century.

[2] *Kyrillos von Skythopolis*, ed. Schwartz, 244.

[3] Joshua the Stylite, *Chronicle*, 13.

[4] Rather than the Ghassānids, who are mentioned as a possibility in "Last Days," 150 note 2. For a Lakhmid invasion of Phoenicia Libanensis, which carried them to the outskirts of Emesa in 527, see my *Martyrs of Najrān: New Documents*, Subsidia Hagiographica 49 (Brussels, 1971), 242.

b. The events of 498 are much more important and extensive. According to the main source, Theophanes,[5] the year witnessed a general invasion of Oriens by three groups of Arabs: (1) The Tented Arabs invaded the province of Euphratensis but were worsted at Bithrapsa in Syria by the distinguished commander of troops in the area, Eugenius. These Arabs were allied to Persia and were under the command of Naaman. (2) A second group of Arabs under Jabala had overrun Palestine before the arrival of Romanus there, but the latter beat them and put them to flight. Then, after hard-fought battles, he freed the island of Iotabe from Arab rule and returned it to Rome. (3) A third group of Arabs under Ogaros, son of Arethas, were beaten by Romanus, who also took many of the Arabs captive, including Ogaros.[6]

The passage in Theophanes is a mine of information on Arab history and Arab-Byzantine relations in the fifth century. The account is distinguished by a specificity that rarely attends such accounts: the names of the two Roman commanders, those of the three Arab ones, and the names of the provinces where the Arab-Byzantine encounters took place, including two very specialized toponyms, Bithrapsa and Iotabe. But the passage also raises a host of questions which must be answered.[7]

I. The First Operation

1. Theophanes assigns this operation to the year 498, to which he also assigns the operations of Jabala and Ogaros. There is no need to doubt his accuracy on this point. Evagrius, who based his account on the contemporary historian Eustathius of Epiphania, also puts all these operations together as occurring simultaneously, or at any rate in one year.[8] Nöldeke[9] cast some doubt on the date 498 because, according to the Arab historian, Hishām, Nuʿmān, the Lakhmid king who mounted the offensive, reigned for four years and died in 503. Nöldeke argued that the reign is too short to accommodate a regnal year before 499. But the discrepancy involves only one year, and the period of four years as a duration or an interval may involve the years 498 and 503, depending on exactly when in the year he started his reign and when he died. Besides, Theophanes was obviously using a document or an account based on a document, and consequently he is likely to be more accurate on the year of the

[5] Theophanes, *Chronographia*, I, 141.

[6] In Theophanes, the third operation comes before the second, but the text clearly shows that it should be placed third.

[7] The best and most up-to-date analysis of this passage is that of Sartre, in *TE*, 155–62.

[8] Evagrius, *HE*, III, 36.

[9] Nöldeke *PAS*, 169 note 1. Nöldeke is aware of the reference to this invasion in Evagrius (*GF*, 10 note 2) but seems unaware that this is important evidence for the year 498 based on the primary source, Eustathius of Epiphania. On Eustathius, see *PLRE*, II, 435 (note 10).

operation than Hishām is on the regnal year of a Lakhmid king.[10] However, the difference is trivial, and an approximation such as ca. 500 should be good enough for dating these important Arab offensives along the *limes orientalis* in the reign of Anastasius.

2. There seems to be some uncertainty about the provincial or territorial jurisdiction of the Roman commander, Eugenius, who scored the victory against the Arabs, and also about his military rank.[11] This is probably because two provinces are involved, Euphratensis and Syria, and he is referred to as *stratēgos*, while Romanus, the *dux* of Palestine, is referred to as *archōn*. Surely Eugenius was the *dux* not of one of the two provinces but of both, hence his description as *stratēgos* to distinguish him perhaps from Romanus who was the *dux* of only one province, Palestine. This is clinched by the *Notitia Dignitatum*, where the military command of Euphratensis and Syria are united, and military authority is vested in one *dux*, who is called *dux Syriae et Euphratensis*.[12]

3. If there is some uncertainty about the Roman *dux*, there is none about the Arab adversary, al-Nuʿmān,[13] the Lakhmid king who reigned for some four years (498–503). He was the son of al-Aswad, the very king during whose reign Amorkesos left the service of Persia and was made phylarch of Palaestina Tertia by Emperor Leo. This makes it clear that the Arabs who attacked the two Roman provinces were the Lakhmids of Ḥīra and allies of the Persians. Theophanes speaks of al-Nuʿmān in Byzantine terms as a *phylarchus*, but the Persian connection of the Lakhmids as "allies," ὑπόσπονδοι, is made clear by Theophanes.[14] This recalls the Byzantine definition of a phylarch as an Arab chief in treaty relationship to Byzantium.[15]

4. What inspired the Lakhmid Arabs to make this invasion of the Euphratesian region of Oriens in this particular year? Technically, peace had reigned between the two empires since the treaty of 442, and so there must have been a reason for this offensive, especially as it was mounted by Arabs who were described as allies of Persia and so were not acting on their own.

[10] Just as Malchus used a document in his detailed account of Amorkesos. Both documents were archival and probably derived ultimately from the *scrinium barbarorum*.

[11] Thus a question mark precedes his description as *dux Euphratensis* in *PLRE* II, 417, which furthermore suggests a possible identification with the Eugenius of the following entry (no. 6), the *dux utriusque Armeniae* in 503.

[12] *Notitia Dignitatum*, 70. Perhaps not unlike the Roman commander, the ἡγεμών, who led the troops of both Phoenicia and Palestine against Queen Mavia in the fourth century, and who most probably was a *comes rei militaris*; see *BAFOC*, 150 and note 49.

[13] This is a large historical figure in the history of the Lakhmids and of Arab-Byzantine relations. He played a prominent part in the Persian War of Anastasius' reign, and will be discussed in some detail in *BASIC*; see *PLRE*, II, 770.

[14] οἱ δὲ νικηθέντες Περσῶν ὑπόσπονδοι ἦσαν τῆς Νααμάνου τοῦ φυλάρχου φυλῆς.

[15] Stein's account of the Lakhmid invasion suggests that he did not think the king took part in it; *HBE*, II, 91.

The reason probably was similar to that which may have inspired the operation of 491–492. The year 498 witnessed the second accession of the Persian king, Kawad.[16] This would have been an occasion for him to renew demands for the payment of the annual subsidies for the upkeep of the Caspian Gates, which had been denied by Anastasius when Kawad had demanded them before. It is thus possible that Kawad wanted to celebrate his second regnal year or accession by some such military operation after a demand for the payment was rejected by Anastasius. So he conveniently ordered his client king to mount this offensive against Roman territory to signal his displeasure. If the Lakhmid king became king of Ḥīra in the same year, he too would have found it convenient to celebrate his own accession by a military operation against the age-old enemy, Byzantium.

5. There is the question of identifying the toponym Bithrapsa, Βίϑραψα, where Eugenius defeated the invading Lakhmids. This, strangely enough, has never been attempted by any of those who have written on this Arab-Byzantine encounter, although it is of some importance for understanding the invasion.

Bithrapsa is none other than Ruṣāfa, or Sergiopolis. The identity of this toponym has been concealed behind the word *Bith*, the first syllable in Bithrapsa, which is Semitic *Bēth* preceding the proper name of the locality Ruṣāfa. The full Semitic form of Sergiopolis is Bēth Reṣāpha. This compound word appears in the lexicon as an entry meaning "forte lapides in ordine dispositi aquae transeundae causa,"[17] but surely in its context in Theophanes it is a proper noun.[18] The addition of Bēth at the beginning may indicate that the chronographer meant the district of Ruṣāfa (Sergiopolis); this can be supported by the use of the term[19] χωρίον to describe it. The second part of the compound, it should be pointed out, has undergone metathesis, which is common in the transliteration of Arabic and other Semitic names.

6. The identification of Bithrapsa as Ruṣāfa raises further questions, one of which is the defense of this region by the Roman military establishment. The various military units at the disposal of the *dux* of Syria and Euphratensis

[16] Kawad's long reign (488–531) was interrupted by an interregnum, that of this brother Zamasp, who ruled from 496–498. Thus the year 498 represents the second regnal year of Kawad and his re-accession to the throne. For Kawad see *PLRE*, II, 273–74 (under Cavades) and for Zamasp, see ibid., 1195 (under Zamasphes).

[17] See R. Payne Smith, *Thesaurus Syriacus* (Oxford, 1879), I, 497.

[18] The first part of the compound Bēth-Reṣāfa, also appears in a mutilated and confusing form in such a toponym as Bizonovias, one of the bishoprics of Ruṣāfa ca. 500, which Musil has argued persuasively is none other than Bēth-Zenobia. See A. Musil, *Palmyrena*, American Geographical Society, Oriental Explorations and Studies 4 (New York, 1928), 268.

[19] A term that can mean district. This is not inappropriate contextually, since it indicates that the battle took place in the district around the city, Ruṣāfa. If *Bēth*, the first part of the compound, means "district," the compound would have parallels in such compounds as Bēth-ʿArabāyē and Bēth-Aramāyē in the Land of the Two Rivers.

are listed in the fifth-century *Notitia Dignitatum*. How many of them were still stationed there or survived after Leo's disastrous expedition against the Vandals is not clear. However, it is noteworthy that among the units listed for Syria are two units of *equites sagittarii indigenae* and one unit of *equites promoti indigenae*, which are both likely to be Rhomaic Arabs. In Ruṣāfa itself there was a unit of *equites promoti indigenae* which is also likely to be Arab.[20] These could have fought the Lakhmids in the district of Ruṣāfa under Eugenius.[21]

7. The identification of Bithrapsa as Ruṣāfa (Sergiopolis) throws much light on the choice of this spot as a military goal for the Lakhmid host. It had two attractions for king Nuʿmān: (*a*) He was well known for his anti-Christian outbursts, and Sergiopolis was a famous holy place in Oriens, the shrine of St. Sergius, revered throughout Oriens and especially by the Christian Arabs.[22] As it was among the nearest Christian shrines to the Persian border, it must have attracted the attention of the Lakhmid king, but this alone would not account for the mounting of the offensive. (*b*) It was the wealth of the shrine that must have attracted the rapacious Nuʿmān. The element of surprise may have influenced him to select Sergiopolis as, in the campaign of 420–422, it had influenced the Lakhmid Mundir, who recommended a campaign along the Euphrates rather than in well-defended Mesopotamia.[23]

8. Finally, what does this campaign against the famous Christian shrine of St. Sergius signify in the larger sense? It is unlikely that the Lakhmid king was acting alone, especially in the conduct of a campaign that trespassed on Roman territory and violated the peace treaty that had been observed since the end of the second war of Theodosius' reign in 442. It is not impossible that it was inspired by Kawad himself, for a reason other than the payment of the annual subsidies. The Persian king had toyed with Mazdakism, which cost him his throne and drove him into exile among the Ephthalites for some two years, 496–498. On regaining the throne in 498, and returning to the embrace of Mazdaism, the orthodox Zoroastrianism of the Magi, it is possible that he wanted to advertise his strict adherence to orthodoxy and the end of his

[20] See below, 467.

[21] On the seeming non-participation of Arab federate troops in the repulse of the Lakhmids, see below, 131.

[22] The Lakhmid Arabs had a long record of anti-Christian outbursts, and this may very well have been one of them. The career of Nuʿmān himself begins with an attack on Sergiopolis and ends with another attack against another Christian holy city, Edessa. On Ruṣāfa, see Musil, *Palmyrena*, app. 6, 260–72, still valuable; *Resafa I. Eine befestigte Anlage vor den Stadtmauern von Resafa*, by M. Mackensen *et alii*, with a preface by T. Ulbert (Mainz, 1984); T. Ulbert *Resafa II: Die Basilika des heiligen Kreuzes in Resafa-Sergiopolis* (Mainz, 1986).

[23] For this, see above, 29. Eugenius' victory recalls that of Vitianus in the war of 420–422. The invasion of Sergiopolis was to be repeated in the following century, both by the Lakhmid king Mundir, and by the Persian king, Chosroes; Procopius, *Wars*, II, xx, 10–16.

romance with Mazdakism by sponsoring a campaign, through his client king, against the holy shrine of the religion that was hateful to the Magi because of its universalistic claims and the spiritual conquests it was making in Zoroastrian Persia.[24]

II. The Second Operation

The second operation, that of Romanus against Jabala, presents a number of problems.

1. This is the first of two operations that Romanus conducted against the Arabs, one against Ogaros and another against Jabala. There is no problem about identifying the Roman commander, clearly the *dux* of Palestine, a distinguished officer who is associated with the Arabs twice, once in 498 when he defeated them and again in 503 when he fought with the Arab phylarch al-Aswad under Areobindus and against the Persians.[25]

2. The first problem that this second operation presents is its place in the passage. Theophanes clearly states that it antedated the third operation, the other one that Romanus conducted against Ogaros, and yet he places it after, not before, that one. The only plausible explanation for this is his desire to give it prominence by placing it at the end of the passage. Furthermore, if he had described Ogaros' operation after Jabala's, he would have separated the operation against Jabala from that against the island of Iotabe, and he clearly did not wish to do this because he conceived of them as two parts of one operation involving Jabala and his group.[26] Thus the operation involving Jabala and Iotabe is the longest part and the one that interested Theophanes most; he therefore first disposed of what to him was relatively unimportant and then proceeded to give emphasis to the operation against Jabala by placing it last. This also enabled him to go beyond the military facts and indulge in an account of the financial gains that Romanus scored by his reconquest of Iotabe.

3. The identity of the Arab chief whom Romanus defeated and put to flight in Palestine is hardly questionable. He is the Ghassānid Jabala, the father of Arethas, whom Procopius mentions by name and patronymic.[27] His relationship to the Amorkesos who first occupied the island of Iotabe is not so clear. He could be lineally or collaterally related to him; he could belong to

[24] Kawad may also have thought that the campaign would induce in Anastasius a more receptive mood for paying the annual subsidies.

[25] For Romans, see *PLRE* II, 948 (no. 7). His campaign with Aswad under Areobindus presents problems which will be treated in *BASIC*.

[26] This receives corroboration from what has been established about the identity of Amorkesos of the reign of Leo, namely, that he was a Ghassānid.

[27] On Jabala, see Shahîd, "Ghassān and Byzantium," 244 notes 241–242 and *Martyrs*, 272–76. He will be discussed again, genealogically and otherwise, in *BASIC*.

the same Ghassānid clan or to another. But he is a Ghassānid, and this is the important genealogical fact. It remains to be seen whether in addition to operating in Palestine he was also in possession of Iotabe as Amorkesos had been. Theophanes does not say this. He only says that Romanus was free to deal with the Arabs of Iotabe after beating Jabala in Palestine. The statement is general, merely suggesting that there was a relationship between the two operations, but leaving open the question of which Ghassānid chief was in charge of Iotabe. The chances are that Jabala was in charge of operations against the Romans, but it is not clear whether he operated in Palaestina Tertia alone or in Iotabe as well.

4. The most important question that must be raised in relation to this operation is the circumstance that led to it. Emperor Leo had come to an agreement with Amorkesos some twenty years before, and the sources reflect no subsequent ruffling of relations. Presumably the arrangement worked smoothly; what, then, occasioned this sudden change in 498?

The sources are silent, but it is practically certain that the financial policy of Anastasius is responsible for it. As is well known, Anastasius retrieved the financial situation after it had reached the brink of ruin because of the costly expedition of Leo against the Vandals. His careful spending and personal attention to matters of detail restored the economy of the state. Surely the extraordinary arrangement that Leo had with the Arab chief would have attracted his attention, and so he was probably determined to wrest the island of Iotabe from Arab hands and restore it to Roman rule. He must, then, have issued orders for its return. Thus it is practically certain that it was not Amorkesos' phylarchate over Palaestina Tertia that irked Anastasius but his rule over Iotabe and the financial loss to the empire that it entailed.[28]

But why would Anastasius wait seven years before deciding to drive the Arabs out of Iotabe? He was preoccupied with the Isaurian problem, and it was only in 498 that the last of them, Longinus of Selinus, was beaten, captured, and tortured at Nicaea. Perhaps it was only then that Anastasius felt he could deal with the Arab problem. But the more plausible explanation would be that the year 498 witnessed the death of Amorkesos, the old phylarch whom Leo had confirmed in the possession of Iotabe; his death must have confronted the Romans with the usual problem of the renewal of the *foedus*. Anastasius took advantage of this moment to refuse to renew what he thought was a *foedus iniquum* as far as Rome was concerned, struck between the

[28] One could wonder whether it is altogether impossible that Anastasius may also have wanted the Ghassānids, Orthodox since the reign of Leo, to adopt Monophysitism. By 498 he had dethroned Euphemius and appointed Macedonius to the patriarchal see of Constantinople (in 496). Stein has some perceptive comments on the island of Iotabe in this context, for which see *HBE*, 91 note 5.

empire and an Arab chief in the aftermath of Leo's expedition against the Vandals, and negotiated under duress. So he refused to renew it, just as he refused to pay the annual subsidies to the Persian king for the upkeep of the Caspian Gates. He may well have considered that the money that Rome paid to Persia and the money that the Arab lord of Iotabe collected belonged to the same order of extortion from, and loss to, the Byzantine treasury.

5. This analysis of the antecedents of the second operation makes the course of events left unrecorded in the sources intelligible. They may be reconstructed as follows. After some twenty years of Ghassānid rule in Iotabe and Palaestina Tertia by Amorkesos, Anastasius refused to renew the treaty. The Arab *foederati* were outraged and decided to revolt.[29] They assaulted the Romans in the province of Palaestina Tertia, where their forces were deployed.[30] They seem to have scored some initial successes against the predecessor of Romanus, who apparently was not yet *dux* of Palestine when Jabala overran it.[31] Romanus was dispatched to deal with this dangerous development. He first beat Jabala handsomely on the mainland in Palaestina Tertia, then crossed over to Iotabe and dislodged the Ghassānids from the island. According to Theophanes, it was only after fierce battles that Romanus was able to free the island from Arab rule.[32]

III. The Third Operation

The third operation, that of Romanus against Ogaros, is less important than the second, but also presents some problems.

1. The first is the identity of the Arab Ogaros, who must be Ḥujr, the Kindite chief, since his patronymic is given. This Kindite prince was the son of Ḥārith, son of ʿAmr, the Kindite king, well known to Byzantium around 500 and for more than a quarter century to come.[33] The genealogical state-

[29] For two precedents of revolts in the 4th century, related to the dissolution of the *foedus* by the death of the Arab federate chief, see *BAFOC*, 142 ff. and 205 ff.

[30] Cf. their revolt late in the 6th century, in the Provincia Arabia when they occupied Bostra; see Nöldeke, *GF*, 29–30 and Sartre, *TE*, 191.

[31] The Saracen raids against the monasteries of Palestine of which Cyril of Scythopolis speaks are likely to have been either a raid by local Saracens or, more likely, the Kindite invasion—the operation recorded by Theophanes, for which see the following section. The Ghassānids were already Christian and it is quite unlikely that they would have attacked monasteries. For the raids, see *Kyrillos*, 67, lines 21–27 and 68 lines 1–2.

[32] Cf. the annexation of Nabataea by Trajan in A.D. 106 after the death of the Nabataean king, Rabbel. For a perceptive analysis of the mystery of the annexation see Bowersock, *Roman Arabia*, 79–82. The language of Theophanes, who speaks of fiercely fought battles (μάχαῖς ἰσχυραῖς ὁ Ῥωμανὸς ἠλευθέρωσεν) recalls that of Ammianus Marcellinus on the annexation of Arabia by Trajan after an armed conflict, "incolarum tumore saepe contunso," *RG*, XIV, 8.13); but on this point, see Bowersock, op. cit., 81.

[33] For Ḥārith/Arethas, and Ḥujr/Ogaros, see *PLRE*, II, 139, 794. On Kinda, see G. Olinder, *The Kings of Kinda* (Lund, 1927) and, more recently, my article in *EI*², s.v.

ment on Ḥujr and his father, Ḥārith is unusual in a Byzantine source. This clearly indicates that it came from a document, probably going back to the *scrinium barbarorum*.[34] According to Theophanes, Romanus captured Ḥujr together with other Kindites. This may well have been the case, but his statement that Ḥujr had died a few years later is certainly untrue.[35] Ḥujr was the father of the foremost poet of pre-Islamic Arabia, Imru' al-Qays; as is well known, he was killed much later by the Arab tribe Asad.[36]

2. His father, Ḥārith (Arethas), lived for at least another twenty-five years and was very active in the military, political, and religious life of the Byzantine limitrophe. And yet he appears only genealogically in the Theophanes passage; it is his son, Ḥujr, that undertakes the operations against the Romans. The explanation is probably that Ḥārith ruled over a vast area in Arabia and so had to delegate authority to his sons.[37] Ḥujr at this time (ca. 500) was apparently in charge of the tribes that were adjacent to the *limes Arabicus*; hence his involvement. The chronographer's account does not specify where Ḥujr operated against the Romans, as he did in the case of Jabala. But since Romanus, who captured him, is described as the *dux* of Palestine, it is natural to assume that he attacked Palestine, Romanus' territorial jurisdiction.[38]

3. Finally, how was the invasion of Palestine by Kinda related to that of the Ghassānids under Jabala? It has been suggested that there was some rivalry

[34] One segment of this genealogical line given by Theophanes is most likely a confusion, but a most valuable one, since it throws much light on the *foedus* of 502 which Anastasius struck with the Arabs; it will be discussed in detail in *BASIC*.

[35] See Theophanes, *Chronographia*, I, 143. This passage in Theophanes belongs chronologically to the 6th century and is more related to the one that comes later in Theophanes on the *foedus* of 502. Both will be discussed in detail in *BASIC*.

[36] See *PLRE*, II, 794 on Ḥujr; also R. Nicholson, *A Literary History of the Arabs* (Cambridge, 1966) 104–5. *PLRE* rightly prefers the Arabic tradition, which assigns to him a later death.

[37] As pointed out rightly by Sartre in *TE*, 157. This also is consonant with what the sources say on his division or delegation of authority among his sons and his distributing them among the tribes under his rule, see *BAFOC*, 44 note 55.

[38] The Saracen invasion of Palaestina Prima during Anastasius' reign, recorded by Cyril of Scythopolis (above, note 31), may be assigned to this year, and it is perfectly possible to relate it to this Kindite offensive, which thus will corroborate that it was against Palestine that Ogaros directed his attack. The Ghassānids of Amorkesos were most probably Christian at this time, but the Christianity of the Kindites is not yet attested around 500; so they could have attacked monasteries and other Christian establishments. The raids recorded by Cyril of Scythopolis passed through two stages. Although both are assigned by him to the reign of Anastasius, Aigrain is inclined to think that the second took place around 530 and was conducted by the Lakhmid Mundir. The first, however, he associates with the invasion of 498; see his "Arabie," col. 1196. Archeologists have seen confirmation of these raids in the construction of forts in certain towns, such as Oboda of the Negev; see A. Negev, quoted by Sartre, *TE*, 159 note 138.

between the two Arab groups.[39] This is possible, but it could not have reached the point of hostility between Ghassān and Kinda.[40] Kinda and Ghassān were two South Arabian tribes who mad moved in the Ḥimyarite orbit of the Arabian south and then pursued a more comfortable political and military self-expression in northern Arabia.[41] Enmity was recorded between the Ghassānids and the Lakhmids and between the latter and the Kindites, but not between Kinda and Ghassān.[42]

What, then, is the explanation for the invasion of Oriens by the Kindite Ḥujr immediately after Jabala was worsted by Romanus? Kinda, poised near the limitrophe, may have naturally involved itself in the general commotion, or, equally likely, might have become involved after an appeal from Ghassān to come to their rescue.

IV. General Observations

1. *Prima facie*, that three operations took place in 498, and that they were led by three well-known figures in pre-Islamic Arab history, may give the impres-

[39] Sartre, *TE*, 156.

[40] Ibid., 157. Later in this century, when both Kinda and Ghassāan had been installed within Oriens as *foederati*, some friction might conceivably have arisen between the two, but even this is uncertain. It may be suggested by a passage in Cyril of Scythopolis, where there is a record of a feud between two phylarchs, Arethas and Aswad; see *Kyrillos*, 75, lines 7–11. But this is contingent on the identity of al-Aswad; his tribal affiliation may or may not have been Kindite.

It is possible that the phrase in Evagrius οὐκ ἐς τὸ συνοῖσον σφισι may have led Sartre to think of rivalry, since he translates the phrase as *n'agissant pas de concert* (*TE*, 160, line 15). I am inclined to translate it, "not without detriment to themselves." The tone of the passage, in which the historian is rejoicing in the defeat of the Arab groups and the victory of the Romans, favors this latter interpretation; and so it is understood by the Latin translator in PG, 86 (2), col. 2675: *non sine suo ipsorum damne*. I take συμφέρειν in the phrase to mean "be useful, profitable" and *not* "to work with, assist." For the phrase in Evagrius, see *Ecclesiastical History*, ed. J. Bidez and L. Parmentier, Book II, chap. 36, 135. This chapter refers to the events of 502, described much more accurately and informatively by Theophanes, *Chronographia*, I, 143.

[41] For these two tribal groups, see the present writer in *EI*² s.vv. "Ghassān," "Kinda."

[42] The enmity between Ghassān and Lakhm is well established. Al-Nuʿmān, who mounted the first operation discussed in this chapter, was the son of al-Aswad, who had massacred the Ghassānid princes of Ḥīra, referred to in the chapter on Leo. The enmity between Kinda and Lakhm is also notorious; the Arethas mentioned in this chapter, the father of Ḥujr, was finally killed by the Lakhmid Mundir around 530, as recounted by Malalas, *Chronographia* 434–35. Intermarriages involving the royal houses of these tribal groups are not necessarily reflective of alliances or friendships. The Lakhmid Mundir who killed Arethas, the Kindite just referred to in this paragraph, was married, according to the famous Hind inscription in Ḥīra, to the daughter of the latter, but this did not discourage him from killing his father-in-law. Nöldeke suggests that Mundir only pursued and defeated Arethas, but those who actually killed him were Arabs from the tribe of Kalb; *GF*, 11, note 2. For the Hind inscription, see Rothstein, *DLH*, 24. On the other hand, marriages between Kinda and Ghassān seem to reflect good relations; Imru' al-Qays, the poet and prince of Kinda, refers to the Ghassānids as his maternal uncles in tones that strongly indicate that he rejoiced and took pride in the fact; see his *Dīwān*, ed. M. Ibrahim (Cairo, 1964), 311.

sion that they were orchestrated. However, as noted above, the first operation may be related to the return from exile of the Persian king Kawad; the second may be related to the financial policy of the Byzantine emperor Anastasius; while the third in all probability was a response to an appeal from the Ghassānids who, after their defeat, invoked the aid of their South Arabian friends, the Kindites. Thus the first offensive was mounted independently of the second, while the second and third were not synchronous, but two separate operations, one of which followed the other, however related they may have been.

2. After the offensives of 498, the sources are silent on the Ghassānids for some four years, but not on the Kindites. In 502 a Kindite prince, Maʿdi-Karib, mounted an offensive against the three provinces of Oriens—Syria, Phoenicia, and Palestine—so swiftly that Romanus was unable to overtake him when he chose to retreat with a great deal of booty.[43]

What conclusions can be drawn from this silence? Since Ghassān emerges a little later as the dominant federate Arab group, it cannot be said that it disappeared or was crushed completely.[44] The conclusion may safely be drawn that, unlike Kinda, Ghassān was already within the *limes* and already had federate status; thus its brush with Romanus was an internal affair between Byzantium, the central government, and one of its federate groups, and so it went unmentioned in the sources. Kinda, on the other hand, was a Peninsular power which, compared to Ghassān, was a latecomer in Oriens. Its first encounter may be dated to this year, 498, unlike the Ghassānids who started some twenty-five years earlier with the phylarchate of Amorkesos in 473. The position of Kinda vis-à-vis Byzantium as a Peninsular group is further reflected in the geographical indications provided by the passage in Theophanes which describes the offensive mounted in 502 by Maʿdi-Karib. He attacked three provinces of the limitrophe—Syria, Phoenicia, and Palestine—and this suggests a Peninsular power attacking the oriental *limes* of Byzantium from northern Arabia. For the same reason, Kinda is mentioned in the *foedus* of 502, while Ghassān's inclusion needs to be argued for.[45]

3. It is noteworthy that those who actually conducted the second and third military operation were not the chiefs of Ghassān and Kinda but their sons or grandsons, younger officers who were acting on behalf of their elders. This gives a glimpse of the style of these two warrior tribes in conducting their military expeditions. The chief did not always take the field personally,

[43] Theophanes, *Chronographia*, I, 143. This passage properly belongs to the 6th century; it will be discussed in *BASIC*.

[44] For its appearance as the new dominant federate group in 502–3, see Shahîd, "Ghassān and Byzantium."

[45] As will be done in *BASIC*.

but delegated authority to younger members of the ruling clan. But when the peace or the *foedus* was concluded, it was *not* with these younger chiefs but with the old one, Arethas himself, as in the *foedus* of 502.

4. What is striking in the accounts of the operations of 498 and 502 is the complete silence[46] of the sources on the Arab allies of Byzantium who were especially employed for this purpose. The defense of the Orient is undertaken everywhere against the Lakhmids in the north and against Ghassān/Kinda in the south by Roman troops under the command of the two dukes, Eugenius and Romanus.

In Chapter 4 it was argued that the expedition against the Vandals most probably thinned the ranks of the Arab *foederati* in Oriens, including the principal federate group, Salīḥ. The silence of the sources on any federate presence toward the end of the century could confirm the view that Arab federate power had been in decline, principally because of the Vandal expedition. Salīḥ was declining[47] for a number of reasons, and the silence of the sources is evidence for it. Thus the way was prepared for the employment of a new federate group—the Ghassānids—whose star had been steadily rising since the exploits of Amorkesos in the reign of Leo.

Appendix I

The Edict of Anastasius

Sometime during his reign Anastasius issued an edict that is attested epigraphically in various parts of Oriens and Libya. It has survived only in fragments, but was clearly an important document dealing with the frontier provinces and their military administration, regulating relations between the *duces* and the various categories of troops stationed there—the *comitatenses*, the *limitanei*, and the *foederati*. Neither the date nor the full content of the edict is known, which is especially unfortunate for Arab-Byzantine relations, since it must have contained some precious references to the Arab *foederati* in Oriens.

Of the fragments that have survived, that recovered at Qaṣr al-Ḥallabat by the Princeton University Archaeological Expeditions to Syria and that recovered at Bostra, commented upon by Maurice Sartre, are the most relevant here.

1. Qaṣr al-Ḥallabat[1] belonged to the Provincia Arabia, and there are fragments[2] that refer to camels and dromedaries, two animals associated with the Arabs of the frontier forces, which counted among them Arab *dromedarii*, as indicated in the

[46] Rothstein erroneously thought the Arab allies of Byzantium were involved in the campaign of Nuʿmān against Ruṣāfa in the first operation; see *DLH*, 74.

[47] That the fortunes of Salīḥ were on the wane was correctly noticed by Sartre in his section on this period, *TE*, 155–62.

[1] For this version of the edict, see *Syria: Publications of the Princeton University Archaeological Expeditions to Syria, in 1904–5 and 1909*, ed. E. Littmann, D. Magie, and D. R. Stuart (Leiden, 1921), Division III, Section A, pp. 24–42.

[2] Ibid., frag. no. 40, p. 38 and no. 53, p. 40.

Notitia Dignitatum. More important is a fragment that attests Arab phylarchal presence in the Provincia, welcome in the reign of Anastasius as an epigraphic confirmation of what the literary sources have established.[3] It is the only instance of its kind for the reign. In view of the importance of the reign of Anastasius for the rise of new phylarchal supremacies, as vouched for by the literary sources, it is certain that this reference in the fragment is to the Byzantine institution of the phylarchate and not the Arab institution, namely, that of shaykhdom.[4]

2. The fragment[5] recovered at Bostra has no explicit reference to phylarchs or *foederati*, but its commentator has very appropriately made use of the data of Arab-Byzantine relations in the last quarter of the fifth century in solving one of the problems that it presents. Sartre has drawn attention to the fact that Clysma, mentioned in the fragment, belonged both geographically and administratively not to Palestine but to Augustamnica II. And yet its *commerciarius* remunerated the *dux* of Palestine. This curious arrangement had not been noted by the previous editor of the edict, and Sartre offers a convincing explanation, deriving from the fact that the *commerciarius* at Clysma had control over the revenue of Iotabe, which belonged to Palaestina Tertia; hence he could return part of this revenue to the *dux* of Palestine.[6]

The occupation of Iotabe by Amorkesos and its continuance in Arab hands from 473 to 498 thus throw light on the curious arrangement. The careful French scholar is reluctant to draw conclusions on the date of the edict from the termination of the Arab occupation of the island.[7] However, his argument involving the Arab occupation of Iotabe and the important date 498 is attractive, even seductive, and suggests that dating the edict could somehow be related to this year. It is possible to argue that if it was issued after the reoccupation of the island by Byzantium in 498, the chances are that there would have been no reference to Clysma in relation to the *dux* of Palestine. Thus the non-reference to Iotabe and the reference to Clysma could suggest that the edict was issued prior to 498.

3. The Edict of Beersheba, which will be discussed in the following chapter, is also relevant to discussing the edict's date.

It has been argued that the Edict of Beersheba might be a local version of the Edict of Anastasius, adapted to conditions in the Negev. It contains a precious reference to the *koinon* of *archiphyloi* and also to one of the phylarchs whose name has been conjectured "Petros," the phylarch of the Palestinian Parembole in Palaestina Prima, who began his phylarchate in 485 and continued in office until the early sixth century. Thus his phylarchate, unfortunately, is too long in duration and encompasses both the period before and after 498 in the reign of Anastasius. Hence, it is not

[3] Ibid., frag. no. 52, p. 40.

[4] Cf. the editor's note on Strabo's phylarchs, ibid., p. 40.

[5] See *Inscriptions grecques et latines de la Syrie*, ed. Maurice Sartre (Paris, 1982), XIII, fasc. 1, 107–19. This is the latest discussion of the edict, and has references to previous ones. It has not included one which appeared simultaneously in 1982, that of D. L. Kennedy in *Archaeological Explorations on the Roman Frontier in North-Eastern Jordan*, British Archaeological Reports, International Series 134 (Oxford, 1982); for the general treatment of Qaṣr al-Ḥallabat, see pp. 20–72; for the new fragments of the edict, see pp. 41–47.

[6] Sartre, *TE*, 115–17.

[7] Ibid., 117.

helpful for dating the edict, but it is a further argument for the proposition that the Edict of Beersheba is one version of the Edict of Anastasius, as has been persuasively noted by Sartre.[8]

Appendix II

Laudes Imperatoris Anastasii: Priscian and Procopius of Gaza

The Latin sources could possibly have references to the Arab offensives against the empire in the reign of Anastasius. Unfortunately, the references are not explicit and the dating is debatable, but it is possible that they refer to events in the first part of the reign of Anastasius.

1. In his *Panegyricus* on Anastasius,[1] the rhetorician and biblical scholar Procopius of Gaza (ca. 475–ca. 538) speaks of barbarian attacks during his reign in language that suggests that he had the Arabs in mind. Since Procopius lived in Gaza, that is, in a region close to the arid zones of Palaestina Tertia, exposed to Arab attacks, it is quite possible that this was a reference to the events of 498 recorded by Theophanes. It was understood in this manner by the commentator on the *Panegyricus*.[2]

2. In his *Panegyricus* on Anastasius,[3] the early sixth-century grammarian Priscian speaks of attacks against the empire during his reign in language that could suggest the Arabs, especially the phrase *latronum more*, which brings to mind the common description of the Arabs and other barbarian raiders of the imperial frontier as *latrones*. There is also reference to the broken treaty, *violato foedere*. The editor takes these verses (254–60) to be a reference to the Arabs and titles the passage *Arabes Scenitae repressi*.[4]

In view of its mention of the Euphrates, it is possible that this was a reference to the Lakhmid attack against Sergiopolis in 498. But, for the same reason, it could refer to the Persians and the Persian War of Anastasius' reign which began in 502. There is no explicit reference to the Persians in the entire work, and the Persian War was an important event, more important than the Lakhmid attack and, what is more, violated the treaty that had obtained since the second Persian War of the reign of Theodosius II. But the Arabs participated in this war and must have been at least implied in these verses of Priscian.[5]

The two possible Latin references to the Arabs do not add anything to those recorded in the literary sources. But their inclusion in the two panegyrics means that these operations of 498 were major ones which were deemed worthy of inclusion in contemporary literary works that sang the praises of the *autokrator*.

[8] Ibid., 119. D. van Berchem had argued that the Edict of Beersheba was issued by Theodosius II; see *L'armée de Dioclétien et la réforme constantinienne* (Paris, 1952), 35. His discussion of the edict may be found on 33–36.

[1] See *Panegyricus* (Bonn, 1829), 14, p. 497.

[2] See ibid., p. 605.

[3] See *Panegyricus* (Bonn, 1829), p. 525, lines 254–60.

[4] See Ibid., p. 523.

[5] Alan Cameron has argued that the *Panegyricus* of Priscian was composed in 503; see "The Date of Priscian's *De Laude Anastasii*." *GRBS* 15 (1974), 313–16.

VII

Three Greek Documents on Palaestina Tertia

Three documents on the fifth century remain to be discussed. Because they are undated, it has not been possible to discuss them in the course of the preceding chapters, each of which is devoted to one particular reign. The documents are: the *Sancti Nili Narrationes*; the Edict of Beersheba; and the papyri from Nessana. All are important, especially the second and the third, since the data they provide rest on the firm ground of epigraphy and papyrology.

I. *Sancti Nili Narrationes*

The *Narrationes de Caede Monachorum et de Theodulo Filio* have been generally rejected as a work by St. Nilus the Ascetic, bishop of Ancyra (d. ca. 430), and are considered Pseudo-Nilus. Their authenticity has also been impugned; according to some, they are not a history but a romance based on a letter by Nilus the Galatian.[1] The part that involves the Arabs has been viewed with the same suspicion that has haunted the work as a whole.[2]

It is difficult to subscribe to this view. Just as the Arabica in a similar work, the *Ammonii Monachi Relatio*, have been examined and found authentic,[3] so are they in the *Narrationes*. The latter most probably derive from facts and documents known to the Sinaitic writer, who describes the local scene both in the Peninsula and in its chief town, Pharan, and who incorporated these

[1] See Quasten, *Patrology*, III, 496–97.

[2] See R. Devreesse, "Le christianisme dans la péninsule sinaïtique, des origines à l' arrivée des musulmans," *RB* 49 (1940), 220–22.

In this article Devreesse is inconsistent in his treatment of the two Sinaitic documents, *Ammonii Monachi Relatio* and the *S. Nili Narrationes*. He concedes historicity to the Arabica in the *Relatio* but not to those in *Narrationes*, presumably because he could not relate this material to a historical source like Sozomen, who functioned as such for the Arabica in the *Relatio*. Methodologically, this is unacceptable, since the non-availability of a source to base the Arabica of the *Narrationes* upon may simply reflect the inadequate state of what has survived on the Arabs in the sources or what was recorded. The Sinaitic monk who wrote this account may have used such sources, possibly on the Arabs of Sinai, unavailable to others since then. If so, he has preserved some valuable data incidentally.

[3] See the two sections in *BAFOC*, 297–319.

details in the body of a larger literary work in which fact and fiction are curiously mixed.[4]

The *Narrationes*, in which the fortunes of Nilus and his son Theodulus are described, are composed of seven parts.[5] The Arabs are involved in *Narrationes* III–VII, but the most important are III and VI. The former is on the religion and customs of the Arabs, and has attracted the attention of anthropologists and historians of religion.[6] It is, therefore, *Narratio* VI that awaits analysis, and it is the most important one for Byzantino-arabica.[7]

I

The *Narrationes* relate the story of Nilus and his son, Theodulus.[8] Nilus becomes a hermit on Mount Sinai in the early part of the fifth century, during the reign of Theodosius II. When the hermitages are attacked by Saracens, Nilus escapes, but Theodulus is captured. Finally, father and son find each other at Elusa in the Negev.[9] Before they meet there, Nilus travels to Pharan, and it is at this Arab oasis and town of southwest Sinai that *Narratio* VI is set. It involves the relations between the Pharanites and the Arab phylarch in the north of the Peninsula concerning the treaty between two parties that was violated, *inter alia*, by the massacre of the monks. The account falls into three parts:[10]

1. After the massacre of a senator (βουλευτής) from Pharan,[11] an entire caravan, and many monks in the vicinity, the senate of Pharan sends couriers

[4] The task of defending the essential reliability of the Arabica in the *Narrationes* has been made superfluous by Philip Mayerson, who is not only an armchair philologist but also a field worker who knows the arid regions of Sinai and the Negev intimately, and to whose views on the Arabica in the *Narrationes* I generally subscribe. See his two articles, "The Desert of Southern Palestine according to Byzantine Sources," *Proceedings of the American Philosophical Society* 107.2 (1963), 161–64, and "Observations on Nilus' *Narrationes*: Evidence for an Unknown Christian Sect?," *Journal of the American Research Center in Egypt* 12 (1975), 51–58.

[5] The text may be found in PG 79, cols. 589–694. V. Christides has looked into new manuscripts of the *Narrationes*, for which see "Once Again the 'Narrationes' of Nilus Sinaiticus," *Byzantion* 43 (1973), 43 note 1. Prof. M. Papathomopoulus of the University of Ioannina has announced that he is preparing a critical edition of the *Narrationes*.

[6] See J. Henninger, "Ist der sogenannte Nilusbericht eine brauchbare religionsgeschichtliche Quelle?" *Anthropos* 50 (1955), 81–88. This position was taken by Christides, op. cit., 46–50, 39 note 1.

[7] *Narratio* VI takes up cols. 656–80 in PG 79.

[8] For resumes of the seven *Narrationes*, see PG 79, col. 590 and extensive ones in P. Mayerson, "Observations" 58–71.

[9] There are many moving episodes in the adventures of Theodulus, and it is partly these that have inclined scholars to view the reliability of the *Narrationes* with suspicion.

[10] For this most relevant part of the *Narratio* VI, see PG 79, cols. 661–69.

[11] His name is given Μαγάδων (col. 664). This could be a name derived from the Arab root *M-J-D*, signifying "glory" plus the suffix *ūn*, which appears in such Arabic names as Khaldūn and ʿAbdūn.

to the king of the barbarians (ὁ τῶν βαρβάρων βασιλεύς) in order to complain of the violation of the treaty (σπονδαί) between them.

2. The couriers bring the king's answer in writing (γράμματα κομίζοντες παρ' αὐτοῦ); he confirms the peace (εἰρήνη); asks those who have suffered injuries to come to him, especially the relatives of those who were taken prisoners; adds that if anyone wants to take revenge on the killers, he is prepared to bring them to justice; and promises to return all the booty taken after the massacre. Furthermore, he states that he did not wish to undo the terms of the peace (λύειν γὰρ οὐκ ἤθελε τοὺς τῆς εἰρήνης θεσμοὺς) because of the obvious material advantages that accrued to him and his people from a state of peaceful coexistence with Pharan.

3. The Pharanites then sent the king envoys with gifts in order to renew the treaty that had been violated. On the twelfth day they reached the camp (παρεμβολή) of Ammanes (Ἀμμάνης), "the king of the barbarians," who receives the envoys cordially.

II

The preceding is roughly the bare skeleton of events that unfolded in Sinai, and they provide material for some important problems of Arab-Byzantine relations, especially in the region of Palaestina Tertia during the reign of Theodosius.

1. The first raid of the Saracens, which brought about the massacre of some of the monks of a monastery near Mount Sinai, clearly implies the persistence of a number of large pagan pockets within the Christian empire. The Sinai Peninsula must have been an ideal region for them in view of its aridity and inaccessibility. Christian missionary activity thus could not have penetrated the Peninsula, especially as only one century had elapsed from the reign of Constantine. Even in the sixth century the Byzantine heartland, Anatolia, had many pagan pockets in the reign of Justinian.[12] Such raids support what has been said on the rise of internal *limites*.[13] In a vast, arid, and inaccessible area such as Sinai, the problem of security became important—for the safety of the Rhomaic city-dwellers, for the institutions of the new religion, namely, isolated monasteries and churches, and for the pilgrim routes that led to the Holy Places.

2. The city of Pharan, about which the *Ammonii Monachi Relatio*[14] is

[12] For the work of John of Ephesus in wiping out paganism in Asia Minor during the reign of Justinian, see *Historia Ecclesiastia*, ed. E. W. Brooks, CSCO, Scriptores Syri, ser. 3, tom. 3 (Louvain, 1936), pars 3, chap. 36, textus pp. 169–70, versio, pp. 125–27.

[13] For these, see *BAFOC*, 479–83, especially the *limes Palaestinae*, 480–81. The mobile phylarchal rather than static limital system would have been the more appropriate form of security for such outlying areas as Mt. Sinai.

[14] See *BAFOC*, 303–5.

informative for events in the latter part of the fourth century, appears almost as an autonomous city. It has its senate, and the name of one of its citizens is known, Magadon. But more important is that it is the city, not the Roman authorities of Palaestina Tertia or Oriens, that concluded the treaty (the σπονδαί, *foedus*) with the Arab chief, Ammanes. This is unusual and admits of one of three explanations: (1) This was an arrangement that was a continuation of a previous one, which obtained before A.D. 106 when Nabataea became the Provincia Arabia. (2) The author of the *Narrationes* was very elliptical in his description of the negotiations between the two parties and simply omitted reference to the official Roman representatives or to Roman participation in these transactions. Thus ultimately the *foedus* was, indeed, between the Arab chief and the Roman state, but since it was the Pharanites who were directly affected by it, they acted as though they were the representatives of the latter. (3) The Sinai Peninsula being what it is, there may have been pockets of Arab rule and sovereignty that the imperial government did not control, and consequently Pharan, in its desire for security, may have concluded the treaty with the Arab chief on its own.[15]

3. The Arab chief involved in these transactions is called in Greek Ἀμμάνης (Ammanes). It rings authentic as an old archaic Arab name that may have been prevalent in the fifth century. It could be related to the Arabic root *A-M-N* meaning "to be faithful, reliable, safe, trustworthy," and its morphological pattern is that of the intensive form in view of the double "m" in Ammanes. There is also the possibility that the first two letters (Am) are the definite article *al*, the L having been assimilated to the following M. If so, the name could be al-Mānī, from the root *M-N-Y*, "to divide," or al-Mānicʿ, from the root *M-N-*ʿ, meaning "to protect," all of which are appropriate for an Arab chief in charge of security. It is tantalizing to think that the name could be a mutilated form of Dahmān, which appears in the onomasticon of the kings of Salīḥ, the dominant Arab federate group in Oriens in this century.[16]

4. The camp of the Saracen chief is located to the north of Pharan—a twelve-day journey.[17] It is appropriately called a "parembole," the same term

[15] See P. Mayerson, "The Desert," 162. It is not impossible that this unusual arrangement between Pharan and the Arab chief took place in a period that was especially propitious, namely, a period of drastic changes in the history of the region and of Arab-Byzantine relations. Toward the end of the century, in the reign of Theodosius I, Egypt was separated from Oriens and a new group of Arab federates appeared, the Salīḥids, superseding the old ones, the Tanūkhids.

[16] If so he must have been an early Salīḥid chief since the one attested in the sources with that name appears late in the century; see my article "The Last Days of Salīḥ," 154 note 1. It is interesting that the patronymic of this late Salīḥid king is Ibn ʿImliq, the Amalecite. The Amaliqa, Amalec, had roamed these regions in biblical times.

[17] For the journey from Pharan to the camp of the Saracen chief and the futility of locating Ammanes's camp, see Mayerson, "The Desert," 163–64.

that was applied to the camps of such Arab *foederati* as those of Aspebetos in the Desert of Juda. The distance of a journey of twelve days raises the important question of the jurisdiction of this chief. To have such a large area under him could imply that he was a powerful one. His station in the north of the Peninsula, not far from Elusa, seems justified, since the Negev, and not Sinai, was the more important region of Palaestina Tertia to defend.

A further question arises as to his status. He is referred to at times as βασιλεύς (king), at others, ἡγούμενος (leader),[18] but these are the nontechnical terms of the literary sources. It is practically certain that he was technically a phylarch; other phylarchs are attested in the Negev in this period.[19]

5. It is not entirely clear from the account whether or not Ammanes was a Christian. The references to the Saracens who perpetrated the massacre as *barbaroi* and the application of the same term to the group of which Ammanes was chief could suggest that he was not a Christian. This need not necessarily be so. The marauding Saracens were not from Ammanes' group. They were Saracens who roamed the southern part of the Peninsula, but over whom he apparently had jurisdiction. This does not make him a pagan. The Greek author of the *Narrationes* obviously had no sympathy for the indigenous peoples of the region and thus simply applied to them the Greek term *barbaroi*, applicable to all non-Greeks. This becomes evident in his application of the term to the people of Ammanes, who emerges from the *Narratio* as an amiable and just chief. Thus the term "barbarian" could not have been used pejoratively of him but simply as one of the two conjugate terms that Greek authors operated with as they viewed the world divided between Greek and non-Greek. The chances are that Ammanes was a Christian, like many of the Arab phylarchs who were in the service of the Christian Roman Empire; his Christianity was not brought out by the Greek Christian author of the *Narrationes*, who wrote under the influence of the massacre of the monks by a people to whom Ammanes belonged in the larger context of Saracens.[20]

[18] See PG 79, cols. 661, 664.

[19] Perhaps his relations with Pharan on the one hand and with the imperial government on the other may be reconciled by realizing that he could have been a phylarch of Byzantium in the northern part of Sinai near the Negev while having a special arrangement with the distant Pharanites, who found it more convenient for security reasons to have their own *foedus* with the phylarch.

[20] The Christianity of the chief is irrelevant to the dating of the *Narrationes*. It might be supposed that because Obedianus (ʿUbayda) of the *Ammonii Monachi Relatio* became a Christian the *Narrationes* may be anterior in time to the *Relatio*, since Ammanes should have been a Christian if he followed Obedianus. But Obdedianus was not a phylarch; he was a citizen of Pharan, and Pharan in the 4th century of the *Relatio* had no phylarch around it. Thus there is no difficulty in dating the *Narrationes* to the 5th century, as a work which follows the *Relatio* chrono-

6. Finally, there is the reference to the *foedus* between Pharan and Ammanes. Rarely are the terms of a *foedus* between Byzantium and her Arab allies stated. But in the *Narrationes* there are some hints as to what these terms might have been. Unfortunately, the references are to the amends that Ammanes was making because of the massacre, such as retribution and return of the property that had been taken. It is possible that such amends were mentioned in the *foedus*. But it is practically certain that it was a simple one, which entailed duties on the part of the phylarch, namely, protection of life and property for the Pharanites and some material rewards in kind or money for the phylarch. The fact that Ammanes replies to the Pharanites in writing is tantalizing: in his camp there were those who could read and write, possibly including himself, and thus the *foedus* must have been a written one. What language the two parties (who were Arab) used in this written exchange remains unknown and raises some important problems concerning the possible use of the Arabic language in Sinai in the early part of the fifth century.[21]

II. The Edict of Beersheba

An important reference to the phylarchal system in Oriens comes in the Edict of Beersheba in Palaestina Tertia, an ordinance that regulated tax payments.[22] In one of the surviving fragments there is a reference to ". . . the *archiphylos* of the most sacred *koinon* of the *archiphyloi* of the *Saltus Constantinianus*": . . .ϱου ἀϱχιφύλου τοῦ ἱεϱο[τά _] [τ]οῦ κοινοῦ τῶν ἀϱχιφύλων τοῦ Κωνσταντινιανοῦ Σάλτου τῶν συντελ'.[23]

This precious reference to phylarchal presence in Oriens has not been adequately discussed.[24] Its problems are many, and the fragmentary nature of the edict and the fact that its date is unknown compound the difficulties of drawing definitive conclusions on this reference to phylarchal presence. The solution of its problems, however, especially regarding the term *koinon*, will throw much light on the structure of the Arab phylarchate in Oriens. Although certainty is impossible, the various interpretations should be explored.

logically. As has been argued, the chances are that Ammanes was a Christian. He was possibly a successor (not necessarily immediate) of the phylarch in the *Relatio* whose death signaled the termination of the *foedus* and prompted the raid on the monasteries.

[21] For the language of the letters sent by the Arabs of Najrān to the Arab king of the Ghassānids at Jabiya, see Shahîd, *Martyrs*, 39–40, 242–50. Najrān's Arabic literary life is not unknown. This is not the case with Pharan; hence the difficulty of drawing conclusion on the language employed in the exchange of letters between the town and the Arab chief.

[22] See A. Alt, *Die griechischen Inschriften der Palästina Tertia westlich der ʿAraba* (Berlin-Leipzig, 1921), 4–13.

[23] Ibid., 12.

[24] It was discussed by Alt in only a cursory manner; see "Limes Palaestinae," *Palästina Jahrbuch* 26 (1930), 75–76.

A

1. The one solid spot in the inscription that could lead to fruitful interpretation is the reference to the *Saltus Constantinianus*, an imperial estate located in Palaestina Prima. Other than this bare information, which comes from George of Cyprus, nothing is known about this *saltus*.[25] However, it is informative on the location of the *koinon* of phylarchs, namely, that it was in Palaestina Prima, and this is good enough as a starting point.

2. The second problem is to pinpoint this phylarchal pocket in Palaestina Prima. If the inscription goes back to the fifth century, then these *archiphyloi* could very well have been the phylarchs of the Palestinian Parembole. If so, this will solve the problem of the location of the *Saltus Constantinianus*. These phylarchs were stationed in the Desert of Juda, east of Jerusalem and west of the Jordan, and so the *Saltus* most probably was in that region.

3. Support for all this—that the phylarchs were those of the Parembole and that the *Saltus* was in the Desert of Juda—may come from the first word, . . . ϱου, of line 2 of the three lines that mention the *archiphyloi* in the inscription. The editor suspected that this word represents the name of the phylarch, and this could very well be the case. What is needed is an Arab phylarch the last syllable of whose name ends with -ϱου. There were two phylarchs of the Parembole named "Petros."[26] It is unlikely that it was the first one, but it is possible, even likely, that it was Petros II. His phylarchate

[25] See A. H. M. Jones, *Cities*, 281. M. Avi-Yonah has suggested that the *Saltus Constantinianus* lay at the western end of the *limes Palaestinae*; see *The Holy Land* (Grand Rapids, Michigan, 1966), 162. Since it was he who revised the chapter on Palestine in Jones' *Cities* (p. v), which appeared in 1971, he presumably changed his views on the location of the *Saltus* and concluded, speaking of the *Saltus Constantinianus*, "nothing is known of the former," 281. The location of the *Saltus* is important. If it was in the western part of the *limes Palaestinae*, this would invalidate the views put forward in the following three paragraphs (3–5) of this chapter, views related to the suggestion that it was in the Desert of Juda. It does not, however, invalidate the most important conclusion to be drawn from an analysis of this inscription, expressed below, paragraph 7.

Avi-Yonah must have been influenced by Alt in his view on the location of the *Saltus Constantinianus*. This is not clear from his footnote (ibid., note 255) where he refers to Georgius Cyprius, *Notitia Dignitatum*, and the *Onomasticon* of Eusebius: none of these sources locates the *Saltus* at the western end of the *limes Palaestinae*. However, he used Honigmann's edition of Georgius Cyprius, in which the editor refers to Alt's article, "Limes Palaestinae," 76–78, where indeed Alt argues for this location, but Avi-Yonah is also aware that his conclusion is purely conjectural.

[26] On the phylarchs of the Palestinian Parembole, see below, Chap. 10, sec. I.B. The superlative adjective which describes the *koinon*, ἱερότατον, "most sacred," admits of various interpretations. If the *koinon* turns out to be truly that of these phylarchs, then this may reflect their staunch adherence to Christianity and the fact that they were protecting the Christian establishment in the region against Saracen raids. The *Saltus* may also have been a bishopric; hence the epithet "most sacred" for its *koinon*; see Jones, *LRE*, II, 877. The Palestinian Parembole was also a bishopric, and "most sacred" would be applicable to it.

extended from 485 to the early part of the sixth century. This will then date the inscription, in general terms, toward the end of the fifth century.

4. This dating could receive much support from the fact that toward the end of the fifth century or the beginning of the sixth Anastasius issued the edict that was discussed in the preceding chapter. This has survived epigraphically in various parts of the empire, and, like the Edict of Beersheba, it has survived in fragments. It is, therefore, possible that this Edict of Beersheba is one of the many versions of the Edict of Anastasius.[27] The various versions of this latter edict are not identical because local variations were introduced into each version, relating it to the province in which it was made public. The so-called Edict of Beersheba could very well have been the version that suited the needs of Palestine.

5. The orthography of the term phylarch presents a problem. The normal one is φύλαρχος and not ἀρχίφυλος. The point may have no significance whatsoever, but this is an official inscription, and accuracy is expected, especially when an officer related to the Roman administration is involved. It is not impossible that the orthography may reflect a difference in status and function between *archiphylos* and *phylarchos*: the former may have signified an Arab shaykh living in Roman territory and possibly paying taxes on behalf of his community of Arab pastoralists living on imperial estates, while the latter may have signified the well-known office of phylarch, a *foederatus* with the empire who received the *annona* in return for military service. The legal status of these *archiphyloi* may have been *vectigales* paying tribute and not *foederati*.[28]

6. An important problem which the inscription raises is the function of this *archiphylos*. The contents of the edict clearly point in the direction of a fiscal duty: the *archiphylos* is a tax collector for the authorities, collecting the taxes due from the use of the *Saltus Constantinianus*. Whether this was the only function he performed remains an open question.

7. The most tantalizing, and possibly the most significant word in the inscription is *koinon* (κοινόν), the company, association, or group. As it appears in the edict, the *koinon* is a tax unit, and the *archiphylos* who appears as the representative of this *koinon* is in charge of collecting dues for the government. A parallel is the *koinon* of Zoora in the first fragment of the edict.[29]

Was this an isolated case of a *koinon* or *archiphyloi* in Oriens? The chances are that there were other *koina* in other parts of the diocese. This may be supported by a suggestion of Alt concerning the reference to another *saltus* men-

[27] This has been persuasively suggested by M. Sartre (see Chap. 6, app. 1, above).

[28] On the ὑπήκοοι of Byzantium in the 6th century, see above, Chap. 5 note 21. The Arab *archiphyloi* in the edict are described as συντελ(εστῶν), that is, the group or association responsible for the collection and payment of taxes.

[29] Alt, *Inschriften*, 5.

tioned in the line preceding the first line that deals with the Arab *archiphylos*. Only the word *saltus* has survived in the line, and the editor suggested it refers to the *Saltus Gerariticus* in Palaestina Prima south of Gaza. It is thus possible that there was another *koinon* or *archiphyloi* related to this *saltus*.

B

The status of these *archiphyloi* remains undecided, whether they were tributary shaykhs, Arab chiefs, or whether they were phylarchs in the technical sense of Arab federate chiefs who received the *annona*, such as the phylarchs of the Palestinian Parembole.

1. The following support the first suggestion: the orthography, which may be significant; reference to the *Saltus Constantinianus*; and the function of the *archiphylos* as συντελεστής (tax collector).

2. In support of the second suggestion, it may be said that the orthography is *not* significant and that the reference to the *archiphylos* as a tax collector is only natural, since the edict happened to be an ordinance that regulated tax payments. But this was only one of the many dimensions of his duties, the others being related to internal security within the *limes* and participation in the wars of the empire.

Whatever the truth may be, it is amply clear that these *archiphyloi* were organized into a *koinon*: that Byzantium did not deem it fit to leave the Arab chiefs uncontrolled or unorganized, and so brought them together into a *koinon*. If so, it is possible that it would have done the same with the much more important *phylarchoi*, the federate chiefs in treaty relationship to the empire. Thus, each province may have had a *koinon* of *phylarchoi*. This may derive some support from a passage in Malalas[30] which speaks of the "*phylarchoi* of the provinces" suggesting that each province had its own phylarch or group of phylarchs. But stronger confirmation comes from Egypt, where the shepherds of Aphrodito and the bargemen-soldiers of Philae were organized in such *koina* for imperial defense.[31] This may not be an exact parallel of a *koinon* of phylarchs, but it fortifies the suggestion of the existence of the latter in Oriens. Such a *koinon* of *phylarchoi* may have existed in such a large region as Palaestina Tertia,[32] perhaps in the Negev, not far from where the two arms of the *limes Palaestinae* met.[33] Papyrology may have just preserved reference to a member of such a *koinon* of phylarchs in the Negev, "the newly appointed phylarch" of fragment 60 of the Nessana Papyri.[34]

[30] Malalas, *Chronographia*, 435.

[31] See J. Gascou, "L'institution des bucellaires," *Bulletin de L'institut Français d'Archeologie Orientale* 76 (Cairo, 1976), 153.

[32] Since it existed in such a small province as Palaestina Prima which, moreover, had such a weak and small phylarchal presence.

[33] As conceived by Alt, "Limes Palaestinae," 75–84.

[34] As will be argued in the following section.

III. The Nessana Papyri

Excavations at Nessana have revealed the intimate life of its inhabitants and have made it the best documented of all the old Nabataean sites of the Negev. The excavations resulted in the publication of three volumes, the first of which dealt with the archeology of the site and its inscriptions, the second with its literary papyri, and the third with the non-literary papyri.[35] The first volume has two valuable chapters on the Greek and the Nabataean inscriptions. These reveal clearly the Nabataean substrate in the structure of Nessana's population, and how, after the annexation of Nabataea by the Romans in A.D. 106, its Nabataean inhabitants were Romanized, Hellenized, and Christianized. The second volume reveals the cultural life of the community of Nessana under Christian and Graeco-Roman influences. These two volumes document the life of the sedentaries of Nessana, the *Rhōmaioi*. The third volume, edited by Casper J. Kraemer, provides some important data for Arab-Byzantine relations. It is, of course, concerned with the *Rhōmaioi* of Nessana, but there are references to the Saracens in the fifth and sixth centuries.[36] The most important is fragment 160, but before commenting on it, three other papyri that deal with the *Rhōmaioi* of Nessana will be taken up.

1. Papyrus 21 is about a division of property. It involves a soldier of the camp, Flavius Sergius, a *stratiōtēs* who wants to divide his property among his four children.

If the papyrus had not given the name of his father and grandfather, Elias and Taim Obodas, it would have been impossible to decide whether or not Flavius Sergius was an Arab. But he was a Romanized Arab who assumed the name Flavius Sergius and thus concealed his ethnic origin. This confirms what has been said about the ethnic origin of the units in the *Notitia Dignitatum* that were stationed in localities where the Arab complexion of the region suggested that the units had strong Arab elements in them, since they were locally recruited.[37] No list has survived of the names of the members of the units stationed in most of these localities. Hence the importance of a papyrus such as this, which confirms what has been suggested.[38]

2. Papyrus 51 is a letter from Moses, the bishop of Ayla, to Victor, son of Sergius of Nessana. Its interest is that the messenger who carried the letter

[35] *Excavations at Nessana*, I, ed. H. D. Colt (London, 1962); II, ed. L. Gasson and E. L. Hettich (Princeton, 1950); III, ed. Casper, J. Kraemer (Princeton, 1958).

[36] For the prosperity of Nessana in the 5th and 6th centuries, see ibid., I, 16 and III, 14–19, 24–26.

[37] See below, Part 3, sec. I.

[38] See also Papyrus 22, which refers to an Arab *stratiōtēs* by the name of Flavius Ghanm, and many instances of this in other papyri which involve military matters. Especially relevant are Papyri 35 and 37, which have established that the Nessana unit was a camel corps, with many Arab names. It is also evident from Papyrus 35 that the camp had a church and a priest with the Arab name Faysan.

of the bishop from Ayla to Nessana is described as a Saracen.[39] It probably denotes a nomadic Arab. Because of their knowledge of the region and their ability to endure the rigors of traveling in that arid country, nomads or pastoralists were used as messengers.

3. Papyrus 80 is an account of offerings to the church of St. Sergius at Nessana. Its interest consists in the names of the donors. It presents a perfect spectacle of the process of assimilation to the Graeco-Roman onomasticon, revealing how the sons of recognizably Arab fathers were assuming non-Arab names. The father of a certain Sergius is ʿĀ'idh, and the father of George is Raqīʿ. The priest of the church has a recognizably Arabic theophoric name, Saʿd-Allah. Of interest is the attestation of the rare name Jaḏīma as one of the donors, the namesake of the famous Arab king of the third century.[40]

4. The index of Volume II is useful for examining the extent of the Arab element in the town and the region. The list of Arabic names and of Arab tribes[41] is especially revealing, as is the appearance of the *praenomen* Flavius before many Arab names.[42] The Arabs were thus very familiar with the *praenomen* Flavius, which was very common in the region, and it was most probably this that led them to describe the Romans as the "sons of the Yellow," Banū al-Aṣfar.[43]

5. The most important and relevant papyrus in the whole collection, however, is fragment 160, with its reference to the phylarch (νέῳ φυλάρχῳ), since this directly concerns the federate rather than the Rhomaic Arabs.

The editor is inclined to think that "phylarch" in this fragment means "chief" (shaykh). It is practically certain that this is not the case. The phylarchal system, which has been studied here and in the preceding volume, was diffused in various parts of Oriens, especially Palestine. The Arab phylarchs in the Byzantine frontier system performed important functions, particularly those pertaining to internal security in this arid and inaccessible region. The adjective νέος in the sense of "newly appointed" clinches the point that what is in question in this fragment is not a shaykh but a Byzantine phylarch in the technical sense. This was one of the areas of the so-called *limes Palaestinae*, and that internal *limes* had its Arab phylarchs and *foederati* as auxiliaries to regular Roman troops which manned its forts. The reference to the phylarch in this fragment is especially welcome because it is precise. It associates him not with

[39] For other references to the Saracens as nomads in the region see Papyrus 89. For the six different ways in which Ayla is spelt, see note 1 to Papyrus 51.

[40] For Jaḏīma, see *BAFOC*, index, p. 617. Just as this papyrus has this rare reference to Jaḏīma, Papyrus 95 has a tantalizing reference to a Samaritan. Could he have ended up there after one of the two Samaritan revolts of 484 and 529?

[41] See *Nessana*, II, 352–55, 340–41.

[42] See ibid., 340.

[43] On the term Banū al-Aṣfar, see Shahîd, *Martyrs*, 274.

a provincial region but with a town. Nessana is not far from Beersheba, and it is quite likely that this phylarch of Nessana belonged to the *koinon* of phylarchs mentioned in the Edict of Beersheba. The *koinon* may have been the Arab component of the Roman defense system in the area where the two lines of the *limes Palaestinae* met—the one that ran from the Dead Sea to the Mediterranean and the other from the Dead Sea to the Gulf of Eilat.[44]

[44] As conceived by A. Alt, for which see Kraemer's commentary on Papyrus 39, 122–23. The date of this fragment is unknown. The editor conjectured the 6th–7th centuries. I am inclined to think that it is earlier than the 7th century and probably belongs to the end of the 6th.

Ecclesiastical History

The facts of the ecclesiastical history of the Arabs in the fifth century derive principally from the Greek sources. These inform us on the wide diffusion of Christianity among the Arabs in Oriens from Euphratensis in the north to Palaestina Tertia in the south; on the Arab episcopate, both Rhomaic and federate, and the participation of the Arab bishops in the three ecumenical councils of the fifth century; and on Arab monasticism and the possible rise of a simple Arabic liturgy. They also provide precious data on the religious development of the non-Christian Arabs and the reality of Ishmaelism among them in pre-Islamic times.

These sources range from historians such as Theodoret and Sozomen, to hagiographers such as Cyril of Scythopolis, to documents such as the *Acta* of the ecumenical councils. They will be analyzed in this order.

VIII

Theodoret of Cyrrhus

Theodoret of Cyrrhus[1] is one of the principal sources[2] for the study of Byzantium and the Arabs in the fifth century. Of his voluminous works, in which he ranged over practically every field of sacred science, three are important for our purposes: the *Historia Ecclesiastica,* the *Historia Religiosa,* and the *Graecarum Affectionum Curatio.* The first was analyzed in the preceding volume in this series;[3] *the Historia Religiosa* and the *Curatio* will be examined here. They are especially important because of the paucity and aridity of the sources for these relations in the fifth century and because of their exceptional quality and reliability. Theodoret was writing contemporary history and was, in fact, an eyewitness of some of the events he recounted.

I. *Historia Religiosa*

The *Historia Religiosa*[4] (Φιλόθεος ἱστορία), composed about 444, is a history of thirty monks who lived near Antioch, some of whom Theodoret knew personally. Twenty of these "athletes of Christ" were dead when he wrote, but the rest were still alive and "still engaged in the contest." There are references

[1] See Quasten, *Patrology,* III, 536–54. In addition to some excellent works by ecclesiastical historians on Theodoret, there are two important studies of the region of northern Syria where Theodoret flourished and about which he wrote: G. Tchalenko, *Villages antiques de la Syrie du Nord*, 3 vols. (Paris, 1953–58); and on the capital of the region, Antioch, J. H. W. G. Liebeschütz, *Antioch: City and Imperial Administration in the Later Roman Empire* (Oxford, 1972). There is also Peter Brown's fundamental and influential article which draws repeatedly on the *Historia Religiosa,* "The Rise and Function of the Holy Man in Late Antiquity," in *Society and the Holy in Late Antiquity* (London, 1982), 103–52. The latest on Theodoret is R. M. Price's introduction to his translation of the *Historia Religiosa,* for which see *A History of the Monks of Syria*, Cistercian Studies Series 88 (Kalamazoo, 1985).

[2] Just as Cyril of Scythopolis is the main informant on Arab-Byzantine relations in the south of Oriens, especially in Palestine, so is Theodoret for the north of the diocese.

[3] The material on the Arabs in the *Historia Ecclesiastia* deals with the 4th century and Queen Mavia. His chapter on Mavia is on a lower level of reliability than those written by Socrates and Sozomen; on this, see *BAFOC,* 184–85.

[4] The Latin form of the title will be used in this chapter. For the standard edition and commentary see P. Canivet and A. Leroy-Molinghen, *Histoire des moines de Syrie,* SC, 2 vols. (1977, 1979) (hereafter *HMS*). The companion volume is indispensible for the study of Syrian monachism in Theodoret: P. Canivet, *Le monachisme syrien selon Théodoret de Cyr,* Théologie historique 42 (Paris, 1977) (hereafter *MST*).

to the Arabs in the *Lives* of three of these monks: Simeon Stylites, Eusebius, and Simeon Priscus.

The *Life* of Simeon Stylites

Most of the references to the Arabs in the *Historia Religiosa* come in the *Vita*[5] of Simeon Stylites, the first of the pillar saints,[6] who died in 459 after living on the top of his last great pillar at Telanissos for some thirty years. His encounters with the Arabs took place there.

1. In Section 11 of the *Vita,* Theodoret testifies to the fame of Simeon, which attracted ethnic groups not only from within the empire but from without.[7] The Ishmaelites are specifically mentioned, and the implication is that they came from across the *limes.* The term "Ishmaelites" is his usual term for the Arabs, and it is clear that they are not the *foederati* of the fifth century who lived within the *limes.* These could have been Arabs of the Syrian desert outside the *limes,* or they could have come from nearby Persian territory.

Especially important is his reference to the Homeritae (Ḥimyarites) who, too, were attracted by his fame. The Homeritae of South Arabia were not yet converted to Christianity in this period. Since only one city in South Arabia was, namely, Najrān, it is therefore practically certain that this reference to visitors from South Arabia indicates the great Arab Christian center of Najrān, which was converted early in the fifth century.[8] Simeon's fame may have reached Najrān through Ḥīra, whence it derived its Christianity; Ḥīra was not too far from Telanissos, and its king, Nuʿmān, is reported to have come to these regions for edification or religious instruction.[9]

2. Section 13 is devoted mostly to the Arabs/Ishmaelites, who came to the pillar saint in great numbers (πολλὰς μυριάδας), sometimes two or three hundred or a thousand at a time. In addition to recording the great number of conversations among the Arabs, the passage is important anthropologically. The Arabs loudly renounce their ancestral errors, smash the idols worshiped by their forefathers, abjure the rites and orgies of Aphrodite,[10] whom they had long worshiped, participate in the divine mysteries (the Eucharist), say

[5] The *Vita* of Simeon Stylites in Theodoret is the best and the most reliable, since Theodoret was a contemporary and an eyewitness, and the miraculous element in it is more sober than the other two; see P. Peeters, "S. Symeon Stylite et ses premiers biographes," *AB* 61 (1943), 30–42. Antony's Greek *Vita* and the Syriac one are discussed below, App. 1.

[6] On the pillar saints, see H. Delehaye, *Les saints stylites,* Subsidia Hagiographica 14 (Brussels, 1923); on Simeon, see pp. i-xxxiv. For Telanissos, see *MST,* 172–75 and map, p. 24.

[7] See *HMS,* II, 182.

[8] On the conversion of Najrān, see below, Chap. 13, sec. III.

[9] See below, App. 1.

[10] See *HMS*, II, 190.

goodbye to the customs of their fathers, and abstain from eating the meat of the wild ass and the camel.[11]

Especially important is that the Ishmaelites also received laws from the sacred tongue of the Saint (νόμους παρὰ τῆς ἱερᾶς ἐκείνης δεχόμενοι γλώττης. What these laws were can only be guessed at—no doubt Christian and biblical legislation for a newly converted people. Interpreted literally, the passage would suggest that the laws were given orally, but they must have been written down after they were delivered, presumably by the interpreter, since the presumption is that Simeon was not an Arab and did not speak the language of the Ishmaelites.[12]

3. Section 14 is devoted exclusively to the author's experiences with the Arabs around the pillar of the saint.[13] Presumably Theodoret wanted to relieve Simeon of some of the pressure that crowds of would-be converts had exerted on him, and so he came to help out. The saint had ordered the Arabs to approach Theodoret for receiving the sacerdotal benediction from him; because of their enthusiasm they rushed so vehemently that Theodoret would have been crushed by them had not the saint cried out and dispersed them.[14] This passage testifies that Theodoret's account of many of these episodes was based on personal observation.

4. In Section 15 Theodoret gives an account of the relation of two Arab tribes (φυλαί) to the saint.[15] One tribe sent a request that Simeon formulate a special prayer and benediction for its chief (phylarch, φύλαρχος). Another tribe in the same area objected to this request on the grounds that the phylarch of that tribe was wicked, while their ἡγούμενος was righteous and consequently should be the beneficiary of the saint's prayer and benediction. The disputing tribes sprang on each other, and Theodoret tried to part them, saying that the two chiefs could receive the prayer and benediction simultane-

[11] As is pointed out by the editor in a footnote (ibid. note 4), the passage recalls the Arabs of Ammianus Marcellinus. For Aphrodite among the Arabs of this region, see ibid., note 2. The customs they renounced must have included polygamy and circumcision. It is natural to suppose that giving up eating camel meat was done in obedience to Deut. 14:7.

[12] This reference to Simeon's giving laws to the Arabs is of considerable interest and is relevant to the discussion of the problem of the Code of Laws which St. Gregentius is said to have given South Arabia after its conversion; see I. Shahîd, "Byzantium in South Arabia," *DOP* 33 (1979), 33–35. The use of the technical term νόμοι rather than some other word, is significant.

[13] See *HMS*, II, Sec. 14, p. 192. A close examination of the passage in the section that follows (Sec. 15, p. 193), shows that Sec. 14 is about the Arabs in spite of the fact that they are not mentioned by name.

[14] He must have been shaken by the experience, since in the passage he refers to them as barbarians.

[15] Ibid., pp. 192, 194.

ously. When they would not listen to him, the saint, from the top of his pillar, quieted them.

The section throws much light on the phylarchal and federate situation in the north of Oriens:

a. It is noteworthy that Theodoret does not call the Arabs in this passage Ishmaelites, a term that he applies as a Biblical scholar to the Arabs outside the *limes*. The Arabs in this passage are clearly *foederati*[16] and, what is more, Christian Arabs who had already been converted.

b. The section incidentally attests phylarchal and federate presence in one of the provinces in the north. Since Telanissos was in Syria Prima, the presumption is that the phylarchs were assigned to this province. This is welcome information since phylarchal presence in the fifth century, though attested, lacks geographical and provincial specificity.

c. It may be safely concluded from this section that the province had more than one phylarch. What is more, one phylarch seems to have been higher in rank than the other, since he is called *hēgoumenos* (ἡγούμενος) while the other is called φύλαρχος.[17]

d. The request of the other tribe that its own righteous chief should be the recipient of the saint's prayer and benediction reflects some maturity in the tribe's understanding of the Christian religion, namely, that the righteous deserve to be rewarded and the wicked punished, and indirectly testifies to the faith of the Arabs in the saint's power to help even soldiers, as these *foederati* were. As Theodoret himself observes, the episode shows the Arabs' faith in the saint, since they would not have quarreled among themselves if they had not thought his blessings possessed great power.

5. In Section 16 Theodoret tells the story of an Arab phylarch who brings to Simeon a man who had been struck by paralysis in Callinicum.[18] The saint asks the paralytic to abjure his ancestral impiety, which he does, and then asks him whether he believes in the Trinity. When the latter answers in the affirmative, the saint tells him to rise and carry the phylarch—who was corpulent—back to his tent.

As in the preceding section, Theodoret incidentally records certain facts important to Arab-Byzantine relations:

a. Theodoret does not use biblical language but that of imperial Rome to

[16] As has been realized by the editors, ibid., p. 193, sec. 15 note 1.

[17] For a parallel, see the application of the term ἡγεμών to the Kindite chief Qays who was given the ἡγεμονία, a large command in the Palestines, during the reign of Justinian; see Shahîd, "Byzantium and Kinda," 68–70.

[18] See *HMS*, II, 194, 196.

describe the Arabs: they are Saracens, and their chief is phylarch. So the Arab personage in question in this section is an Arab phylarch of Byzantium.

b. The section is even more precise geographically and toponymically than the preceding one, as it involves not a province but a city, Callinicum. This could suggest that the province from which the phylarch came was Euphratensis,[19] where Theodoret's episcopal see—Cyrrhus—was located, and that the phylarch crossed the provincial borders to come to Syria Prima, where Telanissos was located, to see Simeon.

c. Finally, the episode reflects the faith of the phylarchs in the power of the saint and that they were instruments of evangelization among those of their congeners who were not Christian.

6. In Section 18 Theodoret recounts another of Simeon's miracles.[20] A prominent Ishmaelite who had become a Christian had vowed to God to be a vegetarian, and Simeon was his witness. Later he broke his vow; when he tried to eat a bird that he had killed, it suddenly turned into a stone. Horrified by this prodigy, the Ishmaelite came hurriedly to the saint to announce his transgression and invoke Simeon's aid and prayers to absolve him from his sin. Many witnessed the prodigy and saw that the bird had indeed been turned into stone.

The Arab in question does not seem to have been a phylarch who had any imperial connections. He is referred to biblically as an Ishmaelite and is further described as a barbarian, but the episode reflects the faith of the Ishmaelites in the power and efficacy of the saint's prayers.

7. In Section 21 Theodoret recounts the story of an Ishmaelite queen (βασιλίς) who was sterile and who sent some of her notables to invoke Simeon's aid against her sterility.[21] His prayers were answered and, since access was forbidden to her as a woman, she sent her child to the saint with a request for his blessing.

Was this queen a *foederata* or an Arab queen living outside the *limes*? If the former, what was her identity and tribal affiliation? It is impossible to

[19] Alternatively, the phylarch could have belonged to Syria, where Telanissos was located, while friends of the paralytic brought him from Euphratensis to be cured by the saint whose fame had reached far and wide. The tenor of the passage, however, suggests more that the phylarch was assigned to Euphratensis and that he brought the paralytic along with him from his province. The reference to the phylarch's tent is not decisive for one province to the exclusion of the other, as it is likely to have been pitched not far from the saint's pillar temporarily in order to accommodate the phylarch while he was attending to the healing of the paralytic.

[20] This account is related in Lietzmann's edition of the various *Vitae* of Simeon, although it is missing in many manuscripts; see *HMS*, I, 74, where it is pointed out that it is missing in MSS. FPHCXVD. For Lietzmann's edition, see below, App. 1, note 1.

[21] See *HMS*, II, 202, 204.

give definitive answers. The Tanūkhids, the Arab *foederati* of the fourth century, come to mind—with their Queen Mavia and the possibility of the survival of a matriarchal system among them in the fifth century—but it is far from certain that this was a Tanūkhid queen. The use of the term Ishmaelite suggests a queen outside the *limes,* from one of the powerful tribes of northern Arabia such as Kalb. It is also noteworthy that the section that recounts her story comes after that on the Persian Great King, and is thus separate from those sections that deal with the Arab *foederati.* It is clear from the account that she was the ruler of her Arab group and not merely the wife of the ruler,[22] since there is no mention of her husband, who, it is natural to suppose, would have approached the saint on behalf of his wife as Zokomos, the first phylarch of Salīḥ, had done.[23] It is also noteworthy that her infant son is referred to as king (βασιλεύς), however proleptically. Hence a ruling dynasty is involved in this episode. The chances are that the Arabs in question lived outside the *limes,* and were not *foederati,* but had heard of the fame of Simeon as a healer-saint. The section is important in documenting the existence of an Arab matriarchy or the survival of matriarchy among the Arabs in this late period.

The *Lives* of Eusebius and Simeon Priscus

There are two important references to the Arabs in the *Lives* of Eusebius and Simeon Priscus. They are important because Theodoret discusses Ishmael and the descent of the Arabs, converted and non-converted, from him.

The *Life* of Eusebius

The first reference is in the *Life* of Eusebius,[24] the abbot of the monastery of Teleda, which lay to the east of Antioch and to the west of Beroaea.[25] One of the monks in his monastery was an Arab or Ishmaelite named Abbas.[26] He had lived the ascetic life in the desert with another famous

[22] Note that in speaking of the wife of the Persian king, he refers to her not as a βασιλίς but as his wife (τὴν δὲ ὁμόζυγα, ibid., 202, line 3.

[23] On Zokomos and his sterile wife, see above, 3–4.

[24] See *HMS,* I, 320, 322.

[25] For Teleda, see *MST,* 165–72.

[26] The editors of *Historia Religiosa* render the name of this Arab, which in Greek is ʼΑββᾶς, as Abba. Clearly the editors thought that the *sigma* in the Greek form is the usual *sigma* that ends Hellenized Semitic names. But Abbas is an Arabic name, and the chances are that the *sigma* in the Greek form is the third radical of the Arabic root *ʿ-B-S*, from which ʼΑββᾶς is derived. ʼΑββᾶς is therefore most probably Arabic ʿAbbās, the intensive form of the *nomen agentis,* signifying "the one who frowns"; the same name appears in the tecnonymic of the founder of the Muslim Arab dynasty, the Abbāsids. If so, this would be one of the very rare attestations of the name, and it is not inappropriate for the monk who indulged in the extremes of ascetic exercises as described by Theodoret. It is not commented upon in *MST* (p. 239) as the other Semitic names are.

anchorite, Marosas, and then, in 406, they joined the flock of Eusebius of Teleda.[27] Abbas spent thirty-eight years at the monastery. Theodoret recounts many of his austerities and records that he became *hēgoumenos* of the monastery and the model for all its inmates in the rigors of the ascetic life.[28]

The interest of this notice of Abbas, the Arab *hēgoumenos* in the *Historia Religiosa,* is that it was Abbas who caused Theodoret to give his perception of what may be termed the new Ishmaelite, the Arab descendant of Ishmael after his conversion to Christianity. Theodoret expresses his vision of the spiritual metamorphosis of the new Ishmaelite in three parts: (1) In ancient biblical times, his ancestor Ishmael had been rejected from the House of Abraham; (2) but the new Ishmael is Isaac's brother, who thus received with him his portion of the paternal inheritance of Abraham; and (3) even more than the Abrahamic inheritance, he gained entrance to the kingdom of heaven.

Theodoret's description of the metamorphosis of Abbas, the new Ishmaelite, is reminiscent of that of Cyril of Scythopolis,[29] when the latter reflected on the conversion of the Saracens. But while Cyril was a pious monk and a hagiographer, Theodoret was an eminent theologian, in fact the last great theologian of Antioch. He had a more profound perception of the spiritual conversion of the Ishmaelites, especially as he was also a distinguished Biblical scholar, who in his exegetical work commented on the relevant verses in Genesis concerning Ishmael.[30]

The *Life* of Simeon Priscus

The second reference comes in the *Life* of Simeon Priscus,[31] the famous solitary who established himself on Mount Amanus, whence he moved to Mount Sinai. Before living on Mount Amanus he had lived in a cave, and his miracles had attracted many of the neighboring barbarians. These are described by Theodoret as Ishmaelites: "those who proudly derive their descent from their ancestor Ishmael live in that desert" (οἰκοῦσι δὲ τὴν ἔρημον ἐκείνην οἱ τὸν 'Ισμαὴλ σεμνυνόμενοι πρόγονον).

Who these Arabs were is not entirely clear. But the following conclusions may be safely drawn from Theodoret's short account:

1. They lived not far from Antioch or Cyrrhus, since Simeon's cave

[27] See *HMS,* I, 321 note 4. On the possibility that the first convent where Marosas and Abbas had lived before coming to Teleda was Necheile, see *MST,* 168 note 84.

[28] Theodoret wrote his *Historia Religiosa* in 444 and Abbas was still alive at Teleda when Theodoret wrote about him; for Abbas, see *HMS,* I, 320, 322.

[29] See below, Chap. 10, app. 2.

[30] As pointed out by the editors of *HMS,* Theodoret was an eminent biblical exegete; see Quasten, *Patrology,* III, 539–42; for his thoughts on Gen. 21:9-21, see his commentary on Gal. 4:21-30 in PG 82, cols. 489–92 and on Rom. 9:6-9 in PG, cols. 152–53.

[31] See *HMS,* I, 351.

before he moved to Mount Amanus must have been in the region of either of these two cities; Theodoret received information from Simeon's own mother,[32] who was an Antiochene, while his other informant, the monk Jacob,[33] was an eremite in Cyrrhestica.[34]

2. These Arabs are not described as *Saracenoi* or as having a phylarch, the terms that would have given them the status of *foederati*. They are called barbarians, and Theodoret describes them in genealogical terms as descendants of Ishmael, terms that he uses for non-federate, still pagan Arabs.[35]

3. The most important feature of Theodoret's description of these Arabs is the reference to their eponymous ancestor, Ishmael. It is not the usual reference to the Arabs by Church historians as Ishmaelites, but to their ancestor himself. And the reference is not just about their descent from a figure in ancient times of some two millennia before, but about Ishmael as a living figure in the consciousness of the fourth- or fifth-century Arabs, as their eponymous ancestor whom they revered and from whom they were proud to be descended. The idiom of Theodoret is clear in his use of σεμνυνόμενοι.

This is a valuable datum, since it is the only reflection in ecclesiastical history by an outside observer of the Arabs' perception of their own self-image and their pride in their descent from Ishmael, contrary to his biblical status as an outcast, "outside the promise." It is significant for the problem of the Arab self-image in Islamic as well as pre-Islamic times.[36]

In view of the great importance of this startling statement in Theodoret, it is important to discuss the authenticity of the passage. It has been pointed out that Theodoret's *Lives of the Monks* in his *Historia Religiosa* are possessed of a high level of authenticity and reliability, and this is especially true of the references to the Arab neighbors of Theodoret himself, in either Antioch or Cyrrhestica, who, as a biblical people descended from Abraham's firstborn, had aroused his curiosity as an exegete. What is the provenance of this important datum on the Arabs and their pride in Ishmael?

1. Did he unconsciously construct it himself, drawing on his knowledge of the biblical narrative about them? This is completely out of the question

[32] Ibid., 365. See also the footnote on the same page on Simeon's death toward the end of the 4th century.

[33] Whose *Life* Theodoret wrote, *HMS*, II, 70–121.

[34] It is also possible that the statement on the Arabs' pride in their descent from Ishmael does not reflect what Theodoret heard from either of these two informants, who reported to him on the Arabs associated with the 4th-century Simeon, who attracted them by his miracles. The statement may reflect what he himself ascertained about them in the 5th century in view of his proximity to them, his interest in them as potential material for conversion, and his curiosity about them as a biblical people.

[35] They may have become Christian later, but when Theodoret noticed them they were still pagan and were attracted by the fame of Simeon as thaumaturge.

[36] On this important issue, see below, 171–72.

since this Arab perception of Ishmael is not at all biblical, and in fact runs contrary to the biblical account. Theodoret, who knew Genesis well and had written a commentary on it, cannot be accused of this flagrant hermeneutical solecism.

2. There is the possibility that he took it from another Church historian of the fifth century who was also interested in the Arabs and who preserved some of the most precious data on them—Sozomen. This must be examined, since Sozomen has an important passage on the religious history of the Arabs as Ishmaelites.[37] But an examination of the relevant part of the passage shows that this possibility, too, is completely out of the question. As a preliminary observation, the old view that Theodoret used Sozomen, among other Church historians has been challenged by L. Parmentier, the editor of Theodoret's *Historia Ecclesiastica*.[38] So it is far from certain that he used Sozomen as a source when he wrote his passage on the self-image of the Arabs in the *Historia Religiosa*.

Even if he did use Sozomen, Theodoret's account of the Arab self-image is very distant from that presented by Sozomen. In addition to the employment of a different term to refer to Ishmael,[39] there is the much more important, even decisive, fact: in Sozomen the Arabs are portrayed as ashamed of their descent from Ishmael through Hagar, the bondwoman; to hide this fact they adopted the name Saracen to suggest that they were descended from Sara, the legitimate wife of Abraham.[40] In Theodoret the self-image is the opposite: the Arabs as Ishmaelites are proud of their eponymous ancestor.

3. Thus the passage in Theodoret represents an independent tradition and is not derivative from Sozomen. It emerges as an authentic passage transmitted by a primary source, Theodoret, who most probably ascertained the fact himself because of his interest in this biblical people who were his neighbors. As will be seen in a later chapter, this crucial passage can be connected with others that come from the pre-Islamic Arabic tradition.[41]

II. *Graecarum Affectionum Curatio*

The Arabs are mentioned in another of Theodoret's writings, the *Graecarum Affectionum Curatio* (Ἑλληνικῶν θεραπευτικὴ παθημάτων), that is, *The Cure*

[37] On Sozomen's importance for the history of the Arabs in the 4th century, see *BAFOC,* 274–83; on the analysis of the passage on the Ishmaelite course of Arab history in pre-Islamic times, see below, 168–69.

[38] See Quasten, *Patrology,* III, 551.

[39] While Theodoret in the passage quoted above refers to Ishmael as πρόγονος, Sozomen refers to him as προπάτωρ; see Sozomen, *Historia Ecclesiastica,* ed. J. Bidez, 299, lines 2–3.

[40] See ibid., lines 3–5. On this fanciful etymology, which probably goes back to St. Jerome, see *BAFOC,* 280.

[41] On this see below, Chap. 13, app. 5–6.

of Pagan Maladies, or *The Truth of the Gospels Proved from Greek Philosophy.* The title reveals its subject matter, and the work is considered to be the best refutation of paganism and the last of the Christian apologies.[42]

This work contains an account of the Arabs which is as startling as that in the *Historia Religiosa.* It is a completely different image from that projected by Theodoret's fellow-Antiochene, Ammianus, since it is flattering and contains a strong note of approval. In the *Historia Religiosa* the Arabs are presented in a favorable light as the new Ishmaelites in the context of the biblical concepts of Jew and Gentile; in the *Curatio* they are presented in the context of the pagan world of Antiquity peopled by Greek and Barbarian. It is, therefore, important to examine this passage and find out what lay behind it.

The passage occurs in the fifth discourse,[43] "The Nature of Man":

> Καὶ οἱ Νομάδες δέ, οἱ ἡμέτεροι πρόσχωροι—τοὺς Ἰσμαηλίτας λέγω, τοὺς ἐν ταῖς ἐρήμοις βιοτεύοντας καὶ μηδὲν τῶν Ἑλληνικῶν ξυγγραμμάτων ἐπισταμένους—ἀγχινοίᾳ καὶ ξυνέσει κοσμοῦνται καὶ διάνοιαν ἔχουσι καὶ ξυνιδεῖν τἀληθὲς δυναμένην καὶ διελέγξαι τὸ ψεῦδος.
>
> As to our neighbors, the nomads (I mean the Ishmaelites who live in the desert and who have not the least conception of Greek letters), they are endowed with an intelligence, lively and penetrating, and they have a judgment capable of discerning truth and refuting falsehood.

The context within which this judgment on the Arabs occurs is a discussion of the unity of the human species in spite of differences in sex and language, a unity affirmed by Scripture. In the passage immediately preceding this one, Theodoret speaks of the various peoples, Greek and barbarian, in a comparative context and tries to show that no people is superior to another. In this comparison the Arabs come after the Persians and the Indians and before the Egyptians and the Romans. The passage on the Arabs is very striking. Instead of referring to such virtues as military prowess—appropriate to the Arabs as raiders of the Roman *limes*—Theodoret describes them in complimentary intellectual terms which, moreover, are clear and very specific. As Theodoret was a responsible author who did not use epithets gratuitously, he must have had something in mind when he went out of his way to describe the Arabs with such specificity. Three possibilities arise:

1. It was suggested in the preceding section that the Arab self-image

[42] On the *Curatio,* see Quasten, *Patrology,* III, 542–44. The standard edition with commentary, translation and introduction is that of P. Canivet, *Théodoret de Cyr, Thérapeutique des maladies helléniques,* SC (Paris, 1957), 2 vols.

[43] In Section 72, Canivet, *Thérapeutique,* I, 250. The theme of the fifth discourse is that man is made in the image of God.

described in the *Life* of Priscus was probably a fifth-century echo of Arab sentiment concerning their ancestor Ishmael, whom they revered and of whom they were proud, and which Theodoret heard directly from them. In this passage in the *Curatio* he speaks of them as "our neighbors," and he certainly had intimate and personal knowledge of them, as the *Life* of Simeon Stylites clearly indicates. Such intellectual virtues as he attributes to them in the passage may have been displayed while he was arguing with them about Ishmael, in whom he was interested both as an exegete and as a missionary. If the Arabs were proud of their ancestor, who for Theodoret, the biblical scholar, was an outcast, then he might have heard in his dialogue with them while trying to convert them that Ishmael was Abraham's firstborn, that the first patriarch prayed for him, and that he prophesied that his descendants would be a great nation. Perhaps this is what Theodoret had in mind when he wrote this passage. This also explains the roots of Arab pride in their eponymous ancestor.

2. The Council of Ephesus in 431 presents a clue to the second possibility. At that council an Ishmaelite Arab distinguished himself, namely, Petrus, the first bishop of the Palestinian Parembole, who was on the side of Cyrillian Orthodoxy and who took an active part in the negotiations with Nestorius.[44] Theodoret was present at Ephesus and sided with John of Antioch against Cyril. It is, therefore, likely that in writing about the Arabs in the *Curatio* he had in mind the part played by Aspebetos/Petrus in the proceedings of the Council of Ephesus, especially in the negotiations conducted by him as part of the delegation that was sent to Nestorius. But this depends on when the *Curatio* was written. It has been placed about 437, that is, six years after the council; thus, chronologically, it is possible that Theodoret had Petrus in mind. On the other hand, the editor of the *Curatio*, P. Canivet, thinks that it was written even before Theodoret became the bishop of Cyrrhus in 432. If so, Petrus would be out of the question as the inspiration of the spirited passage.[45]

3. A third possibility is presented by the accounts of the ecclesiastical historians of the revolt of Queen Mavia against Emperor Valens in the seventies of the fourth century. Theodoret recorded it in his *Historia Ecclesiastica*. Relevant in this context is the dialogue between Mavia's Arab bishop, Moses, and Lucius, the Arian patriarch of Alexandria, when the former was brought to him for consecration as bishop. Moses wins the upper hand and reduces Lucius to absurdity.[46] This dialogue, as recorded in Theodoret and in Sozo-

[44] On Petrus I, see below, 181–84.

[45] On the date of the composition of the *Curatio*, see Quasten, *Patrology*, III, 544.

[46] On this see *BAFOC*, 152–58. For Theodoret's own account, see his *Historia Ecclesiastica*, IV, 20.

men, could have been in the mind of the former when he wrote this passage on the Arabs in the *Curatio*. The dialogue between the Saracen bishop and the patriarch has survived, and so it is possible to relate it to the virtues that Theodoret ascribes to the Arabs. Furthermore, there is another element in the *Curatio* account that could point to the Moses episode. Theodoret speaks of the Arabs as possessing no Greek books; Moses in all probability was a simple Arab anchorite who had no deep knowledge of Greek theology extracted from books. Theodoret is supposed to have finished the *Historia Ecclesiastica* in 449–450, but he certainly had knowledge of these events before he decided to write it and completed his work.[47]

It is impossible to tell which of the three possibilities inspired Theodoret to write his passage in the *Curatio* on the Arabs. Perhaps more than one factor was operative. The chronology of his works is relevant to deciding this issue only as it pertains to Petrus and the Council of Ephesus.

In the larger context of the history of the Arabs and of Arab-Byzantine relations before the rise of Islam, this passage throws light on two important problems: (1) It shows that the *pre*-Islamic self-image of the Arabs as Ishmaelites can be evidenced in the northern part of Oriens;[48] and (2) it corroborates what was said in *BAFOC* on the whereabouts of the Tanūkhids, if Theodoret was indeed thinking of Bishop Moses when he wrote the passage in the *Curatio*. In that case, the Arab Ishmaelites he referred to as his neighbors would be the Arabs of Mavia. This gives some geographical precision to where the Arab *foederati* of Mavia and the Tanūkhids were stationed, in the region of Antioch or Cyrrhus in the northern part of Oriens.[49]

Appendix I

The Greek *Vita* of Simeon Stylites

The *Vita* of Simeon Stylites written by Theodoret and included in his *Historia Religiosa* is the most reliable of the various *Vitae* of the saint. However, the Greek *Vita* of Antonius and the Syriac version have important data for Byzantino-arabica.[1]

This *Vita*[2] was written by a disciple of Simeon Stylites called Antonius. There are a number of references to the Arabs, whom the author refers to as "Saracens."

[47] For the composition of the *HE* in 449–450, see Quasten, *Patrology,* III, 551.

[48] On this self-image involving Ishmael in the Arabian Peninsula, see below, Chap. 13, sec. I.

[49] See *BAFOC,* 465–76.

[1] The three *Vitae* have been assembled by H. Lietzmann, *Das Leben des Heiligen Symeon Stylites*, TU 32, 4 (Liepzig, 1908). The Syriac version was studied by H. Hilgenfeld, who provided a German translation of the *Vita.* References to the two *Vitae* in this appendix are to the texts in Lietzmann's and Hilgenfeld's work (hereafter *Das Leben.*) For the latest on Simeon's biography, see A. Vööbus, "Discovery of New Manuscript Sources for the Biography of Simeon Stylite," in *After Chalcedon,* Orientalia Lovaniensia Analecta18 (Louvain, 1985) 479–85.

[2] In addition to what Lietzmann has said on this *Vita* in *Das Leben,* see the observations of

1. In Section 17 the *Vita* speaks of a crowd of Saracens who came to Simeon and whom he turned to the fear of God. This is confirmed by what Theodoret says in his *Vita* of Simeon, and thus may be accepted as a true statement.[3]

2. In Section 18 the *Vita* recounts the episode of the king of the Saracens. He comes to the saint, whose fame had reached him, in order to receive his prayers. While Simeon was speaking to him, a worm fell before the Saracen king. When he took it up, the vermin was transformed into a pearl. This compelled the king to convert, since he thought the miracle was due to the saint's powers. After saying so to the saint, the king was dismissed by Simeon with blessings.[4]

There is nothing like this episode in Theodoret's *Vita*, but relieved of the miraculous element, the account may have a germ of truth about Arab chiefs in the region coming to see the Saint. The "king" could not have been the Salīḥid king in Oriens since the Salīḥids were already converted, but he could have been an Arab chief in northern Arabia who was attracted to Simeon by his fame as a wonder-worker.

3. In Section 22 a queen (βασίλισσα) of the Saracens who has been taunted by her husband for her sterility comes to Simeon, who promises that the Lord will grant her a child. The queen gives birth to a daughter, but for five years the child can neither speak nor walk. She and her husband bring her to the saint and, after staying around the pillar for seven days, they depart. As they are leaving they look back at the pillar, and their daughter is immediately cured.[5]

This brings to mind Section 21 of the *Vita* of Simeon by Theodoret, which tells the story of the sterile queen with some obvious differences, and also Section 16, which tells the story of the Arab phylarch and the paralytic he brought to Simeon.[6] Perhaps Antonius conflated the two episodes. It is noteworthy that in Antonius' *Vita* the queen reigns over Saracens, not Ishmaelites, and her husband does not seem to be the ruler, since he is not referred to as king. If authentic, the episode could testify to the survival of the matriarchal system among the Arabs in the fifth century.

4. In Section 29 the hagiographer recounts his announcement of the saint's death to the bishop of Antioch and to Ardabur, the *magister militum* in Oriens.[7] When the news of his death (459) became known, the Saracens appeared with their weapons and camels and wanted to possess themselves of his body.

Peeters in "S. Symeon Stylite," 43–48 (with many reservations) reprinted in *Orient et Byzance*, Subsidia Hagiographica 26 (Brussels, 1950); on the Greek *Vita* of Antonius, see 107–12.

[3] See *Das Leben*, 42.

[4] See ibid., 44–46.

[5] See ibid., 56.

[6] See above, 151.

[7] See *Das Leben*, 66–68. Ardabur was present with six hundred soldiers, and this prevented the Arabs from seizing the body of the saint, whom they wanted to bury in their territory. His body was transported to Antioch, where he was laid after the Antiochenes had persuaded Emperor Leo that a city without walls, as theirs was, needed the relics of the saint for protection.

Ardabur, the Alan, was *magister militum per Orientem* from 453 to 466. This was his second encounter with the Arabs, whom he had fought in the vicinity of Damascus in 453, as discussed above, Chap. 3. For Ardabur, see *PLRE*, 135–37.

While the other references to the Arabs in the *Vita* are of moderate interest and of doubtful quality, since the much more reliable account of Theodoret is available for similar episodes, this last reference to the Arabs in the *Vita* of Antonius is a hard datum which may be promoted into a solid fact. Since Theodoret concluded his *Vita* before Simeon's death, it is naturally not to be found there; hence the *Vita* by Antonius provides further valuable data on his death and the desire of the Arabs to have his body. The account has the ring of authenticity, and it reflects in a concrete manner the Arabs' affection for the saint and his influence on their lives.

Appendix II

The Syriac *Vita* of Simeon Stylites

The Syriac *Vita* is on a much higher level of authenticity than the Greek *Vita* of Antonius.[1] It has a precious, detailed description of an encounter in the vicinity of Damascus between Antiochus, the *dux* of Phoenicia Libanensis, and al-Nuʿmān, the Lakhmid king of Ḥīra.

> Es kam zu ihm Antiochus, der Sohn des Sabinus, als er zum Dux in Damaskus gemacht war, und sprach zu seiner Heiligkeit vor jedermann: Naʿman kam herauf in die Wüste neben Damaskus und veranstaltete ein Gastmahl und lud mich ein. Denn zu jener Zeit war noch keine Feindschaft zwischen ihm und den Römern. Als wir nun beim Mahle waren, brachte er das Gespräch auf den Herrn Simeon und sprach zu mir: "Der, welchen ihr den Herrn Simeon nennt, ist der ein Gott?" Ich sprach zu ihm: "Er ist nicht ein Gott, sondern ein Diener Gottes." Wieder sprach Naʿman zu mir: "Als man bei uns von dem Ruf des Herrn Simeon hörte, und die Araber von unserer Seite anfingen zu ihm hinauf zu ziehen, kamen diese Großen meines Heerlagers und sprachen zu mir: Wenn du sie zu ihm hinaufziehen läßt, so gehen sie hin und werden Christen und hängen den Römern an und werden aufsässig gegen dich und verlassen dich. Da schickte ich und rief und versammelte mein ganzes Heerlager und sprach zu ihnen: Wenn sich jemand untersteht und hinaufzieht zu dem Herrn Simeon, werde ich ihm mit dem Schwerte das Haupt abschlagen und seiner ganzen Familie. Nach diesen Worten gab ich ihnen Befehl und ließ sie gehen. Aber um Mitternacht, als ich im Zelte schlief, sah ich einen herrlichen Mann, dessen gleichen ich noch nicht gesehen hatte, und bei ihm waren fünf andere. Als ich ihn sah, wurde mir anders zu Mute, meine Kniee wankten, und ich fiel vor ihm nieder aus Ehrfurcht. Da sprach er zu mir im Zorn mit harten Worten: "Wer bist du, daß du das Volk Gottes zurückhaltst von dem Knecht Gottes?" Und auf seinen Befehl spannten mich die vier Männer an Händen und Füßen aus, und der andere gab mir eine harte und schmerzhafte Züchtigung, und niemand befreite mich aus ihren Händen, bis er sich meiner erbarmte und mich loszulassen befahl. Dann zog er sein Schwert, welches er bei sich trug, zeigte es mir und versicherte mir mit kräftigen Schwüren: Wenn du es wieder wagst, auch nur einen Menschen

[1] On the value of this *Vita*, see Peeters, "S. Symeon Stylite," 48–71. This article was published later with corrections in his *Orient et Byzance*; for the part relevant to the Syriac *Vita*, see 112–26.

vom Gebet bei dem Herrn Simeon abzuhalten, werde ich dir mit diesem Schwert deine Glieder in Stücke zerschlagen und ebenso deiner ganzen Familie! Da stand ich früh am Morgen auf und versammelte das ganze Heerlager und sprach zu ihnen: Wer auch immer hinaufziehen will zu dem Herrn Simeon, um dort die Taufe anzunehmen und Christ zu werden, der möge hinaufziehen ohne Angst und Furcht. Ferner sprach Naʿman zu mir: "Wenn ich nicht dem König der Perser untertan wäre, so würde auch ich zu ihm hinaufziehen und Christ werden. Aber den Schrecken und die Züchtigung spürte ich mehr als einen Monat lang und konnte nich aufstehen und hinausgehen. Siehe, nach meinem Befehl gibt es Kirchen und Bischöfe und Presbyter in meinem Heerlager, und ich sprach: Wer auch immer ein Christ werden will, mag es werden ohne Angst; aber wenn einer ein Heide sein will, so ist das ebenfalls seine Sache." Alle, welche ihn erzählen hörten, priesen Gott, wie er den Triumph seiner Verehrer in jedem Lande erhöhte.[2]

1. The chronology of this passage[3] can be established with reasonable precision in view of the internal indications in the text, involving as they do, a well-known Byzantine *dux*[4] and the reign of the Persian king, Yazdgard. The meeting must have taken place in the second decade of the fifth century, after Simeon established himself at Telanissos and before the death of Yazdgard in 420.

The passage is a gift to the historian of the Lakhmid dynasty, who has no chronological indications to use for establishing the regnal years of the Lakhmids following the death of Imru'al-Qays of the Namāra inscription. After almost a century of a vacuum as far as regnal years are concerned, this is the first solid spot in the sources. It allows one to assign al-Nuʿmān to the second decade of the century and describes him in an important meeting with the Byzantine *dux* of Phoenicia.[5]

2. The journey of a Lakhmid king who was the client king of Persia to Byzantine territory and his encounter with the *dux* of Phoenicia Libanensis may sound extraordinary, but the following facts make it possible: (a) The Lakhmids, especially in this period of peace between Persia and Byzantium, were independent rulers in many ways, and al-Nuʿmān could easily make the journey to Oriens without arousing the suspicion of the Great King. (b) The Lakhmids were well connected with the tribes of the region, such as the Tanūkhids of Oriens, and they themselves, represented by Imru'al-Qays, had in part emigrated to Byzantine territory in the fourth century; even in the sixth century the Lakhmid al-Mundir could claim the *strata* in Phoenicia as his own. The Lakhmids could, then, have maintained some presence in the region since the days of Imru'al-Qays and his defection to the Romans.[6]

[2] Trans. by Hilgenfeld, in Lietzmann, *Das Leben,* 146–47.

[3] Ibid., 248–49.

[4] For Antiochus, son of Sabinus, *dux* of Phoenicia Libanensis, see *PLRE,* II, 104, s.v. Antiochus (no. 9). It was he who described to Simeon his encounter with al-Nuʿmān.

[5] See Rothstein's section on al-Nuʿmān, which utilizes Nöldeke's work, in *DLH,* 65–68.

[6] On the Lakhmids in Oriens, see *BAFOC,* 48; index, 618, s.v.

3. His army chiefs speak to Nuʿmān about the conversion of his Arabs after their visit to Simeon and suggest that this leads them to leaving him and turning against him. Nuʿmān reacts angrily: he assembles his army and threatens them with death if they visit Simeon. This scene, described by Nuʿmān himself to Antiochus, calls for the following comments:

a. These chiefs would have had memories of the conversion of Imru'al-Qays, the Lakhmid king of the fourth century, and his defection to Byzantium.[7] The warnings of these chiefs reflect the fact that adoption of Christianity in those days implied allegiance to Byzantium, the secular enemy of Persia, thus testifying to the power of Christianity to draw them to the Byzantine political orbit.

b. His angry reply and his threats to those who visited Simeon recall a similar scene in the sixth century,[8] when the pagan Lakhmid king of Ḥīra threatened the Christians in his army. It also testifies indirectly to the fact that Christianity had made inroads into Lakhmid territory and into the Lakhmid army itself.

4. Nuʿmān's confession to Antiochus that if he had not been Persia's client he would have become Christian is the most explicit statement on the predicament of the Lakhmid kings vis-à-vis the Great King concerning Christianity. The Persian king viewed the conversion of his Lakhmid client as a betrayal, a gesture to the enemy and amenability to Byzantine influence.[9] Thus the confession documents the connection between the Christian religion and political loyalty to Byzantium, the guardian state of that faith. The conversion and defection of Imru'al-Qays in the fourth century would only have drawn attention to the relationship that obtained between religious persuasion and political allegiance.

5. Nuʿmān's statement that "in his camp (ḥīra) there were churches, bishops, and presbyters" is important for the state of the progress of Christianity in the realm of the Lakhmids. It is absolutely certain that what appears in the German version as *Heerlager*, Syr. *Ḥertā*, Arabic *ḥīra*, is not the common noun *ḥīra* meaning "camp" (*Heerlager*), but the proper noun Ḥīra, the capital of the Lakhmids. The two usages appear in this section of the *Vita*,[10] but undoubtedly in this sentence it can only mean the city, since it is inconceivable that Nuʿmān would have carried with him while on the march bishops and, what is more, churches! This is also corroborated by the fact that Ḥīra in his reign became or was an episcopal see.[11]

The ultimate value of the section on Nuʿmān in the *Vita* is that it corroborates the Arabic tradition on his fate—his renunciation of his kingdom and his becoming a wanderer, Arabic *al-Sā'iḥ*, which epithet describes him in the sources. Thus the

[7] See ibid., 31–45.

[8] For this scene, see Shahîd, *"Byzantino-arabica,"* 119.

[9] See the letter which the last Lakhmid king who adopted Christianity had to write to the Great King asking for his permission to do so, in Abū al-Baqā' Hibat-Allāh, *Kitāb al-Manāqib al-Mazyadiyya fī Akhbār al-Mulūk al-Asadiyya*, ed. S. M. Daradika and M. Khuraysat (Amman, 1984), I, 267.

[10] As they do in the *Letter* of Simeon of Bēth-Arshām; see I. Shahîd, *Martyrs*, 109, line 40.

[11] See Rothstein, *DLH*, 24. The name of the bishop was Hosea.

Syriac source confirms the essential soundness of the Arabic tradition on the Lakhmids, going back to Hishām al-Kalbī.[12]

a. There are two elements in the account of the *Vita* that suggest Nu'mān was a susceptible man: the dream he had of Simeon and the fact that he acted according to the behest of the latter when he appeared to him in a dream. The last remark of Antiochus may have left a lasting impression on him, especially coming from a soldier like himself, namely, that a Christian will have no anxiety or fear. This encounter with Antiochus and the fame of Simeon are the background for understanding what the Arabic tradition on his fate—his renunciation of his kingdom and his becoming a afford no detail other than elaborating on what a poet of Ḥīra, ʿAdi ibn Zayd, says in one of his poems.[13] It is thus possible that the Stylite of Telanissos changed the life of the lord of Ḥīra.

b. The warrior king of Ḥīra must, then, have been under Christian influence both in his own city and during the expedition that brought him to Syria and to the pillar saint. Yet it is possible to detect another influence on him, which finally drove him to renounce the world. The historian al-Masʿūdī states that the name of his mother was al-Hayjumāna, which almost certainly is Greek *hēgoumenē* (ἡγουμένη).[14] Now this, among other things, could signify the *hēgoumenē* of a monastery. His mother probably came from a Christian family which had in it a member who was a *hēgoumenē*, hence the name in the tribal group. If so, this would be another element in the influences that worked on Nuʿmān and turned him to Christianity of the ascetic type—the renunciation of the world.[15]

Appendix III

The Arab *Foederati* and Ecclesiastical Law

Chapter IX in the *Curatio,* on the Laws, has a section (14) that has an important reference to the Arabs, called, as usual in Theodoret, the Ishmaelites.[1]

Theodoret was comparing civil law with that of the Church and arguing for the superiority of the latter. He had first discussed the laws of the Greeks and then proceeded to discuss those of the Romans. According to him, the Romans forced their

[12] Much progress has been made since Nöldeke and Rothstein evaluated this tradition almost a century ago; see *BAFOC,* 349–66 on Hishām al-Kalbī. See also P. Peeters' observation on Nöldeke's article on Imru'al-Qays of the Namāra inscription in *Orient et Byzance,* 121.

[13] Rothstein, *DLH,* 67.

[14] Ibid., 65, although Rothstein is unaware of the signification of the term as "abbess." Hence he could not see its relevance to the discussion of Nuʿmān's renunciation of the world.

[15] Chronologically this is possible and makes the story of his renunciation credible. He is a mighty warrior around 420, then suddenly in 422 he is out of the picture and his son Mun̲dir fights the first war of the reign of Theodosius II. This sudden departure chimes well with the view that he renounced the world. It is also possible that the two are related in the following manner: Nuʿmān's adoption of Christianity would have brought him in trouble with the shah just as Imru' al-Qays may have done before. So after deciding to become Christian, he simply renounced the world, wandered away, and disappeared in the desert, as many a Christian anchorite did in those days.

[1] See *Curatio,* II, 339–340.

laws on the subject peoples, but the latter did not accept them.[2] Finally he enumerates the peoples not subject to the Romans but friendly states and groups, who, he says, do not make use of the laws of the Romans when they make their accords with them. These are the Ethiopians, "the innumerable tribes of the Ishmaelites," the Sanni, the Abasgi, and the other barbarians.[3]

It is clear that this is a reference to the Arab *foederati* along the oriental *limes*, since they are distinguished from those who were subjected to the Romans, referred to in the two preceding sentences of Section 14, and they are described in terms that point to their federate or allied status: οὐχ οἱ ἄλλοι βάρβαροι. ὅσοι τὴν Ῥωμαίων ἀσπάζονται δεσποτείαν, κατὰ τοὺς Ῥωμαίων νόμους τὰ πρὸς ἀλλήλους ποιοῦνται ξυμβόλαια. The description of the number of the Arab federate tribes with a superlative is important in this reference: τὰ πάμπολλα φῦλα τοῦ Ἰσμαήλ. This confirms that the number of Arab *foederati* employed by Byzantium in the fifth century was considerable and also what has been said about the *foederati* of the fourth century[4] and those of the fifth[5]—that they belonged to various Arab tribal groups, of which the Tanūkhids and the Salīḥids, were only the dominant groups.

After saying that the *foederati* did not adopt the laws of the Romans, Theodoret leaves out the question of what laws they did adopt. But the following section[6] in the *Curatio* (15) could throw some light on this question. In this section he explains that the laws of Christianity spread among the Romans and their tributaries and among all the races and the nations of the earth. The Arabs are not included explicitly but only implied and subsumed under the general phrase "men of all the nations and the races." They must be included, since of all the barbarians who had relations with the empire they were the closest to Theodoret, and he had mentioned them in the preceding section. This is testimonially confirmed by a passage in the *Historia Religiosa* where he speaks of Simeon.[7] In that passage he describes the coming of the Ishmaelites to the saint and his giving of Christian laws to them. The status of these Ishmaelites is not given, but they were clearly not *Rhōmaioi* and so must have been Arabs who lived along the *limes,* federate and non-federate Arabs who were roaming in those regions. As mentioned earlier, the laws must have been ecclesiastical ones that regulated their behavior. The passage in the *Historia Religiosa* that precedes the one on the giving of the laws contains a series of practices that the Arabs were asked to give up upon being converted by Simeon; so the passage gives a series of "Thou shalt not" injunctions.

The *Curatio* was written[8] either about 437 or, according to P. Canivet, before 423. Thus the religious laws of which Theodoret speaks and which governed the

[2] This must be an exaggeration; on the enforcement of Roman law on the Nabataeans of the Provincia Arabia and on the Edessenes of Arabia in Mesopotamia, see *RA,* 99 note 29 and *BAFOC,* 242.

[3] On these barbarians, see Canivet's footnote, *Curatio,* II, 340 note 1.

[4] See *BAFOC,* 381–95.

[5] See below, Chap. 12, sec. IV.

[6] *Curatio,* II, 340.

[7] *Historia Religiosa,* sec. 13; for an analysis of this passage, see above, 149–50.

[8] See Quasten, *Patrology,* III, 544.

conduct of the Arab tribal groups along the *limes orientalis* and of the *foederati* were laws that may be dated to the first half of the fifth century. Whether this continued to be the case in the second half of the century or even in the sixth is not entirely clear, but it is likely to have been so. The *Codex Theodosianus* was promulgated in 438, that is, before Theodoret wrote his *Curatio*. It was translated later into Syriac, or rather an adaptation of it, and became known in Oriens as the *Syrian-Roman Lawbook*.[9] The life of the *foederati*, as a military group, was much simpler than that of the *Rhōmaioi* in Oriens, and thus most of the laws of the Codex Theodosianus, applicable to the Syriac-speaking *Rhōmaioi*,[10] were irrelevant to them. The Arab *foederati*'s laws most probably continued to be a combination of the ecclesiastical laws of which Theodoret spoke,[11] breathing the new spirit of Christianity in legislation, and the old Arab tribal code which governed the life and conduct of the Arab tribal groups in pre-Islamic times.[12]

[9] Evangelos Chrysos has noted that it speaks of the *Chrysargyron*. Since this was abolished by Emperor Anastasius (491–518), he concluded that the *Lawbook* was a work of the 5th century. For this view, namely, that the *Lawbook* unfolds Roman law, see references in A. Vööbus, "Important Manuscript Discoveries for the Syro-Roman Law Book," *JNES* 32 (1973), 321 notes 9–10. For other views, see ibid., notes 2–8. Vööbus' article is a useful review of scholarship on the *Lawbook*.

[10] Just as the *Lex Romana Visigothorum* of Alaric II was prepared for the benefit of the Roman subjects of the Visigothic king of Gaul.

[11] Perhaps the history of the Goths could afford a parallel. In his account of their conversion by Ulphila, Philostorgius says that Emperor Constantine would often speak of Ulphila in conversation as the Moses of his day (*Historia Ecclesiastica*, ed. L. Bidez, GCS 21 (1913); revised by F. Winkelmann (1972), Book II, chap. V, p. 18, 11–12. The phrase "Moses of his day" admits of more than one interpretation, but the natural one is that which conceives of Moses as a lawgiver. After translating the Bible for them, Ulphila could well have compiled a small code of Christian laws to guide their conduct, since he wanted them not only to read the bible but also to behave as Christians. This could derive some support from the passage in Theodoret (*Curatio*, sec. 15) which speaks of the spread of Christian laws among the nations, of whom the Goths (Scythians) are explicitly mentioned. If so, Ulphila and Simeon would have been the lawgivers of the Goths and the Arabs respectively.

[12] For this, see the section on the pre-Islamic period in E. Tyan, *Histoire de l'organisation judiciaire en pays d'Islam* (Leiden, 1960), 27–61. Also the chapter on the pre-Islamic Arabs in Nicholson, *A Literary History of the Arabs*, 82–101. The union of the Christian and the Arab ideals is well illustrated in the moving story of Ḥanẓala and Sharīk, for which see ibid., 44. Nicholson, however, does not give the story in its entirety and so omits the reference to Ḥanẓala as a Christian. When the king asked him why he kept his word and fulfilled his promise after an entire year had elapsed and when he could have acted otherwise, Ḥanẓala answered that he was an adherent of a religion (Christianity) that prevented him from choosing the vile alternative; for this, see the account given in Cheikho, *Shuʿarāʾ al-Naṣrāniyya*, 91. The final statement in the account, that after hearing Ḥanẓala's reason the king adopted Christianity, may be rejected as unhistorical. On the union of Christian and non-Christian ideals in the converted Arabs of pre-Islamic times, see *BAFOC*, 338, 560.

IX

Sozomen

Sozomen is one of the major sources for the Arab *foederati* in the fourth and fifth centuries and for the Christianization of the Arabs in Oriens.[1] In addition, he is a major source for the religious history of the Arabs as the sons of Ishmael in the Arabian Peninsula. The relevant section in Book VI, chapter 37, of his *Ecclesiastical History*[2] is precious on what may be termed Ishmaelism among the Arabs in the fourth and fifth centuries.

I. *Historia Ecclesiastica*

The section on the Arabs as biblical Ishmaelites comes between Sozomen's account of Mavia and Zokomos, and thus is a digression. It may be summarized as follows:

1. The Arabs were called by the ancients "Ishmaelites" after their progenitor, Ishmael, the son of Abraham.

2. The later and more recent name of the Arabs is Saracens. It was the Ishmaelite Arabs themselves who adopted this name in order to conceal the opprobrium attaching to their origin because their mother, Hagar, the mother of Ishmael, was a slave girl. In calling themselves Saracens, they allied themselves with Sarah, the legitimate wife of Abraham.[3]

3. The Ishmaelites, like the Jews, practice circumcision and also refrain from eating pork. They also observe many other Jewish rites and customs.[4]

[1] On his contribution to the history of Queen Mavia of the 4th century, see *BAFOC*, 274–77. For his contribution to the history of the Arab *feoderati* in the 5th century—the Zokomids/Salīḥids through his preservation of the name of the eponym Zokomos, see above, 3–9.

[2] See *HE*, 299, lines 1–20.

[3] This etymology for "Saracens" is without basis in fact and is as erroneous as the one suggested by the last of the Church Fathers, John of Damascus, who argued for an etymology of "Saracen" exactly the contrary of the one suggested by Sozomen, for which see PG 94, col. 764. The former etymology may also be found in the work of Jerome, for which see *BAFOC*, 280. Erroneous as they are, these etymologies are not devoid of significance, since they reflect the special interest which Christian churchmen and thinkers took in the Arabs. Unlike many other ethnic groups they were trying to convert, the Arabs were an Abrahamic people but "outside the promise." For the term "Saraceni" and its various etymologies, see *RA*, 123–41.

[4] It is not clear whether Sozomen is speaking of the Judaizing or the non-Judaizing Ishmaelites. The two practices mentioned are observed by Muslims and one of them, abstinence

4. The Ishmaelites and the Jews are so much alike in what they practice that if the former deviate from the latter, it must be ascribed to the lapse of time, their separation from the Jews, and their contacts with neighboring peoples who influenced the development of other practices which departed from "the ancestral Ishmaelite way of life."[5]

5. But afterwards, contact with the Jews enabled the Ishmaelites to gather the facts of their origin and to return to their kinsmen. Consequently they allied themselves to Jewish laws and customs.[6]

6. Since that contact, many of the Ishmaelites, until the present day, regulate their way of life according to the Jewish fashion.[7]

This section on the Ishmaelite Arabs falls naturally into three parts: (*a*) the distant biblical past, briefly touched upon in (1) above, and briefly mentioning the Arab/Abrahamic connection through descent from Ishmael, the son of Abraham; (*b*) the middle period, which elapsed from biblical times to Sozomen's own day, spanning a period of some two millennia from the patriarchal period (2000–1500 B.C.) to the third, fourth and fifth centuries of the Christian era; (*c*) conditions of and views about the Ishmaelites that pertain to the author's own times or those close to him—the fourth and the fifth centuries. What Sozomen says in the first and second parts is of some interest to the student of the ecclesiastical historians. These parts provide material for understanding the framework within which they expressed their thought as well as the historical method they employed, but they have little value as sources for data on the Arabs. The first part draws on the biblical narrative, while the second is clearly a construction on the part of Sozomen.[8] The history of the Arabs in this middle period is long, diffuse, and obscure, and the ecclesiastical historian, it is practically certain, had no reliable sources for the sketch he gave of the Arabs' spiritual development. But it is not without merit. His short and rather involved account[9] may be explicated and amplified as follows:

The Israelites and the Ishmaelites are two peoples descended from two different mothers, Sarah and Hagar respectively. However, they are the children of one father, Abraham, from whom they derived their monotheism. Hence the similarity or near identity of the beliefs and customs of the two peoples—the Israelites and the Ishmaelites—in the patriarchal period. They

from pork, is specifically enjoined in the Koran, evidence of Ishmaelism in the Koran and Islam.

[5] *HE*, 299, lines 11–12: τὴν Ἰσμαὴλ πατρῴεαν διαγωγήν.

[6] Ibid., lines 17–19. The vague adverbial phrases in Sozomen do not indicate the period during which this contact took place.

[7] Ibid., lines 19–20.

[8] But it is practically certain that he used Josephus, whom he mentions in the preface of his *Ecclesiastical History*, Book I, chap. 1.

[9] For the original Greek, see *Historia Ecclesiastica*, 299, lines 5–19.

later parted from each other. Moses legislated only to the Israelites, not to the Ishmaelites, and with him a new religious phase began for the former, namely, Judaism. The Ishmaelites were further separated from the Israelites by the corruption of their Abrahamic monotheism[10] through contact with many other peoples. At this stage in their religious development they again came in contact with the Jews, and thus rediscovered their distant Abrahamic past and inclined toward Jewish laws and customs. This was their religious state when Sozomen wrote about them in the fifth century.

As noted earlier, this was an intelligent speculation on his part. He had before him the biblical account, possibly Josephus, and the religous complexion of the Ishmaelites of his own times, many of whom were still pagan. Consequently he drew some inferences on the middle period from the two sets of facts—the biblical and those he noted and ascertained himself about his Ishmaelite contemporaries. He was thus able to draw a sketch of the development of their religious journey in this middle period—first as a wandering away from the Abrahamic tradition and then as a rediscovery of, and a return to, that tradition.

Although inferential, the truth of this account must be accepted in its broad outlines, unless one does not accept the truth of the biblical narrative. Although less important than the third part of Sozomen's account because of its speculative nature, it is nevertheless of considerable interest to the study of the religious history of the Ishmaelites in the seventh century with the rise of Islam, since there is a striking resemblance between this account and the Koranic one on the religious history of the Arabs in this middle period.[11]

Infinitely more important is the third part, which speaks of the Ishmaelite-Israelite rapprochement and the Ishmaelites' assumption of Jewish laws and customs, summarized above in (4)–(6). It raises and solves important problems in the religious and cultural history of the Arabs and the Arabian Peninsula. But first the reliability of Sozomen's account must be discussed.

The question of Sozomen's reliability when he treats contemporary problems and topics has been examined in detail in connection with his chapter on Queen Mavia of the fourth century.[12] It has been shown that he is

[10] The monotheism of Ishmael is easily inferrable from the Biblical narrative in Genesis. He was named by the angel of God himself and for him the first monotheist prayed. Furthermore, he seems not to have distanced himself from his father, since he shared with Isaac the honor of burying Abraham, to the exclusion of the patriarch's other sons from Ketturah, as stated in Genesis.

[11] But in the Koran, the third and last stage represents the return of the Arabs to the true Abrahamic monotheism and not to Christianity or Judaism, as is the case in Sozomen. The middle period answers to what in the Koran is technically called *al-Jāhiliyya*, for which see, *EI*[2], s.v.

[12] See *BAFOC*, 275–77.

very trustworthy, collecting his data carefully and often indicating the method that he used. Especially relevant and significant in this context is his account of the many bishops of the Arabs, in which he says "I have learnt this from the Arabs."[13] Many of his statements are, then, based on personal observation. It is practically certain that this third part of his account of the religious history of the Ishmaelites derives from the same type of source. (*a*) The final statement in the account is presented as a fact[14] and not merely speculation. Coming from a responsible and extremely careful historian, it suggests that it was the result of direct and intimate knowledge of the Ishmaelites whom he describes as living in his time in the Jewish manner. (*b*) Sozomen was a native of Bethelia, near Gaza, and this is the region of the Negev which had a strong Arab complexion, like the Provincia Arabia across the Jordan. He was also close to the Sinai Peninsula. Thus Sozomen was close to all the areas where Arab pastoralists roamed and, what is more, regions close to the Desert of Paran where, according to the Bible, Ishmael himself lived. It it therefore, conceivable that an Ishmaelite tradition survived in these regions (*c*) The Arabs, or the Ishmaelites he speaks of as Judaizing, were thus likely to have been inhabitants of this desert region in the southern part of Oriens, the traditional seat of biblical Ishmael. But it is equally likely, perhaps even more likely, that the Ishmaelites whom he has in mind were those of the Arabian Peninsula, notably those of western Arabia. In this period, the fourth and fifth centuries, the religion that was making progress in Oriens in the shadow of the Christianized Roman Empire was naturally Christianity, not Judaism, which was actually under fire.[15] Thus the Judaization among the Arabs that Sozomen speaks of must have taken place in large part in the Arabian Peninsula, especially in western Arabia where there was a very strong Jewish presence in the fifth century.[16] Southern Palestine, where Sozomen lived before moving to Constantinople, contained the northern termini of the trade routes that crossed western Arabia from the south. Thus Arabs or Ishmaelites from western Arabia were not unknown in southern Palestine, even in Gaza itself,[17] and caravans brought in ideas as well as wares and mechandise from western Arabia. It is, therefore, not difficult to see how a historian with the intellectual curiosity of Sozomen could have acquired his information on the Judaizing Arabs of the fifth century in western Arabia, especially as he was a

[13] Ibid., 276.

[14] See *HE*, 299, lines 19–20.

[15] For this, see M. Avi-Yonah, *The Jews of Palestine* (New York, 1976), chap. 9, pp. 208–31.

[16] For this, see below, 371.

[17] Where, according to tradition, the Prophet's great grandfather, Hāshim, is buried; on Hāshim see *EI*, s.v.

Christian interested in the progress of the Christian mission among the barbarians and had a natural interest in this particular group among the descendants (through Ishmael) of the first patriarch. In the preface to his *Historia Ecclesiastica*,[18] he expressed surprise that the Jews had not accepted Christianity, while the Gentile world did, or did so more readily. So he must have been doubly surprised and disappointed to learn that some of the Ishmaelites converted not to Christianity but to Judaism.

After establishing Sozomen's reliability we must now examine more closely the third part of his account.

Two concepts involving the Arabs clearly emerge from it: Ishmaelism and Judaism; the problem is to determine the degree to which the Arabs were attached to either one.

1. The last statement in the account—that the Ishmaelites "regulate their way of life according to the Jewish fashion"—is the clearest with its use of "Jewish" ('Ιουδαϊκῶς) rather than "Hebrew," which he had used ethnically a few lines earlier.[19] This is Mosaic Judaism to which he asserts some of the Ishmaelites belonged. And it is clear that he is not thinking merely of Ishmaelites imitating the Jews or behaving like them superficially, but that they actually Judaized and belonged to Judaism as a religion. This is confirmed by the preceding statement that they "allied themselves to Jewish laws and customs." For the ecclesiastical historian, as for St. Paul, Judaism is a legalistic religion, and accepting the Jewish laws of Moses, about whom he had talked earlier, entailed belonging to Judaism.

That there were Ishmaelite Arabs in the fifth century who had adopted Judaism is a most welcome datum from Sozomen. It is the needed external Greek contemporary source for confirming the many statements in the Arabic historians on the Judaism of some pre-Islamic Arab tribes. The two sets of sources thus become complementary, the Greek source vouching for the Judaism of the Ishmaelites in general terms, the Arabic specifically naming the various Judaizing tribes.[20]

2. More important is whether or not Sozomen expressed or implied in his account the existence of Ishmaelism, that is, the consciousness of the Arabs that they were descended from Ishmael, Abraham's firstborn, who to them was not only an ancestor but also a figure whose laws and precepts they followed.

In his account of the middle period of the religious history of the Ishma-

[18] *HE*, Book I, chap. 1.

[19] Ibid., 299, line 12.

[20] Such as Kinda, for which, see Ibn Ḥazm, *Jambara*, 491; and parts of al-Aws and al-Khazraj, of Juḏām, and of Balḥārith for which, see Yaʿqūbī, *Tārīkh*, I, 257.

elites, Sozomen does express such views,[21] but, as mentioned earlier, this part is most likely his own construction. Besides, it deals with the distant past. What is more important is whether or not the Arabs he speaks about retained some of this Ishmaelism in the fifth century and how much they retained of it even when they converted to Judaism. Unfortunately, Sozomen is not explicit on these matters: he simply describes their being drawn to Judaism and is silent on their possible retention of Ishmaelism. The tenor of the account in its entirety, however, could point to the conclusion that they did retain one facet of their Ishmaelism, namely, the genealogical one—their consciousness that they were descended from Ishmael, their eponymous ancestor, and thus emerged as Ishmaelites of the Mosaic faith.

Sozomen's silence must not be construed as entailing the non-existence of Ishmaelism in its more extended connotation. That there were Arabs who regarded Ishmael not only as their distant ancestor but also revered him is clearly reflected in patristic thought, in Theodoret.[22] So what may be implied in Sozomen's account is clearly expressed in Theodoret who, like Sozomen, was writing of contemporaries and who had a special interest in the Arabs who lived near him, which enabled him to ascertain what he says on their Ishmaelism. Thus the two Christian writers complement each other on the Ishmaelite Arabs, Sozomen vouching for the Judaism of some, and Theodoret vouching for the Ishmaelism of others. The two testimonies are extremely valuable for the religious history of the Arabs before the rise of Islam. Theodoret's is the more important of the two, since it confirms the many statements in the Arabic historians on Ishmaelism in Arabia before the rise of Islam and in Arabic pre-Islamic poetry.[23] These Arabic sources have for some time been haunted by the ghosts of authenticity; thus the testimonies of Theodoret and possibly Sozomen are welcome confirmatory evidence.

II

The data extracted from both Sozomen and Theodoret on the cultural history of the Arabs before the rise of Islam and on Arab-Byzantine relations are precious with regard to three major themes: the middle period in the religious journey of the Arabs, the conversion of many of the Arabs tribes to Judaism, and the existence of Ishmaelism in the centuries before the rise of Islam. It is, therefore, important to fortify these conclusions drawn from the Greek sources with further observations on the subject.

1. Josephus: It is almost certain that Josephus was one of Sozomen's sources for the middle period of Arab religious development. He is mentioned

[21] See above, note 5.

[22] On Theodoret and the Ishmaelites, see above, 154–56.

[23] Further on this, see below, Chap. 13, sec. I.

in the preface of the *Historia Ecclesiastica*, although not as a source on the Arabs but as testimony for the truth of Christianity. Sozomen must have been aware of what Josephus said of Ishmael in his *Jewish Antiquities*. It is interesting to note that Josephus speaks of Ishmael's circumcision at the age of thirteen. More important, because it is a personal observation about conditions in his own time, is that the Arabs perform the ceremony in the same year.[24]

The reference in Josephus to a book he intended to write, entitled "Customs and Causes" (Περὶ ἐθῶν καὶ αἰτίων) is important. Apparently this work was never completed, but probably "had taken shape in the author's mind and was actually begun."[25] If this book existed in some form, it could have been known to Sozomen; it is the type of book that would have contained some information on the Arabs as the sons of Ishmael. It is tantalizing to think that Sozomen may have derived his information on the Ishmaelites from this source. This would elevate his section on the middle period from construction to something based on the work of a respectable historian who was a keen observer of the Arab scene. What is more, it would advance the account of the Ishmaelites of this middle period from the fifth to the first century of the Christian era, when Josephus wrote. Consequently, if Josephus was his source, what Sozomen says would be valid for the first century, thus coming closer to patriarchal times and the biblical narrative.

2. Diodorus Siculus: In Book III of his *World History*, Diodorus discusses Arabia and speaks of the Βανιζομενεῖς, whom he mentions before his reference to a sanctuary in northwestern Arabia.[26] It has been argued[27] that the Greek term Βανιζομενεῖς is equivalent to Banū Ismāʿil, the sons of Ishmael, the biblical people. The view is well argued, and the phonetic difficulties are resolved by the process of dissimilation from "m" in Ishmael to "n" in Βανιζομενεῖς. With the evidence presented earlier, this argument on the meaning of Βανιζομενεῖς in Diodorus receives fortification. Diodorus lived and wrote in the first century before Christ, and if the identification is true, this would place the concept of the descent from Ishmael in the first century B.C.[28] and thus advance it even closer to patriarchal times.

[24] See *Jewish Antiquities*, I, 214, Cf. I. Ephʿal's footnote on this point in "'Ishmael' and 'Arab(s)': a Transformation of Ethnological Terms," *JNES* 35 (1976), 232 note 35. The idiom of Josephus suggests that his observation was based on personal knowledge of the contemporary Arab scene. Circumcision at the age of thirteen is still practiced in various parts of the Muslim world, but it was also practiced at other ages; see *Khitān*, *EI*², s.v.

[25] On this work of Josephus, see the footnote of the editor of the *Jewish Antiquities* in the Leob Classical Library, I, 13 note b.

[26] See Diodorus' *Library of History*, Book III, sec. 44; Loeb ed., vol. II, 216, lines 8–13.

[27] See H. Holma, "Que signifie, chez Diodore de Sicile, le nom propre arabe Βανιζομεν(εῖς)?" *Orientalia* n.s. 12 (1944), 358–59.

[28] F. V. Winnett suspected the biblical name, Ishmael, in two inscriptions discovered at Taymāʾ for which, see *Ancient Records from North Arabia* (Toronto, 1970), pp. 93, 96, but see I. Ephʿal, "'Ishmael'," 230–31.

3. The Sons of Hagar: In addition to the phrase "the Sons of Ishmael," there is another phrase which denotes the Arabs, namely, "the Sons of Hagar." It seems a natural appellation for the same people in the biblical context, and the Arabs used matronymics as well as patronymics. Its first attestations are in the Bible itself.[29] The term "Hagarenoi" was later used by ecclesiastical historians to denote the Arabs as much as the term "Ishmaelites." This biblical term for the Arabs may have been revived because it clearly affiliated them with Hagar, and not with Sarah, since the term "Saracenoi" was etymologized by one ecclesiastical historian as "descendants of Sarah."[30]

The term "Hagarenoi" has been recently etymologized not as "Sons of Hagar" but as an old Arabian tribe, unrelated to the biblical Hagar.[31] This is possible but unlikely, since it appears in the Bible in close proximity to "Ishmaelites", which suggests that the "Hagarenoi" were an Arab people related to the Ishmaelites, perhaps a clan or subdivision of the more generic "Ishmaelites." Besides, the Arabic phrase Banū Hāgar, the "Sons of Hagar," is attested in an important pre-Islamic ode, which suggests that Hagar did give rise to a matronymic which was used on the eve of the rise of Islam.[32]

4. Conversion to Judaism: In the *Historia Ecclesiastica*, the statement that many Arabs adopted Judaism in the fourth and fifth centuries stands alone. In a period that witnessed the triumph of Christianity and a successful mission to convert the world to the new faith, the statement is startling, but a close examination of the religious map of the Arabian Near East in this period could explain this phenomenon and consequently give support to the reliability of Sozomen's account.

This was the period of grave difficulties for the Jews of Oriens and Palestine. Imperial legislation starting with Constantine had been unfavorable to the Jews in many ways. Indeed a Jewish historian calls this period (363–439) "The Great Assault on the Jews and Judaism."[33] It ended with the abolition of the Jewish patriarchate, and there is reference in a law of 429 to the *excessus patriarchatum*.[34] The period lasted until the Council of Chalcedon[35] in 451. It is quite possible that the Jews of Oriens and Palestine looked to the Arabian Peninsula as a haven, which possibly acquired special importance in their minds as a biblical land close to the Holy Land, where they would be free to practice their religion without imperial legislation against them. Thus

[29] See I Chron. 27:31; Ps. 83:6.

[30] For this etymology given by Sozomen, see above, note 3.

[31] J. S. Trimingham, *Christianity*, 10–11; but see the more reliable articles in *The Interpreter's Dictionary of the Bible*, s.vv. "Hagar" and "Hagarite."

[32] On this, see below, Chap. 13, sec. I.IV.

[33] See Avi-Yonah, *Jews of Palestine*, 208.

[34] Ibid., 228.

[35] Ibid., 232.

in a sense the Christianization of Oriens in these two centuries may have led in part to the spread of Judaism in western Arabia.

The situation in the Arabian Peninsula, especially western Arabia, was very favorable for the Jewish Diaspora and for a Jewish mission there. (*a*) Already the Peninsula had been a region to which the exiles fled after the destruction of the Temple. And as has been correctly suspected, since the time of the Babylonian king Nabonidus Jewish communities were established in Ḥijāz; there were many prosperous and powerful groups in the fifth century. In fact the religious complexion of Ḥijāz in the context of the struggle of the two religions for Arabia was much more Jewish than Christian, in spite of the inroads that Christianity had made there. (*b*) Judaism was not only longer and more firmly established in the Peninsula but also more widespread in western Arabia. There was a strong Jewish presence both in Ḥijāz and in South Arabia, whether it was officially sponsored by the kings of South Arabia[36] or simply represented by a powerful and large Jewish community. This was a country whose rulers were hostile to Byzantium and consequently were unsympathetic to its official religion, which was also that of their enemies across the Red Sea—the Ethiopians.

Set against this background of a strong Jewish presence in western Arabia in the fourth and fifth centuries, the statement in Sozomen on the Arabs adopting Judaism acquires even greater credibility. The Jews of the Arabian Diaspora may have engaged in proselytization, since imperial legislation of this period suggests that they engaged in it in Oriens.[37] The Arabs themselves may have been attracted to Jewish monotheism without proselytizing efforts on the part of the Jews. And if the South Arabian state embraced Judaism in the fifth century, the conversion of some of the Arab tribes that moved in its orbit to Judaism becomes understandable. Notable among these was Kinda,[38] which moved far and wide in the Peninsula and perhaps spread

[36] Depending on whether J. Ryckmans or A. F. L. Beeston is right in interpreting the evidence. The former believes that the kings of South Arabia adopted Judaism in the 5th century, while the latter denies it. For their respective views, see J. Ryckmans, "Le christianisme en Arabie du sud préislamique," in *L'Oriente cristiano nella storia della civiltà*, Accademia Nazionale dei Lincei (Rome, 1964), 426 ff; and A. F. L. Beeston, in *L'Arabie du sud*, I, 276–78.

[37] On the *Novella* of Theodosius II of the year 438, see Avi-Yonah, *Jews of Palestine*, 215; see also 147–48.

[38] On Judaism in Kinda, see Ibn Ḥazm, *Jamhara*, 491. Conversely, the Judaism of Kinda could give support to the proposition that the South Arabian state adopted Judaism. Kinda was a client of Ḥimyar in South Arabia, and the most natural explanation for its adoption of Judaism is the assumption that they adopted the religion of their overlords, in much the same way that the Arab clients of Byzantium adopted Christianity. It is noteworthy that Ibn Ḥazm reports on Kinda's Judaism immediately after speaking of Ḥimyar's adoption of it, and indeed limits his statement on the Judaizing Arabians to Ḥimyar and Kinda. Perhaps even the adoption of Christianity by Arab Najrān was partly a reflection of a desire on the part of the

Judaism with it. The process of conversion carried with it the realization that the Arabs and the Jews were descended from the patriarch Abraham. Thus Judaism was the agent of the Arabs' awareness of their descent from Ishmael. For those Arabs who were already aware of their Abrahamic and Ishmaelitic descent, this was a reminder; for those who were not, it was a revelation.

III

The concept of the "sons of Ishmael" is biblical; it is therefore important to discuss the views of biblicists and Semitists on the subject. The best and most recent study[39] traces the problem from biblical times to the period of the rise of Islam in the seventh century A.D.

In this work I. Ephʿal observes that the terms "Ishmael"/"Ishmaelite" are not used in the Bible after the mid-tenth century, during the Davidic monarchy; that the term "Arab" appears in the Bible for the first time in the second half of the eighth century, only after "Ishmaelite" had become obsolete; and that the two terms were never used concurrently in the Bible. He concludes that the use of "Arab" and "Ishmaelite" interchangeably is unjustified. The presumed kinship between the sons of Israel and the sons of Ishmael developed during the period of wandering in the wilderness when the Israelites sojourned at Kadesh Barnea, "apparently the center of the Ishmaelite confederation," while "the list of the Sons of Ishmael is not based on historical fact but is more in the nature of an ethnological *midrash* on Ishmael."[40]

The dialogue among biblical and Semitic scholars on this thorny problem involves F. Delitzsch, C. Thompson, J. Lewy, and F. Winnett, who saw in the Assyrian and North Arabian inscriptions a confirmation of the view that the Ishmaelites of the Bible were an Arab people.[41] This aspect of the problem is only remotely relevant here, but the following observations may be made on it:

1. On the question of kinship between the two peoples, it is difficult to dismiss the parts in Genesis which affirm this as unhistorical. The patriarchal part (chaps. 12–50), unlike the one that precedes it (chaps. 1–11), is not primeval history. While to some, Adam and Noah may appear as types, Abraham is a person and so are Hagar and Ishmael, who are presented with extremely intimate and significant details. To reject one portion of Genesis

Najrānites to express their independence from Ḥimyar, which according to one view, officially adopted Judaism; above, note 36.

[39] See I. Ephʿal, "'Ishmael' and 'Arab(s)'" 225–35; and idem, *The Ancient Arabs* (Leiden, 1982).

[40] For these views and conclusion, see ibid., 226, 227, 229.

[41] The first three scholars dealt with the Assyrian inscriptions, while the fourth discovered the north Arabian at Tayma': see ibid., 227–31.

and accept another in the history of Abraham presents obvious methodological difficulties.

2. As noted byEphʿal, the tribes mentioned in the Assyrian inscriptions as evidence of the Arabness of the Ishmaelites present difficulties to the views of the four Semitic scholars mentioned above. But Nebaioth, the first of the twelve tribes and sons of Ishmael, is a better link between the two concepts of Ishmaelism and Arabness.[42] This is a well-known people who survived well into Roman times and whose Arabness cannot be doubted. According to the biblical narrative, the other eleven names in the Ishmaelite list are Nebaioth's brothers. If he is Arab, so are the other eleven. According to this reasoning, the twelve sons of Ishmael could turn out to be Arab tribes.

3. The prominence given to Nebaioth of all the sons of Ishmael—the first to be mentioned and the eldest—suggests that the biblical sons of Ishmael were a vast confederation[43] of Arab tribes in northwestern Arabia, among whom the dominant tribe was that of Nebaioth. This seems to correspond with the historical reality about the Nabataeans of later times—their power and wide diffusion over a vast area in northwestern Arabia. Consequently, in the period from biblical to Macedonian times they must have absorbed the other eleven tribes of the confederation, which merged into the Nabataeans, although tribal traces remained, as in Duma (Dumāt al-Jandal). This endows the Nabataeans with a very distant antiquity, extending back to the time of the Israelite wandering, and this may well be the truth about them.

The correct ethnic identity of the biblical sons of Ishmael is a matter for biblicists and Semitists to decide. What matters in dealing with the pre-Islamic period, which may be termed the second inter-Testamental period, is what the Arabs, or a portion of them, *believed* regarding this concept. The Arabs of Koranic times in the seventh century believed that they were descended from Ishmael, and so they are the sons of Ishmael. Thus it is the cultural concept that is important here, not the historic reality of Ishmaelite

[42] That the Nabaiati of the Assyrian inscriptions, the Nebaioth of the Old Testament, and the Nabataean Arabs of the 4th and subsequent centuries are one and the same people has been convincingly demonstrated by E. C. Broome; for his article which gave the coup de grâce to the opposite view, see "Nabaiati, Nebaioth, and Nabataeans: The 'Linguistic Problem,'" *JSS* 18 (1973), 1–16.

[43] The Ishmaelites may after all, turn out to be neither Arab nor even one ethnic group. But they are a political and social entity as a confederation, and this is what is striking in the biblical narrative. The twelve tribes of Ishmael are not left in the biblical narrative with their individual names but are grouped together and given one name explicitly, the patronymic which unites them together—Ishmaelites. There is no doubt that what is involved here is the question of a political entity—an extensive and powerful Arab *ḥilf*, a confederation, if not an ethnic entity—and this is the one certain datum which can be extracted from the biblical narrative.

descent. That this belief in the descent of Ishmael among the Muslim Arabs of the seventh century does go back to pre-Islamic times has been established by the examination of some ecclesiastical texts. The Arabic texts pertaining to this problem will be discussed later.

Appendix I

Some Arab Bishops and Monks

In addition to the valuable chapter in Sozomen on the Christianity of the Arab *foederati*, on the Arabs as the sons of Ishmael, and on the Judaizing Arabs, there are important references to what he calls the bishops of the *Arabioi* and to some Arab monks.

I

In his chapter on the customs of different nations and churches Sozomen says that among the Arabs there are many bishops who serve as priests over villages.[1]

1. The statement clearly indicates that he actually spoke with the Arabs themselves on this point, and thus his information derives not from hearsay but personal knowledge.[2] Sozomen examined the Arab scene, which apparently interested him; this raises the value of his account of the Arabs in the important section of his work which has just been analyzed.

2. Those he observed are described as *Arabioi*, not *Saracēnoi*. It is practically certain that they are thus not the *foederati* he discussed in connection with Queen Mavia but Arab provincial *Rhōmaioi*. Sozomen, who was from Bethelia, would have met them personally, since these Arab *Rhōmaioi* lived not far from his native town in the Negev of Palaestina Tertia and also in the Provincia Arabia across Wādi ʿAraba. It is even possible that his use of *Arabioi*, not *Arabes*, may reflect a subtle difference, designed to distinguish the Arabs of the Provincia from the Arabs of the Peninsula. Thus *Arabioi* in the usage of the Greek historians of the period may be limited to the Rhomaic inhabitants of the Provincia Arabia. This conclusion is supported by the usage of Sozomen himself in the same passage, when he refers to the provinces of Cyprus and Phrygia in gentilic rather than in territorial terms.

3. The statement in Sozomen on the large number of bishops among the Arabs is confirmed by the large number of *kōmai* (κῶμαι) in Arabia listed in the *Descriptio Orbis Romani* of George of Cyprus, a work of the sixth century, but naturally reflecting the continuance of the situation as it was in the fifth century when Sozomen wrote. Their number is striking.[3]

4. The large number of bishops over the villages and the cities of the Arabs reflect the progress that Christianity was making among them in Sozomen's time. It

[1] *HE*, Book VII, chap. 19, p. 330, lines 14–15.

[2] The reliability of Sozomen's account has been discussed in a different context in *BAFOC*, 276.

[3] For the list of Arab *kōmai* see S. Vailhé, "La province ecclésiastique d'Arabie," *EO* 2 (1898–99), 169.

is also quite likely that these bishops were ethnically Arab. If so, they would have formed a part of the Arab episcopate in Oriens in the fifth century.

II

In Book VI of the *Historia Ecclesiastica* there are several chapters that deal with Christian monks and the spread of monasticism from Egypt to Oriens.

1. In two of these chapters Sozomen discusses some monks of Syria and Edessa respectively. In the first, Chapter 33, he lists the names of some famous monks, some of whom have Greek names, while others have distinctly Semitic ones. It is not always easy to determine whether a particular Semitic name is Arabic because of common roots with the cognate language, Aramaic, but Abdaleus (Ἀβδαλέως) is certainly Arabic ʿAbdalla with the Greek sigma at the end, and the chances are that Abbos (Ἀββῶς) is also Arabic ʿAbbūs.[4]

Chapter 34, mentions Gaddanas (Γαδδάνας) and Azizus (Ἀζίζος) as monks of Edessa. The second is certainly the Arabic name ʿAziz with the Greek sigma at the end, while Gaddanas could also be an Arabic name, morphologically a *nomen agentis* in the intensive form, derived from one of several Arabic roots.[5]

It is not easy to determine exactly when these monks lived. But it is amply clear from the context of his chapters on the monks that his references may be dated ca. 400. A statement in Chapter 34 suggests that their *floruit* may be extended to the middle of the fifth century. He says that God has given them longevity for furthering the interests of religion and specifically says that some of them survived to his own days.[6]

2. In addition to the short list of Arab monks that Sozomen gives, which documents what has been said elsewhere on the rise and spread of monasticism among the Arabs, there is a valuable statement that witnesses to the importance of monasticism for the propagation of Christianity among the Arabs. In praising the ascetic life of the monks, he says that they were actually instrumental in leading most of the Saracens, among others, into the straight path of Christianity.[7]

Appendix II

Ishmaelism: A Cautionary Note

Ishmaelism has been discussed here in two chapters and will be discussed in two more, "Ishmaelism" and "Byzantium and Mecca." In view of the importance of this concept in the history of the Arabs, especially to Koranic studies, a cautionary note is necessary to guard against any misapprehension.

1. This concept has been extracted from the works of two Greek authors, a

[4] For these two names, see *HE*, p. 289, lines 8, 9.

[5] For these two Arabic names, see ibid., line 27. Khaddān is known in the pre-Islamic Arabic onomasticon in connection with the death of Ḥujr, the father of the Kindite poet Imru' al-Qays. It appears in the second hemistich, which refers to that death: "maniyyatu Ḥujrin fī jiwāri ibn-Khaddāni"; see G. Olinder, *The Kings of Kinda*, 78.

[6] See ibid., 291, line 4.

[7] See ibid., lines 7–9.

church father, Theodoret, and an ecclesiastical historian, Sozomen. Both vouch for the reality of Ishmaelism in the genealogical sense among the Arabs of pre-Islamic times. They also go beyond this to suggest that the Ishmaelite consciousness of the Arabs went beyond the genealogical level to the "cultic." The Arabs venerated Ishmael and took pride in their descent from him, as if he was alive in their consciousnes, not a dead, remote figure of some two thousand years before; he also provided them with a model and a way of life.[1]

2. The two Greek sources that recorded these data on Ishmaelism were contemporary with this component in Arab cultural life. They were also primary sources for what they reported, since they knew the Arabs intimately, conversed with them, and were interested in them, both historically and theologically as a biblical people, descended from Abraham's firstborn. Their qualifications and credentials for the data they provide on Ishmaelism, both genealogical and cultic, are above suspicion.

3. In the chapters "Ishmaelism" and "Byzantium and Mecca," the Arabic sources on Ishmaelism in this proto-Byzantine period will be examined. They are full of legendary accounts, which have been eliminated in the preceding discussion. The confrontation of the two sets of sources—the Greek and the Arabic—on Ishmaelism was made in full conformity with Nöldeke's law: accept from the Arabic sources for pre-Islamic times only those elements that can be supported by the Greek. The confrontation has been effected on the two levels of Ishmaelism, the genealogical and the cultic, but the thrust is on the first.

4. I have been a minimalist in entertaining the references in the two Greek authors to the two levels of Ishmaelism. I accept without hesitation the genealogical one, namely, that some Arabs in the proto-Byzantine period *believed* in their Ishmaelite descent, but suspend judgment on the second, the cultic, because exactly what this meant in the cultural life of the pre-Islamic Arabs is not entirely clear from the laconic statements of the two authors. Nevertheless, I have presented the data from the Arabic sources pertaining to the second level for two reasons: (*a*) to accommodate the maximalist who accepts the data from the Greek authors on the two levels of Ishmaelism, a legitimate alternative to my conservative interpretation; and (b) to provide a framework in anticipation of possible future discoveries, both literary and epigraphic, which may confirm this position.

5. My conservative position is clearly reflected in the Preface and the Synthesis, where only the first level of Ishmaelism, the genealogical, is presented. The other level is relegated to the analytic part of the book, where it is discussed in the four chapters mentioned above.

[1] The Ishmael of Abrahamic times is not my concern; hence literature on him by biblical scholars is not included here. Only the concept of descent from Ishmael in the proto-Byzantine period is my concern, and not so much its validity as belief in it on the part of the Arabs or some of them. What biblical scholars and Semitists have said on the sons of Ishmael in early times falls outside the range of the present work. It is, therefore, sufficient to discuss recent articles that sum up biblical scholarship on the subject in the context of the new data extracted from the Greek sources and confronted with those from the Arabic, for example, I. Ephʿal's article, "'Ishmael' and 'Arab(s)'," and that of F. Winnet, "The Arabian Genealogies in the Book of Genesis," *Essays in Honor of Herbert Gordon May*, ed. H. T. Frank and W. L. Reed (New York, 1970).

X

Cyril of Scythopolis

Cyril of Scythopolis is a major source for the history of Arab Christianity in the fifth century, especially in Palestine.[1] We owe him our knowledge of the church of the Parembole in the Jordan Valley, and of other aspects of Arab Christianity and presence in Oriens.

I. The Parembole

This Arab enclave in the Holy Land was both a phylarchate and an episcopate; therefore the fortunes of the phylarchs as well as the bishops of the Parembole will be discussed here.[2]

A. The Episcopate of the Parembole

Petrus I

Petrus was the first phylarch-bishop of the Palestinian Parembole.[3] He was converted to Christianity when St. Euthymius miraculously cured his son, Terebon, who had had a dream that led his father to carry him from the Provincia Arabia to the Judaean desert where the two saints, Euthymius and Theoctistus, lived.[4] He was the first to be baptized[5] by Euthymius after his son was cured; he then changed his name to Petrus, which became his baptismal name.[6] The saint kept him and the other baptized Saracens in his cave for some forty days, gave them religious instruction, and then dismissed them.

[1] The standard edition is that of E. Schwartz, *Kyrillos von Skythopolis*, TU 49 (1939) (hereafter *Kyrillos*); useful are the footnotes in A. J. Festugière, *Les moines d'Orient* (Paris, 1962), II; see also the analysis of the Church of the Saracens in F. Thelamon, *Païens et chrétiens*, 123–47; the old work of R. Génier, *Vie de saint Euthyme le grand*, is still valuable.

[2] After Aspebetos and Terebon I, the phylarchs and the bishops of the Parembole are mentioned very briefly by Cyril. Hence reference to the phylarchs as well as the bishops of the Parembole, even when they belong to the 6th century, are included here. The episode involving the phylarchs Arethas and Aswad of the 6th century (*Kyrillos*, 75) will be discussed in *BASIC*

[3] For Petrus as phylarch Aspebetos, see above, Chap. 2, sec. IV.

[4] For the dream of Terebon and the circumstances of the miraculous healing, see *Kyrillos*, 19–21.

[5] In a small baptistry that Euthymius ordered constructed in a corner of his cave for baptizing the Saracens of Aspebetos after the miracle. It was still to be seen when Cyril wrote his account of St. Euthymius; ibid., 21.

[6] His adoption of the baptismal name Petrus may have been significant, reflecting his Arabic name, which might have been Sakhr or Jandala.

After Euthymius left his cave and founded his monastery, Petrus brought more Saracens to the saint for conversion. Petrus then engaged in some construction work: with the help of masons whom he brought with him he constructed a cistern, a bakery (*mancipium*), three cells for the saint, and an oratory or a church in their midst. For his part, Euthymius laid out for the Saracens, who wanted to be close to him, the plan of a church between his monastery and that of Theoctistus, and asked them to build their church according to his plan with the tents surrounding it. This was the first church of the Saracens of Petrus, and Euthymius assigned to it a presbyter and deacons.[7]

After the establishment of this church, the number of Saracens who flocked to the Parembole and its church increased considerably.[8] This made Euthymius decide to create a new diocese in the Jordan Valley composed of the Saracen community, which he had provided with the lower ranks of the clergy after its conversion. His choice fell on Petrus himself, and he wrote to Juvenal, the bishop of Jerusalem, recommending to him the consecration of Petrus as the first bishop of the Parembole. Petrus went up to Jerusalem, and Juvenal consecrated him there.

1. The date cannot be determined with absolute precision, but it must have been around 427, since it took place shortly before 428 or 429, when Juvenal consecrated the church in the lavra of St. Euthymius.[9]

2. The question may be raised whether this consecration violated the rights of the bishop of Caesarea, the metropolis of Palestine. Perhaps it did, but the strong ecclesiastics involved in the consecration, the formidable combination of Euthymius and Juvenal, must have made any opposition from Caesarea pointless. The metropolitan of the city probably acquiesced in this eminently realistic and appropriate decision to have the Saracen Petrus consecrated by the closest bishop to him, Juvenal.[10]

3. That a phylarch was chosen as the bishop of the new diocese should cause no surprise. Petrus was a zealous Christian who for years had led the converted Saracen community and had increased its numbers since his arrival in Palestine. His outstanding qualities must have attracted the attention of Euthymius, as they were to attract the attention of Juvenal later, and thus he was the natural choice to lead a community of Saracens who probably at this

[7] See *Kyrillos*, 24–25. This first church of the Saracens in the Jordan Valley is located between the monastery of Theoctistus in Wādi-Dabur and that of Euthymius in Sahel; Génier, *Euthyme*, 104.

[8] Génier makes Petrus the moving spirit behind the increase in the number of Saracens in the Parembole and of their conversion; Génier, *Euthyme*, 102. This is not explicitly stated by Cyril, but Petrus' missionary zeal is implied.

[9] See Honigmann, "Juvenal of Jerusalem," *DOP* 5 (1950), 218–19.

[10] Honigmann points out that the "Parembolae apparently belonged to the municipal area of Jerusalem"; ibid., 219.

stage spoke nothing but Arabic. It is almost certain that the priest and the deacons whom Euthymius had assigned to the community were also Arab ecclesiastics, recruited locally in Palaestina Prima. This ensured perfect communication between pastor and parish.

4. Thus Petrus appears as the first in a line of Parembole bishops that survived well into the sixth century.[11] But he was also the first phylarch of this small community, and this raises the question whether or not he continued to hold the phylarchate after his consecration, and thus held the episcopate and the phylarchate simultaneously. He probably continued to hold the phylarchate for a few years more until his son, Terebon, was of age to shoulder that responsibility.[12] The latest possible *terminus* is 449, the date of the Latrocinium when Auxolaus, and not Petrus, was the bishop representing the Parembole.

5. Four years or so elapsed between Petrus' consecration as bishop of the Parembole and his participation in the Council of Ephesus in 431. He no doubt continued his missionary work in the Jordan Valley, and relations between him, Euthymius, and Juvenal must have matured. It was in this period, after Euthymius had received eleven new inmates, that he asked Petrus to build small cells for them and to furnish and adorn the church of the lavra. Thus the lavra of St. Euthymius owes its construction to the energy of this Saracen phylarch/bishop. This church was consecrated on May 7, 428 or 429 by Juvenal, who came down from Jerusalem for the occasion.[13]

The climax of his career was his participation in the Council of Ephesus, which also represented the climax of his association with both the saint and the bishop of Jerusalem.[14] Before his departure for Ephesus he visited Euthymius, who exhorted him to side with Cyril of Alexandria and Acacius of Melitene[15] against Nestorius, and do what seemed right to them. Petrus followed his advice, and on his return from Ephesus visited Euthymius and informed him of all that had taken place at the council.[16] Thus the last reference to Petrus in Cyril of Scythopolis is to his orthodoxy at Ephesus. In subscribing to the definition of faith at Ephesus he recalls another Arab bishop, Pamphilius of the fourth century, who subscribed to the Orthodox definition of faith at Nicaea.[17]

The hagiographer is primarily interested in saints, not in the bishops of

[11] Thus the birth of the new diocese of the Parembole is hailed by Cyril who, in the middle of the 6th century, was aware of the long line of its bishops; *Kyrillos*, 25, lines 8–9.

[12] On this, see above, 47–49, but cf. Génier, *Euthyme*, 112.

[13] *Kyrillos*, 26

[14] On his activities at Ephesus, see below, 214–16.

[15] It is noteworthy that Euthymius was a native of Melitene and that Acacius had been his tutor there before his elevation to the episcopate.

[16] *Kyrillos*, 33.

[17] For Pamphilius, see *BAFOC*, 330–34.

the Parembole. Consequently Petrus' fortunes after Ephesus are not recorded, although his death is mentioned incidentally in the section of the *Vita Euthymii* on the Council of Chalcedon,[18] in which another bishop, John, participated. But he was already dead in 449, because in the same section Cyril mentions Auxolaos as the representative of the Parembole at the Latrocinium, which took place in that year. Thus Petrus must have died sometime between 431 and 449. It is practically certain that he was buried in the Parembole, either in the church that Euthymius planned for the Saracens or in the monastery of St. Euthymius which he had built.

After Petrus I

Petrus I is the only bishop of the Parembole about whom the hagiographer is expansive. The other four are shadowy figures, and Cyril mentions only the first two:

1. Auxolaus,[19] who participated in the Council of Ephesus (449).
2. John,[20] who participated in the Council of Chalcedon (451).
3. Valens,[21] who took part in the Council of Jerusalem (518).
4. Petrus[22] II, who signed the sentence against Anthimius at the Council of Jerusalem (536).

All the bishops of the Parembole were Orthodox, except for Auxolaus; he died soon after the Latrocinium, and the Parembole returned to Orthodoxy. Whether these bishops were all Arab is difficult to tell. The presumption is that they were. Petrus I certainly was, and the Greek or Latin names of these bishops do not argue against their Arab origin, since it was customary to assume such names on consecration.

Hagiographic literature is relatively informative on the first three of the five bishops of the Parembole but practically silent on the two, Valens and Petrus II, of the sixth century, just as it is not informative on the phylarchs of the Parembole. Only their names are known, and they are mentioned as participating in Church councils. Whether they were related genealogically to the line of the phylarchs is also unclear.

The later history of the Parembole episcopate is unknown. It is possible that it survived until the Persian conquest. But in any case it is safe to infer that there were bishops of the Parembole about the middle of the sixth century. The phylarch Terebon II was then flourishing, and it is inconceivable that the episcopate disappeared while the phylarchate survived. The two insti-

[18] *Kyrillos*, 41, lines 11–12.
[19] Auxolaus is discussed below, 216–17.
[20] John is discussed below, 217–19.
[21] J. D. Mansi, *Sacrorum conciliorum nova et amplissima collectio*, VIII, col. 1071.
[22] Ibid., col. 1174.

tutions were inseparable from the time of their founder, Petrus I, who thus was the first to unite in his person the episcopate and phylarchate of the Parembole.

B. The Phylarchate of the Parembole

The Saracens flourished in the Parembole for some two centuries and had other phylarchs and bishops, but Petrus I remains the most important figure. However, in view of the paucity of source references to the phylarchs after Petrus, it is desirable to gather together the few that have survived (almost exclusively hagiographical) to this Arab phylarchal presence in Palaestina Prima. As Petrus I has been treated extensively both as phylarch and bishop,[23] this section will deal exclusively with the phylarchs who came after him.

Terebon I

Of the phylarchs who came after Petrus I, the one on whom Cyril of Scythopolis is informative is his son, Terebon I. There are important references to him, related to both the political life of the Parembole and the religious life of the Christian community in the Jordan Valley.

1. The first question that arises, is that of Terebon's dates. It was argued earlier that he was probably too young to assume the phylarchate after his father, Aspebetos, was consecrated bishop of the Parembole around 427, but that he took office a few years later, possibly when his father died. It was also argued that he was the phylarch not of Arabia but of Palaestina Prima, of the Parembole in the Jordan Valley.[24] If the hagiographer is silent on the year in which he assumed the phylarchate, he is not on the year and manner of his death, which took place around 485, as will be discussed below. Thus he must have been in office as phylarch of Palestine for almost half a century.

An important episode concerning him is related by the hagiographer for the years 459–460.[25] Circumstances forced him to cross provincial boundaries and travel from the Parembole to Bostra in the Provincia Arabia. The intrigues of a co-phylarch in Arabia landed him in prison, where he languished until Euthymius came to his rescue and wrote to Antipatrus, the bishop of Bostra, for help toward his release. The latter did so and sent him back to Palestine with a *viaticum.* The episode is important and informative on various matters: (1) as has been argued before, it clearly implies that Terebon was not the phylarch of Arabia but of Palestine; (2) it documents phylarchal presence in the Provincia Arabia at this time, 459–460; (3) it gives a glimpse

[23] For this see above, Chap. 2, sec. IV.

[24] For this, see above, 48.

[25] See *Kyrillos*, 52–53.

of strife in Oriens between phylarchs who belonged to different tribal groups; and (4) it brings out the influence of powerful ecclesiastics on the course of secular affairs. The saint of the Jordan Valley writes to the metropolitan bishop of Bostra to intervene with the governor of Arabia for the release of a Palestinian phylarch put in jail in a province not his own. The nature of the offense that caused the governor to put the Roman phylarch in jail remains unknown and something of a puzzle.[26]

Finally, it is clear from the account of the fortunes of Terebon that the phylarchate of the Parembole was hereditary, since Terebon succeeded his father, Petrus, and he in turn was succeeded by members of the same house. It is noteworthy that on his conversion he did not change his Arabic name to a Christian (Greek or Latin) one, as his father had done when he adopted the baptismal name Petrus.[27] What his contribution during his long phylarchate was to the security of the monastic establishment can only be guessed, since he had a special relationship with Euthymius and must have been its guardian in the Jordan Valley.[28]

2. Although Terebon was a phylarch and thus belongs to the secular history of the Parembole, more is known about his relation to the Church and Christianity than about his secular history. This is not surprising, since the relationship between the phylarchate and the episcopate was very close, and Petrus I united the two in his own person. The following are the significant episodes related by Cyril about Terebon; all are important for giving a glimpse of the attachment of these phylarchs to Christianity.

a. Before his baptism by Euthmius, half of his body had been paralyzed; obeying a dream-vision of Euthymius who beckoned him, he went to the saint and was cured by him.[29] If his healing made such a great impression on others, it must have made an even greater impression on him. The miraculous story was alive in the consciousness of his grandson, Terebon II, who told it to Cyril more than a century later. Since he had been afflicted with paralysis while he was still in Persian territory, it is possible that his father's decision to

[26] See also above, Chap. 4, app. 2.

[27] By contrast, the names of all the bishops of the Parembole are Christian Greek, or Latin, which was natural.

[28] The fortunes of the episcopate and the phylarchate of the Parembole during the insurrection of 451–453 are unknown. During this period the monk Theodosius was in charge of Jersualem, which Juvenal had fled after his return from Chalcedon. *Comes* Dorotheus hurried back from Moabitis, where he was battling Saracen invaders of Palaestina Tertia, to restore order. Jerusalem, according to the *Notitia Dignitatum*, had stationed in it the *Equites Mauri Illyriciani*. Whether Dorotheus invoked the help of Terebon and the *foederati* of the Parembole is not clear, but at least he must have given some protection to the Orthodox monastic community from Monophysitic encroachments. In the course of these two years Euthymius took refuge at Rouba; *Kyrillos*, 44. For Jerusalem in this biennium, see Honigmann, *Juvenal*, 247–57.

[29] For an account of this, see *Kyrillos*, 18–21.

leave for Roman territory was partly inspired by desire to have his son cured by the miraculous powers he had heard Christian saints were possessed with.

b. After being himself the object of a healing miracle by the thaumaturge Euthymius, Terebon's wife, a Saracen like himself, was also the object of a miracle. He brought her to the saint and implored him to pray that she might conceive; this the saint did, and prophesied that she would bear three sons. One of these was Petrus II, the father of Terebon II, the phylarch who, around 550, told Cyril this story, confirmed by the testimony of others.[30] Cyril's account also makes it clear that one of the three sons born to Terebon's wife was Petrus II, the father of Terebon II. This makes it practically certain that he was the intervening phylarch who ruled after the death of Terebon I, around 485, and before Terebon II, who flourished about the middle of the sixth century.

c. After the return of Euthymius from Rouba, where he took refuge for two years, (451–453), another miracle involving Terebon I occurred. The phylarch was worshiping in the church of the lavra of Euthymius[31] and was standing near the altar with his hands on the "chancel" of the presbyterion when he suddenly saw fire descending from the sky over the altar; the fire covered Euthymius like a veil from the commencement of the doxology until its end.[32] Seized with fear, Terebon retreated to the narthex of the church where he belonged, and, in obedience to Scripture (Lev. 15:31), never again ventured to lean on the "chancel" of the presbyterion.

The miracle sheds light on the piety of the phylarch, his *pietas* toward Euthymius, and the possibility that he unconsciously permitted himself to leave the narthex of the church and proceed further to the chancel because the church was built by his father, Petrus! The account incidentally testifies to the strength and soundness of the oral tradition, which had preserved the history of the phylarchs of the Parembole: Cyril says that he heard this from one of the anchorites, Kyriakus, who had heard it from Terebon I himself. Terebon II was the chief informant of Cyril on the history of his house; this indicates that the traditions of the family were kept alive by word of mouth from father

[30] Ibid., 35–36. The miracle must have happened sometime between the Council of Ephesus (431) and the Latrocinium (449), since this is its place in the narrative of Cyril. Terebon's wife is referred to as a *Saracēnissa*. Whether one or both of his anonymous sons attained to the phylarchate after Petrus II is not clear.

[31] On this miracle, see *Kyrillos*, 45.

[32] On this miracle, see also Festugière's valuable footnotes on church service and architecture; *Moines*, 99 notes 79–83. On the miracles in Cyril's work, see B. Flusin, *Miracle et histoire dan l'oeuvre de Cyrille de Scythopolis*, Études augustiniennes (Paris, 1983), perceptively reviewed by L. Rydèn in *BZ* 77 (1984), 301–2. "Chancel" in the above text is used in the strict sense of a barrier that separated the sanctuary from the faithful, the iconostasis of later times; Festugière, *Moines*, 99 note 81.

to son for more than a hundred years.[33] This does not preclude, of course, that there were also written records in the possession of the house of Petrus.

d. The last mention of Terebon I in Cyril's work comes in the *Vita* of Kyriakus, in connection with the separation of the monasteries of Euthymius and Theoctistus by Paul, who became *hēgoumenos* after the death of Abbot Longinus.[34] This account relates that Terebon I was about to die, and the year is given as twelve years after the death of St. Euthymius, thus 485. Before his death, Terebon I left to the two monasteries a sufficient endowment (ἱκανὰ πράγματα), but Paul appropriated both the endowment and the corpse of Terebon. As a result of Paul's arrogance and high-handedness, the two monasteries became separated. Paul gave two hundred *nomismata* for the other monastery to acquire a hospice (ξενοδοχεῖον), which the monks of the monastery of St. Euthymius did.[35]

The passage is valuable for determining the date of Terebon I's death, the end of his phylarchate, and the beginning of that of his son, Petrus II. It is also testimony to the piety of Terebon I and his attachment to the monastery of St. Euthymius, the saint to whom he owed the restoration of his health, the birth of his children after his wife was cured of her sterility, and his release from the prison of Bostra. He had been his contemporary for almost a half century.

The significance of Paul's possession of his corpse is not clear. Perhaps it helped him lay claims to all the property of Terebon I which, according to Cyril, he appropriated. Perhaps he wanted to curry favor with the successor and son of Terbon I. In any case, the body of the phylarch was deemed important enough to be held by the *hēgoumenos*,[36] and he probably kept it for burial in the monastery.

Not much is known about the phylarchs of the Parembole after the death of Terebon I in 485. The barest outline, however, is available and yields the following.

[33] Cf. the survival of the tradition of Queen Mavia's victories in the 5th century, which Sozomen heard some hundred years after they had taken place; see *BAFOC*, 444, It is also noteworthy that Terebon I was the informant of Kyriakus, who in turn was the informant of Cyril concerning the miracle (above, note 30); see *Kyrillos*, 45.

[34] For this account, see *Kyrillos*, 226. This was missed by both Génier and Aigrain in their accounts of Terebon and the Parembole; see Aigrain, "Arabie," col. 1195, where he also misdates the death of Terebon I and the accession of his son Petrus; it was in 485, not 483.

[35] The reference to 200 *nomismata* suggests that the endowment Terebon I left was not property but money, or partly money. It is tantalizing to think that part of this came to him from the central government, as *annona foederatica*.

[36] Cf. the attempt of the Saracens to have the corpse of St. Simeon Stylite, discussed above, Chap. 8, app. 1.

It is established that Terebon I died in 485. The presumption is that his son, Petrus II, immediately acceded to the phylarchate of the Parembole, but it is not clear how long he ruled as phylarch. The other *terminus* is the middle of the sixth century, when Terebon II was the phylarch of the Parembole and was informing Cyril on the history of his family.[37]

As far as the phylarchs of the Parembole are concerned, there is reference to only two shadowy names, Petrus II and Terebon II.

Petrus II

Petrus II is not explicitly attested as a phylarch by Cyril; he is merely referred to as the eldest son of Terebon, who had two other sons who are not named.[38] Nevertheless, Petrus II can be considered the phylarch who succeeded Terebon I.[39] The phylarchate was in the house of Aspebetos, and Petrus II was the son of Terebon I, established as phylarch, and the father of Terebon II, also established as phylarch. It is, therefore, natural to assume that he also became phylarch after the death of his father in 485. He could not have been the bishop, Petrus II, who participated in the Council of Jerusalem in 536, as this date is too late for him. Furthermore, the fact that Cyril mentions him by name implies that he was not unknown, and so he must have been either a phylarch or a bishop, but most probably a phylarch; otherwise there would have been a long lacuna in the history of the phylarchate from Terebon I in 485 to Terebon II around 550. Besides, if he had been bishop, the hagiographer Cyril would certainly have said so.

Petrus II would have been the phylarch of the Parembole in the reign of Anastasius, and yet he is never mentioned in contexts relating specifically to that period, such as the devastating raids on the Parembole[40] around the year 500. The omission is puzzling, but a key to understanding it may be found in the fact that the Orthodox phylarch of the Parembole was living under an emperor inclined toward Monophysitism. It is possible that there was friction between the phylarchs and the central government that led to their withdrawal from the service, in much the same way that the Monophysite Ghassānid phylarchs[41] withdrew during the reign of the Chalcedonian Justin I.

[37] Cyril entered the lavra of St. Euthymius in 544, where he stayed until 554; during this period he collected the material for his *Lives*. In 555 he entered the lavra of St. Sabas, where he wrote the *Life* of St. Sabas. As the phylarch Terebon II was one of his informants, he must have come in contact with him around 555. On Terebon II, as the informant of Cyril, see *Kyrillos*, 18, lines 13–15 and 36, line 10. For Cyril and the composition of the Lives, see *Kyrillos*, 408–15 and Festugière, *Moines*, III, 9–16.

[38] *Kyrillos*, 36.

[39] As does Aigrain, "Arabie," col. 1195.

[40] See below, Sec. v.

[41] This will be discussed at length in *BASIC*.

Some support for this may be derived from the language of the hagiographer when he speaks of the Saracen invasion of the Parembole around 500 in the reign of Anastasius.[42] After the destruction of the tents of the Parembole, they are restored, but instead of saying that the phylarch of the Parembole effected the restoration, the hagiographer uses the non-technical term οἱ πρῶτοι, which could suggest that the Parembole at the time had no official phylarch.[43]

Terebon II

Nothing is known about him except that he was Cyril's informant on the history of the Parembole, its phylarchs and bishops. Cyril, however, refers to him as the "renowned phylarch in this region" (ὁ κατὰ τὴν χώραν ταύτην περιβόητος τῶν Σαρακηνῶν φύλαρχος). Either he was celebrated for his piety, loyalty, and endowment of other monastic establishments, which would have been in conformity with the tradition of his house, or he revived the Parembole militarily after a period of eclipse when, for instance, in the reign of Anastasius, it could not defend itself against Saracen raids.[44]

The sources are silent on the phylarchs of the Parembole after the last reference to Terebon II in the 550s. But this should not argue for their disappearance. On the contrary, one could infer from the positive reference to "the renowned phylarch, Terebon" that they survived until the Persian invasion of the seventh century. The emergence, around 530, of the powerful Ghassānid phylarchate, which watched the oriental *limes* in its entirety throughout the sixth century, would have protected them against invasions from the Arabian Peninsula such as were mounted in the reign of Anastasius, and would have made their participation superfluous. Consequently their history now most probably has to be sought within the framework of the history of Palestine as a Holy Land, related to the symbiosis between Parembole and monastery and the protection of the latter in the Jordan Valley from local Saracen raids. Furthermore, the phylarchs would have had unruffled relations with the emperors of the sixth century from Justin I onward since these, like themselves, were Orthodox. Thus the simplest way to explain their disappearance from the sources is that they had no historians after Cyril. And had it not been for the incidental references to them in the pages of his *Vitae*, the history of this attractive Arab enclave in the Holy Land would have remained a closed chapter. Finally, it is possible that the religiosity of the phylarchs of the

[42] See *Kyrillos*, 67. The term φυλάρχειν however, appears in Cyril a few years later. If used with technical accuracy, it would imply that the phylarchate of the Parembole had by then been restored; see below, 204.

[43] Ibid., 18, lines 14–15.

[44] Ibid., 67–68.

Parembole allied them more with Christianity than with military duties, and thus conceivably their martial spirit faded, especially since military challenges from the Arabian Penninsula were contained by the covering shield of the powerful Ghassānid phylarchate.[45]

II. The Arab Monks of Palestine

The association of Aspebetos' family with Euthymius also resulted in Arab involvement in monasticism in Palaestina Prima. The two most important members of the Arab monastic establishment were Maris and Stephanus, both of whom were *hēgoumenoi* of Euthymius' monasteries. Maris became the head of the first lavra of Euthymius, which he gave to Theoctistus, his intimate associate;[46] Stephanus became the head of the second. A third Arab, Elias, became patriarch of Jerusalem. Cyril of Scythopolis is the chief informant on all three.

Maris

Maris was Aspebetos' brother-in-law, and emigrated with him and his group from Persia. His life was also touched by St. Euthymius.

1. After the saint healed Aspebetos' son, Maris was baptized by Euthymius.[47]

2. After the forty days that the converted community stayed in the *koinobion*, during which they were instructed in the Christian faith, Maris decided to stay in the lavra. He renounced the world and never left the lavra, having become one of its monks. He gave all his wealth, which was considerable, for the construction and enlargement of the monastery,[48] which thus represents the first recorded instance of an Arab religious endowment in the Holy Land.[49]

3. After the death of Theoctistus, Euthymius' companion, in 466, Maris became the *hēgoumenos* of the lavra. Euthymius, who had come to the lavra and stayed there for his companions' last days, considered the aged Maris worthy of leading the monastic community and appointed him to the hegoumenate. He died two years after his appointment. Euthymius came and deposited his remains in the tomb of Theoctistus.[50]

[45] Cf. what happened to Dāwūd, the religious Salīḥid king, for whom see below, 257–58.

[46] Not related to Aspebetos.

[47] See *Kyrillos*, 22.

[48] Ibid.

[49] Cf. the religious endowments of the Arabs of Mesopotamia, *BAFOC*, 420–21; also those of Muʿayn, the Arab commander in the army of Shāpūr II, in A. Musil, *The Middle Euphrates* (New York, 1927), 18 note, 14; 345.

[50] See *Kyrillos*, 55a; also Festugière's note on the exact death of Theoctistus on 3 September 466; *Moines*, 108 note 115. The name "Maris" is a Semitic name, and must be either Syriac

Stephanus

Stephanus is described by Cyril not as *Saracēnos* but as Ἄραψ; he, too, became the *hēgoumenos* of the *koinobion* of St. Euthymius. The followng facts are recorded by Cyril.

1. In 514 on the death of Simeon, the *hēgoumenos* of the *koinobion* of St. Euthymius, Stephanus became the new leader of the monastic community. When his brother Procopius died, he inherited his property and gave it to the monastery.[51]

2. He remained *hēgoumenos* for twenty-one years and died in 535, having enlarged and enriched the *koinobion* from his own inherited property and left it six hundred *nomismata*.[52]

3. The last mention of him in the *Life* of Euthymius comes in the chapter that recounts the theft of gold from the monastery. Cosmas and Chrysippos, the guardians of the cross, had given the *koinobion* portions of the True Cross. During his hegoumenate, Stephanus had inserted one of them in the cross of gold, adorned by gems, that he had ordered for the monastery.[53]

Cyril's description of Stephanus as Ἄραψ and not Σαρακηνός suggests that he was a Roman citizen,[54] hailing from the Provincia Arabia or some limitrophe province in Oriens where the Arab element was dominant. This is corroborated by the fact that his brother is called Procopius and was priest of the church at Caesarea. They must have been Hellenized Arabs, possibly of the Provincia Arabia, and had it not been for the incidental biographical comment of the hagiographer on his ethnic origin, no one would have suspected that the *hēgoumenos* of the *koinobion* of Euthymius, who had the name Stephanus, was an Arab. This suggests that many of the ecclesiastical and secular figures who appear in the sources with Greek and Roman names could have been Arabs.

Elias

Like Stephanus, Elias is described by Cyril as coming from Arabia;[55] as a result, all ecclesiastical historians have referred to him as an Arab, which

---

or Arabic. If the final letter is the Greek *sigma* which attaches to proper nouns, then his name would be Mari, a Christian name celebrated in the Land of the Two Rivers, whence Maris came; it could also be Arabic from the root *m-r-y*. If the final *sigma* is a radical and not the Greek letter, then the name could be derived form the root *m-r-s*, and it can be either Māris or Maris.

[51] See *Kyrillos*, 68.

[52] Ibid., 68–69.

[53] Ibid., 69.

[54] Ibid., 68, line 7.

[55] He does not actually say that he was Arab, as he had said about Stephanus, but there is no doubt that "Arab" (Ἄραψ) would have described him accurately: that is, a Roman

is practically certain. The following facts are extracted from Cyril's *Vita Euthymii*:

1. Elias was educated in one of the Nitrian monasteries in Egypt together with his companion Martyrius the Cappadocian, but the turbulence generated in Egypt by the fiercely Monophysitic patriarch of Alexandria, Timothy Aelurus, drove the two from the Nitrian Mountains to seek refuge in the lavra of Euthymius in 457. The saint took special interest in them and prophesied that both of them would become partiarchs of Jerusalem.[56]

2. Euthymius used to take them with him to the desert of Koutila on January 14 and stay there until Palm Sunday, in company with other anchorites, notably Gerasimus. As the cells of the lavra of Euthymius were very narrow and uncomfortable, Elias went down to Jericho and built a cell outside the city. Here, in the time of Cyril, were to be found holy men and celebrated monasteries.[57]

3. The last association of Elias with Euthymius is in the section that describes the death of the saint (January, 473), which reverberated in Palestine. Both Elias and Martyrius wept, even after the saint was buried. The patriarch of Jerusalem, Anastasius, who had come for the funeral, asked them to come to see him often in Jerusalem.[58] Patriarch Anastasius came again to the lavra of Euthymius, after the ceremony of the translation of his relics that took place on May 7, 473. Immediately afterward he took Martyrius and Elias back with him to Jerusalem and ordained them priests of the church of the Anastasis.[59]

Cyril also recounts the following in his *Vita* of St. Sabas (439–532), which describes Elias' career after the death of Euthymius:

1. In 494, after the death of Patriarch Sallustius, Elias was elected patriarch of Jerusalem. He built a monastery near the episcopal mansion and gath-

---

citizen of Arab origin coming from one of the provinces that were ethnically Arab, such as the Provincia Arabia; "Saracen" would have implied that he was not a Roman citizen. Schwartz takes Arabia to mean the Provincia Arabia (*Kyrillos*, Register, p. 282, s.v. Arabia). On the other hand, Arabia here may have been the Ptolemaic nome in Egypt, visited by and known to St. Egeria as such. In support of this, it may be said that Elias had gone to one of the Nitrian monasteries in Egypt for his education, and if he had been from the Provincia Arabia, the chances are he would have gone to a monastery in Palestine, where monasticism had spread widely. There is no way of telling which Arabia is meant. If the latter, it would be a remarkable survival of old administrative nomenclature relevant to the discussion of Arabia Nova among Late Roman historians; see Bowersock, *Roman Arabia*, 145, 146. For the Arabian provenance of Elias, see *Kyrillos*, 51, line 5; further on Elias, see below, App. 4.

[56] See *Kyrillos*, 51.

[57] Ibid. Other references to Elias the anchorite in the desert of Rouba may be found, ibid, 56, lines 26–28; 57; line 19.

[58] See ibid., 60.

[59] Ibid., 61–62.

ered around him the ascetics of the church of the Anastasis, who had been scattered until then around the Tower of David, assigning them cells and providing them with all the necessary resources.[60]

2. At a later date he laid the foundation of the New Church of the Mother of God (Theotokos) in Jerusalem. About 530 St. Sabas, during his visit to Constantinople, asked Justinian to complete the building of the church.[61]

3. His relations with St. Sabas, whom he knew from the days of Euthymius, remained close after his election to the patriarchate of Jerusalem.

(*a*) A certain monk, Jacob, wanted to found another lavra on the same ground as that of the lavra of Sabas. After he repented and gave up the attempt, Elias sent men from Jerusalem to dismantle his establishment.[62] (*b*) He figured in Sabas' attempt to have John Hesychastes ordained in Jerusalem, in the period 497–498. After learning that he had already been consecrated a bishop, he allowed him to remain a solitary.[63] (*c*) In 501 he went to the lavra of St. Sabas, dedicated its Great Church of the Mother of God (which had been recently constructed by St. Sabas), and built a sacred altar.[64] (*d*) When Sabas disappeared from his lavra into the desert and inmates of the lavra missed him and took him for dead, they went to Jerusalem and invoked the aid of Elias, patriarch of Jerusalem since 494, to appoint a new *hēgoumenos* for them. But Elias would not, assuring them that no harm had come to the saint. His confidence was justified when Sabas appeared in Jerusalem for the Feast of the Dedication of the two basilicas, the Martyrium (Golgotha) and the Anastasis. Elias asked him to return to his lavra, but Sabas refused, and

[60] Ibid., 115–16. On this *spoudaeon*, see J. Wilkinson, *Jerusalem Pilgrims before the Crusades* (Warminster, Eng., 1977), 161 s.v. "Spoudaeon of the Anastasis." Dr. Wilkinson tells me that on this site now stands the Lutheran Church of the Redeemer, as stood in Crusader times the Church of St. Mary the Latin.

[61] See *Kyrillos*, 175 on the νέαν τῆς Θεοτόκου ἐκκλησίαν. R. Janin attributes to him the building of another church in Jerusalem, that of St. Helena; *DHGE*, 15, s.v. Elie (no. 22), for which see below, App. 5. Elias left the church unfinished and S. Vailhé suggests this was due to lack of funds; S. Vailhé, "Répertoire alphabétique des monastères de Palestine," *ROC* 5 (1900), 27. But the patriarch's record of building suggests that he was a good administrator who suffered from no lack of funds, and he helped others financially in their building programs. The most plausible explanation is that he started it just before his exile in 516. It was later built and completed by Justinian at the instance of St. Sabas when he visited Constantinople in 531, and the dedication took place in 543. Procopius gave a detailed description of the difficulties encountered in the building of the church and also of its splendors after it was completed; see *Buildings*, V.VI. For this church, see Wilkinson, *Pilgrims*, 166, s.v. "New St. Mary"; and H. Vincent and F. M. Abel, *Jerusalem* (Paris, 1922), I, 912–19. For recent archeological work involving this church, see N. Avigad, *Discovering Jerusalem* (Nashville, 1983), 229–46.

[62] See *Kyrillos*, 130.

[63] Ibid., 207.

[64] See ibid., 117.

informed him of the revolt of sixty of its inmates. Elias' firmness won the day, and Sabas agreed to return. Elias sent the monks of the lavra a letter assuring them that their *hēgoumenos* was alive and staying with him and advising them in strong terms to obey him. Thus Elias' intervention ensured the return of Sabas to his lavra.[65] (*e*) On his return to the lavra, the rebellious sixty inmates separated themselves from the community and moved to a place south of Tekoa, where they built a few cells and called this the New Lavra. After learning its location, Sabas visited them and found the community in disarray. He asked Patriarch Elias to build a regular convent for them. Elias gave him a pound of gold, and Sabas stayed some five months with the community of deserters, during which he used the money to build a bakery and a church in 507. Elias was again involved with the New Lavra when its *hēgoumenos* Agapetos discovered that four of its monks held heretical views. After consulting with Elias and obtaining his permission, he expelled the monks from the monastery.[66] (*f*) In 511 he sent Sabas, with other *hēgoumenoi* of the monastic establishment in Palestine, to Constantinople in order to present the case for Orthodoxy before the Monophysite emperor Anastasius and to guard the peace of the church of Jerusalem and Palestine against imperial displeasure. He also sent a letter to Anastasius.[67] (*g*) The final encounter of Elias and Sabas took place in Jerusalem in 515, in connection with the case of the monk Abraamius, who had been excommunicated by Platon, the bishop of Karateia. Both came to Sabas at the Great Lavra, and he decided to take them to Jerusalem and present their case to Elias. When he asked whether the excommunication could be annulled, Elias answered that it was uncanonical to annul the excommunication order of a fellow bishop, especially if he was still alive. He recommended that Abraamius return to his bishop and be absolved by him, which was what happened.[68] (*h*) Elias was evidently responsible for the erection of monasteries in the region of Jericho during the period of his patriarchate in Jerusalem. These are referred to in the text of Cyril as "the monasteries of the blessed Elias" and "the monasteries of Archbishop Elias."[69]

[65] Ibid., 121–22. The text of his letter is preserved on p. 122.

[66] Ibid., 123, 124–25.

[67] See ibid., 139–41. The letter of Elias to Anastasius may be found on p. 141. Elias' involvement in the Christological disputes of the period between the Chalcedonians and the Monophysites has been told many times in standard histories of these controversies; there is no need to repeat them in this book. A lucid resume may be found in R. Janin's article on Elias in *DHGE* 15, s.v. Elie (no. 22).

[68] See *Kyrillos*, 246. This tells something about Elias, his correctness and scrupulous adherence to canon law, although he was the archbishop and presumably could override the bishop of Krateia.

[69] Ibid., 161, lines 7–8 and 171, lines 19–20.

Owing to the recalcitrance of Alexander, its *hēgoumenos*, one of these became the Monastery of the Eunuchs.[70]

4. Finally, after a bitter struggle with the imperial government and with the rising tide of Monophysitism, the emperor decided to depose Elias. He instructed Olympius of Caesarea, the *dux* of Palestine, to give Elias the choice between deposition and submission. Elias refused and was driven from his episcopal seat and exiled to Ayla[71] on the Gulf of Eilat in 516.

5. In June, Sabas and Stephanus, the *hēgoumenos* of the lavra of Euthymius, and Euthalius, the *hēgoumenos* of the monasteries of Elias in Jericho, went to Ayla to visit Elias, who announced to them the death of Emperor Anastasius and prophesied his own imminent death. Before he died he gave directions for governing the monasteries he had founded and supervised during his two-year exile in Ayla.[72]

III. The Languages of the Liturgy in Palestine

Cyril of Scythopolis provides some data relevant to the problem of celebrating the liturgy in the various languages of the Christian Orient. In addition to the Greeks, the Armenians celebrated the liturgy in their own language. Also, the *Vita Theodosii* by Theodore of Petra speaks of the celebration of the liturgy in the languages of the Bessoi, the Armenians, and the Greeks.

The first reference to Armenian occurs in Cyril's *Vita Sabae*.[73] The account indicates that Armenian was used for the celebration of part of the liturgy in the monastery of St. Sabas.[74] The Armenian monks were allowed to read the Gospel and the rest of the Office in Armenian, but were asked to join their Greek-speaking colleagues in the celebration of the Holy Mysteries.[75] Some of the Armenians began to include in the Trisagion the words of Peter the Fuller[76] ("who has been crucified for us"), which was unacceptable to the Orthodox Sabas.[77]

More information is in the *Life* of another desert saint, Theodosius, written by Theodore of Petra.[78] One chapter[79] describes the psalmody, at night

[70] Ibid., 171, lines 21–25.

[71] Ibid., 150–51.

[72] Ibid., 161.

[73] Ibid., 117–18. The year is 501, after the dedication of the Great Church of the Lavra by Patriarch Elias; see Festugière, *Moines*, III. 2, p. 44.

[74] *Kyrillos*, 117, lines 20–21, 23.

[75] For the use of τὸ μεγαλεῖον to mean "Gospel lesson" or "reading of the Gospel," "Gospel reading," see Festugière, *Moines*, III.2 (Sabas), p. 44 note 61.

[76] On his heretical views, see ibid., note 62.

[77] Thus, the recommendation to use Greek was clearly due to fear of doctrinal deviation. When the Armenians used Greek, the saint could understand what they were saying.

[78] For this, see the critical notes of Festugière on H. Usner's edition, ibid., III, 91.

[79] Ibid., 127.

and several times during the day, in different languages in the four churches that the saint built in the interior of his monastery. In the first, Greek was used; in the second, the Bessoi[80] used their own language; the third was reserved for the Armenians, who are described as "continually occupied in singing hymns in their own languages."

Each community celebrated the Mass in its own language from the beginning until the reading of the Gospel, then they all gathered in the Great Church of the Greek-speaking monks and participated in the Sacred Mysteries. The account confirms that of St. Sabas' *Life* on the use of Armenian by the Armenian monks in the Judaean desert and reveals the use of another native language for the same purpose, that of the Bessoi, a Thracian people.

The hagiographers do not mention the use of Arabic in these monasteries; there was no community of Arab monks to justify its use, and hence no reference is made to it. Only two[81] monks in these monasteries are known to have been Arab: Maris, who became the *hēgoumenos* of the lavra of St. Euthymius or Theoctistus for two years (466–468), and Stephanus, who was the *hēgoumenos* of the same lavra from 514 to 535. Maris was *hēgoumenos* for some fifty years, during which he stayed at the monastery and must have learned Greek; Stephanus was a Romanized and Hellenized Arab who, like many of his countrymen in Arabia or other provinces of the limitrophe, knew the ecclesiastical and imperial languages of Byzantium.[82]

The case is different for the churches of the Parembole under the direction of bishops such as Aspebetos/Petrus I. A simple form of Arabic liturgy may have been used by that community of Arab *foederati*. In support of this contention the following observations may be made.

A

The *Vitae* of Sabas and of Theodosius provide material for discussing the existence of a simple Arabic liturgy.

1. They attest the existence of various liturgical languages, even some of the lesser-known ones, such as Armenian and the language of the Bessoi, about which little is known. They also attest the desire of these groups to express their inmost religious thought through the medium of their own languages.

[80] On the Bessoi, see Festugière's note 291, on p. 124 of his *Life* of Sabas; *Moines*, III.2. They are considered a Thracian people. They were numerous enough to found monasteries at Shoubiba, according to John Moschus, and in the Jordan Valley according to Cyril, for which see ibid. They were also to be found in Sinai and they used their language, see *BAFOC*, 320 note 143.

[81] Further research may reveal one or two more, such as Thallelaios!

[82] For these two monks, see above, 191–92.

2. These ethnic groups celebrated the liturgy in their own languages, in spite of their knowledge of Greek, which is attested by the two *Vitae*.

3. Finally, in a lyrical passage of the *Vita* of Theodosius,[83] the hagiographer praised the effect induced in the hearer by the celebration of the glory of God through the use of many languages in the monastery. Thus the early Church not only encouraged but also gloried in the liturgical expression of the Christian faith through a multiplicity of languages.

B

The relevance of these three observations to the possible existence of a simple Arabic liturgy for the Arab *foederati* of the Parembole is obvious.[84] It is hard to believe that, of all the languages of the Christian Orient, Arabic was the only one not used for liturgical expression. It had reached a high level of expressiveness in pre-Islamic times, which is reflected in poetry that exemplifies the Arabs' desire for articulation of their innermost thoughts. Although many Arabs knew Syriac and Greek, they, like the Armenian monks and the Bessoi, desired to express themselves liturgically in their own languages. But did the Church of the Parembole have an Arabic liturgy?

1. The Church of the Parembole was an organized Arab church; the congregation was entirely Arab, its members being the *foederati* who emigrated from Persia. Its bishop was also Arab, Aspebetos/Petrus I. His consecration as the first bishop of the Parembole could not have been accidental and without significance. The suggestion came from Euthymius, who baptized the community of Arabs and understood that they needed an Arab bishop. It is practically certain that the priest and the deacon Euthymius assigned to them[85] were also Arab, probably recruited from local Arabs who were Romanized and Hellenized in the Provincia Arabia or Palestine but whose native language was Arabic, in much the same way that Stephanus and Elias were. It is impossible to believe that if all these constituents of the Church of the Parembole were Arab, the liturgy was not celebrated in Arabic, especially since the newly arrived community did not know Greek and had not had time to learn it, although some, such as Petrus I, must have. Even if they did know Greek, this would not preclude an Arabic liturgy, just as the knowledge

[83] See Festugière, *Moines*, III.3, 127. It is noteworthy that the writer was the bishop of Petra, the all-Arab city in which St. Epiphanius notes that Arabic was used for the celebration of the pagan liturgy; see *BAFOC*, 291–92. As Vailhé pointed out, there were many monasteries in Petra, the metropolis of Palaestina Tertia, and many of its monks are mentioned in the *Apophthegmata Patrum*; see S. Vailhé, "Repertoire," 42.

[84] For other observations see *BAFOC*, 435–43.

[85] When John Chrysostom sent presbyters, deacons, and readers to the Scythians (Goths) he made sure that these spoke Scythian (Gothic): see Theodoret, *HE*, V, xxx.

of Greek on the part of the Armenians and the Bessoi did not preclude their celebrating the liturgy in their own languages. Since Gospel reading was an integral part of the liturgy, the presumption is that in the Jordan Valley in the fifth century there was an Arabic Gospel, or at least that portion of it which was part of the lectionary used for liturgical purposes.

2. The background of the community of Christian Arabs that formed the Church of the Parembole in the Jordan Valley is also relevant. What was said about the Tanūkhids of the fourth century, the first *foederati* of Byzantium, may also be said of them. They also came from the Land of the Two Rivers, where the tradition of literary Arabic was strong; consequently Arabic could have been used in the Jordan Valley for liturgical expression. This particular community most probably belonged to the tribal group Tamīm,[86] which was known for the number of poets it produced in pre-Islamic times. Tamīm was prominent in the cultural life of Ḥīra, represented by the family of the famous Christian poet ʿAdi, son of Zayd, of the sixth century, whose family had settled in Ḥīra and had attained social and political prominence.[87]

3. Finally, was this simple form of the Arabic liturgy developed after the arrival of the Arab *foederati* from Persia and their conversion, or was it the liturgy of some Arab group in Oriens, such as the Tanūkhids of the fourth century?[88] It is impossible to tell. But whatever the provenance of this liturgy, the chances are good that when Euthymius recommended the consecration of an Arab as the first bishop of the Parembole, he also recommended the use of an Arabic liturgy. This was in conformity with the practice of the early Church in this small region of the Jordan Valley where the liturgy was recited in such minor vernaculars as that of the Bessoi.

IV. Saint and Saracen in the Desert of Juda

In the work of Cyril of Scythopolis a number of Saracens cross the path of St. Sabas and that of Euthymius posthumously. These encounters provide further documentation for the peculiar relationship between the desert Saracen and the desert saint/monk. They also raise questions about the extent of the Arab presence in the monastic Desert of Juda.

St. Sabas

There are four episodes involving encounters with St. Sabas (439–532), the principal saint of the region[89] after the death of Euthymius in 473.

86 For the possible Tamīmi origin of the Arabs of the Parembole, see above, 42–43.
87 For the family of ʿAdi ibn Zayd, see Shahîd, "Conference of Ramla," 118–19.
88 For this, see *BAFOC*, 435–43.
89 He founded his famous lavra in the Judaean desert in 478, was ordained a priest

1. While still in the desert of Rouba, he came upon four Saracens who were starving and about to die. He fed them with the little he had. Before departing, they learned from him where in the desert his cave was. A few days later they returned and brought him bread, cheese, and dates.[90]

2. Again, while he was still living in the desert of Rouba, six Saracens schemed to attack Sabas and his companion Anthus and capture them as prisoners. To that end they sent one of them in advance. But fear never visited the two monks; instead they prayed, and the earth opened and engulfed the Saracen; his companions were terrified and fled. Thenceforth the saint was never afraid of Saracen ambushes.[91]

3. After spending the fourth year of his wandering in these deserts, and guided by a vision, Sabas settled in the cave of Siloam when he was forty years old, in 478. It was accessible only by climbing a rope. Four Saracens came, and he let them visit him by dropping the rope for them. After they saw that he had nothing in the cave, they admired his poverty and virtue and a few days later returned with bread, dates, cheese, and whatever they could lay their hands on.[92]

4. The last episode involving Sabas and the Saracens occurred after his death. Some camels were bringing corn bought at Machairus to the hospice of the lavra when one of the camels fell into the ravine. The Saracen cameleer invoked the aid of the dead saint, who came to the rescue of the fallen camel. It was lifted from the ravine and led back to the hospice to discharge its load. As a result of this miracle, the Saracen cameleer returned every year to the lavra of St. Sabas and worshiped at the saint's tomb. In gratitude to Sabas he gave the *oikonomos* of the lavra one *trimision*.[93]

St. Euthymius

In addition to these four episodes, there are three others that involved St. Euthymius, all of which took place in the period 543–553, that is, long after his death in 473. While the Saracens that encountered St. Sabas were left

against his will in 490, and finally was made by the patriarch of Jerusalem in 492, the superior of all the monks of Palestine.

[90] The staple food of the desert Arabs; see *Kyrillos*, 96.

[91] Ibid., p. 97

[92] For this, see ibid., 97–99. The Saracens are referred to as barbarians. The cave of Siloam became the famous monastery of St. Sabas, known even today as Mar Sabas. It is possible that the Saracens involved here are the same as those mentioned in the first encounter. They are four and return with the same three items of food. It is noteworthy that they are referred to as barbarians, presumably because they are not Christian Saracens.

[93] For this episode, see ibid. The passage in Cyril is noteworthy for the association of the Arabs with camels, with such phrases as the "Saracenn camels" and the "Saracen cameleer." See Festugière's notes on the *trimision*, *Moines*, 116, note 273.

anonymous by the hagiographer, two of the three involved with St. Euthymius are known by name, thus providing information on the Arab onomasticon of this region and period.[94]

1. One day two "barbarians" came to the monastery of St. Euthymius, led by a Christian Saracen, Thaʿlaba. With them was another "barbarian," who was possessed by a demon. The three "barbarians" had come to water their camels and, finding the door to the monastery cistern closed, one of them broke it with a stone and as a result was possessed. Thaʿlaba passed by them and, after learning what had happened, advised them to bring the possessed man to the monastery. There the monks brought the possessed barbarian into the funerary chapel and placed him near the tomb of St. Euthymius. Shortly afterward he was cured of his malady, and a few days later he was deemed worthy of baptism.[95]

The following is noteworthy: (*a*) The term "barbarian" is used for non-Christian Saracens (*b*) It is clear from the account that the desert of the Jordan Valley still had many Saracens who were not Christianized, and these are referred to as barbarians. The three "barbarians" were related to those "barbarians" who spread confusion and terror in the region during the strife between the two phylarchs, Arethas and Aswad (*c*) The story of the three barbarians was told to the monks of the lavra by Thaʿlaba. The presumption is that he spoke Greek, unless he spoke Arabic and an Arab or Arabic-speaking monk of the lavra translated for him. But the natural interpretation is that he could speak Greek and was understood without an interpreter. (*d*) Thaʿlaba was described as a descenant of those Arabs whom Euthymius had baptized; thus the small group of Arabs in the Jordan Valley remained so loyal to the memory of the saint who converted them that a century later they still came to his lavra. (*e*) Finally, Thaʿlaba was described in the next episode as living in Lazarion/Bethany, and it is known from the same episode that he had a brother and a niece. Thus there was an Arab family living in Lazarion in the sixth century.[96]

2. The second episode involves the same Thaʿlaba, who brings to the lavra of Euthymius his own niece, who was troubled by an impure spirit. She

[94] All these episodes come immediately after a reference in Cyril to the strife between the two phylarchs Arethas and Aswad, which is dated by Schwartz to 543–553; see his Register in *Kyrillos*, 259, s.v. "Arethas." This episode will be discussed in *BASIC*.

[95] See ibid., 75.

[96] It would be pleasant to think that this Thaʿlaba is related to the Arabs who mounted the offensive against the *limes* ca. 500 in the reign of Anastasius, as Génier suggests, *Euthyme*, 115, 117. But Thaʿlaba is a common Arabic name. Génier suggests that these Christian Arabs in Lazarion and Bethabudis were refugees from the vicinity of the Parembole, from Saracen incursions such as noted in this chapter. They could have been, although the name Bethabudis, which goes back to Cyril himself, sounds strongly Arabic and suggests an Arab village in the vicinity of Jerusalem.

stayed there for three days, during which Thaʿlaba rubbed her body with holy oil from the tomb of St. Euthymius. On the third day she was completely cured, and Thaʿlaba took her back with joy to Lazarion.[97]

3. Another Arab, named ʿUrqūb, was also living in Lazarion. His son, who pastured sheep in the desert, was possessed by a demon, and his face was contorted. He was brought to the lavra of St. Euthymius and placed near the tomb of the thaumaturge saint. After a few days he was relieved of the demon that possesed him, and his face returned to normal.[98]

4. The last episode involved a woman from the village of Bethabudis who was seized by a demon. Her husband brought her to the lavra; she stayed three days and nights outside it, since women were not allowed to enter; on the third day she was cured. Each year she returned to offer thanks.[99]

The name of the woman is not given, but that of her village is recognizably Arabic. The chances are that this woman from an Arab village was Arab, and this is possibly corroborated by the fact that her name is not given. If it had been a Greek name with which Cyril was familiar, he would have given it; it may have been so strange and unpronounceable for him that he omitted it.[100]

V. The Parembole and Saracen Invasions

The sources record invasions of the Parembole by the Saracens who, after penetrating the *limes Arabicus*, reached Palaestina Prima across the Jordan Valley. Such deep penetrations indicate that these were major military operations. They therefore deserve a separate treatment, especially as there has been some confusion[101] in the attempt to identify them, and this has resulted in some erroneous views on the later history of the Parembole.

[97] See *Kyrillos*, 75–76.

[98] Ibid., 76. Greek Ἀϱγώβ is a resoundingly Arabic name, ʿUrqūb. The account discloses that Lazarion could have among its inhabitants shepherds of the neighboring desert. "ʿUrqūb" and his son join Thaʿlaba, his brother and his niece, as a little Arab colony in Lazarion.

[99] See ibid., 76.

[100] So Strabo in his *Geography* omitted mentioning Arab names because of the difficulty of pronouncing them; *Geography*, XVI.iv.18.

[101] On the part of the three specialists on this subject—Génier, Aigrain, and Charles. Their confusion is due to failure to notice the important raid conducted by Mund̲ir, the Lakhmid king, against Palestine ca. 504, recorded in the *Vita* of Hesychastes, and concentrating solely on the *Vitae* of Euthymius and Sabas. As a result, they erroneously identified the second raid or invasion with a Lakhmid one that took place much later, in 529, and was directed against Syria Prima as far as Antioch and never reached Palestine (Theophanes, *Chronographia*, 178). For the views of these three authors, see Génier, *Euthyme*, 115–16; Aigrain, "Arabie," col. 1196; and H. Charles, *Le christianisme*, 46. Charles' view on the late survival of the phylarchs of the Parembole, at least toward the middle of the 6th century, are sound and correct those of Génier.

It will be argued that: (1) all the invasions recorded by Cyril which affected the Parembole, and to which there is specific reference, took place during the reign of Anastasius; (2) that they may be identified with three major thrusts by the three major Arab military groups during his reign—Kinda, Ghassān, and Lakhm—ca. 500; and (3) that the little phylarchate of the Palestinian Parembole was affected adversely by all of them but did not disappear as a result and continued well into the latter part of the sixth century and most probably into the seventh.

Of the three recorded invasions, the first two are found in one paragraph in the *Vita Euthymii*,[102] and *both* are clearly dated to the reign of Anastasius (491–518).

a. The first one entailed the dismantling of the tents (σκηναὶ) of the Parembole.[103] The tents are mentioned specifically, not the built structures. The Arab chiefs[104] had other tents further to the west, near the monastery of Martyrius, and also a church.[105] This invasion most probably can be identified with that recorded by Theophanes for the first time ca. 500 involving Kinda and Ghassān.[106]

b. The second invasion was more severe. The invaders attacked again in the vicinity of the monastery of Martyrius, killed some of the Saracens, enslaved others, while the rest dispersed to various villages. Great confusion and destruction took place in the region.

The use of the adverb πάλιν suggests that this was a second phase of the same attack by the same group of invaders and that it took place shortly after the first.[107] The sources provide a probable identification, namely, the second invasion by the Kindite Maʿdī-Karib, mentioned by Theophanes,[108] which may be assigned to the year 502.

The Parembole, and the entire region, must have suffered heavily. It was a phylarchate designed to deal with local disorder, not with the onslaught of

[102] *Kyrillos*, 67–68.

[103] In the paragraph the hagiographer continued to observe the distinction between βάρβαροι and Σαρακηνοί, reserving the first to non-Christian Arabs, the second to Byzantinized Christian Arabs; see V. Christides, "Arabs as *Barbaroi* before the Rise of Islam," *Balkan Studies* 10 (1969), 315–24; idem, "Pre-Islamic Arabs in Byzantine Illuminations," *Le Muséon* 83 (1970), 167–81.

[104] Noticeable is the term applied here to three chiefs as οἱ πρῶτοι, not *phylarchoi*. Perhaps the term is more inclusive, subsuming chiefs who were not technically phylarchs. On the possible implication of the term, see above, 190, and below, 204.

[105] Another evidence for a church built by the Arabs in the Jordan Valley. The site of the Arab settlement near Martyrius is now Mrasras, according to Féderlin's research cited by Génier, *Euthyme*, 113–14.

[106] For these raids, see Theophanes, *Chronographia*, 141.

[107] At least after they had built the church referred to in *Kyrillos*, 67, line 24.

[108] See Theophanes, *Chronographia*, 143.

the most powerful groups in Arabia, who in this period attacked the empire and forced it to conclude the well-known treaty.[109]

c. The third invasion, unlike the first, is better documented in Cyril.[110] The identity of the invader is stated—Munḏir, the Lakhmid king, son of Shaqīqa—and the date is rather clearly inferable,[111] after the fall of Amida, which took place in January 503, and after he had just become king, that is, after the death of his father Nuʿmān before the walls of Edessa, in August– September 503.

The passage where all this is stated occurs in the *Vita* of Hesychastes; it repays careful study. (1) The desert (τὴν ἔρημον ταύτην) in which the *barbaroi* of Munḏir scattered must be the Rouba desert (τὸν ἔρημον τοῦ ῾Ρούβα), whither Hesychastes retired from the Great Monastery of St. Sabas; the troops of Munḏir possibly came from south of the Dead Sea.[112] (2) Much more important is the description of those who defended the monasteries and who alerted them against the attack: τῶν φυλάρχειν τε καὶ φυλάττειν τὴν ἔρημον ταύτην τεταγμένων. This is one of the very rare occasions when the verb φυλάρχειν is used, and it is not quite clear whether it is used with technical accuracy to indicate the phylarchs or as a literary locution to mean the heads of the tribes, recalling the οἱ πρῶτοι used in the passage that described the first invasion, analyzed above. It is possible that the term is being used with technical accuracy and that the hagiographer, for stylistic reasons, chose to express himself in this fashion. On the other hand, it could be argued that if the technical sense of phylarch was intended, he would have used the noun phylarch, as he did before (and after) in connection with the phylarchs of the Parembole. Supporting this view is the use of the plural on two occasions in this passage, and also in that which described the first invasion, with its οἱ πρῶτοι. The Parembole was a very small Saracen phylarchal circumscription, and it is quite unlikely that it had more than one phylarch. Thus the plural form could suggest the non-technical use of the term, meaning the heads of the various tribes who lived in the region. The evidence is ambivalent and admits of being interpreted either way.[113]

[109] For the peace treaty, see Shahîd, "Ghassān and Byzantium", 232–55.

[110] See *Kyrillos*, 211.

[111] And it must be sometime after the fall of Amida in 503, before the end of the Persian War.

[112] For reference to the desert, see *Kyrillos*, 211, line 18; for the Rouba desert, see ibid., 209, line 10. It is noteworthy that Cyril maintains the distinction between pagan Arabs as *barbaroi* and Christian Arabs, who defended the monasteries and whom he does not so describe.

[113] Cf. above, 189–90. Also, Cyril was a friend of the Parembole and its phylarchs, and if they had been on hand during these invasions he would have noted their efforts.

This invasion of Palestine by Munḏir has not been mentioned by those who have written on the Parembole. Other problems related to it will be discussed in *BASIC*.

The last mention of Saracen invasions in Cyril is in his *Vita* of St. Sabas.[114] After the Samaritan revolt of May, 529, Sabas went to Constantinople in April, 531 or 532 and made some requests of Emperor Justinian,[115] one of which was the building of a fort (κάστρον) in the desert south of the monasteries which he had built because of the raid of the Saracens. Justinian acceded to the requests and wrote to Summus, the *dux* of Palestine, who supplied a garrison to guard the monasteries as well as a thousand *nomismata* for building the fort.[116]

The Saracen raid referred to may have been a local one in the wake of the Samaritan revolt of 529. On the other hand, since it was deemed necessary to build a fort as a result, the raid may have been more than local. Its exact date is not given. If it was during the 520s, when the Ghassānids withdrew from active military service because of doctrinal difficulties with Justin I, it could have been a serious raid from the Arabian Peninsula or even mounted by the Lakhmids, who in the twenties were raiding far and wide in the oriental limitrophe.[117]

As has been noted above, there is no mention of the phylarchs of the Parembole in the account of Saracen invasions in the *Vita* of Sabas. Again, it is difficult to assess the significance or non-significance of his silence in this context. This was a period of great phylarchal reorganization in the whole of Oriens, which found expression in the *basileia* of the Ghassānid Arethas ca. 530 and the concentration of federate power, or most of it, in his hands. This may have operated to the disadvantage of the phylarchs of the Parembole, who, moreover, as Chalcedonians may not have viewed favorably the advancement of a Monophysite phylarch such as Arethas at their expense. This may have conduced to some friction, either with the Ghassānids or with the central government, and caused their temporary withdrawal from the service. Their inactivity, then, may account for Cyril's silence.

This interpretation may be pure speculation; and yet on two important occasions within the span of thirty years, from around 500 to 530, the phylarchs of the Parembole were conspicuous by their absence in an area which was supposed to be theirs to defend. The conclusion is almost inevitable that whatever the underlying cause may have been, all was not well with the Parembole and its phylarchs. In spite of the obscurity that shrouds their disappearance, this serves as the most satisfactory background for understanding the sudden and startling description of Terebon II some twenty years later,

[114] *Kyrillos*, 175.
[115] On the chronology, see Festugière, *Moines*, 102 note 230.
[116] *Kyrillos*, 178.
[117] The Lakhmid campaigns against Oriens in the 520s will be discussed in *BASIC*.

in mid-century, as the "renowned phylarch in this region" by the hagiographer. The presumption is that his "renown" rested on his having returned the Parembole to its former eminence after a protracted period of obscurity in the service of the monastic establishment of the Jordan Valley.

The reference to the building of a fort in the list of Sabas' requests to Justinian is noteworthy. The saint asked that it be erected south of his monasteries. This would make it face the Rouba desert, a large area west of the Dead Sea, from which Mund̲ir's forces attacked around 503–504. The Parembole was to the north—the triangle consisting of the two lavras and Bi'r al-Mazraᶜa—apparently not adequate to defend the monasteries to the south, facing the desert of Rouba. Sabas, then, may have wanted the additional protection of regular Roman soldiers against possible threats from the south. The fortifications in the Jordan Valley and the rise of the Parembole may be viewed as evidence that Palestine needed an internal[118] *limes* for security. Students of the Roman frontier have focused on the internal *limes* in the Negev and Sinai,[119] but the Jordan Valley, with its diminutive Parembole and forts, may be added to that of Palaestina Tertia as a line of fortification.

It remains to comment on the broader significance of these Saracen invasions of Palaestina Tertia in the reign of Anastasius.

These invasions, especially the first two, are a valuable commentary on the well-known passage in Theophanes that speaks of the general assault of the Arabs all along the *limes orientalis*. Theophanes reflects the seriousness of the military operations and the ferocity of one when he speaks of Romanus' dislodging Jabala the Ghassānid from the island of Iotabe. Cyril's account is welcome because the seriousnes of the invasion is clearly expressed and implied, and it is given geographic precision. That these invasions represent a remarkably powerful Saracen military thrust against Byzantinum is evidenced by the deep dent they made in the Byzantine defense system when they penetrated the *limes Arabicus*, crossed either the Jordan or Wādī ᶜAraba, and reached Palaestina Prima. And it is to Cyril that this intelligence is owed.

In the larger context of Roman frontier studies, these invasions have an important place. The whole military thinking behind the erection of the *limes Arabicus* was the containment of the Saracens. Hence the two ingredients in the makeup of the *limes* were the Roman regular soldiers manning it and the Peninsular Saracens, raiders of the frontier. Within this framework, the place of these invasions is clear. They are an important test of the efficacy of the *limes Arabicus* and the degree of its military readiness to deal with the problem

[118] Not in the technical sense in which this term has been used; see "The Two *Limites*," *BAFOC*, 479–81. It is used here in the sense of an inner line of fortification.

[119] See ibid., 480–81.

it was designed to solve. Important is the possible existence of what has been termed the "enigmatic gap"[120] in the *limes*, and the extent to which knowing Saracens exploited it.

Appendix I

Greek Hagiography and the Arab Oral Tradition

The accounts that Cyril gave of the fortunes of the Parembole, spanning almost a century and a half, were based on oral traditions transmitted to him directly by the last attested representative of the line, Terebon II, and going back to the time of the first Parembole phylarch, Aspebetos/Petrus I.[1] They have been confirmed by the archeological research of Féderlin, and so through this triad of Arab informant (Terebon) Greek recorder (Cyril), and French explorer (Féderlin)[2] their authenticity is beyond doubt. The same is true of the oral traditions that Sozomen recorded a century before Cyril, which are confirmed by the independent Arabic tradition on Queen Mavia, which undoubtedly goes back to the same source.[3]

This sheds light on the problem of the transmission of pre-Islamic Arab history in the works of Islamic writers such as Hishām al-Kalbī, the most famous and important of them, who used epigraphy as an auxiliary, and sometimes as the main source of his information.[4] The accounts of Arab historians on the pre-Islamic past are confirmed by comparing them with the Greek hagiographical and ecclesiastical sources that used the Arabic oral tradition, the general soundness of which is proven beyond doubt. As a hagiographer, Cyril was interested in one aspect of the history of the Parembole, and so was Sozomen in his account of the Arabs of Queen Mavia. The tribal groups themselves were naturally interested in all aspects of their respective histories, and so would have preserved them. Terebon II probably told the history of the Parembole in its entirety to Cyril, who naturally chose only what was suited to hagiography. It is practically certain that Terebon and the house of Aspebetos also had some written records on the history of the Parembole and their tribal group, since with their settling down and adopting the faith of a scriptural religion such as Christianity, they would have been a literate group. The same applies to the fourth-century Tanūkhids, whose records on tribal history must have been the basis for what were later called the *Dīwān* or the *Kitāb al-Qabīla*[5]—the traditions of tribal history based on its poetry.

[120] For this phrase, see P. Mayerson, "The Saracens and the Limes," *BASOR* 262 (1986), 35. S. Thomas Parker denies there was such a gap in the *limes Arabicus*; see below, 546–47, a.

[1] In addition to Terebon II as the informant of Cyril, there was also Terebon I, who informed Kyriakus, who in turn informed Cyril on the miracle of fire which engulfed St. Euthymius; *Kyrillos*, 45. The monks corroborated what the phylarchs told Cyril, as in the case of Terebon II's accounts; see ibid., 18.

[2] See Génier, *Euthyme*, 104–11.

[3] See *BAFOC*, 444.

[4] For Hishām al-Kalbī, see *BAFOC*, 349–66, and below, Chap. 12, sec. i.

[5] On these (the *Dīwān* and the *Book of the Tribe*), see *BAFOC*, 354, 448–57.

Appendix II

The Image of the Arabs in the *Vitae* of Cyril of Scythopolis

Arab figures in the *Vitae* of Cyril are described by a variety of names: Arabs, natives of Arabia, Saracens, Ishmaelites, and Hagarites. The first is apparently applied to Arabs who were *Rhōmaioi*, such as the *hēgoumenos* Stephanus, the second also to *Rhōmaioi* from the province of Arabia, such as the patriarch Elias. The last three names, however, repay careful study for our theme.[1]

The most common word designating the Arabs is the term "Saracens," applied to those who were not Roman citizens (*Rhōmaioi*) but who were outsiders from across the *limes*, whether raiders of the imperial territory or *foederati* in a special relationship to the empire. The use of this term affords the best chance of examining the image of the Arabs in fifth-century Byzantine hagiography. The term is often applied in a neutral sense, principally to describe the pastoralists—*foederati*[2] or raiders from without—who came within Cyril's purview. When he is in a hostile mood because of destructive raids that affected the life of a monastic establishment, he uses the term *barbaroi*, clearly in a pejorative sense, especially when they are not Christians.[3]

It is, however, the use of the term for the Arabs of the Parembole which shows that the hagiographer conceives of the transformation of the Arabs through the catalysis of Christianity in three phases. One of his statements refers to the "old wolves of Arabia becoming members of the spiritual flock of Christ."[4] More technical, and important to what may be called a theology of the Arabs, is the passage in which Cyril describes the great cultural and spiritual metamorphosis[5] which the Arabs of the Parembole experienced after their conversion by Euthymius. In the conceptual apparatus of the hagiographer, these are the terms and the stages:

(1) Before they were converted they were *barbaroi*[6] and *Saracēnoi* (2) Then the terms *Hagarenoi* and *Ishmaelitai* were applied to them, naturally coming from a hagiographer who could not conceive of the Arabs except in the biblical terms of being the descendants of Hagar and Ishmael. The implication of these terms is well known: they are a people outside the Promise, children of the slave girl Hagar. (3) The third name applied to them, which reflects their new status after their baptism, is "descendants of Sarah"; they are "no longer *Hagarenoi* and Ishmaelites but have become descendants of Sarah and inheritors of the Promise, transferred by baptism from slavery to liberty."[7] The hagiographer's mature judgment draws on the thought of the Old[8]

[1] For the image in the 4th century, see *BAFOC*, 560–64.

[2] The term is applied consistently to the phylarchs of the Parembole, in spite of their conversion, because the term became a technical one to describe the *foederati* and to distinguish them from the Arabs who were *Rhōmaioi*; it was applied to Terebon I after his conversion and even when he was worshipping in the church; see *Kyrillos*, 45, line 9.

[3] See V. Christides, "Arabs as *Barbaroi*," 315–24; idem, "Pre-Islamic Arabs in Byzantine Illuminations," 167–81.

[4] *Kyrillos*, 24, lines 20–22.

[5] Ibid., 21, lines 8–10.

[6] Ibid., 19, lines 11, 12, 15.

[7] Ibid., 21, lines 8–10: ἀπέλυσεν οὐκέτι ᾿Αγαρηνοὺς καὶ ᾿Ισμαηλίτας, ἀλλὰ τῆς Σάρας ἀπογόνους καὶ τῆς ἐπαγγελίας κληρονόμους γεγονότας διὰ τοῦ βαπτίσματος ἀπὸ δουλείας εἰς ἐλευθερίαν μετενεχθέντας.

[8] For this, see Gen. 12.

and New Testaments[9] but goes beyond it in declaring the Saracens as part of the New Israel of God. Thus it is only through baptism that the Arabs could win freedom from the state of spiritual bondage to which they were consigned by Old Testament thought.[10]

Appendix III

Two Bishops of Jerusalem in the Third Century

The election of an Arab, Elias, as patriarch of Jerusalem, only some thirty years after the death of the first one, Juvenal, raises the question whether the Holy City had other bishops who were Arabs.

In his *Ecclesiastical History* Eusebius mentions the names of two bishops of Jerusalem in the third century who may turn out to be Arab. He is silent on their ethnic origin, but their names are suggestive.[1] The first is Mazabanes (Μαζαβάνης), bishop of Jerusalem from 253 to 264; the second is Zabdas (Ζαβδᾶς), bishop of Jerusalem from 297 to 301.

These names are neither Christian nor Graeco-Roman, such as bishops were wont to assume, but Semitic. Both are Aramaic in form, and one of them, Zabdas (the same as Zenobia's general), is derived from the root "to give" that is common to Arabic, Hebrew, and Aramaic.[2] The bearers of these names must, therefore, have been either Aramaeans or Arabs. It is impossible to tell from the names alone which of the two peoples they belonged to, but a case can be made for their being Arab.

Both are attested in the inscription of Palmyra, that Arab city whose Arabs used Aramaic for their public inscriptions and whose onomasticon was deeply influenced by Aramaic. It is, therefore, possible that these two bishops were Palmyrene Arabs: (1) The Palmyrenes maintained a presence in Palestine under Odenathus, and occupied it under Zenobia[3] until 273. It is possible that Palmyrene Arabs settled in Palestine in this period of some thirteen years, which might explain how one of them, Zabdas, became bishop of Jerusalem.[4] (2) The name of the architect of the Church of the Holy Sepulcher in the time of Constantine the Great was Zenobius, a Palmyrene-sounding

[9] See Gal. 4:30–31.

[10] This is, of course, not consonant with the self-image of the Arabs who, in pre-Islamic times, considered themselves descended from Ishmael and took pride in the fact; see above, 154–56, for analysis of the passage on Ishmael in Theodoret. This could also apply to the Arabs of the Parembole before their immigration to Palestine, if they truly belonged to the Tamīm tribe; according to the Arabic sources, this group or some portion of it, namely, Banū al-ʿAnbar, were considered to be Ishmaelite Arabs; see above, 42–43, and below, Chap. 13, sec. I note 1.

[1] Eusebius, *Ecclesiastical History*, VI.39; VII.xxxii. 29.

[2] See J. K. Stark, *Personal Names in the Palmyrene Inscriptions* (Oxford, 1971), 16 ff, 74, 85 f, 143; 30, 94. The other one could conceivably be derived from an Arab root that gave the Arabic proper noun Zabbān. I thank Prof. Franz Rosenthal for his comments on the Aramaic form of these two names.

[3] On this, see Avi-Yonah, *The Jews of Palestine*, 126–27.

[4] Starting from 260, when Odenathus was put in charge of the Roman Orient. But this does not explain the episcopate of Mazabanes, which began in 253. Christianity, however, had invaded Palmyra, which even became an episcopal see. It is, therefore, not unlikely that a Christian Palmyrene Arab become bishop of the Holy City.

name, which suggests some association of the Palmyrenes with Jerusalem.[5] (3) These bishops did not assume Graeco-Roman or Christian names on their consecration, which suggests that they had a strong sense of Arab identity, such as the inhabitants of a city with a distinguished past—Palmyra—might have had. All this does not make Zabdas and Mazabanes Arabs, but suggests it as a possibility.[6]

Appendix IV

Elias, the Patriarch of Jerusalem

The career of this Arab patriarch of Jerusalem raises some questions, two of which will be treated here.

1. Little is known about his background other than the bare statement that he came from Arabia, either the Provincia in Oriens or the old Ptolemaic nome in Egypt. But the account of Nicephorus Callistus provides us with the name of his father, Passarion.[1] This was also the name of the famous chorepiscopus and archimandrite of a monastery in Jerusalem, Juvenal's friend, who accompanied him for the consecration of the Church of Euthymius' lavra in 428 or 429. He was a renowned saint, and it is practically certain that Elias' father was named after him, since Passarion was a rare name and probably attained celebrity only because it was the saint's name.[2] This leads to the conclusion that Elias came from a Christian family, which then must have been thoroughly Christianized and Hellenized, in much the same way that the family of the Arab Stephanus, the *hēgoumenos* of the lavra of Euthymius from 514 to 535 was, judging from his name and that of his brother, Procopius.[3] That his father was given the name Passarion may throw light on the inclination of Elias to monasticism quite early in his life, since Passarion was the superior of all the monks in the Diocese of Palaestina Prima.

2. The Arabic *Chronicle* of Eutychius, in its account of Elias, credits him with building churches, one of which was the church of St. Helena.[4] This is startling, since no one else credited him with this foundation. The statement in Eutychius

[5] On Zenobius the architect, see Philostorgius, ed. Bidez, fr. 13, GCS, p. 202; Theophanes, *Chronographia*, 33, line 11. The name was also known in Arab Elusa in Palaestina Tertia, whence came Zenobius, Libanius' teacher.

[6] Hence the categorical assertion on the Arabness of these bishops is unjustified; see J. S. Trimingham, *Christianity among the Arabs*, 75. Even more unjustified is the assertion that Alexander, the bishop of Jerusalem during the principate of Philip the Arab, was also Arab; ibid., 58. I have read all the references in the *HE* of Eusebius to Alexander but have found nothing to support the view that he was Arab. Perhaps Trimingham used other sources which he did not indicate.

[1] Nicephorus Callistus, *Historia Ecclesiastica*, PG 147, xxxii, col. 180B; also *BAFOC*, 139 note 5.

[2] On Passarion, see Honigmann, *Juvenal*, 219 note 55.

[3] On Stephanus, see above, 192.

[4] Eutychius, "Annales," PG 111, col. 1057. In this Latin version, Euthychius says of Elias, "struxitque ecclesias (inter caeteras) ecclesiam Helenae quam non perfecit." For the Arabic version, see CSCO, Scriptores Arabici, vol. 50, p. 186, lines 7–8. The translation is accurate.

must, therefore, be untrue: Euthychius is a late author[5] who cannot compete with Cyril, the contemporary Greek source who wrote specialized studies on the ecclesiastical figures of Palestine in the fifth and sixth centuries, is a primary source on Patriarch Elias and his activities, and attended in 543 the dedication of the church of the Theotokos after it was completed by Justinian[6] at the request of St. Sabas, as recorded by Cyril himself.[7] Since it is inconceivable that Cyril would thus have omitted mention of Elias' building of such a church as St. Helena's if this did take place, the chances are that this is a confusion with Elias' church of the Theotokos. This is corroborated by the fact that Eutychius adds that Elias did not finish it, which is what Cyril says about Elias' church of the Theotokos. It is unlikely that Elias would have simultaneously started two churches which he did not finish. It is, therefore, practically certain that what Euthychius had in mind was the church of the Theotokos.[8]

Appendix V

Arab Structures in Palaestina Prima

The Arabs of the fifth century, as noted earlier, made a modest contribution to ecclesiastical building in Palaestina Prima. This was the work of four men who figured prominently in the ecclesiastical life of the region between Jerusalem and the Jordan—in the Desert of Juda: Aspebetos/Petrus; Maris, his brother-in-law; Stephanus, the *hēgoumenos* of the lavra of Theoctistus; and Elias, the patriarch of Jerusalem.

1. Petrus I. After Euthymius founded his monastery, Petrus built him a cistern, a bakery, and three cells; between these cells he also built the conventual church. The site was Khān al-Aḥmar. Later, when eleven more monks joined the community, Petrus built more cells and provided the church with furniture. This church was consecrated by Juvenal in either 428 or 429. Petrus also built the church of the Parembole, which Euthymius had laid out for him, in Bir al-Zarʿa.

2. Maris. Petrus' brother-in-law and the second after Petrus to be baptized became, toward the end of his life, the *hēgoumenos* of the lavra of Theoctistus in Dayr al-Dawākis.[1] Prior to that he gave away all his wealth for the construction and enlargement of the monastery of Theoctistus.[2]

[5] On Eutychius, see Sezgin, *GAS*, I, 329–30.

[6] See *Kyrillos*, 216.

[7] Ibid., 175.

[8] Besides, there is no mention of a church of St. Helena in the list of Jerusalem churches, such as that in F. M. Abel, "Jerusalem," *DACL* 7, cols. 2344–53, or in J. Wilkinson, gazeteer, s.v. "Jerusalem," pp. 160–62. It is, therefore, strange that the attribution of the building of a church dedicated to St. Helena is accepted by R. Janin in his article in *DHGE* 15, s.v. Elie (no. 22).

[1] For these sites, see "La *parembole*," in Génier, *Euthyme*, 94–117, and the map opposite p. 94.

[2] Aspebetos and Maris were the builders of the two principal monasteries associated with the figure who spread monasticism in the desert of Juda. Their activities as builders are hardly consonant with the image that is often projected of the Parembole as a camp inhabited by a group of nomads.

3. Stephanus. While *hēgoumenos* of the lavra of Euthymius, from 514 to 535, enlarged and enriched the lavra.

4. Elias, the patriarch of Jerusalem (494–516). The first structure he built was a modest cell outside Jericho, even while he was an inmate of the lavra of Euthymius during the first years of their association. Upon his election as patriarch he built a monastery in Jerusalem, near the episcopal mansion. He also laid the foundations there of the Church of the Theotokos, but did not finish it. He gave Sabas money to build a new lavra for the sixty rebellious inmates, and Sabas used the money to build them a bakery and a church within the lavra. Thus Elias' main contribution to church building in the Holy Land was the Church of the Theotokos in Jerusalem.

Appendix VI

On the Term "Parembole"

The Greek term παρεμβολή, which has attained some prominence because of the extraordinary career of Aspebetos/Petrus, its appearance in conciliar lists, and its frequent use by Cyril of Scythopolis, deserves further discussion.

In the previous volume, I discussed the term in a paragraph[1] which is quoted here because of its relevance to the fifth century. A few more observations will also be made in light of the detailed discussion of the Palestinian Parembole.

"Greek authors who had occasion to refer to the Arab military establishments or encampments use for them the term παρεμβολή, rather than the more formal and strict στρατόπεδον or κάστρον. This is significant and might afford a clue to a better understanding of what these military encampments were. The prefix παρά-, as well as the verb παραβάλλω ('put in beside or between, insert'), can convey the notion of an annex or a subordinate structure; and it is possible that the Arab encampments were built beside or between other establishments, possibly the camp of the regular Byzantine troops, to ensure cooperation between these regular troops and the Arab auxiliaries in the event of a military operation.[2] It is also possible to infer from the verb παραβάλλω that these establishments were less solid or permanent than the ordinary *castra*, and this notion is clearly conveyed by its application to the establishments of the nomads.[3] The παρεμβολή was thus a movable camp, which could, however, develop into a more permanent establishment;[4] this semantic dimension of movability is confirmed by the Sabaic inscriptions where verbs of motion are used with the term *ḥīra*."

[1] See *BAFOC*, 496.

[2] The *parembole* of the phylarchs of Palaestina Prima which was founded by the Arab chief Aspebetos was built in close proximity to the lavra of St. Euthymius.

[3] See the inscription found in the Ḥawrān region, carved for the στρατηγὸς παρεμβολῶν νομάδων, *PPUAES*, III, A5, p. 347.

[4] *Parembole* has found its way into the idiom of Zacharia Rhetor, where it appears as *farīmbūlā*; see Zacharia rhetor, *HE*, CSCO, ser. 3, vol. 6, text, p. 197; it appears to be a *hapax legomenon* in Syriac. It is also used in the *Martyrium Arethae*; see *ActaSS*, tomus decimus, p. 742. The term appears in the New Testament, Acts 21:34. The Authorized Version wrongly translates it as "castle," but the New English Bible translates it correctly, "barracks," as had the Peshiṭta before with its *mashrīthā*.

In addition to these attestations, there are others provided by the various conciliar lists examined below[5] and also that tantalizing reference to Job (καὶ υἱοῦ Ἰώβ, ἐθνάρχου Χριστιανοῦ πάσης τῆς παρεμβολῆς) in the *Martyrium Arethae*,[6] datable around 520. It is noteworthy that in the conciliar lists the plural form (παρεμβολαί) is used in the subscription. This could imply that the number of Saracens in these camps increased and led to the establishment of new ones.[7] It is practically certain that the Arabic equivalent of the Greek term was *ḥīra*, which gave its name to the famous city of the Lakhmids in Iraq. The Saracens of the Palestinian Parembole had come from that region in the Land of the Two Rivers, where the term *ḥīra* was very much in use. In its plural form, the Arabic term would have been *ḥiyār* or *ḥīrān*, both well-known morphological patterns of the plural and also attested toponyms in Oriens.[8]

The site of the Palestinian Parembole was excavated early in this century by Féderlin,[9] who located it at Bir al-Zarʿa, southeast of Khān al-Aḥmar. The final question is whether the site, the military camp of these Arab *foederati* of Palaestina Prima, was mentioned in the *Notitia Dignitatum*. This document does not list the *foederati* and their camps, with the exception of the two units of Saracens in Phoenicia Libanensis,[10] but it is possible that the Parembole *foederati* were the *Cohors prima salutaria inter Aeliam et Hierichunta* listed for Palestine.[11] The fact that no particular site is given as the station of this *cohors* could give support to the view that it was a mobile unit, such as the Parembole *foederati* were.

[5] See below, Chap. 11.

[6] See Shahîd, "The Conference of Ramla," 118.

[7] See Génier, *Euthyme*, 104–11.

[8] See *BAFOC*, 402, 403, and 490–98, on the etymology of *ḥīra*.

[9] Génier, *Euthyme*, 104–11.

[10] See below, 466.

[11] *Notitia Dignitatum*, 74. The Parembole was exactly between Jerusalem (called Aelia in the *ND*) and Jericho.

XI

The Arab Episcopate in Oriens: The Conciliar Lists

Despite the paucity of sources about the Arab episcopate in the fourth century, a modest list has been compiled, which includes the names of three bishops.[1] The same source problem plagues the attempt to draw a clear picture of the Arab episcopate in the fifth century, but conciliar lists do provide the names of Arab bishops.[2] These lists also contain the names of Rhomaic and federate bishops.[3]

I. The Arab Federate Bishops

A

There were three ecumenical councils in this century—Ephesus, the Latrocinium, and Chalcedon—and the conciliar lists of all three have survived.

The Council of Ephesus (431)

The Arab *foederati* are represented at Ephesus by one bishop, the former ally of Persia, Aspebetos of the Palestinian Parembole, who after his conversion assumed the Christian name Petrus. His active participation is fully attested in the *Vita Euthymii* of Cyril of Scythopolis and in the *Acta* of the Council of Ephesus.[4] He was sent to the council by St. Euthymius, who

[1] See *BAFOC*, 330–40.

[2] The principal source is the *Acta Conciliorum Oecumenicorum*, edited by E. Schwartz and continued by J. Straub (hereafter *ACO*). The "Index Prosopographicus" referred to here is the Pars Secunda of the Index Generalis Tomorum I–III of *ACO*. R. Devreesse sensed the rise of an Arab hierarchy in the 4th century and discussed some of the bishops of the conciliar lists in *Le patriarcat d'Antioche* (hereafter *PA*); on Devreesse, see *BAFOC*, 340–42; E. Honigmann's article is basic for the study of the conciliar lists; see "The Original Lists of the Members of the Councils of Nicaea, the Robber-Synod and the Council of Chalcedon," *Byzantion* 16 (1944), 20–80; R. Génier and H. Charles, respectively, touched on Arab participation in the councils in *Euthyme* and *Le christianisme*. More recently the subject was treated in a general fashion by J. S. Trimingham, in *Christianity*, reviewed by I. Shahîd in *JSS* 26 (1981), 150–53.

[3] On the Rhomaic bishops (i.e., bishops of the Arab provincials) in the 4th century, see *BAFOC*, 344–45.

[4] The detailed account of the role of Petrus in the Council of Ephesus may be found in Génier, *Euthyme*, 145–52. His account is perceptive rather than enthusiastic in favor of Petrus, and is documented in the sources. Charles' comments are ungenerous to Génier's sound scholarship and he is unjustified in equating sympathetic understanding with writing *con amore*: see Charles, *Le christianisme*, 42–43.

For other discussions of Petrus in this book, see the Index. For all the references to him in the *Acta* of the Council of Ephesus, see *ACO*, Index Prosopographicus, 388.

advised him to take his lead from Cyril, the archbishop of Alexandria, and Acacius, the bishop of Melitene, in combating Nestorius. Petrus' participation involved the following activities: (1) He was elected one of the four bishops forming a delegation that was sent by the council to communicate with Nestorius, and it was he who reported to the assembled fathers the failure of the mission. (2) He was also chosen as one of the delegates who conferred with John, the Patriarch of Antioch, and he reported on the failure of the mission to persuade John to join the assembly. (3) He was one of the bishops who subscribed to the articles of faith and the condemnation of Nestorius.

Petrus' active participation raises some questions. His episcopal see, the Parembole, was very small. Given this fact and his recent conversion to Christianity, it seems odd that he was saddled with these responsibilities. However, his metropolitan bishop, Juvenal, was a strong ecclesiastic, who at Chalcedon, was able to create for himself a new patriarchate at Jerusalem, thus changing the patriarchal map of Christendom. This is perhaps consistent with his interest in some visibility for his suffragan bishop. Perhaps most important was the personality of Bishop Petrus. From his antecedents, as recounted by Cyril of Scythopolis, it can easily be concluded that he was an extraordinary figure. It must have been this personality that induced the council or Juvenal to recommend him for this active part, in much the same way that Euthymius had done before, when he recommended to Juvenal that the phylarch was worthy of the episcopate.

The participation of only one Arab bishop, who led a small Arab Christian community, raises the question of the non-participation of other Arab groups in Oriens, especially the Salīḥids, the dominant Arab federate group. (1) It had been a long time since an Arab bishop of the *foederati* participated in a synodical or conciliar gathering. The last attested bishop was Theotimus, who participated in the Synod of Antioch in 363; none participated in the Council of Constantinople in 381, possibly because the Tanūkhids were in their second revolt.[5] Since half a century separated Constantinople from Ephesus, the practice of inviting the bishop of the *foederati* may have lapsed, especially after this second revolt. (2) Further, one would expect that Salīḥ would be represented as the dominant federate group, which, moreover, was very attached to Christianity. It is also possible that involvement in Christian monasticism, which spread widely among the Arabs in the fifth century, may have disinclined the Salīḥids from participating actively in theological disputes, and consequently they did not send a representative.[6]

[5] On Arab participation in the councils of the 4th century, see *BAFOC*, 330–35; for the second Tanūkhid revolt, see ibid., 205–16.

[6] For the involvement of Salīḥ with monasticism, see below, 297–300. Some twenty years later the Salīḥids may have been represented in a church council; see below, App. 1.

Of all the bishops of the *foederati* in the fifth century, the picture of Petrus is the clearest. He is not merely a name in a conciliar or synodical list, as some of the federate bishops are, but appears as an active participant in the deliberations at Ephesus. His own words are extensively preserved in the acts of the council, as in the case of the dialogue between Moses, the Arab bishop of Mavia, and Lucian, the Arian patriarch of Alexandria in the fourth century.[7]

The Latrocinium of Ephesus (449)

The Arab *foederati* were represented at the Latrocinium by a bishop of the Parembole with the uncommon name Auxolaus. He was one of the group of bishops whom Juvenal took with him from Palestine to the council. Auxolaus championed the heterodoxy of the council, which was presided over by Dioscorus, and voted for the orthodoxy and rehabilitation of Eutyches, as well as for Flavian's deposition. On his return to the Parembole he was rebuked for this by Euthymius. Auxolaus died soon after, and the hagiographer connected this to his having sided with Dioscorus.[8]

How is one to explain Auxolaus' doctrinal position? On the one hand, he was simply following Juvenal's lead. He had come with him to Ephesus as one of his suffragan bishops, and he naturally voted with his metropolitan when the latter sided with Dioscorus in declaring the orthodoxy of Eutyches and asking for his rehabilitation as a priest and as the head of his monastery. There is no record that Euthymius had briefed Auxolaus as he had earlier done with Petrus. So, without clear signals from Euthymius, Auxolaus naturally gravitated to the position of his powerful superior, Juvenal, when away from the influence of the revered saint. As noted above, Juvenal had a very strong personality. The bishop of the diminutive Christian Arab community of the Parembole understandably followed his lead. As early as the first council in 431 Juvenal had shown signs of wanting the three Palestines to be ecclesiastically independent of Antioch.[9]

Thus not much can be said for the view that Auxolaus' doctrinal position indicated that of the community and was the first manifestation of the Arabs'

[7] The inference to be drawn from the quotations from Petrus cited in the *Acta* is that the Arab bishop learned Greek and became fluent in it. This must have been the case in view of the fact that he was also sent to *negotiate* with Nestorius, and it is impossible to believe that he would have been given this assignment if he had not been fluent in the language.

[8] For an account of Auxolaus' mission to the Latrocinium and his return to the Parembole after it, see Génier, *Euthyme*, 180–82. For references to him in the *Acta* of the council, see the Index Prosopographicus, 65. See also Schwartz' comment, *Kyrillos*, 361.

[9] On how the bishops of the three Palestines formed one bloc at the Council of Ephesus in 431 under the direction of the ambitious bishop of Jerusalem, see Devreesse, *PA*, 133 and note 1 for pp. 45–46.

propensity toward Monophysitism.[10] But, as suggested above, no general conclusions on the doctrinal propensity of the Arabs can be drawn from this isolated episode. An examination of the circumstances attending Auxolaus' vote shows that it was shared by many others and was cast in a hierarchical context involving the powerful prospective patriarch of Jerusalem, Juvenal.

Auxolaus's participation raises three further questions.

1. Was he an Arab, or was he simply the bishop of the Arab Parembole? His name is not decisive. On their consecration, Arab ecclesiastics assumed Graeco-Roman names and gave up Arab ones, which smacked of paganism. The Arab Petrus, first bishop of the Parembole, would have passed as a non-Arab in the conciliar list, had it not been for information on his Arab background in the *Vita Euthymii*. Auxolaus, too, was probably an Arab. His name is uncommon; not a single ecclesiastic in the councils seems to have had it. It could have been the translation of his Arabic name or some other Arabic name.[11]

2. It is noteworthy that Auxolaus is described not as bishop of the Parembole (ἐπίσκοπος Παρεμβολῶν) but as ἐπίσκοπος Σαρακηνῶν ὑποσπόνδων, reflecting the fact that he was the bishop of the *foederati*. This confirms the continuance of the small Arab community in the Jordan Valley as allies and not assimilated *Rhōmaioi*. This description also makes certain that *civitas* was not extended to them even after sharing an experience as Byzantine as participating in a church council.

3. Finally, was Auxolaus the only representative of the Arab *foederati* in Oriens at the Second Council of Ephesus? Apparently he was. Arab representation at both councils came only from bishops of the Palestinian Parembole —evidence of the active part which it took in the religious life of the empire, no doubt owing to its association with Juvenal of Jerusalem.

The Council of Chalcedon (451)

The Council of Chalcedon was attended by two, possibly three, bishops of the Arabs.

John

The Parembole sent John, the successor of Auxolaus, as representative to the Council of Chalcedon. After the council he brought its definition of faith to Euthymius, who accepted it.

[10] As some did; see Charles, *Le christianisme*, 43. Petrus is much more important than Auxolaus, and yet Charles devoted two paragraphs to the latter (pp. 43–44) and only one to Petrus (pp. 42–43).

[11] Such as Zayd al-Qawm, the literal translation of Αὐξόλαος. For another Arab bishop who had the Arabic name of ʿAbdalla, see below, Sec. II. This was, of course, a theophoric name not inappropriate for a Christian Arab.

The participation of John in the council is clearly documented in the *Vita Euthymii* of Cyril of Scythopolis.[12] The lists of the Council of Chalcedon, however, present problems of identification for the Arab bishop. A bishop named John[13] appears in the list of bishops who attended the first session on October 8, 451; he is described as "John of the Saracens" (Ἰωάννου Σαρακηνῶν). Another list of subscriptions has a John, also described as "John of the Saracens," Ἰωάννης ἐπ. Σαρακηνῶν [Ταιηνῶν Σ], who signed with the bishops of Osroene, not of Palestine.[14] This subscription has created a controversy about the identity of the Osroenean bishop: Was he another Arab bishop who was the namesake of the Palestinian one from the Parembole, or a different one belonging to Osroene?

Schwartz argues that this was John of the Parembole,[15] but Devreesse rejects this on the grounds that the bishopric of the Parembole was "Palestinian" and not "Arab."[16] Honigmann, however, returns to the position of Schwartz and argues persuasively for identifying this John with that of the Parembole and gives personal differences with his patriarch, Juvenal, as an explanation for his signing with the bishops of Osroene.[17]

Honigmann is probably right in identifying the two Johns and in concluding that the ecclesiastic in question was the bishop of the Parembole. Furthermore, it may be pointed out that there is reference to only one John in each of these lists of Chalcedon. Since the bishop of the Parembole is indisputably attested in the *Vita Euthymii* as having taken part in the council, and since no Arab bishop of Osroene is attested elsewhere, the chances are that the John of the lists is the John of the Parembole. On the other hand, these lists vary in what they include, and it is possible that they left out a reference to

[12] See *Kyrillos*, 41.

[13] See Schwartz, *ACO*, II, i, pt. 2, p. 134.

[14] See E. Honigmann, "Original Lists," 53; Devreesse, *PA*, 138. The description of John as "of the Taienoi" in addition to "Saraceni" comes from the Syriac version, where the Arabs are normally referred to as Ṭayāyē.

[15] See Schwartz, *ACO*, II, vi, p. 36; on John, see also the Index Prosopographicus, 251.

[16] Devreesse, *PA*, 215. It is not entirely clear what he means by this distinction. Auxolaus, the Parembole bishop of Palestine who attended the Latrocinium, is described as the bishop of "the allied Saracens" (ἐπίσκοπος Σαρακηνῶν ὑποσπόνδων). So John, who is described as "the bishop of the Saracens," could also have come from the Palestine Parembole, as indicated in the *Vita Euthymii*. The fallacy in Devreesse's reasoning is also noted by Honigmann, "The Patriarchate of Antioch," *Traditio* 5 (1947), 148.

[17] For his commentary on the reference to "John of the Saracens," see Honigmann, "Original Lists," 70–72. In support of Honigmann's view, it might be pointed out that Euthymius disapproved of the part played by Juvenal in the Latrocinium, as is clear from his indignation at Auxolaus on his return from Ephesus. And it is natural to assume that when John attended the Council of Chalcedon, he was aware, as Euthymius must have been, of the doctrinal position of Juvenal. But this is weakened by the fact that his colleague, Stephen of Jamnia, who came back with him to see Euthymius, sat with the Palestinian bishops.

one of the two Johns. As has been shown here and in the preceding volume, the Arab federate presence in Oriens was extensive, and those who have argued for the identification of the two were not fully aware of this fact. The Arab bishop who signed with those of Osroene could have been the bishop of an Arab group in that province. The Arab element in Osroene was quite strong, and the name Osroene itself derives from that of the Arab tribal group that lived there.[18]

The same problem arises with reference to another ecclesiastic, Timotheus, who, according to Honigmann,[19] was one of the members of the σύνοδος ἐνδημοῦσα[20] of 448. In Latin he appears as *Timotheus episc. Saracinorum civitatis provinciae Palaestinae*, which has led some scholars to consider him a bishop of the Saracens in Palestine.[21] Honigmann again argues persuasively that the Latin is a corrupt version of the Greek original and should read *episcopus (s)Ar(a)cinorum civitatis*.[22] What is involved is Arca in Phoenicia, not *Saracenus*.

What emerges with certainty from these arguments is that the John who represented the Christian Arab church at Chalcedon was John, the third bishop of the Parembole in Palestine. Was he, like Petrus, ethnically Arab? This is impossible to determine from his name, and his background is little known. More important is the fact that his participation and his return from Chalcedon with the definition of the faith signals the return to Orthodoxy of the Arab church of the Parembole in Palestine, slightly troubled by the heterodoxy of Auxolaus, the second bishop of the Parembole, who participated in the Latrocinium of 449.

Eustathius

The second clearly identifiable Arab participant at the Council of Chalcedon after John of the Parembole is Eustathius. Unlike "John of the Saracens," there is no problem about his provincial affiliation; he belonged to Phoenicia Libanensis. His participation is reflected in two different documents: (1) His name appears twice in the *Acta* of the Council of Chalcedon,[23]

[18] On this, see Shahîd, *RA*, 3–4.

[19] Honigmann, "Original Lists," 66.

[20] This local synod which condemned Eutyches was held in 442; see Honigmann, "Juvenal," 231.

[21] See Schwartz, Index Prosopographicus, 489, and W. Ensslin, in *RE*, VI A, col. 1361.

[22] Honigmann, "Original Lists," 66–67. His argument rested on the fact that the two predecessors of John at the Parembole—Petrus and Auxolaus—are known, and so there is no room for a Timotheus. But Palestine may have had more than one Arab bishop. Palaestina Prima is unlikely to have had another bishop, but Tertia may have had. Even so, Honigmann is most probably right; see his "Juvenal," 228.

[23] For these two references to Eustathius in the *Acta* of Chalcedon, see Honigmann, "Original Lists," 58 and Schwartz, *ACO*, II, i, pars 2, p. 138.

once as Εὐστάθιος ἐπὶ Σαρακηνῶν and again as Εὐσταθίου ἔθνους Σαρακηνῶν. (2) A few years later Eustathius Saracenorum appears in the *codex encyclicus*, a collection of letters sent in 458 by the provincial synods to Emperor Leo in defense of Chalcedon. Eustathius signed with the bishops of Phoenicia Libanensis, the metropolitan bishop of which at that time was John of Damascus.[24]

What is his identity and what Arab group did he represent? The Arab presence in Oriens was extensive; the diocese had many groups of Arabs, both federate and non-federate. However, since Eustathius is described as being assigned to Phoenicia Libanensis, there are two possibilities:

1. It has been suggested that Eustathius was the bishop of the thirty thousand Arabs who were said to have been converted to Christianity in the region of Heliopolis in Phoenicia Libanensis.[25] But this suggestion has been open to such strong objections that it is necessary to look elsewhere.[26]

2. Surely this must be an important group of Arabs, important enough to be represented at an ecumenical council meeting in distant Chalcedon. They are referred to as *ethnos* (ἔθνος), the term which, in its Latin form *gens*, is used in official Byzantine terminology to refer to the Arab *foederati* of Byzantium in the fifth century. Arab federate presence in Oriens was spread out and represented by various tribal groups. But the most distinguished Arab federates in the fifth century were the Salīḥids, and the chances are good that Eustathius was their bishop.

Since the Salīḥids were undoubtedly the main Arab federate group in Oriens in the fifth century, it is natural to suppose that they would have been selected to send a general representative of the Arab *foederati* to the council.[27] Their representation was also relevant to the policy of both the Byzantine *imperium* and *ecclesia*. The empire had a taste of federate heterodoxy with the Arianism of the Germans, and it must have been anxious that its Arab *foederati* be of the right doctrinal persuasion. Since their conversion earlier in the century, the Salīḥids had been orthodox and zealous Christians, and the new orthodoxy, centering around the Christology of the fifth century, naturally interested them.

[24] For this, see E. Honigmann, "Studien zur *Notitia Antiochena*," *BZ* 25 (1925), 64–65. By an oversight, Devreesse (*PA*, 215) said that the letter was addressed by Leo to Eustathius. This is corrected by Honigmann, in "The Patriarchate of Antioch," 147.

[25] See Vailhé, "Notes de géographie ecclésiastique," 14–15; see also Honigmann, "Studien zur *Notitia Antiochena*," 68, and above, 17–19.

[26] See Charles, "Le christianisme," 47–48. It is so unlikely that the well-established *foederati* of Byzantium in the 5th century would have been left unrepresented in favor of a group of recent converts.

[27] The participation of the Arabs of the diminutive Parembole at the council, represented by John, was due to the energy of Juvenal and the association of the Parembole with a celebrated saint, Euthymius.

The *Notitia Dignitatum* could throw some light on the identity of the Arabs who were represented by Eustathius at Chalcedon and corroborate the view that they were the Salīḥids. Two Arab units are described in it as assigned to the defense of Phoenicia Libanensis: *Equites Saraceni indigenae*, stationed at Betroclus, and *Equites Saraceni*, stationed at Thelsee.[28] As noted earlier, the *Notitia* does not list the units of the Arab *foederati* in Oriens; it lists only the regular units of the Roman army whose members were *Rhōmaioi* (Roman citizens). Thus the listing of two non-citizen Arab units in Phoenicia suggests that they were distinguished enough to merit inclusion in the document.[29] Since this is the century when the Salīḥids were the dominant federate power in Oriens,[30] it is natural to suppose that these two units were Salīḥids.[31] If they were stationed in Phoenicia Libanensis, it is natural to assume that a reference in the *Acta* of Chalcedon to a bishop of the Saracens whose province was Phoenicia is a reference to the bishop of the Salīḥids.

What was Eustathius' ethnic origin, and what was his episcopal see? Again there is no way of telling from his name whether or not he was Arab. The chances are that he was, but more important than his ethnic origin is that he was a bishop of the Arab *foederati* around the middle of the century. He thus may be added to the badly documented hierarchy of the Arab federate church in the fifth century. It is possible that he had no fixed see but moved about in Phoenicia Libanensis performing his episcopal duties. On the other hand, it is possible that Thelsee, the locality where the *Equites Saraceni* were stationed, functioned as his episcopal see. This may receive some support from the fact that Thelsee has been identified with Ḍumayr (Ḍmeir), a town long associated with the Arabs.[32] In the Byzantine period it is closely associated with the Ghassānids of the sixth century, an association that has been epigraphically confirmed.[33] Thus it was an old Arab establishment and would have been a natural place for the episcopal see of an Arab bishop in the fifth century.

[28] For a discussion of the Arab units in the *Notitia Dignitatum* see below, Part 3, sec. I. The two units referred to as *Saraceni* are discussed in *RA*, 59 note 33 and *BAFOC*, 486 note 81. I am now more inclined to think that they are Salīḥid.

[29] The only other reference to *Saraceni* in the *Notitia* is to *Equites Saraceni Thamudeni*. But the Thamudeni had long been in the service of Rome, and the unit was possibly Rhomaic by this time. Besides it was stationed in the *limes Aegypti*, which did not form part of Oriens in the 5th century.

[30] It was argued earlier that the decline of Salīḥ started with their participation in the expedition of Leo against the Vandals in 468; see above, Chap. 4, sec. VI.

[31] The two units could have constituted only a contingent of Salīḥids, who must have had other units stationed in other parts of Oriens.

[32] See A. Musil, *Palmyrena*, 252, app. 4; and R. Dussaud, *Topographie historique de la Syrie antique et médiévale* (Paris, 1927), 270.

[33] For the fort built to its south by the Ghassānid Munḏir, see ibid.

B

The lists for the Rhomaic bishops at Ephesus and Chalcedon, especially the latter, are complete or nearly so. Each ecclesiastical province in the empire sent its group of bishops with their metropolitan, and this is reflected in the conciliar lists. The representation of the Arab federate church was understandably meager, and when more than one bishop attended, as was the case at Chalcedon, it was for a very special reason. Thus the quest for the other members of the Arab federate episcopate has to consider documents other than the conciliar and synodical lists. These have left out many Arab bishops who must have flourished in the course of the twenty years or so that elapsed from the first Council of Ephesus to Chalcedon, and naturally there were bishops in the years before Ephesus and the half century after Chalcedon.

1. These "missing" bishops must be sought in other sources for the fifth century.[34] It is by the merest chance that anything is known about the important Arab federate bishop Petrus. Our knowledge of him is owed not to an ecclesiastical but to a secular historian, Malchus. This gives an indication of how much federate ecclesiastical history was not recorded or has been lost.

There are, however, other ways of assessing the extent of the Arab federate episcopate in the fifth century through understanding their history and how they were deployed, grouped, and governed in the many provinces of Oriens.[35] Although precise information is lacking, it may be safely assumed that each province of Oriens, especially those of the limitrophe, had Arab federates. The dominant power was Salīḥ, but there were others, belonging to various tribal affiliations and not united under Salīḥ. It follows that each tribal group is likely to have had its own bishop. Malchus, when speaking of Petrus, the bishop of Amorkesos, calls him "the bishop of the tribe" (ἐπίσκοπον τῆς φυλῆς).[36] In view of the strong Arab tribal feeling of solidarity, each tribe probably had its own bishop, just as each had its own phylarch.[37] Since these tribes were many their bishops were correspondingly many, and this is consonant with what Sozomen says on the number of bishops among the Arabs.[38]

The rise of the Arab federate episcopate was a novel form of control and discipline in the life of the Arab tribe, which it had not had in its pagan

[34] Sozomen testifies to the considerable number of bishops whom the Arabs had in the 5th century; see *HE*, VII, 19.

[35] On the tribal structure of Arab federate power in Oriens in the 4th century, see *BAFOC*, 381–88; for the 5th century, see below, Chap. 12, sec. IV.

[36] See the discussion of Petrus, above, 72–74.

[37] The most explicit reference to this is in the history of Queen Mavia and her insistence on a bishop of her own tribal group; see *BAFOC*, 152–58.

[38] See above, 178. Sozomen does speak of villages (κῶμαι), but the federates did live in villages; Arab federate influence extended to these, as when Leo put Amorkesos in charge of many of them.

Peninsular days. While the phylarch had jurisdiction over the federate soldiers, as the old *sayyid* had, the bishop's spiritual authority had a wider range; it affected the entire tribe, including women, children, and the phylarch himself. Thus the bishop may now be added to other forms of control and influence within the Arab federate tribal structure which developed in the shadow of Byzantium.[39]

2. The organization of the Arab federate *ecclesia* must have been along the following lines.

Just as the phylarch of a particular province answered to the *dux* of that province, so the bishop of a federate Arab group must have answered to the metropolitan bishop of the province. This is clearly illustrated in the case of the bishops of the Parembole in relation to Juvenal of Jerusalem, who even subscribed to his doctrinal views at the councils, and in the case of Eustathius, who signed the letter addressed to Leo in 458 with his metropolitan, the bishop of Damascus.

The number of Arab federate bishops in each province remains a problem, as does the number of phylarchs. Large provinces, such as Palaestina Tertia, probably had more than one bishop. For instance, Petrus was the bishop of the Arabs of Amorkesos, whose jurisdiction was in the Trans-ʿAraban region. It is difficult to assume that he also functioned as bishop for the rest of Palaestina Tertia, which extended to the Negev and Sinai.[40] It is, therefore, practically certain that in large provinces there was more than one bishop and that they were assigned along tribal lines. That only one bishop represented the province of Phoenicia when Eustathius signed with his Phoenician colleagues does not argue that it had only one Arab bishop. In fact the reference to Eustathius raises the question of seniority in the Arab episcopal hierarchy. It is possible that since provinces had more than one bishop each, there was some sort of senior bishop among the college of Arab bishops answering to the metropolitan in the province, and that this senior bishop represented the Arab episcopate of the province at the councils.

[39] In the Peninsular stage it consisted of the *sayyid*, the poet, and the orator as the most important. Within the *limes*, the bishop was added; the *sayyid* developed into a phylarch, and the *kātib* (scribe) possibly appeared; see below, 415. On the spiritual authority of the bishop over his tribal flock, see the account of the submission of the Christian poet Akhtal, the laureate of the Umayyads, to his priest and bishop: Cheikho, *Shuʿaraʾ al-Nasrāniyya*, 172.

[40] Thus, although the names of the federate bishops of Palaestina Tertia contemporaneous with Petrus may not be known, it is safe to assume that there were bishops, especially in the Negev where an inscription speaks of a *koinon* of phylarchs; see above, 141. A strong phylarchal presence implies a correspondingly strong episcopal presence, or at least some form of it. In sparsely populated places, where federate presence was numerically weak, presumably the community had a priest, while episcopal duties were discharged by the bishop of the neighboring city, such as Pharan or Elusa.

Finally, did these federate bishops have their own episcopal sees, as did the Rhomaic bishops of each province? They must have, although they were not recognized as such in references to them in the lists, except in the Parembole of the phylarchs of Palestine, where they are referred to as "bishops of the Parembole." The federate bishops probably had to travel wherever the *foederati* were ordered by the military administration. As has been suggested above in discussing Thelsee,[41] they might have had headquarters from which they set out to wherever their episcopal duties called them.

II. The Arab Rhomaic Bishops

In addition to the Arab federate episcopate, there was a second Arab one, composed of *Rhōmaioi*, not *foederati*.

As pointed out in *Rome and the Arabs*, the Diocese of Oriens had an Arab zone separable from the Aramaean and the Greek zones, which retained some of its ethnic and cultural identity.[42] It comprised the limitrophe provinces. Many, perhaps most, of the bishops in the provincial lists of the limitrophe must have been Arab. Just as the Roman *imperium* recruited the *limitanei* who manned the frontier locally, so the *ecclesia* recruited its members from the provincial natives, especially as Christianity spread there so quickly in the first Christian centuries, and the Arabs figured so prominently in the early theological disputes.[43] But these Arab ecclesiastics, like their secular compatriots, assumed Graeco-Roman names, especially on the occasion of episcopal consecration, since their old Arab names were pagan. How, then, can one identify the Arab bishops?

First, one could isolate from the conciliar lists the provinces that may be considered limitrophe, such as Palaestina Tertia, Arabia, Phoenicia Libanensis, Syria, Euphratensis, Osroene, and Mesopotamia. This can lead to the fallacy of arguing from the general to the particular, which must be avoided. Faced with a provincial list of bishops of Palaestina Tertia or Arabia containing Graeco-Roman names, it would be impossible to argue that this or that particular bishop was an Arab. But it would be safe to conclude on the basis of the ethnic and cultural identity of the limitrophe provinces that many or at least some of the bishops who were assigned to that region were Arabs, leaving aside the question of which among them were such.[44]

Second, one could isolate from the lists the names of bishops which are

[41] See above, notes 32–33.

[42] For the Arab zone in Oriens, see *RA*, 3–16.

[43] For this, see G. Kretschmar, "Origenes und die Araber," *Zeitschrift für Theologie und Kirche* 1 (1953), 258–79.

[44] If Arabia in the 3rd century sent to Athens itself the two sophists Callinicus and Genethlius to teach rhetoric there (Bowersock, *Roman Arabia*, 135–36), it is not extravagant to say that it also put the talents of its inhabitants at the disposal of the local *ecclesia*.

unmistakably Arab.[45] This is the easier and more obvious course, although it produces few results; yet it afford opportunities for examining names that certainly betray the Arab identity of the bishops.

Ephesus (431)

The *Acta* of the Council of Ephesus provide the names of three bishops that are recognizably Arab:

1. Abdelas (Ἀβδελᾶς) is Arabic ʿAbdallah, "the servitor of God," with a Greek ending.[46] He is, appropriately, the bishop of Elusa, an Arab city whose Saracens were converted by St. Hilarion in the fourth century.[47] The subsequent Hellenization of this name is evident, and the onomastic metamorphosis may be presented as follows: Abdelas is translated as Θεόδουλος, and finally is completely assimilated to a Greek name, Apellas (Ἀπελλᾶς).

2. Saidas (Σαΐδας) is clearly Arabic Saʿīd, "the happy, the fortunate."[48] He is the bishop of Phaeno in Palaestina Tertia, like Elusa, a region where the Arab ethnic complexion is quite strong.

3. Natiras (Νατίρας) is clearly Arabic and most probably Naḏīr, "consecrated, vowed."[49] It is noteworthy that he is the bishop of Gaza; the name may have been appropriately chosen by the bishop on his election to that see. The association of the city and the region with Samson, a Nazarite, could suggest the reason he chose it.

Constantinople (449)

In November 448 a local synod (σύνοδος ἐνδημοῦσα) met in Constantinople and condemned Eutyches, the influential monk and archimandrite of a monastery in Constantinople, after his "Monophysitic" confession. In April of the following year a committee inquired into Euthyches' appeal. Among the members of this committee were two Palestinian bishops, one of whom was Natiras of Gaza who had participated in the Council of Ephesus eighteen years before.[50]

The Latrocinium (449)

The *Acta* of the Latrocinium of Ephesus provides one name that is recognizably Semitic—Arabic or Aramaic—but most probably Arabic, since the bishop who bore that name was the bishop of Phaeno in Palaestina Tertia, an

[45] It is noteworthy that those who retained their Arabic names are not the Arab bishops of the federates but the *Rhōmaioi*, the bishops of the Byzantine *ecclesia*.

[46] See the Index Prosopographicus s.v. "Theodulus," p. 477.

[47] See *BAFOC*, 288–93.

[48] See the Index Prosopographicus, 423.

[49] Ibid., 335.

[50] See ibid.; also Honigmann, "Juvenal," 230–31.

almost exclusively Arab area. His name is Caioumas (Καϊούμας),[51] which could be Arabic Qayyūm, Qayūm, or Qā'im.

Chalcedon (451)

The *Acta* of the Council of Chalcedon provides the names of three recognizably Arab bishops:

1. Aretas ('Αρέτας)[52] is an Arabic name borne by the bishop of Elusa in Palaestina Tertia. The region was heavily Arab.

2. Natiras (Νατίρας)[53] was the bishop of Gaza who had attended Ephesus in 431 and Constantinople in 449. Consequently he is the only Arab bishop who attended three councils in the fifth century; he thus recalls Juvenal, his metropolitan bishop, who also attended three.

3. Caioumas (Καϊούμας),[54] as already mentioned, is most probably Arabic, and not Aramaic. At the Council of Chalcedon this name was borne by the bishop of Marciopolis. This city is situated in Osroene which, if not exclusively Arab, was very strongly so. Since it is attested as the name of an Arab bishop in Palaestina Tertia, the chances are that Caioumas, the bishop of Marciopolis, also was Arab.

4. Gautus (Γαῦτος) is also an Arabic name, Ghawth, known in the Arabic onomasticon.[55] He appears in the lists as a bishop from the province of Arabia, the bishop of the city of Neila (ἐπίσκοπος πόλεως Νείλων). His episcopal see presents a problem since it is not clear where in the Provincia Arabia this was.[56]

The Arab substrate in the Rhomaic church is thus a fact in the ecclesiastical history of Oriens. It should not, however, be concluded that it constituted an *ecclesia in ecclesia* within the Patriarchate of Antioch, or that the Arab origin of these bishops interfered with their loyalty to it. There was no tendency toward separatism. The importance of discovering their Arab origin lies elsewhere, in the area of federate-imperial relations, in the symbiosis that must have obtained between the Arab *foederati* and the larger society within which they were living in Oriens.

[51] See the Index Prosopographicus, 83.

[52] Ibid., 49.

[53] Ibid., 335.

[54] Ibid., 82.

[55] Ibid., 205.

[56] The commentators have had great difficulty identifying Neela/Neila, the episcopal see of Ghawth, as is clear from the marginal note on Neile in E. Honigmann, *Le Synecdèmos d'Hiéroclès* (Brussels, 1939), 722:2 (p. 44), where it appears as Νείλα Κώμη. But it is clearly in the Auranitis, either Khirbet el-Nile, as identified by R. Dussaud, or Moushennef, as identified by Waddington, probably the former; see R. Dussaud *Topographie historique*, 342, 359.

III. The Arabs and Orthodoxy

One of the themes of this series is that of heresies and national movements and their relation to the Arabs. In the preceding volume the problem was discussed for the fourth century.[57] Since Arab bishops participated in the councils of the fifth century, which dealt with christological controversies, some discussion of this problem is necessary.

The Arab *foederati* of the fourth century were solidly Orthodox. Their loyalty to the empire was firm, but they did challenge the central government by their revolt, which was in behalf of Orthodoxy and against the heretic emperor, Valens. But in the fifth century there was no challenge to imperial authority nor any trace of federate unrest. The *foederati* lived in perfect harmony with the central government from the reign of Arcadius to that of Anastasius.

The conciliar lists have revealed that the Arab bishops, both Rhomaic and federate, voted on the side of Orthodoxy at the first Council of Ephesus and at Chalcedon. What is more, Petrus, the bishop of the Parembole, played an important role in the deliberations at Ephesus against Nestorius. A dissonant note was sounded by the heterodox Auxolaus at the Latrocinium of 449, but he was not a representative; he died soon after, and the Parembole returned to strict Orthodoxy. The circumstances were exceptional, and, as was argued earlier, Auxolaus was only following his metropolitan bishop.

Why did the Arab bishops generally vote in the interest of Orthodoxy? The question admits of a categorical answer, especially as pertains to the bishops of the Parembole at the three councils of the fifth century. They followed the strong lead given by the powerful metropolitan of Jerusalem, Juvenal, as the course of events clearly demonstrates. The figure of St. Euthymius was also in the background. The same applies to Eustathius, the bishop of the Saracens of Phoenicia, who also voted and signed with his metropolitan bishop, Theodore, at Chalcedon and later followed his metropolitan, John of Damascus, in 458 when he signed the letters sent to Emperor Leo.

This raises the question of the nature and role of leadership in the religious controversies of the century. One scholar has noted that this "played a significant role in the development of the loyalty which determined the direction of popular opinion."[58] In the case of the Arab bishops, leadership did not

[57] See *BAFOC*, 8, 82 note 33, 201–2. The two basic works involved in this controversy are E. L. Woodward, *Christianity and Nationalism in the Later Roman Empire* (London, 1916) and A. H. M. Jones, "Were the Ancient Heresies National or Social Movements in Disguise?" *JTS*, n.s. 10 (1959), 280–98. See the recent treatment by T. E. Gregory, *Vox Populi* (Columbus, 1979).

[58] Gregory, *Vox Populi*, 209.

exercise its influence on the "urban crowds" but on the individual bishops, who seem to have had a sense of regional solidarity. Surely some of them were intellectually convinced of the soundness of their doctrinal position, but the presumption is that strong metropolitan leadership exercised by a powerful and dominating ecclesiastic, such as Juvenal, was the decisive factor,[59] even with bishops who were not docile.

Just as the metropolitan exercised leadership over his Arab suffragan bishops, so did these exercise influence over the phylarch of the *foederati* and through him, and perhaps without his mediation, over the *foederati* of the Parembole themselves. The Arab *foederati* of the fifth century, those of the Parembole and those of the Salīḥids whom Eustathius probably represented at Chalcedon, were Orthodox. They were not theologians and perhaps understood little of what was told them about the conciliar decisions. Their loyalty to their bishops and phylarchs bound them to Orthodoxy. This was a new kind of loyalty for the Arabs who, in pagan times, had been used to loyalty toward their tribes and tribal chiefs.

Juvenal was important to the Arab church in Palestine. It has been argued on good grounds[60]—his name and his knowledge of Latin—that he was of Roman extraction. Consciousness of his Roman birth may explain his autocratic ecclesiastical administration. He may even have been descended from a noble Roman family, just as some of the great popes of the Middle Ages were.[61] Thus two Romans—Juvenal and Leo—dominated the two councils—the Latrocinium and Chalcedon.

The ambition of his life was to end his subordination to the see of Caesarea, elevate his own see to an archbishopric or patriarchate over the three Palestines, and become independent of the Patriarchate of Antioch. All this he finally achieved at Chalcedon.[62] These ambitions gave some prominence to the Arab church of Palestine. Juvenal took with him to the three councils the bishops of the Arab Parembole. It was he who consecrated the first bishop of

[59] Possibly reflected in the description of Juvenal as "our bishop Juvenal" by suffragan Saidas of Phaeno in Palaestina Tertia; see Honigmann, "Juvenal," 222.

[60] Ibid., 211, 223. Honigmann's is the most authoritative study of the first patriarch of Jerusalem.

[61] Such as Gregory I and Innocent III.

[62] Thus creating an anomalous situation: the ecclesiastical diocese—the Patriarchate of Antioch—was no longer coterminous with the civil Diocese of Oriens. The civil and military administration of the three Palestines remained part of Oriens, with Antioch as capital. However, by his excision of the Palestines from the jurisdiction of Antioch, Juvenal insured for the region the continuance of Orthodoxy for all time, with the exception of the two years 451–453, when it was under the rule of the Monophysitic monk Theodosius; see Honigmann, "Juvenal," 247–57. Cyprus formed part of the Diocese of Oriens but its church asserted its independence from the Patriarchate of Antioch and its claim was recognized by the Council of Ephesus in 431.

the Parembole, Petrus, and who gave him such a prominent role at the Council of Ephesus in 431. He shepherded the fortunes of the Church in the three Palestines from his see in Jerusalem for more than a third of a century and insured the visibility of the Arab bishopric of Palestine at the councils. By making the three Palestines into a patriarchate, he set the stage for an Arab, Elias, to become the highest ecclesiastic in pre-Islamic times, namely, Patriarch of Jerusalem, toward the end of the century.[63]

The questions posed by Woodward and Jones, referred to earlier, have been answered in the negative. The Arab *foederati* of the fifth century were neither heterodox nor separatist. They were Orthodox and loyal to the empire. It was in the sixth century, when the *foederati* became Monophysites, that Woodward's views can be discussed in relation to the Arabs.[64]

Appendix I

Eustathius and the Salīḥids

Earlier in this chapter[1] it was suggested that Eustathius, the Arab bishop who participated in the Council of Chalcedon, was most probably the bishop of the Salīḥids. As the Byzantine sources on the Salīḥids lack geographical and chronological precision, this datum is a welcome addition to their history.

The reference to the *Saraceni* over whom Eustathius was bishop as *ethnos* (ἔθνος), *gens*, confirms the suspicion that these *foederati* of Byzantium were not *cives*, but remained non-Romans. If they had been *cives*, they would not have been referred to as *gens*, or ἔθνος.[2] They are not referred to in the conciliar list as *foederati*, but this is not unprecedented. In fact, it is paralleled by the non-reference to Petrus and John as bishops of the Arab *foederati*, although they both were: the first is referred to as the bishop of the Parembole and the second as the bishop of the Saracens. Only Auxolaus is referred to as the bishop of the *foederati* (ὑπόσπονδοι).

The subscription of Eustathius to the canons of Chalcedon suggests that Salīḥ was Orthodox, as it had been since it became employed by the Romans as *foederati* early in the century, in the reign of Arcadius. The Salīḥids were and remained zealous Christians. Why, then, did they not participate in the Council of Ephesus, which condemned Nestorius? As mentioned earlier, the *foederati* had not been represented at a council for a long time after the Tanūkhids revolted in the fourth century, while the participation of the bishops of the Parembole was due to the energy of the patriarch of Jerusalem, Juvenal, with whom they were ecclesiastically affiliated. When Oriens was rocked by the christological controversies, the Salīḥids were naturally involved, and so took part in the Council of Chalcedon.

[63] On Elias, see above, 192–96.

[64] See *BAFOC*, 82 note 33, and the forthcoming *BASIC*.

[1] See above, 219–21.

[2] For a *novella* of Theodosius II, issued in 443 and referring to the Arab *foederati* as a *gens*, see above, Chap. 2, sec. v.

With so little known about Salīḥ's whereabouts in Oriens and where it operated, the geographical and chronological precision provided by the conciliar list of Chalcedon is welcome. It suggests that the Salīḥids occupied an important position in the Roman defense system in Phoenicia Libanensis. They were deployed or partly deployed there[3] possibly because it was centrally located in Oriens between the southernmost Palaestina Tertia and Mesopotamia. But another reason may also have been behind the stationing of the Salīḥid cavalry there. The *Acta* of Chalcedon and the novella of Theodosius II in 443 find the Salīḥids flourishing as soldiers in the imperial service and as Orthodox Christians. But it was not long before their decline started, possibly with their role in Leo's expedition against the Vandals.[4]

The participation of the Salīḥids in the Council of Chalcedon was politically more important than that of the Arabs of the Parembole in the three councils. The latter were a small group who counted in the ecclesiastical history of Palestine but not in the political and military history of Oriens. The Salīḥids, on the other hand, did count in the history of the diocese, hence the significance of their participation, especially in a period when doctrinal persuasion was politically important to their relations with the Orthodox central government. It is also noteworthy that, in the long list of participants at Chalcedon, the only group of *foederati* that participated were the Arabs.

Appendix II

Two Greek Inscriptions

The Arab episcopal presence in Oriens, as noted above, was not limited to those bishops, federate and Rhomaic, who attended the meetings of the ecumenical councils. There were other bishops on whom the sources are silent or for whom they are not extant. The detection of Rhomaic bishops of Arab origin is especially difficult because of their assumption of Graeco-Roman names.

The excavation of the ex-Nabataean urban establishment in Palaestina Tertia[1] has not added many names of Arab bishops. Since most of the names of the ecclesiastics are Graeco-Roman, there is no way of telling whether or not they were Arab. The inscriptions of Sobota have yielded the name of only one Arab priest, Salmān,[2] while those at Magen have yielded the name of a priest named ʿAbdullah.[3]

[3] On their settlements in the Provincia Arabia, see below, Chap. 12, app. 1.

[4] On this, see above, Chap. 4, sec. VI.

[1] For Palaestina Tertia and a bibliography especially devoted to it, see K. C. Gutwein, *Third Palestine* (Washington, D.C., 1981). The inscriptions from Oboda (Avdat), Sobota (Shivta), Mapsis (Mamshit), and Elusa (Haluza, Khalasa) are brought together in A. Negev, *The Greek Inscriptions from the Negev* (Jerusalem, 1981).

[2] Negev, op. cit., 59.

[3] See V. Tsaferis, "Mosaics and Inscriptions from Magen," *BASOR* 258 (1985), 28. In the same inscription occurs the name of the bishop Petrus, but there is no way of determining his ethnic origin. On p. 27 is the name of a lector in the church with an Arab name in the diminutive, Ẓunayn (Zenenos). Magen appears on the map on p. 1 to the southeast of Khān Yūnus.

PART TWO
THE ARABIC SOURCES

XII

Oriens

I. Hishām al-Kalbī

The Arabic sources for the *foederati* of the fifth century are not as informative as they are for those of the fourth and the sixth.[1] Nevertheless, the data that they provide are significant. It is important to examine the principal source from which all these data are derived, namely, Hishām al-Kalbī, and account for the paucity of the information provided by him. In the process, other problems related to Hishām's account will be treated, and this will shed more light on the principal historian of the Arabs before the rise of Islam.[2]

Salīḥ

1. The paucity of the data for the history of the fifth-century *foederati*, the Salīḥids, may be explained as follows.

a. Some of the Arab *foederati* of Byzantium stayed on in Bilād al-Shām (now Arab and Muslim Oriens) after the Conquests in the seventh century, but the Salīḥids, or most of them, apparently emigrated to Anatolia together with other *foederati*. Thus, while the Tanūkhids and the Ghassānids maintained a presence in Bilād al-Shām after the Muslim Conquests and took an active part in the making of Islamic history,[3] the Salīḥids did not have a

[1] The same is true of the Greek and Latin sources; for the reasons behind their paucity, see above, xxiv–xxv.

[2] For a treatment of Hishām in general and for his value to the history of the *foederati* of the 4th century, the Tanūkhids, see *BAFOC,* 349–66; this chapter is devoted to an examination of his work as a source for the history of the *foederati* of the 5th century. For the long list of those medieval authors who wrote on the Arabs before the rise of Islam, see Sezgin, *GAS*, I, 258–74. The list makes even clearer the prominent position of Hishām among them, since he emerges not only as a genealogist, as most of them were, but the foremost historian of pre-Islamic Arabia. For the genealogical arrangement, see F. Rosenthal, *A History of Muslim Historiography* (Leiden, 1968), 95–98; for early Arab and Muslim historiography, see ibid., and A. A. Dūrī, *The Rise of Historical Writing among the Arabs*, ed. and trans. L. I. Conrad, introduction by F. M. Donner (Princeton, 1983). The fundamental work on Hishām remains W. Caskel's *Ǧamharat al-Nasab,* 2 vols. (Leiden, 1966), (hereafter *GN*) which, however, does not give attention to the Byzantine profile of Hishām's work. The treatment of Hishām's work in the three volumes of this series fills this gap.

[3] For Tanūkh *post* Tanūkh, see *BAFOC,* 455–57; for Ghassān *post* Ghassān, see I. Shahîd, "Ghassān *post* Ghassān," in *The Islamic World from Classical to Modern Times: Essays in Honor of Bernard Lewis* (forthcoming).

strong presence there and were represented by only a few major figures.[4] Consequently Hishām could gather information about the Tanūkhids and the Ghassānids from their family and tribal records or from their descendants, but he could not do the same for the Salīḥids. And, as will be argued here, the few data he could gather about them were most probably taken from a hostile source—his own tribe, Kalb.[5]

b. The Salīḥids who stayed on in Bilād al-Shām, must have been few and historically insignificant. Some of them carried a name that did not reveal their tribal affiliation, such as Ḥawtaka,[6] while others probably allied themselves with other, more powerful tribes and lost their identity. Thus Hishām most probably could not find a Salīḥid prominent enough to arouse his curiosity[7] for writing the history of Salīḥ; nor were the Salīḥids associated with an event that made him go out of his way to record their history.[8] Salīḥ disappeared and dispersed, as was reflected in an Arabic verse of later Islamic times which made them an example of tribal dispersion.[9]

2. Hishām wrote a number of monographs on the various Arab tribes. Did he write one on the Salīḥids, or did his research find expression in some other form?

a. He could have written a short monograph on the Salīḥids in their role as Arab *foederati* of Byzantium in pre-Islamic times. He did write a book on the *foederati* of the fourth century, namely, *Akhbār Tanūkh wa Ansābuhā*, and he is, not unlikely, the author of a book on the *foederati* of the sixth century, namely, *Akhbār Mulūk Ghassān*.[10] Since he wrote on these two groups of *foederati*, he may well have written also on the Salīḥids. If so, his book has not survived nor has reference to it.[11]

b. Alternatively, his account of Salīḥ may have formed part of one of his monographs, such as *Nawāqil Quḍāʿa*, which dealt with tribal groups that changed their tribal affiliations.[12] As mentioned earlier, this may have hap-

[4] On this, see below, Sec. VII.

[5] See below, 235–37.

[6] For this group, Banū Ḥawtaka, see Ibn Durayd, *Ishtiqāq,* 546.

[7] As Aḥmad ibn abī-Du'ād must have stimulated Hishām's interest in the federate tribal group Iyād, for which see below, 237–40.

[8] Or as the relation of Hishām to the Abbāsid al-Mahdī inspired him to write a monograph on the 4th-century *foederati,* the Tanūkhids, for which see *BAFOC,* 360–62.

[9] For the verse (or rather, the hemistich) *fa inna Salīhan shattata Allāhu shamlahā,* which speaks of the *tashtīt* of Salīḥ, its dispersion, see al-Subkī, *Ṭabaqāt al-Shāfiʿiyya al-Kubrā,* ed. M. al-Ṭanāḥī and H. al-Ḥulw (Cairo, 1964), I, 272. The hemistich comes in an account too good to be true, but its authenticity is irrelevant since what matters is the image of Salīḥ in the perception of the Arabs which the hemistich reflects.

[10] On both these monographs, see *BAFOC,* 360 and note 34.

[11] His book on Tanūkh has also not survived and even reference to it would not have survived had it not been for the interest of the Shiʿite writer al-Najāshi, for whom see ibid.

[12] For this, see Ibn al-Nadīm, *Fihrist,* ed. G. Flügel (Beirut [reprint], 1964), p. 96. On the Nawāqil, see W. Caskel, *GN,* I, 59–62.

pened to Salīḥ after the Muslim Conquests. Another book of Hishām was *Futūḥ al-Shām*,[13] the *Conquest of Shām*, which dealt with the Arab Conquest of Oriens. Salīḥ was one of the federate tribal groups that fought with Byzantium against the Muslim Arabs, and so it might have been noticed by Hishām in this context.

c. Although the two preceding possibilities have to be entertained, the chances are that Hishām's only account of the tribe was that which formed part of his major work, *Jamharat al-Nasab*, which was a comprehensive account of all the Arab tribes and tribal groups. If further research does not reveal new manuscripts that prove Hishām's authorship of a special monograph on Salīḥ, the *Jamhara* will represent the extent of his interest in the history of this federate group.

3. His sources for the history of Salīḥ can only be conjectured, unlike those for the history of other tribal groups, such as Iyād, about which he stated that a member of the tribe, ʿAli ibn Waththāb, informed him on its history.[14]

The natural sources would have been family or tribal records which each tribe kept and which were read or recited "in evening gatherings (*majālis*) of the tribe or governor, or in the mosque, and were customarily regarded as the collective property of the families or tribes."[15] In the case of Salīḥ, this would have been difficult to imagine in Islamic times, since most of them had disappeared by then.[16] However, Salīḥ's history may have been included in that of the large tribal group Quḍāʿa, to which it belonged, or in that of other groups to which it affiliated itself; but this must remain a remote possibility.

b. Two well-known sources on which Hishām depended are Abū Mikhnaf and ʿAwana ibn al-Hakam.[17] But neither would have been helpful, since they dealt with the Islamic period. The latter was closer to Hishām; like him, he was a Kalbite and wrote on the Umayyads and Bilād al-Shām, and so may have mentioned the Salīḥids.

c. Since Salīḥ was related to Kalb, Hishām's tribe, in the larger tribal context of Qudāʿa, it is possible that he received information on Salīḥ from the tribal accounts of Kalb. Such accounts of Salīḥ may be found in the treatment of the dispersion of Qudāʿa, to which Kalb belonged.[18] These accounts,

[13] See Sezgin, *GAS*, I, 436.

[14] For this, see Ibn al-Nadīm, *Fihrist*, 95, where it is stated that this Iyādī was the informant of Hishām's father, Muḥammad, on the history of his own tribe. The same informant is quoted by Hishām on Iyād, for whom see Bakrī, *Muʿjam ma Istaʿjam*, I, 75, 76.

[15] See Dūrī, *Rise of Historical Writing*, 42.

[16] Bakrī mentions Iraqi localities in which Salīḥ dwelt in his days. Whether Salīḥ lived in those regions after its dispersion and whether Hishām could have met some members of the tribe there and then remains possible but unlikely. See Bakrī, *Muʿjam*, I, 203, s.v. Anqira.

[17] See A. A. Dūrī, *Rise of Historical Writing*, 52.

[18] For a detailed account of the dispersion of Qudāʿa, see Bakrī, *Muʿjam*, I, 22–26. The account in Bakrī comes from *Aghāni* and ultimately goes back to al-Zuhrī.

however, refer to the distant past of Salīḥ, when it was still a Peninsular tribe, and tell of its wandering to the Land of the Two Rivers and thence into Oriens. What is relevant here is not the distant past but Hishām's account of federate Salīḥ in Oriens in the fifth century.

It is practically certain, then, that Hishām did not receive his information on Salīḥ directly from any member of the tribe or records belonging to it, but from the accounts and informants of three other tribes which had important relations with Salīḥ—Kalb, Kinda, and Ghassān. This is supported by the fact that the three clusters of data about Salīḥ that are most informative, precise, and valuable are related to these three tribes: (*a*) It was a member of his own tribe, Kalb, that felled the Salīḥid king Dāwūd (David). It is, therefore, natural that accounts of the battle which witnessed the victory of Kalb over the Salīḥids should have been preserved by Kalb, and with them many significant details about Dāwūd, such as his excessive religiosity, his court poet, his daughter, who replied to the verses of the Kalbite who took pride in the killing of her father, and finally the monastery associated with this Salīḥid king.[19] (*b*) Hishām wrote a monograph on Kinda,[20] the powerful tribe whose power spread far and wide in the Arabian Peninsula in the fifth century and which had important relations with the Salīḥids—mostly hostile, as in the famous battle of Baradān, between the Kindite Ḥujr and the Salīḥid Ziyād ibn al-Habūla.[21] Thus his knowledge of the battle involving Salīḥ was derived from his accounts of Kinda, which had a strong presence in Islamic times and whose scholars kept records of the achievements of their tribe. (*c*) Finally, Hishām is one of the important sources for the history of the Ghassānids and was not unlikely the author of the monograph on them, *Akhbār Mulūk Ghassān*.[22] They overcame the Salīḥids and established themselves as the new *foederati* of Byzantium in the sixth century.[23] One may, then, assume that Hishām knew about this first phase in the history of the Ghassānids as *foederati* and with it their relations with Salīh; indeed one of the most detailed accounts of Salīḥid history in Hishām is his description of Salīḥ's last days as *foederati* and of the rise of the Ghassānids. Like the Kindites, the Ghassānids had a strong presence in Oriens in Islamic times and would have been well informed on their rise as *foederati*, the rise that coincided with the last days of the Salīḥids. That Hishām's account of Salīḥ is uneven in its coverage, treating only these three episodes, confirms this conclusion. Their intertribal charac-

[19] On all this, see below, 257–62.
[20] On this *Kitāb Mulūk Kinda*, see Ibn al-Nadīm, *Fihrist,* 96.
[21] On the Day of al-Baradan, see below, 262–64.
[22] This will be treated in detail in *BASIC.*
[23] On this see below, Sec. V.

ter, involving Kalb, Kinda, and Ghassān, is a pointer to the sources whence he derived his information.

Iyād

One of the most important of Arab federate tribes in the service of Byzantium was Iyād. Since this group will be discussed in detail later, this section will be limited to its appearance in, and relation to, Hishām's historiography.[24]

While Hishām's interest in Salīḥ and the reflection of this in his works is faint and unclear, it is extensive and clearly indicated in the case of Iyād. It is reflected in at least two monographs on Iyād, and possibly in other works of his which dealt with tribal groups within which Iyād was included, or in events in which it took part: (1) a monograph on Iyād ibn Nizār; (2) the *dīwān* (poetic works) of the Iyādi poet Laqīt; (3) the monograph on the dispersion of the Arabs, *Kitāb Iftirāq al-ʿArab*; (4) a monograph on the dispersion of the sons of Nizār, *Kitab Iftirāq Wuld Nizār*; and (5) of course, *Jamharat al-Nasab*.[25] This immediately raises the question of the reasons behind Hishām's interest in Iyād and his monographs on it.

Hishām had many reasons to be interested in this tribal group. It had played an important role in the history of the Arabs before the rise of Islam, politically, militarily, and culturally.[26] Furthermore, unlike other federate tribes, Iyād maintained a strong presence in the lands of the Islamic caliphate, and Hishām was also a historian of the Arabs in Islamic times. Nevertheless, his special interest in Iyād needs further explanation, and the key must surely rest in the fact that Hishām was an acquaintance of Aḥmad ibn abi-Du'ād, the famous chief judge of the caliph al-Ma'mūn and, after him, al-Muʿtaṣim.[27] He belonged to Iyād and the court poets remembered this in their odes and

[24] For the real possibility that Iyād was already a federate tribe in Oriens in the 5th century, see below. Sec. IV.

[25] For these works, see Sezgin, *GAS*, I, 269–70. The author suspects that the second and the fourth monographs may have been one.

[26] The tribe also had important connections with the two dominant federate groups in Oriens in the 5th and 6th centuries, Salīḥ and Ghassān respectively, and Hishām wrote on both groups.

[27] Hishām lived long enough to see Ma'mūn enter Baghdad in 819, and so he knew him for the last two years of his life. Hishām must have died in 821, although another account dates his death in 819. Surely the former date is the correct one, since al-Ma'mūn commissioned him to write the genealogical work *al-Farīd,* and it is unlikely that he asked him to do so on his entry into Baghdad in 819; Aḥmad ibn abī Du'ād moved into the circle of al-Ma'mūn and became close to him shortly after the latter's entry into Baghdad, and so Hishām met Aḥmad in the last two years of his life. His books on Laqīṭ and Iyād must have been among the last he wrote. For Aḥmad ibn abī Du'ād at the court of Ma'mūn in these first two years of Ma'mūn's caliphate and the last of Hishām's life, see the chapter on Aḥmad ibn abī Du'ād in Ibn Khallikān, *Wafayāt al-Aʿyan,* ed. Iḥsān ʿAbbās (Beirut, 1977), I, 84.

sang the praises of the famous tribe. Just as Hishām's special interest in the Tanūkhids of the fourth century was aroused by his relation to the caliph al-Mahdī,[28] so was his interest in Iyād enhanced, it is practically certain, by its affiliation with the powerful and celebrated *qāḍī* (judge) to whom the great littérateur of the age, al-Jāḥiẓ, dedicated one of his most important books, *al-Bayān wa al-Tabyīn*.[29]

The discovery of the stimulus for Hishām's monographs on Iyād, namely, the *qāḍī* Aḥmad, makes possible the following observations:

1. The *nasab* (genealogical affiliation) of many of the Arab tribes became a matter of considerable interest and importance in the Islamic period for various reasons. One of them was the appearance of the Prophet Muḥammad from the large tribal group Muḍar, (son of Nizār) which derived its descent ultimately from Ishmael. Some Arab tribes were considered non-Ishmaelite, and it was natural that in Islamic times members of the Christian Iyād were interested in the affirmation of their Ishmaelite origin through Nizār.[30] Hence a book by the chief genealogist and historian of the period on the subject would have been welcome to the powerful *qāḍī*.[31]

2. His other monograph, on the Iyādī poet Laqīṭ, is even more interesting and revealing of the influence of the *qāḍī* on Hishām, and is more important for the Byzantine profile of Iyād's history.

a. That Hishām should have chosen one of the poets of Iyād for a monograph may seem at first surprising, but when it is remembered that Aḥmad ibn abī Du'ād himself composed poetry, Hishām's choice ceases to cause surprise. But Laqīṭ was not the most famous Iyādī poet. Another one by the name of Abū Du'ād[32] was, and choice of the one and the rejection of the other for a monograph does call for an explanation.

Hishām wanted to evoke the memory of an Iyādī poet whose career would be flattering to the chief *qāḍī*, Aḥmad. But the principal Iyādī poet would

[28] See *BAFOC*, 422–32.

[29] It is, therefore, not accidental that Jāḥiẓ should go out of his way to praise Iyād for its oratory and to single it and Tamīm out from all the Arab tribes for a glowing tribute to their orators. For the same reason, he gives special attention to a celebrated Iyādī of pre-Islamic times, Quss ibn Sāiʿda, who won the admiration of the Prophet Muḥammad. He hails him as a pre-Islamic Arab monotheist, quotes the Prophet on Quss, and gives the text of the latter's sermon: for Jāḥiẓ on Iyād and Quss, see his *al-Bāyan wa al-Tabyīn,* ed. ʿA. Hārūn (Cairo, 1961), I, 42–43, 52, 308–9.

[30] For the Iyādī Aḥmad ibn abī Du'ād, it also implied closeness to the tribe of his caliph and patron al-Ma'mūn who, through his father, Hārūn al-Rashīd, belonged to the tribe of the Prophet, Quraysh. As Aḥmad's claim to descent from Iyād was contested by some of his enemies, it is almost certain that Hishām would have affirmed it in his monograph.

[31] In view of this, chances are that the monograph entitled *Iyād ibn Nizār* is not identical with *Kitāb Iftirāq Wuld Nizār* but is a separate one written to affirm Iyād's descent from Nizār; see note 25, above.

[32] On this Iyādī poet, see *EI* and Sezgin, *GAS*, II, 167–68.

hardly have served this purpose. His teknonymic was close to the patronymic of the *qāḍī*; his real name, Jāriya, was hardly flattering, and his patronymic, bin Hajjaj, would have reminded the reader of what, from the point of view of the Abbasids, was the infamous governor of the Umayyads, al-Hajjaj ibn Yusuf. Furthermore, Abū Du'ād was in charge of the stables of the Lakhmid king al-Mundir, and this would have been inappropriate for an ancestor of the influential *qāḍī*. On the other hand, Laqīṭ's[33] career was much more attractive and provided analogies to the career of the *qāḍī* himself: he was secretary for Arab affairs in the Sasanid chancery; his patron and overlord was the Persian Chosroes; he lived in Ctesiphon. All these facts would have pleased the Iyādī *qāḍī* of Abbāsid times who, too, had for his patron the Abbāsid caliph in Baghdad, not far from Ctesiphon, and al-Ma'mūn was half-Persian. Thus Laqīṭ's career would have suggested to the reader that the tribe of Iyād had in pre-Islamic times produced public figures of whom the chief *qāḍī* of al-Ma'mūn could be proud, and that the assumption of high office was not new to the distinguished tribe of Iyād. Al-Ma'mūn patronized Hishām, and Aḥmad ibn abī Du'ād was favored by Ma'mūn. Hishām wrote *al-Farīd* for Ma'mūn, and most probably he also composed the monograph on the Iyādī poet Laqīṭ in this context of court and court-related patronage.

b. Important as the monograph on Laqīṭ is in this context, it is even more important because it throws light on a crucial datum found in Hishām's *Jamharat* on the Salīḥid federate king Dāwūd, the client of Byzantium in the fifth century, namely, that his court poet was an Iyādī named ʿAbd al-ʿĀṣ. The significance of this will be discussed later.[34] What is important here is to argue that it is a solid spot in the account of Salīḥ that cannot be doubted.

Hishām was very well informed about Iyād. His own father had started a work on its genealogy derived from an Iyādī, ʿAli ibn Waththāb,[35] while Aḥmad ibn Du'ād, the highly literate *qāḍī*, may have supplied him with more data from family and tribal records. Hishām was also well informed about the poets of Iyād, especially in pre-Islamic times. Iyād had a number of distinguished poets then, one of whom was Laqīṭ, whose *dīwān* Hishām collected. Another was Abū Du'ād, the court poet of the Lakhmid king of Ḥīra, the famous al-Mundir, about whom Hishām was undoubtedly well informed since the latter was an authority on Ḥīra, the Lakhmids, and especially Mundir, about whom he wrote a monograph and after whom he named his own son; his teknonymic was Abū al-Mundir. Thus, when Hishām says in the *Jamharat* that the poet of the Salīḥid king Dāwūd was the Iyādī ʿAbd al-ʿĀṣ, he cer-

[33] On Laqīṭ, see *EI*, s.v. Lakīṭ, and Sezgin, *GAS*, II, 175–76.

[34] See below, Chap. 14, sec. IV.B.

[35] For this, see *Fihrist*, 95, where his name appears as ʿAdi ibn Rathāth, while in Bakrī he appears as ʿAli ibn Waththāb; see *Muʿjam*, I, 75.

tainly knew what he was saying, and the statement has to be accepted without hesitation as authentic.[36]

3. This raises the question of the authorship of the *dīwān* of Iyād, the collection of poetry written by members of the tribe, and whether Hishām was involved in it.

The *dīwān* is mentioned by al-Āmidī[37] in his list of the *dīwāns* of the Arab tribes, all of which have been lost with the exception of one—that of the tribe of Huḏayl. Al-Āmidī died in 370 H. (A.D. 980–981), and so the *dīwān* was extant in the tenth century. But it is clear from a statement by Ibn Qutayba, who died in 888, that he consulted the *dīwān*, and thus it was already in existence in the ninth century.[38] The other author who has given a list of the *dīwāns* of the Arab tribes in his work, namely, Ibn al-Nadīm (d. 385 H., A.D. 995) does not mention the *dīwān* of Iyād in his list, but it is much shorter as it consists of only twenty-nine *dīwāns*.[39] Unlike al-Āmidī, he mentions the compilers of these *dīwāns*, among whom al-Sukkarī holds the first position for having compiled twenty-eight. Al-Sukkarī died in 888, and so Ibn Qutayba could have consulted an Iyādī *dīwān* compiled by him. Since Hishām died early in the ninth century, Ibn Qutayba could have used the material compiled by Hishām on Iyād, especially his *dīwān* of the Iyādī poet Laqīṭ.

The possibility that it is Hishām rather than al-Sukkarī who could be credited with the compilation of the *dīwān* is also real, and may even be stronger. Ibn al-Nadīm goes out of his way to mention the compilers of the various *dīwāns* in his list and gives prominence to al-Sukkarī. So, if the latter was indeed the compiler of the *dīwān*, the chances are that Ibn al-Nadīm would have said so, but he does not, nor does he mention the *dīwān*. Hishām, on the other hand, was heavily involved in the history and poetry of Iyād and the chances that he was the author of the *dīwān* are good and may be supported by the following facts. (*a*) His own father Muḥammad had written on the *nasab*, the genealogy of Iyād, material which Hishām inherited. (*b*) Hishām's interest in Iyād has been commented upon, and was reflected in a number of monographs.[40] Thus it is quite likely that one who was so interested in the history and poetry of Iyād also compiled its *dīwān*, the *dīwān* which Ibn Qutayba consulted as *Dīwān Iyād*. This possibility can be fortified by the realization that one of Hishām's monographs is on Iyād.[41] If this

[36] Iyād thus appears as a tribe which produced three poets related to kings, Laqīṭ and Sasanid Chosroes, Abū Du'ād and Lakhmid Munḏir, ʿAbd ʿal-ʿĀṣ and Salīḥid Dāwūd.

[37] For the list, see N. al-Asad, *Maṣādir al-Shiʿr al-Jāhilī* (Cairo, 1982), 543–44.

[38] Ibid., 549–50.

[39] Ibid., 545–47. The list of al-Āmidī contained sixty *dīwāns*.

[40] See above, 237.

[41] For this monograph, which is mentioned only in *Mishkāt*, see Sezgin, *GAS*, I, 270 (no. 9).

monograph had the title *Kitāb Iyād*, it could have been the *dīwān*, since the verse collection of an Arab tribe was often referred to as *kitāb* and not *dīwān*. It is, therefore, possible that this monograph of Hishām was what al-Āmidī in the tenth century called the *dīwān* of Iyād. If this monograph did not contain poetry exclusively, it must have contained some of it.

It is practically certain that this *dīwān* of Iyād, whether composed by al-Sukkarī or Hishām, contained the poetry of ʿAbd al-ʿĀṣ, the court poet of King Dāwūd. Its loss is therefore regrettable, especially as Iyād was associated with the use of the Arabic script in pre-Islamic times[42] and, thus the material that reached Hishām on its history and poetry consisted of *written* records preserved by the tribe since pre-Islamic times. Consequently, the data it provided on Iyād and federate Iyād would have been extremely reliable.

As has been said before, Hishām is the principal historian of pre-Islamic Arabia and also of the Arab *foederati* of Byzantium in the three centuries before the rise of Islam.[43] All later historians who include in their works accounts of the pre-Islamic and the federate Arabs draw on Hishām: (*a*) his own pupils, to whom he transmitted directly his information, such as Ibn Ḥabīb, Khalīfa ibn Khayyāṭ, and Ibn Saʿīd;[44] (*b*) those to whom his own son, ʿAbbas, passed on the accounts written by his father, such as Ibn Durayd, Ṭabarī, and Balāḏurī;[45] and finally (*c*) the much later historians, who did not receive information from father or son but derived it from the works of those who did, and thus were indirectly dependent on Hishām. Hence all important accounts of the Arab *foederati* of Byzantium derive ultimately from Hishām.

A work titled *Kitāb al-Lubāb fi al-Jāhiliyya* is ascribed to Hishām. It is one of the few works ascribed to him, and is described as represented by a

[42] On this see below, Chap 14, app. 4.

[43] See *BAFOC*, 349–66 for a general evaluation of Hishām and for a discussion of his historiography with regard to the *foederati* of the 4th century, especially the Tanūkhids. In this volume an intensive study of Hishām's treatment of the 5th-century *foederati*, especially Salīḥ and Iyād, is presented as a contribution to a better understanding of this important figure in Arab historiography.

[44] The most detailed account of the last phase of Salīḥ's federate existence and the first of Ghassān's may be found in Ibn Ḥabīb; see his *al-Muḥabbar*, ed. I. Lichtenstädter (Heyderabad, 1942; reprinted Beirut, n.d.), 370–72. It is also noteworthy that Khalīfa ibn Khayyāṭ singles out Hishām of all the authorities he depends on for his accounts of Arab-Byzantine relations in the Muslim period of the Orthodox caliphs and the Umayyads. These relations had attracted Hishām's attention for the pre-Islamic period, and he naturally kept his interest in them after the rise of Islam. For Khalīfa's historical work, see *Tārīkh Khalīfa Ibn-Khayyāṭ*, ed. Akram al-ʿUmarī (Beirut, 1977).

[45] For this see W. Atallah, *EI*[2], s.v. al-Kalbī. The short paragraph on his son ʿAbbas in this article confirms the suggestions concerning the confusion surrounding him and his name and makes it even more necessary to refer to the three Kalbis (the father, the son, and the grandson) as Muḥammad al-Kalbī, Hishām al-Kalbī, and ʿAbbas al-Kalbī; see *BAFOC*, 460–61. Hishām presumably called his son "Abbas" to reflect his pro-ʿAbbasid sympathies, just as his own father called him after the name of the Umayyad caliph Hishām, in order to reflect his Umayyad sympathies.

"few fragments of various lengths which have been preserved, vestiges of lost works."[46] This work has survived only in a few fragments, and its ascription[47] to Hishām, if correct,[48] suggests that he had transcended the atomic approach to pre-Islamic Arab history, which consisted in writing the accounts of individual tribes. A book with such a title suggests that Hishām conceived of the entire pre-Islamic period as a genuine period in the history of the Arabs and consequently treated it as such. In so doing, he was no doubt following the Koranic conception, reflected in his using the Koranic term "Jāhiliyya." But even if he did not write *Kitāb al-Lubāb* Hishām had a conception of the pre-Islamic period as one clearly defined in the history of the Arabs. He was, *inter alia*—and as his father before him had been—a Koranic and Muhammadan scholar, who was naturally influenced in his periodization of Arab history by Koranic and Muhammadan conceptions. Later works on the *Jāhiliyya*, such as *Nashwat al-Ṭarab fī Tārīkh Jāhiliyyat al-ʿArab*, ultimately derived from Hishām's work.[49]

II. The Identity of the Fifth-Century *Foederati*: The Salīḥids

The identity of the fourth-century *foederati* of Byzantium in Oriens, the Tanūkhids, had to be argued for, since they were left anonymous in the Greek

[46] See Atallah, "al-Kalbī."

[47] I have been unable to obtain a microfilm of these fragments. The only fragment from this work known to me is printed as a footnote by the editor of Ibn Durayd's *al-Ishtiqāq*, 545 note 7, where the full title of the book is given. Yet the footnote is confusing. It consists of two parts or long sentences. The first (from *al-Lubāb*) presents a confused account of the Ghassānids and the Salīḥids, while the second (from *Jamhara*) may provide some valuable information on the kings of Salīḥ and how they were related to one another. There are two references to Hishām in the fragment, the first to him as the author of *Kitab al-Lubāb*, the second to him as the author of the *Jamhara*. The quotations from the *Lubāb* and from the *Jamhara* are put together by a commentator on the original manuscript of *al-Ishtiqāq* and not by the modern editor, ʿA. Hārūn.

[48] The confused account, referred to in the preceding note, which purports to emanate from *al-Lubāb*, makes its ascription to Hishām doubtful.

[49] For *Nashwat al-Ṭarab* and its 13th-century Andalusian author Ibn Saʿīd, see the work of Manfred Kropp, below, Chap. 13, app. 3 note 10. For the sources of Ibn Saʿīd and the discussion of the mysterious Baihaqi and his Kamā'im, see ibid., I, 78a–86a. Such sources as indicated by Ibn Saʿīd are late, and *ultimately* the source of all of them is Hishām.

The editor of *Nashwat al-Ṭarab* limited himself to a part of *Nashwat,* namely, the one that dealt with the South Arab tribes, referred to as al-ʿArab al-ʿĀriba. An examination of the rest of the manuscript of *Nashwat,* which deals with the northern Arabs, al-ʿArab al-Mustaʿriba, yields information of little value to the historian. Salīḥ is hardly mentioned, except in connection with its battle-day, al-Baradān, the account of which is not instructive. There is, however, a chapter on Iyād, and the author quotes two attractive verses composed by the son of the famous Iyādī poet Abu Du'ād on the death of his father. Ibn Saʿīd wrote more as a man of letters than as a historian. For the Tübingen manuscript of *Nashwat al-Ṭarab,* see Kropp, ibid., I, 97a–110a.

and Latin sources for that century.[50] By contrast, the identity of the fifth-century *foederati* is documented in a Greek source, and this leaves no doubt that the dominant group of Arab *foederati* of the fifth century were the Salīḥids, as the foremost historian of pre-Islamic Arabia, Hishām al-Kalbī, states.

The Greek source is Sozomen, the historian who has been so valuable for writing the history of the Arab *foederati* in both the fourth and fifth centuries. In the chapter that described the conversion of the Arabs/Saracens ca. 400, the ecclesiastical historian spoke of the conversion of one of the chiefs after the prophecy of a monk that his sterile wife would bear him a child came true.[51] By the merest chance, Sozomen not only told the story but also gave the name of the Arab chief, Zόκομος, and in so doing he enabled the Arab *foederati* of the fifth century to be identified. Gutschmidt was the first to see in Greek Zόκομος Arab Ḍujʿum, the eponym of the Zokomid royal house, the Ḍajaʿima of the Arabic sources, who ruled the Salīḥids. The identification was followed by Nöldeke's endorsement, and both identification and endorsement have to be accepted.[52]

There are intermittent references to the Arab *foederati* in the fifth century in the Greek and Latin sources, although they are not referred to specifically by the names Salīḥid or Zokomid. But incontestably authentic Arabic sources, deriving from Hishām al-Kalbī, leave little doubt that these Salīḥids were the Arab *foederati* of the fifth century.[53] Just as a Greek source, Sozomen, has determined for the historian of the *foederati* the *terminus a quo* of their Byzantine connection (around 400), so an Arabic source, Hishām al-Kalbī, has determined the last phase of their status as the dominant Arab federate group in Oriens in the fifth century. An unusually detailed description of this last phase appears in an account which goes back to Hishām and which may be dated to the reign of Anastasius (491–518).[54] Furthermore, Hishām's accounts can be authenticated by being interlocked with a Greek source, The-

[50] See *BAFOC*, 368–72.

[51] Sozomen, *Historia Ecclesiastica*, VI, xxxviii. The Salīḥid attachment to Christianity and to monasticism derive from this episode.

[52] For this, see Nöldeke, *GF*, 8, where the phonology of the transliteration of Arabic Ḍujʿum to Greek Zόκομος is explained. Since the name is so unusual in Arabic and denotes only this well-known federate group, there is no chance whatsoever that the identification can be applied to another Ḍujʿum.

[53] In the sequence of dominant federate groups enumerated by Hishām—Tanūkh, Salīḥ, Ghassān—Salīḥ comes after Tanūkh. Since it has been established that Tanūkh was the dominant group of the 4th century, Salīḥ is inevitably the 5th-century one; see *BAFOC*, 369. Salīḥ's 5th-century federate status can be determined independently of this sequence, through references in Sozomen and Hishām to the first and last phase of its federate status.

[54] See Ibn Ḥabīb, *al-Muḥabbar*, 370–71. Ibn Ḥabīb was Hishām's pupil and derived from him his information on the Arab *foederati*; see the preceding section on Hishām. For an

ophanes.[55] In both sources mention is made of the appearance of the Ghassānids on the scene of Arab-Byzantine relations, and they form a link between the two accounts, since the fall of the Salīḥ in Hishām's account is related to the rising power of the Ghassānids. Hishām supplies important inter-Arab data between Salīḥ and Ghassān, while Theophanes supplies the crucial chronological indication—around A.D. 500. Thus the life-span of the Salīḥids as the dominant federate group of the fifth century can be determined, and it roughly coincides with that century, extending from the reign of Arcadius (395–408) to that of Anastasius (491–518).

The establishment of the identity of the fifth-century *foederati* clears the ground for raising some relevant questions concerning these Salīḥids:[56]

A

1. The truth about the genealogical history of Salīḥ is shrouded in obscurity; it is even more obscure than that of the fourth-century Tanūkhids. There is, however, much consensus that it ultimately derives from the large tribal group, Quḍāʿa, which was settled in Oriens and northern Arabia from ancient times.[57] As mentioned earlier, Ḍajaʿima (Zokomids) is the name of the royal house, while the term Salīḥid is the large tribe to which the Zokomids belonged and which it ruled.[58]

Salīḥ's affiliation with the large tribal group Quḍāʿa is important for

analysis of the last phase of Salīḥ's existence, see Shahīd, "The Last Days of Salīḥ," 145–58. In this article Yaʿqūbī's account rather than Ibn Ḥabīb's is analyzed, but the latter is fuller and will be used below in sec. V.

[55] For an analysis of Theophanes' account, see ibid., 152 note 8.

[56] This chapter is devoted to the Salīḥids alone, the dominant federate group. For other federate Arab tribal groups in Oriens in the 5th century, see below, sec. IV.

[57] For a discussion of Quḍāʿa, see below, Chap. 13, app. 2. For the affiliation of Salīḥ to Quḍāʿa ultimately, see Ibn Ḥazm, *Jamhara,* 450, and Ibn Durayd, *Ishtiqāq*, 545. The genealogical segment which connects Ḍujʿum with Salīḥ is as follows: Ḍujʿum ibn Saʿd ibn Salīḥ, while that which connects Salīḥ with Quḍāʿa runs as follows: Salīḥ ibn Ḥulwān ibn ʿImran ibn Ilḥāfī ibn Quḍāʿa; see *Jamhara,* 450. Without inscriptions it is impossible to vouch for the *accuracy* of these derivations, but the truth of the affiliation to Quḍāʿa in general may be accepted.

[58] Hence its adoption in this volume for the name of the dominant federate group rather than "Zokomid," which is also the practice of the Arab historians in whose works the two names are sometimes used interchangeably. "Salīḥ" is also the more euphonious of the two names in Arabic, since it has not the palatal and guttural sounds of Arabic Ḍujʿum. As is clear from the preceding footnote, Ḍujʿum is the grandson of Salīḥ; the royal house is named after the former, the tribal group after the latter. One account makes Salīḥ a more distant ancestor of Ḍujʿum: see Bakrī, *Muʿjam,* I, 26. The employment of the two names "Zokomid" and "Salīḥid" has understandably been confusing to scholars who have researched this period and dynasty, but this footnote clears up the confusion; see M. Sartre, *TE,* 145, 148. A parallel would be Ghassānid and Jafnid, the former standing for the tribal group, the latter for the royal house.

studying the problem of the other Arab tribes along the *limes orientalis*. The rise of Salīḥ as the dominant federate tribal group may have opened a new chapter in the history of the Quḍāʿa group after a century or so of Tanūkhid supremacy in Oriens. It is not impossible that other tribes within the Quḍāʿa group became, through Salīḥ, more involved in the Byzantine connection, and may even have acquired federate status. Some of these tribes will be discussed later on, but they may be enumerated here: Balī and Bahrā'; Juhayna and ʿUḏra; Balqayn and Kalb. According to the Arab genealogies, each of the three pairs was descended from one ancestor, and the three ancestors were descended ultimately from Quḍāʿa.[59]

2. Whence did Salīḥ come into Byzantine Oriens? Its original abode in ancient times is of no importance to our theme, but its immediate past—before it became the dominant federate tribal group in Oriens—is relevant and may be treated briefly as follows:

a. The best and most detailed account of Salīḥ's original abode and wanderings in the Peninsula before it reached Oriens assigns it to Tihāma, the coastal plain of Ḥijāz, whence it moved into northern Arabia and the regions adjacent to Oriens.[60] It is impossible to check on the accuracy of the data given in this account. However, the account contains some features that have the ring of authenticity, and it can be interlocked to a certain extent with incontestably reliable Greek sources for the later period. The account speaks of three Salīḥids: (*a*) Ubāgh, the lord of ʿAyn Ubāgh, who fell in battle against a chief of the tribe of Bahrā';[61] (*b*) al-Ḥidrijān, who led Salīḥ into Oriens and settled not far from Palestine with Banū Uḏayna;[62] and (*c*) Ḍujʿum, who,

[59] For a genealogical account of Quḍāʿa and more details on the six tribes, see Ibn Ḥazm, *Jamhara,* 440–60. The rising importance of Salīḥ through its Byzantine connection may be reflected in the fact that a clan of al-Namir ibn Wabara from Quḍāʿa by the name of Labwān affiliated itself with Salīḥ; ibid., 455. For some of these six tribes, see below, Sec. IV.

[60] See Bakrī, *Muʿjam,* I, 25 quoting Ibn Shabba. For the origin of the term Quḍāʿa and the abode of this tribal group in ancient times, see above, notes 57 and 59. Arab genealogists in Islamic times were inclined to conceive of most or all of the Arab tribes as Ishmaelites, since this Ishmaelite affiliation related to Quraysh and the Prophet Muḥammad. The attempt to assign a Ḥijāzī origin in Tihāma to Quḍāʿa which is rather unlikely, seems to derive from the same motive, assigning a place of origin to the Arab tribes not far from Mecca, the city of the Prophet.

[61] The name appears in the genealogical table of Hishām al-Kalbī (see the stemma for the Salīḥids at the back of this volume). ʿAyn Ubāgh is the name of a famous battle-day in the 6th century between the Ghassānids and the Lakhmids, but this does not necessarily invalidate this reference to an earlier encounter near ʿAyn Ubāgh. The Lakhmid-Ghassānid encounter was too famous to be mistaken by the authority on this account; see Bakrī, *Muʿjam,* I, 21.

[62] Ibid., 23. The name Ḥidrijān is archaic; what is more important, it appears in the 7th century as the name of the Salīḥid chief (Ibn al-Ḥidrijān), who fought the Muslim troops at Dumāt al-Jandal; Ṭabarī, *Tārīkh,* II, 378. Thus there is no doubt about the name's Salīḥid identity. Cf. the reappearance of the name Ḍujʿum, the Zokomos of Sozomen, two centuries

leading a group of Salīḥids, marched with Labīd, the son of al-Ḥidrijān, into Roman territory and allied himself with the descendants of Uḏayna.[63]

The account retains echoes of archaic names which are distinctly Salīḥid and which recur in later Salīḥid history. Furthermore, the historical context within which the wandering of Salīḥ in this period is set lends plausibility to the account. It is the world of the third century, that of the imperial crisis, the period of the ascendancy of the Arab kingdom of Palmyra in the East, and the Byzantine-Sasanid conflict. The movement of an Arab tribe such as Salīḥ into Roman territory and its dealing with the Palmyrene Arabs[64] under such circumstances is thus perfectly possible.[65]

b. More important are its fortunes in the fourth and fifth centuries, in the Byzantine period. The Arabic sources suggest that this was an old Arab tribe that had lived in North Arabia and, when its opportunity came, became the dominant federate group. Here the Greek sources have to be the guide; they are helpful and valuable, and seem to confirm the general tenor of the Arabic sources on the whereabouts of Salīḥ around or slightly before 400. Just as Sozoman solved the important chronological problem for the inception of Salīḥ as a federate power by recording the name of the chief Ζόκομος, so Ptolemy helps pinpoint the area whence this particular clan of the Salīḥids—the Zokomids of the Byzantine connection—hailed. One of the toponyms he mentions in northern Arabia is Ζαγμαΐς.[66] It is practically certain

---

later in Theophylactus Simocatta, as a Salīḥid chief in the Byzantine army (Ζώγομος); noted by Nöldeke, *GF*, 8. Uḏayna in Banū Uḏayna is Arabic for Odenathus, the well-known ruler of Palmyra, Zenobia's husband.

63 Bakrī, *Muʿjam,* I, 26. Note that these are descendants of those mentioned in (*b*); so this Salīḥid migratory wave belongs to a later generation.

64 Ṭabarī mentions that Salīḥid troops fought for Zenobia; see *Tārīkh,* I, 618.

65 A tradition going back to Ibn Saʿīd and quoted by Ibn Khaldūn (*Tārīkh,* II, 521) makes a branch of the Salīḥids the lords of al-Ḥadr (Hatra) in Mesopotamia. This probably involves a confusion with another tribal group. Who the Arabs who ruled Hatra were remains a mystery; for the view that they were Tanūkhids, see Bakrī, *Muʿjam,* I, 23–24.

The tradition that links Salīḥ with Ḥadr and Mesopotamia may have something to be said for it but, if so, this must be a branch of Salīḥ different from the one that later became the federate one, which, as will be argued presently, came from Wādī Sirḥān. What could commend this tradition is the names of the two Salīḥids, Ḥidrijan/Ḥadrijān and Ubāgh. The first could possibly be a compound of Ḥadr (the Arab city) and the Persian suffix *gān,* which serves to form nouns that indicate relation, similitude, and origin. According to this archaic and strange name, Ḥadrijān could mean "he of Ḥadr/Hatra." Ubāgh is a strange-sounding name in Arabic. Yaqūt suspected it was not Arabic (*Muʿjam,* I, p. 61, s.v. Ubāgh), and it is very close to Persian *bāgh,* garden. Thus the names could argue that these two Salīḥid personages had lived in the area of Persian domination in Mesopotamia. But this is pure speculation, and the names could very well be archaic Arab names the etymology of which presented a problem to later Islamic genealogists and etymologists.

66 For this toponym in Ἀραβία ἐρημός, see Ptolemy, *Geographia,* ed. C. Müller (Paris), Vol. I, part 2, p. 1016. The credit for this identification must go to O. Blau; see his "Die Wanderung der sabäischen völkerstämme im 2. Jahrhundert," *ZDMG* 27 (1868), 664. The rest of his views on the pre-federate history of Salīḥ cannot be accepted.

that this is Ḍujʿum.[67] Personal names and names of places are often identical in this region, and this must be an instance of such onomastic and toponymic identity.[68] In addition to Ptolemy's confirmation of the general area which the Arabic sources say the Zokomids came from, there are the facts of Salīḥid toponyms in Oriens after their elevation as the dominant federate group. Most, if not all, of the toponyms associated with Salīḥ are in the southern and not the northern part of the limitrophe and, consequently, suggest an exodus from Wādī Sirḥān, the northern end of which opens toward the Provincia Arabia. Finally, according to the genealogists, as noted earlier, Salīḥ was closely related to Kalb as one of the many subdivisions of Quḍāʿa, the two having been descended from one ancestor. Since Kalb was certainly settled near Wādī Sirḥān and Dūmat, the chances are that Salīḥ, too, was settled in the same Wādī.[69] Thus the correct identification of the toponym in Ptolemy with Ḍujʿum argues for a successful penetration[70] of the *limes orientalis* from Wādī Sirḥān by an Arab group who became the *foederati* of Byzantium in the fifth century.[71]

The travels of a reliable modern explorer of Arabia, Ḥamad al-Jāsir, give further confirmation to the association of the Salīḥids with Wādī Sirḥān. According to his accounts, one of the small streams that flow into Wādī Sirḥān from the west is called Ḥidrij/Ḥidraj. This recalls the Salīḥid figure Ibn al-Ḥidrijān/Hidrajān who around 630 fought the Muslims at Dūmat al-Jandal at the southern end of Wādī Sirḥān. In his chapter titled "Ancient Remains in the District of al-Jawf/Dūmat al-Jandal," al-Jāsir also tells a story,

[67] An accepted alternative orthography for Dujʿum. The consonantal sequence *d-j-ʿm* is so uncommon in Arabic that the identification of Ḍajʿam/Ḍujʿum with Zagmais is certain, since the latter has three of them in the right order; as to the *ʿayn,* Greek naturally does not reflect it.

[68] Accepted by one who has the right to be heard on this subject, the indefatigable traveler, A. Musil. As one who traveled in this region, he identifies the toponym in Ptolemy with a village in Wādī Sirḥān, Ẓagʿām. He warns the reader that this must be the case, in spite of the fact that Ptolemy places Zagmais to the east of Wādī Sirḥān, and does this also in the case of "Tedion" or "Pedion," which is not where he places it; see A. Musil, *Arabia Deserta* (New York, 1927), 507.

[69] It may not have been altogether accidental that in the period of the Muslim Conquests the Salīḥids are to be found fighting the Muslim invasion at Dūmat; Ṭabarī, *Tārīkh,* III, 378.

[70] Thus recalling its penetration by the Midianites of biblical times whom Gideon smashed, and also the historic march of Khālid ibn al-Walīd through the same *wādī,* the march which made possible the Muslim Arabs' annihilating victory over Byzantium, the battle of Yarmūk in 636.

[71] For the most recent statement on the importance of Wādī Sirḥān in the Roman defense system, see Bowersock, *Roman Arabia,* 118–121, 156–59. Important Latin inscriptions have been found at both Azraq and Dūmat (Jawf) at the northern and southern entrances of the *wādī.* A systematic exploration of it and the area of Dūmat will undoubtedly reveal Arabic inscriptions for this early Byzantine period, too, since the Arab *foederati* must have patrolled it for Byzantium together with Byzantine troops. The Ghassānid involvement in the *wādī* will be treated in *BASIC*.

still current among the inhabitants of that region, involving the tribe of al-Dayāghim and a verse fragment which speaks of the Rūm (Romans). The name of the tribe, "Dayāghim," is very close (especially in Arabic) to Ḍajaᶜim (plural of Ḍujᶜum/Zokomos), and it is, therefore, possible that memories of the Zokomids have survived in the region of Wādī Sirḥān, with which they were associated in Byzantine times. If so, this would indeed be a very remarkable survival.[72]

B

A problem related to that of their place of origin is where in Oriens the Salīḥids settled as *foederati*. All the sources that have toponymic data on Salīḥ are late Islamic sources and thus present the usual problem of whether or not the toponym they assign to, or associate with, these pre-Islamic tribal groups went back the pre-Islamic past or whether it only reflected the contemporary topynymic reality in the Islamic period. In the case of the *foederati* of the fourth century, there are three inscriptions which give some precision to the attempt of locating these *foederati*; the Arabic Namāra inscription and the two Greek inscriptions found outside Anasartha.[73] For the Salīḥids of the fifth century, the inscriptions remain to be discovered.[74] One can only present the toponymic data provided by the Arabic sources and relate them to certain facts about the Salīḥids which may be helpful for solving the problem.

The toponymic picture presented by the sources is an extensive one, stretching from Chalcis (Qinnasrīn) near the Euphrates to the Balqā᾽ district in the south, in the Provincia Arabia.[75] It is difficult to believe that the Salīḥids occupied all these places *simultaneously* during their supremacy in the fifth century. But the conclusion arrived at in the last section will go a long way toward solving this problem. Since the Salīḥids came from Wādī Sirḥān, the presumption is that they were established as *foederati* with their base in the Provincia Arabia. Thus the toponyms associated with them in the Provincia, and generally in the south, are likely to be the original settlements of the Salīḥids and represent the area where their power was based. The toponyms to the north may be explained as follows: (*a*) Since they were the dominant federate group, it is quite likely that the Byzantine authorities extended their power to the north and allowed them to settle in provinces other than the

[72] See Ḥamad al-Jāsir, *Fi Shamāl Gharb al-Jazīra* (Riyad, 1981); for Wādī Ḥidrij, see p. 610, for Dayāghim and Rūm, pp. 141–42.

[73] For these see *BAFOC*, 31–45; 222–38.

[74] For the Arabic Usays inscription associated with the Ghassānids of the 6th century, see below, Sec. VII. Although not a Salīḥid inscription, it is the first and so far the only *possible* epigraphic evidence for federate Salīḥ. It will be discussed in detail in *BASIC*.

[75] Or, as Ibn al-Athīr says, it is from Palestine to Qinnasrīn; see *Al-Kāmil*, (Beirut, 1965), I, 510.

original one, Arabia. (*b*) After their fall as the dominant power, it is possible that the Ghassānids who fought with them displaced them in the Provincia and thus caused them to emigrate to a more northerly province.[76] (*c*) Finally, the seventh century was that of the Muslim Conquest of Oriens. This, together with the movement and arrival of new Arab tribes in Oriens from the Peninsula during the times of the Conquests, of the Orthodox Caliphs, and of the Umayyads, must have led to upheavals, displacements, and a drastic change in the tribal landscape in Oriens in the first centuries of the Muslim era. All this may have caused the Salīḥids to move from their original abodes and seek new ones.

In spite of the difficulties noted for Salīḥid toponymy in the preceding paragraphs, it is possible to present this toponymy in the Roman period, the proto-Byzantine period, and the period of the Arab Conquests. However, this presentation depends on the literary sources of late Islamic times, and in only one instance is it related to a fairly recent epigraphic discovery.

a. *The Roman period.* (1) Ibn al-Athīr speaks of their settlements as extending from Filasṭīn to Qinnasrīn.[77] He uses the terms Filasṭīn (Palestine) and Qinnasrīn (Chalcis) as terms for the two junds (military districts) of Oriens/Shām in Islamic times. (2) It is quite likely that Ibn al-Athīr was paraphrasing the statement that goes back to Ibn Shabba[78] that in the third century the Salīḥids allied themselves with the Palmyrenes, who settled them in Manāẓir al-Shām, from al-Balqa' to Ḥuwwārīn to al-Zaytūn.[79] For frontier studies, the important term in the account is Manāẓir al-Shām, which suggests the watchtowers of the *limes*. It is interesting that Bakrī, who has preserved this account from Ibn Shabba, says that the latter states that the Salīḥids were still in these places in Shām "to this day" (A.D. 875/876).[80] (3) Iṣfahānī associates a Salīḥid, Ubāgh, with ʿAyn Ubāgh in this early Roman period, although apparently before Salīḥ made the Roman connection through the Palmyrene Arabs.[81] (4) Finally, mention should be made of Ptolemy, whose Zagmais has made possible the identification of the place from which Zokomids hailed.

[76] Such as Jabal Usays where the inscription referred to (above, note 25) was found. If so, Jabal Usays in Phoenicia may be considered Salīḥid area, but the brevity of the inscription does not permit one to draw the conclusion categorically.

[77] Ibn al-Athīr, *al-Kāmil,* I, 510.

[78] See Bakrī, *Muʿjam,* I, 26.

[79] In the provincial terms of the Byzantine period in Oriens/Shām, the Salīḥids would have been settled in places in the Provincia Arabia, Phoenicia Libanensis, and possibly Syria Salutaris, depending on where Zaytūn was. Balqā' is the well-known district which has survived to this day in Jordan; Ḥuwwarīn is Evaria; Zaytūn is unknown in this form to the geographers. It may be al-Zaytūna of the Umayyad caliph Hishām; see Yāqūt, *Muʿjam,* III, 163.

[80] For Ibn Shabba, see *al-Fihrist,* 112–13.

[81] Bakrī, *Muʿjam,* I, 23. The account is that of Iṣfahānī, who is mentioned on p. 21.

b. *The Byzantine period.* (1) Ibn Khaldūn refers to Moabitis (which for him was part of al-Balqā') as the region where the Salīḥids settled when they entered Oriens/Shām.[82] (2) Hamdani associates them with the Rayʿan al-Maḏāhib, al-Balqā' and al-Muwaqqar; two of these localities, and possibly all, are in Trans-Jordan.[83] Elsewhere, he associates them with al-Balqā', Salamiyya, Ḥuwwarīn, and al-Zaytūn.[84] (3) There are references to three toponyms in connection with the inter-Arab wars of the Salīḥids: al-Baradān, the name of the battle between them and Kinda, al-Qurnatayn, and Ḥārib in the Jawlān, near which Dāwūd fought and died against the tribe of Kalb.[85] (4) Dayr Dāwūd, the monastery of David, built by the Salīḥid king, was a Salīḥid establishment in the north near Ruṣāfa.[86] (5) In the description of the last days of Salīḥ, Yaʿqubī refers to the Salīḥids as settled in Balqā', and Ibn Ḥabīb speaks of the final battle between the Salīḥids and the Ghassānids as having taken place at al-Muḥaffaf.[87] (6) An inscription that *may* involve a rebellious Salīḥid chief in 530 associates them with Jabal Usays southeast of Damascus.[88] (7) The sixth-century pre-Islamic poet, al-Nābigha, finds one of their chiefs in Bostra or Burqat Hārib.[89] (8) Finally, in the Gazetteer for

[82] See Ibn Khaldūn, *Tārīkh,* II, 580. It is not clear what his source is, possibly, Ibn Saʿīd.

[83] See Hamdānī, *Ṣifat Jazīrat al-ʿArab,* ed. M. al-Akwaʿ (Riyad, 1974), 334. For al-Muwaqqar, see Yāqūt, *Muʿjam,* V, 226. Rayʿan without al-Maḏāhib appears in Bakrī, *Muʿjam,* II, 688–89, but judging from a verse by Kuthayyir where it is described as Ḏāt al-Maṭārib, the toponym as given by Hamdānī may be Rayʿan al-Maṭārib. Since it comes in a verse by Kuthayyir, it is likely to be in northern Ḥijāz or southern Oriens/Shām. According to al-Sukkarī, cited by Bakrī, it is either a mountain or a town.

It would be pleasant to think that the Salīḥids were associated in some way also with Madaba and that they contributed to its rise and development as an important Christian center, to which its splendid mosaics which have survived, testify; see below, App. 1.

[84] Hamdānī, op. cit., 319. Salamiyya is located northeast of Emesa and southeast of Ḥamā (Epiphania).

[85] For al-Baradān see below, 262–64. This is outside Oriens in the Arabian Peninsula and thus is not a Salīḥid toponym in the sense that they were settled there. For al-Qurnatayn and Ḥārib, see below, 260. That the battle was fought in the Jawlān region suggests that the Jawlān in Palaestina Secunda was in the 5th century (as it was to continue in the 6th under the Ghassānids) a region where the Arab *foederati* were settled.

[86] For Dayr Dāwūd, see below, 262.

[87] See Yaʿqūbī, *Tārīkh* (Beirut, 1960), I, 206; Ibn Ḥabīb, al-Muḥabbar, 371. The toponym Muḥaffaf is "Mukhaffaf" in Yaʿqūbi, op. cit., 207. It is somewhere near Bostra, judging from the account of Yaʿqūbi, but does not appear in Bakrī or Yāqūt. The morphological pattern of the toponym and the possibility that there has been some transcriptional error pertaining to the diacritical marks and to some letters strongly resembling one another could suggest that the place may be al-Mushannaf, northeast of Bostra; see Dussaud, *Topographie,* Map 14, B4.

[88] On this inscription, see below, Sec. VII.I.

[89] See Ahlwardt, *Divans,* 164. Burqat Ḥārib is not an entry in Bakrī or Yāqūt. But it must be in the vicinity of Bostra. The verse is attributed to Nābigha, but may belong to some other pre-Islamic poet.

Jordan there are two toponyms that strongly suggest a Salīḥid presence: a village called al-Salīḥī and a valley called Wādī al-Salīḥī.[90]

c. *The period of the Conquests*. (1) The Salīḥids fight the Muslims at Dūmat al-Jandal at the southern end of Wādī Sirḥān. They also form part of the contingent of federate Arabs (at Zīza in Trans-Jordan) whom Byzantium mobilized to repel the Muslim invaders.[91] (2) Some of them apparently moved to the north after the fall of Oriens/Shām and lived near the Tanūkhids, not far from Qinnasrīn.[92]

The foregoing section on the toponymy of the Salīḥids has confirmed what was said earlier on the region whence they came, namely, that it was not Mesopotamia but northern Arabia, in or near Wādī Sirḥān. The most important toponyms associated with them assign them to the southern part of Oriens—to the Provincia Arabia and further to the north in Phoenicia Libanensis, and to the south in Palaestina Tertia. The south[93] of Oriens was the natural region in which a people who had marched into Oriens through Wādī Sirḥān settled.[94] It is this region that beckoned the pastoralists of northern Arabia and Ḥijāz, which needed protection, and this was especially the case in view of the relative peace that reigned between Byzantium and Persia. The dominant *foederati* were not needed in the north to fight the Persians, but in the south to guard the approaches into Oriens from the Arabian Peninsula. As to their being found in a few places not in the south, this is easily explicable by the course of events which probably led to their finding or seeking new areas for settlement in the sixth and seventh centuries: the rise of the Ghassānids in the sixth century as the dominant federate group; the Persian occupation of Oriens in the second and third decades of the seventh century; and the Muslim Conquests in the same century.

[90] See *Jordan: Official Standard Names,* U.S. Army Topographic Command (Washington, D.C., 1971), 323. This is very important, since the two toponyms must be survivals from ancient Salīḥid times in the 5th century. Excavations at the two places are likely to shed important light on the Salīḥids. It is also decisive evidence that this was indeed the region where they settled in the south of Oriens. Further on this, see below, App. 1.

[91] Ṭabarī, *Tārīkh,* III, 378, 389.

[92] Balāḏurī, *Futūḥ al-Buldān,* ed. S. Munajjid (Cairo, 1956), I, 172.

[93] Thus the Salīḥid supremacy in the 5th century signals the shift in the center of federate power in Oriens from the Tanūkhids of the 4th century, who were settled in the north of Oriens.

[94] Thus they were the guardians of the *wādī.* Amorkesos, the Ghassānid phylarch of Leo's reign, entered the *limes* from northern Ḥijāz into Palaestina Tertia, but the Ghassānids of the succeeding generation, who replaced the Salīḥids, may have entered Oriens through Wādī Sirḥān.

III. The Kings of Salīḥ

Unlike the kings of Tanūkh[95] and of Ghassān,[96] those of Salīḥ, the Zokomids,[97] have not survived in a list that has been preserved in the later Islamic sources. There are only scattered references to them in the various historical and literary sources.[98] Fortunately, in Hishām al-Kalbī's *Jamharat al-Nasab*, there is a genealogical tree for the Salīḥids.[99] The accounts of Hishām on the various members are skeletal but, together with the genealogical tree, they serve as a basis for the investigation of the fortunes of members of the dynasty. The genealogical tree in the *Jamharat* is not extensive.[100] This, coupled with the archaic names, argues for its essential authenticity, however inaccurate it may be in matters of detail and in family relationships. Furthermore, its authenticity is enhanced by the rise in the reputation of the foremost historian of the *foederati*, Hishām.

What concerns us here is phylarchal or federate Salīḥ, mainly the descendants of Zokomos/Ḍujʿum, the eponym of the royal dynasty.[101] With the exception of Zokomos, the first phylarch in the service of Byzantium, the rest of its members and the genealogical tree have to be discussed within the framework of the Arabic sources alone. There are no confirmatory Greek sources with which to interlock the discussion. Much care has therefore been employed in the process of recovering the facts about these phylarchs/kings. Fortunately, the sources are fairly reliable and some of them are pre-Islamic

[95] For these, see *BAFOC*, 373–81.

[96] For the lists of Ghassānids kings, see Nöldeke, *GF*, 52–62.

[97] That is, the descendant of Zόκομος/Ḍujʿum (according to some Arabic sources, the grandson of Salīḥ), the first Salīḥid phylarch in the service of Byzantium in the 5th century, and the founder of the dynasty. Like the Ghassānid federate chiefs of the 6th century, the Zokomids were both phylarchs and kings. On the confusion of the list of Tanūkhid kings with the Salīḥid in Ibn Qutayba, see *BAFOC*, 411 note 2. On the missing list of Salīḥid kings in the sources, see Ibn Khaldūn, *Tārīkh*, II, 520.

[98] That such a list of Zokomid kings or extensive accounts of them did exist in medieval Islamic times is clear from the repeated reference to the Zokomids as kings and to individual members of the family as such. There is a reference to the eponymn Ḍujʿum in one of the sources as "Ḍujʿum al-Mulūk," "Ḍujʿum of the kings," i.e., Royal Ḍujʿum, the ancestor of the kings which recalls the description of Kinda, the important south Arabian tribe, as Kindat al-Mulūk, Royal Kinda. The reference to Ḍujʿum al-Mulūk is even more restricted since it is applicable to Ḍujʿum and his descendants, while Kinda is a tribe and the phrase implies kings from various clans of Kinda. The phrase is striking and clearly suggests that the learned South Arabian author in whose work it occurs had before him sources still extant which told the story of the Zokomid kings; for this reference see Nashwān ibn Saʿīd al-Ḥimyari, *Shams al-ʿUlūm*, ed. ʿAzimuddin Ahmad, Gibb Memorial Series 24 (Leiden, 1916), p. 64.

[99] For this tree in its entirety, see Caskel, *GN*, Band I, 326.

[100] Thus corresponding with the fact that the lifespan of the dynasty was not more than a century or so.

[101] For this tree, comprising both the Zokomids and other Salīḥids, see the stemma at the back of this volume.

verses, which are on a higher level of authenticity than the prose sources of later Islamic times.[102] Finally, the Arabic manuscripts of Hishām's works are now available for inspection, and these provide new and important material for the work of reconstruction.[103] Thus what is presented in this chapter is the result of all that can be done within the framework of the Arabic literary sources—an intensive study which will serve as a foundation for an epigraphic-literary confrontation once the relevant inscriptions have been discovered.[104]

I. The Zokomids

The number as well as the duration of the Zokomid phylarchs/kings is difficult to ascertain from the genealogical list, but it is clear that the duration of their supremacy as the dominant federal group is roughly coterminous with the fifth century, from the reign of Arcadius (395–408) to that of Anastasius (489–518). Uncertainty attends the identity of the last Salīḥid ruler, but there is no doubt whatsoever about the first, namely, Ḍujʿum, with whom this presentation must then begin.

Ḍujʿum/Ζόκομος

According to the genealogists, he was the son of Saʿd and the grandson of ʿAmr/Salīḥ. His name was Ḥamāṭa (the name of an Arabian tree) and Ḍujʿum was his nickname (the powerful, mighty man).[105] The Arabic sources have little to say on him other than that he was the founder of the dynasty, but his fame must have spread so far and wide that some of his descendants bore his name,[106] in spite of its uneuphonious quality.[107] He is the only phylarch/king of Salīḥ about whom the Greek sources have something to say. The notice of him by Sozomen is precious and welcome as it solves the problem of the inception of the dynasty ca. 400 in the reign of Arcadius.[108] Zokomos/Ḍujʿum thus initiates the lines of Arab phylarchs of the fifth century. Sozo-

[102] Thus it is possible to refine on and advance the presentations of Caskel on Salīḥ and the individual members of the dynasty. His monumental work on the *Jamharat* is fundamental but he approached the subject as a genealogist and had no special interest in the Byzantine profile of the history of the Arab tribes.

[103] For instance, the important datum on ʿAbd al-ʿĀṣ, the Iyādī court poet of Dāwūd, the Salīḥid king; see below, 434.

[104] On this optimistic view of the role of future epigraphic discoveries, see below, note 191.

[105] For Zokomos/Ḍujʿum, see Caskel's "Register" in *GN*, II. For the etymology and the meaning of his name and nickname, see Ibn Durayd, *al-Ishtiqāq*, 545.

[106] On Ζώγομος in Theophylactus Simocatta, see Nöldeke, *GF*, 8.

[107] Hence the use of the Greek form of his name, Zokomos, in this chapter. Emperor Zeno did well to spare posterity his polysyllabic Isaurian name, Tarasicodissa.

[108] On this, see above, 4.

men's account, which speaks of the conversion of Zokomos and with him of "all his subjects," implies that he was already a powerful man even before he effected the Byzantine connection—which, however, made him and his followers even more powerful. Zokomos/Ḍujʿum had two sons, ʿAmr and ʿAwf: phylarchal or federate Salīḥ consists of members descended from these two sons—the ʿAmrids and the ʿAwfids.

A. The ʿAmrids

This is the less important of the two branches, counting among its members only two names, al-Mundir and Sabīṭ. If ʿAmr is added to the list, then only three members of this branch are known. It is about one of them, Sabīṭ, that the Arabic sources have some important information.

ʿAmr

In his account of the conversion of Zokomos, Sozomen spoke of the birth of a son to Zokomos after a "certain monk of great celebrity" prophesied it on condition that Zokomos believed in Christ. It is, thus, not impossible that the son left anonymous in Sozomen is one of the two sons of Zokomos according the genealogical table, ʿAmr and ʿAwf. Of the two, the first is more likely to be the son referred to in the ecclesiastical historian, since ʿAmr is a name of good omen and, what is more, may be related to the birth of a son of Zokomos under the circumstances Sozomen described.[109] The following two observations may be made in connection with this son of Zokomos. As has just been suggested, he may have been none other than the ʿAmr of Hishām's genealogical tree.

1. Sozomen has left the monk who uttered the prophecy also anonymous. Since the Zokomids lived across the Jordan in the Balqā' region and since this monk is described as "a certain monk of great celebrity," it is not unlikely that he was one of the solitaries of the Judaean desert in Palaestina Prima, west of the Jordan, a member of the monastic establishment which counted Hilarion and Euthymius, the propagators of Christianity among the Arabs whose fame attracted such Arab chiefs as Aspebetos in the 420s.[110] If so, this establishes a Salīḥid connection with Palestine, and leads to the second observation.

[109] Various significations can be attached to the root from which the name ʿAmr is derived, all of which make it appropriate for a child born after his father had despaired of his sterile mother.

[110] On Aspebetos, see above, Chap. 2, Sec. IV. Of course, Hilarion is too early and Euthymius too late for Zokomos to have made his trip to either of them since, as has been suggested earlier, the birth of his child may be assigned to the reign of Arcadius (395–408). Hilarion died in 371, and Euthymius came to Jerusalem in 405, but his reputation spread after that date.

2. There is a locality north of Jerusalem called Dayr ʿAmr, the Monastery of ʿAmr. This could originally have been a Salīḥid foundation built by ʿAmr to commemorate his miraculous birth, prophesied by one of the monks of the Holy Land. Dayr ʿAmr is a Christian locality and the name ʿAmr is an old Arab name which, as a Christian name, most probably goes back to pre-Islamic times.[111] The ʿAmr who founded the monastery or after whom it was named is not likely to have been a Tanūkhid, since they lived in the north of Oriens and their physical relationship to Palestine is not attested.[112] The Ghassānids built outside Palestine. They were Monophysites who were not on good terms with the Orthodox Chalcedonian hierarchy of Palestine[113] and the only possible foundation that could be associated with them is another locality, also near Jerusalem, by the name of Dayr Ghassānī, the Dayr or Monastery of the Ghassānids. Finally, in support of a Salīḥid origin for this Dayr ʿAmr, it may be pointed out that there is the analogy of Dayr Dāwūd, the Monastery of Dāwūd, in the north of Oriens, undoubtedly a Salīḥid foundation built by one of their kings.[114] Thus it is perfectly possible that Dayr ʿAmr in Palestine is a Salīḥid foundation that goes back to the fifth century. Its name has survived since then, just as that of Dayr Dāwūd has in northern Syria.

Sabīṭ

Nothing is known about his father, Mundir, except his name. But the sources have something to say on this grandson of ʿAmr. He figures prominently in accounts of the last days of Salīḥ in Oriens and their struggle with the Ghassānids. He is left anonymous by Yaʿqūbī, who only speaks of "the official of the king of the Romans" who came to collect the tax from Ghassān. But the more authoritative and ample account of Ibn Ḥabīb, the pupil of Hishām, supplies his name and his genealogy: Sabīṭ, son of al-Mundir, son of ʿAmr, son of Zokomos.[115] He also describes him as a *jābī* (tax collector). It was his murder by the Ghassānid Jidʿ that brought about the Ghassānid-Salīḥid war which ended with the victory of the Ghassānids and their rise to power as the dominant federate group in Oriens.[116]

The new light shed on the last days of Salīḥ by the publication of Ibn Ḥabīb's *Muḥabbar* and the new data it provides on the Zokomid Sabīṭ calls for the following observations:

[111] After the rise of Islam it became predominantly an Arab Muslim name. So a monastery built by or for a ʿAmr almost certainly goes back to pre-Islamic times.
[112] For this, see *BAFOC,* 395–407.
[113] This will be discussed in *BASIC.*
[114] On Dayr Dāwūd, see below, 297–99.
[115] See Ibn Ḥabīb, *al-Muḥabbar,* 370–71.
[116] Further on this, see below, Sec. v.

1. His father's name may be significant. Mundir is a new name among the Salīḥids which became popular later with the Ghassānids in the sixth century. It may be related to the verb *andara*,[117] "to utter warnings," but it is equally possible that it is derived from the verb *nadara* "to make a vow." This may be the truth about the name, in view of the strong Christian complexion of the Zokomids, especially since Mundir was probably the son of the same ʿAmr that was born after Zokomos had vowed that he would become Christian if a son was born to his wife. So ʿAmr himself may very well have made a vow or reflected something connected with a vow he had made by calling his son al-Mundir or al-Mundar, "the vowed one."

2. His own name is unique among the Salīḥids, and is uncommon in the Arabic onomasticon. It could be related to the root (*s-b-ṭ*) meaning smooth hair, but Sabīṭ as a proper noun is apparently unknown to the lexica in this sense. It is, therefore, possible that this is an Old Testament name, related to Arabic Sibṭ (which appears later in Islamic times), signifying one of the twelve sons of Jacob, an onomastic expression of *imitatio Veteris Testamenti*. This is not impossible in view of the strong Christianity of the Salīḥids and the fact that one of them assumed or was given the Israelite name David/Dāwūd, the descendant of one of the Israelite *asbāṭ*.[118]

3. His function as a member of the royal house of the Zokomids was that of a *jābī* (tax collector), who collected taxes from the Arab tribes allowed to settle within Oriens by the Romans. This datum on Sabīṭ is very valuable for giving a glimpse of the conditions under which the Arab tribes settled within the empire and of the functions of the Arab phylarchs of Byzantium: they not only fought but also collected taxes for the empire from their fellow Arabs. The passage in Ibn Ḥabīb also gives a glimpse of how the Zokomids were functioning as a family, with various members performing various functions. Thus one member was collecting taxes while another was fighting for the chief Salīḥid phylarch and king.[119]

4. His genealogy presents some chronological difficulties. According to the table, he is of the same generation as al-Habūla, Dāwūd's father.[120] The

[117] The derivative verbal form *andara*, from which the *nomen agentis* al-Mundir is formed, does not have the meaning "to vow" in the lexica. But this is not decisive, since *andara* in 5th-century Christian Oriens may have had this meaning. Some support for this may be derived from the fact that the Greek inscriptions of later times which have preserved this name vocalize it as al-Mundar and not al-Mundir, that is, the *nomen patientis*, the passive, which yields the meaning "the one who was vowed." Al-Mundar makes no sense as a passive if derived from *andara* ("to warn"), but it does when derived from *nadara* or *andara* in the sense of "to vow."

[118] It may be even possible to add another Israelite name, Solomon, among the Salīḥids; see below, 302 note 334.

[119] Such as Ziyād and Ḥārith, if they were really coevals or contemporaries during the kingship of Dāwūd. For Ziyād and Ḥārith and their campaigns, see below, Sec. III.B.

[120] Ibn Khaldūn makes Sabīṭ, whom he calls Sabṭa, the grandson of Dāwūd; see *Tārīkh*,

line descended from ʿAmr was obscure, and it is perfectly possible that one or two names fell out of the genealogical line of the ʿAmrids or were unknown to the genealogists, who were more informed about the line of ʿAwf, from which Dāwūd was descended.

B. The ʿAwfids

This is the more important branch of the Zokomids, counting among its members three on whom the sources are informative. Of ʿAwf's son, also called ʿAmr, as of his brother, nothing has been reported (or is not extant if it was reported). He had three sons, Habāla, Ḥawthara, and Habūla, who begat Dāwūd, Mandala, and Ziyād, respectively. Mandala begat Ḥārith, and the other sons have offspring in the genealogical table. They were the last dynasts of the Salīḥids just before their fall, after which their descendants ceased to play a historical role; hence the lack of interest on the part of historians in their fortunes. The sources are silent on Habāla, Ḥawthara, and Habūla, but are informative on the two sons, Dāwūd and Ziyād, and on the grandson Ḥārith. By far the most important of these three, and the one on whom the sources are most informative, is Dāwūd.

Dāwūd

Dāwūd is the best known of all the kings/phylarchs of Salīḥ, owing to a biographical notice of him in Hishām's *Jamharat al-Nasab* which amplifies the scanty information available in later works such as the *al-Ishtiqāq* of Ibn Durayd.[121] In addition to this short notice, there are various valuable references scattered in the *Jamharat*, all of which makes possible a reasonable reconstruction of the main features of his reign.

The text of the *Jamharat* may be translated as follows:[122] "And he was a king who used to engage in raiding expeditions. Then he became a Christian, repented, loathed the shedding of blood, and followed the religious life (*ta-ʿabbada*). He built a monastery and used to carry the water and the mortar on his back, saying 'I do not want anyone to help me,' and so his clothes became wet, and he was nicknamed *al-Lathiq*, 'the bedraggled.' When he became

II, 583. For the two verses that remember his death by the sword of the Ghassānid Jidʿ, see below, Sec. VIII note 14.

[121] See *Ishtiqāq*, 545. For the entry on Dāwūd deriving from the *Jamharat* see Caskel, *GN*, II, 232. Much water has flowed under the bridge since Caskel wrote, and this chapter on Dāwūd will gather together all the pieces of evidence on this Salīḥid king. See also below, Sec. VIII.

[122] This is a literal translation of the account in the *Muqtaḍab* of Yāqūt where the biographical notice—deriving from the *Jamharat*—is clear and more detailed. See below, Sec VIII.

averse to bloodshedding and killing, his position weakened and he became himself the target of raids until he was killed by Thaʿlaba ibn ʿĀmir al-Akbar (from the tribe of Kalb) and Muʿāwiya ibn Ḥujayr (from the tribe of al-Namir ibn Wabara)."

This valuable text, brief as it is, serves as a basis for studying in detail the career of this best known of the Zokomid kings:

1. The first question one must raise concerns his name, the biblical Dāwūd/David and the significance of his assumption of this name. All the names of the other Zokomids, the Tanūkhids, and the Ghassānid kings were Arabic and not biblical. The name is very striking in the Arabic pre-Islamic onomasticon. If it was a given name, then this reflects the strong attachment of his father to the biblical tradition. If it was assumed by him, then it may reflect an attempt on his part to conceive of himself as the Arab David, self-named after the warrior-king of ancient Israel. The seat of the Salīḥids was al-Balqā' in biblical Ammonitis, the region that witnessed the death of Uriah the Hittite before the walls of Rabbath Ammon, and David was involved in his death. The Christian Salīḥid king may thus have remembered the episode that inspired David to write the famous Psalm of Mercy and decided to call himself by the name of the Israelite king. If so, the name tells something about Dāwūd and his self-image, but it has also concealed his Arab name. What exactly in David's career attracted the attention of Dāwūd (or his father) cannot be answered in view of the paucity of the sources.

2. Dāwūd started as a *ghāzi* (warrior). His expeditions must have been conducted against the Arabs of the Peninsula in view of the peace that reigned between Byzantium and Persia in the fifth century. These expeditions probably extended to Ḥijāz and northern Arabia and also involved conflict with the rising power of Kinda in the Arabian Peninsula. His career as an Arabian warrior is reflected in the fact that he was considered a *jarrār*, that is "leader of a thousand" (chiliarch).[123]

3. The statement in the *Jamharat* that he became Christian must be a mistake, since the Zokomids had been Christian since the conversion of their eponym Zokomos, in the reign of Arcadius around 400. But the further statement is correct and cannot be viewed with suspicion, namely, that he became very religious and indulged in such humble acts as carrying water and mortar for building his monastery. Dāwūd's renunciation of the world is consonant

[123] Ibn Ḥabīb, *al-Muḥabbar,* 250. This is probably a reference to him before he became king and while he was still a commander in the army of the Salīḥid king, whoever he was. The short chapter in Ibn Ḥabīb on the *jarrārūn* from Quḍāʿa could represent the manpower contributed by these federate tribes to the defense of the Byzantine frontier. In addition to Salīḥ, there is reference to Kalb and ʿUḏra and chiliarchs from both of these federate tribes; ibid., 250–51.

with what is known about the mood of Christianity in fifth-century Oriens, which witnessed the spread of monasticism and the rise of the desert saints, including the Stylites, who were instrumental in the conversion of the Arabs and in influencing the life of Arab rulers.[124] Dāwūd is one of these rulers. The details about his acting as his own mortar carrier in building his monastery is perfectly credible and has parallels in the history of the period.[125]

4. Dāwūd, "the bedraggled" ("al-Lathiq"),[126] did not entirely renounce the world and take to a monastery. In spite of losing interest in his previous function as a warrior and raider, he remained federate king of Salīḥ. It was in this capacity that he met his fate in battle. There are many references to the last battle fought by Dāwūd, which may now be gathered together since they raise many important questions.

a. His two killers are identified in Hishām's genealogical work. One was Thaʿlaba, the son of ʿĀmir al-Akbar, and the other was Muʿāwiya, the son of Ḥujayr.[127] Not only are their names known but also their clans and the larger tribes to which the clans belonged. The first, Thaʿlaba ibn ʿĀmir, came from a clan that later became the clan of ʿĀmir or Banū ʿĀmir, after their eponym ʿĀmir. The other came from the clan of Mashjaʿa or Banū Mashjaʿa.[128] The first clan belonged to the tribe of Kalb and the second to that of al-Namir ibn Wabara, tribes related to each other and ultimately belonging to the large tribal group, Quḍāʿa.

b. The death of Dāwūd is remembered not only in the prose accounts of

[124] On Nuʿmān, the Lakhmid ruler who renounced the world, see above, Chap. 8, app. 2.

[125] That this was not an isolated phenomenon is clear from examples of other Near Eastern rulers whose religiosity drove them to indulge in similar acts of piety; Shahîd, *Martyrs,* 229. Unjustifiably, Caskel (*GN,* II, 232) is inclined to disbelieve it.

A striking parallel for Dāwūd's act of humility is afforded by the career of an American president. Four years after he left office, Jimmy Carter volunteered "to spend a week renovating an abandoned building in Manhattan's run-down and crime-infested Lower East side. . . . He is expected to don overalls and to do carpentry work . . . ."; *The Washington Post,* 3 Sept. 1984. I am grateful to Stephen Anderson for photocopies of this material.

[126] The term that described Dāwūd the builder was Arabic al-*Lathiq,* "the wet, the bedrabbled, the bedraggled." It is interesting that in one of its significations it is considered a South Arabian word in some of the *lexica* (*Tāj al-ʿArūs,* VII, p. 59). As its application is derisive and pejorative, it may well have been the term applied to him by those whom the Salīḥids replaced, namely, the Tanūkhids or those who replaced them, the Ghassānids, both originally hailing from South Arabia.

[127] On these two killers, see below, 309–10.

[128] Another source knows of a group called Banū Mashjaʿa, the "sons of Mashjaʿa," whom Khālid ibn Walīd found in the vicinity of Damascus during the Conquest of Oriens. They are described as belonging to Quḍāʿa, and so may have taken the name of the killer of Dāwūd after he "distinguished" himself as a regicide; for this group, see al-Azdī, *Tarīkh Futūḥ al-Shām* (Cairo, 1970), 75–76.

Hishām al-Kalbī but also in a verse composed by his own daughter,[129] which also speaks of the two clans ʿĀmir and Mashjaʿa but introduces within the clan of Mashjaʿa a smaller group, "the group of Ibn Qārib."[130] The two sets of sources, the verse and the prose accounts, raise the question of whether the death of Dāwūd was the result of a personal feud or a hostile tribal alliance against the power of the Salīḥid king. A close examination of the manuscripts of Hishām al-Kalbī clearly indicates that the two clans of the two tribes formed a close alliance, that they launched an offensive against the central power of the dominant federate group, and that Thaʿlaba and Muʿāwiya were the names of the ringleaders within the alliance. What lay behind the alliance is not clear, but the verse gives us a precious glimpse of intertribal federate warfare in the limitrophe and identifies two important tribes, al-Namir and Kalb, as involved with the Salīḥids in the political and military history of the Arab phylarchate of Oriens in the fifth century.[131]

c. The place where the encounter took place is also known, through a verse fragment composed by one of the regicides himself, the Kalbite, Thaʿlaba ibn ʿĀmir.[132]

The first question that the verse raises is the exact locality at which Dāwūd met his fate. Al-Qurnatayn is most likely Karnaim, the biblical town, capital of al-Bathaniyya (biblical Bashan), present-day Shaykh Saʿd. Ḥārib is Mount Ḥārib in the Jawlān (biblical Golan) overlooking the Sea of Galilee.[133]

[129] On this see below, Sec. VIII.

[130] On this small group, see below, Chap. 12, sec. VIII.II.

[131] In *BAFOC*, 196–97, was suggested that Queen Mavia of the 4th century belonged to the tribe of Kalb on the ground that Banū Māwiya ("the sons of Māwiya") were a Kalbite group. The tribal affiliation of this Mavia, the matriarch of this group of Kalbites, however, was Bahrā' and not Kalb; see Caskel, *GN*, II, 405, s.v. B. Māwiya (2). Mavia thus became a Kalbite by her matrimonial connection and was a Kalbite only in this sense. The death of Dāwūd at the hand of a Kalbite thus justifies what was said in *BAFOC* on friction between Salīḥ and Kalb. The 4th-century queen could, of course, have been a Kalbite with no connection to the group called Banū Māwiya, referred to in *BAFOC*. The tribal affiliation of Queen Mavia must remain hypothetical until the discovery of some relevant inscriptions.

[132] For the fragment, consisting of three verses, see Yāqūt, *Muʿjam,* 331, s.v. al-Qurnatayn. The regicide glories in what he did, saying: "We are those whose blades felled down Dāwūd between al-Qurnatayn and Ḥārib." Caskel was unaware of this important and informative fragment, a welcome addition to the dossier on Dāwūd. It may be added to others that deal with the same theme—the death of tyrants and kings at the hands of tribesmen, such as Kindite Ḥujr and the Lakhmid ʿAmr ibn Hind.

[133] For Shaykh Saʿd/Karnaim, see Dussaud, *Topographie,* 329. Wetzstein thinks that Ḥārib, too, is in Bathaniyya, since it is near Ṣaydā', which he locates in that region; see J. G. Wetzstein, *Reisebericht über Hauran und die Trachonen* (Berlin, 1860), 117.

The identification of Qurnatayn with Karnaim is justified phonetically, morphologically, and possibly semantically. If the *nun* of *Qurnatayn* is really a *ya,* this reading would give Qaryatayn instead of Qurnatayn. This would also be in Oriens, a town northeast of Damascus. It is unlikely that al-Qaryatayn is meant, since it is rather far from Ḥārib (unlike Karnaim) and the description of the battlefield would not have been specific enough in the verse. Both

That the battle took place either in the Jawlān or the Bathaniyya is consonant with the fact that the Salīḥids were stationed in the Provincia Arabia and possibly in some provincial zones adjacent to Arabia, such as Palestine and Phoenicia.[134]

This *yawm* (battle-day) between Salīḥ on the one hand and Namir and Kalb on the other is not listed among the *ayyām* (battle-days) of the Arabs.[135] But it was even more important than many others that are considered as such. While the others mostly deal with skirmishes and encounters within the Peninsula whose significance is relatively small, this one involved the death of a Byzantine client-king. Together with one or two more *ayyām*, it brought about the downfall of the phylarchate of Salīḥ toward the end of the fifth century and ended its century of dominance in Oriens.

5. The genealogical table for Salīḥ makes Dāwūd issueless since it makes no mention of any son. The table stops with him and his cousins, Ziyād and Mandala, and his nephew Ḥārith. Whether this implies that he sired no sons or whether they simply did not reign is not clear. Whatever the case may be, he clearly had a daughter, which Hishām al-Kalbī's patriarchal attitude in matters of genealogy caused him to omit from the list. The daughter was a poetess, and unfortunately she is left anonymous. However, students of Zokomid history should be grateful to her for the poem she composed on the death of her father, a verse of which has survived to inform posterity on the two regicides.[136]

Dāwūd also had a court poet, ʿAbd al-ʿĀṣ, from the tribe of Iyād, a matter of considerable importance in the cultural history of the Salīḥids and the Arab federates in Oriens. Furthermore, the presence of this poet at the court of the Salīḥid king could argue that Iyād was already a federate tribe in the fifth century.[137]

---

al-Qurnatayn and al-Qaryatayn in this context have to be distinguished from other sites in Arabia that were not related to the conflict involving Salīḥ and in which other tribes are involved. Reference to Ḥārib and to Dāwūd make certain that it was not the Arabian localities that were referred to in the verse.

[134] It is noteworthy that the battle did not take place *extra limitem*. The Salīḥids, as well as other federate tribes, were settled within the *limes*, some apparently on both sides and others outside it in what may be termed the invisible frontier of Byzantium's sphere of influence. In the 6th century, the Ghassānids were established in the Jawlān, and their capital Jābiya was in that region. This raises the question of whether or not the Jawlān or part of it was already occupied by the Salīḥids in the 5th century.

[135] It should not be confused with the well-known Yawm al-Qurnatayn, fought in the Arabian Peninsula far from Bathaniyya and the Jawlān; see Bakrī, *Muʿjam*, III, 1068, s.v. al-Qurnatan.

[136] See above, note 35; for more on this Salīḥid princess, see below, Chap. 14, sec. IV.B.II.

[137] Further on ʿAbd al-ʿĀṣ, see below, Chap. 14, Sec. IV.B.I.

6. Finally, the most solid spot in Salīḥid toponymy is associated with Dāwūd. Mention has already been made of the monastery he built,[138] Dayr Dāwūd. It was his engaging in the construction of this monastery that earned him the nickname al-Lathiq, the "bedraggled." The Salīḥids were settled in the Provincia Arabia in the south of Oriens, and so the question arises why Dāwūd chose the north for building his monastery. Perhaps he wanted to be as far away from the center of Salīḥid military power as possible. Furthermore, the region where Dayr Dāwūd was located was close to the desert of Chalcis, which had already emerged in the fourth century as a region of monastic establishments, well known to St. Jerome.[139] With the appearance of St. Simeon the Stylite in the north, that region became even more celebrated for its monastic foundations and figures. Finally, the Dayr which Dāwūd built was not far from Sergiopolis/Ruṣāfa, the great center of pilgrimage in Syria, the shrine of the celebrated St. Sergius, the patron saint of Arab military groups even in Islamic times.[140] Perhaps Dāwūd, a soldier before he opted for the ascetic life, wanted to be near the military saint.

Thus Dāwūd emerges from a study of the various references to him in the sources as more than a mere name in a genealogical table, as other Salīḥids are. Unfortunately the years of his reign are not known, and there are difficulties in reconciling the genealogical datum that he is the last king of Salīḥ with other data in the sources relating to the last phase of Salīḥ's history as the dominant federate group. But it is also clear that if he was not actually the last king or ruler, he was among the last, and his reign thus represents the beginning of the end of Salīḥ's supremacy in Oriens.

Ziyād

The other member of the dynasty who is well known to the Arabic sources is Dāwūd's cousin Ziyād,[141] sometimes considered his brother. In view of the strong Christian complexion of the dynasty, his may have been a theophoric name, Ziyād-Allāh, and if so the name could imply that he was not the eldest son of his father.[142]

Quite unlike Dāwūd, who renounced the world, Ziyād appears in the sources as very much of this world, a military figure associated with one of the famous battle-days of the Arabs, Yawm al-Baradān. He also appears as one of

[138] On this dayr, see below, 297–99.

[139] See *BAFOC* 284–88, 293–95.

[140] Such as the Taghlib. The relations of the Ghassānids of the 6th century to Ruṣāfa and St. Sergius will be fully discussed in *BASIC*.

[141] Sometimes it is spelled *Ḏiyād*.

[142] Just as Assyriologists have argued, after examining the component parts of the name "Sennacherib," that the king was not the eldest of his father's sons. The root from which Ziyād is derived (*z-y-d*) means "to increase, multiply."

the *jarrārūn*, the chiliarchs of the Arabs in pre-Islamic times.[143] The reference to him in that capacity is a solitary one in the sources, but many, copious, and bewildering are the references to him as one of the protagonists of Yawm al-Baradān, which deserves some attention because of its historical importance.

According to most of the sources the battle was fought between Ziyād and Ḥujr (Ākil al-Murār), the king of Kinda, and ended, after an initial success by Ziyād, with his defeat and death. The accounts of this *yawm* are perhaps the most detailed[144] for any of pre-Islamic Arabia,[145] and yet there is much uncertainty about the identity of Ziyād's antagonist, the location of the toponym al-Baradān, and the date of the battle.

1. Most of the sources conceive of the antagonist of Ziyād as Ḥujr (nicknamed Ākil al-Murār), the founder of the branch of Kinda called Banū Ākil al-Murār, who established the power of Kinda in central Arabia and became the eponym of the dynasty well known to Byzantium.[146] It was his grandson, Ḥārith (Arethas), whose two sons Ḥujr and Maʿdi-Karib were attacking the Roman frontier[147] around 500 and with whom Byzantium concluded a treaty in 502. Some of the sources suggest that the antagonist was not Ḥujr but his father, al-Ḥārith,[148] and there are other possibilities. The most plausible suggestion would be the great grandson of Ḥujr, also called Ḥujr; the identity of names is in favor of this suggestion.

2. The medieval Arabic geographical dictionaries place al-Baradān in a variety of regions in the Arabian Peninsula, and this is the major difficulty in identifying the place where Yawm al-Baradān was fought. However, it is generally accepted that the site of the battle is the one that Yāqūt identifies with a spring in the district of al-Samāwa,[149] toward Iraq and on the road from al-Kūfa to Syria, as modern topographers and toponymists have argued.[150] This is far from where Salīḥ was settled in the Provincia Arabia, and its distance from the Balqāʾ region raises the question of why Ziyād was campaigning in that distant region outside the *limes*. The key to this question is the rising power of Kinda in Arabia and the threats and challenges it was

[143] Ibn Ḥabīb, *al-Muḥabbar,* 250.

[144] For two very detailed versions of this *yawm,* see Iṣbahānī, *Aghānī,* (Beirut, 1962) XVI, 277–81 and Ibn al-Athīr, *al-Kāmil,* I, 506–11.

[145] For a succinct and informative account of these peculiarly Arab battle days, see E. Mittwoch's article in the new *EI*,[1] 793–94.

[146] For this, see Shahīd, "Kinda," *EI,*[2] V, 118–20; the family tree of Ḥujr Ākil al-Murār is on p. 118.

[147] Theophanes, *Chronographia,* I, 141–43.

[148] See Iṣbahānī, *Aghānī,* XVI, 280.

[149] For Baradān, see Yāqūt, *Muʿjam,* I, 375–76. For the spring in al-Samāwa, see ibid., 375.

[150] See Musil, *Arabia Deserta,* 359 and note 91.

posing to Oriens. Ziyād's presence in al-Baradān must, therefore, be due to the fact that he marched through Wādī Sirḥān or some other route which would have brought him to North Arabia, where the encounter with Kinda took place. The Salīḥids were the guardians of Wādī Sirḥān, and its southern end near Dūmat was not far from the region where turbulent tribes lived and whence they could molest the Roman frontier.

One of the toponyms associated with Yawm al-Baradān is that of ʿAyn Ubāgh,[151] itself the name of a famous battle-day, generally considered a battle fought between the Ghassānids and the Lakhmids in the sixth century.[152] Yet ʿAyn Ubāgh is associated with the Salīḥids,[153] and it is not impossible that there was a Ghassānid participation in this battle-day on the side of Kinda, since the two rising powers are associated with each other in their thrusts against the *limes*.[154] Whether or not the Ghassānids participated in the battle must remain hypothetical, but what is certain is the participation of Kinda against the Salīḥids and that the *yawm* is the famous one in which Salīḥ was involved.[155]

3. The chronological problem is almost insoluble without the recovery of some solid data from new sources. Ḥujr, the Kindite victor of Yawm al-Baradān, may be assigned to the middle of the fifth century.[156] But the *yawm* witnessed the death of Ziyād who, according to the genealogical tree of Hishām, is either the last or the penultimate Salīḥid. This is too early for the fall of Salīḥ, which a confrontation of the Arabic with the Greek sources places at the end of the fifth century.[157] The difficulty may be resolved by entertaining the possibility, already suggested earlier in this section, that the Kindite involved in the battle was not Ākil al-Murār but his great grandson and namesake, the son of Arethas who around 500 was campaigning against Byzantium and presumably also against her *foederati*, the Salīḥids.[158]

[151] See Ibn al-Athīr, *al-Kāmil*, I, 507.

[152] See Nöldeke, *GF,* 19 and note 2.

[153] See below, 269–70.

[154] What could give some support to the Ghassānid participation is the fact that in one of the pre-Islamic verses of al-Nābigha of the 6th century, this *yawm* of ʿAyn Ubāgh is considered one of the old battle days of the Ghassānids and not a recent one. For the verse, see Ahlwardt, *Divan*', p. 168, frag. 22.

[155] It is noteworthy that accounts of this *yawm* reflect an image of *royal* Salīḥ with its Byzantine connection: (*a*) Ziyād is described as having a canopy; (*b*) he is saluted by the phrase "O! Best of Fityān," the royal salute which became that of the Ghassānids of later times; (*c*) reference to *al-Quṣūr al-Ḥumr* in Shām/Oriens, a clear reference to the *castra* and *castella* of the *limes*; for these references, see Ibn al-Athīr, *al-Kāmil,* I, 507, 508.

[156] On this, see G. Olinder, "Āl-al-Ǧaun of the Family of Ākil al-Murār," *Le Monde Orientale* 25 (1931), 208. Epigraphers are inclined to date him even earlier—to the first half of the 5th century—on paleographical grounds, as J. Pirenne does; see G. Ryckmans, "Inscriptions sud-Arabes," *Le Muséon* 69 (1956), 152.

[157] See below, Chap. 12, sec. v.

[158] In a well-known passage, that discriminating historian Ibn al-Athīr, expressed incre-

It remains to relate the career of Ziyād to that of his relative Dāwūd in the context of the dynasty of phylarchs in the service of Byzantium. From the discussion above, Ziyād may either have been one of Dāwūd's generals during his lifetime or he may have acceded to the kingship or supreme phylarchate after Dāwūd renounced the work or died. The two battle days in which Dāwūd and Ziyād were involved throw light on the tribal groupings that brought about the downfall of Salīḥ—Kalb and Kinda, and, as has been argued, possibly Ghassān. The natural presumption is that Ziyād's death came after that of Dāwūd.

Ḥārith ibn Mandala

The last ʿAwfid of pre-Islamic times known to the sources and closely related to both Dāwūd and Ziyād is al-Ḥārith ibn Mandala, their cousin. A short notice of him in Ibn Durayd's *Ishtiqāq*[159] may be translated as follows: "And among (the Zokomids) may be counted al-Ḥārith ibn Mandala; he went on a raiding expedition but did not return; it was on this occasion that ʿĀmir ibn Juwayn composed (the following verse): 'By God I will not give Ẓulāma/ẓulama to a king or a commoner, until Ibn Mandala returns.'" Much can be extracted from this short notice.

1. There is general agreement that the poet[160] who composed the verse belonged to the tribe of Ṭayy and was a contemporary of the Lakhmid king, Mundir (505–554). The *floruit* of al-Ḥārith may therefore be assigned to the first half of the sixth century, after the rise of the Ghassānids as the dominant federate group in Oriens. But it is possible that ʿĀmir composed the verse before the accession of the Lakhmid Mundir which thus may assign Ḥārith to the last years of the fifth century.

2. The establishment of Ḥārith's *floruit* in the first half of the sixth century makes him a Salīḥid figure who survived the fall of the dynasty as the

---

dulity that Ziyād and Ḥujr could have been contemporaries and hence the antagonists at the battle of al-Baradān. But he gave the wrong reason—the fantastic duration of the Ghassānid dynasty as conceived by some Arab historians; see *al-Kāmil,* I, 510.

[159] See *Ishtiqāq,* 546.

[160] For ʿĀmir ibn Juwayn and his encounter with the Lakhmid Mundir, see Abū ʿAli al-Qāli, *Dayl al-Amālī wa al-Nawādir* (Beirut, 1926), 177–78. The establishment of the *floruit* of al-Ḥārith makes certain that associating him with *yawm al-Baradān* must be a mistake, since this took place in the 5th century and Ziyād, not al-Ḥārith, was the Salīḥid who fought it. For this mistake, see H. al-Marsafī, *Al-Wasīla al-Adabiyya* (Cairo, 1872–73), 271–73. The information contained in this work on the encounter between Ḥārith and Ḥujr the Kindite, however, has some potentially valuable data for *yawm al-Baradān,* such as that it took place in the reign of the Sasanid king Bahrām Gūr (420–438) and that Ḥujr the Kindite was away campaigning against Najrān when the Salīḥids attacked Najd. The reign of Bahrām Gūr is rather early for *yawm al-Baradān,* and so the source could have confused it with a later reign.

dominant federate power in Oriens.[161] Ḥārith appears as a general in the federate army to whom was assigned a raiding duty in Arabia.

3. The reference to Ẓulāma in the verse of ʿĀmir ibn Juwayn provides valuable data for understanding federate Arab history *extra limitem* in the Arabian Peninsula. The word "Ẓulāma" can be a common noun meaning "what has been wrongfully taken away," and there is some support for this interpretation of the word in the verse.[162] But it could also be a proper noun, and in fact the biographical dictionary knows of a Ẓulāma in Arabia, and a literary source speaks of it as a location seized by the tribe of Asad from a subdivision of the tribe of Ṭayy, by the name of Nabhān.[163] So it is perfectly possible that the Ẓulāma mentioned in the verse is none other than this one. The exact course of events that led to the expedition of Ḥārith ibn Mandala is not clear, but what can be safely inferred is that the federate expedition led by the Salīḥids counted the Ṭayy tribe as the allies of the federate Arabs in Oriens.[164]

4. It is fortunate that Ḥārith's patronymic is given—Ibn Mandala.[165] It is unique or almost unique in the Arabic onomasticon.[166] Although it may be related to the root *n-d-l* (to snatch away), it is more likely related, as Ibn Durayd cogently suggests, to *mandal*, the aromatic smoke of which is used as incense.[167] As the Salīḥids were ardent Christians, it is possible that this member of the Salīḥid royal house, the father of Ḥārith, was given the name Mandala as a nickname for having donated to the church some incense—or better a censer, since the morphological patterns of the name suggests the noun of instrument. This is consonant with the fact that the use of incense in

[161] On Sulaymān, possibly another Salīḥid leader (ca. 530), see below, 302 note 334.

[162] From the fact that the phrase in which the word occurs seems to be a set phrase, since it recurs in the poetry of Imru' al-Qays; see Ahlwardt, *Divans*, 131, verse 58; and in *Dīwān Shiʿr Ḥātim al-Ṭāʾī*, ed. ʿA. S. Jamāl (Cairo, 1975), 44.

[163] For Ẓulāma as a village taken unjustly from Nabhān by Asad, see Bakrī, *Muʿjam*, I, 281, s.v. Ḏū Bahdā.

[164] After what is called *ḥarb al-fasād*, many clans of Ṭayy moved within Oriens and lived in the vicinity of Aleppo/Beroea: Ibn Ḥazm, *Jamharat*, 399. Ghassānid relations with Ṭayy will be discussed in *BASIC*.

[165] His own name, Ḥārith, is a newcomer in the Salīḥid onomasticon, but is a well-known royal name among the Kindites and the Ghassānids (never among the Lakhmids); it goes back to Nabataean times.

[166] Balāḏurī knows of a Traditionist from Kufa by the name of Mandal; see *Futūḥ al-Buldān*, I, 200.

[167] Ibn Durayd, *Ishtiqāq*, 546, perhaps Arabic *mandal* derives from Mandalay, whence it may have been brought. India was the country of exotica and aromata. In the poetry of ʿAdi ibn Zayd there is reference to the aromatic wood coming from India, "al-Hindī." For the verse of this pre-Islamic 6th century poet of Ḥīra, see the *dīwān*, ed. M. J. al-Muʿaybid (Baghdad, 1965), 51, line 1. The aromatic wood *al-Mandalī* appears in the poetry of the Umayyad poet Kuthayyir; see Yāqūt, *Muʿjam*, I, 293.

the Christian churches of the East is dated precisely to the fifth century; Mandala must be a fifth-century figure since his son belongs to the early part of the sixth. His donation of a censer to the church could be paralleled by the donations of other religious federate leaders of the fifth century: Dāwūd built a monastery,[168] and the phylarch/bishops of the Palestinian Parembole furnished and appointed churches.[169] Thus Mandala emerges as a royal Salīḥid figure, a cousin to Dāwūd and Ziyād but closer to Dāwūd in his religiosity than to the warrior Ziyād.

Habūla/Habāla

The genealogical tree and the sources sometimes assign different fathers to Dāwūd and Ziyād, namely, Habūla and Habāla or vice versa. As an examination of the root *h-b-l* from which the two names are derived will presently show, it is quite unlikely that two fathers are involved. It is much more likely that there was only one father who, moreover, bore the more likely form Habūla and that Dāwūd and Ziyād were brothers, not paternal cousins.[170]

The name al-Habūla is striking; it is not attested elsewhere in the Arabic onomasticon, and it is certainly not the name of the Zokomid but a nickname given him. The root from which al-Habūla is derived, the verb *habila* in Arabic, has two meanings: (1) the one who loses a child, the bereaved; (2) the fool. Either signification could be the base of the nickname al-Habūla, and either could be related to important facts about this Salīḥid:

(1) The significance "the bereaved" could have been applied to him after the tragic death of his son Dāwūd, and possibly Ziyād, who, as has been argued above, is likely to have been his son, rather than his nephew. The loss of the two sons could explain the morphological pattern of Habūla, with the final "tā" functioning as an intensive.[171]

(2) The signification "the fool"[172] could be related to his Christianity. It

[168] And also acquired the nickname al-Lathiq. His cousin could easily have acquired the nickname Mandala.

[169] St. Euthymius asks the Arab phylarch/bishop Aspebetos/Petrus to furnish and appoint the church which the latter had built in the Judaean Desert in Palaestina Prima; above, 183.

On the dedication of a censer by an Arab in pagan times, see G. W. Bowersock, "A New Antonine Inscription from the Syrian Desert," *Chiro* 6 (1976), 353 and note 13.

[170] The point has no great significance, and the argument in this section on Habūla/Habāla could easily apply to one or to two persons, but it is more appropriate and cogent when applied to one.

[171] The full form in transliteration is al-Habūlat. The lexicons give the form *al-Habūl,* without the feminine *ta* and apply it to women, but in 5th century Arabic it is perfectly possible that it was applicable to men. The final *ta* in the name is most likely to be the intensive, as in *raḥḥālat, ʿallāmat.*

[172] For the semantic development of the root *h-b-l* from "bereaved" to "fool," see *Tāj al-ʿArūs* (Beirut, 1966), VIII, 163.

is possible that this member of the Christian dynasty indulged in acts of self-renunciation so extravagantly that to the unsympathetic observer they seemed to be those of a fool, in much the same way that his son Dāwūd was given the pejorative nickname "al-Lathiq."

In support of this Christian signification for al-Habūla, one may refer to the Epistle of St. Paul to the Corinthians, which has the well-known phrase μωροὶ διὰ Χριστόν, "fools for Christ's sake" (I Cor. 4:10). The term σαλός replaced μωρός in this sense, and it first appears in the *Lausiac History* of Palladius, an ascetic who visited Palestine and wrote the *Lives* of solitaries, finishing his *History* in 420. Thus it is perfectly possible for al-Habūla to be the equivalent of μωρός and σαλός in St. Paul's sense.[173] The fifth century witnessed the rapid spread of monasticism in Oriens and also some of its extreme forms, as represented by Simeon the Stylite, so close to the Arabs. The Salīḥids were ardently Christian, and it is quite possible, even likely, that one of them merited the epithet al-Habūla for his extreme religiosity. His son Dāwūd's Christianity earned him the nickname al-Lathiq, and one of his collateral descendants acquired the nickname Mandala, possibly for the same reason.

II. Other Salīḥids

There are three or four names of other Salīḥids, non-Zokomids, which deserve to be discussed briefly. They are less important than the Zokomids, but in view of the paucity of the sources on the Salīḥids, it is worthwhile discussing them in the hope that a few more facts may be extracted about these Arab *foederati* of the fifth century.

Salīḥ

The name of the eponym is striking and literally unique in the Arabic onomasticon, both pre-Islamic and Islamic. Etymologists connect it with one of the meanings of the root *s-l-ḥ* meaning "weaponry."[174] But in view of its uniqueness and the fact that this tribal group was Christian, it is not impossible that this name was a loanword from Syriac *Shlīḥa*, "apostle," reflecting the

[173] For a recent discussion of these terms, see the succinct account in L. Rydén, "The Holy Fool," in *The Byzantine Saint* (Birmingham, 1980), 106–13, with its bibliographical orientation including other works by the author; also Rydén, "The Life of St. Basil the Younger and the Date of the Life of St. Andreas Salos," in *Harvard Ukrainian Studies* (1983), 568–86. The etymology of the term *salos* is obscure, and its derivation from Syriac *sakla* is apparently ruled out (Rydén, "The Holy Fool," 107 and note 4). It is possible that it is a loan word from Persian, which has the term *sālūs,* meaning "hypocrite, deceiver," and that in the process of naturalization in Greek the Persian word experienced semantic development from "deceiver" to "fool"—from one who fools others to one who is fooled himself.

[174] Ibn Durayd, *Ishtaqāq*, 537.

religious affiliation of the group.[175] It is noteworthy that "Salīḥ" is not the given name of the eponym, which is ʿAmr, but his adopted name, his nickname (*laqab*).[176] His adoption of a Syriac word as his *laqab* is not surprising, since historical personages among the Arabs of pre-Islamic times adopted foreign nicknames.[177] Furthermore, Salīḥ was living or located in a region of *Oriens Christianus* where Syriac was the language of cultural dominance.[178] The term appears often in Christian Arabic for "apostle."

Ubāgh

According to Hishām, one of the many sons of Salīḥ was Ubāgh, sometimes vocalized Abāgh.[179] As has been noted above, it is quite likely that this is a Persian word and that the name represents a real historical personage whose provenance was the Mesopotamiam region, which Salīḥ had been associated with. The name formed part of two toponyms, one of which is mentioned in the sources as being Mesopotamian, while the other is in Oriens or near it, and both toponyms called ʿAyn Ubāgh are associated with Salīḥ.[180] As a Persian word it is either Abāgh ("a mark of burning") or Bāgh ("gar-

[175] The Arabic for "apostle" is *rasūl.* Perhaps it was avoided in favor of the Syriac term, lest there should be a confusion with *rasul,* meaning "ambassador." Note that an Arabic Islamic dynasty appeared in Yaman in the 13th century which had the name Rasūlids, and claimed descent from Ghassān. This is usually taken to mean "ambassador," but in much later times, the reigning dynasty in Yaman, until the 20th century, called itself "al-Rasūliyya" after Muḥammad, Prophet and Apostle.

It is noteworthy that in certain versions of the name "Salīḥ," deriving from Hishām al-Kalbī, its orthography ends in a long *aliph,* almost recalling Syriac *Shlīḥā;* see Yāqūt, *Muʿjam,* IV, 175 s.v. ʿAyn Ubāgh. If this etymology for Salīḥ turns out to be the correct one, it will mean that Zokomos was not the first to be Christianized. He will then have to be the head of a clan among the Salīḥids that remained pagan until converted ca. 400.

[176] Cf. the *laqab* of the last king of Tanūkh, al-Ḥawārī, "disciple," not "apostle"; see *BAFOC,* 378–79.

[177] Cf. the Byzantine titles and honors of the Ghassānid kings and the Iranian titles assumed by the Arabs close to Persia.

[178] Cf. the assumption of the name Māriya by a Ghassānid princess; it has been argued that it is Syriac "mistress" and not Mary/Maryam; see Nöldeke, *GF,* 22 note 2.

[179] See Yāqūt, *Muʿjam,* I, 61; Bakrī, *Muʿjam,* I, 95.

[180] For the Mesopotamian toponym and personage, see Ibn Khaldūn, *Tārīkh,* I, 503, where Abāgh/Ubāgh appears corrupted as "Abān," son of Salīḥ, and presumably assimilated to the Arabic name "Abān." He is referred to as "Ṣāḥib al-ʿAyn," "the lord or master of the ʿAyn Ubāgh"; for a more archaic form of the name in Hishām, see Yāqūt, *Muʿjam,* IV, 175, also associated with the ʿAyn. For the toponym in Oriens in Roman territory or close to it, see the account of *yawm al-Baradān,* in Ibn al-Athīr, *Kāmil,* I, 507. The existence of two toponyms with the name ʿAyn Ubāgh could suggest that the name given by the Salīḥids to the toponym in the Mesopotamian period of Salīḥ's history was again given to another toponym in Oriens or near it in Byzantine territory after the tribal group crossed to Roman territory, a practice with precedents in the history of the Arab *foederati* who joined the Romans after having lived elsewhere.

den"),to which the Arabic plosive sound, the *hamza*, was added initially, and so it appears as Abāgh or Ubāgh.[181]

Dahmān b. al-ʿImliq

This analysis of the names and careers of the Salīḥids will not be complete without reference to Dahmān b. al-ʿImliq, who appears in the account of Yaʿqūbī[182] for the last days of Salīḥ as the chief of Salīḥ when Ghassān settled within the empire.[183] It may be that Nöldeke is right in thinking that this is a corruption of Dāwūd al-Lathiq. But Dahmān b. al-ʿImliq seems rather distant graphically and phonetically from Dāwūd al-Lathiq. The following observations may be made in support of the reality of Dahmān b. al-ʿImliq as a historical personality.

1. Although Dāwūd may have been the Salīḥid king of this period with whom Ghassān treated, Dahmān could have been a member of the dynasty in southern Oriens, one of the many phylarchs of Salīḥ. Indeed, in the *Narrationes* of St. Nilus there is reference to a phylarch by the name of Ammanes (ʼΑμμάνης),[184] which does not sound or look too remote from Dahmān, given the difficulty of reproducing Arabic names in Greek.[185]

2. Dahmān may not have been a Salīḥid but one of those phylarchs in the south of Oriens, in Arabia or Palaestina Tertia, who had persisted from olden times. The Ghassānid thrust ca. 500 encompassed southern Oriens, as well as the island of Iotabe and possibly Sinai (if Amorkesos of the Greek sources turns out to be a Ghassānid).[186] The Ghassānids could very well have negotiated with a phylarch in Sinai or southern Trans-Jordan who was not Salīḥid but was allied to the Romans and so could have conveyed their request for settlement to the principal Salīḥid phylarch.

The names Dahmān and ʿImliq are noteworthy. The first is very rare and old, and can be related to the root *d-h-m* (black).[187] More important is ʿImliq, singular of ʿAmāliq. The name is undoubtedly the biblical Amalik who were to be found exactly in those southern regions. The Arab genealogists and historians knew the term, and applied it to those tribes in Oriens who lived in the area in older times. What is even more relevant in this context is their

[181] See F. Steingass, *Persian-English Dictionary*, pp. 4, 148.

[182] See Yaʿqūbī, *Tārīkh*, I, 206.

[183] See Nöldeke, *GF*, 8 note 3.

[184] On Ammanes, see above, Chap. 7, sec. II.

[185] Arabic Dahmān could easily have become Ammanes (ʼΑμμάνης). The soft "h" that closes the first syllable of "Dahmān" followed by a consonant could not have been reproduced in Greek. Instead, by process of assimilation the "m" that begins the last syllable assimilated the "h" and produced the double "m" of the Greek form. As for the "d" that begins the first syllable, it could have dropped out in much the same way the "d" of "diabolus" has dropped out, yielding the Arabic form "Iblīs."

[186] On Amorkesos of the reign of Leo, see above, Chap. 4.

[187] See Ibn Durayd, *Ishtiqāq*, 176; also Caskel, *GN*, II, 233–34.

application of the term to the Arabs of Palmyra, of Odenathus and Zenobia.[188] This application enables the Dahmān b. al-ʿImliq of Yaʿqūbī to be set within this context: (1) he may have belonged to the old tribe that had survived in the same area since biblical times; or (2) he may have belonged to the Salīḥ of the third century which, as has been argued before, was allied with Palmyra's Arabs and were in fact settled along the frontier, including the southern part of Palestine.[189]

In spite of the real possibility that Dahmān ibn al-ʿImliq is a real historical personage with that name, the chances are that Nöldeke is correct in suspecting that he was none other than Dāwūd al-Lathiq.

Concluding Remarks

The foregoing discussion of the genealogical tree in Hishām's *Jamharat* has yielded some conclusions, the validity of which ranges from the possible to the probable to the certain. The last generation or so of Zokomids—Dāwūd, Ziyād, Sabīṭ, and Ḥārith—are in the full light of history and not mere names from a genealogical list. Although matters of detail and precision remain controversial, there is no doubt about the historicity of the accounts concerning the four.

As to the rest of the names in the genealogical tree, there is no way of arguing cogently for their historicity. They have, however, been analyzed and examined within the framework of the literary sources—the only ones available—in the hope that future epigraphic discoveries will validate these conclusions and thus make these names available to the historian for reconstructing with confidence the history of the dynasty in its entirety. Epigraphy has so far confirmed data extracted from the literary sources on Tanūkh[190] of the fourth century and Ghassān of the sixth. The chances are that it will also confirm the data on the Salīḥids of the fifth century, and thus will vindicate the essential reliability of the Arabic tradition.[191]

IV. The Arab Federate Tribal Groups in Oriens

The Arab tribes that were involved in the Arab-Byzantine relationship in the three centuries before the rise of Islam have been enumerated[192] and those

[188] See Ibn Khaldūn, *Tārīkh,* II, 504.

[189] See above, 249.

[190] See *BAFOC,* 375 and note 90.

[191] Excavations in Wādī Sirḥān and Wādī al-Salīḥī in Jordan should yield some relevant inscriptions. Whoever thought that Ayyub and Ḥajjāj, historical personages of the pre-Islamic period (6th century) mentioned in literary sources written much later in Islamic times, could be confirmed by reliable and contemporary Greek sources with their Ἰώβ and Ἀγγαῖος? See Shahîd, "The Conference of Ramla," 117–18. For epigraphic confirmation of the Arabic literary sources, see *BAFOC,* 375 note 90.

[192] See *BAFOC,* 382–83.

who had federate status in the fourth century have been identified.[193] For the fifth century, in addition to Salīḥ, the dominant federate group in Oriens, the sources indicate that two other tribes were involved in the Arab-Byzantine relationship: Iyād and ʿU̱dra. The first is a newcomer from the Mesopotamian region, while the second is an old tribe belonging to the Quḍāʿa group, which had lived in Ḥijāz and on which the Arabic sources on the fifth century are quite informative. Its earlier relationship to Byzantium is not entirely clear, but in the fifth century it was moving in the Byzantine orbit.

There were other tribes along the *limes,* the most important of which was Kalb, the tribe that played an important role in the sixth and the seventh centuries. Its Christianity and its Byzantine connection cannot be doubted, but how far back this relationship goes is not documented in the sources. The chances are that this powerful tribe guarding the entrance to Wādī Sirḥān must have moved in the Byzantine orbit from early times. Other tribes, such as the mysterious Bahrāʾ, have an unequivocal presence in the sixth and seventh centuries (although there is no indication as to when Bahrāʾ established its federate status). This chapter will then concentrate on the two tribes, Iyād and ʿU̱dra, for which a fifth-century Byzantine connection is documented in the sources.[194] The Byzantine profile of the other tribes will be postponed to the following volume on the sixth century.[195]

Iyād

Iyād, it is certain, was a federate Arab tribe in Oriens in the sixth and seventh centuries.[196] But this took place after a long period of wanderings in the Arabian Peninsula and in the Land of the Two Rivers.[197] This raises the question of when Iyād, or part of it, went over to Byzantium. The Arabic sources, though expansive on Iyād, are not united in their accounts concerning this problem. They suggest two different periods, either the fourth or the sixth century and relate the emigration to friction with the Sasanids. It is impossible to reach entirely satisfactory conclusions without the aid of inscrip-

[193] Ibid., 383–85.

[194] Iyād has been discussed in the chapter on Hishām al-Kalbī and the reign of Theodosius II. This chapter examines more data on it as a federate tribe, and it will be discussed again below, in Chap. 14. ʿU̱dra has been discussed in Chap. 13, sec. II ("Byzantium and Mecca") from one point of view—the aid rendered by it to Quṣayy toward the conquest of Mecca.

[195] The fortunes of tribes that have been discussed in this volume—such as Iyād—will also be treated in *BASIC* as more information on them in the 6th and 7th centuries becomes available.

[196] See *BAFOC,* 382.

[197] The Arabic sources that tell the story of these wanderings have been collected in the bibliography of the article on Iyād in *EI.*

tions, especially as the Iyād may have emigrated into Byzantine territory more than once.

A

Arguments may be put forward for either century. Nöldeke was inclined to date the emigration to the sixth century.[198] This conclusion does not preclude an earlier and partial emigration to Oriens.[199] Nöldeke drew his conclusion more than a century ago, and the important datum on the presence of the Iyādī poet ʿAbd al-ʿĀṣ at the court of the Salīḥids was unknown to him. It is, therefore, necessary to raise the question anew. It will be argued that there was probably at least a partial emigration to Oriens in the fifth century, a prelude to the strong Iyādī presence in Oriens in the sixth and seventh centuries, which may have been due to a new emigration in the sixth, as Nöldeke suggested.[200]

1. According to Hishām, there was a poet from the tribe of Iyād attached to the Salīḥid king of the fifth century Dāwūd al-Lathiq. It is also clear from the passage in Hishām that the group to which this poet, ʿAbd al-ʿĀṣ, belonged was also in Oriens, having affiliated themselves with the Tanūkhids.[201] Thus it is not the case of a single Iyādī in Oriens at the court of the Salīḥid king but of a group of Iyādīs and possibly more who emigrated to Oriens. This establishes an Iyādī presence in Oriens in the fifth century.[202] Whether this presence will tip the scale in favor of a fourth-century presence, of which that of the fifth-century may be seen as a continuation, cannot be determined. It is sufficient gain in understanding the tribal structure of the federate shield to know that there was an Iyādī constituent not only in the sixth and the seventh, but also in the fifth century.

2. References to Iyādī settlements come from those Arabic sources that

[198] In an article that appeared in 1882 on the Iyādī poet Laqīṭ ibn Yaʿmur, *Orient und Occident,* 689–718.

[199] Such as suggested by the account of Masʿūdī, with its references to Sābūr (Shāpūr); for which, see Masʿūdī, *Murūj al-Ḏahab,* I, 295–96. See also M. Morony, *Iraq after the Muslim Conquest* (Princeton, 1984), 216–17.

[200] This will be discussed in *BASIC.*

[201] The poet was discussed in the chapter on the Arabic MSS, below, 307. His pedigree appears in the genealogical work of Hishām discussed there, *Kitāb Nasab Maʿadd wa al-Yaman al-Kabīr,* on p. 21 B. It is given as follows: Zuhr ibn Iyād gave birth to Ḥuḏaqa al-Shalak(?); Ḥuḏaqa ibn Zuhr begat Ḏubyān and Aws and Ḥārith. The poet ʿAbd al-ʿĀṣ was descended from them. His full name is given as ʿAbd al-ʿĀṣ ibn ʿAwf ibn Ghatafān ibn Ahyab ibn Ḏubyān. Thus Hishām was well informed about the poet and his ancestry.

[202] It is tantalizing to think that Iyādis were among those included in one of the conditions of the treaty between Byzantium and Persia after the end of the first Persian War of the reign of Theodosius II in which it was stipulated that neither empire should receive the Arab allies of the other.

speak of their emigration after their war with the Sasanids in the sixth century and later, during the period of the Muslim Conquests. In the introduction to his geographical dictionary, Bakrī combines two accounts. The first states that in the sixth century Iyād settled in Emesa and *aṭrāf al-Shām,* the "extremities or boundaries of Oriens" and also in "arḍ al-Rūm," almost certainly Anatolia, in a place called QRY(?).[203] The second refers to the Muslim period and provides the following data: In the period of the Conquests, the Iyād together with other Christian Arab tribes left Oriens with the last Ghassānid, Jabala ibn al-Ayham, and settled in Bilād al-Rūm (Anatolia); they are to be found there with the Ghassānids until the present day (about 800), and their *madīnat,* city, is called Madīnat al-ʿArab, "the City of the Arabs." The account also says that some remained in the various *junds* (military districts) of al-Shām and in its cities, but that they lost their influence and prestige there.[204]

B

Reference to Iyādī settlements within Oriens south of the Taurus are much less important than reference to their settlement in Anatolia. The Arab presence in pre-Islamic Anatolia, represented by an Iyādī colony, would indeed be remarkable, and the Arabic sources vouch for it. In support of an Arab emigration to Anatolia in pre-Islamic times, and not only after the Conquests, the following observations may be made:

a. The reference to Ancyra as the new abode of Iyād after their war with the Sasanids in the sixth century is supported by a reference in the account which tells of the death Imru'al-Qays on his way to Constantinople and mentions Ancyra[205] as the place where he died around 540. The reference could be purely coincidental if Ancyra was a station on his journey to Constantinople. On the other hand, it could imply that the Arab poet, while

[203] Bakrī, *Muʿjam,* I, 71, quoting al-Qāli and his authorities. The reference to Emesa may be true since in the 6th century the Kindite poet Imru' al-Qays mentions (in his "Caesar Ode") Arab communities in the cities of Oriens which he visited. Among them was a certain Arab by the name of Ibn Jurayj or Jurayḥ in Emesa who apparently did not treat him well. This could have belonged to a small Iyādī community in the city of Emesa which had important Arab associations since Roman times. The not very clear QRY is most likely Ancyra in Anatolia, about which more will be said presently. For Emesa in the "Caeser Ode," see Ahlwardt, *The Divans,* 131.

[204] Bakrī, *Muʿjam,* 175. It is important to note that the account comes from Hishām al-Kalbī, the historian who wrote much on Iyād and researched its history. In addition to what was said earlier on Hishām's interest in Iyād (above, 237–41) his special interest in Ḥīra may have enhanced his curiosity about Iyād, since some Iyādīs lived near Ḥīra and built monasteries there.

[205] On this, see R. Nicholson, *A Literary History of the Arabs,* 104. This will be treated at greater length in *BASIC.*

journeying in a strange land like Anatolia, wanted to stay with an Arab community which was settled there.

b. Even more important than the prose accounts is a precious fragment of a pre-Islamic poet by the name of al-Aswad ibn Yaʿfur al-Nahshalī, from the tribe of Tamīm.[206] He was the court poet of al-Nuʿmān, the last Lakhmid king of Ḥīra. In one of his fragments, he laments the fall of the Lakhmids, which took place around 602, and also the misfortunes of Iyād. After recounting their glories, represented by two palaces and two important Iyādī personages, he says that they settled in Anḳira.[207] This was a pre-Islamic poet about whose fragment there is no doubt, but it raises two questions.

a. What century was the poet thinking of when he said that Iyād left its abode around Ḫira? He certainly was talking about the Lakhmids around 600, when the dynasty fell, and he did live much longer after that date.[208] As to the Iyād, it is not clear whether he was referring to their departure in the sixth century or earlier.

b. The other problem that the fragment raises is the identity of the toponym "Anḳira" to which it refers as the new abode of Iyād. It is described as a place where "the waters of the Euphrates flow to them, coming from mountains." Some Arab commentators thought that Anḳira was a place near Ḥira but others, including Yāqūt, thought it could only be Anatolian Ancyra.[209] The rival "Anḳira," near Ḥira, is an obscure place, practically unknown. Furthermore, the description of Anḳira in the poem, involving the Euphrates and mountains, makes it certain that Anatolian Ancyra is meant, since there are no mountains near Ḥīra.[210]

The reference to Anatolian Anḳira in a pre-Islamic poem as the new abode of an Arab tribe is important. It calls for a short reference to another Anatolian city, which also could have had a ṣettlement of Arabs, namely, Arabissos, the etymology of which strongly suggests an association with the Arabs, who even may have given the city its name.[211] The obscurity that shrouds the name may thus be slightly dispelled by the Iyād episode and the real possibility that this pre-Islamic period witnessed the emigration of Arab

[206] On the poet, see Sezgin, *GAS*, II, 182–83.

[207] For the fragment, see *Mufaddaliyyāt*, ed. A. Shākir and ʿA. Hārūn (Cairo, 1943), II, 17.

[208] Since the fall of the dynasty is attested at around 602.

[209] See Yāqūt, *Muʿjam*, I, 271–72. Yāqūt's judgment is on p. 272.

[210] Some doubted the Anatolian identity of Anḳira on the ground that it is far from the Euphrates, but the source is a poem and its author was not a topographer or a cartographer who had a precise knowledge of the distance of Anḳira from the Euphrates. See Bakrī, *Muʿjam*, I, 204. The Euphrates or one of its tributaries is not far from Larissa, which is about 200 miles from Ancyra (Anḳira).

[211] For more on Arabissos, see below, App. 4.

tribes from Sasanid territory and that the Byzantine city welcomed them as valuable allies in the struggle with Persia. Iyād may thus have settled in Ancyra first and then moved to Arabissos, or some other group of Arabs may have moved into Anatolia in earlier times and settled in Arabissos.

The Iyād became important in the military annals of Arab-Byzantine relations, but they were even more important in the cultural history of the Arabs. Most of the data on their cultural role pertain to the period of their Mesopotamian history, when they were living in Sasanid territory. The dimensions of that cultural role are three—Christianity, the rise of the Arabic script in Mesopotamia, and poetry.[212] All three are relevant for examining their cultural presence in Oriens, reflected most clearly in the Iyādī poet ʿAbd al-ʿĀṣ at the court of King Dāwūd.[213]

ʿU<u>d</u>ra

The most important clans of ʿUḏra for Byzantine history are those of Rizāḥ and Ḥann, the sons of Rabiʿa ibn Ḥarām.[214]

ʿUḏra's role as Byzantium's ally in extending aid to Quṣayy in his expedition against Mecca, the role of Rizāḥ in Hijāz and Western Arabia, and the etymology of the eponym of the clan of Ḥann will be discussed further in later chapters,[215] using data that go back to Hishām al-Kalbī and al-Zubayr ibn Bakkār.

The loss of the *dīwāns* of the Qabā'il[216] (the poetry or verse collections of the tribes) is a great loss, since these would have been a mine of information on the tribes and their Byzantine connection. The only one that has survived is that of Huḏayl, which is not very relevant to the Arab-Byzantine relation-

[212] For references to all these cultural constituents, see Bakrī, *Muʿjam,* I, 67–76. For the script, see pp. 79, 72, 75; for their Christianity, see ibid., 69 on the three monasteries which they built in Mesopotamia, Dayr al-Aʿwar, Dayr al-Jamājim, and Dayr Qurra; there is also reference to Dayr al-Sawā; as to their poetry, they counted among them many poets; the most important in pre-Islamic times was Abū Duwād al-Iyādī who moved in the circle of Munḏir, the Lakhmid king (505–554); Sezgin, *GAS,* II, 167–69.

The most explicit statement on the association of the Arabic script with Iyād in Mesopotamia comes from Ṭabarī in the section on the Muslim Arab conquest of Iraq. After his pact with the people of Anbār, Khalid asks its inhabitants, whom he noticed writing Arabic, whence they learnt the Arabic script, and they answered that they had learnt it from Iyād; see Ṭabarī, *Tārīkh,* III, 375.

[213] For this, see below, Chap. 14, sec. IV.B.

[214] While much is known about Rizāḥ, next to nothing is known of Ḥunn/Ḥann, other than the fact that he was the eponym of the most important clan within ʿUḏra. That the clan bore his name suggests that he was not an obscure figure.

[215] For a discussion of the name of the clan, see below, App. 5.

[216] On these *dīwāns* see Sezgin, *GAS,* II, 36–46.

ship, but even so has provided some valuable data.[217] As a substitute for the loss of the *dīwān* of ʿUḏra, however, there is the *dīwān* of the celebrated ʿUḏrite love poet of the seventh century, Jamīl ibn Maʿmar.[218] His *dīwān* has some very valuable data for the Byzantine connection of ʿUḏra; when these are considered together with the data extracted from Hishām and Ibn Qutayba, a clear picture of ʿUḏra as a federate tribe emerges. The data that can be extracted from this *dīwān*,[219] may be divided into two groups: those that pertain to ʿUḏrite love and involvement in Christianity, and those that pertain to the tribe's political and military history, involving the Salīḥids and, indirectly, Byzantium.[220]

A

1. In one of the verses[221] in which Jamīl speaks of his ʿUḏrite love for his beloved Buthayna there occurs the phrase "the Covenant of God with (or for) her love." This association of God's covenant with love is more reminiscent of Christianity than of Islam.[222]

2. In another verse, he makes reference to a poet of ʿUḏra who died of his chaste love for ʿAfrāʾ, referring to him as "ʿUrwa the ʿUḏrite."[223] This confirms that the tradition of chaste ʿUḏrite love formed a continuous chain among the poets of the tribe, and that they were aware of themselves as forming a distinct "school" of love poetry in the history of Arabic literature.

3. That this type of love was already well defined not only among the critics but also among the poets, who were themselves smitten by it, is clear from another verse, in which the phrase "ʿUḏri al-ʿālāqa" ("ʿUḏrite connection or relationship") occurs.[224]

4. The phrase "ʿIbād Allāh" occurs twice in the *dīwān*. Although the

[217] On the Christian toponyms in Oriens supplied by this *dīwān*, see *BAFOC*, 403–4.

[218] On Jamīl, see Sezgin, *GAS*, II, 406–8.

[219] The *dīwān* has not survived, only fragments of his poetry have, scattered in various works. These were collected in *Dīwān Jamīl* by Ḥusayn Naṣṣār (Cairo, 1967). Hishām al-Kalbī apparently was interested in accounts of such lovers as Jamīl and collected information on them, as may be inferred from a statement in *Fihrist*, 306.

[220] Before discussing these two sets of data, it might be mentioned that the *dīwān* covers the toponymic scene of Ḥijāz and both sides of the Jordan; such toponyms are Ramlat Ludd (p. 26), Qurā Ludd (p. 93), Ḥismā (p. 35), al-Sharāt, Aḏruḥ, al-Urdunn, and Tabūk (p. 49). It is also noticeable that the word "awbāsh," which occurs in the verse composed by the daughter of Dāwūd on his death, an unusual word in Arabic verse, occurs in the *dīwān* (p. 31).

[221] *Dīwān*, 74. The verse reads: *Laqad jadda mīthāqu l-Ilāh biḥubbihā wamā lillaḏī la yattaqī Allāha min ʿahdi*.

[222] Note also the use of al-Ilāh instead of Allāh for God, which had been the Christian form, as in the Hind inscription of pre-Islamic times; see Rothstein, *DLH*, 24.

[223] *Dīwān*, 76. For ʿUrwa, see below, 311.

[224] *Dīwān*, 183.

term is known in Islamic times, it has a distinctly pre-Islamic ring, audible in the poetry and slogans of the Christian Arabs. It was the slogan of the Christian Tanūkhids in pre-Islamic times and occurs in the poetry of the Christians of Najrān.[225]

5. Finally, Buthayna's teknonymic was Umm ʿAbdulmalik.[226] The name ʿAbdulmalik ("the servant of the king") later became an Islamic name, after *malik* appeared in the Koran as one of the names of God. However, it remained uncommon, assumed by Muslims such as the Umayyad caliph. But it first appeared in the Arabic onomasticon as a Christian Arab name: witness its assumption by the Kindite chief who fought the Muslims at Dumat al-Jandal in the period of the Conquest.[227] The "king" in this name, it is practically certain, was not God but a secular king, most probably the Byzantine *basileus*. Its assumption was an expression of loyalty on the part of the federate Arabs toward their Byzantine overlord.[228]

The conclusion that may be drawn from these few data is that the ʿUd̲rites retained in their consciousness even in this first Islamic century memories of their pre-Islamic Christian past. This awareness of antiquity is reflected in a phrase in Jamīl's *dīwān* that describes his tribe as "ʿĀdiyya"[229] ("a tribe that goes back to the days of old ʿĀd," an old Arabian tribe the name of which became a symbol of antiquity in which the Arabs took pride).

B

The political and military place of ʿUd̲ra in Ḥijāz may be summarized by saying that its strategically central position there gave it considerable power and influence, and so did its marriage relationship, which enhanced its political influence in northwestern Arabia: (1) When it settled near Wādī al-Qurā it had a treaty with the Jews of that *wādī* which secured for it some advantages. (2) the mother of the Azd Arab tribes of Medina itself was a lady from ʿUd̲ra by the name of Qayla bint Kāhil. (3) In Mecca, Quṣayy was the half-brother of

[225] See *BAFOC*, 418, and the verse in the poem of ʿAbd Yagūth, in Cheikho, *Shuʿarāʾ al-Naṣrāniyya*, 79.

[226] *Dīwān*, 214.

[227] The name of the Kindite chief was Ukaydir ibn ʿAbd al-Malik. Thus it appears as his *patronymic*, making it certain that it is a pre-Islamic name. In this case and all cases in pre-Islamic times it was not a theophoric name, which it became in Islamic times, when *al-Malik* became one of the *al-Asmāʾ al-Ḥusnā*, "the most beautiful names of God" in the Koran.

[228] Just as the name Flavius was assumed by al-Mund̲ir, the Ghassānid king of the 6th century, who also expressed his loyal sentiments toward the *basileus* in terms that translated literally ʿAbd l-Malik. This will be discussed in *BASIC*. To the same order of loyalty belongs the assumption of the name "Qayṣar" in the modern Near East by members of the Arab Orthodox community, who looked up to the Russian Czar as the protector of Orthodoxy in the Ottoman period.

[229] *Dīwān*, 217.

Rizaḥ, the chief of ʿUḏra; Rabīʿa ibn Ḥarām, Rizaḥ's father, had married Quṣayy's mother while on a journey which took him to Mecca.[230]

In the *dīwān* of Jamīl there is a long poem, "the rhyme in F," which might be called *al-fāʾiyya*. It has extremely important references to two major connections of ʿUḏra, Byzantium and Mecca:

1. One of the verses of this *fāʾiyya* has survived in a later Islamic work, the author of which specifically ascribes it to Jamīl. The verse speaks of a *shamṭāʾ*,[231] a term that describes a *katība*, a military division which belonged to the Zokomids and which warded off evil and the enemy from ʿUḏra. The verse repays careful study.[232]

The verse occurs in that passage of the *fāʾiyya* where the poet takes pride in the exploits and glories of his tribe, ʿUḏra.[233] He mentions Quḍāʿa, the large tribal group to which ʿUḏra belonged, by name. More revealingly, he points out the glorious record of ʿUḏra in pre-Islamic as well as in Islamic times, but the balance is definitely in favor of the pre-Islamic past, and it is striking that he uses the term *mulk* ("kingship") and applies it to ʿUḏra in that period.[234] He also takes pride in the fact that ʿUḏra never succumbed to any tribe, an allegation that is confirmed by al-Nābigha in his poem addressed to the Ghassānid Nuʿmān, in which he refers to his defeat at the hands of ʿUḏra.[235]

But it is the verse that speaks of the Zokomids that is a mine of information. It describes the Zokomid military unit as "a magnificent division from the House of the Zokomids, that bristles with armor, thrusts with its spears, wards off the enemies from us, and fights ferociously."[236]

a. The verse clearly speaks of both the power of the Zokomid division and, more importantly, of the fact that it defended ʿUḏra. This immediately

[230] See ʿUḏra in *EI* for all these data.

[231] Arabic *shamṭāʾ* is derived from the root *sh-m-ṭ*, which signifies "grizzled in the hair, having whiteness mixed with blackness." Applied to a military division it signifies that it bristles with weaponry, the sheen of spears and swords representing the whiteness.

[232] See Nashwān ibn Saʿīd al-Ḥimyari, *Shams al-ʿUlūm,* 64. The learned South Arabian scholar obviously had before him the *dīwān* of Jamīl, which was still extant, and so has preserved for posterity this historically precious line. He prefaces it with a statement on the Zokomids as the kings of Oriens before the Ghassānids.

[233] See *dīwān,* 137, either after verse 6 or, better still, after verse 10. The poem, the longest of all Jamīl's poems, has been put together from fragments and versions scattered in a variety of sources; see ibid., 131.

[234] Thus he may have recalled the days of Rizāḥ or Hawḏa, who called Rabb al-Ḥijāz the "lord of Ḥijāz"; see below, 310–11.

[235] See Nöldeke, *GF,* 38 and note 2.

[236] The Arabic version of the verse, as vocalized by the editor, reads: *Wa shamaṭāʾu(a) min rahṭilal-Dajāʿimi fakhmatin/ṭiʿānun(in) taḏubbu al-nāsa ʿannā wa taʿsifu*. The word *ṭiʿānun* (or *ṭaʿānun*) suggests that the Zokomids in the division were spearmen; *taʿsifu* signifies "taking with power or strength" or "acting tyrannically," appropriate in this military context.

raises the question of interfederate relations. The verse clearly says that the Salīḥids—the dominant federate group in Oriens in this period—put one of its divisions at the service of another tribe, ʿUḏra. The occasion is not clear, but ʿUḏra was apparently threatened by some invasion from a powerful Arab group and forced to invoke the aid of the Salīḥids.

b. The verse confirms that the Salīḥids had at their disposal a powerful army organized in the Roman manner, with divisions that were respected by enemies. Their troops were often referred to by the technical term *jaysh* (army).[237]

c. It has been argued in this volume that the Salīḥids[238] were stationed in the Provincia Arabia, having reached Oriens from Wādī Sirḥān. This verse confirms this conclusion, since the Salīḥids could easily come to the aid of the ʿUḏrites in Ḥijāz from that province.

d. This verse leaves no doubt that ʿUḏra was indeed a federate tribe in a special relationship to Byzantium, either directly or through the Salīḥids. This has been argued inferentially,[239] but this clear association of the dominant federate group with ʿUḏra clinches the point. The Salīḥids naturally rushed to the rescue of ʿUḏra, important for the security of Byzantium in the invisible frontier of indirect Byzantine presence in Ḥijāz.

e. Another version of the first hemistich, "and a division of our *amlāk* (kings or possessions) belonging to Zokomos," could yield even more important data on interfederate relations.[240] "*Amlāk*" in this verse can only mean kings, and this could imply that the Zokomid kings were also made kings of the federate tribes in Ḥijāz, such as ʿUḏra.[241] This could receive some confirmation from a statement in the Arabic sources that the Rūm, the Byzantines, put Quḍāʿa, to which Salīḥ belonged, over the Arabs of *bādiyat al-ʿArab* in the region adjoining the frontier.[242] It could also confirm another statement in

[237] See Ibn Ḥabīb, *Al-Munammaq* (Heyderabad, 1964), 454.

[238] See above, Chap. 12, sec. II.A.

[239] See below, Chap. 13, sec. II.

[240] See *Shams al-ʿUlūm*, 65.

[241] *Amlāk* as the plural of *milk, mulk,* meaning possession, makes no sense here, and it is doubtful whether it was even in use in this period. It is clearly the plural of *malik* (king). It is noteworthy that in the early Islamic and also pre-Islamic period, this plural form, *amlāk,* and not *mulūk*, was apparently the common plural of *malik,* king; see the 6th-century Arabic inscription of Hind, where the term appears in the Arabic version of the title of the Persian "king of kings"; Rothstein, *DLH*, 24.

This reference to the Salīḥids as the kings of ʿUḏra could not have been technical and accurate, since the kingship of the dominant federate group over other federates took place only around 530, when Justinian made the Ghassānid Arethas king and supreme phylarch. But Jamīl was simply reflecting the close military and political relationship that obtained between Salīḥ and ʿUḏra, which called for help on occasion.

[242] Ibn Khaldūn, *Tārīkh,* II, 520.

the Arabic sources—that after the fall of the Salīḥids, the last of them, Ziyād, marched with what remained of his tribe to Ḥijāz, where he was killed.[243] Friendly connections with tribes such as ʿUḏra could make this course possible and the statement credible.

2. The poem described above as *al-fāʾiyya* ends with a couplet in which Jamīl takes pride in the fact that ʿUḏra afforded protection to Quṣayy with their spears, and that they actually marched with him to Mecca, surrounded it, and insured victory.[244]

The two verses are a valuable document for ʿUḏra's participation in the conquest of Mecca. This has been known from prose sources which are late, going back most probably to Zubayr ibn Bakkār.[245] Now this participation is vouched for by one of the ʿUḏrites themselves who, moreover, lived or died around 700, that is, two hundred years before Zubayr ibn Bakkār. This enhances the value of what the later Islamic sources have transmitted and establishes that they derived their information from tribal and family records.

Thus Lammens' original interpretation of the terse statement in Ibn Qutayba to the effect that Quṣayy conquered Mecca with the "help of Qayṣar (Caesar)" is fully confirmed and justified by this couplet in the *fāʾiyya* of Jamīl. It is a pity that Jamīl does not mention whether or not Rizāḥ personally marched to the rescue of his half-brother Quṣayy, but the chances are that he did. A statement in one of the Arabic sources confirms the military status and exploits of Rizāḥ when it describes him as one of the *jarrārūn* of the Arabs in pre-Islamic times, that is, those who were important enough to command a thousand soldiers,[246] a number that could suggest a Roman officer, a chiliarch.

The dominant position that ʿUḏra enjoyed in pre-Islamic times is fully reflected in an episode involving Jamīl and the Umayyad caliph Marwān ibn al-Ḥakam (683–685). While traveling with Jamīl, the caliph asks him to recite some poetry of his (in the *rajaz* meter), hoping that the poet would sing his praises. Instead Jamīl recited some poetry that glorified his own tribe, ʿUḏra.[247] That a tribesman such as Jamīl should refuse to accede to the request of the caliph is noteworthy, even startling; but what was said in the

[243] Ibid.

[244] See *Dīwān,* 139. Noteworthy is Jamīl's employment of the phrase "yawm Mecca" ("battle-day of Mecca") adverbially, for the struggle between Quṣayy, aided by ʿUḏra, against Khuzāʿa for the possession of Mecca. The phrase may be used to denote Quṣayy's conquest of Mecca, and thus may be added to the long list of the Arab *ayyām,* the battle-days of the Arabs in pre-Islamic times.

[245] See below, 356–57.

[246] See Ibn Ḥabīb, *Al-Muḥabbar,* 250–51.

[247] See *Dīwān,* 141, 199.

preceding section on the part played by ʿUdra in the establishment of the power of Quṣayy in Mecca fully explains it. Jamīl most probably considered that the rule of the Umayyads must have been partially due to the contribution of ʿUdra in establishing their ancestor Quṣayy in Mecca.

This dominant position of ʿUdra in Ḥijāz in pre-Islamic times is fully confirmed by the fact that the very powerful Ghassānids, the *foederati* of Byzantium in the sixth century, found it difficult to control them: witness the disastrous campaign of the Ghassānid king Nuʿmān against them in the second half of the sixth century.[248]

V. The Fall of the Zokomids

The preceding discussion of the kings of Salīḥ, especially the last generation, makes it possible now to examine the problem of the fall of the Salīḥids as the dominant federate Arab group in the service of Byzantium. The problem is important for discovering the pattern of the rise and fall of these Arab-Byzantine client-kingdoms.[249] What is more, the sources for the fall of the Salīḥids have traces of the texts of the *foedera* which Byzantium struck with these Arab groups.[250] These rare documents are valuable for understanding the nature of imperial-federate relations.

The problem is due for a reexamination[251] since more trustworthy sources are now available, each of which contributes toward writing the history of the fall of the Salīḥids. Furthermore, the Arabic sources cohere with one another on the one hand and with the Greek sources on the other. Some matters of detail will remain controversial, but the main features of the fall of the Salīḥids can be recovered and presented in a satisfactory fashion.

The story of Salīḥ's fall is roughly the story of its relations with Ghassān, the newcomers from Arabia who finally replaced them as the dominant *foederati* in the sixth century. These relations spanned the last decade of the fifth century, and may be divided into three stages.

1. The crossing of the *limes* by the Ghassānids around 490, when they were allowed to settle within imperial territory. The Salīḥids were guardians

[248] This will be discussed with some detail in *BASIC*. For the time being, see Nöldeke, *GF*, 38.

[249] By comparisons and contrasts with the fall of the Tanūkhids in the 4th century and the Ghassānids in the 6th. The former has been elucidated in *BAFOC*; the latter will be in *BASIC*.

[250] Unlike the sources for the Tanūkhids, where no texts are available. Only the Greek sources have a word to say on the *foedus* with Queen Mavia, namely, her insistence on the ordination of a bishop who was Arab; *BAFOC*, 152–58. The other conditions or terms of the *foedus* have had to be inferred.

[251] The fall of the Salīḥids was treated in 1958 in Shahîd, "The Last Days of Salīḥ." Ibn Ḥabīb's *Muḥabbar* was not available to me at that time; only his account through Ibn Khaldūn was. The main conclusions on the fall of the Salīḥids expressed in this article still hold, and are the foundation on which this chapter is based.

of the *limes* for Byzantium, and the Ghassānids had to pay the tribute as a condition for their settlement.

2. The conflict between the Salīḥids and the Ghassānids concerning the payment of the tribute, a conflict which developed into open hostilities in which the Ghassānids were the victors.

3. The formal conclusion of the *foedus* between Byzantium and the Ghassānids in 502, according to which the latter replaced the Salīḥids and emerged as the principal Arab federate group in the sixth century.[252]

I

Of the variety of sources which will be drawn upon for the reexamination of the problem of the fall of the Salīḥids, two stand out: *al-Muḥabbar* by Ibn Ḥabīb and *Tārīkh* by al-Yaʿqūbi:

1. Hishām al-Kalbī is the original source from whom later historians of Salīḥid-Ghassānid relations derive. The closest to him, and the one who must have preserved the original account in its relatively purest and most adequate form, was Ibn Ḥabīb,[253] his own pupil. The following data may be extracted from the account which has survived in his *al-Muḥabbar*.[254] (*a*) The Salīḥids appear as representatives of Byzantium in collecting taxes from the Arabs who were settled within the Salīḥid area. These Arabs were principally from the Muḍar group.[255] (*b*) When the Ghassānids arrived in Salīḥid territory, the latter asked them to pay tribute, which the Ghassānids refused to do. In the war that ensued, the Ghassānids were worsted, whereupon they agreed to pay the tribute. (*c*) The chief of the Ghassānids at this time was Thaʿlaba ibn ʿAmr, and the Ghassānids each paid annually, a dinar, a dinar and a half, or two dinars according to their worth or standing.[256] (*d*) A quarrel developed between the Ghassānid Jiḏʿ ibn ʿAmr and the Salīḥid tax collector, Sabīṭ ibn al-Munḏir,[257] and each group shouted their war slogans.[258] In the battle

[252] For some translations from the Arabic and for the arguments behind the conclusions presented in this chapter, see ibid., 145–53. Modifications of certain matters of detail, now made clearer with more sources available and by a more intensive study of the problem of the fall of Salīḥ since the publication of this article in the fifties, will be made in the course of this chapter.

[253] For Ibn Ḥabīb, see *Fihrist*, 106–7.

[254] See al-*Muḥabbar*, ed. I. Lichtenstädter, 370–71.

[255] Muḍar is the very large Arab tribe group, some of whom lived in Ḥijāz not far from the Byzantine border. Thus the Salīḥids were living in Roman territory, and Arabs who wanted to settle in that area were considered tributaries.

[256] This will be discussed later on in this section.

[257] The names of the chiefs are important. Thaʿlaba is the Ghassānid chief; Jidʿ, who has the same patronymic, apparently was his brother, and so was a member of the ruling clan who was assigned certain duties; such was also the case of Sabīṭ, the Salīḥid tax collector, who was also a member of the ruling clan, working presumably for King Dāwūd or some other Salīḥid chief.

[258] It is a pity that these slogans have not been preserved. In his chapter on the religions

which took place at al-Muḥaffaf,[259] the Salīḥids were badly beaten. (*e*) The king of the Romans then wrote to Thaʿlaba, recognizing the prowess of the Ghassānids because of their victory over his Salīḥid allies, whom he had considered very powerful and warlike. (*f*) Finally, he suggested a *foedus* of mutual assistance involving Byzantium and the Ghassānids in case the Arabs (of the Peninsula) attacked either party, but on condition that the Ghassānids would not interfere in the war between Byzantium and Persia.[260]

Such is the account of Ibn Ḥabīb. In addition to his having preserved traces of the texts of the two *foedera*, the sequence of events and the identity of the contestants are best preserved in this account, so he has to be followed on such matters. However, as will be clear in the course of this chapter, other authors have also preserved data not preserved by Ibn Ḥabīb, each historian having his own predilections and interests to guide him in the selection or rejection of data from the original version of Hishām.

2. The most important of these is al-Yaʿqūbī, who has been used as the main source in the treatment of the fall of Salīḥ.[261] Yaʿqūbī retells the story of Ghassānid-Salīḥid relations twice, and the following data may be extracted from the two versions.[262] (*a*) The Ghassānids' first encounter with Salīḥ took place in the Balqā' in the Provincia Arabia (Ammonitis), and this is where they apparently settled after they were permitted to do so. (*b*) The chief of Salīḥ who wrote to the "king of the Romans," Nūshar, about permission for

of the Arabs before the rise of Islam, Yaʿqūbī gives the slogan of Ghassān, presumably in the Peninsular stage: *labbayka rabba Ghassān, rājilihā wa al-fursān*, "At your service, O Lord of Ghassān, its infantry and cavalry." But the military character of the *talbiya* (the declaration of compliance or obedience) is clear, and this may well have been their war slogan at this stage when they had their encounter with Salīḥ. For this slogan, see Yaʿqūbī, *Tārīkh*, I, 256. Later in the 6th century their slogans took on a more Christian and biblical form, invoking Jesus and Job, as may be inferred from a verse by al-Nābigha; see Ahlwardt, *Divans*, 4. This is a difficult verse and will be discussed fully in *BASIC*.

259 On the location of this toponym, see above, Sec. II note 87.

260 This *foedus* has been examined in detail in Shahîd, "Ghassan and Byzantium," 232–55, and will be discussed again in *BASIC*, in a different context.

It is noteworthy that another version of this treaty, also derived from Hishām al-Kalbī, has been preserved by the much later historian Ibn Khaldūn, who does not say anything about Ghassānid neutrality in the Byzantine-Persian war of the reign of Anastasius. However, Hishām's account as preserved by Ibn Khaldūn does present Dāwūd al-Lathiq as the Salīḥid king whom the Ghassānids encountered when they crossed the *limes*, and makes his Ghassānid counterpart Thaʿlaba. It also makes Sabīṭ, the tax collector, Dāwūd's grandson, and his counterpart, Jidʿ, the brother of Thaʿlaba, but this statement on Sabīṭ and Jidʿ is likely to be a confused account. However, Ibn Khaldūn has preserved some valuable echo of the Persian-Byzantine conflict and uses it as the background for explaining the Roman emperor's apprehensions and hence his willingness to ally himself with the Ghassānids. But he paraphrased the text of the *foedus*, unlike Ibn Ḥabīb who gives a version which purports to be the actual text. For Ibn Khaldūn on the Salīḥid-Ghassānid conflict, see *Tārīkh*, II, 582–83.

261 In Shahîd, "Last Days of Salīḥ."

262 Yaʿqūbī, *Tārīkh*, I, 204–5 and 206–7.

the Ghassānids to be settled within the *limes* was called Dahmān ibn al-ʿImliq.[263] (*c*) The area that witnessed the quarrel between the Ghassānids and the Salīḥids apparently was in the northern part of the Provincia Arabia and the southern part of Phoenicia Libanensis. This is based on the reference to the *ʿāmil* (governor or representative) of the Romans in Damascus, and to the wars in Bostra and then al-Muḥaffaf/Mukhaffaf. (*d*) Ṣāḥib al-Rūm[264] fought them, but when he experienced their military prowess, he made a treaty with them, accepting the Ghassānids' condition that only one of them should be their king.[265]

Yaʿqūbī's account is most valuable for its onomastic and toponymic precision, and settles the question of the period of Salīḥ's fall by indicating that the name of the Byzantine emperor during whose reign this took place was Anastasius (491–518). He is also informative on the terms of the *foedus,* involving the Ghassānid condition that only one of them should be their king. This implies that the treaty had more conditions than are preserved in Ibn Ḥabīb and that Hishām must have mentioned more than one or two conditions. Thus, much light is shed on the original and fundamental account of Ibn Ḥabīb which, however, makes no mention of the Roman emperor or the Salīḥid king.

3. Ḥamza al-Iṣfahānī[266] adds two data which contribute to precision in the story of Salīḥid-Ghassānid relations. (*a*) The tax collector was indeed Sabīṭ, the Salīḥid, and that this was his assignment in the allocation of responsibilities among members of the Salīḥid royal house. The account suggests that tax collecting was an important function of the federate Arabs of Byzantium. (*b*) He states explicitly that Jidʿ was indeed the brother of the *sayyid,* Thaʿlaba, the lord of Ghassān at this time.[267]

[263] On the identification of Dahmān with Dāwūd, see above, 270–71. The further statement in Yaʿqūbī that he wrote to the king of the Romans at Antioch must be a confusion. Some other Roman lived in Antioch, such as the *comes Orientis*. Nūshar is undoubtedly Anastasius, as understood by Nöldeke a long time ago; see *GF*, 9.

[264] Yaʿqūbī, *Tārīkh*, 207. Normally the phrase Ṣāḥib al-Rūm denotes "the King of the Romans." In "The Last Days of Salīḥ" (151–53), I referred to the involvement of the Romans in the war against Salīḥ, based on the interpretation of "Ṣāḥib al-Rūm" in the normal manner. But it need not be so. A closer examination of the text of Yaʿqūbī shows a distinction between the "Ṣāḥib al-Rūm" and "Malik al-Rūm" (the king of the Romans), and so the former may well have been the Salīḥid chief in charge of conducting operations against the Arabs (ibid., 205, 207). Ibn Ḥabīb's account supports this interpretation, since there is no mention of the Romans as actually participating in the Salīḥid-Ghassānid conflict.

[265] This is a valuable addition, reflecting the strong sense of identity which the Ghassānids always had. Some thirty years later, Justinian made the Ghassānid chief king of all the Arabs in Oriens.

[266] For Ḥamza, this 10th-century historian, see F. Rosenthal, *History of Muslim Historiography*, Index, s.v. Ḥamza al-Iṣbahānī, p. 626, and F. Sezgin, *GAS*, I, 336–37. These data are taken from his *Tārīkh* (Beirut, 1961), 98–99.

[267] The relationship of Jidʿ to Thaʿlaba had to be inferred from their having the same patronymic, which is not decisive.

4. ʿAlī ibn Hasan al-Khazrajī[268] adds a few details on Jid̲ʿ, who thus emerges as a colorful figure. According to al-Khazrajī, he was a wily, one-eyed, and deaf *sayyid.* His account of the encounter with the Salīḥid representative of Byzantium may be summarized as follows. When the Salīḥid came to collect the taxes from the Ghassānids, Jid̲ʿ told him that "we are a hungry people and we have nothing to give to the king. But take this sword as a pawn until such time as we have something to give to the king." The Salīḥid responded in a vulgar, unseemly manner. As Jid̲ʿ was deaf, he could not hear what the arrogant Salīḥid said, but as the people around him laughed, Jid̲ʿ understood what he had said. He immediately unsheathed his sword and cut off the head of the Salīḥid, a circumstance that gave rise to the proverb "Take from Jid̲ʿ what Jid̲ʿ chooses to give" (*khud min Jid̲ʿin mā aʿtāka*).[269]

II

The various stages in the period of ten years or so that witnessed the fall of Salīḥ may now be related to the data extracted from the Arabic sources for establishing the truth about the kings of Salīḥ in the last section. Both sets of data may also be related to the Greek sources to shed more light on the process of Salīḥ's disintegration and fall.

1. The last generation of Salīḥids or Zokomids appear to be Dāwūd and his brother or cousin, Ziyād, both belonging to the ʿAwfid line, and Sabīṭ who belonged to the ʿAmrid. The genealogical list and the sources conceive of Dāwūd as the last Zokomid king, and he apparently was still alive around 490 when the Ghassānids crossed the *limes.* So he must have witnessed at least the first stage of Ghassānid-Salīḥid relations during this last decade. Dāwūd fell after an attack by a coalition of Kalb and al-Namir ibn Wabara, somewhere between al-Qurnatayn and Ḥārib.[270]

2. Ziyād presumably became king after the death of Dāwūd. He is associated with the battle-day of al-Baradān, in which he is said to have died. And yet the account of Ibn Saʿīd, preserved by Ibn Khaldūn, suggests that he remained alive, that he was the last Salīḥid chief after the fall of the Zokomids, and that he marched with what remained of his followers to Ḥijāz, where he was killed by the Kindite Ḥujr.[271] Ziyād is not mentioned in the

[268] A late Yamanite historian (d. 1409), who wrote the history of the Rasūlid dynasty in Yaman in medieval times, and who himself was related to the Ghassānids. See his *Kitāb al-ʿUqūd al-Luʾluʾiyya* (*The Pearl Strings*), ed. M. ʿAsal, Gibb Memorial Series 3.4 (Leiden, 1913), 12, 14.

[269] Perhaps roughly equivalent to "Do not look a gift horse in the mouth."

[270] On this see above, 260–61. The Salīḥid toponymy, indicated in the authentic pre-Islamic verse that recorded the place of the bloody encounter, suggests that the statement in Yaʿqūbī on the Salīḥids' fighting the Ghassānids in Bostra, near Damascus and al-Muḥaffaf, is credible.

[271] See Ibn Khaldūn, *Tārīkh*, II, 580.

accounts of the historians of the fall of Salīḥ examined in the preceding section, and yet he is mentioned in Ibn Saʿīd, whose account could not have been altogether a fabrication. The account coheres with what is known about Ziyād as one of the last Salīḥids and as involved with Kinda in a battle that he lost. It has been suggested[272] that the Ḥujr who beat him at the battle of Baradān was not the son of ʿAmr, of the mid-fifth century, but his great grandson, the son of the Arethas who was raiding the Byzantine frontier around 500. This resolves many of the difficulties that involve Ziyād and the fall of the dynasty. Ziyād may have been the Salīḥid who fought the Ghassānids at al-Muḥaffaf/Mukhaffaf, just as he fought the Kindites at al-Baradān. The sources do not mention Kinda in the accounts that recorded the fall of Salīḥ, but they may have been selective in their presentation of the data.

3. That Kinda could very well have participated in the general operations that led to the fall of the Zokomids is strongly suggested by the Greek sources. That precious passage in Theophanes[273] speaks of a general offensive by both Kinda and Ghassān against the Roman frontier. The date of the offensive—around 500—and the appearance of the name Ḥujr as that of a Kindite commander engaged in war with Byzantium support the hypothesis that both Ghassān and Kinda were involved in the fall of the Zokomids.

4. The problem of the fall of the Zokomids has to be related to the part played by Amorkesos of the reign of Leo in the history of this region in the last quarter of the fifth century, especially as it has been argued in this volume that he was most probably a Ghassānid. If this turns out to be true, then the Arabic sources on the fall of the Ghassānids analyzed in this chapter must have been speaking of the generation of Ghassānids that came after him and who were related to him lineally or collaterally. His sphere of influence was Palaestina Tertia and northern Ḥijāz, while that of the Salīḥids was Arabia. So the Salīḥid-Ghassānid conflict may have been the result of a push on the part of the Ghassānids of Amorkesos north toward the region that was Salīḥ's preserve, or it may represent an entirely new Ghassānid wave from the Peninsula coming through Wādī Sirḥān and only related to Amorkesos through common descent from the Azd, the large tribal group.

5. Some matters of detail about the fall of Salīḥ will remain controversial, and their resolution must await epigraphic discoveries. Nevertheless, there is no doubt that the confrontation of the Arabic and the Greek sources has resulted in a large measure of coherence in their presentation of the data for the fall, and that the general conclusions on the stages of the fall as well as the chronology must be judged valid. What is more, the fall of the Zokomids can be comprehended more fully in light of the fact—established in previous

[272] See above, 263.
[273] Theophanes, *Chronographia*, I, 141.

chapters—that the Ghassānids made deep inroads into Byzantine territory in the reign of Leo and thus weakened the Salīḥids, and that the latter had most probably been participants in Leo's disastrous expedition against the Vandals in the late 460s, which can account to a great extent for the diminution of their numbers. Other matters may also be brought to bear on the weakening of the Salīḥids, even before they fell to the onslaught of the Ghassānids: for example, the peace that reigned between the two world powers, which did not keep the Salīḥids on military alert and in a perfect state of military readiness. Thus the elucidation of Salīḥid history throughout the fifth century provides a background for the problem of the fall and enables one also to understand the antecedent problem of their decline and disintegration.

One of the most important features of the sources for the Salīḥid-Ghassānid conflict is the fact that they speak of two *foedera*, struck between Ghassān and Salīḥ and later between Ghassān and Byzantium. Both refer to the writing of treaty texts, which bears on the problem of the Arabic script in the fifth century.[274]

1. The first *foedus* between Ghassān and Salīḥ pertained to the condition of settlement, but only one of these conditions is mentioned, no doubt because it was the one that later led to the conflict between the two Arab groups, namely, that pertaining to the tax. Ibn Ḥabīb does not give the actual text, but only a paraphrase of one of the conditions. He speaks of a dinar, a dinar and a half, or two dinars to be extracted from each Ghassānid according to his worth or station (*ʿāla aqdārihim*). The meaning is not clear, but presumably it refers to either their age or their wealth.

It remains to be seen whether these figures are correctly transmitted, but the principle involved is clear. Arabs could not settle within the *limes* and not pay tax if they were not *foederati*. Also the term used is *kharj,* sometimes corrected as *kharāj*,[275] the technical term used in Islamic times for the land tax. Whether or not this term was used in pre-Islamic times is not clear; if not, then the Muslim historian was using a contemporary term anachronistically.[276] It is important in this account that the king of Salīḥ writes to the king of the Romans about the terms before they are accepted; this is the only instance in which a Salīḥid is associated with writing.

Arab-Byzantine relations, especially when they were imperial-federate, required that the two parties understand each other perfectly, particularly on important occasions such as this one, when a *foedus* was being struck. It is

[274] The accounts of both treaties may be found in Ibn Ḥabīb, *al-Muḥabbar*, 371.

[275] As in M. Hamīdullāh, "Die Neutralität im islamischen Völkerrecht," *ZDMG* 89 (1935), 71. And yet the account suggests that what was involved was the poll tax.

[276] Arabic *kharaj* is possibly Greek Χορηγία; if so, the term is likely to have entered Arabic in pre-Islamic times.

unreasonable to suppose that the Arab federates were expected to understand Greek, which the newcomers did not. So it is practically certain that Arabic was used as one of the two languages in such a transaction, the other being Greek.

2. The second *foedus* between Ghassān and Byzantium is in part quoted verbatim. Its political and military clauses are beyond the scope of this volume, since it is dated to 502 and deals not with Salīḥ but with Ghassān and Byzantium. However, there are two, possibly three, references to writing in this account. The king of the Roman sends a letter to the Ghassānids, saying that he would write an agreement with them if they found the terms acceptable. The terms were acceptable to Thaʿlaba, and as a result the agreement was written down. Again, as in the first *foedus,* it is unnatural to assume that in a bilateral agreement such as this, the Ghassānids, who were newcomers from Arabia, would have been expected to understand the Greek of the *foedus.* The presumption, then, is that there was an Arabic version, written possibly by the Arab federates already in Oriens, or perhaps by a scribe attached to the tribal group.[277]

VI. Arab Monasteries

After spreading from Egypt in the fourth century, monasticism especially flourished in Oriens in the fifth[278] and sixth centuries. Both the *Rhōmaioi* and the *foederati* among the Arabs were deeply influenced by it. Monks and monastic establishments associated with the *foederati* are less difficult to identify.[279] This chapter is therefore devoted to the collection and interpretation of data on federate monasticism in the fifth century, both in Oriens and in the Byzantine sphere of influence in western Arabia.

I

The strong ties that linked the federates of the fifth century to monasticism go back to the rise of the Salīḥids, the dominant group of *foederati* in

[277] Such as the one mentioned in an Arabic inscription found at Umm al-Jimāl, Jordan, and known as Umm al-Jimāl II; see Syria, *PPUAES*, Division IV, Semitic Inscriptions, Section D (Leiden, 1949), pp. 1–3, especially the very competent commentary of Littmann on *Kātib* (scribe) on p. 2. Besides, the Ghassānids had come from the sedentary Arabian south, the society of which was literate. Once in Oriens they must have used the script of the region, deriving from Nabataean and Syriac, as argued below, Chapter 14, sec. II.III.A.

[278] On monasticism in Syria, see P. Canivet, *MST*, 42, with its bibliography.

[279] Such as Aziz in Sozomen (*HE*, IV, 34) and possibly Gaddan in the same chapter. Canivet has examined the ethnic background of monks in Theodoret and suggests that Abbas was an Ishmaelite (Saracen/Arab). This could be Arabic ʿÁbbās; see Canivet, *MST*, 239. On Abbas, see above, Chap. 9, app. 1.

Oriens in this century. As discussed in a previous chapter, the Salīḥids owed their conversion to Christianity and their Byzantine connection to a monk who cured the wife of Zokomos of her sterility.[280] The Salīḥids naturally kept their devotion to monks throughout their supremacy in Oriens. Sozomen, who provided this precious datum on the Salīḥids, is also informative on the process of the conversion of the Saracens in general in Oriens, which he ascribes to the monks rather than to the priests.[281] Sozomen's statement can be verified and made meaningful by an examination of the data related to the *foederati* of Oriens in the fifth century and the two important federate groups that are associated with monasticism, the Tanūkhids and the Iyādis.

A

The Tanūkhids were the dominant group of *foederati* in the fourth century, but after the rise of the Salīḥids they stayed on in Oriens. Even before their emigration from the Land of the Two Rivers, they were known for their devotion to Christianity and for having founded some monasteries, such as Dayr Ḥanna in Ḥīra.[282] The Arabic sources are much more informative on the pre-Islamic Arabs in the eastern half of the Fertile Crescent than on those of Oriens; hence the data on monasteries there are more plentiful.[283] But it is practically certain that the Tanūkhids of Oriens, in both the fourth and fifth centuries, continued their attachment to monasticism and must have endowed many monasteries (as they had done in Persian territory). An echo of their attachment to monasticism is reflected in the insistence of Queen Mavia that an Arab *hermit*, Moses, should be the bishop of the *foederati*.[284] The *martyrion* ascribed to a certain Mavia near Anasartha is probably a Tanūkhid foundation.[285]

The Iyādīs, too, had come from the Land of the Two Rivers, where they had written an important chapter in the history of Arab Christianity and the rise of the Arabic script.[286] Their attachment to monks and the monastic way of life is even better documented than that of the Tanūkhids, since no less than three monasteries are associated with their name—the monasteries of al-Aʿwar, al-Sawā, and Qurra, all in the vicinity of Ḥīra.[287] As argued, the chances are that a portion of Iyād emigrated to Oriens in the fifth century,

[280] See above, 3.

[281] Sozomen, *HE*, IV, 34.

[282] See *BAFOC*, 419.

[283] As may be seen from a perusal of the list of monasteries in the Land of the Two Rivers compared to those in Oriens.

[284] See *BAFOC*, 152–58.

[285] Ibid., 222-27.

[286] On Iyād, see above, Sec. IV.

[287] See Yāqūt, *Muʿjam*, II, 498, 516, 526.

where one of them, ʿAbd al-ʿĀṣ, became the court poet of the Christian Salīḥid king, Dāwūd. As the Arabic sources on Iyād in Oriens are much less informative than they are on Iyād in Persian territory, it is not surprising that Iyād's monastic foundations in Oriens are not recorded. But it is almost certain that the dedicated Iyādīs, who had endowed at least three monasteries in and near Ḥīra, in the land of the Fireworshippers, did not lose their interest in endowing others after their emigration to the territory of the Christian empire.

A confirmation of the attachment of the Christian Arabs to monasticism comes from the Syriac and Greek sources. The *History* of Aḥūdemmeh recounts the conversion of the Arabs, including the Tanūkhids, in sixth-century Mesopotamia and pays a special tribute to the attachment of the converted Arabs to the monasteries which they endowed and their devotion to fasting and the ascetic way of life.[288] In fifth-century Oriens, the example of the bishopric of the federate Arabs of the Parembole in Palaestina Prima in the desert of Juda confirms their attachment to monasticism. Maris, the brother-in-law of Aspebetos, the Arab phylarch-bishop of the Parembole, donated all his property to the monastery of St. Euthymius and finally became its *hēgoumenos*.[289] This example is taken from the history of the little Parembole, but its size is irrelevant. What happened in this diminutive federate Arab bishopric-phylarchate must have happened elsewhere in Oriens among the other and more numerous federate groups, as will be discussed presently.

B

The sources, for obvious reasons, are not informative on the federate Arab monastic establishment, which, in view of the attachment of the Arabs to that form of the expression of Christian life, must have been considerable. There are only a few references scattered in the sources to the various regions in which monasticism flourished, so the references to Arab monasteries will be noted and discussed below by region.

Oriens

The references to the Arabs and Arab monastic life in Oriens are mostly to the two large regions in the south and in the north: the former is represented by the two Palestines, Prima and Tertia; the latter by Syria Prima and Euphratensis.

[288] On this, see *BAFOC*, 419–22. It is worth quoting the author of the *History* on Arab devotion to the ascetic life: "mais ils aimaient le jeûne et la vie ascétique plus que tous les chrétiens, au point de commencer le saint jeûne des quarante jours une semaine de plus avant tous les chrétiens"; *Histoire de Mar Aḥudemmeh*, PO 3 (1909), 28.

[289] See above, 191.

1. Palaestina Tertia, or Salutaris, was the natural region in which the Arabic monastic establishment must have grown. It comprised Sinai and the Negev and, together with Gaza and the desert of Juda in the Jordan Valley, was the bridge over which monasticism crossed from its homeland, Egypt, into Oriens.

As far as Palaestina Tertia is concerned, it is natural to assume that the beginnings of monastic life established in the fourth century by St. Hilarion, the apostle of the Arabs in the Negev, should have continued.[290] There was a strong monastic community in Rhaithou, whose head was the Arab holy man, Moses, and he may have drawn other Arabs from the ʿAraba Valley—such as Joseph and Paul, natives of Ayla and Petra respectively. These are all fourth-century figures, and the presumption is that in the fifth century Rhaithou continued as the chief Arab monastic center in the Sinai Peninsula.[291] To these data from the non-Arabic sources may now be added the fact supplied by the Arabic sources, that at Ayla there was a monastery by the strikingly Arab name of Dayr al-Qunfuḏ, "the Monastery of the hedgehog."[292] Ayla was by this time an Arab town, and surely the inmates of the monastery were mostly Arabs. What is important is the fact that this monastic foundation was the work of the tribe of Balī, which lived not far from Ayla. Arab federates normally built outside the city walls, as was the case for Mavia's *martyrion* outside Anasartha[293] and the Ghassānid Munḏir's structure outside the walls of Sergiopolis. But this rule apparently had its exceptions, resulting from the important fact that the Arab *foederati* in Oriens were settled among *Rhōmaioi* who themselves were Arabs or had been independent before Rome annexed their territory—such as the Nabataean, the Palmyrene, and the Edessene Arabs. The *foederati* and the *cives* had a natural affinity to each other, in spite of the difference in the degree of their acculturation or assimilation to the Roman and Byzantine systems.

Palaestina Prima witnessed a diminutive Arab monastic establishment in only a part of it—the desert of Juda, near the Jordan. St. Chariton carried the seed of monasticism there and founded Pharan[294] around 330, and no region could be holier and more appropriate for eremites than the desert of Juda,

[290] See *BAFOC*, 288–93.

[291] On Rhaithou, see ibid., 297–305. In Yāqūt, Rhaithou appears as Rayat, see *Muʿjam*, III, 22.

[292] See below, Sec. VIII.II.

[293] See *BAFOC*, 222–27, but compare one structure within the walls of Anasartha, ibid., 227–33.

[294] On Pharan in the desert of Juda, see S. Vailhé, "Répertoire alphabétique," 42. The name recalls the Pharan in Sinai, associated with Hagar and Ishmael as related in Genesis. How this monastery was called after the same toponym that Ishmael is associated with has not been commented upon.

lying between the holy city and the holy river, with moving biblical associations. It was in this region that the small Arab federate community of the refugee Aspebetos settled after they fled from Persian territory. In this region the great influence on the Arabs was St. Euthymius, just as St. Hilarion had influenced the Arabs of the Negev in the fourth century in Palestine. Arab federate life in the desert of Juda is remembered through the church of Aspebetos and his participation in the Council of Ephesus, where he was the spokesman of Cyrillian Orthodoxy. But his brother-in-law, Maris, who was converted by St. Euthymius, endowed the monastery of St. Euthymius and finally became its *hēgoumenos*. This could not have been an isolated case among the federate Arabs, and the chances are that other Arabs acted similarly. Two other Arab monks distinguished themselves in this region: Stephanus, who became the *hēgoumenos* of Euthymius' second lavra, and Elias, who finally rose to be patriarch of Jerusalem.[295] Thus in this small area three Arab monks distinguished themselves, and this could not have been a phenomenon peculiar to this region. The chances are that other Arabs played a similar role in the annals of monasticism in Oriens, but while Palestinian monasticism found an eloquent historian in Cyril of Scythopolis, without whom little would have been known about monasticism in Palaestina Prima, the other regions in Oriens were not so fortunate.

2. The data on the Arab federate monastic establishment in the north of Oriens are not as good as they are on the establishment in the two Palestines; but it must have existed. Just as St. Euthymius exercised great influence on the life of the federate Arabs in the south of Oriens, so did St. Simeon the Stylite on the Arabs in the north. The north, however, was dotted with monasteries, and the desert of Chalcis already in the fourth century witnessed the flowering of an eremite community, among whom Jerome spent some time. Then there was the region around Ruṣafa/Sergiopolis (southeast of Qinnasrīn/Chalcis), named after the military saint who was especially revered among the Arabs. There are lists of monasteries for northern Syria, but it is difficult to identify specifically Arab monasteries only from an examination of the names. There were at least three, including that of Dāwūd, and it is difficult to believe that there were only these three.[296] If the Salīḥid king who lived in the south, in the Balqā' across the Jordan, thought fit to build a monastery in the north, attracted presumably by the fame of its saints (either Simeon or Sergius), the chances are that the Arabs of the north acted in a similar fashion.[297] The combined fame of the two saints made the north of Oriens a singularly attractive region for pious Christians, and it drew pilgrims

[295] On these three figures, see above, Chap. 10, sec. II.

[296] These Syriac lists and the three Arab monasteries are described later in this section.

[297] On the monastery of Ruṣāfa, see Yāqūt, *Muʿjam*, II, 510.

even from the far side of the Mediterranean world. Consequently, it must have attracted the attention of the Arabs who were devoted to these two particular saints.[298] Only excavations in the "dead cities" of the region can advance knowledge of the Arab contribution to the monastic establishments.

Arab monasticism is also attested in the Ḥijāz, that sphere of Byzantine influence in the pre-Islamic period. This is a region that was related geographically to Palaestina Tertia and also politically, through the Arab *foederati* in the region, of whom the most important were Judām and ʿUdra. The few references in the sources make it possible to extract the following data.

1. The region of Madyan (biblical Midian) must have been a monastic center, since this is irrefutably attested in the verse of one of the poets of the Umayyad period, Kuthayyir ʿAzza, who speaks of the "monks of Madyan."[299] These naturally must have settled in that region in pre-Islamic times, and the chances are they did so in the century that witnessed the flowering of monasticism in Oriens. Ayla was the last Byzantine bishopric in the south, and the appearance of monasticism in the neighboring region of Madyan must have been an extension of Christianity from that city of Palaestina Tertia. The spread of monasticism in Madyan could easily be related to its biblical associations with Moses, Jethro, and Sepporah. This was the territory of Judām, and it is possible that the monks belonged to this federate tribe.

2. The southernmost region of Ḥijāz in which monasticism is attested is Wādī al-Qurā ("the Valley of the Towns") near Medina. The association is documented or recorded in the verse of an Umayyad poet who speaks of "monks in the lower part of Wādī al-Qurā."[300] Just as the monks of Madyan could very well have been of the tribe of Judām, so these monks could have belonged to the tribe of ʿUdra, which lived not far off. That the language of the poet is more explicit on these than on the monks in Madyan suggests that they did belong to the tribe of ʿUdra.

3. In the northeastern part of Ḥijāz there was the station of Kilwa. Unlike Madyan and Wādī al-Qurā, the evidence for a monastic establishment there does not derive from Arabic or other literary sources but from its ruins,

[298] The Ghassānid federate king Mundir of the 6th century also had his headquarters in the south of Oriens, as did Dāwūd. He too was attracted by Sergius. Near his tomb in Sergiopolis/Ruṣāfa, Mundir built his *praetorium* or *ecclesia extra muros*, and he also repaired the cisterns of the city, no doubt as an act of piety; see Nöldeke, *GF*, 51.

[299] On the Umayyad poet Kuthayyir ʿAzza, see *EI*^{2}, s.v. More precision is possible through the identification of Madyan not only with the region but also with the "town of Madyan," which lies inland from the eastern shore of the Gulf of Eilat, known to Josephus, Ptolemy, and Eusebius. In Islamic times it is referred to as Madyan Shuʿayb; see C. E. Bosworth's article in *EI*^{2}, s.v.

[300] On this poet and his verses, see below, 359.

examined in the early 1940s. The explorer even derived the name Kilwa from Greek *kellion*, and concluded that the "distintegrated stone structures . . . must have been ruins of cells or hermitages." She also refers to a "cross of an unusual type and . . . a Maltese Cross," and to Byzantine pottery which she found there. The location was known to the tenth-century Arab geographer al-Muqaddasī, who describes it as a station on the way from ʿAmman to Medina west of the southern end of Wādī Sirḥān. When exactly this monastic compound was founded is not entirely clear but, the chances are good that it, too, was established in the century that witnessed the flowering of monasticism in Syria.[301]

Thus these regions, far apart from one another, testify to the wide diffusion of monasticism in Ḥijāz. The literary sources, mainly the geographical dictionaries of Bakrī and Yāqūt, have some specific references to a few monasteries:

1. *Dayr Ḥismā*. According to Bakrī, the Ḥismā, the region between Hijāz and Shām, belonged to the tribe of Judām. A reference to a Dayr occurs in an Arabic verse, but where exactly in the region of Ḥismā it was is not indicated in the Arabic sources.[302]

2. *Dayr Ḍamḍam*. Reference is found in the same source,[303] and in the same verse, and the presumption is that it too, is in Madyan or northern Ḥijāz. Ḍamḍam is an old Arabic name, attested in the West Arabian onomasticon, and it appears in the "suspended ode" of the pre-Islamic poet ʿAntara as belonging to the tribe of Ḏubyān.[304] Unlike Dayr Ḥismā, its Arab character is clearly indicated in the Arab name, Ḍamḍam.

3. *Dayr Saʿd*. Finally, there is a reference to a Dayr Saʿd, which was located between Shām/Oriens and the region where the Ḥijāzī tribe of Ghaṭafān was settled.[305] The reference is not precise but it may be safely assumed that it, too, was in Ḥijāz and that its founder, judging from the name, was an Arab.

South Arabia

The Byzantine mission to South Arabia during the reign of Constantius in the fourth century succeeded in founding three churches in the country, but there is no mention of monasteries. These could easily have been founded subsequent to the founding of the churches and to the Byzantine mission,

[301] For all this information on Kilwa, see A. Horsefield, "Journey to Kilwa, Transjordan," *The Geographical Journal* 102 (August 1943), 71–77, especially 73–74.

[302] Bakrī, *Muʿjam*, II, 446–47, s.v. Ḥismā.

[303] Ibid.

[304] See Ahlwardt, *Divans*, 49, line 2.

[305] See Yāqūt, *Muʿjam*, II, 514–15.

since the monastery followed the church as an expression of Christian life in the fourth, fifth, and sixth centuries.

That South Arabia was not a stranger to monasticism may be confirmed by a letter written by Jerome[306] from Bethlehem about the beginning of the fifth century, addressed to a Roman lady, Laeta, on the education of her daughter Paula. Jerome speaks of welcoming crowds of monks who came to the Holy Land from India, Persia, and Ethopia; "de India, Perside, Aethiopia, monachorum quotidie turbas suscipimus."[307] The reference to India presents a problem, since it is not always clear whether India proper is meant or South Arabia, which is often referred to as India. The likelihood is that South Arabia is meant here, in view of the mission of Theophilus Indus a half century earlier, while it is difficult to believe that crowds of monks could have come to the Holy Land from India proper around the beginning of the fifth century.

Further confirmation of the existence or spread of monastic life in South Arabia comes from Hishām al-Kalbī. He speaks of an Arab poet of South Arabia by the name of al-Barrāq who was associated in his early years with a monk in that region. Just as the reference in Jerome to monks in South Arabia has for a background the mission of Theophilus Indus, so this statement pertaining to the middle of the fifth century has for a background the conversion of Najrān in South Arabia by Ḥannān/Ḥayyān in the first quarter of the century,[308] as well, of course, as the statement in Jerome.

The account of Hishām is even more important for the problem of an Arabic pre-Islamic Bible, but its value is diminished by the uncertainty that attends the source from which his account derives.[309]

Other Monasteries

In addition to monasteries that can be assigned to specific regions such as Oriens, Ḥijāz, and South Arabia, there are other pre-Islamic monasteries which are either definitely Arab or possibly so. There is no way of telling who founded them or when they were founded, but they are all pre-Islamic.

Definitely Arab are Dayr Ibn Āmir, Dayr Arwā, and Dayr Ḥabīb.[310] No indication is given as to their location, but their names argue for their

[306] Monasticism is well attested in South Arabia in the 6th century; see I. Shahîd, "Byzantium in South Arabia," 74–75.

[307] See PL 22, col. 870. For Laeta, see the footnote of the editor of Jerome's letters in *Select Letters of St. Jerome* (Loeb), p. 338. Monasticism in South Arabia could receive further confirmation from a letter sent by Paula and Eustochium, her daughter, to Marcella in Rome and written in 386; see PL 32, col. 489.

[308] On this, see below, Chap. 13, sec. III.

[309] For Hishām's account, the poet Barrāq, and the reference to a Gospel in this account, see the detailed discussion below, Chap. 14, sec. IV.II.

[310] For these three monasteries, see Yāqūt, *Muʿjam*, II, 496, 497, 504. The last, Dayr Ḥabīb, appears in the Syriac list, for which see the following section.

being Arab monasteries. Another, Dayr Kaʿb,[311] is described as being in Shām/Oriens, but where in Oriens is not clear.

Possibly Arab are such monasteries as Dayr al-Bāʿiqī, at which, according to Yāqūt, the Prophet Muḥammad is supposed to have met the mysterious monk Baḥīra in this pre-Prophetic phase of his life; Dayr Buṣrā, in the capital of the Provincia Arabia; Dayr Fīq in the Jawlān, a region associated with both the Salīḥids of the fifth and the Ghassānids of the sixth century; and Dayr Khunāṣira (Anasartha),[312] near which were found two inscriptions involving Christian Arab ladies.[313]

Undoubtedly, the most important Arab monastery of the fifth century is Dayr Dāwūd. It was noticed both in the Arabic and possibly in the Syriac sources. As it was built by Dāwūd, the king of the Salīḥids, it has a special significance in the history of this federate dynasty and in the history of Arab monasticism. The laconic reference to it in the sources is not helpful in answering the many important questions regarding this most solid spot in Salīḥid toponymy.

1. The first question that must be raised is where in Oriens it was located. Reference to it in the Arabic sources, such as Ibn Durayd,[314] is not helpful at all but its possible inclusion in the Syriac lists is. These are not contemporary fifth-century, but sixth-century documents and what is more, Monophysite; hence they present new problems, but are the only sources at our disposal.

These Syriac sources consist of four letters, the relevant portions of which are the subscriptions of the Monophysite clergy, which state the names of the monasteries they belong to.[315] Dayr Dāwūd appears in the second and third

[311] For Dayr Kaʿb, see Bakrī, *Muʿjam*, II, 594.

[312] For Dayr al-Bāʿiqī, Dayr Buṣrā, Dayr Fīq, and Dayr Khunāṣira, see Yāqūt, *Muʿjam*, II, 499, 500–1, 525, and 507. Dayr Buṣrā was still functioning in Islamic times and its inmates were Arabs from Banū al-Ṣādir; it will be discussed further in the chapter on poetry.

Of these four *dayrs*, al-Bāʿiqī is least known, and its location is not stated by Yāqūt. It is an important monastery, since it is among those which the Islamic tradition associates with a visit by the Prophet Muḥammad, the two others being Dayr Buṣrā and Mayfaʿa (Umm al-Rassās). But since the name is so unusual, it is possible to locate the *dayr* at or near Qaṣr al-Bāʿiq, which lies 20 km southwest of Bostra. For Qaṣr al-Bāʿiq (Qaṣr el-Bāʿek), see Dussaud, *Topographie*, 360 note 8 and Map II; for more recent discussions, see Parker, *Romans and Saracens*, 146 and notes 72, 73, with reference to the work of G. W. Bowersock. Parker reports that "the fort at Bāʿiq is directly adjacent to the *via nova Traiana* and was erected in 412," a welcome and relevant fact, since it places the locality on the caravan route to Bostra, which Muḥammad in the pre-Prophetic phase of his career would, as a caravan leader, have traversed; this makes his visit to Dayr al-Bāʿiqī, reported in the Islamic sources, probable.

[313] For these two inscriptions, see *BAFOC*, 222–38.

[314] See Ibn Durayd, *al-Ishtiqāq*, 545.

[315] See E. Honigmann, "Nordsyrische Klöster in vorarabischer Zeit," in *Zeitschrift für Semitistik und verwandte Gebiete* 1 (1922), 15–33; and E. Littmann, "Zur Topographie der Antiochene und Apamene," ibid., 163–95.

lists.[316] The first problem that must be addressed is the determination of which of the two *dayrs* that bear the name of David is the Salīḥid monastery and where it was located. One of the two is located near Qinnasrīn, as is stated in the Syriac document. The location of the other is not indicated, and this may argue that it was the more famous one, which needed no further specification to guide the reader to its location. The abbot who put his subscription just before that of the abbot of this Dayr Dāwūd was the abbot of the monastery of Melōṭā, which is located south of Ruwēḥā, not far from Maʿarrat al-Nuʿmān.[317] If the subscriptions followed a geographical order of location, the chances are that Dayr Dāwūd was not far from the *dayr* of Melōṭā, but there is no certainty about this conclusion.

The locations of these two *dayrs* are not far from each other, and they are close to Qinnasrīn/Chalcis; one of them may have been in Qinnasrīn itself. These are Monophysite monasteries, while the Salīḥids of the fifth century were Orthodox and the presumption is that they remained so even in the sixth century, although the *dayr* may have been occupied by the Monophysites in the sixth century after the fall of the Salīḥids. Dāwūd may have been attracted by the desert of Chalcis, which had attracted Jerome before him in the fourth century. On the other hand, the location of this *dayr* may be sought elsewhere than in Chalcidice, especially as it is far from certain that either of these two convents is to be identified with the Salīḥid *dayr.* That indefatigable scholar-traveler, A. Musil, who roamed and combed this area, located Dayr Dāwūd—or Dayr al-Lathiq, as he calls it—halfway between Isriye and Ruṣāfa/Sergiopolis, at the present-day al-Turkumāniyya. Of this locality he writes that there "is a structure built of roughly-hewn stone; above the well-preserved door it is ornamented with a cross. In ruins for the most part, it seems to have been a monastery in times past."[318] He is likely to be right, since he based his conclusion on an unequivocal statement in Ṭabarī describing the march of the last Umayyad caliph Marwān II from al-Qasṭal via Surija and Dayr al-Lathiq to al-Ruṣāfa.[319] The locations of these toponyms are known, and

[316] In Honigmann's article (op. cit.), Dayr Dāwūd appears first in List II, no. 38, p. 22; a second time in List III, no. 56, p. 26; and a third time in List III, no. 38, p. 27, where it is stated that it is associated with Qinnasrīn/Chalcis. Honigmann has cogently argued that the first and third occurrences, which carry no. 38, are one and the same since their abbot was the same Joḥanan, and are to be distinguished from the second *dayr* (no. 56), the abbot of which was Ḥannīna.

[317] See Honigmann's commentary on this, ibid., p. 28, no. 55. The abbot who signed after Ḥannīna of Dayr Dāwūd was the abbot of the *dayr* of Gurgis, the location of which is unknown; Littmann, "Topographie," 181.

[318] See Musil, *Palmyrena*, 153–54.

[319] See his footnotes, ibid., 154, note 41. It was also fortunate that Musil drew a plan of the monastery; ibid., 153. Musil remembered Dayr Dāwūd elsewhere in Palmyrena; see 50 note 12, where he locates al-Turkumāniyya halfway between Isriye and Ruṣāfa. The locality,

what is important is the reference to the *dayr* not simply as Dayr Dāwūd but as Dayr al-Lathiq, which clinches the point that it is the *dayr* of the Salīḥid king.

It is therefore certain that present day al-Turkumāniyya is the site of Dayr Dāwūd. The analysis of the Syriac lists has been necessary at least to rule out one of the two *dayrs* described as Dayr Dāwūd, namely, the one associated with Qinnasrīn. The possibility is still open that the other *dayr* in the Syriac lists, which is not assigned to any location, may well be the *dayr* of the Salīḥid king. If so, the list is informative, since it indicates that the *dayr* was functioning as a monastery in the sixth century, that it had been possessed by the Monophysites, and that one of its abbots was called Hannīna.

There are references in the Syriac lists to two other Arab monasteries: the *dayr* of the Ṭayāyē (the Arabs) and Dayr Ḥabīb. Both belong to the sixth century and are Monophysite; whether they were founded in the previous century and whether they were Orthodox cannot be determined.[320]

2. The religiosity of the Salīḥid king, noted in the sources and commented on earlier in this volume, is the obvious background for his building Dayr Dāwūd. The monastery associated with his name raises several questions, none of which, because of the state of the sources, can be answered with certainty.

The first question is whether or not he actually became a monk. If he did, he may have followed the example of his neighbor,[321] Empress Eudocia, who after leaving her husband, Theodosius II, in Constantinople came to the Holy Land and lived in Jerusalem.[322] Dāwūd was living across the Jordan in

---

according to Musil, acquired its name after the Turkomans held the surrounding territory in the 13th century.

That Dayr Dāwūd was located in the northern half of Oriens and not in Arabia is further confirmed by the fact that it is *not* mentioned in the Syriac list of subscriptions pertaining to the region of Damascus and Ḥawrān, examined by Nöldeke; see his "Zur Topographie und Geschichte des damascênischen Gebietes und der Haurângegend," *ZDMG* 29 (1875), 419–44.

There is an important reference to Dayr Dāwūd in Ṭabarī's recounting of the events of the Hijri year 127 (744–745). The Muslim historian mentions that the last Umayyad caliph, Marwān, passed through the *dayr* on his way to Ruṣāfa/Sergiopolis. Thus the *dayr* survived till at least the middle of the 8th century, some three hundred years after its foundation, roughly in the middle of the 5th century. It is interesting that its name is not Dayr Dāwūd, but Dayr al-Lathiq, the *laqab* of the Salīḥid king "Dāwūd, the bedraggled." For this reference see Ṭabarī, *Tārīkh*, VII, 315.

[320] For "the monastery of the Ṭayāyē," see Honigmann, "Nordsyrische Klöster," List I, no. 8, p. 18, and his commentary on p. 19. It was noted in *BAFOC*, 434. For "the monastery of Ḥabīb," see Honigmann, op. cit., List III, no. 64, p. 27 and his commentary on p. 28; also Littmann, "Topographie," 183. The two monasteries will be discussed in *BASIC*.

[321] He need not have been exactly her contemporary to have followed her example. He may have reigned slightly after her death, but her memory would have been alive in the region.

[322] The standard work on Eudocia is now K. G. Holum, *Theodosian Empresses*.

the Balqā region, and surely the pilgrimage of the empress and her residence in Jerusalem must have been known to the Christian federate Arab king. Such examples of renunciation could have been inspiring to him. On the other hand, he may have built the monastery as an act of piety inspired by imperial and other models, acts which the Ghassānids of the sixth century were to indulge in on a large scale.

Since something is known about the circumstances of his death at the hands of the two tribesmen in rebellion against the Salīḥids,[323] the chances are that he was not a monk when he died, although he may have wanted or prepared to become one. If so, he might have been buried there, which may explain the names Dayr Dāwūd or al-Lathiq, which persisted long after his death. If the *dayr* at al-Turkumāniyya can be identified with that mentioned in the Syriac list, then the chances are that Dāwūd may have been revered by his Arab followers, since the name of the *dayr* has before Dāwūd the Syriac word "Mār." As mentioned earlier, the monastery was Monophysite in the sixth century; if the identification is correct, then Dāwūd's *dayr* became so in the century following his death.

Why the Salīḥid king chose this spot for the building of his monastery is not entirely clear, but two reasons suggest themselves. He may have wanted to be far away from the seat of his secular duties as king of the federates in the Balqā , and this region was far, or far enough.[324] He may also have wanted his *dayr* to be near the shrine of the St. Sergius, the patron saint of the Arab federates and, what is more, a military saint who may have had a special attraction for an old soldier such as Dāwūd was.[325]

The Nabataean and Palmyrene Arabs of Roman times developed architectural forms and expressions peculiar to themselves in Petra and Palmyra, adaptations from those of the higher civilizations that surrounded them. Art historians have suspected that the Christian Arabs of this proto-Byzantine period also developed some peculiarly Arab styles in their architecture, and this was predicated of the Ghassānids of the sixth century.[326] Whether the same can be predicated of the Salīḥids of the fifth century remains to be seen.

[323] See above, 259.

[324] Although he may have wanted to be as far as he could from the seat of his secular duties, he may also have wanted the *dayr* to be near an area where he could have some Arab protection. It is noteworthy that two Saracen units listed in the *Notitia Dignitatum*, were stationed in Phoenicia Libanensis, one of which was at Betroclus and the other at Thelsee; on these two units, see below, 466.

[325] The Ghassānid federate king of the 6th century, Mundir, apparently was equally attracted by the shrine of St. Sergius at Ruṣāfa; see above, note 298.

[326] For instance, see E. Herzfeld, "Mshatta, Ḥīra and Bādiya," *Jahrbuch der preussischen Kunstsammlungen* 42 (1921), 113–16.

Only one structure can with certainty be attributed to them: Dayr Dāwūd. Fortunately, the plan of this *dayr* has been preserved,[327] but whether this solitary example of the Salīḥid architectural effort can justify drawing any conclusions must be left to the art historian to decide.[328]

In *Rome and the Arabs* I disentangled the strictly Arab component from the capacious terms "Syrian" or "Semitic," and in *Byzantium and the Arabs in the Fourth Century* I drew attention to the fact that in this proto-Byzantine period in the history of Oriens the Arab component became complex, consisting as it did of Rhomaic and federate Arabs. Art historians interested in the Arab component in the Syrian art of this period might care to reexamine previous views[329] and consider whether they admit of modifications in the light of these conclusions on the coexistence of two categories of Arabs in Oriens. Needless to say, this component, if it obtained, is a matter of considerable importance to the discussion of early Muslim architecture in Bilād al-Shām.[330]

VII. Salīḥ *post* Salīḥ

The *foedus* struck between Byzantium and Ghassān in 502 elevated Ghassān to the position of dominance among the Arab *foederati* in Oriens, but it did not decree Salīḥ out of federate existence; it simply demoted it. The Salīḥids remained in Oriens as a federate group till the end of this proto-Byzantine period and well after the Muslim Conquest. Their fortunes in these two periods are the subject of this section.

I

The sources are not very informative on the Salīḥids in this period of a century and a half or so that elapsed from the reign of Anastasius (491–518) to that of Heraclius (610–641). But they are relatively more informative than on the Tanūkhids, the *foederati* of the fourth century, possibly owing to the friction between the Ghassānids and the Salīḥids, which was noticed in the

[327] See Musil, *Palmyrena*, 153. Cf. the *martyrion* erected for the Arab girl Chasidat in the 4th century; *BAFOC*, 227–38. The first two lines of a Greek inscription (ibid., 227) give a glimpse of some of the architectural features of this *martyrion* built at Anasartha.

[328] The data become much more plentiful for the Ghassānids of the 6th century, to be discussed in *BASIC*.

[329] Such as those of Herzfeld; above, note 326.

[330] The problem of a specifically Muslim art and its formation has been raised by O. Grabar, *The Formation of Islamic Art* (New Haven, 1973). Works on Syrian architecture in this proto-Byzantine period include H. C. Butler, *Early Churches in Syria: Fourth to Seventh Centuries* (Princeton, 1929); J. Lassus, *Sanctuaires chrétiens de Syrie* (Paris, 1947); and the relevant portion of C. Mango's *Byzantine Architecture* (New York, 1976), with its attractive illustrations. To these may be added G. Tchalenko's masterly study of the villages of this region, although written from a different viewpoint: *Villages antiques de la Syrie du Nord*.

sources while there was no conflict between the Ghassānids and the Tanūkhids, who were related by tribal affiliation (al-Azd).

It is possible to divide the history of Salīḥ in this period into five phases:

1. The first phase extends from the treaty of 502 to the year 529. Nothing is reported in the sources on the Salīḥids or any other federate group except the Ghassānids, and the presumption is that the Salīḥids coexisted peacefully within the phylarchate of Oriens, constituting one of its federate groups and not directly responsible to any other federate group, but only to the *dux* of the province or the *magister militum* in Oriens.

2. The second phase extends from 529 to about 580. In 529 Justinian made the Ghassānid Arethas, son of Jabala, *basileus*—king over all the Arab federates[331] in Oriens. This placed the Salīḥid troops under the supervision of the Ghassānids, and it was only natural that Salīḥid-Ghassānid relations would sour. There is an echo of this in the Greek sources. The Byzantines lost the battle of Callinicum to the Persians in 531, immediately after the *basileia* of Arethas, and friction was suspected between the Ghassānids and some of the Arab federates in the Byzantine army during the battle.[332] Another echo may possibly be detected in an Arabic inscription found in the region of Jabal Usays.[333] The reading and the interpretation of the inscription are not certain, but it may record a military operation against a threat to the authority of the Ghassānids, dated as it is, immediately after the elevation of Arethas to the *basileia*.[334]

The sources do not mention the Salīḥids after this, but they may have figured in two difficult periods of Byzantine-Ghassānid relations: in the 520s, when the Ghassānids withdrew from the service because of the Chalcedonian policy of the house of Justin;[335] and in the 570s, when relations were ruffled between Arethas' son Mundir and the Chalcedonian emperors of the decade.[336] The Salīḥids could very well have figured prominently in the course of these relations because of their Orthodoxy, which they shared with their Chalcedonian Byzantine overlords. John of Ephesus, the principal Byzantine source on the Ghassānid federates, was a Monophysite; hence his apparent silence on whatever the Salīḥids may have done or achieved in this period.

3. The third phase may be said to have lasted for some thirty years, from

[331] Procopius, *Wars*, I, xvii, 47.

[332] See Shahîd, "Procopius and Arethas," 43–48.

[333] Southeast of Damascus.

[334] For this inscription, see A. Grohmann, *Arabische Paläographie* (Vienna, 1971), II, 15–17; also the map, p. 15, for the location of Usays. "Sulaymān" is the *crux* in the inscription, and it is not clear whether it is the name of a person (probably a Salīḥid) or of a place (a fort). The Usays inscription will be discussed in detail in *BASIC*.

[335] Shahîd, *Martyrs*, 99 ff.

[336] Nöldeke, *GF*, 27 ff.

around 580 until around 610, that is, from the exile of the supreme Ghassānid phylarch and king, Mundir, until the Persian invasion of Oriens. The first decade of this period witnessed the exile of Mundir and the imprisonment of his son and successor Nuʿmān,[337] and Salīḥid power may have revived with the fall of the group which had beaten them early in the century and replaced them as the dominant federate group, especially as it was the doctrinal persuasion of the non-Chalcedonian Ghassānids that brought about their downfall.

It is with this as a background that one must interpret the startling reappearance of the name Zokomos in the Greek sources.[338] An Arab phylarch by that name appears as an ally fighting with the Byzantine army in 586, during the siege of Mardīn. Coming after the humiliation of the two Ghassānid kings and the suppression of their power, this attestation of a Zokomid phylarch as participating in the Persian War of Maurice's reign can only have one interpretation—that the power of the Salīḥids was revived by Chalcedonian Byzantium.

This revival of Salīḥid power could derive some support from the Arabic sources. A verse ascribed to the pre-Islamic Arab poet al-Nābigha,[339] whose *floruit* may be assigned to this period, speaks of his having visited a Salīḥid from Āl Ḍujʿum, the House of Ḍujʿum (Zokomos), in either Bostra or Burqat Hārib.[340] The Zokomid comes in for praise in the verse, and the clear implication is that the Zokomids were not living in eclipse in this period, even after the Ghassānids were somewhat rehabilitated towards the end of the century.

4. The fourth period may be said to extend from 610 to 628, that is, the period of the Persian invasion and occupation of Oriens. What happened to the Salīḥids in this period is not clear. They may have joined the Ghassānids when they withdrew with the Byzantine army across the Taurus after the Persian victory, or they may have stayed in Oriens. The sources are absolutely silent on their fortunes in this period.

5. The fifth and final phase of this proto-Byzantine period, during which the Salīḥids were still *foederati* of Byzantium, is the period of the Muslim

337 Ibid.

338 As in Theophylactus Simocatta; see Nöldeke, *GF*, 8.

339 For the verse, see Ahlwardt, *Divans*, 164. For al-Nābigha, see Sezgin, *GAS*, II, 110–13.

340 The two toponyms coming from a contemporary pre-Islamic source are especially valuable, since they confirm the accounts of the later Islamic prose writers that the Salīḥids lived in this region around Bostra in the Provincia Arabia. The second toponym could very well be Burqat Ḥārib and not Burqat Hārib, which is unknown to the geographical dictionaries. Ḥārib is mentioned in the verse that spoke of the death of King Dāwūd: Ḥārib, in the Bathaniyya or the Jawlān. It may be inferred from the verse of al-Nābigha that the Zokomid chief whom the poet visited was affluent and had residences in both places.

Conquest of Oriens. The Salīḥids are attested fighting with the Christian Arab federates on the side of Byzantium against the Muslims.

They appear in two places. (1) at Dūmat al-Jandal[341] together with other federate Arabs such as Kalb, Ghassān, and Tanūkh, and led by Ibn al-Ḥidrijān, who joined forces with al-Ayham, the Ghassānid, against the Muslim commander Iyād ibn Ghanm but was worsted by him; (2) near Zīza,[342] in Trans-Jordan with other federate Arabs—Kalb, Tanūkh, Lakhm, Judām, and Ghassān—against Khālid ibn al-Walīd.

Their final appearance in this period takes place in the north, whither they were presumably moved after the Muslim victories in the south. They are to be found in the *ḥāḏir* (military encampment) of Qinnasrīn/Chalcis, together with the Tanūkhids. When the Muslim commander Abū ʿUbayda asked those in the *ḥāḏir* to accept Islam, the Salīḥids refused and remained Christian.[343]

II

Unlike some other federate Arabs, the Salīḥids, with only one solitary exception, did not attain prominence in Islamic history.[344] This was only natural, since they remained Christian and isolated within the new Islamic order. Besides the obscurity that attended their fortunes, they were also dispersed throughout the Fertile Crescent and possibly in Egypt.

1. The historians and geographers found them settled in various places in Abbāsid times. (*a*) Some of them were to be found in Iraq, living near Kūfa together with part of the tribe of Ṭayy,[345] the old Christian tribe of pre-Islamic times which was most probably an ally of Salīḥ during its federate days.[346] (*b*) Others were to be found in Bilād al-Shām, from al-Balqā to Ḥuwwārīn to al-Zaytūn,[347] and also closer to the Mediterranean, in Laodi-

[341] See Ṭabarī, *Tārīkh*, III, 378.

[342] Ibid., 389.

[343] Balāḏurī, *Futūḥ al-Buldān*, I, 172.

[344] The name Ḥidrijān is attested in one of the famous battles of early Islam, the battle of Ṣiffīn (657) between the two contestants for the caliphate, ʿAli and Muʿāwiya; see M. Hinds, "The Banners and Battlecries of the Arabs at Ṣiffīn," *Al-Abḥāth* (Beirut, 1971), 21. It appears there as the *shiʿār* (sign or battlecry) of an Arab group that looked upon Ḥidrijān as their eponymous hero and sought inspiration by invoking his name. Since the name is so rare and is attested in the onomasticon of the Salīḥids, it is tempting to consider it as such. If so, then a group from Salīḥ may be said to have fought at the battle of Ṣiffīn. The group is listed as one that fought under ʿAli, not Muʿāwiya, but as Hinds observes, the reference to it is "possibly misplaced" (ibid., 30 note 17). The group, then, is likely to have been enrolled in the *jund* system of Umayyad Shām/Oriens, and thus would have fought under Muʿāwiya, not ʿAli.

[345] See Bakrī, *Muʿjam*, I, 203, s.v. Anqira. The account comes from ʿUmar ibn Shabba, a trustworthy writer of the 9th century.

[346] On this *ḥilf* (alliance) between Salīḥ and Ṭayy, see above, 266.

[347] See Hamdānī, *Ṣifat Jazīrat al-ʿArab*, 319.

caea.[348] (*c*) Finally, some Salīḥids by the name of Banū Ḥawtaka ("the sons of Ḥawtaka") were to be found in Egypt.[349]

2. The only Salīḥid known to have risen high in the new order was Usāma ibn Zayd, who was one of the *mawālī* of the Umayyad caliph Muʿāwiya[350] and who served a number of Umayyad rulers. He was put over the *Kharāj* (revenues) of Egypt in the caliphates of al-Walīd and Sulaymān and became the *kātib* (secretary) of Yazīd ibn Abdulmalik.[351] He also served the caliph Hishām in this capacity.[352]

Usāma must have been a remarkable personage to have served four Umayyad caliphs.[353] He clearly was judged a capable administrator, since he was put in charge of the *Kharāj* of such an important province as Egypt. And this is all the more remarkable since he was a Christian. But this was the period of the Umayyads, whose tolerance enabled them to enlist in the service of the new Muslim state the talents of fellow Arabs who had been trained for such important administrative functions or who came from families that had performed such functions in the Byzantine period.[354]

It was not altogether inappropriate that Usāma should have figured so prominently in the Umayyad administration, especially as a *kātib* in Umayyad Oriens, since it was the Salīḥids who most probably gave an impetus to the rise of the Arabic script in pre-Islamic times; at least it was in their period of supremacy in Oriens that that script was developed.[355]

Usāma the Salīḥid was apparently considered an important figure in the

[348] Yaʿqūbī, *Kitāb al-Buldān*, BGA, VII, 324–25.

[349] Ibn Durayd, *Ishtiqāq*, 546. Apparently their descendants are still living in Egypt. The editor of *Ishtiqāq*, ʿA. Hārūn, writing in 1958, says that there is a village near Aswān in Egypt which has the name al-Ḥawātika; ibid., note 1. But this depends on whether a word in the manuscript of Hishām al-Kalbī should be read Miṣr (Egypt) or Muḍar (the tribal group in Arabia); see below, Sec. VIII note 376.

[350] For references to his serving the various Umayyad caliphs, see Muḥammad al-Jahshiyārī, *Al-Wuzarāʾ wa al-Kuttāb*, ed. M. Saqqā, I. Abyārī, and A. Shalabī (Cairo, 1938), 51–52, 56. His Salīḥid origin cannot be doubted, since it is attested by the earliest sources, such as Jahshiyārī and Masʿūdī; hence his "Tanūkhid" origin as stated in Taghrī Birdī, a very late writer, cannot be accepted; ibid., 51, note 4. His description as a *mawlā* (client) of Muʿāwiya must *not* be understood, of course, in the sense of *mawla ʿatāqa* (ibid., 42), a *mawla* who was freed after being a slave, but one who affiliated himself out of loyalty with the Umayyad Muʿāwiya, who was known for his interest in the service of the Christian Arabs and who himself married a Christian lady from Kalb, the mother of his son and successor, Yazīd.

[351] On *kharāj*, see *EI*, s.v. Kharaj. Presumably *kharāj* in this context is elliptical for *dīwān al-Kharāj*, "the bureau of revenue."

[352] The information comes from Masʿūdī, *Al-Tanbīh wa al-Ishrāf*, ed. ʿA. al-Ṣāwī (Cairo, 1938), 279.

[353] His durability in the service of four Umayyad caliphs is the best defense of the integrity of this Salīḥid *kātib* against the calumnies of contemporaries for which, see al-Jahshiyārī, op. cit., 51–52 and 56.

[354] The family of John of Damascus provides an obvious parallel.

[355] See below, Chap. 14, sec. II.

annals of the new Muslim Era, even in Abbāsid times, since he was deemed important enough to be remembered as one of the prominent personages who died[356] in the year 153 after the Hijra (A.D. 770).

VIII. Two Arabic Manuscripts

The fundamental work on Hishām remains that of Werner Caskel. In the first of the two massive volumes which he devoted to the study of Hishām's genealogical work, Caskel described almost all the manuscripts of Hishām's *Jamharat al-Nasab*, explained the transmission of the text, worked out the *stemma,* and discussed later works that depended on Hishām, such as Ibn Hazm's *Jamharat al-Nasab* and Ibn Durayd's *al-Ishtiqāq.*[357] In the second volume he studied the history of the various Arab tribes discussed in Hishām's *Jamharat* and compiled an extensive and detailed *Register,* composed of short entries on the Arab personalities who figure in the work.[358]

Yet a specialized and detailed study, such as the present volume, which concentrates intensively on one group of Arab tribes and their Byzantine connection, cannot depend entirely on Caskel's work. A return to the Arabic manuscripts whence Caskel derived his information and reached his conclusions is imperative. There is no substitute for the Arabic texts themselves, which unfortunately Caskel did not publish. This section is devoted to the examination of the Arabic texts of two manuscripts of Hishām's work which, furthermore, Caskel did not use. As will be evident, Caskel missed certain data, avoided discussing others, and did not give variant or alternative readings of certain passages.

The two manuscripts are: (1) British Library, Additamentum 22376, a manuscript of *Kitāb al-Nasab al-Kabīr,* titled *Kitāb Nasab Maʿadd wa al-Yaman al-Kabīr.*[359] It is possibly another version of the manuscript used by

[356] For this, see *Tārīkh Khalīfa ibn Khayyāṭ*, 426. Khalīfa ibn Khayyāṭ mentions that Usāma was in charge of the *khātam* (seal department) during the caliphate of Yazīd ibn ʿAbdul-Malik (ibid., 335) and of the *karāj* and *jund* (revenue and army pay) during the caliphate of Hishām (ibid., 362).

[357] See *GN*, 82–132. The Iraqi scholar Jawād ʿAlī attempted an evaluation of the manuscripts of the *Jamharat* but did not have all the necessary documents before him. However, his evaluation of British Museum Additamentum 23297 is valuable and has been confirmed by Caskel; see J. ʿAlī, *"Jamharat al-Nasab li Ibn al-Kalbī," Majallat al-Majmaʿ al-ʿIlmī al-ʿIrāqī* (Baghdad, 1950), I, 337–48.

The multivolume work of J. ʿAlī in Arabic on the history of the Arabs before the rise of Islam, *Al-Mufassal fī Tārīkh al-ʿArab Qabl al-Islām*, has not been laid under contribution in this series because it is too general to be profitably used in the writing of its very specialized volumes. The same observation applies to J. S. Trimingham's *Christianity among the Arabs in Pre-Islamic Times*, only occasionally referred to in this volume.

[358] The contribution of his collaborator, G. Sternziok, should not be forgotten. He participated in the preparation of the Register and compiled the Tables of the first volume.

[359] And thus should be distinguished from another manuscript, British Museum Addimentum 23297, which Caskel used: see *GN*, I, 88.

Caskel;[360] it is similarly an Escorial manuscript acquired by the British Museum, but apparently not exactly identical with the one used by Caskel, since it contains information not to be found in his two volumes.[361] (2) A manuscript from the Yahūda section of the Garrett Collection of Arabic Manuscripts in the Princeton University Library, 2864, which became known to the learned world only after Caskel published his work, and possibly after he died.[362] It is a manuscript of Hishām's *Mukhtaṣar Jamharat al-Nasab*, a version of which was used by Caskel.[363] It is from these two manuscripts that the relevant new data for Salīḥ and the other federate tribes are extracted.

Kitāb al-Nasab al-Kabīr
British Library Add. 22376

This is the first of the two manuscripts which remained unknown to Caskel and it has the following valuable data:

1. In the section on Iyād (fol. 21ʳ), there is a reference to an Iyādī poet by the name of ʿAbd al-ʿĀṣ ibn ʿAwf as being in the retinue of the Salīḥid king Dāwūd. The MS reads "he was with Dāwūd al-Lathiq al-Salīḥī, while they[364] were with Tanūkh." ʿAbd al-ʿĀṣ was thus some sort of a laureate or court poet for Dāwūd. This is one of the most precious data provided by this MS of Hishām for the cultural history of the Salīḥids.[365]

2. In the section on the tribe of Kalb (fol. 80ʳ) the MS names one of the two killers of Dāwūd and refers to Dāwūd and his monastery: "and Thaʿlaba[366] is the *fātik* (the assassin) that killed Dāwūd ibn Habūla al-Salīḥī, who

[360] Escorial 1698, which is written in Naskhi script, for which see ibid., 82.

[361] Such as the precious datum on ʿAbd al-ʿĀṣ, the court poet of King Dāwūd. On the other hand, Caskel may have missed this datum or its importance, and so the two manuscripts may be identical. In his Register (*GN*, II, 122), there appears the name ʿAbdal ʿAṣī b. ʿAuf. If this is the Iyādī poet, then Caskel missed the significance of the reference to him, since there is no account of who he is and such accounts appear for the important names in his Register; furthermore, he did not discuss him with Iyād and Salīḥ in *GN*, II, 29–30, 86, respectively.

[362] For a description of this manuscript, see R. Mach, *Catalogue of Arabic Manuscripts (Yahuda Section) in the Garrett Collection, Princeton University Library* (Princeton, 1977), p. 385, no. 4487. The old number of the MS is 2864; see below, Sec. VIII.III.

[363] For the version of the *Mukhtaṣar* from the Turkish library, Ragib Pasha 999, used by Caskel, see *GN*, 198.

[364] "They" in the sentence refers to an Iyādī clan by the name of Zuhr, which Hishām has just discussed, saying that they affiliated themselves with Tanūkh; he repeats the statement on this affiliation while referring to the Iyādī poet. This raises the question of which Tanūkh he refers to—Syrian Tanūkh or Mesopotamian Tanūkh. The presumption is that he refers to Syrian Tanūkh, since the poet became attached to the Salīḥid king, who lived in Oriens. This is a matter of some importance for determining when Iyād went over from Persian Mesopotamia to Byzantine Oriens. The reference in this sentence to the Iyādī poet clearly indicates that at least a part of Iyād was already in Oriens in the 5th century (the group descended from Zuhr to which the poet belonged). The full name of the poet as given in the manuscript is ʿAbd al-ʿAṣ ibn ʿAwf ibn Ghatafān ibn Ahyab ibn Ḍubyān.

[365] See above, note 361.

[366] His full name is given as Thaʿlaba ibn ʿĀmir ibn ʿAwf.

had built a monastery and used to carry the water and the mortar on his back; consequently he was called 'the bedraggled'." Then follow three verses, composed presumably by Thaʿlaba on the occasion. The first one is most important, specifying with two toponyms exactly where Dāwūd was killed—between al-Qurnatayn and Ḥārib.[367]

3. In the section on the tribe of al-Namir ibn Wabara (fol. 91ʳ) the MS names the other killer of Dāwūd, Muʿāwiya, and gives his patronymic, Ibn Ḥujayr. Then follows another patronymic for this second killer, Ibn Qārib; it is not clear how the two are to be related to each other.[368] The clan al-Namir, to which this second killer belonged, was called Mashjaʿa. More important is the information that the MS provides on tribal alliances, namely, that the two clans of al-Namir ibn Wabara—Mashjaʿa and al-Ghawth (the sons of al-Taym ibn al-Namir)—were allies of Kalb. This is important for understanding the circumstances that led to the death of Dāwūd.

4. The section on Salīḥ (fol. 91ᵛ) has two important data. (1) There is first the verse composed by the daughter of Dāwūd on his death, which has various versions. It reads: "Aṣābaka ḏuʾbānu al-halīfayni ʿĀmirin/wa-Mashjaʿata al-awbāshi rahṭi ibni-Qāribi." This translates: "The wolves of the two allies, ʿĀmir and Mashajaʿat, the group of Ibn Qārib, have hit you or felled you down." This version, with the reading *al-ḥalīfayni*, is the best.[369] (2) There are also two verses composed on the death of the Salīḥid tax collector Sabīṭ and his death by the sword of the Ghassānid Jidʿ, a welcome addition to the poetry composed on the fall of the Salīḥids.[370]

[367] Also left out by Caskel, who may have been disinclined to quote the verse because of the difficulty of reading it in the manuscript. The last word is left without the diacritical marks, which must have made the verse untranslatable. But surely the last word should be read "fa-Ḥāribi," a well-known toponym in the Jawlān or Bathaniyya. Besides, the three verses are quoted by Yāqūt in his *Muʿjam* (IV, p. 331), and the last word is clearly "Ḥārib," although in Yāqūt it is preceded by the preposition "bi." Yāqūt was not clear about the location of one of the two toponyms in the verse, al-Qurnatayn. He thought it was the one in the Arabian Peninsula and associated it with the famous battle-day *Yawm al-Qurnatayn*. But this one involving the Salīḥids was in Oriens, as has been explained before.

[368] Possibly this second patronymic is taken from the verse composed by Dāwūd's daughter which mentions the group of Ibn Qārib. However, the reference is to a group called "rahṭ ibn Qārib" to which the second killer belonged. But he may have been endowed with this other patronymic for some reason; see below, App. 6.

[369] Caskel chose a version that reads: *Aṣabaka ḏuʾbānu al-halīfi ibniʿĀmirin*. This version divides "al-ḥalīfayni" (the two allies) into two words, *al-ḥalīfi* and *ibni* (the *ḥalīfi* (ally) *ibni* (the son of); thus Caskel translates "die Wölfe von al-Halīf b. ʿĀmir." He also translates the second hemistich, *wa-Mashjaʿata al-Awbāshi rahti ibn Qāribi*, as "von den zusammengelaufenen Mašǧaʿa, der rahṭ des I. Qarib"; but "Mašgaʿata al-Awbāsh" cannot be translated as "von den zusammengelaufenen Mašǧaʿa," since the pejorative element in *Awbāsh* is lost. He also capitalizes "Al-Ḥalīf," but not "rahṭ," which may suggest that he thought "ḥalīf" was a proper noun, the full name of the killer being al-Halīf ibn ʿĀmir; see Register in *GN*, II, 232, s.v. Dāwūd b. Habāla. This verse and its correct interpretation are discussed below.

[370] They read: *Alam yaʾtīka wa al-anbāʾu tanmī bī-ẓahri al-ghaybi ma lāqā sabītu / Bglq(?) iḏ samā Jidʿun ilayhi wa-Jidʿun fi arūmatihī wasītu*. The first word in the second verse is not

5. In the section on the tribe of Balī (fol. 93ʳ), there is reference to two clans, ʿAdī and Qunfuḏ. The latter is important, since the name of this clan could throw light on one of the monastic establishments in Oriens.

According to al-Bakrī,[371] there is a monastery by the name of Dayr al-Qunfuḏ at Ayla in Palaestina Tertia. Since the tribe of Balī lived near Ayla, the chances are that the Balawī clan of Qunfuḏ built it. There are parallels, such as the building by the tribal group Iyād of monasteries in Ḥīra, near which they lived.[372]

Kitāb Mukhtaṣar al-Jamharat
Princeton 2864

The other manuscript which remained unknown to Caskel, the Princeton version of *Mukhtaṣar al-Jamharat,* provides the following valuable data on Salīḥ and the federate tribes:

1. There is some important background information (fol. 155ᵛ) on the Kalbite killer of Dāwūd. His father was called ʿĀmir; his mother was called Raqāsh and belonged to the tribe of Bahrāʾ. Their children, of whom the killer Thaʿlaba was one, were called Banū Raqāsh ("the sons of Raqāsh"). The Banū ʿĀmir multiplied prodigiously and became a clan, Banū ʿĀmir, within Kalb. The eponym was ʿĀmir al-Akbar.

2. More relevant information on the tribe of Kalb is provided (fol. 156ᵛ). The toponym Qurāqir obviously belonged to them, and this fixes one of the locations where they were settled in pre-Islamic times.[373] They are also referred to as being all Christians with the exception of one clan, MDRT.[374]

3. Background information on the other killer of Dāwūd is also provided (fol. 165ʳ). The larger tribal group to which he belonged was al-Namir ibn Wabara. His own clan was called Mashjaʿat. The eponym of this clan together with al-Ghawth, the eponym of another clan, were the sons of al-Taym

---

clear. It could read "bijilliqa"; if so, this would yield the important fact that the encounter between the Salīḥid tax collector and the Ghassānid killer took place in Jilliq, a mysterious toponym associated with the Ghassānids of the 6th century. This is not far from the area where the two fought, and would, if correct attest the toponym, almost a hundred years before its appearance in the poetry of Hassān ibn Thābit.

[371] Bakrī, *Muʿjam,* II, 593–94. The monastery survived until Umayyad times, judging from the verses quoted by al-Bakrī. His statement that Qunfuḏ was the name of Ayla is, of course, untrue and there is no evidence for it. Bakrī was unable to explain the name and so he suggested it was another name for Ayla, never referred to as such in the sources.

[372] For the monasteries of Aʿwar, al-Sawā, and Qurra, built by Iyād in Ḥīra or its environs, see Yāqūt, *Muʿjam,* II, 499, 517, 526.

[373] The toponym made famous by Khālid ibn Walīd's march from Iraq to Syria before the fateful battle of Yarmūk. It is modern Qulbān (Qarāqir) on the eastern boundary of Wādī Sirḥān for which see Philip K. Hitti, *A History of the Arabs* (London, 1937) p. 149, n. 4.

[374] This word is not entirely clear in the MS. Its consonantal, unvocalized skeleton appears as MDRT. Perhaps it should be vocalized Madarat.

ibn al-Namir. These two clans were allied firmly to Kalb, and this alliance is expressed in very strong terms (*yadun, waḥilfun wa nuṣratun*), a most valuable datum for understanding the circumstances that surrounded Dāwūd's death.

Another clan, collateral with Mashjaʿat and al-Ghawth in its descent from al-Namir, was Labwān ibn al-Namir ibn Wabara. It is reported (fol. 165ᵛ) that it affiliated itself with Salīḥ. This is important information, relevant to the death of Dāwūd. Unfortunately, it is not stated whether the affilation with Salīḥ took place before or after his death and how it may be related to the assault on the Salīḥid king, but it is valuable enough to indicate that friction obtained in the Arab federate camp.

4. The manuscript is not informative on Salīḥ but two readings in its account are welcome. One (fol. 165ᵛ) speaks of Dāwūd as *taʿabbada,* which is not very clear in other accounts. It occurs in the phrase "taʿabbada fi naṣrāniyyatihi": "as a Christian he devoted himself to the worship of God." The first hemistich of the verse composed by Dāwūd's daughter (fol. 166ʳ) reads, "Aṣabatka ḏu'bānu al-ḥalīfi ibni ʿĀmirin." The first word is better Arabic than the "aṣābaka" of other accounts and goes better with the subject, "ḏu'bān". "Al-ḥalīfi," used in this hemistich, is not, as will be argued, as good as "al-ḥalīfayni," used in *Kitāb al-Nasab al-Kabīr* and discussed above.

5. Important data are provided on the tribe of Balī, settled in northern Ḥijāz (fol. 169ʳ). (*a*) One of its tribesmen is called Fārān/Farrān and his son is called Qismīl, two most uncommon names in Arabic which could suggest some biblical influence.[375] (*b*) To Fārān belonged the "maʿdin Farrān" ("the mine of Fārān") in Ḥijāz. (*c*) Some of the tribesmen from Balī used to work as *quyūn* among the tribe of Sulaym, forging iron. (*d*) A story is told of a contest in pre-Islamic times between a Balawī tribesman, called Ḥamza, and Zinbāʿ ibn Rawḥ, father of his more famous son, Rawḥ, from the tribe of Juḏam. The Balawī won because of the many *darāhim* (drachmas) which he strew on the ground. (*e*) One of the Balawīs was born in al-Balqā' evidently in pre-Islamic times, and the Balawīs are associated with the Balqā' and Urdunn (Jordan) in Umayyad times (fols. 168ᵛ–170ʳ).

6. Important data are provided on the tribe of ʿUḏra (fols. 172ʳ–172ᵛ). (*a*) Its chief Rizāḥ, who helped Quṣayy occupy Mecca, appears as a powerful chief among the whole of Quḍāʿa. He writes an important chapter in the history of the tribal structure of Ḥijāz by terminating the affiliation of some tribes[376] with Quḍāʿa and sending some of them outside Ḥijāz. (*b*) A ʿUḏrite

[375] Namely, Ismaʿil (Ishmael) and the toponym associated with him in Genesis, Paran. Arabic does not have the sound "p." Its reading as Farrān and derivation from the verb "farra" is pure guesswork; see Ibn Durayd, *Ishtiqāq*, 550.

[376] The tribes are: Nahd, Jarm, Ḥawtaka, and Banū Rifāʿa ibn ʿUḏra. Rizāḥ is said to have sent (*alḥaqa*) Nahd to Tathlīth, which is a *wādī* in the south, located north of Najrān and

named Hawd̲a, was called the "lord of Ḥijāz" (*rabb al-Ḥijāz*).[377] The manuscript makes clear that he was a pre-Islamic figure, since he was praised by the pre-Islamic poet of the sixth century, al-Nābigha al-D̲ubyāni.[378] The phrase "the lord of Ḥijāz" is striking, and could imply that ʿUd̲ra was the most powerful tribe of Ḥijāz in the fifth century, possibly owing to its Byzantine connection, attested and reflected in the account of Rizāḥ and Quṣayy. (*c*) Rizāh had a brother Ḥunn, the eponym of a famous clan of the ʿUd̲ra tribe. This is a most uncommon name, and since its vocalization is not certain, it might be Ḥann or Ḥannā. It appears in the form Ḥannā in another manuscript of Hishām;[379] the *aliph,* the long a̲, also appears in the name of the father of Buthayna of the seventh century.[380] It is therefore not impossible that this was some version of the Christian name John which was assumed by the Christianized tribe of ʿUd̲ra.[381] (*d*) Finally, there is a short account of the ʿUd̲rī poet ʿUrwa ibn Ḥizām. He is described as *qatīl al-ḥubb,* one who died of love (for ʿAfrā, his paternal cousin); the account concludes "and she is the one for whose sake he died with the permission of God"). Since, according to one tradition, he died in the caliphate of ʿUthmān, he could easily have been born in the late pre-Islamic period.[382]

---

west of al-Faw. The verb *alḥaqa* which can mean "affiliate" must here mean "sent them to," since Tathlīth is not a tribe but a *wādī*. There is some difficulty about Ḥawtaka and whether he sent them to Miṣr (Egypt) or affiliated them with Muḍar (the tribal group). One diacritical mark makes all the difference (below, note 379). The reference to Tathlīth in faraway South Arabia suggests a parallel, that of a place and not a tribe, but Tathlīth is within the Arabian Peninsula, while Egypt is a Byzantine province. However, his Byzantine connection could have enabled him to negotiate sending the tribe away to Egypt, especially if the tribe rebelled against the hegemony of ʿUd̲ra, the client of Byzantium in Ḥijāz and hence indirectly against Byzantium. It is pertinent to remark that another north Ḥijāzi tribe, Thamūd, appears in Egypt and is listed in the *Notitia Dignitatum*, for which see below, Part 3, sec. I.

[377] This ʿUd̲rite figure is mentioned by Ibn Durayd, *Ishtiqāq*, 547, but no indication is given of his *floruit*.

[378] See *Dīwān*, ed. M. Ibrāhīm (Cairo, 1977), 195. The phrase "lord of al-Ḥijāz" appears in this poem, whence Ibn Durayd took it. Its appearance in the poem of a contemporary, al-Nābigha, enhances the value of the phrase.

[379] In the *Muqtaḍab* of Yāqūt for which see, *GN*, I, 160. The form Ḥannā with a long *aliph* at the end of the word, as the name of the brother of Rizāḥ, appears on p. 142 of the *Muqtaḍab*. Also in this MS (ibid.), Ḥawtaka appears affiliated with Muḍar (the tribe) and not Miṣr (Egypt), and Muḍar is clearly written with the diacritical mark.

[380] See Ibn Ḥazm, *Jamharat*, 449, where the name of Buthayna's father appears as Ḥabā, which makes no sense. The chances are that the name "Ḥannā" survived in the tribe of ʿUd̲ra in the 7th century. Buthayna's father appears as the grandson of Hawd̲a ibn ʿAmr, "the lord of Ḥijāz."

[381] It still survives among Christian Arabs as the Arabic version of John. It is pertinent to remark that in this very period it appeared in the form of Ḥannan, assumed by another Arab who was converted to Christianity—the merchant from Najrān, Ḥayyan/Ḥannan on whom, see below, Chap. 13, sec. III.I.

[382] For ʿUrwa, see Sezgin, *GAS*, II, 264–65. The possibility that he was born in the late

The preceding section has identified some valuable data from the two manuscripts on the Salīḥids and also on some other federate tribes, such as Balī and ʿUḏra.

1. There is no doubt that the reading of the verse of Dāwūd's daughter quoted above is correct, but before discussing it it is necessary to refer to another reading, if only to dispose of it and leave no doubt whatsoever about what the correct version is.

The controversial hemistich in the verse is the first one, which speaks of how Dāwūd was felled by a murderer from the clan of ʿĀmir (belonging to the tribe of Kalb). As is often the case, the diacritical marks are left out; hence the possibility of more than one reading for a word. One such case was discussed in the preceding section—*al-ḥalīfayni,* similarly, the word *ḏuʾbān,* which is usually translated "the wolves," can easily be read *dūnāni,* the dual of *dūn,* meaning a lowly, mean person. If so, what follows can only be read *al-ḥalīfu bnuʿĀmirin.* This yields better poetry, since it reflects the contempt of the aristocratic Salīḥid princess toward the plebeian tribesmen who murdered her father, a king. The word *dūnāni* is consonant with the term *awbash* in the second hemistich, which likewise expresses the contempt of the princess toward the "bunch of rabble" who had murdered her father. Attractive as this reading is, the data supplied by Hishām on the historical situation that obtained at the time argues against this interpretation and favors the other. Furthermore, the verse would then lose some of its symmetry, since the nouns in apposition to *dūnāni* would be an individual (Ibn ʿĀmir) in the first hemistich and a group in the second (the clan Mashjaʿat).

The correct reading of the verse must be the one suggested before, which tells the death of Dāwūd at the hands of two allies, the clan of ʿĀmir from Kalb and that of Mashjaʿa from al-Namir ibn Wabara. The order and symmetry in the reference to two clans, in apposition to "the wolves," commends this interpretation, and so does the historical information provided by Hishām on the alliance of Mashjaʿa and ʿĀmir as two *ḥalīfs,* allies.

2. More important than the personalities involved in the murder of the Salīḥid king are the circumstances that attended the act. Hishām is not very specific, but he does provide the precious data on tribal alliances related to this incident. According to him the two clans of al-Namir ibn Wabara, Mashjaʿa and al-Ghawth, were staunch allies of Kalb. He also mentioned that a clan within al-Namir ibn Wabara, Labwān, affiliated itself with Salīḥ. No certainty can be predicated of what exactly happened, but it is possible that

pre-Islamic period is important, since he would thus be the earliest of the ʿUḏrite group of poets whose work has survived. He could thus constitute a link with ʿUḏrite poetry in the pre-Islamic period, and fortify the argument that this type of chaste poetry arose under the stimulus of Christianity.

al-Namir ibn Wabara was divided in its allegiance and alliances, two clans with Kalb and one with Salīḥ, and that this may have led to the little "civil war" in the Arab tribal camp. The chances are that Kalb was also a federate tribe in this period but not under Salīḥ, in spite of the fact that the latter was the dominant federate group in Oriens. Hence the war of the two clans against Salīḥ was not necessarily against Byzantium but was interfederate. Whatever the truth about the causes of the interfederate war turns out to be, the defeat of Dāwūd under these circumstances gives a glimpse of how the federate shield was vulnerable to tribal strife. A faint echo of the image of Salīḥ as the upholder of law and order in Oriens may be detected from two words in the verse. Although the pejorative words *d̲u'bān* (wolves) and *awbash* (rifraff) may reflect the contempt of the bereaved princess toward the murderers of her father, they could also reflect that the two clans were a disorderly, hungry rabble and howling wolves who killed the king who, at least by implication, stood for law and order. Whether the term *al-ḥalīfayni* reflects the fact that the allied relationship involved Salīḥ too remains an open question. In any case, the episode reflects the difficulty of the Salīḥid king in holding the federate tribes together.

The data on Balī and ʿUd̲ra are most valuable and will now be analyzed.

1. It is practically certain that by the fifth century Balī was a Christian tribe moving in the Byzantine orbit. The data collected in the preceding section may be interpreted as follows. (1) Its Christianity is reflected concretely in the monastery of Qunfud̲ in Ayla, and this implies that the tribe had close relations with that Christian center and seat of a bishop. The onomasticon of Balī, with its Fārān and Qismīl also suggests some biblical connection. (2) The mine they were in possession of may explain their importance, since its iron would have been used by the Balawites for making swords. Both the source of iron and the weapons would have made them attractive as federates. (3) The episode of the *darāhim* (drachmas) could suggest that they were also recipients of the *annona foederatica,* which in their case may have been paid money, not in kind. The tribesman Ḥamza may even have been a phylarch in the Balqā' region. (4) Their association with the Balqā' in pre-Islamic times implies that at least some of them were actually within the *limes,* since this was part of the Provincia Arabia. This may be confirmed by the fact that the commander of the Arab federates at the battle of Mu'ta against the Muslim army was one of the Balī, a commander by the name of Mālik.[383]

[383] See *BAFOC*, 384. It is of interest to note that Balī (or parts of it) in later times settled in the Islamic Occident, in Andalusia north of Cordova; Ibn Ḥazm, *Jamharat*, 443. He also adds that they speak only Arabic and not Latin, and are very hospitable.

Key

Photographs of some of the folios of the two manuscripts discussed in the preceding section follow. It is desirable to present them since these two manuscripts have not been used in the preparation of what so far has appeared in print of Hishām's *Jamharat*. Number I is from the British Library, Ms. Add. 22376 (by permission of the British Library); numbers II–V are from Princeton University Library, the Garrett Collection of Arabic Manuscripts, Yahūda Section, Ms. 2864 (by permission of Princeton University Library).

I. Fol. 21^r is the source for ʿAbd al-ʿĀṣ, the "poet laureate" of the Salīḥid king Dāwūd (above, 307).

II. Fol. 156^v documents the wide diffusion of Christianity among members of the Kalb tribe (above, 309).

III. Fol. 165^r is the source for the alliance of two clans from al-Namir ibn Wabara with Kalb, which brought about the downfall of Dāwūd (above, 309–10).

IV–V. Fols. 165^v–166^r: these two consecutive pages contain the account of Dāwūd's Christianity, his *dayr*, and his death (above, 257–62). On the first page is the reference to the tribal structure of the federate shield, involving Labwān and Salīḥ (above, 309–10).

داوود واسمه حارثه بن حمران (وح) بن بحر بن عصلم بن مهلان بن
منيه بن حذاقه بن زهر بن اياد واخواه مازيه ومن بني اميه بن حذاقه
الذي ينسب اليه دير الاعور وموضع الذي يقول ابو داوود و
دار الداروون ... اله ... ل ... داراً
ومنهم الذي ينسب اليه دير قره و دير السوا و ولد الشلك بن
زهر ذبيان والوس و الحرث منهم عبد العاص بن عوف بن غطفان بن
اميه بن ذبيان الشاعر كان مع داود اللتف الساحي وهم في تنوخ
وولد دعمي بن اياد نزار افصى و غيلان امهما رمله بنت اشذ بن ربيعه
فولد افصى بن دعمي يقدم و يرد والحرث امهم زينب بنت غيلان و
امها عمره بنت طابخه بن خندف و يقال ليرد و غيلان تماماً
اياد فولد الحرث بن افصى صبح و ركنه و محلاً وهم في تنوخ
فولد ركنه بن الحرث معرض و ولد صبح بن الحرث بن افصى والحرث
من يقدم علي بن الحرث بن مرب بن مردول ومنهم الحر بن ثابت بن
عبد الله بن ثابت بن جسان و ولد يقدم بن افصى عود مناه
و منصور وابادوس و مالك امهم اسما بنت عميره بن اسد بن ربيعه
بن نزار فولد منصور بن يقدم النبيت و عمرو و
سعد (٨٥) فولد النبيت بن منصور و منبه وهو النعمن و
ساهره ولحيان فولد منبه بن النبيت قسي وهو ثقيف فيما
يقال والله اعلم وكنه وثعلبه والحرث و الحموث ومالك ومنهم
اميه بنت سعد بن هذيل فمن ينسب ثقيف الي اياد فهذا نسبهم
ومن نسبهم الي قيس فهو قسي بن منبه بن بكر بن هوازن يقولون
كانت اميه عند منبه بن النبيت فتزوجها منبه بن بكر فجات بقسي
معها من الايادي و صبح بن الحرث بن منبه بن النبيت في تنوخ
و ولد ابودوس بن يقدم بن افصى بن دعمي بن اياد جدي منهم
قس بن ساعده بن عمرو بن شمر بن عدي بن مالك بن جدي صاحب
الكلام بعكاظ و ولد عود مناه بن يقدم بن افصى بن دعمي بن اياد
الطمثان و بجل و ذهل فولد الطمثان بن عود مناه و ايله و عمرو

ابن لام الطائي تذكر قول ابي عياش الكلبي

رماحي كبلت بشر الاوس · ولولا آل من سعدى لطاحا ·

فنحن الوالبية يوم بشير · ولا تذكر لوالبة الجلاحا ·

واخوه عبد عمرو واسمه بكر وفد على النبي صلى الله عليه وسلم ومن

ولده الابرش واسمه سعيد بن الوليد بن عبد عمرو بن جبلة

صاحب هشام بن عبد الملك والنعمن بن جبلة وهو ابو الشقرا

الذي مدحه نابغة الذبياني

ولولا ابو الشقراء مازال ماتح · يعالج خطافا باحدى الجرائر

قال الكلبي اذا اختصمت بنو القين وكلب في قراقر

لكل يد عمه فقال عبد الملك اليس النابغة الذي يقول

يظل الاماء يبتدرن قديحها · كما ابتدرت كلب مياه قراقر ·

يعني بالكلب بهذا البيت ومن بني الجلاح جهبل بن سيف

يسكنون حضرموت وجهبل الذي ذهب بموت النبي صلى الله

عليه وسلم الى حضرموت فنعاه لهم وله يقول امرء القيس بن عابس الكندي

شمت البغايا يوم اعلن جهبل · بنعي احمد النبي المهتدي ·

فخضبن بطون وعصعص بعض ابنا الحارث بن عوف بن عامر

الاكبر هو ولاء بنوا شحة وهي امراة من ولد عامر

المذمم بن عوف بن عامر الاكبر بن عوف مالك وهو

الرماح سمي بذلك لطول رجليه وقد راس وعوف

وهو الشغا وامهما عدسة بنت مالك بن عامر بن عوف

بها يعرفون وابوهما عامر المذمم المذكور ومن اخوتهما

ابو عمرو والحارث ابنا مدرة اختهما بها يعرفون يعني

اخت عدسة وكلب اسلم كلها غير مدرة كانوا

نصارى من بني بكر بن عامر المذمم بن عوف بن عامر الاكبر

حملة وصلة ابنا بغثر كانا من اشراف اهل الشام

ابن امرئ القيس بن ثعلبة بن مالك ايضا فمن بني زبان الاطنابة
بنت قيس ام عمرو بن الاطنابة الشاعر واخوها الارقم
ابن قيس بن شهاب بن حارثة بن سعد بن زبان كان
فارسا وهو الذي اسر نابغة بني ذبيان وابنة العايذ
بنت الارقم ام اخي نزار بن شريك ومن بني كنانة
ابن القين ابو الطمحان الشاعر وهو حنظلة بن الشرقي
وابو عبد الرحمن وهو ذو الشكوة كان جسيما قاتل يوم
اجنادين مع ابي عبيدة بن الجراح فقتل ثمانية من الروم
فقال ابو عبيدة رضي الله عنه
افعل كفعل الضخم من قضاعه في طاعة الله ونعم الطاعه
قال ابو عبد الرحمن المدني انما سمي ذا الشكوة لانه كانت تكون
معه شكوة اذا قاتل ومنهم مليكة بنت امرئ القيس
كانت تلقب البرصا لبياضها تزوجها الطفيل بن مالك
ابن جعفر بن كلاب وولدت له عمرا وعبد الله ويزيد
يقال لولدها بنو القينية يقال انها سبية ولها حديث
ومن بني النمر وبرة مشجعة بطن والغوث بطن
ابنا التيم بن النمر وهما بطنان عظيمان مع كلب يد واحد
ونصرة وعاملة بطن ابن التيم كانوا اشم درجوا
عتيك بطن ابن امرئ مناة بن مشجعة البطن وعوف
وصعب بطنان ابنا امرئ مناة عامر وذهل وحبيب
بطون كلهم وهم بنو عتيك ومن بني مشجعة افلح
ابن يعبوب الشاعر الذي يقول لزهير بن معوية
قضاعة بن مالك بن حمير تيتة بن النمر بن وبرة
دخلوا في بني تغلب وهم على نسبهم وعاضرة بن النمر
... بن النمر دخلوا في سليم بن منصور يقولون عاضرة

وعانية بعا سليم ولبوان بن النمر دخلوا في سليح ومن
عوف شجعة المقدم ذكره الجلندح بن حضرمي الشاعر
والغربي بن مسعدة الشاعر هؤلاء بنو التيم بن النمر
وولد خشين بن النمر شترا وفيه العدد والشلم مكلبيين قليل
فمن بني مر ابو ثعلبة وهو الاشتر بن جرهم بايع رسول الله
صلى الله عليه وسلم بيعة الرضوان وضرب له بسهم يوم خيبر
وارسله الى قومه فاسلموا واخوه عمرو بن جرهم اسلم على
عهد النبي صلى الله عليه وسلم وولد جعثمة بن النمر ام مناة
وسبيعا دخل سبيع في خزاعة على نسب فيهم فولد ام
مناة اللبوة فولد اللبوة عصية دخلوا في بني جشم
ابن معوية بن بكر بن هوازن منهم رهط ابي الاحوص العقيلي
الذي يروي عن عبد الله بن مسعود واسم ابي الاحوص عوف
ابن مالك فولد عصية كعبا فولد كعب جشم بن معوية على
كعب فتزوج ابنته ماوية فولدت لجشم غنمة وعديا
وعامرا انتقلوا عصية بن جشم هؤلاء بنو النمر بن
وبرة بن تغلب بن حلوان بن عمران بن الحاف بن قضاعة
نسب سليح فولد سليح بن حلوان
سعدا وناسكا والنخع بن صليح وضعفة ومراجا
فولد سعد حماطة وهو ضجعم بطن وهم الضجاعمة وكانوا
الملوك بالشام قبل غسان منهم زياد بن هبولة بن
عمرو بن عوف بن ضجعم الذي اغار على حجر آكل المرار
وداود اللثق بن هبالة اخي هبولة بن عمرو بن عوف
ابن ضجعم وكان ملكا يغير فتنصر وكره الدماء وتعبد
فبنى ابنه فيلثق شابه وقال لا اريد ان يعينني
احد بغشيتي اللثق فلما كره الدماء والقتل ضعف امره

وجعلوا يخيرون عليه حتى قتله ثعلبة العايك بن عامر
الاكبر بن وايل بن شجعة بن التيم بن النمر بن وبرة
فقالت بنت داود
اصابتك ذو بان الحليف بن عامر ، وشجعة الآباء من هاطر بن قارب
ومنهم الحارث بن مندلة بن حوشة بن عمرو بن عوف
ابن ضجعم الذي يقول له عامر بن جوين الطائي
فو الله لا اعطي مليكا ظلامة ، ولا سوقة حتى يؤوب ابن مندله
حفظي مندلة غير معجمة عن ابي عمرو وابي عبيدة
والمنذر بن بسيط بن عمرو بن ضجعم الذي قتله جذع
ابن عمرو الغساني والضيزن بن معوية بن الاجرام
ابن سعد بن سليح كان ملكا بالجزيرة وولدت ابنته
في بني السفاح وهي النضيرة بنت السفاح وهي صاحبة
الحضر واليهم ينسب مرج الضيازن بالجزيرة
هؤلاء بنو سليح بن حلوان
نسب جرم ولد زبان وهو علاف بن
حلوان جرما بطن وعوفا وهو كان بطن وناجية
بطن وقدامة فجدة ولد بجدة فسمي جدة ابنا
جرم وولد قدامة الاعجب فطرودا فولد الاعجب
الهون وحزما بطن ولاينا بطن وولد حرب بن
حرب بهم وولد الهون بعد ذلك حين هانت حرب بهم
ولانت وولد لابن حين اصطلحوا وتلاءم امرهم
فسمي كل بذلك فمن بني حرب بن الاعجب العدر
الشاعر بن تمام بن حسيل وقد يك الشاعر بن
قرة بن حنظلة بن خصيفة سبيلة بطن وعمارة
ابنا الهون بن الاعجب شيع بطن بن عميرة بن الهون

منهم ادبس

2. More important than Balī is ʿUdra, both culturally[384] and politically, and its importance in this century turns largely around the personality of Rizāḥ. The interpretation of his historical role must be related to two significant events in which he actively participated—his dealings with four tribal groups in western Arabia, described above, and his support of Quṣayy's occupation of Mecca.

a. Rizāḥ must have been a very powerful and influential chief to have succeeded in changing the affiliation of four tribes and sending one of them as far as Tathlīth[385] in the South. What was behind this dispersion of four tribes so far and wide? It is possible that these tribes united together in some political and military action against ʿUdra or Byzantium,[386] perhaps during the Persian War of the reign of Theodosius II. The Arab *foederati* of Persia, the Lakhmids, may have stirred up some trouble for Byzantium in Ḥijāz, and Rizāḥ, Byzantium's ally, punished this confederation of hostile tribes by dispersing them. It may also have been related to an entirely different circumstance, namely, the dispersion of the Azd, the large and powerful South Arabian tribal group. Rizāḥ may have seen in them a threat to ʿUdra and its group of tribes in Ḥijāz. Whatever the truth behind the dispersion of these tribes, it was an important event in the history of the Ḥijāz and its tribal structure and it clearly reflects the power of the ʿUdrite chief.

b. The elucidation of the role and position of Rizāḥ sheds more light on what turned out to be the more important event historically, the assistance he extended to Quṣayy for the occupation of Mecca; within the context of Rizāḥ's wide-ranging operations in Ḥijāz, the two events are mutually illuminating. In addition to helping his half-brother Quṣayy, Rizāḥ must have been aware of the intrusion of the Azd group into Mecca, represented by the Azdite tribe of Khuzāʿa. Hence his willingness to help Quṣayy dislodge it from its dominant position in Mecca and wrest the custodianship of the Kaʿba from its hand. The conquest of Mecca meant the extension of ʿUdra's influence and, indirectly, that of Byzantium, south of Wādī al-Qurā into Mecca. This practically gave Rizāḥ control of Ḥijāz, since he and his half-brother were in control of some of the most important centers of both halves of the Ḥijāz. Hence the application of the term Rabb al-Ḥijāz, "the lord of Ḥijāz," to the sixth-century ʿUdrite figure Hawda ibn ʿAmr becomes intelligible. It represented

384 Its importance in this sphere is discussed below, Chap. 14, sec. IV.B.IV.

385 It would be remarkable indeed if the units of Thamudeni in the *ND*; stationed in Egypt were none other than the Ḥawtaka tribe he sent to Egypt according to one reading of the manuscript; above, note 376.

386 In much the same way that the two clans of ʿĀmir and Mashjaʿa had rebelled against Dāwūd or fought with him.

an ʿUḏrite hegemony in Ḥijāz, the foundation of which was laid down by Rizāḥ in the fifth century.[387]

Set within this context, the episode of Quṣayy's conquest of Mecca becomes more intelligible and also credible, both militarily and culturally. Rizāḥ, the chief of the Qudāʿa group, was alarmed by the intrusion of the Azd from South Arabia into Ḥijāz. Consequently, he enthusiastically supported his half-brother in the conquest of Mecca and its emancipation from the hands of this intrusive group.[388] Culturally, too, the influence of Rizāḥ and ʿUḏra on Quṣayy becomes clearer. Rizāḥ was not the only half-brother of Quṣayy. There was Ḥunn/Ḥann, too. If his name turns out to be Christian, Quṣayy most probably was influenced by monotheistic ideas during his stay among the tribe which had been converted to Christianity and among others in the north such as Balī which, as has been suggested, could have even retained the biblical name Fārān. The verses ascribed to Quṣayy in which he refers to the two Ishmaelite tribes, Qaydar and Nabīt, cannot then be rejected outright as unauthentic.[389]

From the preceding analysis, Rizāḥ emerges as an important factor in the history of Ḥijāz and, indeed, in western Arabia in the first half of the fifth century.[390]

Appendix I

Further Observations on the Salīḥids in Trans-Jordan

The toponymy and the tribal onomasticon of present-day Jordan confirm what has been established on the Salīḥids, especially their occupation of the central sector of the Provincia Arabia, including Moabitis.[1]

Traces of the Salīḥids have survived in the name of a village, al-Salīḥī, which lies twenty kilometers to the northwest of Amman/Philadelphia on the way to Jarash/Gerasa. Northeast of al-Salīḥī there is a spring, by the name of ʿAyn al-Salīḥi. To the east of the village, there is a valley (*wādī*) by the name of Wādī al-Salīḥī.

Nelson Glueck is, perhaps, the only scholar who has noticed this area. In his

[387] They were so powerful militarily that they beat the Ghassānids (who were Azdite) in the 6th century, as can be understood from a poem by al-Nābigha for which, see Nöldeke, *GF*, 38. ʿUḏra had fought the Khuzāʿa (Azdite, too) in the 5th century in Mecca.

[388] His dispatch of the tribe of Nahd to Tathlīth in the south may have been in response to the movement of the Azd from the south to the north.

[389] On Quṣayy and his verses, see below, Chap. 13, sec. II note 101.

[390] It is not altogether incredible that the trip to Constantinople of Ḥayyān/Ḥannān, the merchant from Najrān, was arranged by Rizāḥ, especially if it came chronologically after Quṣayy's conquest of Mecca through the assistance rendered him by Rizāḥa. Ḥayyan would have heard of the great event that took place in Mecca and of Rizāḥ's influence with Byzantium; on Ḥannān, see below, Chap. 13, sec. III.1.

[1] I should like to thank warmly the following friends and colleagues who have supplied me with information and photographs: Dr. Ra'ūf Abujaber, Dr. Fawzi Zayadine, Mr. Tawfik Kawar, and Mrs. Wadad Kawar.

survey of Trans-Jordan,[2] the name al-Salīḥī appears as "eṣ-Ṣelīḥī" and, of course, he was unaware of the historical significance of the name and that it goes back to pre-Islamic times. Important is his statement that "several Roman, and numerous Byzantine and mediaeval Arabic sherds were picked up there." The "powerful spring" he refers to must be the explanation of the continuous habitation of the region throughout the ages.

Not far from these places associated with the Salīḥids lives a tribal group by the name of al-Salīḥāt, pronounced in the conversational Arabic of Jordan as Sleiḥāt.[3] The name is so uncommon that it can in this case be only the Salīḥīs/Salīḥids, especially as the present-day tribal group in Jordan occupies roughly the same area that the Salīḥids of Byzantine times occupied in the Provincia Arabia.

That they are descendants of the Salīḥids of pre-Islamic times derives considerable support from their former Christianity. This can be established when statements in the sources on such groups as al-Abbad, al-Fqaha, Mheirat, and Sleiḥāt are put together and related to one another.[4]

It has been pointed out that with the exception of the Decapolis the Provincia Arabia was inhabited by Arabs—the descendants of the Nabataeans. And it was within this Arab area of the Provincia that the Salīḥids were settled, in the central sector.

The Arab character of this sector is supported by archeological finds. Inscriptions of the region reveal Arab names.[5] But more important than the appearance of mere names on gravestones is another type of evidence, which suggests that the Arabs of the region participated in the artistic flowering which the region witnessed in the sixth century—the splendid mosaics of the Madaba region, which may, not inappropriately, be called "mosaic country." Especially relevant are the following data, made available by archeology:

1. In the church of St. George in the town of Nebo, which lies to the east of the Dead Sea and to the west of Madaba, an Arabic inscription consisting of one word was

[2] See N. Glueck, "Explorations in Eastern Palestine, III," *The Annual of the American Schools of Oriental Research* 18–19 (1939), 201.

[3] The principal source for the tribal groups of Jordan is a work by the first commander of the Arab Legion in Jordan, Frederick G. Peake, better known as Peake Pasha; see his *History and Tribes of Jordan* (Miami, 1958); there is an Arabic translation of this work with additional data; see *Tārīkh Sharq al-Urdunn wa Qabā'ilihā*, trans. B. Tūqān (Jerusalem, n.d.).

[4] The relevant data for this is on p. 166 of Peake Pasha's book, mentioned in the preceding footnote. These data involve al-Abbad, which are most likely to be al-ʿIbād, the well-known name for the Christians (especially of Ḥīra) before the rise of Islam. Subdivisions of al-Abbad are many, and there are two that are especially relevant: Mheirat and Sleiḥat. The former is said to have been descended from a Christian ancestor before they were converted to Islam. If so, their relatives, the Sleiḥat, must also have been Christian. The Christianity of the Mheirat is still remembered but that of the Sleiḥat is not, presumably because the latter had converted earlier. The Arabic translator of Peake Pasha's book adds (p. 263) some relevant material to the effect that the Bedouins continue till the present day to taunt the Mheirat.

[5] See, for example, F.-M. Abel, "Mélanges," *RB* 36 (1927), 567; and A. Alt, "Zwölf christliche Grabsteine aus Moab," *ZDPV* 51 (1928), 223–25.

found in the mosaic floor of the church: it reads "bi-salām," "in peace."[6] The construction of the church goes back to the first half of the sixth century.

2. In 1986 Fr. M. Piccirillo excavated Mayfaʿa, present-day Umm al-Rasas, which lies 25 kilometers southeast of Madaba. He uncovered the remains of two churches with splendid mosaic floors. (*a*) The first church was dedicated in 587, during the episcopate of Bishop Sergius, and was mosaicized by the priest Procopius. It is referred to by its excavator as "The Church of Bishop Sergius." Arab figures with Arab names appear in the mosaics as benefactors of the church: the son of Ouadia, Baricha, Soleos (possibly Zangon), and Robab. In one of the inscriptions appear the Arabic names Soleos, Casiseos, Abdalos, and Obedos.[7] (*b*) The second church is that of St. Stephen. This is the much more important of the two churches.[8] Among other things, it has a mosaic map comparable to that of the famous Madaba mosaic map. Although its importance is diminished in the context of this volume by its late eighth-century date, it does have some relevant data. For one thing, the name of the mosaicist is preserved—Staurachius, from Ḥesban, the son of Zada.[9] Also, the inscriptions contain many Arabic names: Abdela Ouaias, Obedou, Abosobeos, Alafa, and Gomela.[10]

Thus archeology confirms the Arab character of the region[11] and the participation of the Arabs in its artistic activity as benefactors, priests, and artists. This confirmation raises the question of *federate* Arab participation, especially in the fifth century. The church in the town of Nebo and the church of Bishop Sergius in Mayfaʿa

[6] For this inscription and the dating of the church, see S. J. Saller and B. Bagatti, *The Town of Nebo*, Publications of the Studium Biblicum Franciscanum (Jerusalem, 1949), 171–72.

The inscription is certainly Arabic and this is supported by the fact that the Arabic script is well attested in the 6th century in Oriens and that this is an ethnically Arab area. So it was understood by the two authors of *The Town of Nebo*. J. Milik's contention that it is Christian-Palestinian-Aramaic is therefore unjustified and has been rejected by others, including A. Knauf; see "Bemerkungen zur frühen Geschichte der arabischen Orthographie," *Orientalia* 53 (1984), 456–58 and 457 note 11.

It is relevant in this connection to mention that a monk and priest of the town of Nebo was an Arab by the name of Qayyoum (Kaioum). This, it is true, goes back to the 8th century, but the ethnic character of the town is not likely to have changed from the 6th century. For this reference to the Arab priest see p. 24 of Piccirillo's work, cited in the next note.

[7] See M. Piccirillo, *Um er-Rasas Kastron Mefaa in Giordania*, Suppl. to "La Terra Santa," Nov.–Dec. 1986 (Jerusalem, 1986), 9, 20.

[8] For this church, see Piccirillo, op. cit., 20 ff. The author considers its importance comparable to that of the Madaba church, in which was found the famous mosaic map; for the author's evaluation of the importance and significance of his finds at Mayfaʿa, see ibid., 22, 32.

[9] Ibid., 22. "Zada" is clearly Arabic Zayd or some version of it. The diphthong in the original Arabic name is not reflected in the Greek transliteration; for other Greek versions of Zayd as Ζήτ or Ζήδ, see Shahîd, "The Conference of Ramla," 117, 118.

[10] Ibid., 28.

[11] Thus confirming that the ethnic identity of the Nabataean Arabs of the provincia is masked by their assumption of Christian and Graeco-Roman names, as was argued in *RA*. The Arab character of Mayfaʿa in pre-Islamic times was known to the Arab geographers such as al-Bakrī, as is noted by Piccirillo; see op. cit., 30, also al-Bakrī, *Muʿjam* IV, 1284–85.

are churches of the sixth century, the period not of Salīḥid ascendancy but that of the Ghassānids, who also occupied this region. But the Salīḥids persisted there even after they ceased to be the dominant federate group and, what is more, they wrote an important chapter in the cultural life of the Arabs in Oriens. It is, therefore, not unlikely that this artistic activity goes back to the fifth century, when the Salīḥids flourished in this region.

This conclusion could receive considerable support from the data on the other church in Mayfaʿa, that of St. Stephen. This is a church of the eighth century, but the artistic tradition that it represents goes back to the sixth, as is clearly suggested by the church of Bishop Sergius. Had it not been for the discovery of the church of the sixth century, this would have been only an inference; the successful exploration of Mayfaʿa has made this conclusion certain. But the exciting discoveries in Mayfaʿa represent the results of only the first campaign of excavations in 1986. Future campaigns will most probably reveal more evidence, possibly going back to previous centuries, including the fifth. The Salīḥids, could have participated in the artistic life of the region and may even have given it an impetus through their patronage, as the Ghassānids of the sixth century were to do on a much larger scale.

Appendix II

Umm al-Jimāl

Something was said in the preceding volume on Umm al-Jimāl,[1] the Arab town in the northern part of the Provincia Arabia. Since then some studies on this site have appeared[2] and they raise a question that may appropriately be discussed in an appendix to Salīḥid toponymy.

In one of these studies, reference is made to the Arabic inscription found at Umm al-Jimāl (known as Umm al-Jimāl II) which refers to the tribe of Banū ʿAmr. The author suggests that these were the Ghassānids of the sixth century who established a presence in Umm al-Jimāl.[3] This is possible, although a patronymic such as Banū ʿAmr, involving the very distant Ghassānid ancestor ʿAmr is unlikely, since in the sixth century these were divided into the smaller clans known as Banū Jafna, Āl-Imruʾal-Qays, and Banū Thaʿlaba.

An alternative interpretation of the patronymic could relate this tribal group to the Salīḥids and the Zokomids among whom were also ʿAmrids, (Banū ʿAmr).[4] The Salīḥids were settled in the Provincia Arabia where Umm al-Jimāl was located, and they are represented till the present day by two toponyms—the village al-Salīḥī and the Wādī al-Salīḥī near Amman in Jordan.[5] So it is possible that the Banū ʿAmr referred to in this Arabic inscription were the Salīḥids, but this is far from certain.

[1] See *BAFOC*, 415–16.

[2] See E. A. Knauf, "Umm El-Jimāl: An Arab Town in Antiquity," *RB* 91 (1984), 576–86; and B. De Vries, *Umm El-Jimal in the First Three Centuries A.D.*, British Archaeological Reports Monograph 8 (Oxford, 1986), 227–41.

[3] E. A. Knauf, op. cit., 583.

[4] See above, Sec. III.I.A.

[5] See above, App. I.

The author further relates the Banū ʿAmr of the Umm al-Jimāl inscription to the l-ʿAmrat, the tribal group that appears in many of the Safaitic inscriptions in northern Jordan, suggesting that the later form ʿAmrat is a plural of ʿAmr.[6]

This, too, is possible. An alternative interpretation of ʿAmrat in these inscriptions is to construe ʿAmrat as a feminine singular[7] rather than a masculine plural. Matriarchies were not unknown to the Arabs of this period[8] and Queen Mavia was a well-known figure in the annals of Arab-Byzantine relations in the fourth century.

The author also draws attention to the fact that an Arab tribe, also by the name Banū ʿAmr (υἱοὶ Ἄμβϱ(ε)ι), lived in the town of Madaba[9] as early as the second century B.C. Madaba was not one of the Greek cities of the Decapolis; hence the Semitic and Arab elements in it were strong, going back to biblical times, and the reference to Banū ʿAmr in it confirms its Arab and Semitic character.

Appendix III

The *Jamharat*

After this manuscript was completed I was able to consult a portion of Hishām's *Jamharat* in printed form. It consisted of the first part of the *Jamharat*, devoted principally to the genealogy of Quraysh, the tribe of the Prophet Muḥammad, but not to any of the tribes of *foederati* that are treated in *BAFIC* and for which I had to consult the manuscript of the *Jamharat* in its entirety. This first portion of the *Jamharat* appeared in two different editions, both published in 1983, in Damascus and Kuwait.[1] It is hoped that the remaining portion of the *Jamharat* will appear in print before long.[2] Both editions are based on the manuscripts of the *Jamharat* that W. Caskel used, but neither editor is aware of the Princeton manuscript, the *Mukhtaṣar*, which was consulted for the writing of the section "Two Arabic Manuscripts" in this volume.

An important datum may be noted in the printed edition of the *Jamharat*. While speaking of Lu'ayy, one of the ancestors of the Prophet, Hishām says that he had a brother called Taym, who was a *kāhin*.[3] This is significant, and may be related to what has been said on the possibility that the name Lu'ayy had a religious connotation, which recalls epigraphic *lawī'*, *lawī'at*.[4] This conclusion is now fortified by the

[6] E. A. Knauf, op. cit., 584, and the article of J. T. Milik, "La tribu des Bani ʿAmrat en Jourdanie de l'époque grecque et romaine," *ADAJ* 24 (1980), 41–54.

[7] The personal name ʿAmrat is attested in the Arabic onomasticon of pre-Islamic times. It is tantalizing to think that ʿAmrat in Qusayr ʿAmra, the famous Jordanian structure, is the name of an Arab woman.

[8] See *BAFOC*, 196 note 17.

[9] Knauf, op. cit., 584.

[1] *Jamharat al-Nasab*, I, ed. ʿAbd al-Sattār Farrāj (Kuwait, 1983); *Jamharat al-Nasab*, ed. Mahmud F. al-ʿAẓm (Damascus, 1983). I am very grateful to Dr. Ṣalāḥ Hāshim for making his own copy of the former available to me.

[2] It is unfortunate that the editor of the Kuwait *Jamharat* has died; hopefully this will not interfere with the completion of that edition.

[3] See *Jamharat* (Kuwait ed.), 81.

[4] See below, Chap. 13, sec. II note 91.

new datum from Hishām on his brother Taym. Hishām says he was a *kāhin*, which may be translated either as "priest" or "soothsayer." Furthermore, Taym is a theophoric name: before it experienced ellipsis, it was Taym-Allāh or Taym-Allāt.

Hishām also speaks of one of his own ancestors, ʿAbd al-ʿUzzā, who visited one of the Ghassānids and brought some horses with him as a present.[5] The datum may be added to others on the relations between Ghassān and Kalb, the tribe of Hishām.

There is also a tantalizing reference to the *barīd* (Latin *veredi*), horses. One of the sons of ʿAbd Manāf was called Abū Qays and he is described as *rākib al-barīd*, "the one who mounts the post."[6] *Barīd* is one of the Latin words that entered Arabic in pre-Islamic times from the language of the Roman imperial administration, from the institution of the *cursus publicus*, the state post.[7] It is not clear whether *barīd* in this phrase is the imperial Byzantine one or the Meccan. It is not impossible that Abū Qays may have worked for the *cursus publicus* in this Arabian region of indirect Roman rule and influence, which extended deep into the south of Ḥijāz. It is more likely that Abū Qays used the *cursus publicus* by imperial permission in order to transact some business within the empire related to Meccan-Byzantine relations. In the sixth century, Imru' al-Qays, the pre-Islamic poet, mentions in one of his poems that he had mounted the imperial *barīd* on his journey to Constantinople; he uses the phrase *wa-rakibtu al-barīda*[8] ("and I mounted the *barīd*"), employing the same verb from which is derived *rākib*, as in the phrase *rākib al-barīd*, applied to Abū Qays. The possibility that the imperial post reached Mecca may not be remote when the episode of ʿUthmān ibn al-Ḥuwayrith is examined. The account speaks of a letter sent by the emperor to Mecca and also that the emperor had ʿUthmān ride a mule on which there was a golden saddle;[9] this sixth-century figure in the history of Meccan-Byzantine relations will be discussed in *BASIC*. It is noteworthy that Abū Qays was the brother of the maternal grandfather of the Prophet Muḥammad, who before his Call had led the caravans for fifteen years in Ḥijāz, into Palaestina Tertia, and the Provincia Arabia.

This attestation of *barīd* (*veredi*) recalls another loanword in pre-Islamic Arabic which reached it from the language of the imperial administration, namely, Greek ζωγραφία, which also reached Mecca in this period.[10]

[5] See *Jamharat* (Kuwait ed.), 28. "Horses" (*afrāsan*) appears as "bows" (*aqwāsan*) in the text. But surely the former reading is the correct one, and so it is in Ṭabarī, *Tārīkh*, II, 66. The editor has misread *afrāsan* as *aqwāsan*; the consonantal skeletons of the two words are almost identical in the Arabic script. There is really no substitute for working with manuscripts!

[6] See *Jamharat* (Kuwait ed.), 239.

[7] For the *cursus publicus*, see F. Dvornik, *Origins of Intelligence Services*, 122–29.

[8] For this, see L. Cheikho, *Shuʿarāʾ al-Nasrāniyya*, 39.

[9] For this, see Zubayr ibn Bakkār, *Jamharat Nasab Quraysh*, ed. M. M. Shākir (Cairo, 1961–62), 425–26.

[10] See below, Part 3, sec. IV note 74.

Appendix IV

On the Etymology of Arabissos

As indicated in the discussion of Iyād, the obscurity that surrounds the etymology of the Anatolian city Arabissos[1] could be dissipated by suggesting that its etymon is the ethnic term Arab. Anatolian toponymy is difficult and complicated, so no certainty can be claimed for this endeavor, only possibility or probability.

1. The case for the ethnic term "Arab" as the most natural etymon rests on phonology. Although one other etymon may be suggested, it is not as perfect as "Arab" is on phonological grounds. Arabissos with an Arab etymon has a parallel in "Arabia in Mesopotamia," the region which acquired its name from the Arab tribes who had emigrated into the neighboring region of Mesopotamia. It was known as Arabia as early as the time of Xenophon and as late as that of Septimius Severus.[2]

2. It is supported historically in this proto-Byzantine period of the three centuries or so which elapsed before the rise of Islam by references in the Arabic sources to the emigration of Arab tribes in Anatolia. As explained in this chapter, the tribe of Iyād is said to have emigrated in this period to Ancyra, and it has been suggested that this tribe or some other tribe might have also settled in the place that came to be known later by the name of Arabissos. It is also possible to see some connection between the fall of the Arab city of Edessa to Emperor Gordian in the third century and the emigration of some of its Arabs to the vicinity of Arabissos; and Edessa is not far from Arabissos.

3. There is significant reference to the Islamic period in the Arabic sources. One states that after the Arab conquest of Oriens/Shām, the Christian Arab federates withdrew north of the Taurus into Anatolia and settled in a city called "madīnat al-ʿArab," "the city of the Arabs." This naturally points to Arabissos.[3] The clear

[1] Not much is known about Arabissos before the 6th century, when it became a city of the newly created province of Third Armenia, governed by a *comes Justinianus*. Even so, Jones' statement that nothing is known about it is startling; see his *Cities of the Eastern Roman Empire*, 182. *RE* has not much on it, but see now F. Hild and M. Restle, *Kappadokien* (Vienna, 1981), 144–45; L. Zgusta *Kleinasiatische Ortsnamen* (Heidelberg, 1984), 86–87. It also receives much attention in N. Adontz, *Armenia in the Period of Justinian*, trans. N. Garsoïan (Lisbon, 1970), see Index, p. 312.

[2] On "Arabia in Mesopotamia," see Shahîd, *RA*, 7–8. The Roman province of Osroene also received its name from the Arab tribe Osroeni; ibid., 8.

[3] See Bakrī, *Muʿjam*, I, 75. In Islamic times the Ghassānid Arabs were to be found in Kharshana (Charsianon); see Istakhrī, *Masālik al-Mamālik,*, ed. M. J. de Goeje, BGA (Leiden, 1870), II, 45. The transliteration of "Arabissos" with the Arabic ṣound ʿayn rather than the plosive initial hamza in Balāḏurī (*Futuḥ al-Buldān*, I, 185–86) is significant, and supports the view that the etymon is ethnic, "Arab." It gives an indication as to how the toponym was pronounced in the first half of the 7th century and that this is how the Arabs of the frontier heard it. The description of "Arabissos" in Balāḏurī could also support the view that it was inhabited by Arabs. It is described as lying between Arab Shām and Rūm, Romania or Byzantine Anatolia. It is also stated that its inhabitants were supplying information to Byzantium about the Muslim Arabs in Shām. One could infer that Byzantium used the services of these inhabitants, who were so conveniently near the frontier, to gather information about the

implication of the statement is that the city was already known as "madīnat al-ʿArab," an appellation that goes back to pre-Islamic times. Even if the Arabic source is in error (which is unlikely in this case) when it translates the Anatolian toponym in which the Arab federate settled as "madīnat al-ʿArab," the fact remains that the Arab federates chose to settle or were settled there, and this suggests that the place had some association already with the Arabs and that this was a consideration in its choice. In the light of this datum on the federate Arabs in the seventh century, the chances are that Arabissos had been settled in this proto-Byzantine period by Arabs who gave the city its name.

Mention has been made of the possibility that "Arab" in Arabissos may not be the ethnic term, but some other homophonous word which has nothing to do with the Arabs. One such word has been suggested—Hittite "Arawa," which means "free." This is unlikely, and against this etymon the following observations may be made.

1. The second part of the compound word "Arabissos," -issos/-assos, is the old Luvian appurtenance suffix, replacing the genitive in Luvian grammar. This is the ubiquitous morpheme that appears in so many toponyms in Greece, Asia Minor, and even Syria.[4] Apparently it was alive in the proto-Byzantine period, since it appears in the old name of Emperor Zeno, Tarasicodissa.

2. The word "Arawa"[5] would indeed be an extraordinary survival of a Hittite word in an Anatolian toponym of this period. What argues against it, perhaps decisively, is historical geography: "Arabissos" is not attested before the fourth century A.D., and the revival of a Hittite word in this period is quite inconceivable; besides, it would stand isolated in the toponymy of Anatolia.

Thus the balance of arguments is in favor of the ethnic term "Arab" as an etymon of the toponym Arabissos. This is some gain for Byzantino-arabica in both pre-Islamic and Islamic times, and the existence of a little Arab colony north of the Taurus in pre-Islamic times is of some significance. Its importance for examining one of the most important problems of Arab-Byzantine relations in the sixth century will be discussed in *BASIC*.[6]

Muslims in Shām; they could do so because they were Arabs, familiar with the language of the Muslim Arabs and with conditions in Shām/Oriens, which had been their original abode before they crossed the Taurus and settled in Anatolia after the Muslim Conquest. Balāḏurī does not say that the inhabitants of Arabissos were Arab, possibly because his statement on Arabissos was an incidental remark coming in the wake of the long discussion on Cyprus. Presumably the inhabitants were a mixed group ethnically, although Arabissos may have started as an Arab colony. Other ethnic groups must have outnumbered the Arabs eventually. Arabissos was the birthplace of Emperor Maurice in the 6th century.

[4] As in Telanissos, associated with St. Simeon Stylite.

[5] See J. Puhvel, *Hittite Etymological Dictionary* (Berlin-New York, 1984), I, 119–20.

[6] I thank Prof. Jaan Puhvel for answering my queries on the Luvian and Hittite dimensions of the etymology of Arabissos, and particularly for acting as the devil's advocate when I asked him to suggest a homophone of the ethnic term "Arab" from the world of Hittite Anatolia. I have also discussed the etymology of Arabissos with Prof. Robert Browning, and I thank him for some fruitful conversations on this problem.

Appendix V
On the Name "Ḥunn"

The very real possibility that the eponym of the ʿUḏrite Ḥunn carried the Christian name John is important. Hence it is desirable to bring together the various observations on this problem, scattered in this chapter.

The Christianity of ʿUḏra cannot be denied, and it clearly goes back to at least to the fifth century. Ḥunn/Ḥinn/Ḥann was the brother of Rizāḥ, whose Byzantine connection is established. It is not unnatural that his brother assumed a Christian name, John, as many Christian Arabs of the period did.[1] The following may be adduced in support of this contention.

1. The name itself is most uncommon for an Arab clan, both semantically and morphologically. In a warlike society, such as that of the tribes of pre-Islamic Arabia, such a sentimental name, related to *ḥanīn* and *ḥanān* ("yearning" and "mercy, tenderness," respectively), sounds suspicious.

2. Philologists and genealogists clearly had difficulty in vocalizing the name satisfactorily in Islamic times, when the truth about the correct etymology of the name had been lost.

3. The most plausible explanation for this strange name is that it is none other than the name John, which the Christian chief assumed on his conversion, or was given by his father Rabīʿa, who was probably a Christian.

4. This is supported by the fact that in Yāqūt's *Muqtaḍab* its orthography suggests the Christian name Ḥannā because of its long final *aliph*, and also by the fact that the same name, with a long *aliph*, survived into the early Islamic period of the 7th century, assumed by the father of Buthayna, the beloved of the poet Jamīl.[2]

5. In its morphological pattern it was assimilated either to the Arabic adjectival form *faʿl* (*Ḥann*), or to the verb *faʿala* (*Ḥanna*). The names of some other Arab tribes were morphologically patterned after verbs, such as Taghlīb and Yashkur.[3]

6. A version of the name appears assumed by a contemporary of Rizāḥ in western Arabia, Ḥannān, the merchant from Najrān who introduced Christianity to that city.[4] In this case it assumed an intensive form *faʿʿāl*.

7. The name John most probably appears in the patronymic of a Christian poet of the sixth century, the Taghlibite Jābir ibn Ḥny, who, according to tradition,

[1] Such as a chief of the Christian tribe of Kalb who was called Romanis/Romanus, clearly after the well-known Christian saint; see *Al-Manāqib al-Mazyadiyya*, ed. S. Daradika and M. Khuraysāt (Amman, 1984), I, 287. Arabs in the Persian sphere of influence adopted and assumed Persian names, such as Bisṭām, and Qābūs.

[2] On these two points, see Chap. 12, sec. viii, notes 379 and 380.

[3] It is noteworthy that in the pre-Islamic verse of Nābigha, in which the name of the tribe appears as Ḥunn, the variant Ḥannā (John) can very well be substituted and the verse does scan with this substitution. It is also likely that the Arabic name Ḥunayn is none other than the diminutive of Ḥannā (John). The most famous carrier of this name is the celebrated Christian Arab of Ḥīra in Islamic times, the famous translator of Greek thought into Arabic, Ḥunayn ibn Isḥāq. For the verse of Nābigha, see Ahlwardt, *Divans*, 15, no. 13, line 1.

[4] On this, see above.

accompanied Imru' al-Qays on his journey to Constantinople.[5] The consonantal skeleton of the name of his father (HNY) has been variously read by editors and scholars.[6] Surely the reading Ḥunayy, the most popular, is the least likely, a *hapax legomenon* in the Arabic onomasticon and almost unintelligible in the semantic order of Arabic. Consequently, Ḥannā (John) is the reading most likely to be correct. This is supported by the fact that his tribe, Taghlīb, was a well-known Christian tribe, and remained so well into Islamic times. Jābir gave expression to his Christian sentiment in a well-known verse.[7]

8. In the early seventh century, "John" appears in Arabic in two forms: (*a*) as "Yūḥannā," carried by the master of Ayla, Yūḥannā ibn Ru'ba, with whom the Prophet Muḥammad concluded a treaty;[8] and (*b*) as "Yahya," the Qur'ānic form for John the Baptist.[9] Clearly the Arabic language had difficulty in naturalizing the name of the evangelist, and it was not alone in encountering these difficulties.[10]

Appendix VI

On the Appellation "Ibn Qārib"

One of the killers of Dāwūd, the Salīḥid king, was Thaʿlaba, who belonged to the tribe of Kalb; the other was called Muʿāwiya, and belonged to the tribe of al-Namir ibn Wabara. The full name of the second killer is Muʿāwiya, son of Ḥujayr, but sometimes he is also referred to by another patronymic, Ibn Qārib. This patronymic appears in the MSS of Hishām and also found its way into medieval printed works which drew on Hishām.[1] More importantly, it appears in the verse composed by the Salīḥid princess on her father's death.[2] Hence this patronymic deserves some attention, and there are two explanations for it.

1. It is possible that it is not really a patronymic of the killer but of someone else who belonged to his tribal group and who furthermore gave that group its name, Rahṭ Ibn Qārib ("The group of Ibn Qārib"), the smaller group within Mashjaʿa to which Muʿāwiya belonged; Ibn Ḥujayr was his real patronymic.

2. Alternatively this could be a part of the killer's name. Qārib is a most uncommon name in the Arabic onomasticon, and it can have one of two meanings: either "a

[5] For this poet, see *Al-Mufaddaliyyāt*, ed. A. Shākir and A. Hārūn (Cairo, 1941), II, 8.

[6] On the various readings, see ibid.

[7] The verse may be translated: "And Bahrā' has alleged that our swords are swords of Christians that do not wade into blood"; see ibid., 11. Taghlīb's Christianity is an established fact; their patron saint was Sergius. The editor's denial (ibid.) of the poet's Christianity cannot be accepted.

[8] See Balāḏurī, *Futūḥ al-Buldān*, I, 71.

[9] On how "Yūḥannā" became "Yaḥyā" in the Qur'ān, owing to the position of the diacritical marks, see A. Jeffery, *The Foreign Vocabulary of the Qur'an* (Baroda, 1938), 290–91. This hypothesis is confirmed by the fact that one editor did actually read HNY in the patronymic of Jābir, the Taghlibī poet, as Yaḥyā. See *Al-Mufaddaliyyāt*, II, 8, the long footnote.

[10] In Armenian it is Hovannes, in Italian, Giovanni, in Spanish, Juan, and so on.

[1] See Ibn ʿAbd Rabbihi, *Al-ʿIqd al-Farīd*, ed. A. ʿAmin, A. al-Zayn, and I. al-Abyārī (Cairo, 1982), III, 373.

[2] See above.

boat," which is out of the question here,[3] since Namir ibn Wabara was not a seafaring tribe, or "the one who sheathes his sword, who returns it to its *qirāb* (sheath)." This could be a soubriquet for his father (Ḥujayr), and this could suggest that he was a peace-loving tribesman whose sword rested in his sheath most of the time, and so quite unlike his son, the regicide who unsheathed his sword and killed the Salīḥid king. Thus the name could tell something about the family background of the regicide. Alternatively Ibn Qārib may have been a soubriquet rather than a patronymic for Muʿāwiya himself, signifying "the one who leaves his sword in his sheath," that is, a coward who does not use his sword. This is a possible taunt in pre-Islamic Arabia in which the martial quality of the man was his virtue. What the princess would then be saying is that her father fell by the sword of one not known for his prowess in war, but a coward who let his blade rust in its scabbard.

[3] Arabic *qārib* is a loanword, Greek καράβιον.

XIII

Western Arabia

This chapter treats western Arabia, especially the Byzantine mission, in three areas: Mecca, Najrān, and Ḥimyar. It is prefaced with a section on Ishmaelism, which was discussed earlier with regard to ecclesiastical history. Now its reflections in the Arabic sources are treated, as well as its expressions in western Arabia, especially in Mecca.

I. Ishmaelism

As pointed out earlier, the Arabs in the few centuries before the rise of Islam *believed* (or at least a part of them did) that they were descended from Ishmael and that the biblical appellation "sons of Ishmael" applied to them. The earlier discussion drew on the Greek sources Theodoret and Sozomen, and reflected the Ishmaelite image of the Arabs as perceived by the Christian outside observer.[1] The concept of the "sons of Ishmael" will now be treated as it is reflected in the Arabic sources, as the self-image of the Arabs themselves in Arabia, mainly in western Arabia.

The historical period that is involved is what might be termed the "second inter-testamental period," that is, the period that elapsed between the Christian Revelation—the New Testament and the first century—and that of the Muslim Revelation—the Koran in the seventh century.[2] In the fifth century, more than two millennia had elapsed since the appearance of Ishmael as a figure in the Bible who gave rise to the concept of "Ishmaelites" and "sons of Ishmael." By this time the old biblical tribes and their names had disappeared or were assimilated into other tribes, but the concept of Ishmaelism[3] either remained alive or was resuscitated. From our point of view, this topic is important and relevant to the theme "Mecca and Byzantium" and, more explicitly, to the question why neither of the monotheistic religions which

[1] For this, see above, Chaps. 8–9.

[2] I. Ephʿal traced the concept of the "sons of Ishmael" in the period antedating this, the Period of the Second Temple, or the "first inter-Testamental Period," for which, see sec. II of his article, "'Ishmael and ʿArab(s)'."

[3] Ishmaelism is a convenient term to use; its orthography distinguishes it from Ismailism, the sect of later Islamic times, for which see *EI*.

were competing for supremacy in the Arabian Peninsula was able to establish itself strongly and significantly in Mecca.

I

Accounts of Ishmaelism and the "sons of Ishmael" appear in various Arabic Islamic authors. A coherent account is provided by the historian Yaʿqūbī in his *Tārīkh*; although fact is mixed with much fiction, a kernel of truth is evident.[4] In this narrative Ishmael is associated with Abraham and his monotheism. Many achievements are ascribed to him. He marries a woman from the tribe of Jurhum, which for some time had the upper hand in Mecca, but the sons of Ishmael remained responsible for the Kaʿba. Yaʿqūbī then enumerates the main tribal groups descended from Ishmael and finally comes to the tribe of the Prophet Muḥammad, Quraysh, and his ancestors, with special prominence given to Quṣayy and his achievements in Mecca, and he carries the story to the time of ʿAbdul Muṭṭalib and the year of the Elephant. In another chapter he writes more expansively on the adulteration of the pure Ishmaelite monotheism in Mecca through the tribe of Khuzāʿa and one, ʿAmr ibn Luḥayy, who brought the idols into the Kaʿba. This was the situation when Muḥammad appeared, restored the old, pure Abrahamic monotheism, and smashed the idols.

Ecclesiastical history and patristic thought have vouched for the reality of Ishmaelism in the two or three centuries before the rise of Islam. This facilitates the task evaluating the Arabic tradition on Ishmaelism and isolating certain elements in it which may be described as hard facts or spots. Nöldeke's law must be followed in such an evaluation—the acceptance of elements in the Arabic tradition only when they can be interlocked with or related in some way to Greek and Latin sources the reliability of which is incontestable.[5] With the help of such elements or hard spots it is also possible to detect authentic rings in the Arabic tradition which are not always possible to relate to the classical sources. Nöldeke's law, however, must remain the guide until Semitic inscriptions in northwestern Arabia and Ḥijāz have been discovered, which will accelerate the process of evaluating the Ishmaelite tradition and

[4] The European edition of Yaʿqūbī is probably more accessible than the Beirut one: for the former see *Historiae* (Leiden, 1883), I., 252–94 on the Sons of Ishmael and 294–99 on Arabian religions. For the latter edition, see *Tārīkh al-Ya ʿqūbī* (Beirut, 1960), I.; the chapter on the Sons of Ishmael may be found on pp. 221–53, the one on the Arabian religions on pp. 254–57. Al-Azraqī has much material but it is diffused and scattered in various chapters, and tends to be concentrated on the Kaʿba; see M. al-Azraqī, *Akhbār Makka*, ed. R. Malḥas (Mecca, 1965), passim. This edition is based on three new manuscripts and has thus superseded the old European edition of Wüstenfeld. A good account may also be found in Masʿūdī, *Murūj*, 161–78.

[5] On this see *BAFOC*, 4–7.

relate it to a new set of incontestable sources.[6] In this light, the following aspects of Ishmaelism in the Arabic sources may be presented.

1. Ishmael appears in the Arabic sources as a religious figure and a monotheist, and his monotheism may (for the maximalist) be supported by the biblical tradition. In Genesis he is the object of God's care and Abraham's prayer, and is actually called Ishmael by God himself or his angel.[7] It is natural to suppose[8] that Ishmael was apprised of this by his mother Hagar, and that he followed the monotheism of his father Abraham. It is noteworthy that he continued to live in the desert of Paran, not far from where the first patriarch and monotheist lived and, what is more, that his filial *pietas* is reflected in his participation with his brother Isaac in the burial of Abraham in the cave of Machpelah.[9]

2. Closely related to this Ishmaelite monotheism is what the Arabic tradition calls "Dīn Ibrāhim," "the religion of Abraham," in which Ishmael believed as did the Ishmaelite Arabs. This is roughly consonant with what Sozomen says about the Ishmaelite religion before it was adulterated by the polytheism and paganism of their neighbors, distinguishing it from that of the Israelites, for whom alone Moses legislated. The implication of Sozomen's statement is that the Ishmaelites continued to believe in monotheism of the Abrahamic variety. Thus the Ishmaelite Arabs preserved their identity, and accentuated it through their continuing belief in Abrahamism, the monotheism of the first patriarch, as opposed to Mosaic Judaism, which addressed the Israelites.

3. Less fugitive and more tangible than the concept of Ishmael as a religious figure and guide to many Arabs is the genealogical concept, that of the descent from Ishmael. Both Sozomen and Theodoret knew of it and documented it for both the north and south of Oriens and western Arabia. Two problems are involved.

a. The reality of this concept as a matter of belief, if not historical truth—is attested in the Arabic sources, which in this case must reflect a genuine historical tradition, since it is supported by the Greek sources.

[6] As the inscription of Nabonidus the Babylonian King, found at Taymā, has shed so much light on the history of Ḥijāz in the 6th century B.C. and has made practically certain that the Jewish communities of Ḥijāz settled there as early as that century.

[7] See Gen. 16, 17, 21, 25. The Arab tradition also knows why Ishmael was so called; see Masʿūdī, *Murūj*, II, 164.

[8] At least by those who believe in the reliability and historicity of the Genesis narrative.

[9] This Ishmaelite monotheism is something of a puzzle. If it was inspired by contacts with the Jews of western Arabia it would be remarkably selective, in that the Arabs would have accepted Abrahamic monotheism from the Jews and rejected Mosaic monotheism. The alternative explanation would be to assume a native form of monotheism which goes back to antiquity, possibly to biblical times, which is also equally puzzling. So is the reference to Ṣuḥuf Ibrāhim, for which see Koran, sura 87, verse 19, probably *The Testament of Abraham*.

Genealogical Ishmaelism was viewed with suspicion as a late Islamic fabrication because of the confusion in Islamic times which made it such a capacious term as to include the inhabitants of the south as well as the north of the Arabian Peninsula. But shorn of this extravagance, the concept is much more modest in its denotation, and in the sober sources it applies only to certain groups among the Arabs of pre-Islamic times. Some important statements to this effect were made by the Prophet Muḥammad when he identified some Arabs as Ishmaelites and others as not.[10]

b. The belief of the Arabs in their descent from Ishmael raises the question of the genesis of this view. Was it a concept which they owed to contact with the Jews of Arabia, whose antiquity in the Arabian Peninsula and in Ḥijāz in particular most probably goes back to the sixth century B.C.? This is possible, and has been argued by some scholars.[11] Or was it spread by Christianity when it entered the Arabian Peninsula at a later time than Judaism? The Old Testament formed part of the Christian Bible and the Ishmaelite descent of the Arabs would have become known to the converted Arabs either from Christian missionaries or preachers.

Either alternative is possible but both encounters difficulties. The Arabs were a people who took pride in their tribal allegiance and affiliation. They could from time to time change this allegiance and affiliate themselves with other tribes for various reasons, but these Arab tribes were ultimately related to them and this usually happened as a result of certain economic or political exigencies.[12] It is, therefore, difficult to believe that they would have accepted the adulteration of their ethnic origin and violation of their ethnocentricity only to find that this genealogical dislocation allocated them *not* to the Chosen People but to descent from a slavewoman by the name of Hagar.

According to the Arabic sources, Ishmael thus emerges as both a religious figure and an eponymous ancestor for some of the Arabs of western Arabia. These are the two important components of Ishmaelism, also adumbrated by the contemporary church historians, Theodoret and Sozomen.

4. Within the genealogical component in Ishmaelism, the Arabic sources give prominence to two of the sons of Ishmael who are enumerated in Genesis, Nebaioth and Kedar.[13] This is striking and raises the question why these two

[10] See below, note 45.

[11] See S. Goitein, *Jews and Arabs* (New York, 1955), 22, where he also argues that the Hebrew term *dodanim* ("cousins"), applied by the Jews to the Arabs, was a pun on the name of Dedanim, the Arab tribe mentioned in Isa. 21:13. Sozomen also thought so, but also considered that both the Arabness of the Ishmaelites and their being cousins of the Jews were biblical facts.

[12] Tribes who changed their allegiance and affiliated themselves with other tribes are called *Nawāqil* for whom, see W. Caskel, *GN*, I, 59–62.

[13] Gen. 25:13–14.

should have been selected as the two branches through whom, according to the historians, the Arabs multiplied.[14] They appear in Arabic as Nābit or Nabīt, and Qaydar or Qaydār.

The key may be provided by the biblical narrative. Prominence is given to Nebaioth as the eldest, the one who represented primogeniture. Further prominence is given to Nebaioth in the genealogy of Esau, who marries one or two of Ishmael's daughters. The bride, Mahalath or Bashemath, is referred to as the sister of Nebaioth,[15] and so he is singled out of all the sons of Ishmael in spite of the fact that the other eleven brothers were also brothers of the bride. Kedar is also given some prominence, since he is listed as coming immediately after Nebaioth and thus is closest to the representative of primogeniture. Thus it is possible that what determined the prominence given to these two sons of Ishmael as progenitors of the Arabs was the authority of the Bible.

This view is not entirely satisfactory, since it assumes Arab dependence on the Bible in such matters of genealogy. Furthermore, the selectiveness of the Arabic genealogical tradition regarding the sons of Ishmael raises other difficulties which the prominence given to these two in the Bible does not entirely explain. The more natural explanation is that these two sons of Ishmael lived in northwestern Arabia—in Ḥijāz, in Sinai, in eastern Trans-Jordan—and that theirs were historically the two most prominent among the twelve Ishmaelite tribes.[16] And the two are closely associated, as in their alliance against the Assyrian king Assurbanipal in the seventh century B.C. Moreover, their historical presence in the area is attested late: the Kedar as late as the fifth century B.C., through reference to Geshem, the Kedarite who obstructed the work of Nehemia in rebuilding the wall of Jerusalem; the Nabataeans as late as the second century A.D., when Nabataea became (in 106) the Provincia Arabia. Perhaps Kedar had been incorporated within the Nabataean state, which thus emerged as the strongest and the most enduring representative of the Ishmaelite presence in northwestern Arabia until the second century A.D. Thus a link can now be established between the Nabataeans of the second century and the Arabs of the few centuries before the rise of Islam; the strand of continuity in the Ishmaelite tradition thus points to a Nabataean provenance. If so, this adds a new dimension to the sigificance of Nabataean history.[17]

[14] See for instance Ṭabarī, *Tārīkh*, I, 314; also Azraqī, *Akhbār Makka*, 81.

[15] See Gen. 28:9 for Mahalath and 36:3 for Bashemath.

[16] For the less well known but historically very important tribal group Kedar, see *The Interpreter's Dictionary of the Bible* (New York, 1962), s.v.

For the latest on the Ishmaelite Arabs involving Qidar/Kedar and the Nabataeans in North Arabia and Palestine, see E. A. Knauf, "Supplementa Ismaelitica," *BN* 30 (1985), 19–28.

[17] This may be at the basis of their strong sense of identity, which enabled them to endure for a long time before they were incorporated in the Roman Empire, and might also

5. The tribe of Jurhum is involved in the Arabic accounts of the sons of Ishmael. This was an old Arab tribe, which played an important role in the history of two cities with which Byzantium had relations, Najrān and Mecca,[18] the former of which had been Jurhum's abode before they emigrated to the latter.

According to these Arabic accounts, the tribe of Jurhum gave protection to Hagar and her child Ishmael, who cemented the relationship by marrying a lady related to a Jurhumite, al-Muḍāḍ ibn ʿAmr.[19] The tribe was involved in the worship which centered around the Kaʿba and one of them even rebuilt that temple. Finally, they were ousted from their custodianship of the Kaʿba and from Mecca, according to one tradition, by a new tribal group from the south, Khuzāʿa.[20] Only what is relevant to the Ishmaelite connection of Jurhum during their Meccan period will be discussed in this section.

a. There is no question about the historical reality of Jurhum, since it is attested in the Greek source.[21] That it went back to biblical Ishmael may be safely rejected, while its *floruit* as an important tribe in the affairs of Najrān and Mecca in western Arabia may be assigned to a period within the few centuries before the rise of Islam.[22]

b. The name that is involved in the marriage of Ishmael to the Jurhumite woman is important. It is al-Muḍāḍ, although the sources are not unanimous as to whether he was her father or grandfather. It is practically certain that this was a historical personage, since he is mentioned in one of the authentic verses of the pre-Islamic poet al-Aʿshā as having built or rebuilt the Kaʿba.[23] Ishmael certainly did not marry his daughter or granddaughter, but an Ishmaelite of this period may have done so. The question arises as to the significance of this marriage and why the sources projected it to the distant past of biblical times. One explanation is that the marriage represented a symbol of symbiosis between the two groups of North and South Arabians. It was an attempt on the part of the latter to establish a link between themselves and the Prophet Muḥammad by suggesting that Ishmael married a South

---

explain the force with which they resisted annexation by the Romans, if Ammianus Marcellinus is to be trusted on this point; see *RG*, XIV, 8.13; but see the chapter "The New Province" in Glen Bowersock, *Roman Arabia*, 76–89.

[18] This role will be discussed later in this chapter.

[19] According to Yaʿqūbī, the lady was called al-Ḥanfāʾ and was the daughter of al-Ḥārith, son of Muḍāḍ, the Jurhumite; according to Azraqi she was called Raʿlat and was the daughter of al-Muḍāḍ son of ʿAmr; for these two statements see *Historiae*, 253 and *Akhbār Mekka*, 86, respectively.

[20] On Jurhum, see the entry in *EI*², s.v.

[21] Ibid. It is also attested in Sabaic epigraphy; see below, 548.

[22] On its origins and provenance, see T. Fahd, "Gerrhéens et Ǧurhumites," in *Studien zur Geschichte und Kultur des vorderen Orients, Festschrift für B. Spuler*, ed. H. Roemer and A. Noth (Leiden, 1981).

[23] On this, see the next section of this chapter.

Arabian lady and thus the blood of the latter flowed in the veins of the sons of Ishmael, including the Prophet.[24]

c. Finally, the name al-Muḍāḍ is reminiscent of the biblical name Almodad,[25] the first son of Yoktan, son of Eber. Even if al-Muḍāḍ as a Jurhumite name turns out to be fictitious, the appearance of the name in the genealogies of this South Arabian tribe is significant, and indicates that the biblical table of nations had made progress not only among the Arabs of the North—the sons of Ishmael—but among the peoples of South Arabia. As is well known in later Islamic times, to balance ʿAdnān, the ancestor of the North Arabs, the South posited as their ancestor Qaḥṭān, who was identified with biblical Yoktan. And this identification made some sense, since in the Bible Yoktan was the ancestor of some South Arabian tribes. Almodad as the first son of Yoktan appears to balance Nebaioth as the first son of Ishmael.

II

A return to the genealogies of the Arabic sources touched upon earlier is now necessary in light of this discussion of the concept of the "sons of Ishmael" in the same sources. After the rise of Islam the genealogies were worked out in an extensive fashion to cover the Peninsula in its entirety, including non-Arab groups; hence great confusion has reigned. In their most extravagant and confused form, the genealogies conceive the Peninsula as peopled entirely by Arabs and Ishmael as the ancestor from whom both South and North Arabians were descended.[26] A better understanding of the concept of the sons of Ishmael, along with the clearer picture of the ethnography of the Arabian Peninsula made possible by epigraphic discoveries in North and South Arabia, permit a return to sanity and a re-drawing of the genealogical landscape of Arabia, which will show how the Arabs were related to one another and to the other inhabitants of the Peninsula in the context of the biblical genealogies, with all their inaccuracies.[27]

1. The South Arabian inscriptions—the Sabaic—have made amply clear

[24] The projection of this into the distant biblical past may be an expression of pride on the part of Jurhum and an attempt to present themselves as the true Arabs (*al-ʿArab al-ʿĀriba*), since according to this tradition, Ishmael spoke no Arabic and learned the language from Jurhum, a reflection of the well-known South Arabian pride and vanity in later Islamic times. See also A. K. Irvine, "Ḳaḥṭān," *EI*².

[25] See Gen. 10:26 and I Chron. 1:20.

[26] For an example of this extravagant claim, see Ibn Hishām, *Sīrat al-Nabī*, ed. M. ʿAbdulhamīd (Cairo, 1937), 1, 4–5.

[27] For a substantial and important article on the biblical Arabian genealogies, see F. V. Winnett, "The Arabian Genealogies in the Book of Genesis," *Essays in Honor of Herbert Gordon May*, ed. H. T. Frank and W. L. Reed (New York, 1970), 171–96; and "Pre-Islamic Arabic Genealogies," in R. R. Wilson, *Genealogy and History in the Biblical World* (New Haven, 1977), 129–32.

that the language of these inscriptions, in spite of slight dialectal differences, is quite distinct from the language of the Arabs, the *ʿarabiyya*, although related to it as a Semitic language. And so the Semitic peoples who wrote these inscriptions are related to the Arabs but quite distinct from them; they appear in the sources of Islamic times as Ḥimyar. Thus the two principal large ethnic groups in the Arabian Peninsula in the few centuries before the rise of Islam were the Arabs and the Ḥimyarites, or Sabaeans.[28]

2. The Arabs lived mainly in Central and North Arabia, and are known to history as the nomads (Saracens), the oases dwellers, and the inhabitants of the various cities they founded or occupied, both in western Arabia and in the limitrophe of the Fertile Crescent. But there were Arabs who also lived in the south of the Peninsula and who, in spite of their proximity to the Ḥimyarites, were quite distinct from them. They are the people often referred to in the Sabaic inscriptions as Aʿrāb; but there were also better known and more sedentary large tribal groups, which played an important role in the history of both the south and the north of the Arabian Peninsula. Such were Maḏḥij, the Azd, and Kinda. The northern and the southern Arabs, among other things, shared the same language, the *ʿarabiyya* of pre-Islamic times, but the two groups were aware of differences between them in spite of their being one Arab people. This feeling went back to pre-Islamic times and persisted well into the Islamic period.

3. The biblical genealogical concepts were applied to the Arabs and the Arabians. In spite of certain inaccuracies, there is some sense in which they are correct. The concept of "the sons of Ishmael," for instance, was applied mainly to the northern Arabs and, what is more, not to all of them. In so doing, the inspired writer of Genesis may have reflected an important political fact about the tribes subsumed under "the sons of Ishmael," namely, that they formed a confederation in the distant, past history of the Arabs.[29] Careful Arab writers understood that only part of the northern Arabs could be included under the term "sons of Ishmael" and indeed they narrowed it down in Islamic times to descendants of two of the sons, Nebaioth and Kedar.[30] Also the Arabs living in the South, including the three large tribal groups, Azd, Maḏḥij, and Kinda, were conceived of by genealogists as related to one another, as indeed they were.[31] In Islamic genealogies the eponymous ances-

[28] On this, see I. Shahîd, "Pre-Islamic Arabia," *CHI*, I, 6.

[29] See above, 176–77.

[30] See above, 336.

[31] In some Arabic genealogies they are made to be the descendants of Kahlān, who may or may not have existed; but the genealogical table that makes the Arabs of the South his descendants is sound in that through this ancestor, real or fictitious, it sharply distinguished the Arab inhabitants of the South from the non-Arab, who are correctly made the descendants of another ancestor, Ḥimyar.

tor of the South Arabs was, along biblical lines, conceived of as Qaḥṭān, the closest to the biblical Yoktan—according to the Bible, the ancestor of many South Arabian tribes.[32] The phonetic resemblance between Qaḥṭān and Yoktan seemed to justify the process of identification.[33] To counterbalance Qaḥṭān, all the northern Arabs, including the sons of Ishmael, were conceived of as the descendants of ʿAdnān, a term that rhymed with Qaḥṭān. Whether Qaḥṭān and ʿAdnān were historical figures is not important.[34] What is important is that in sober genealogies the two groups of Arabs in the Peninsula were understood to be descended from two different ancestors but to constitute one people. Violence was done to biblical concepts when both Qaḥṭānis and ʿAdnānis appeared as descendants of Ishmael,[35] although careful genealogists actually rejected this.[36]

4. The reasons behind the confusion in the work of the genealogists of Islamic times is due to two main factors. These are interesting to explore for the light they throw on certain cultural trends among the Arabs generated by the rise of Islam and the Arab conquests.

a. In pre-Islamic times, it was the non-Arab South, composed mainly of the Sabaeans, that was the more important part of the Peninsula in the history of the Near East. Their high material culture, their wealth, their importance in the international trade of the ancient world, and their flourishing cities were well known to the classical historians. All this came to an inglorious end in the sixth century with the two foreign occupations, the Ethiopian and the Persian. With the rise of Islam, it was the northern Arabs that attained prominence and made history in the Peninsula and elsewhere in the world, while Ḥimyar and South Arabia receded into the background. But early authors from South Arabia tried to remind the world of the vanished glory of their region. One result of their concern was the concoction of the tripartite scheme of classifying the Arabs as *bāʾida* (extinct), *ʿāriba* (true), and *mustaʿriba* (arabizing).[37] In this scheme the South Arabians appear as *ʿāriba*,[38] the "true

[32] See Gen. 10:26–30. But only some of the eleven sons of Yoktan could have been Arab, since the others clearly belonged to the non-Arab inhabitants of the South. In the article cited above (note 27), Fred V. Winnett is unaware of the important and necessary distinction between the Arab and the non-Arab inhabitants of the South; see his section on the sons of Yoktan (pp. 181–89 and 195).

[33] Winnett, op. cit., 181–82, argues that it was not the Muslim genealogists who adapted Arabic Qaḥṭān to biblical Yoktan.

[34] It is important to remember, however, that both belong genuinely to the Arabic pre-Islamic onomasticon since both are attested epigraphically; for ʿAdnān, see Caskel's article in *EI*, s.v.; for Qaḥṭān, see Irvine's article, ibid., s.v. Kaḥṭān.

[35] See above, note 26.

[36] As in Ibn Ḥazm, *Jamharat*, 7.

[37] See Irvine, op. cit.

[38] On the "true" Arabs, see the work of M. Kropp in two volumes, *Die Geschichte der "reinen Araber" vom Stamme Qaḥṭān aus dem Kitab Našwat Aṭ-Ṭarab fī Tārʾīḫ Ǧāhiliyyat al-ʿArab des Ibn Saʿīd al-Magribī*, Inaugural Dissertation (Heidelberg, 1975).

Arabs," and within these "true Arabs" are included the non-Arab Ḥimyarites of the South!

b. Equally important is the central place that the person of the Prophet Muḥammad had in the affection of the Arabs and the Muslims of all the Peninsula after Islam and the Conquests Arabized and Islamized the whole region, including the non-Arab South of the Ḥimyarites. Since the Arabs did not renounce their interest in their lineage and the facts of their descent after the rise of Islam, in spite of the teachings of the new dispensation about the relative non-importance or insigificance of lineage, genealogical proximity to the Prophet and his tribe became important to the Arabs. Hence the attempts of individuals and tribal groups to present themselves as closely as possible in the genealogical tables to the tribal group he belonged to and to appear as ultimately descended from Ishmael—the ancestor of the Prophet.

These two facts—South Arabian pride and desire to be as close to the tribe of the Prophet as possible—are behind much of the confusion in the Arabic genealogies.

5. Unlike the Bible, the Koran has no detailed genealogies of the Arabs or other peoples. It has only some references to tribes and periods, including one reference which is relevant to this discussion of the Arab and Arabian genealogies. The Prophet Muḥammad is also credited with a number of *ḥa-dīṯẖs* or statements, that bear on the problems of Arab genealogies.

a. *The Koran.* In Chapter 22 of the Koran there is a verse that has great bearing on the descent of the Arabs, going back to biblical times. The last verse in this chapter has the phrase "the religion of your father Abraham."[39] In spite of Muḥammad's belief that Ishmael was his ancestor and the ancestor of some of the Arabs, there is no such statement of affiliation in the Koran. The context in which the phrase occurs is a religious and not a genealogical one, and the reference to Abraham is natural since he, not Ishmael, is the first monotheist; but the expression "your father Abraham" remains exceedingly striking. Unlike the concept of the "sons of Ishmael" which applies only to twelve of the tribes of the northern Arabs, that of the "sons of Abraham" can accommodate more Arabs in the North and possibly in the South. In addition to marrying Hagar, through whom were descended the twelve tribes of the North, Abraham married Kettura, through whom were descended other Arabian tribes.[40] Kettura bore seven sons to Abraham, and some of them have been identified as Arab tribes.[41] Thus more northern Arabs become related to one another through the descent from Abraham and his two wives, Hagar and Kettura. It is also possible that the descent from Kettura may include some

[39] See verse 78 in chap. 22 of the Koran, called *al-Hajj*, "The Pilgrimage." See also "The Historical Outlook of Muhammad," in F. Rosenthal, *HMH*, 24–30.

[40] See Gen. 25:14.

[41] See Winnett, "Arabian Genealogies," 189–93.

southern Arabs. One of the sons of Kettura was called Yokshan, and he begat a son called Sheba.[42] Some scholars find it difficult to identify Yokshan with Yoktan,[43] the progenitor of many South Arabian tribes. But the two names are strikingly similar, and Sheba, one and the same son, is ascribed to both of them.[44] Whatever the truth about the possibility of a South Arabian origin for Yokshan, the reference to Abraham rather than to Ishmael as "your father" in the Koran considerably widened the circle of Arabness in the Koranic genealogy, and thus included more Arabs within it than the twelve tribes of Ishmael.

b. *Muḥammad.* In addition to the Koran, there are the Muḥammadan statements on Arab genealogy. Muḥammad accepted the concept of descent from Ishmael but did not apply it to all the Arabs.[45] This was consonant with the biblical tradition which assigned only twelve tribes of the Arabs to descent from Ishmael. As far as the detailed pedigrees which ultimately traced the Arabs through many ancestors ultimately to Ishmael, Muḥammad accepted the line of descent as far back as ʿAdnān and rejected everything that extended from ʿAdnān to Ishmael as a segment of the line of descent that cannot be known.[46]

The genealogical conceptions of the Prophet Muḥammad were thus sober and, generally speaking, in conformity with the biblical tradition.[47] With him the concept of the "sons of Ishmael" reached its climax. However, the very same period that witnessed its reappearance as a vital force, that of the Muslim Revelation in the seventh century, also witnessed the appearance of the Koranic and Islamic concept of the Umma, the Islamic People of God, which neutralized it and made it obsolete in the world-thought of Islam. But the concept remained a unifying element in the work of the Arab genealogists.

III

For those who believe in the soundness of the Hebrew tradition, both biblical and post-biblical, about the sons of Ishmael, including their Arab-

[42] See Gen. 52:2,3.

[43] See Winnett, "Arabian Genealogies," 189. For Yoktan, see Gen. 10:26.

[44] For Sheba, son of Yoktan, see Gen. 10:28; for Sheba son of Yokshan, see Gen. 25:3. Sheba, the son of Yokshan could have been the name of a Sabaean colony in Ḥijāz.

[45] For his thoughts on the Ishmaelite origin of a subdivision of Tamīm, namely Banū al-ʿAnbar, see Ibn Ḥazm, *Jamharat*, 4, 7. The clear implication is that other tribes did not belong to the Ishmaelite group. See also his views on the Ashʿariyyūn of South Arabia as Ishmaelites in Bakrī, *Muʿjam*, I, 54.

[46] On this, see Balāḏurī, *Ansāb al-Ashrāf*, I, 12; and Masʿūdī, *Murūj*, III, 6–7. Sometimes the tradition regarding the Prophet's judgment of the unreliability of the pedigree stops with Maʿadd, son of ʿAdnān, sometimes with his father, Udad.

[47] Needless to say, the view of R. Paret that "originally Muhammad was not well informed about the family relationship between Abraham and Ishmael" cannot be accepted; for a succinct statement of his position on this, see his article in *EI*², s.v. Ismāʿil.

ness, and for those who believe that the Arabic tradition about the sons of Ishmael contains kernels of truth, it is appropriate to summarize the detailed and complex discussion of the many elements and facets of this concept in the two traditions.

1. The Hebrew biblical tradition presents a picture of twelve tribes as the sons of Ishmael, suggesting a political confederation that obtained from the last centuries of the second millenium B.C. to the first centuries of the next millennium.[48] This Hebrew tradition continued in post-biblical times, in the period of the Second Temple and in Josephus. This important author identified the sons of Ishmael with the Arabs, as have many modern scholars, using, *inter alia*, Semitic epigraphy, especially Assyrian, as the foundation for their conclusions.

2. The Arabic tradition also conceives of many of the Arab tribes as the sons of Ishmael and considers the latter as the eponym of some of the Arabs, especially in the north of the Arabian Peninsula. This tradition singles out two of the twelve biblical tribes, Nebaioth and Kedar; these names appear in Arabic in various forms (Nābit, Nabīt, or Nabt for Nebaioth and Qaydār, Qidār, or Qidar for Kedan).[49] It has been suggested in this chapter that this is likely to be a native Arab and Arabian tradition about the descent of some of the tribes of Ḥijāz and North Arabia from these two Ishmaelite tribes, probably the most powerful and historically the most important of the twelve Ishmaelite tribes.

3. One of these two tribes, Nebaioth, is attested until the first decade of the second century A.D.; in A.D. 106 the Nabataeans ceased to exist as an independent Arab state and were annexed by the Emperor Trajan, who formed out of their territory the Provincia Arabia. Thus, the Arabic tradition about the Nābit/Nebaioth, which refers to them not long after the second century A.D., seems to derive from a sound historical tradition which remembered the Nabataeans as an historical and political entity in the region, and may not have been the imaginary construction of Arab genealogists and ethnographers of later times about a distant and vanished past.

4. This Arabic tradition on the Ishmaelite origin of a number of Arab tribes continued through the three or four centuries after the fall of the Nabataeans and before the rise of Islam, and is selective in its denotation of who the Ishmaelite Arab tribes were. Various Muḥammadan traditions have been preserved, which are also selective. From these traditions it emerges that of the descendants of Ishmael through either Nebaioth or Kedar, one, ʿAdnān, is accepted as a genuine historical personality, and that one of his sons, Nizār,

[48] See above, Chap. 9, sec. III.

[49] See Ibn Qutayba, *al-Maʿārif*, 64; the statement is repeated in various other authors.

gave birth to the two large tribal groups Rabīʿa and Muḍar, who are the genuine Ishmaelite Arabs of this second inter-testamental period, between the New Testament and the Koran in the seventh century.[50]

5. Muhammad's tribe, Quraysh, belonged to Muḍar. The strong Ishmaelite tradition in the Arabic sources about the Arabs of this second inter-testamental period suggests that the mysterious early history of the tribe of Quraysh, depicted in the sources as an Ishmaelite tribe, may have to be accepted and that this tradition, which undoubtedly has many legendary and unhistorical data in it, also contains kernels of truth, especially as regards the relations of Quṣayy with northern Ḥijāz—former Nabataean territory.[51]

In the three centuries before the rise of Islam, the tribal and genealogical landscape of Arabia presents a spectacle in which the term Ishmaelite ceases to exist as a denotation for a large tribal group, and with it such terms as the Nabataeans and Kedar also disappear. New large tribal groupings appear, the most important of which are Maʿadd and Quḍāʿa.[52] The first is attested in inscriptions, in genuine pre-Islamic poetry, and in the Syriac sources.[53] The presumption is that the tribes of this confederation, named after the son of ʿAdnān and the father of Nizār, were the old Ishmaelite tribes, which after the breakup of the Nabataean confederation in 106 remained independent of Rome in the Peninsula and retained traces of the old Ishmaelism. The Quḍāʿa, the large tribal group in North Arabia, has been an enigma to Arab genealogists.[54] It is not an Ishmaelite group and has not been so considered by the genealogists. Perhaps it formed after the dissolution of the Nabataean confederation in 106 and was composed of old tribes which had been settled in the area for centuries and of Arabs tribes which had emigrated from the South and so were not Ishmaelites. It is even possible that they were the descendants of the Arab tribe in the Ḥismā/Midian region mentioned in the Assyrian sources as Ḫaiapa,[55] since in the Arab genealogies occurs the resoundingly archaic name of their ancestor Il-Ḥāfī, which can easily be equated with Assyrian Ḫaiapa.[56]

[50] It is convenient to have a term for this period which answers to the Koranic *fatra*, the second al-Jāhiliyya. For references in the Koran to the various eras of Sacred History, see *EI*, s.vv. al-jāhiliyya and *fatra*.

[51] On Quṣayy, see below, 350–55.

[52] Both of which are important to the Arab-Byzantine relationship.

[53] In the Namāra inscription, in the poetry of Nābigha, and in Procopius; for these see, *BAFOC*, 38, 43; Nöldeke, *GF*, 38 note 3; and *Wars*, I, xx, 9, respectively.

[54] The genealogists found it difficult to subsume it under either ʿAdnān or Qaḥṭān; see Ibn Ḥazm, *Jamharat*, 7, 8; also the first paragraph of M. J. Kister's article, *EI*, s.v. Kuḍāʿa.

[55] See Fred V. Winnett, "Arabian Genealogies," 191. Winnett identifies the Ḫaiapa of the Assyrian source with the biblical Ephah, the son of Midian, son of Abraham from Kettura.

[56] For al-Ḥāfī or al-Ḥāf, see Ibn Ḥazm, *Jamharat*, 440. The two consonants are strikingly similar in the Assyrian and the Arabic sources. If the identification is correct, it could

IV

One of the most important Arabic documents—perhaps the most important for the reality of the concept of Ishmaelism among the Arab in pre-Islamic times—is a poem of the sixth century, written by one of the tribe of Awd, which belonged to the large tribal group Maḏḥij and lived in South Arabia near the city of Najrān.[57] Unlike the Arabic Ishmaelite tradition, which is derived from historians who lived in Islamic times, this poem is a primary source which goes back to pre-Islamic times. For this reason and for the light it sheds on Ishmaelism in pre-Islamic times, it deserves some notice.

Although the authenticity of some pre-Islamic poetry has been called into question, both in ancient times by the Arab critics and in modern times by Arab and European critics,[58] there is no doubt that this is an authentic poem of the sixth century and truly reflects the prevailing cultural trends in the region to which its poet, al-Afwah, belonged.[59] For a poem of such antiquity, it is natural that some verses should have dropped out or that the order of the verses should have been ruffled, but otherwise the poem is sound and breathes the spirit of genuine pre-Islamic poetry from beginning to end.[60]

A

More Arabico, the poet takes pride in his tribe and tribal group, Maḏḥij, and in their achievement. What is relevant in this context is his reference to two elements in the Ishmaelite scene in western Arabic of the sixth century, which perhaps may be narrowed down to that of Najrān and Mecca: the tribe of Jurhum and the Ishmaelites, whom he refers to as the "sons of Hagar." The

---

easily argue that the Arab tribes remembered their ancestors of the distant past and that this is a native tradition, since the Arab genealogists had no access to Assyrian inscriptions, which were still buried beneath the earth in early Islamic times. This could give some fortification to the validity of the Arabic tradition which derives the Ishmaelite Arabs of the second inter-testamental period from Nabit and Qaydar (Nebaitoth and Kedar) and suggests that it is a native pre-Islamic tradition that had survived and was not fabricated in Islamic times along biblical lines. As far as I know, the identification of Arabic al-Ḥāfī with Assyrian Ḫaiapa has not yet been made. The same is true of biblical Almodad which, according to Winnett ("Arabian Genealogies," 183) remains unidentified. In this section, attention has been drawn to the existence of a Jurhumite with the name of al-Muḍāḍ; although he does not go back to biblical times, he and his name are important for those concerned with the identification of the members of the table of nations in Genesis.

[57] For al-Afwah al-Awdī, see Sezgin, *GAS*, II, 302–3.

[58] On the problem of the authenticity of pre-Islamic poetry, see *BAFOC*, 443 note 111.

[59] The only dissonant note is that of the 9th-century Arabic Muslim author, Al-Jāḥiẓ (d. 869), whose views will be discussed below.

[60] The poem is included in *Al-Hamāsa al-Baṣriyya*, ed. A. J. Sulaymān (Cairo, 1978), 170–171, where it consists of twenty-two verses. A fuller version of the poem, consisting of thirty verses, is given by A. Maymanī, who collected the *dīwān* of al-Afwah al-Awdī in his *Al-Ṭarā'if al-Adabiyya* (Beirut, 1937), 11–13.

passage that pertains to Jurhum presents some difficulties in interpretation, but the import or tenor of the three verses is clear. The references to Jurhum and the sons of Hagar constitute an important document for the intertribal animosity that inspired some pre-Islamic poetry. Such animosity is often encountered in this poetry, but in this case it is expressed in the unusual context of the feud between the Ishmaelites and the non-Ishmaelite Jurhum.

a. The reference to Jurhum consists of three verses, the second and the third of which sing the praises of South Arabian Jurhum and its prowess in war, especially vis-à-vis the northern Arabian tribal group Maʿadd.[61] The first verse mentions Jurhum by name, and is the one that presents some difficulties. In the first hemistich, the poet says that Jurhum feathered its arrows but suffered as a result.[62] The implication could be that what good they did turned out to be a thankless task.[63] The obscurity may be dispelled if this is a reference to that episode in the history of Jurhum in Mecca when, after building the Kaʿba, they were kicked out and returned to Najrān or to the South.[64] The verse may admit of other interpretations[65] but the reference of Jurhum is clear, as is the poet's pride in it against Maʿadd, the North Arabian tribal group.[66]

b. More important is his reference to Banū Hājar, the "sons of Hagar." The verse opens a passage in the poems[67] in which the poet reviles and belittles the "sons of Hagar" and the North Arab groups under Nizār, the Ishmaelite ancestor of a great tribal group. He does all this while taking pride in his tribe, Awd, and the larger group to which it belonged, Maḏḥij. The importance of this passage is in the phrase Banū Hājar. It is a very rare phrase in the extant corpus of pre-Islamic Arabic poetry, and its use implies that the polemic between the two rival groups of Arabs—the Arabs of the South and the Arabs of the North—was then so sophisticated as to be expressed in the cultural terms of the biblical genealogical concepts.[68] Finally, the phrase

[61] For these verses (10, 11, 12), see ibid., 12.

[62] The verse reads: *rayyashat Jurhumu nablan farama Jurhuman minhunna fūqun wa-ghirār. Fūq* is "the part of the arrow, which is the place of the bow string (i.e., the notch thereof); *ghirār* is the edge for the tip of the blade." For relevant observations and quotations on these two words that throw light on this line, see E. W. Lane, *Arabic-English Lexicon*, pp. 2462 and 2239, respectively.

[63] Expressed in Arabic and made clearer by a well-known Arabic verse: *uʿallimuhu al-rimāyata kulla yawmin falamma ishtadda sāʿiduhu ramāni* ("Every day I taught him how to use the bow and arrow, and when his arm got strong he made me his target.")

[64] On this episode in the history of Jurhum, see below, App. 3.5.

[65] For the relevance to this verse of what the Prophet said involving Ishmael, see below, 349.

[66] And against Nizār of the North Arabian tribal group, considered the son of Maʿadd in the genealogies of the Arabs. The reference to Nizar occurs in verse 21, Maymanī, op. cit., 13.

[67] Verses 13 ff., ibid., 12.

[68] And it suggests that the two north Arabian tribal groups referred to in the poem, Maʿadd and Nizar, were Ishmaelites. The designation "the sons of Hagar" appears also in the

carries strong pejorative overtones, the implication being that the Arabs addressed in the phrase were the descendants of a slavewoman.[69] Thus it is a reversal of what the Ishmaelite Arabs meant when they called themselves sons of Hagar, the Hagarites of the Bible, taking pride in their descent from their *mater* eponyma.[70]

The poem attracted the attention of the Prophet Muḥammad, who, because of the insulting tone of the poet towards Hagar and the Ishmaelites, prohibited his followers from reciting it, as will be explained in the next section.

B

As pointed out by the editor of the collected poems of Al-Afwah, the ninth-century Arab author Jāḥiẓ went against the consensus of critics when he doubted the authenticity of the poem.[71] In view of the importance of the poem, it is necessary to examine Jāḥiẓ' argument against its authenticity closely.

Jāḥiẓ' views derive from the employment of a phrase in one of the verses of the poem, *shihāb al qaḏf* ("the meteor of hurling or pelting"), which he claims or pretends is a borrowing from the Qur'an. Since Al-Afwah was a pre-Islamic poet, the appearance of this phrase leads to the conclusion that the poem was fabricated after Islam and falsely attributed to the pre-Islamic poet. Furthermore, Jāḥiẓ maintains that all the *ruwāt*, the reciters and preservers of poetry, consider it so.[72] His arguments must be totally rejected in light of the following.

Ishtiqāq of Ibn Durayd as a name for Ḍabba, one of the tribes of Yamāma; see *Ishtiqāq*, 100. Since a clan of Tamim, (closely related to Ḍabba), Banū al-ʿAnbar, also claimed descent from Ishmael and was so considered by the Prophet (see above, note 45), it is possible that Ḍabba, too, viewed herself in the same genealogical light. Thus pride in descent from Hagar seems also to have been reflected by a group that lived in the northeastern part of the Arabian Peninsula. The phrase "Khayl Hājar" ("the horse or cavalry of Hagar") appears in an ode by the Umayyad poet of the 8th century, Jarīr. The verse in which it occurs was included by al-Marzubānī in his *Muwashshaḥ*, and the commentator explains that the referent of Hagar in the verse is the clan of the tribe, Ḍabba. Thus the designation survived until at least the 8th century, or did so in the consciousness of the poet Jarīr. For this verse, see M. Marzubāni, *al-Muwashshaḥ*, ed. A. M. al-Bajāwi (Cairo, 1965), 199–200.

[69] It is not clear whether the biblical concept of the descent of the South Arabians from Yoktan had reached the poet and his group. The poem in its present form may not be complete and in the missing lines the poet may have contrasted the descent of the South Arabs from Yoktan with that of the North Arabs from the slave woman Hagar.

[70] Matronymics were not uncommon in pre-Islamic Arabia, and within the tribe of Kalb there were twenty two-groups with eponymous ancestresses, including "the sons of Mavia," for whom see *BAFOC*, 196 note 17. For Banū al-Hayjumāna, "the sons of al-Hayjumāna," see Ḥamza, *Tārīkh*, 89; also for Hayjumāna as Gr. *hēgoumenē*, see above, Chap. 8, app. 2.5, and below, Chap 14, sec. I note 9.

[71] See al-Maymanī, op. cit., 3, where he says that of Jāḥiẓ *ka'annahū kharaqa al-'ijmāʿ*.

[72] See Jāḥiẓ, *Kitāb al-Ḥayawān*, VI, 275, 280–81. The verse is quoted on p. 275, and reads: *ka-shihabi al-qaḏfi yarmīkum bihi fārisun fi kaffihī lilḥarbi nār*.

1. The statement that the *ruwāt* rejected it has no basis in fact. None of the Arabic works that deal with and quote this poem has considered it spurious.[73] It is noteworthy that he fails to name a single one of the scholars who reject it, as he does when he discusses another poem.[74]

2. A careful examination of the alleged Koranic thought in the verse does not necessarily yield the conclusion that Jāḥiẓ drew from it. In its Islamic, Koranic amplitude, that thought involves meteors (shooting stars) and devils who were hit by them as God's punishment for their engaging in illicit activities.[75] There is no reference whatsoever in the verse to the devils; the phrase simply means "the meteor, or shooting star, or hurling." The object of this activity is left implied, and may or may not be the devil—Koranic or other; Jāḥiẓ' categorical claim that it is the Koranic one is unjustified.[76]

3. Even if the verse breathes the same sentiment as the Koran, this is a far cry from its having been borrowed from the Koran. The Koran and Arabic poetry share much in common, the language, the style, and the similies; indeed, pre-Islamic Arabic poetry was the key that provided the Koranic exegetes with solutions for unlocking many a Koranic problem. It is therefore quite possible that both the Koran and the poem of Afwah drew on common Arabian sources and modes of expression in referring to the meteors of heaven. This is especially so in this area; the Arabs of pre-Islamic times had a special interest in the stars, which guided their caravans at night, and had special knowledge of the stars, which was called *ʿilm al-anwāʾ*.[77] The spectacle of shooting stars was familiar to the pre-Islamic Arabs, and it is practically certain that they attributed some significance to the phenomenon and could possibly have related it to their version of pre-Islamic demonology, which was quite developed. Consequently, even if the phrase shared its view of meteors involving the devils and the demons with the Koran, which is far from certain, it does not necessarily follow that it was influenced by it; it is more likely that both the Koranic and the poetic verse draw on common Arabian experience concerning that celestical phenomenon.

[73] One who was both an eminent critic and poet did not "buy" what Jahiz had to say on the authenticity of the poem or the line; see Abu al-ʿAlāʾ al-Maʿarrī, *Risālat al-Ghufrān*, ed. ʿA. Abd al-Raḥmān (Cairo, 1963), 297.

[74] See Jāḥiẓ, *Kitāb*, 278.

[75] For the Koran on devils and meteors, see chap. 15, *al-Ḥijr*, verses 16–18; chap. 37, *al-Ṣaffāt*, verses 6–10; chap. 67, *al-Mulk*, verse 5.

[76] His argument is cast in the form of a simple perhaps naive question: "By what means did al-Afwah know that the meteors he sees are the meteors of hurling and pelting, while he is a pre-Islamic poet, and none but the Muslims ever said so (about meteors)"? In the question, he uses the Koranic term *rajm* in order to strengthen his case that the verse is a Koranic borrowing, whereas Afwah did not use this term; he used only *qadf*. As the following section will show, this view of meteors could not have been only Islamic.

[77] On this science of the stars among the pre-Islamic Arabs, see Al-Shahrastāni, *al-Milal wa al-Niḥal*, ed. A. al-ʿAbd (Cairo, 1977), 583.

An examination of the context in which Jāḥiẓ rejected this poem as unauthentic will reveal that the distinguished writer was carried away by his zeal, and so judged the poem spurious. As the chapter in which his criticism appears indicates,[78] Jāḥiẓ was engaged in responding to those anti-Arab and anti-Muslim groups who had attacked the Koran, and in that particular chapter the Koranic references to the stars and meteors was the battleground. Carried away by his desire to defend the Koran, Jāḥiẓ became extravagant in his rejection of the authenticity of many poems that included references to the stars. No doubt he had some justification for rejecting some of these poems, or at least for declaring the invalidity of the arguments of the anti-Muslim or anti-Koranic groups who cited them as evidence for what they were saying. He was especially justified in the case of admittedly *mukhdram* poets, that is, poets who lived both in pre-Islamic and Islamic times, and so could have heard the Koranic verses on these meteors. But he went too far, and in the process rejected what is undoubtedly a poem of a well-known pre-Islamic poet. Moreover, the verse in Afwah's poem is irrelevant to the argument of the anti-Koranic group. Instead of noting or commenting on its irrelevance, Jāḥiẓ declared it unauthentic.

A third and final argument for the authenticity of the verse (and the entire poem) derives from certain Muḥammadan traditions. One says that the Prophet Muḥammad prohibited the recitation of this poem of al-Afwah because of its sentiments against Ishmael;[79] another that whenever he heard one of its verses recited he cursed al-Afwah.[80] This is strong evidence against Jāḥiẓ, which he does not refer to or dispose of. It is difficult—if not impossible—to believe that these Muḥammadan *ḥadīths* (traditions) were fabricated.[81] The conclusion that not only the poem but also the Muḥammadan *ḥadīths* were fabricated involves a series of unjustified suppositions which are unsupported by facts and are the result of pure speculation, while the case for the poem's authenticity rests on internal and external evidence.[82]

[78] Jāḥiẓ, *Kitāb*, 272–81.

[79] See Abdul Rahim al-ʿAbbāsī, *Maʿāhid al-Ṭansīs ʿalā Shawāhid al-Talkhīs*, ed. M. Abdul-Hamīd (Beirut, 1947), IV, 95. The author cites the verse in the poem involving Jurhum quoted above (note 62), but there is no reference in the verse to Ishmael unless by implication, which was clear to the Prophet at the time but since then has become obscure. The poem in its present form is clearly not complete, so it is possible that there was a verse that referred specifically to Ishmael but which is not extant.

[80] See Abū al-Baqā' Hibat Allāh al-Ḥillī, *Al-Manāqib al-Mazyadiyya fī Akhbār al-Mulūk al-Asadiyya*, ed. S. Daradika and M. Khuraysāt (Amman, 1984), I, 332). The verse in question is the one in which Banū Hājar are referred to (discussed above, note 67): *Yā banī Hāgara sāʾat khuṭṭatan an tarūmu al-nisfa minnā wa-nujār*. The last word has many variants.

[81] As many of them clearly were.

[82] The discovery of an important Arabic manuscript at the Yale University Library, *Muntahā al-Ṭalab min Ashʿār al-ʿArab*, has made substantial additions to the corpus of pre-Islamic poetry, for example, the flyting poem in response to that of al-Afwah al-Awdī, by a

II. Byzantium and Mecca

Arab-Byzantine relations involving Mecca turn largely about Quṣayy, whose *floruit* may be assigned to the first half of the fifth century,[83] Muḥammad's ancestor in the fifth generation and the largest figure in the history of the city before Muḥammad. The Arabic sources credit Quṣayy with far-reaching measures and reforms pertaining to the tribe of Quraysh, the city of Mecca, and the Temple of Kaʿba. Before discussing the strictly and explicitly Byzantine profile of his career, it is well that a brief treatment of his achievements involving Mecca be attempted, since it was a Meccan, building on the foundation laid down by Quṣayy, who successfully threw down the gauntlet to Byzantium in the seventh century.

I

His career may be presented briefly as follows. Born in Mecca, he lost his father, Kilāb, soon after his birth. His mother, Fāṭima, who belonged to the Azd tribe,[84] married a man from the tribe of ʿUḏra and emigrated with him to the north, near the Byzantine border; after learning of his Meccan origin from his mother, Quṣayy returned to Mecca. He married Ḥubbā, the daughter of the Khuzāʿi chief, Ḥulayl, son of Ḥubshiyya, and thus gained an important position in the city. After the death of his father-in-law, who controlled the arrangements for worship in the Kaʿba, Quṣayy succeeded him in that capacity, either through a tricky bargain with its custodian (Abū) Gubshān or after an armed conflict with Kuzāʿa. Having thus become the master of Mecca and the guardian of the Kaʿba, he proceeded to reorganize the tribal and insti-

North Arabian poet, al-Find al-Zimmāni. Like that of the former, it has the spirit of pre-Islamic Arabia, which confirms its authenticity. The most relevant part of it is a cluster of verses in which the poet refers to Hagar and Ishmael, reflecting his pride in the descent of his tribal group Nizār from the two biblical figures. For the poem, see *Majallat al-ʿArab* (Riyad, 1975), 877–80; for the three verses on Hagar and Ishmael, see 880, lines 8–10. For this 6th-century Arab poet, see Sezgin, *GAS*, II, 156.

[83] For Quṣayy, see G. Levi Della Vida in *EI,*[2] s.v. Ḳuṣayy. The bibliography will guide the reader, especially the Byzantinist, to the Arabic sources on Quṣayy.

Quṣayy must have been a 5th-century figure, since he was the ancestor of Muḥammad in the fifth generation and Muḥammad, according to the best of the Arabic traditions, was born in what the Arab historians call "The Year of the Elephant," traditionally given as around 570. The only statement in the Arabic sources which gives a chronological indication for Quṣayy assign his *floruit* to the reign of the Lakmid king Munḏir, son of al-Nuʿmān, a contemporary of the Sasanid king Bahrām Gūr who ruled from 420 to 438. The statement comes in a modern work on pre-Islamic Arabia by M. al-Alūsī, *Bulūgh al-ʿArab fi Maʿrifat Aḥwāl al-ʿArab* (Cairo, 1964), I, 247. Unfortunately, the learned author does not give his source, but the synchronization is very attractive and is probably correct. The author must be quoting an ancient Arabic source.

[84] His descendant, ʿAbdul Muṭṭalib, Muḥammad's grandfather, also married into the Azd, his wife being Salmā from Banū al-Najjār of Medina. Thus Muḥammad had two ancestresses from the Azd, to which belonged the Ghassānids of Oriens and probably the Hārithids of Najrān.

tutional life of Mecca: he gathered together the clans of Quraysh who had been scattered before and settled them in and around Mecca,[85] in the Biṭāḥ and the Ẓawāhir; he built for the *mala'*, the elders of the city, Dār al-Nadwa,[86] where they could assemble and in which every important business in Mecca was transacted; he rebuilt the Kaʿba and gathered together in his own hands the functions associated with it. These were also related to the institution of pilgrimage, which gave Mecca great prestige among the Arabs; before his death he arranged for the religious functions involving the Kaʿba to be kept in the hands of his sons and descendants.

Such is the career of the man[87] of whom Caetani[88] perceptively wrote "egli è per Makkah quello che fu Tesseo per Atene e Romolo per Roma, con la differenza, che egli ha maggiore probabilità di essere un personaggio storico, e non eroe leggendario." The following aspects of his career deserve attention, especially as some of them have indirect relations to future Meccan-Byzantine or Arab-Byzantine encounters.

1. The obscurity that surrounds the early history of his city (Mecca) and of his tribe (Quraysh) may be said to be partially dispelled by reference to a Macoraba in Ptolemy and to a *Dabenigoris regio* in Pliny.[89] If the identification of the phrase in Pliny is truly to the *regio Ḏu Banī Quraysh*, then the antiquity of the tribe can be pushed back to the second half of the first century B.C.

2. A similar obscurity surrounds the background of Quṣayy. The remoter background of his ancestors has two names, Lu'ayy and Elias, both of which suggest some involvement in religion. Elias is the well-known name of the OT prophet,[90] while Lu'ayy may be related to a North Arabian term, attested epigraphically, which could relate him to a religious function.[91]

[85] Thus acquiring the title of Al-Mujammiʿ, the uniter or unifier.

[86] For this see R. Paret in *EI*, s.v. Dar al-Nadwa.

[87] There is really nothing about him to justify suspecting that he was not a historical figure. Even his march from the Byzantine border to Mecca with the intention of regaining control of his native city can be paralleled in the 20th century, by the much more arduous task that faced King ʿAbdul-Azīz ibn Saud when he marched from Kuwait and recaptured his ancestral capital, Riyad. The former married the boss's daughter, while the second carved his kingdom with his sword.

[88] L. Caetani, *Annali del Islam* (Rome, 1904), I, 73.

[89] The game of identification, when it involves Arabic toponyms and ethnonyms on the one hand and Greek and Latin versions of them on the other, is hazardous. But I am inclined to agree with H. von Wissman in his identification of both Mecca and Quraysh with what he found in Ptolemy and Pliny, in spite of some difficulties presented by these identifications; see *RE*, Suppl. 12, s.v. Μακοράβα.

[90] It should be mentioned, however, that Elias comes in the segment of the genealogical table of Muḥammad's ancestry which extends from ʿAdnān to Ishmael, which probably derives from non-Arabic sources and is viewed with suspicion, unlike the segment which extends from Muḥammad to ʿAdnān which is more or less reliable. However, the striking name Elias could be significant. See the geneaological table in Caetani, *Annali del Islam,* opposite p. 38, where the name appears as Al-Yās.

[91] The term is *lawī,* which was thought to mean "priest." This was suggested by D. H.

Quṣayy's own immediate background and residence in the north near the Byzantine border seems confirmed by a number of indications. (*a*) The name Quṣayy appears in the Nabataean inscriptions; although found elsewhere, it is not a common name, so its epigraphic attestation in the Nabataean north is significant.[92] (*b*) The gods which appear in Mecca in this and the following century are *North* Arabian gods; this includes Hubal, the chief pagan god of Mecca, and also the "three daughters of Allah" in the Meccan pantheon, mentioned in the Koran—Allāt, Al-ʿUzzā, and Manāt.[93] How these can be related to Quṣayy's northern sojourn is not clear, especially if he was—as tradition portrays him—a monotheist restoring the religion of Ishmael and Abraham. On the other hand, he may simply have tolerated religious pluralism as a political necessity.

3. According to the Arabic tradition, Quṣayy wrested the guardianship of the Kaʿba and rule over Mecca from the tribe of Khuzāʿa, a South Arabian tribe which belonged to the large tribal group al-Azd, and which presumably had occupied Mecca before the fifth century. The tribe is fully attested in Muhammadan and early Islamic times, and its most important member historically is an enigmatic ʿAmr, son of Luḥayy, to whom is ascribed the introduction of idolatry, into Mecca and the Kaʿba after a period during which a monotheistic tradition going back to Abraham had prevailed.[94] There is no way of unlocking the secrets of this ʿAmr without the solid evidence of epigraphic discoveries, but what has survived of the onomasticon of Khuzāʿa could shed some light.

The name of the daughter of the Khuzāʿi chief whom Quṣayy married is given as a Ḥubbā. This is an archaic name which speaks for itself and has been recovered in the Nabataean inscriptions.[95] More important is the matronymic

---

Müller but later contested by H. Grimme, revived by F. Winnet but again rejected by A. Jamme. For the original dialogue between Müller and Grimme, see H. Grimme, *Le Muséon* 37 (1924), 169–99. For the equation of Lu'ayy with *lawiʾ*, one has to assume that the term underwent metathesis.

[92] See Della Vida, *EI*, col. 520 and the attestations in R. Dussaud, *Les Arabes en Syrie avant l'Islam* (Paris, 1907), 123–24, where a family is involved in the custodianship of the temple of the goddess Allāt in Salkhad. Surprisingly enough, the name "Qasiou, son of Aklabou" appears in the genealogical tree of the family, and this recalls Quṣayy, whose father was called Kilāb. This family, however, lived centuries before Quṣayy.

[93] See P. K. Hitti, *A History of Syria*, 385. The Nabataean connection could receive some confirmation for a tradition which goes back to the caliph ʿAli, that Quraysh were Nabataeans from Kūthā; see T. Fahd, *Le panthéon de l'Arabie*, 215 note 3. But Kūthā is situated in Babylonia, for which see ibid., 215. This valuable book should be consulted for many of the elements that involve Mecca and the Kaʿba discussed in this chapter.

[94] On him see J. Fück in *EI*,[2] s.v.

[95] For this inscription, see R. Dagorn, *La geste d'Ismaël d'après l'onomastique et la tradition arabe* (Paris, 1981), 322. In this inscription and another also discovered at Madāʾin Salīḥ, the name of Hagar is attested; ibid., 322–23.

of her father, Ḥulayl, which is given as Ḥubshiyya or Ḥabashiyya, the Arabic form of "Abyssinian." The presumption is that ʿAmr's mother was an Abyssinian lady, and this may be related to the fact that in the fourth century, which possibly witnessed Khuzāʿa's supremacy in Mecca, the Abyssinians under their king ʿEzana, the Constantine of Abyssinia, invaded South Arabia and occupied it for some time.[96] An event of such importance must have convulsed western Arabia, and the movement of tribes such as Khuzāʿa from the south to the north could be related to this invasion. What cultural effects the invasion of South Arabia by a newly converted Christian Abyssinia had is not clear, but it is not altogether extravagant to suspect that it carried in its wake some cultural influences related to Christianity,[97] as well as the infusion of Abyssinian strains into the ethnographic body of western Arabia, which is reflected by names such as Ḥabashiyya.[98]

4. Of all the measures and reforms which Quṣayy brought about in Mecca, his rebuilding of the Kaʿba and the organization of the worship centering around it were most significant. The center of it all was the institution of the pilgrimage, which made Mecca the religious center for many of the Arab tribes of the Peninsula and thus established its supremacy and prestige in Arabia. But the pilgrimage had another facet to it, for during the pilgrimage months Mecca also became a highly profitable commercial fair.[99] Thus Quṣayy may be said to have laid the foundation of Mecca's power through his organization of its religious and commercial lives, which went hand-in-hand in the course of the following two centuries. In the second of these two centuries Mecca produced the prophet Muḥammad, who had been a caravan leader for fifteen years before his Call around 610.

5. It remains to examine the relations of Quṣayy to Ishmaelism and his contribution to the Meccan pantheon. Did he purify it of idolatry or did he in addition tolerate religious pluralism?

a. The Arabic tradition associates Quṣayy with the restoration of the "religion of Abraham" in the worship of the Kaʿba after it had been adulter-

[96] For this, see *BAFOC*, 90–100.

[97] As it could have done in South Arabia. For Christianity in South Arabia in the first half of the 4th century related to the mission of Theophilus Indus and the Ethiopian occupation, see *BAFOC*, 1200–6.

[98] And also the "Ahabish" of later times in H. Lammens' view, disputed by some, such as W. M. Watt in *Muhammad at Mecca* (Oxford, 1953), 154–57. The problem of the "Ahabish" will be discussed in *BASIC*.

N. Abbot suggested that the Abyssinian occupation of Yaman in South Arabia may have stimulated Meccan trade and contributed to its rise as a commercial center in the 4th century; see *The Rise of the North Arabic Script*, Oriental Institute Publications (Chicago, 1939), I, 11–12.

[99] And this could easily explain why the Quraysh accepted the idols of many of these tribes in their temple.

ated by idolatry, introduced by the Khuzāʿi ʿAmr, son of Luḥayy.[100] This is not altogether unlikely, in view of his sojourn in the Nabataean north which could very well have been the center of Ishmaelism in this second inter-testamental period. Additionally, the Arabic sources ascribe verses to Quṣayy in which he takes pride in his lineal descent from the sons of Ishmael, Qaydar and Nabīt.[101] Such verse as goes back to the first half of the fifth century and treats such subjects is usually suspect in the eyes of Arabic literary critics. But recent research on the beginnings of Arabic poetry, going back at least to the fourth century,[102] and on the possible survival of Ishmaelism among the Arabs in this second inter-testamental period, cannot but exercise some salutary influence by making students of this verse at least entertain the possibility of its authenticity.

b. On the other hand, there is some evidence that Quṣayy was not a pure Ishmaelite monotheist, as the sources portray him. For example, the names of his sons, ʿAbd Manāf and ʿAbd al-ʿUzzā, betray pagan influence, carrying the names of a well-known Arabian god (Manāf) and an Arabian goddess (al-ʿUzza). In defense of his monotheism, it might be suggested that he gave these names to his sons before his conversion to monotheism and that they continued to carry them even after their father's conversion in much the same way that the Umayyad dynasty after its conversion to Islam continued to be called the sons of ʿAbd Shams, the servant of the Sun (goddess). The pagan elements that coexisted with Ishmaelism may also be due to the political necessity of allowing each tribe to have its own idol in order to keep the Kaʿba a center of Arab worship and commerce.[103]

6. Quṣayy laid the foundation of Mecca's position as the Arab religious and commercial center in western Arabia. Since this was the foundation on which Muḥammad built in the seventh century, before he threw the challenge to Byzantium, it is well that Quṣayy's achievement be summed up.

A. Quṣayy established what might be termed the institutional constituents of the new Arab polity that Mecca became. (*a*) He gathered together the various clans of Quraysh in and around Mecca, the tribe that was to produce the astounding number of generals and administrators who ran the nascent Muslim empire fashioned by the successors of Muḥammad. (*b*) He re-built the

[100] This is clearly implied in Ṭabarī when he speaks of Quṣayy as saying that the Quraysh are the "choicest descendants of Ishmael, son of Abraham" *Tārīkh,* II, 255–56. And when he speaks of "Allah," Quṣayy appears again as a pure monotheist in his address to Quraysh (ibid., 260).

[101] See al-Azraqī, *Akhbār Makka,* I, 107.

[102] See Shahīd, *BAFOC,* 443–48; idem, "The Composition of Arabic Poetry in the Fourth Century," in *Studies in the History of Arabia; Pre-Islamic Arabia* (Riyad, 1984), II, 87–93.

[103] For support of this, see Ṭabarī, *Tārīkh,* II, 259.

Kaʿba, reorganized worship at that shrine, and concentrated in his own hands (and after him in the hands of his descendants) all the offices that pertained to that worship. That assured the supremacy of Quraysh among the Arabs and his own house in particular, a matter of some importance in later Islamic political history. (*c*) The organization of worship at the Kaʿba and its climax in the institution of the pilgrimage enhanced both the prestige of Quraysh as the custodians of the Kaʿba and Mecca and also gave the Arab tribes, mostly pagan, a focal point around which they actually discovered their identity.

B. These institutional elements made of Mecca "The Mother of Cities" (*Umm al-Qurā*)[104] in the region, and this primacy was two-dimensional. (*a*) Spiritually, Mecca emerged not only as the great religious center of the Arabs, but also as an independent one. The Arabs were aware of this character of Mecca as a native, indigenous religious center that resisted the temptation of being converted to either of the two monotheistic religions that might have attempted such a conversion; they applied to Mecca and Quraysh the technical term *laqāḥ*[105] ("independent"). It was Quṣayy's great achievement to give to Mecca its strongly distinguishing character as an independent religious center, from which issued the Islamic mission in the seventh century. Had it been otherwise, it would be difficult to imagine that mission in that century. (*b*) Materially, Mecca also emerged as an important commercial center, since the institution of the pilgrimage also entailed that of the commercial fair held in its vicinity, from which great wealth accrued to the Meccan custodians of the Kaʿba. In the time of Quṣayy this trade was probably still intra-Arabian, and it was not until the time of his grandson Hāshim,[106] according to the sources, that it became extra-Arabian, involving, among other powers, Byzantium itself.

II

The Byzantine profile of Quṣayy's career is documented in a sole statement in the *Maʿārif* of Ibn Qutayba (828–889), which reads "then Quṣayy marched to Mecca and he made war against Khuzāʿa with those that followed

[104] On this expression, which is first met with in the Koran, see Fahd, *Le panthéon de l'Arabie,* 222–24.

[105] The term is applied to Mecca and Quraysh in the 6th century, in connection with the episode involving ʿUthmān ibn al-Ḥuwayrith, who wanted to bring Mecca within the Byzantine sphere of influence. M. J. Kister has discussed this term and collected the sources on this episode; see his "Al-Ḥīra: Some Notes on Its Relations with Arabia," *Arabica* (1968), 153–54.

[106] The important role of Hāshim in developing the extra-Arabian trade of Mecca will be discussed in *BASIC,* as will the episode involving ʿUthmān ibn al-Ḥuwayrith. Hāshim's father, ʿAbd-Manāf, was an important figure in Mecca, but the sources say nothing about a Byzantine connection involving him, as they do about his father Quṣayy and his son Hāshim. Patricia Crone challenges the traditional view in *Meccan Trade and the Rise of Islam,* which has been announced by the Princeton University Press as forthcoming.

him and Qayṣar (Caesar) extended aid to him against it (Khuzāʿa)."[107] This cryptic but precious statement is the sole evidence that has survived in the Arabic sources for the Byzantine connection, and also happens to be the first explicit reference in any of the sources to Byzantium's contact with Mecca. Hence it deserves a thorough treatment.

1. The first problem that must be discussed is the reliability of the account. There is no question that it is authentic, coming as does from that judicious author Ibn Qutayba, the polymath and polygraph of the ninth century[108] who in the same historical manual has also preserved from sources no longer extant such other precious statements as those which document the Ghassānid Arethas' campaign against the Jewish oasis of Khaybar in Ḥijāz and the Ghassānid Christian mission to Ḥimyar.[109]

Ibn Qutayba was influenced by the various trends and cultural currents prevalent in the ninth century, and drew inspiration from a wide variety of contemporary written sources. This raises the question of the "source of the source" whence he received this information on Quṣayy's invoking and receiving the aid of Byzantium. It is practically certain that such detailed information on the distant past of Mecca, involving the ancestor of Muḥammad in the fifth generation, must have come from a book specifically and exclusively devoted to Mecca and Quraysh. Such a book existed in the ninth-century *Kitāb Nasab Quraysh wa Akhbārihim,*[110] by al-Zubayr ibn Bakkār (788–870). Ibn Qutayba was al-Zubayr's younger contemporary, and outlived him by nineteen years. Thus it is chronologically quite possible that Ibn Qutayba could have received this information from al-Zubayr's book, just as he incorporated in his work something from another older contemporary, al-Jāḥiẓ, who died in 869. Finally, even if the source of Ibn Qutayba cannot be established with absolute certainty, the authenticity of the statement cannot be impugned because it is of such a nature as not to admit of being fabricated and fastened on the Prophet's ancestor. Pious Muslim authors—and Ibn Qutayba qualified as such—would not have cared to associate the conquest of the Holy City of Islam with the Christian Byzantine Empire if this had not been the case.[111]

[107] See Ibn Qutayba, *Kitāb al-Maʿārif,* ed. Th. ʿUkāsha (Cairo, 1960), 640–41. Lammens was the first to comment on this statement in Ibn Qutayba and to make some pertinent remarks. But his views on the role of the Ghassānids in the Byzantine aid extended to Quṣayy cannot be accepted. Quṣayy's *floruit* antedates the rise of the Ghassānids as the dominant federate group in the service of Byzantium by almost a century; on this, see the various authors cited by Abbott in *Rise of the North Arabic Script,* 11. For Lammens' views, see "La Meccque à la veille de l'hégira," *Mélange de l'Université Saint Joseph, Beyrouth* (1924), 268–70.

[108] For Ibn Qutayba see Sezgin, *GAS,* VIII, 161–65, and *EI,* s.v. Ibn-Ḳutayba.

[109] See *Maʿārif,* 642, 637.

[110] For this book and its author, see F. Sezgin, *GAS,* I, 317–18.

[111] The point was well understood by Lammens, who made some perceptive remarks in defence of the reliability of the account and its laconicism.

There is no doubt that the account in the original source must have been fairly detailed. An indication of its possible extensiveness is afforded by the parallel case of another chief in the sixth century, ʿUthmān ibn Ḥuwayrith, who also was a Meccan and established contacts with Byzantium. In the *Jamharat Nasab Quraysh* of al-Zubayr ibn Bakkār there is a very extensive account, which is luckily available for examination since it comes in the portion of al-Zubayr's book that has survived, dealing with the clan of Quraysh called Banū Asad ibn ʿAbd al-ʿUzzā.[112] Since the chapter on Quṣayy has not survived, one must unlock the secrets of this cryptic statement on the Byzantine aid to Quṣayy inferentially, from other relevant data that are available.

2. The statement in Ibn Qutayba speaks of Qayṣar[113] (Arabic for Caesar), that is, the Byzantine emperor, as the one who extended aid to Quṣayy. It is not impossible that Quṣayy may have reached Constantinople while he was in the north.[114] Two other Arab chiefs of the same century are attested in Constantinople: one of them was the Arab from Najrān in South Arabia in the first half of the fifth century; the other was Amorkesos, the adventurous chief of the reign of Leo in the second half of the century.[115] Whether Quṣayy was so privileged remains an open question; the chances are that he was not. Arab authors normally speak of Qayṣar when they only mean the Byzantine or the Roman authorities in general. This is clinched by references in the sources to the fact that Quṣayy spent his minority in the north near the Byzantine border, where ʿUḏra, the tribe of his father-in-law, was settled. The exploration of Quṣayy's Byzantine connection will then turn about the Byzantine connection of ʿUḏra and its place in the Byzantine defence system.

3. The relevant facts about ʿUḏra may be stated as follows.[116] (*a*) It was an Arab tribe that was settled in Wādī al-Qurā, near Medina and the oasis of Tabūk in north Ḥijāz, and is attested as far to the north as Ayla, the seaport on the Gulf of Eilath; where it was exactly in the fifth century cannot be determined, but this was roughly its area of settlement.[117] (*b*) Thus the tribe controlled the trade route that ran between Ḥijāz and South Arabia on the one hand and the northern regions of the Provincia and Oriens on the other. (*c*) ʿUḏra was thus settled in that area that was most probably adjacent to the boundaries of the Provincia (now Palaestina Tertia), or partly within the Provincia when it settled in Ayla. It was thus one of the Arab tribes that were

[112] See al-Zubayr ibn Bakkār, *Jamharat Nasab Quraysh*, I, 425–38.

[113] On Qayṣar in the Arabic authors, see I. Shahîd and R. Paret in *EI*,[2] s.v. Ḳayṣar.

[114] Especially if his stay in the north before his capture of Mecca was truly near Yarmūk in the Provincia Arabia; see Ḳuṣayy in *EI*, vol. V, p. 519.

[115] On Ḥayyān the Najrānite, see below, Sec. III and on Amorkesos see above, Chap. 4.

[116] For ʿUḏra, see Levi Della Vida, *EI*,[2] s.v.

[117] On the extensive portion of Nabataea that was incorporated in the Provincia Arabia, see Bowersock, *Roman Arabia*, 90–109, 156–59.

technically *foederati* of Byzantium, employed by the Empire for the defence of the southern parts of Oriens.[118]

The foregoing fully explains the nature and extent of the Byzantine stake and involvement in the Quṣayy episode. It is quite unlikely that Byzantium sent regular Byzantine troops with Quṣayy. Much more likely would have been federate or phylarchal aid, extended through the Arab *foederati* of Byzantium, ʿUḏra. Through their Byzantine connection, these would have acquired more advanced techniques of warfare than the Peninsular Arabs, and thus would have been invaluable allies of the youthful Quṣayy in his endeavor to regain his ancestral city.

4. Byzantine aid, however indirectly, raises the further question of what Byzantine interest was served, imperial or ecclesiastical. It is difficult to believe that no Byzantine interest was involved, and equally difficult, in view of the obscurity that surrounds this period in the history of Byzantine-Meccan relations, to ascertain exactly what that interest was. One can only speculate.

a. The determination of Quṣayy's *floruit* could throw some light on this obscure question. As has been mentioned before, he was a contemporary of al-Munḏir ibn al-Nuʿmān and the Persian king Bahrām Gūr, so he lived roughly in the third, fourth, and fifth decades of the fifth century. During this period occurred the two Persian Wars of Theodosius II's reign, the first in 421–422 and the second in 440–442. The theater of war was far from western Arabia, but so little is known about these two wars that it is not impossible that Byzantium might have thought that Persian influence in western Arabia had to be counterbalanced by the extension of Byzantine influence to the region of Mecca through aid to Quṣayy.[119] If so, then Quṣayy's victory over Khuzāʿa may be precisely dated to the period of either of these two Persian Wars.

b. As pointed out earlier in this section, ʿUḏra lay astride some important trade routes between Arabia and Oriens. It is thus quite possible that the motive behind extending aid to Quṣayy was commercial—to secure a longer segment of the trade routes of western Arabia for Byzantium by extending Byzantine influence to the central sector, in which Mecca was located. If so,

[118] See *BAFOC,* 389 note 120. That it was an old tribe going back to remote times is confirmed by Ptolemy's reference to it as ῎Αϑρται, ᾿Αϑροῖται. The identification of these with ʿUḏra is practically certain; cf. Levi Della Vida in the old *EI,* s.v. ʿUḏra, IV, 988. Its Christianity is another pointer to its federate status; see below, notes 40–42.

[119] Parallels to this situation may be invoked from the history of Arab-Byzantine relations in the 6th century: the treaty of Byzantium with the Ghassānids in 502 and the episode of ʿUthmān ibn al-Ḥuwayrith. Both reveal a Byzantium that was interested in Arab affairs in response to fear of Persian influence or a Persian threat; for the first, see Shahīd, "Ghassan and Byzantium," 239; for the second, see H. Lammens, *La Meccque,* 270–79.

this could argue that even in the first part of the fifth century Mecca was already an important station on the West Arabian trade route.

c. Finally, it is not impossible that some ecclesiastical interest might have been served by the aid extended to Quṣayy—the extension of the Christian mission from Byzantine north to Mecca. This is a thorny question. Already under Jurhum, Mecca must have received some form of Christianity which, however, may have been effaced by the period of Khuzāʿa's primacy and the introduction of idolatry.[120] This then may have been a revival of the Christian mission, not altogether unlikely, since further to the south Ḥayyān first introduced Christianity to Najrān roughly during Quṣayy's *floruit* (or slightly antedating it by a few years), after a visit to Constantinople and contacts with the Christians of Ḥīra on the lower Euphrates.[121]

This may derive some support from the fact that ʿUḏra was converted to Christianity in pre-Islamic times and the tribe, or at least parts of it, remained Christian well into the Islamic period. This is clearly indicated in a verse addressed to the famous ʿUḏrite poet Jamīl[122] by another poet, Jaʿfar ibn Surāqa, in which he taunts his tribe, ʿUḏra, that it consists of "two divisions, monks who live in the lower part of Wādī al-Qurā (near Medina) and *ʿarrāfūn*,[123] who live among those who adopted Christianity in Shām (former Oriens from the Taurus to Sinai). The verse reads: *Farīqāni ruhbānun bi-asfali ḏi al-Qurā/wa-bishshāmi ʿarrāfūna fīman tanaṣṣarā.*[124]

The Christianity of ʿUḏra in Umayyad Islamic times is thus established, and this must go back to the pre-Islamic period, since it is inconceivable that this would have happened after the rise of Islam. How far back into pre-Islamic times it goes is an open question, but the chances are that ʿUḏra had become Christianized in the fifth century, and possibly in the fourth. The verse quoted above is informative both on the ʿUḏrite presence in Ḥijāz and Shām and on the existence of Christian monasteries in Wādī al-Qurā.[125]

This may seem inconsistent with what has been said about Quṣayy's keeping Mecca *laqāḥ*, independent in every sense, religiously and politically. But, as has also been pointed out, Quṣayy paid his dues to Arabian paganism

[120] On Jurhum, see below, App. 3.

[121] On this, see below, 360–70.

[122] A well-known Umayyad poet (d. about 701) who was known for his chaste and pure love poetry. On Jamīl, see Sezgin, *GAS,* II, 406–8.

[123] For this technical term describing those who practiced divination in pre-Islamic Arabia, see T. Fahd, *La divination arabe* (Leiden, 1966), 113–19. Christianity had, of course, no *ʿarrāfūn*; nevertheless, the term is used for Christian priests. The poet was engaged in a contest of invectives, hence the pejorative application of the term.

[124] For the verse, see A. Iṣbahānī, *Al-Aghānī,* VIII, 139.

[125] Much more will be said below on ʿUḏra's Christianity and its support of Quṣayy through Rizāḥ, its chief and Quṣayy's half-brother, as more sources are examined in the context of other themes.

by giving two of his sons theophoric names that smacked of paganism. In any case, whatever form of Christianity may have entered Mecca in the wake of Quṣayy's victory over Khuzāʿa and with Byzantine help, it could not have had a far-reaching effect, nor could it have endured for long. In the fifth and the sixth centuries, despite some Christian presence, Mecca remained outside the effective jurisdiction of the Christian *ecclesia*; significantly, there does not seem to have been a functionary representing a Christian hierarchy at Mecca.[126]

A statement in Theodoret's *Curatio*, speaking of the "innumerable tribes of the Ishmaelites" who welcomed the Roman alliance and connection, was discussed earlier.[127] The church father had spoken before of such faraway peoples as the Ethiopians and those in the Thebaïd, who fell in the same category as the Ishmaelite Arabs. It would be pleasant to think that echoes of the Ishmaelite Quṣayy's victory in Mecca in western Arabia, made possible by Byzantium's aid, had reached the Christian ecclesiastic in Cyrrhus[128] when he penned that paragraph, and that he included Quṣayy and the Meccans among the Ishmaelites who were within the Byzantine sphere of influence. This is not altogether impossible, but is probably too good to be true.

III. Byzantium and Najrān

There are three sets of sources for the propagation of Christianity at Najrān: the Arabic, the Syriac, and the Ethiopic. The first consists of some fairly extensive legendary accounts,[129] and of a chapter in a Nestorian *Chronicle*;[130] the second is represented by the *Book of the Ḥimyarites*;[131] and the third by the *Acts* of ʿAzqīr.[132] Of these sources the last three are the most important: the Christian *Chronicle* and the *Book of the Ḥimyarites* tell the story of the introduction of Christianity to Najrān in the first half of the fifth century; the *Acts* of ʿAzqīr tells the story in the second half of the same century.[133] They will be discussed in this order.

[126] On this, see below, App. 4.

[127] For this, see above, Chap. 8, app. 3.

[128] Theodoret was Quṣayy's contemporary.

[129] These have been well analyzed by M. Moberg, and J. W. Hirschberg; see Moberg, *Über einige christliche Legenden in der islamischen Tradition* (Lund, 1930), 15–35; Hirschberg, in "Nestorian Sources of North-Arabian Traditions on the Establishment and Persecution of Christianity in Yemen," in *Rocznik Orientalistyczny* (Krakow, 1939–49), vol. 15, 321–38; also J. Ryckmans, "Le christianisme," 441–42. Legendary as these accounts are, they do reflect the importance of Najrān as the principal center of Christianity in western Arabia.

[130] See, for example, Ibn Qutayba, *al-Maʿārif*, 637. On the Christian *Chronicle* see below, note 134.

[131] *The Book of the Ḥimyarites*, ed. A. Moberg (Lund, 1924) (hereafter *Book*).

[132] For these see below, especially notes 169–70.

[133] Some twenty years have passed since the appearance of Ryckmans' standard article, "Le christianisme." Hence the subject is due for reexamination, especially in a book devoted to

I

The most informative of the sources is the Nestorian *Chronicle*, sometimes referred to as *The Chronicle of Saʿard*, but in its published form as *Histoire nestorienne.*[134] It may be described as informative only in view of the paucity and exiguity of the sources in general. Furthermore, it is cryptic as well as laconic, and the task of scholarship is to extract the facts from statements ambiguously worded and expressed. The French version of this account in the *Chronicle* reads as follows:

> Dans le pays du Nedjran du Yémen il y avait, sous Jazdgerd, un commerçant célèbre dans la région, du nom de Ḥannan. Il alla un jour à Constantinople pour son commerce; il rentra ensuite dans son pays; puis se dirigea vers la Perse. Mais, passant à Ḥira, il fréquenta les chrétiens et connut leur doctrine. Il y reçut le baptême et y resta un certain temps. De là, il revient au pays natal et engagea ses compatriotes à partager ses convictions religieuses. Il baptisa les membres de sa famille ainsi que d' autres personnes de son pays et des régions avoisinantes. Puis, aidé de quelques-uns d'entre eux, il convertit au christianisme le territoire de Ḥamir et ses alentours voisins de l'Abyssinie. Plus tard, un roi juif, appelé Masrouq, régna sur ces pays. Il était né d'une mère juive emenée captive de Nisibe (Naṣibin), achetée par un roi du Yémen. Elle apprit à son enfant la religion juive. Lorsqu'il monta sur le trône de son père, il massacra beaucoup de chrétiens. Barsahdé raconte tout cela dans son histoire.

It is not unlikely that this account derives from that of the *Book of the Ḥimyarites*, which also speaks of a certain Ḥayyān as the one who first introduced Christianity to Najrān.[135] For the correct analysis of the precious passage from the *Chronicle* it is imperative to make a confrontation between these

Arab-Byzantine relations in the 5th century, which witnessed the introduction of Christianity to Najrān. For a short, recent treatment of Christianity in South Arabia, see A. F. L. Beeston, "Judaism and Christianity in Pre-Islamic Yemen" in *L'Arabie du sud,* ed. J. Chelhod (Paris, 1984), I, 271–78. Reservations and objections to Beeston's views have already been expressed by the present writer in *BAFOC,* 100–2.

[134] *Histoire nestorienne,* ed. Addai Scher, PO 4, 5, 7 (hereafter *Chronicle*). This 11th-century *Chronicle* is written in Arabic but derives from old Syriac sources no longer extant; see Moberg, *Über einige Legenden,* xlix-l.

[135] The short section in the *Chronicle* most probably derives from the long second chapter in the *Book,* of which only the title is extant: "Account telling how Christianity began to be sown in the land of the Himyarites." See Moberg, ibid., l. But just as this section in the *Chronicle* illuminates the void left by the disappearance of the text of chap. 2 in the *Book,* so chap. 21 of the *Book* (on the martyrdom of Ḥabṣa and the two Ḥayyāns) amplifies the short section in the *Chronicle.*

two sources,[136] and the results of the comparative studies of J. Ryckmans and J. W. Hirschberg need to be reexamined after the lapse of such a long time.[137] Hirschberg suggested that the Persian king during whose reign Ḥannān/Ḥayyān visited Ḥīra was not Yazdgard I (399–420) but Yazdgard II (438–457); that the introduction of Christianity to Najrān must therefore be assigned to the second half of the fifth century; and, finally, that Ḥannān/Ḥayyān was a Nestorian. Ryckmans, influenced by this dating, was inclined to think that the first penetration of Christianity into Najrān could be assigned to the middle of the fifth century, but disagreed with Hirschberg on the doctrinal persuasion of Ḥayyān/Ḥannān, whom he considered a Monophysite, and concluded that the Ḥannān of the *Chronicle* could not be the Ḥayyān of the *Book of the Ḥimyarites*.

1. This conclusion must be incorrect. The two names are so close to each other graphically, both in Arabic and in Syriac, that the possibility of a scribal error is perfectly possible. Ḥayyān is attested in the *Book of the Ḥimyarites*, from which the *Chronicle* derives, as the name of an Arab from the Arab city of Najrān, and is well attested as an Arab name both in pre-Islamic and Islamic times. On the other hand, Ḥannān is a Christian name, John, arabized and assimilated to the Arabic morphological pattern *faˁˁāl*, and is an appropriate name for a convert to Christianity who was baptized at Ḥīra. So it is possible that both names were his—Ḥayyān before his conversion, Ḥannān after.[138]

The king during whose reign Ḥayyān/Ḥannān appeared in al-Ḥīra must be Yazdgard I. This is clearly stated in the *Chronicle*, which tells the story of Nestorian Christianity in strict chronological order and, in the pre-Islamic period, according to the reigns of the Sasanid kings.[139] Those who thought the king might have been Yazdgard II did so because an entire century separates Ḥayyān of the *Book* from his granddaughter Ḥabṣa, who appears as a martyr around 520. But the Arabs of those days lived to ripe old ages, and counted among them many macrobiotes.[140] Furthermore, Ḥayyān must have been a relatively young man around 420, since he made two long and strenuous journeys from Najrān, to Constantinople and Ḥīra. He could have been alive around the middle of the fifth century or even in its second half. If so, he

[136] Much can be extracted from this confrontation, as well as from the setting of the few available data against the background of Arab-Byzantine relations in the 5th century.

[137] See Ryckmans, "Le christianisme," 444, 450 and Hirschberg, "Nestorian Sources," 333; see also Altheim and Stiehl, *Die Araber in der alten Welt*, IV, 314–17.

[138] Ḥayyān emerges as an important figure in the Christian mission to South Arabia. His name, therefore, deserves to be known correctly.

[139] The *Chronicle* begins its account of the reign of Yazdgard I on p. 316. Fourteen pages later (p. 330) appears the account of Ḥayyān. Thus there is no doubt which Yazdgard the writer of the *Chronicle* had in mind.

[140] On the macrobiote ˁAbd al-Masīḥ ibn Buqayala see below, note 157.

could easily have had a son who was alive around 500 and a granddaughter who was martyred around 520. It is also not entirely clear from the account in the *Book* that Ḥayyān was Ḥabṣa's grandfather. He could have been her great-grandfather. She describes herself as "Ḥabṣa, of the family of Ḥayyān, son of Ḥayyān, the teacher, . . ." or as "the daughter of Ḥayyān of the family of Ḥayyān, the teacher. . . ."[141] She does not say explicitly and clearly that she is the daughter of Ḥayyān, son of Ḥayyān. Instead the term "family" intervenes as an element in the genealogical line, and this could easily suggest that Ḥayyān, her father, was not the son of Ḥayyān the teacher; so he could have been his grandson, especially as namesakes are more likely to be those of father and grandson than father and son. Finally, the argument from a statement in the *Acts* of ʿAzqīr cannot be valid. In these *Acts* the Ḥimyarite king of the second half of the fifth century speaks of Christianity as a religion recently introduced in South Arabia. The *Acts*, in spite of some elements of truth in them, are a hagiographic work full of legendary accounts, and such statements cannot be used for arguing that Ḥayyān's *floruit* was the middle or the second half of the fifth century.[142] The evidence from the sober *Chronicle* must be accepted that Christianity was first preached in Najrān sometime during the reign of the Sasanid king Yazdgard (399–420).

That Ḥayyān's doctrinal persuasion was either Nestorian or Monophysite has to be rejected. It must be remembered that Ḥayyān visited Ḥīra in the reign of Yazdgard, that is, before both the Council of Ephesus (431), after which Nestorianism spread in the East in the Land of the Two Rivers, and the Council of Chalcedon (451), after which Monophysitism appeared as a force in the Orient. Both dates are posterior to the reign of Yazdgard, and thus a Nestorian or Monophysite ascription to Ḥayyān is out, and with it the Nestorian or Monophysite complexion of a nascent Christianity in Nājran in the first quarter of the fifth century. Surely both were represented at Najrān later, and Monophysitism established itself as the dominant Christian denomination in Najrān, possibly late in the century and certainly in the sixth,[143] but at this stage Najrānite Christianity was neither. It must have been the Christianity that prevailed in the East after the two ecumenical councils of the fourth

[141] See *Book*, pp. cxxii, cxxiii.

[142] See Ryckmans, "Le christianisme," 444. This statement in the *Acts* has to be rejected along with others, such as that in the second half of the 5th century Najrān had a full hierarchy of metropolitans, priests, deacons, etc. See ibid., 442, where the author rightly rejects all this.

[143] As Ryckmans rightly points out; ibid., 450–53. But surely these later developments are irrelevant to the argument regarding Ḥayyān's doctrinal persuasion, since he considerably antedates the advent of both Nestorianism and Monophysitism in Najrān and the South Arabian region. Ḥīra did not become a center for Nestorianism until the sixth decade of the 5th century (in 457). The spread of Nestorianism in the Land of the Two Rivers took some time, and even more time before its arrival in faraway Najrān.

century, which established Nicene Christianity, and before the two ecumenical councils of the fifth, which split the Christian Orient and indeed all Christendom.

2. The appearance in Constantinople of a merchant from Najrān raises many important problems for Arab-Byzantine relations in the fifth century.

His designation as a merchant explains why this Arab from Najrān journeyed to the capital.[144] Najrān was a most important commercial center in western Arabia, well known to the Romans since the ill-starred expedition of Aelius Gallus (25–24 B.C.). A well-known merchant in that important caravan city would have been welcome in the capital of an empire which needed and wanted the luxury articles for which Arabia was famous and which Najrān, because of its strategic position, mediated. As pointed out in the preceding volume, the initiative taken by Byzantium during the reign of Constantius in the fourth century was not continued by Julian and his successors—the emperors of the second half of the century, the house of Valentinian and Theodosius the Great.[145] It is perfectly possible that the Byzantium of Theodosius II wanted to reopen its diplomatic and commercial offensive in the world of the southern Semites and so welcomed Ḥayyān in much the same way that the Byzantium of Leo in the second half of the same century welcomed the phylarch Amorkesos.[146]

But what was Ḥayyān's objective in visiting Constantinople? Amorkesos, of the reign of Leo, operated along the Roman *limes*, within the Byzantine sphere of influence, and wanted to become a Byzantine phylarch. But Ḥayyān, hailed from a region very far from the Byzantine sphere of influence. There may have been nothing behind the visit other than the attempt of an ambitious merchant to establish trade relations with the Mediterranean power that bought Arabian goods. But the chances are that other factors were operative, although these can only be the object of speculation in the absence of evidence. Ḥayyān's journey to Constantinople might have been politically inspired. In these Arabian caravan cities a prominent merchant could easily also have been a political leader, as in the case of Hāshim in the Mecca of the sixth century.[147] Ḥayyān could even have been the chief, the *sayyid*, of Najrān.

[144] Cf. the appearance of the Byzantine merchant Sopatrus in Ceylon at the court of the king; see Cosmas Indicopleustes, *Topographie chrétienne,* SC 197 (Paris, 1973), III, 349, 351.

[145] See *BAFOC,* 104, 539.

[146] See above, 77–82. While in Constantinople, Ḥayyān must have been the ward of the *Scrinium Barbarorum,* which may have kept records about Najrān and South Arabia deriving from Ḥayyān's well-informed testimony.

[147] The Arabic sources, which are copious on Mecca, give a glimpse of the interaction of commercial and political leadership and often their union in one person; they provide an analogy of a caravan city such as Najrān and how it was possible for one of its merchants to engage in political transactions. Hāshim, the great-grandfather of the Prophet Muḥammad, will be discussed in *BASIC.* Cf. also what the chief and martyr of Najrān in the 6th century, Ḥārith

This suspicion is strengthened by the fact that after his return from Constantinople he set out to Persia. That journey may also have been inspired by commercial motives, but political motives cannot be ruled out. In short, his journeys suggest a political leader who wanted to deal with the two world powers of the period.[148] In view of the peculiar position of Najrān as an Arab city in the Sabaean south and its northerly location closer to the Arab cities of Ḥijāz, distant from those of the Sabaean/Ḥimyarite south, it is not impossible that in this period (the first two decades of the fifth century) Najrān was trying to move away from the Sabaean orbit and assert its independence.[149] Ḥayyān, an influential Najrānite and possibly its *sayyid*, may have thought the most efficacious way of achieving this independence was to negotiate with the two world powers.

How the thought occurred to Ḥayyān to enter the international diplomatic arena beginning with Byzantium can only be guessed. Two of Najrān's neighbors may have suggested it. It was about this time that Quṣayy established himself in Mecca with Byzantine aid; and across the Red Sea there was Ethiopia, Christianized[150] and moving within the Byzantine sphere of influence. Either or both of these two neighbors could have inspired the Najrānite chief to make the Byzantine connection. The results of Ḥayyān's visit to Constantinople are unknown, but this Byzantine connection may have borne fruit and asserted itself in his efforts to propagate Christianity in the land of Ḥimyar, as will be discussed in the next section of this chapter. Although Ḥayyān derived his Christianity from Ḥīra according to the *Chronicle*, the sight of the great Christian metropolis must have left some impression on the enterprising merchant from Najrān.

3. Ḥayyān's intended journey to Persia was interrupted at Hīra, where he tarried for some time, converted to Christianity, and was baptized.[151] Appar-

(St. Arethas) says about his journeys to and contacts with some of the kings of the neighboring countries; see Shahîd, *Martyrs,* 51.

[148] Ḥayyān's dealing with both empires brings to mind the Ḥimyarite leader Sayf ibn D̲i Yazan of the second half of the 6th century, who first went to Constantinople and then to Ctesiphon, where he invoked the aid of the Persians against the Ethiopians, who had been in occupation of South Arabia for a half century.

[149] Sabaicists have noted the peculiar position of Najrān, which "seems to have been the focus of any rebel groups in times of civil disturbances"; see A. K. Irvine's review of Shahīd, *Martyrs,* in *BSOAS* 36 (1973), 643.

[150] As the political and military power of Rizāḥ, Quṣayy's half-brother, has clearly emerged from the sources examined in this book, it is perfectly possible that the powerful chief of ʿUd̲ra was the one who arranged Ḥayyān's journey to Constantinople, especially since he was well connected with Byzantium. The Ethiopians could also have arranged Ḥayyān's journey. Although the history of Ethiopian Christianity in the 5th century, after the conversion of ʿEzāna in the 4th, is obscure, there is no doubt that politically it moved in the Byzantine orbit.

[151] As the Najrānite Afʿū, the husband of his granddaughter or great-granddaughter was baptized in the same city a hundred years later; for the baptism of Afʿū, see *Book,* p. 23a.

ently after his conversion, he cancelled his journey to Persia, and his conversion may have had something to do with it.

How he fared at Ḥīra is easier to imagine and document than how he fared in Constantinople, since Ḥīra was an Arab city which had close relations with Najrān and, what is more, a large section of the population of Ḥīra were South Arabian tribes related to the Arabs of Najrān.[152] Furthermore, enough is known about the fortunes of Christianity in Persia and at Ḥīra in the reign of Yazdgard to make his conversion intelligible.

Christianity by this time was well established in that great center of Arab culture before the rise of Islam. Ḥīra had a bishop, Hosea,[153] mentioned in the episcopal list, and it is practically certain that this distinction was due to its strategic position as a center for the diffusion of Christianity, especially among the Arabs of the Peninsula and the Persian Gulf. It was in this period that some significant conversions took place among the Arabs of that region. The Lakhmid king Nuʿmān converted to Christianity and became a monk and wandered, known thereafter as al-Nuʿmān al-Sā'iḥ, and so did Aspebetos, who defected from the service of Yazdgard and became the phylarch and the bishop of the Palestinian Parembole.[154] Ḥayyān's conversion may be set within this context and against this background. Perhaps the persecution of Christian Arabs by Yazdgard may have induced Ḥayyān to convert, as it did Aspebetos,[155] and it may in fact have disinclined him to continue his journey to Persia. He returned to his native Najrān to propagate the Christian faith rather than conduct the caravan trade.

Special mention should be made of the fact that if Ḥayyān belonged to the tribe of al-Ḥārith ibn Kaʿb, the dominant tribe of Najrān in this period, he would have found many of his tribesmen settled in Ḥīra, along with members of the larger South Arabian tribal groups such as Tanūkh and Azd.[156]

[152] On Ḥīra, see G. Rothstein, *DLH,* which appeared in 1899. Since then M. J. Kister has written an important article, "Al-Ḥīra," in *Studies in Jāhiliyya and Early Islam* (chap. 3), which has also drawn the attention of scholars to a precious Arabic manuscript which has abundant materials on the Lakhmids and Ḥīra, *Al-Manāqib al-Mazyadiyya*. It has recently been edited; see above, note 80.

[153] Rothstein, *DLH,* 24.

[154] For Nuʿmān and Aspebetos, see above, Chap. 8, app. 2, and Chap. 2, sec. IV. According to *Al-Manāqib,* I, 118, it was a bishop from Liḥyān by the name of Shamʿūn ibn Ḥanẓala that converted Nuʿman.

[155] And as the martyrdoms at Najrān around 520 brought about the baptism of Afʿū, the husband of Ḥayyān's granddaughter for whom, see above, note 151.

[156] The three works cited above (note 152) have plenty of material on this. *Al-Manāqib al-Mazyadiyya* has some information on two important personages in Ḥīra who, according to the author, belonged to Balḥārith: Aws ibn Qallām, who ruled in Ḥīra in the 4th century, and Shamʿūn, who was the bishop of Ḥīra toward the end of the 6th century; *Manāqib,* I, III and II, 506. In *Manāqib* the bishop is anonymous, but in *Aghānī* he is Shamʿūn, and this is likely to be correct in view of the biblical name. For the statement in *Aghānī,* see ibid.

Since these were most probably converted at this time, their Christianity would have inclined Ḥayyān to adopt the same faith.[157]

4. On his return from Ḥīra, the "well-known merchant" became the "apostle" of Christianity in Najrān and the region. His activities as a Christian missionary in the Arabian South may be divided into two parts: in Najrān itself and in South Arabia, "the land of Ḥimyar."[158]

His activities in and around Najrān can also be divided into three parts, beginning with the conversion of his own house or clan. On this point the *Book of the Ḥimyarites* is very informative.[159] His clan is referred to as the clan of Ḥayyān, but this was probably its appellation in the sixth century, after his fame was established as the founder of Christianity in Najrān. His family belonged, as argued earlier, to the larger group Banū al-Ḥārith ibn Kaʿb, more often abbreviated as Balḥārith, and so Ḥayyān must be credited with converting Balḥārith of Najrān, or most of it. The city which appeared in the sixth century as the Arabian martyropolis can thus claim Ḥayyān as its evangelist. The *Book* is also informative on the names of certain individuals who belonged to this family—a younger Ḥayyān, either the son or the grandson of Ḥayyān, and Ḥabṣa, either his granddaughter or great-granddaughter. A sister of hers is also mentioned but remains anonymous, the wife of Afʿū, the Najrānite notable who was baptized, as Ḥayyān was, at Ḥīra.[160]

More difficult is the further statement in the *Chronicle* that Ḥayyān spread Christianity in the "land of Ḥimyar and those parts of it close to Ethiopia" ("Balad al-Ḥabashat"). This may sound like an exaggeration and an extension of the role of Ḥayyān, but a close look at the *Book*, from which the *Chronicle* almost certainly derives, reveals that the "land of Ḥimyar or Ḥimyarites" appears in the account of Ḥayyān's activity in the chapter that has survived on the martyrdom of Ḥabṣa and also in the heading of the third chapter, no longer extant, about the beginning of Christianity in South Arabia.[161] Thus

[157] The well-known Ḥīran figure and macrobiote of the 7th century ʿAbd al-Masīḥ ibn Buqayala counted a Ḥayyān among his ancestors. He was a Ghassānid and thus belonged to the larger group al-Azd. Balḥārith, the tribe of Najrān in the 5th century, belonged most probably not to Madhij but to the Azd (see below, App. 7). If so, there might have been some relationship between ʿAbd al-Masīḥ and Ḥayyān. For ʿAbd al-Masīḥ, see above, Chap. 4, sec. I.

[158] This information on the role of Ḥayyān must be authentic, since it is practically certain that it derives from Afʿū, the husband of Ḥayyān's granddaughter, one of the informants of the author of the *Book of the Ḥimyarites*. His wife would have informed him about the role of her ancestor (or grandfather) Ḥayyān in propagating Christianity in Najrān and Ḥimyar.

[159] This enhances the relationship that obtains between the two documents, and the *Book* amplifies and expatiates on what the *Chronicle* has told so laconically. The *Chronicle,* as said earlier, derives from the *Book.*

[160] On all these members of Ḥayyān's family, see *Book,* pp. cxxii–cxxvii.

[161] See *Book*, pp. 3b and 31a. In so doing, the author is not taking into account the propagation of Christianity by Theophilus Indus earlier in the 4th century, during the reign of Constantinus. But, as will be argued presently, it was probably another part of Ḥimyar that

the account of Ḥayān's activities in the "land of Ḥimyar" has to be accepted. The question is what part of Ḥimyar is included in this statement. In view of what has been said on the special position of Najrān as an Arab city in the Sabaean or Ḥimyarite South, the chances are that Ḥayyān spread Christianity in that part of Ḥimyar that would have been receptive to it and for the same reason that Najrān was, that is, areas that were close to Najrān and possibly also Arab, and which wanted to be independent of Ḥimyar by adopting a different religious persuasion. More precise and clear is the second part of the statement, that Ḥayyān spread Christianity also in that part of the Ḥimyarite South close to Ethiopia; this must be the coast, Tihāma.[162]

The spread of Christianity outside Najrān and in these regions of Ḥimyar is stated by the *Chronicle* to have been effected by a *qawm*, a people or group who helped him spread it there. This raises the important question of the identity of the group referred to. Perhaps the key to the answer is that this is said of his missionary activity in Ḥimyar, not in Najrān, his native city where he presumably needed no help. For the *qawm* to have been effective it must have been a politically and possibly militarily powerful group that could help in this enterprise against the central government.[163] South Arabia had two powerful neighbors, Byzantium and Ethiopia, either of whom could have been

---

Hayyān evangelized. Alternatively, the author of the *Book,* a Monophysite, may not have cared to remember the spread of Christianity in South Arabia by Arian Constantinus.

[162] This can be supported by the fact that it was about this time that the Ḥimyarite king, Abkarib Asʿad brought within his dominion the "Aʿrāb of Ṭawd and Tihāma" which is reflected in the long titulature of the Ḥimyarite kings. The Namāra inscription speaks of Najrān itself as "ṃadīnat Shammar," which could imply that, Najrān, too, had succumbed to the arms of Shammar Yuharʿish some hundred years before. In a different context, Ryckmans speaks also of Ma'rib and Ḥaḍramawt as regions which derived their Christianity from Najrān for geographical reasons; for Abkarib Asʿad, see Ryckmans, *L'institution monarchique en Arabie méridionale avant l'Islam* (Louvain, 1951), 318; for the Namāra inscription and Najrān, see *BAFOC,* 38–43; for the spread of Christianity in Ma'rib and Hadramawt, see Ryckmans, "Le christianisme," 422. One of the four presbyters martyred in Ḥaḍramawt around 520 was from Najrān for whom, see Shahîd, *Martyrs,* 45. The Arabic sources single out Khathʿam, a South Arabian tribe, as a Christian tribe which used to perform the pilgrimage to the Christian Kaʿba of Najrān; perhaps Khathʿam may be considered one of Ḥayyān's spiritual conquests. On Khathʿam, as a Christian tribe, see Bakrī, *Muʿjam,* II, 603. In the period of the persecutions, the Ḥimyarite king Yūsuf sent his general, Sharaḥ'il, against the coastal tribe of Ashʿar, presumably Christian. This, too, could have been evangelized by Ḥayyān. Its territory answers to the description of a land close to Ethiopia in the *Chronicle.*

[163] Note also that the sentence which expresses the help extended to him by this *qawm,* and which begins in the original Arabic text with *wattaṣala bihi* ("they came in touch with him") is left out in the French version. The first words in the sentence suggest that the initiative came from those who extended the help, presumably after they heard of Ḥayyān's evangelizing activities. This implies that they were Christian and that they were in a position to do so. The French version has *quelques-uns d'entre eux* for Arabic *qawm,* whereas the latter simply means "people," "group"; the implication is that the group was not indigenous.

meant. Ethiopia had a physical presence in the Peninsula, represented by Ḥabas͟hat in South Arabia, which might have been involved.[164] This is a very real possibility, although it is attended by difficulties deriving from the uncertain knowledge of the state of Ethiopian Christianity in the fifth century. This leaves Byzantium as the power which helped Ḥayyān, and in support of this it may be pointed out that the *Chronicle* begins its account of Ḥayyān by mentioning his trip to Constantinople. The statement thus establishes his Byzantine connection; the further statement, involving the *qawm*, may be interpreted in the light of the opening one, which would otherwise be irrelevant in an ecclesiastical chronicle, since the trip of a merchant to Constantinople would not be one of its concerns.

It is unlikely that Byzantium would have extended aid to Ḥayyān directly from Constantinople. However, its *foederati* in the Orient and western Arabia could have done so, in much the same way that ʿUḏra helped Quṣayy establish himself in Mecca. And it is not altogether impossible that this aid came from the closest neighbor to the north, Mecca, which in the first half of this century had a Byzantine connection, after Quṣayy returned and captured it, assisted directly or indirectly by Byzantium.[165]

5. Finally, the attitude of the writer or compiler of the *Chronicle* and the viewpoint from which he wrote the *Chronicle* should by now be clear, and *cannot* be drawn upon to argue for the Nestorianism or Monophysitism of Ḥayyān. The author was a Christian before he was a Nestorian, and wanted to tell the story of the propagation of the Christian faith in South Arabia. The "apostle" of its propagation was neither a Nestorian nor a Monophysite, but represented Nicene Christianity, to which the Nestorians claimed to adhere; thus his doctrinal persuasion did not dissuade the author from telling his story. In the second half of the account of Ḥayyān, some reservation may be expressed about those who helped him propagate Christianity and possibly about those who were martyred by Masrūq in the sixth century. As has been argued, those who helped him may have been representatives of Byzantium, the orthodox Cyrillian, Chalcedonian empire which early in the fifth century condemned Nestorius and later in the same century kicked the Nestorians out of its territories.[166] The Nestorian chronicler writing in the eleventh century

[164] On Ḥabas͟hat in South Arabia, see A. K. Irvine, *EI*,[2] s.v.

[165] The validity of this point depends on the proposition that Quṣayy's entry into Mecca antedated Ḥayyan's missionary activities. Quṣayy and Ḥayyān both lived in the first half of the 5th century, and were probably contemporaries, but there is no way of pinpointing the exact period of Quṣayy's return to, and capture of, Mecca.

[166] Ibas, who had supported Nestorius at Ephesus, founded a strong Nestorian school at Edessa. After Chalcedon, Monophysite hostility caused many Nestorians to emigrate to Persian territory. But it was not until 489 that the emperor Zeno expelled the Nestorians from Edessa, whereupon they formed the school of Nisibis in Persia. For Nestorianism in South Arabia, see

thus obscures the identity of those who helped Ḥayyān by referring to them in vague, general terms and of those who were martyred by using another general term, *khalq*.[167] Thus the chronicler may not be very warm in his account of Ḥayyān, but he is not hostile either, for the reasons explained above. Nevertheless, he did mention that the evangelization of Najrān came from Ḥīra, which emerged in the late fifth century and in the sixth as the great Arab center of Nestorian Christianity, and it is just possible that this reflects his Nestorian complexion. In any case, he has rendered "the historian of the roots" a great service in settling the question of whence Najrān derived its Christianity.

II

The study of the history of Christianity at Najrān in the second half of the fifth century is documented in the Ethiopic source, the *Acts* of ʿAzqīr, and possibly in the Arabic and Syriac sources.[168] The problems involved are: a persecution of Christians at Najrān, the doctrinal complexion of Najrānite Christianity, and the consecration of Najrān's first bishop.

A

Of the three sets of sources, the Ethiopic *Acts* of ʿAzqīr is the most important. It is a hagiographic work and, in spite of many data which have to be rejected as legendary and fictional, has considerable historical importance. The *Acts* have been studied by a number of scholars,[169] and the text was published early in this century.[170] However, it is necessary to make some fresh observations in the context of the theme "Byzantium and Najrān."

G. Fiaccadori, "Yemen Nestoriano," in *Studi in onore di Edda Bresciani* (Pisa, 1985), 195–212. In footnote 63, the writer inadvertently misquotes me as writing that Abraha "let South Arabia into the Chalcedonian fold." In the article cited the sentence begins with conditional "if," and I was only entertaining the views proposed by the Sabaicists Lundin and Beeston; see note 19 of my cited article.

[167] Pierre Dib, the translator of the *Chronicle* in which this chapter occurs, caught the exact nuance of Arabic *khalq* when he translated it *beaucoup*. That they were Monophysites is a fact known from the *Book of the Ḥimyarites*. Its translation as "part" is inaccurate; see Hirschberg, "Nestorian Sources," 333.

[168] "Possibly" because these sources are not dated and so it is impossible to tell whether they refer to events before the turn of the century or after.

[169] Such as H. Winkler, C. Conti Rossini, and J. W. Hirschberg; see the last (in "Nestorian Sources," 324–29) for his references to the works of his German and Italian predecessors and his comments on the works. Most recently, A. F. L. Beeston has treated the *Acts* in "The Martyrdom of Azqir," 5–10.

[170] The text of *Acts* with a translation, was prepared by C. Conti Rossini, in "Un documento sul cristianismo nello Iemen ai tempi del Re Šarāḥbīl Yakkuf," *Rendiconti della R. Accademia dei Lincei, Classe di scienze morali, storiche e filologiche*, 19 ser. 5a (Rome, 1910), 705–50.

1. As has been noted by those who have studied this document, the full name of the Ḥimyarite king is given, and is both a stamp of authenticity and an important chronological indication that there was a persecution of Christians at Najrān in the second half of the fifth century.[171] But, as pointed out above, the statement in the *Acts* that Christianity had just been introduced at Najrān before the persecution has to be rejected.[172] Therefore, the *Acts* document the Christianity that had been in existence at Najrān for at least a half century, since Ḥayyān introduced it sometime during the reign of Yazdgard. Christianity in Ḥimyar proper, which was introduced by Theophilus Indus in the fourth century, apparently had died out or was extinguished, but the *Acts* document its persistence at Najrān, thus endowing the city with a continuous Christian tradition throughout the fifth century.

That the new faith of Najrān attracted the attention of the Ḥimyarite dynasty in distant Ẓafār is an indication that it was strong enough to engage in some hostile or militant action that elicited response from the central government, resulting in persecution.

2. The part played by the Ḥimyarite king, Sharaḥbi'l is the central fact of the *Acts*. It calls for the following observations.

The first striking fact is the progress Judaism must have made in South Arabia and, what is more, at its capital in the fifth century. This had been the case in the fourth century, when Theophilus Indus appeared in Ẓafār, but apparently it was not a strong enough factor to dissuade the Ḥimyarite ruler from giving his permission for the establishment of three churches in his dominions. In the *Acts* Judaism appears much stronger; what is more, it is tolerated in South Arabia and the Ḥimyarite king does not view it with disfavor.[173]

Christianity, on the other hand, is not tolerated by the Ḥimyarite ruler, who orders ʿAzqīr to be brought to him at Ẓafār, where he is interrogated and

[171] See Ryckmans, "Le christianisme," 443. On the Ḥimyarite king involved in the persecution, Sharaḥbi'il Yakkuf, and his dynasty, see A. Jamme, *La dynastie de Šaraḥbi'il Yakuf et la documentation épigraphique sud-arabe* (Istanbul, 1961). The martyrdom then must belong to the third quarter of the 5th century.

[172] The statement on the Christian hierarchy which the *Acts* endows Najrān with must also be rejected. But if the data on the elaborate hierarchy is to be rejected, at least ʿAzqīr may be salvaged as the name of the priest of Najrān in the second half of the 5th century. The strange name must be genuine, a corruption of some Arabic name. Beeston suggested *adh-dhakir* in "The Martyrology of Azqir" (p. 6). This is attractive, coming from a competent Sabaic epigrapher and Arabic grammarian; but it is what might be termed "a grammarian's conception" of the enigmatic name. The Arabic pre-Islamic onomasticon is extensive and well attested both in the literary sources and epigraphically, but it does not include *adh-dhakir*.

[173] This is consonant with what has been noted about the strength of Judaism in Ḥimyar in the 5th century; according to some Sabaicists it actually became the religion of the Ḥimyarite rulers; see Ryckmans, "Le christianisme," 429. This view is questioned by Beeston; see "The Religions of Pre-Islamic Arabia," in *L'Arabie du Sud,* I, 268.

finally sent back to be judged by his own people at Najrān[174] and publicly executed. This raises the question of why the Ḥimyarite ruler treated Christianity differently from Judaism. As has been noted before, Najrān was an Arab city, moving in the political orbit of the Ḥimyarite South, and apparently had been annexed or brought within that orbit only in the preceding century. The adoption of a religion other than that of the Ḥimyarite state was bound to be viewed in Ẓafār as giving an impetus to secessionist movements in the Arab area. Moreover, Ḥayyān had been to Constantinople, and the Christianity he finally brought to Najrān and South Arabia was the official religion of the traditional enemy of South Arabia, whether pagan Rome or its successor, Christian Byzantium.[175]

3. Finally, the question arises why it was that this persecution broke out after Christianity had been established for a half century at Najrān. What could have happened to induce the faraway Ḥimyarite king in Ẓafār to take a sudden interest in the religious complexion of Najrān and react in this hostile fashion?

Just as the *Book of the Ḥimyarites* was helpful in shedding some light on the laconic statements of the *Chronicle*, so it is also helpful in a confrontation with this Ethiopic text. In the very same chapter in which Ḥayyān is discussed,[176] his descendant, the martyr Ḥabṣa, the daughter of Ḥayyān (the younger) makes a statement that may turn out to be the clue for understanding the events that the *Acts* describe. While talking to the Jewish Ḥimyarite king, Yūsuf, she says, "Ḥayyān, my father, once burnt your synagogues." Chronologically this is perfect, since a woman who died a martyr around 520 could easily have had a father who was alive in the middle of the second half of the fifth century. The implication of her statement is that Judaism had spread to Najrān and that its Jewish community had some synagogues in the city. The rising tide of Christianity in Najrān clearly created tensions between the two religions, which resulted in some vandalism and arson directed against the synagogues. The Jews of Najrān must then have invoked the help of their coreligionists in the capital, and the result was the intervention of the Ḥimyarite king from his seat in Ẓafār.

[174] It is just possible that this is an echo of Najrān as the seat of the famous arbiter al-Afʿā al-Jurhumī and other arbiters among the Arabs.

[175] Hence Ryckmans' good judgment in treating the evangelization of Najrān separately from that of Ḥimyar in "Le christianisme."

[176] Chap. XXI, pp. 31a–36b. The statement on the burning of the synagogues is on p. 32b. Note the plural "synagogues," which implies that the Jewish community was substantial; cf. the paucity of churches in Najrān even at the time of the persecution. It is noteworthy that the Ḥimyarite king in answering Ḥabṣa speaks of one synagogue only. The presumption is that by around 520 the fortunes of Judaism had ebbed in Najrān and so much so that it had only one synagogue. But the plural in Ḥabṣa's statement may be a scribal error.

B

The doctrinal complexion of the church of Najrān is a matter of some importance. At the time of the great persecution and martyrdoms around 520, that church appears very strongly Monophysitic. At its inception a century before, its Christianity had been that of Byzantium after the two ecumenical councils of the fourth century. How the Najrānite Church developed in the midst of the christological controversies of the fifth century and emerged as strongly Monophysitic in the sixth century is not entirely clear, but an attempt to chart its doctrinal course may be made as follows.

Twenty years separate the Council of Ephesus in 431 from that of Chalcedon in 451. Both the Nestorians and the Monophysites appear as distinct bodies of believers after these two councils, and the Nestorians started earlier. How the nascent Christianity sown by Ḥayyān at Najrān before the two councils were convened was affected in the course of the century by these two movements is not clear. There is no doubt that there were Nestorians in South Arabia and in Najrān. In view of the fact that Nestorianism in the middle of the second half of the fifth century established itself firmly in Persian territory, one would have thought that it would have dominated Najrān, especially as this city derived its Christianity from Ḥīra, a city in Persian territory. Yet it was not Nestorianism that emerged as the dominant Christian confession in Najrān but Monophysitism, the relative latecomer. How this came about may be explained by the following considerations.

a. If Monophysitism came to Najrān from Ḥīra, it is likely to have been mediated by a group acceptable to the Najrānites, such as Balḥārith, some of whom lived in Ḥīra and were related to the Arabs of Najrān by tribal affiliation. This is perfectly possible because, as suggested earlier, Ḥayyān's conversion to Christianity in Ḥīra may have been effected by South Arabian groups close to him in their tribal affiliation.

b. It is possible that Monophysitism came to Najrān from the closest Christian power to Najrān, Ethiopia, which also became Monophysite, although the history of both its Christianity and its particular doctrinal color is not clear in the fifth century.

c. Finally, Byzantium was veering towards Monophysitism in the reign of Zeno (474–491), who issued the Henotikon in 482, and was definitely Monophysitic under Anastasius (491–518). Monophysite Byzantium could easily have influenced Najrān through its Arab *foederati*, especially the Ghassānids. One of these, Amorkesos, was already established as phylarch in Palaestina Tertia as early as 473. He and his bishop Petrus could have played an important role in the affairs of Najrān, especially as the Ghassānids and the Balḥāriths of Najrān were most probably related through their Azd affiliation.[177] There were also the Ghassānids, who established themselves around 502 as the dominant federate group, and these could have influenced or even decided the doctrinal complexion of Najrān as Monophysite, since they were staunchly so.

This seems the most plausible road for Monophysitism to have taken to Najrān, especially in view of the fact that there is some documentary evidence which admits of being interpreted in support of a Ghassānid mediation of Monophysitism. This is a statement in reliable Arabic sources to the effect that Christianity was brought to Najrān by a Ghassānid.[178] This must be dated to the period when the Ghassānids emerged as a power in the Byzantine federate structure, and the Christian confession that the Ghassānids must have brought with them was the Monophysite. The statement cannot be true if it refers to the introduction of Christianity, since this had been done by Ḥayyān early in the century, but must mean the Ghassānid version of Christianity, Monophysitism. Thus understood, the statement becomes acceptable as containing a kernel of truth.

C

Closely related to the problem of Najrān's doctrinal persuasion is that of its first bishop. This has been partially solved by the publication of the new letter of Simeon of Bēth Arshām, in which it is clearly stated that he was Paul I, who suffered martyrdom in Ẓafār around 520. He was certainly the first Monophysite bishop of Najrān, and was consecrated by Philoxenus of Mabboug.[179]

This precious reference throws much light on a number of related problems. The reference in the Arab historians to the appearance of a Ghassānid in South Arabia may be said to have received a historical context with this reference to Philoxenus.[180] The Ghassānids now appear as the link between Mabboug in the far north and Najrān in the far south. They were the dominant group of *foederati* in the sixth century and had been a powerful federate group in the last quarter of the fifth century.[181] Moreover, they were strongly Monophysitic. Philoxenus was an energetic and aggressive cleric and, together

[177] His bishop, Petrus, was most probably a contemporary of ʿAzqīr; if so, news of persecutions at Najrān must have reached Amorkesos and Petrus in Palaestina Tertia.

[178] See Ibn Qutayba, *al-Maʿārif,* 637, also Ryckmans, "Le christianisme," 428 note 78.

[179] See Shahîd, 46–47, and the footnote on Paul I on p. 238.

[180] The two historians are Ṭabarī and Ibn Qutayba. For the reference to the Ghassānid in the former, see *Tārīkh,* II, 89; in the latter, see *Maʿārif,* 637. In spite of some confusion and inaccuracy in the two sources, the kernel of truth is discernible; it consists in realizing that there was a Ghassānid mission in South Arabia. It is practically certain that the account of Ibn Qutayba is more accurate, since the Ghassānids would have sent their emissary to Najrān, the city of their relatives, Balḥārith, and not to Ḥimyar.

[181] See above, 287–89.

with Severus of Antioch, the leading Monophysite figure. It was in this period that the Ghassānids must have become Monophysites. They had come from South Arabia but kept their interest in their country of origin alive, especially in Najrān, where the ruling and dominant tribe of Balḥārith was related to them. Thus the statement in the Arabic sources on the Ghassāid mission to South Arabia becomes credible and clear. The staunch Monophysites sent their emissary to win Najrān and he did,[182] while the Monophysite church in Oriens must have decided that the best way of determining the doctrinal persuasion of Najrān was to give the city a Monophysite as its first bishop. This it did when Paul I was consecrated.

The tantalizing reference in the new letter of Simeon to this first bishop of Najrān raises the following questions.

1. The year of Paul's consecration as bishop is not stated in Simeon's letter. All that is said is that he was consecrated by Philoxenus of Mabboug (Hierapolis). Unfortunately, Philoxenus' episcopate over Mabboug extended from 485 to 519, a period of some thirty-four years, and so he could have been consecrated in either the fifth or the sixth century. Given the silence of the sources, one is forced to suggest ca. 500, midway between the first and the last years of Philoxenus' episcopate.[183]

2. It is equally important to discover the circumstances that led to the establishment of a bishopric of Najrān—or rather that allowed it, in view of the strong opposition of Ḥimyar and the central government in Ẓafār to the rise and propagation of Christianity in South Arabia,[184] an attitude strongly

[182] Thus the role of the Ghassānids in the history of South Arabian Christianity at Najrān was not (as the two historians say) the introduction of Christianity, which had taken place almost a century earlier at the hands of Ḥayyān, but the winning of Najrān to the Monophysite camp. Although Najrān derived its Christian faith from Ḥīra, in Persian territory, it was from Byzantine Oriens that it derived its doctrinal complexion and allegiance to Monophysitism. The fact is also reflected in the number of clerics who hailed from Oriens, such as Sergius and Ananias among the martyred clerics at Najrān, and Elias and Thomas among those martyred in Ḥadramawt; see Shahîd, *Martyrs,* 45, 64.

[183] One item in the chronology of Paul I's episcopate may be mentioned; it is stated in the *Martyrium Arethae* that at the time of the great persecution around 520, Paul I had been dead for two years. So he died toward the end of Philoxenus' life, and this could give his episcopate a long duration, since the earliest possible year of his consecration is 485. One would be inclined to think that the consecration took place in the period 512–518, during which Anastasius moved away from the neutrality that had characterized his religious policy of maintaining the spirit of the Henotikon and definitely entered the Monophysite camp. On the other hand, Philoxenus had been active long before this period and, what is more, is his correspondence with the Arab dynasty of Ḥīra, Abū' Ya'fur around 500. So the energetic Monophysite cleric may have wanted Najrān in the Monophysite fold as early as 500, as presumably he wanted Ḥīra. For his correspondence with Abū Ya'fur, of which Abu-Nafīr must be a corruption, see A. Baumstark, *Geschichte der syrischen Literatur,* 143.

[184] Especially in the 5th century, when the rival religion, Judaism, was strongest in South Arabia and at the court, see above, note 173.

reflected in the *Acts* of ʿAzqīr. Unfortunately, not much is known with precision about Ḥimyar and its king toward the end of the fifth century which could help answer this question. One therefore has to assume that some favorable condition enabled Najrān to have a bishop of its own consecrated, thus establishing a new episcopal see in South Arabia. Although uninformative on how the see of Najrān could have been established, one of the sources does throw light on later developments in its history. In the new letter of Simeon, it is stated that Paul I died a martyr and, what is more, at the hands of the Jews away from the see, in the Ḥimyarite capital Ẓafār.[185] This brings echoes of ʿAzqīr himself—his abduction to the capital and his dialogue with the Jews at the court in Ẓafār—which throw light on the antecedents of Paul's martyrdom. The central government apparently was alarmed by the progress of Christianity at Najrān after it was organized under a bishop, and so (possibly) called ʿAzqīr to appear in Ẓafār, whence he was sent back to Najrān to die as a martyr.

3. It has been suggested that Paul I may have been consecrated ca. 500. If so, his episcopate was of relatively long duration. It is practically certain that the organization of the church of Najrān was his work. In support of this view it may be pointed out that two years after his death, when the persecution broke out around 520, the list of martyrs preserved in the letter of Simeon indisputably documents the existence of an ecclesiastical hierarchy at Najrān. In addition to the bishop, there were archpresbyters, archdeacons, and arch-subdeacons, sons of the covenant, and daughters of the covenant.[186] It is unlikely that this was the work of Paul II because his episcopate did not last for more than two years at most.[187] It is also noteworthy that the hierarchy was drawn from the international community of the Near East—Byzantium, Ethiopia, Persia, and Ḥīra.[188] This fact indicates the importance and connections of this caravan city which in the sixth century became the Arabian martyropolis.

IV. Byzantium and Ḥimyar

After an active interest in the affairs of Ḥimyar and South Arabia in the reign of Constantius in the fourth century, the sources reflect hardly any trace of

185 See above, note 179.

186 See table of contents of the *Book of the Ḥimyarites*, ci-civ, and Shahîd, *Martyrs*, 64.

187 Paul II does not seem to have cut a large figure in the history of Christianity at Najrān, and he hardly receives any notice. Perhaps the lost portions of the *Book of the Ḥimyarites* recorded some of his achievements or said something about him. The only reference to him in Shahîd, *Martyrs* occurs on p. 46.

188 See ibid., 64. Since the ecclesiastical organization of Najrān may, properly speaking, belong to the 6th century, it has been treated briefly in this volume; it will be treated in detail in *BASIC*.

relations between the two powers until the reign of Anastasius, when, according to the ecclesiastical historian John Diacrinomenus, the Ḥimyarites received a bishop from Byzantium by the name of Silvanus.[189] The same historian says that the Ḥimyarites had originally been Jewish and that they were only evangelized in the reign of Anastasius.[190] This statement may be dismissed as inaccurate, and thus the fruitful recovery of the facts of Byzantine-Ḥimyarite relations must turn about the cluster of problems which the reference to bishop Silvanus[191] raises:

A

The first question is the whereabouts of his episcopal see. Najrān has been suggested as a possibility,[192] and in view of the discussion of the episcopal see of Najrān in the last section it is well that this suggestion be discussed first.[193]

Those who suggested that Silvanus was the bishop of Najrān did so before the publication of *The Martyrs of Najrān*, in which the identity of the first bishop—Paul I—is clearly stated. This completely rules out Silvanus, especially in view of the fact that both were Monophysite bishops; if Silvanus had belonged to a different Christian confession the suggestion might be entertained. It might be argued that Silvanus is Paul, the latter being his episcopal name after consecration. This, too, is out, since the background of Paul I is not unknown. In the new letter of Simeon it is stated that he was the brother of the deaconess Elizabeth, who was an Arab from Najrān.[194] Conse-

[189] See below, App. 8.

[190] See *Historia Ecclesiastica*, ed. G. C. Hansen, *Theodorus Anagnostes: Kirchengeschichte*, GCS 54 (Berlin, 1971), 157, lines 13–16.

[191] For the extensive efforts of Byzantium during the reign of Constantius (337–361), see *BAFOC*, 86–106. This of course did not result in the evangelization of Ḥimyar, but it did sow some seeds of the Christian faith and may have affected some of the Ḥimyarites, including the ruler at Ẓafār, according to the historian Philostorgius. The more tangible achievement was the erection of three churches in Ḥimyar. As there is no mention in Philostorgius' account of a bishop assigned to Ḥimyar in the 4th century, John Diacrinomenus' statement on Bishop Silvanus is most probably true; the two accounts are harmonious if John's statement is understood to mean that it was only in the reign of Anastasius that Ḥimyar received a Christian bishop. The strong categorical tone of John Diacrinomenus may derive from his antipathy to the Arian historian Philostorgius and his desire to obliterate the achievement of the Arian mission to South Arabia in the 4th century.

[192] As has been suggested by Aigrain in "Arabie," col. 1241. Ryckmans seems inclined to share this view; see "Le christianisme," 444–45, and note 158 for other authors he mentions; also E. Stein and F. Altheim-Ruth Stiehl, cited by Hansen in *HE*, 157.

[193] The discussion of the first bishop of Najrān here brings out aspects of the problem not discussed in the section above on Byzantium and Najrān, and which can be more fruitfully discussed in this new context.

[194] See Shahîd, *Martyrs*, 47–48. That she was a Najrānite woman is reflected in the sentence which speaks of three young men from her family who discovered her body; ibid., 48.

quently, Paul I was also an Arab from Najrān, and so would have had an Arab name. Moreover, John wrote in Byzantium, not in some city in Arabia; when he says that Ḥimyar received its first bishop in the reign of Anastasius, the presumption is that the bishop was sent to Ḥimyar from Byzantium. The consecration of a bishop (Paul) in faraway Najrān most probably would not have been known to an ecclesiastical author living in Byzantium. What attracted John's attention was that the bishop was dispatched from Byzantium, possibly by the Byzantine emperor Anastasius himself.

B

2. By process of elimination, Silvanus must have been the bishop sent to Ḥimyar. This raises the question of the year, the see, and the occasion, and the best way of trying to answer these three questions is to start with the last.

The dispatch of a bishop from Byzantium to a state such as Ḥimyar, known to have been anti-Christian and anti-Byzantine, especially in the fifth century, was surely extraordinary. It must have taken place at a propitious moment, when the Ḥimyarite state was in a receptive mood to accept a Christian bishop from the traditional enemy—the Roman colossus which, whether pagan or Christian, had had imperial designs against it from the time of the disastrous expedition of Aelius Gallus in 25–24 B.C. The most plausible juncture that could accommodate such an ecclesiastical mission as the establishment of an episcopate in Ḥimyar was the period immediately following the first Ethiopian invasion of Ḥimyar a few years before 520. Little is known about this expedition, but it is clearly recorded in that primary source for the history of Ḥimyarite-Ethiopian relations, *The Book of the Ḥimyarites.*[195] The texts of the chapters in which this important episode was recounted are not extant but the titles of four of them, (4–7) clearly tell the events, which with the help of other sources present the following sequence: the Ḥimyarites persecute the Christians of South Arabia; Bishop Thomas goes to the Ethiopians, informs them, and presumably invokes their aid; the Ethiopians cross to South Arabia and defeat the Ḥimyarites; the Negus adopts Christianity after his victory, as he had vowed before he left Ethiopia; after putting the affairs of the country in order, the Ethiopians go back.[196]

[195] See *The Book of the Ḥimyarites,* pp. ci-cii.

[196] His adoption of Christianity is recorded in Dionysius Tell-Mahrē; for this first Ethiopian expedition and its sources, see Shahîd, *Martyrs,* 258–59.

The discovery and publication in 1974 of a Geʿez inscription in Axum set up by Negus Kaleb throws much light on this first Ethiopian expedition. It has been suggested in a study of this inscription, in which the Negus speaks of his having sent ḤYN against Ḥimyar and built a church there (possibly in Qana'), that this ḤYN is none other than the ḤYWN' of *the Book of the Ḥimyarites,* who appears as a leader of the first Ethiopian expedition against Ḥimyar. This invaluable inscription confirms my conclusions in *Martyrs* (pp. 258–59) that the two Ethiopian

Surely this sequence of events provides the answers to the questions raised earlier in this section. It provides a framework which can be filled with some details available from related sources.

1. The mysterious persecution referred to in the title of chapter 4 in the *Book* is illuminated by the reference in Simeon's letter to the martyrdom of Paul I, bishop of Najrān, in Ẓafār itself, the capital of Ḥimyar.[197] This is the most explicit and concrete evidence for the persecution referred to in chapter 4 of the *Book*, and it is close to 520, approximately the year of the great persecution. This makes it practically certain that the martyrdom of Paul belonged to this persecution and not to an earlier one in the fifth century, such as that of ʿAzqīr. The death of the high-ranking ecclesiastic in the capital must have been sensational, and such as to move Bishop Thomas to take action.

2. Thus the mysterious bishop Thomas, knowledge of whose episcopate is owed only to the *Book of the Ḥimyarites*, could not have been the Silvanus mentioned by John Diacrinomenus and dispatched from Byzantium during the reign of Anastasius. He appears as already installed somewhere in South Arabia or across the Red Sea in Adulis,[198] but not in Ḥimyar proper, which was persecuting the Christians.

3. The mission of Thomas to Axum resulted in the first Ethiopian expedition, which was successful. This brings echoes of the expedition in the preceding century, when the Ethiopian presence paved the way for a Christian presence established by Theophilus in the reign of Constantius, and in the sixth century when, after the successful Ethiopian expedition of Negus Kaleb (Ella Aṣbeḥa), a strong Christian presence was established in Ḥimyar. Noth-

---

invasions were very close to each other. It also solves the problem of the mysterious ḤYWN' of the *Book*. He is a general of Kaleb, sent by him to Ḥimyar. Because the name was unintelligible in the *Book*, I sought to emend the reading (*Martyrs*, 146 note 2). This is unnecessary now, since ḤYWN' appears almost certainly as ḤYN in the Geʿez inscription. For the inscription and the identification of the two, see A. J. Drewes, "Kaleb and Himyar: Another reference to HYWN'," *Raydan, Journal of Ancient Yemeni Antiquities and Epigraphy*, 1 (1978), 27–32. There is a suggestion in this article that ḤYN may be identified with the Arabic name, Ḥayyān. If so, could this ḤYN whom Kaleb sent have been an Arab from Najrạn belonging to the clan of Ḥayyān who had gone over to Ethiopia to invoke aid in much the same way that later in the century another South Arabian, Sayf, goes to Byzantium and Persia and returns to regain his country from the Ethiopians?

197 See ibid., 46. Survivors of this first persecution who were martyred in the second may have included Thomas the Presbyter in Ḥadramawt, whose left hand was cut off; see ibid., 45. Even before the discovery of the new letter of Simeon, J. Ryckmans argued correctly that the first persecution mentioned in the table of contents of the *Book of the Ḥimyarites* must have taken place only a few years before the second, which took place around 520; see Ryckmans, "Le christianisme," 422; for confirmation of this, see Shahīd *Martyrs*, 143–45. The Geʿez Axum inscription is also relevant as it speaks of ḤYN, the general of Kaleb, clearly associated with the "first coming"; see Drewes, "Kaleb and Himyar," 27–30.

198 As surmised by Ryckmans, "Le christianisme."

ing is known about the Ethiopian presence in Ḥimyar in the fourth century other than the imperial titulature of the Negus,[199] but much more is known about the Ethiopian expedition and occupation of Ḥimyar around 520, and it provides an illuminating analogy to what must have happened during the first Ethiopian expedition which took place a few (possibly two) years earlier. The most relevant datum in the history of this second Ethiopian expedition is that the Negus asks the patriarch of Alexandria in Byzantium to send a bishop to the territory newly conquered for Christendom, and the patriarch accedes to the request.[200] This then must be the model of what happened two years earlier. The Negus, now converted to Christianity by his victory, asks for a bishop from the Christian Roman Empire and possibly writes to the *basileus*, Anastasius himself.[201]

4. The bishop sent from Byzantium was Silvanus, who thus arrived sometime in the second decade of the sixth century. But where in Ḥimyar was his episcopal see? It is possible that he was assigned to Mukhā or Ẓafār, more likely to the latter.[202] As explained above, Ḥimyar was now no longer hostile to Christianity, and so could have tolerated a bishop in the capital. It was amenable to Christian influence after the first Ethiopian victory in the sixth century, in much the same way that it was after the later victory of Kaleb. It is thus natural to suppose that the capital of Ḥimyar would have been the episcopal see of the newly arrived bishop.[203] What happened to him and how he fared after his departure from Byzantium is completely unknown. The sources tell nothing about him; he may have been martyred in the great persecution or died shortly after his arrival. That he is not mentioned in the South Arabian sources or others that record South Arabian history is not surprising. The former, principally epigraphic and hostile to Christianity, are naturally silent on matters such as the martyrdom of a Christian bishop, while the latter have not survived except in fragments. Precious as these are, they tell little about Ẓafār, and the chances are that if chapter 7 of the *Book of the Ḥimyarites* has survived it might have said something on Silvanus. But except for its title, with its tantalizing reference to the persecutions at Ẓafār, only some fragments have survived, and they tell of the massacre of the Ethiopians. But

[199] The historicalness of this Ethiopian expedition in the 4th century has been challenged, but there has been no cogent refutation of it, especially when its scope and very short duration are taken into account; see the argument for it in *BAFOC*, 41–42.

[200] See Shahîd, "Byzantium in South Arabia," 89–91.

[201] Such requests on the part of the Negus and addressed to either the *basileus* or one of his patriarchs, provides evidence that Ethiopia moved in the Byzantine cultural orbit.

[202] See Ryckmans, "Le christianisme." For the two churches burnt around 520 at Mukhā and Ẓafār, see ibid., 423.

[203] Especially as it had witnessed some very short time before the martyrdom of Paul I, bishop of Najrān. Its declaration as an episcopal see and the assignment of Silvanus to it would have been only natural.

three leaves of this chapter are missing, and they may have told of Bishop Silvanus. On the other hand, the author wrote his *Book* after the coming to power of the Chalcedonian house of Justin in 518, when Monophysitism was persecuted in Byzantium. Consequently, he may not have been eager to refer to the role of what was now to him Chalcedonian Byzantium in the history of South Arabian Christianity, in spite of the fact that it was under Monophysite Anastasius that Silvanus was sent to South Arabia.[204]

In view of the difficulties that attend the identification of Silvanus with the bishop of Ẓafār, it cannot altogether be ruled out as a last resort that Silvanus was sent to Najrān not as Paul I, who was martyred in Ẓafār, but as Paul II. If so, one has to assume that when John spoke of a bishop sent to Ḥimyar in the reign of Anastasius he included Najrān, as was the practice of Byzantine authors, within the whole South Arabian region, but that he was uninformed about the fact that the South Arabian episcopate started earlier than the consecration of Paul II. His ignorance of Paul I's consecration was perhaps due to the fact that he was not sent from Byzantium, but was a local Najrānite Arab bishop whose consecration remained unknown to the Byzantine historian writing in faraway Constantinople. In support of the identification of Silvanus with Paul II, the following arguments may be advanced: (*a*) Nothing is recorded in the sources about his ethnic origin; he could have been a non-Arab sent from Byzantium or Byzantine Oriens, one who carried the name Silvanus and whose episcopal name after consecration became Paul. (*b*) With the exception of Thomas, who has been ruled out as Silvanus, Paul II is the only bishop mentioned in the sources for this period.[205] (*c*) A pointer in the direction of his Byzantine provenance is the fact that he was consecrated by Philoxenus. This precious datum, preserved in the new letter of Simeon, clinches his Byzantine connection through his consecration in Byzantine Oriens by the powerful bishop of Mabboug/Hierapolis and metropolitan of Euphratensis.[206]

The conclusions presented in this section on Silvanus are tentative and no certainty is attainable, given the state of the evidence. But this is the most that can be extracted from the extant sources, few, exiguous, and sometimes confusing. The range of possibilities encompasses Najrān, Ẓafār, and Mukhā.[207]

[204] On this, see Shahîd, *Martyrs,* 172.

[205] On Paul II, see ibid., 56.

[206] His consecration by Philoxenus is consonant with what is known about the latter as a zealous propagator of Monophysitism in the country villages of Antioch, and in the Patriarchate of Antioch and the Orient in general.

[207] To which Aden may be added.

Appendix I

La geste d'Ismaël

After this chapter was written, Father R. Dagorn's book, *La geste d'Ismaël*,[1] became available to me. The work is a welcome addition to the literature on Ishmael and the Arab self-image as Ishmaelites, and it is well documented and argued. What is more, its preface is written by M. Rodinson, who has enriched the discussion with some modifications of the book's thesis and drawn attention to the relevance of the author's conclusions to a reexamination of L. Massignon's celebrated article, "Les trois prières d'Abraham, père de tous les croyants," and M. Hayek's *Les mystères d'Ismael*, pointing out the implications of these conclusions to some important theological discussions involving the Arabs as the sons of Ishmael. Thus the book is important in what it expresses and what it implies.

I am in agreement with the author in all that he says about the *geste* of Ishmael in Islamic times and the great impetus that the Koran gave to the development of this theme in the Islamic period. But my conclusions in this volume on the sons of Ishmael and Sozomen and the Arabs make it necessary to also mark off an area of disagreement, which pertains to the pre-Islamic period.

1. The dependence of the author on the *onomasticon* for arguing that their descent from Ishmael was unknown to the Arabs before the rise of Islam does present a problem, but is not decisive. The name "Ishmael" appears five more times in the Bible,[2] that is, more often than both Abraham and Isaac! But one would not draw conclusions similar to those of Father Dagorn from the non-recurrence of the last two names. The ancestor of the Prophet Muḥammad in the fifth generation, Quṣayy, was the most important figure in the history of Quraysh and Mecca, and yet none of his descendants carried his name in the course of the two centuries that separated him from Muḥammad, except an obscure son, whom he himself named ʿAbd Quṣayy.

2. Surely M. Rodinson is right in expressing some dissent from the conclusions of the author[3] when he refers to the text of Sozomen, analyzed in detail in a previous chapter in this book, pointing out that the concept of the descent from Ishmael *was* prevalent among some Arabs in *pre-Islamic* times, especially those Arabs who were either converted to Judaism or Christianity or were in touch with Judaeo-Christian communities. Sozomen was a neutral observer of the Arab scene in the pre-Islamic fifth century, and so his testimony cannot be treated lightly or ignored.

3. Even more important than the testimony of Sozomen is that of Theodoret,[4] who speaks not of the Ishmaelites in general but of Ishmael himself and the Arab veneration of their eponymous ancestor. This passage in the patristic author has not been noted by those who have discussed the problem of Ishmael in pre-Islamic times, and is decisive for establishing the fact that some of the Arabs, at least in the three centuries before the rise of Islam, did look up to Ishmael as their revered ancestor.

[1] See R. Dagorn, *La geste d'Ismaël d'après l'onomastique et la tradition arabes* (Paris, 1981). See also above, Chap. 9, sec. III.

[2] See Rodinson's introduction p. v, for biblical figures who assumed the name "Ishmael."

[3] Ibid., xix.

[4] For this, see above, Chap. 8.

4. The precious reference to the "sons of Hagar" in an authentic pre-Islamic poem by al-Afwah al-Awdī[5] clinches the point made by an examination of the passage in Theodoret. Here is an entirely independent tradition coming from the world of pre-Islamic Arabic poetry which echoes what the patristic author affirms. This poem, too, has not been noted by those who have discussed the concept of Ishmaelism in pre-Islamic times, but it forms, together with the passage in Theodoret, solid evidence for the reality of the concept and suggests that it did *not* make its *first* appearance in the Koran.

All that these fragments can show is that there was some consciousness among some of the Arabs, notably those of Ḥijāz, in the three centuries or so before the rise of Islam[6] that they were descended from Ishmael, and that the mysterious Quṣayy probably contributed towards either localizing it or reviving it around Mecca and the Kaʿba.[7]

Appendix II

Maʿadd and Nizār

In this proto-Byzantine period of three centuries which extended from the reign of Constantine to that of Heraclius, the names of the old Ishmaelite tribes disappear as designations for tribes and tribal groups in Arabia.[1] Instead there now appear new names for the tribes of the Arabs of the north. The tribal picture of pre-Islamic Arabia in these centuries appears represented by such tribal groups as Maʿadd, Nizār, Muḍar, and Rabīʿa[2] which are attested in pre-Islamic Arabic poetry and, in the case of Maʿadd, also in the Syriac and Greek literary sources as well as in the Sabaic inscriptions.

The history of these tribal groups presents many problems. In view of the paucity of the sources, it is surprising that a most important source has not been laid under contribution, namely, the Namāra inscription.[3] This is especially valuable because it is a solid piece of evidence, coming as it does from epigraphy, and what is more, it is a very early inscription, dated to A.D. 328. The inscription makes reference to two of these tribal groups, Maʿadd and Nizār, making it certain that these tribal groups did exist at such an early date in the tribal world of pre-Islamic Arabia; it is natural to suppose that they existed for some time before 328. The smaller tribal groups Rabīʿa and Muḍar, which, according to the genealogists, were descended from Nizār, do not appear in the inscription. Since the honorand in the inscription made extensive conquests in Arabia, the absence of any reference to these two groups

[5] For this, see the discussion of Priscus above, Chap. 8, sec. I.

[6] The appearance or survival of a monotheistic tradition in Arabia and Ḥijāz in particular, possibly Ishmaelite, could possibly be fortified by references in the Koran to such religious figures as Ṣāliḥ, the Koranic prophet of Thamūd.

[7] On the picture of Ishmael painted on the wall of the Kaʿba in pre-Islamic times, see below, App. 4.

[1] With the exception of Qaydar/Qidar and Nābit/Nabīt, which, however, appear in pre-Islamic Arabic poetry the authenticity of which has not been decided yet.

[2] For all these tribes and others, see the concise articles in the *EI*, s.vv.

[3] On this, see *BAFOC,* 31–45.

suggests that they were formed after 328. Thus by what the Namāra inscription expresses about Maʿadd and Nizār and by what it implies about Rabīʿa and Muḍar, it is most illuminating.

The solid date 328 makes it possible to raise the question of a genetic relationship between these new tribal groups of the early Christian centuries and the older Ishmaelite groups.

a. The date of the inscription, 328, is not far from a fateful date in the history of the north Arabs, namely, A.D. 106, which witnessed the end the Nabataean kingdom and its annexation by Rome as the Provincia Arabia.[4] The Nabataean kingdom was vast in extent and must have embraced within its territory many of the Ishmaelite tribes of old. The annexation naturally would have made drastic changes in the tribal structure of North Arabia and thus it is possible that these new tribal groups appeared with their new names in this period that followed the fall of Nabataea to the Romans in 106.

b. The date of the Namāra inscription may be related to another date in the history of the Arabs before the rise of Islam, A.D. 272, which witnessed the fall of Palmyra to the Romans, a date as important as 106 and even closer to 328. The powerful rulers of Arab Palmyra had run a vast commercial empire and controlled many tribes settled in North Arabia, lying astride the Trans-Arabian trade routes. The utter destruction of the city by Aurelian, and with it its commercial and political empire, terminated its political control over the tribes of North Arabia. This, too, must have contributed generously to the rise of new tribal groups, which now came into existence and moved in new independent political Peninsular orbits, thus perhaps giving rise eventually to the division of ʿAdnān into the two groups of Rabīʿa and Muḍar, which do not appear in the Namāra inscription and which thus might have taken some time to form after the fall of Palmyra in 272 and the death of the Imruʾ al-Qays, whom the Namāra inscription commemorates in 328.

There remains the problem of Quḍāʿa,[5] the enigmatic tribal group of North Arabia, which became an umbrella title for many tribes that had emigrated to North Arabia, affiliated themselves with it, and thus were considered as belonging to the Quḍāʿa group. But the original Quḍāʿa could easily have been another group of Ishmaelite tribes which formed after the breakup of the Nabataean and Palmyrene kingdoms but were quite distinct from Maʿadd.[6]

[4] This can be fortified by what was said in the last paragraph, namely, that the tribal groups Maʿadd and Nizār must have existed before 328. This brings their existence closer to 106, and thereby to the possibility of a genetic relationship with the old Ishmaelite tribes.

[5] See *EI,* s.v.

[6] The name Quḍāʿa calls to mind that of another tribe, Khuzāʿa. The two are identical morphologically, and semantically are almost so. The derivation Khuzāʿa, from the Arabic verb *inkhazaʿat* (separated) could thus throw light on Qudāʿa and suggest that it too separated from some tribal group, such as the Maʿadd or another one. On Khuzāʿa, see *EI,* s.v.

It is hoped that the observations on these and other tribal groups, made in the course of this book, will contribute towards solving some of the problems that attend Arab genealogical studies. Perhaps the one who knows them best, M. J. Kister, will be able to advance these studies in light of these observations.

Appendix III

Jurhum and Other Tribes in Mecca

Jurhum has been the subject of two important studies in recent times, one by Father R. Dagorn (to which reference has been made in appendix 1, above), and the other by T. Fahd.[1] The two works appeared simultaneously, and consequently their authors were unable to make use of each other's work. It is proposed in this appendix to bring together some data relevant to the study of this enigmatic but very important tribal group in the cultural history of western Arabia in the hope that those who deal with this period and area may find them helpful towards a reconstruction of the history of this tribe and others whose historic role in West Arabia is related to that of Jurhum, such as Khuzāʿa, Iyād, and Liḥyān.

I

In the first part of his article, T. Fahd assembled the relevant classical sources on the Gerrhans, the people of Gerrha. He suggested that they emigrated from the northern part of the Persian Gulf to western Arabia after the rise of a strong Persia under the Sasanids, and that they were the Jurhumites who are associated in the Arabic sources with Mecca and the Ishmaelite tradition in Arabic historiography.[2] There is something to be said for this possibility, and the history of Tanūkh and Iyād, which also emigrated under Sasanid pressure, could afford a parallel.

Father Dagorn's well-titled chapter[3] on Jurhum has exploded the myth of the remote antiquity of the tribe, going back to biblical patriarchal times, the division of Jurhum into the "first Jurhum" and the "second Jurhum," and the matrilineal descent of the Arabs through a woman from Jurhum whom Ishmael is said to have married. His analysis of the prose sources cannot be refined upon[4] but his handling of the two verses from Zuhayr and Aʿsha cannot be accepted.[5]

The following paragraphs present the available sources which contribute to an understanding of the tribe of Jurhum and its history.

1. All discussion of Jurhum must begin with its attestation in an incontestable Greek source, the *Ethnica* of Stephanus of Byzantium, who apparently wrote his

[1] See T. Fahd, "Gerrhéens et Ǧurhumites," 67–78.

[2] In the second part of his article (ibid.), the author discusses the Arabic sources for Jurhum and offers a number of suggestions as to how the final consonant "m" in Jurhum became attached to it (pp. 72–73). In addition to what the author suggests, the "m" may have been picked up in the Sabaic south of Arabia. As a final consonant "m" appears both as an enclitic and as an instance of what is called by Sabaicists *mimation,* although the rules governing the use of the latter are still obscure; for mimation and enclitics in Sabaic, see A. F. L. Beeston, *Sabaic Grammar,* (Manchester, 1984), 30–31.

Fahd's identification (p. 75) of Quṣayy with Qays, the Maʿaddite chief (around 530) mentioned by Procopius, is difficult to accept on phonetic grounds. Furthermore, Quṣayy was the ancestor of the Prophet Muḥammad in the *fifth* generation, and Muḥammad is traditionally accepted as having been born in 570. Qays' *floruit* could fall within that of Muḥammad's grandfather, Hāshim, but not his more distant ancestor Quṣayy, who must be assigned to the first half of the 5th century; see above, Sec. II note 83.

[3] See his chapter "L'énigmatique tribu des Ǧurhum," in *La geste d'Ismaël,* 287–320.

[4] He asks a pertinent question on the non-appearance of any reference to Jurhum in the Koran, but the question admits of answers other than the one he suggests; ibid., 311–13.

[5] See below, App. 6.

dictionary in the reign of Justinian I and who knew of the Γοραμῆνοι. Thus Jurhum is a historical reality in the pre-Islamic past of the sixth century.[6]

2. Of the Arabic sources for the history of Jurhum, the prose works of later Islamic times are practically worthless, since they represent the attempt of later writers in Islamic times to write extensive commentaries and invent a background for the references in the Koran to Ishmael and his association with the Kaʿba, all of which has been conveniently termed "la geste d'Ismaël." But the task of scholarship is to recover from these Arabic sources the hard and solid spots for the history of Jurhum, and these consist of two precious verses from two major pre-Islamic poets, Zuhayr and Aʿshā. These not only attest a Jurhumite presence at Mecca but also involve the tribe in the construction, or reconstruction, of the Kaʿba; they also supply the name of the Jurhumite who engaged in this work, al-Muḍāḍ. Furthermore, they suggest that Jurhum also engaged in the ritual of circumambulating the Kaʿba, the *Ṭawāf*. Thus al-Muḍāḍ of the later Arabic historians emerges from this analysis as a figure known to a pre-Islamic document. It follows from this that he was not a fabrication of later Islamic times. The chances that he was a historical figure in the period slightly antedating the rise of Islam are tolerably good.[7] That his antiquity goes back to Abrahamic times must be thrown out of court without further ado, along with the further datum that makes him Ishmaël's father-in-law.[8] In the rubbish and rubble of the Arabic secondary sources of later times, the verse of al-Aʿsha that gives the name of the Jurhumite who built or restored the Kaʿba is a pearl of great price. Also important but less informative is the reference to Jurhum in the verse of al-Afwah al-Awdi analyzed earlier in this volume.[9]

3. One Arabic author, the thirteenth-century Ibn Saʿīd al-Maghribī, deserves to be noticed here for the information he has preserved on Jurhum.[10] He is a derivative and secondary source,[11] but may have preserved echoes from a good source.

[6] The work of Stephanus has survived only in fragments in the work of the 6th-century Hermolaus and in those of Eustathius of Salonika (d. around 1193); see *Cambridge Medieval History*, The Byzantine Empire, Part II (1967), 295 for the reference to the Γοραμῆνοι; in the *Ethnica,* see Stephanus of Byzantium (London, 1688), 276. On the attestation of Jurhum in Sabaic epigraphy, see below, Addenda et Corrigenda, 548.

[7] On al-Muḍāḍ in a different context, see above, 337–38. For the two verses, see below, App. 5.

[8] There is no doubt that this represents the bias of Yamanite historiography in early Islamic times, with the intention of linking the South Arabs with the northern Ishmaelite Arab tribes, which became the honored branch of the tribes of the Peninsula with the rise of Islam and the call of the Prophet Muḥammad, who derived his descent from Ishmael.

[9] See above, Sec. I.IV.

[10] The most detailed study of Ibn Saʿīd's work on pre-Islamic times, *Nashwat al-Ṭarab fī Tārīkh Jāhiliyyat al-ʿArab,* is the published doctoral dissertation of Manfred Kropp, in two volumes, with a translation, an introduction, and a commentary; see M. Kropp, "Die Geschichte der "reinen Araber" vom Stamme Qaḥṭān aus dem Kitāb Našwat Aṭ-Ṭarab fī Tārikh Ǧāhiliyyat al-ʿArab des Ibn Saʿīd al-Maghribī," *Heidelberger Orientalische Studien* (Tübingen, 1975). It is hoped that Dr. Kropp will publish and study the entire manuscript of *Nashwat al-Tarab* involving the part on the north Arabs. For Ibn Saʿīd see Ch. Pellat in *EI*[2], s.v. Ibn-Saʿid al-Maghribi (III, 926). This source was not consulted nor analyzed by Father Dagorn in his chapter on Jurhum.

[11] On the sources of Ibn Saʿīd, see Kropp, "Geschichte," 1, 78–93. One of his sources,

The most important data to be examined in his work, entitled *Nashwat al-Ṭarab*, which is exclusively devoted to the pre-Islamic history of the Arabs, are the names of the Jurhumite kings and some toponyms.[12] The former, such as ʿAbd al-Masīḥ ("the servant of Christ") are resoundingly Christian, and the question arises whether or not they are genuine. The editor and commentator of Ibn Saʿīd suggests that these are really the names of the Ghassānids of Ḥīra, given to the Jurhumites of Mecca, especially in view of the appearance of the distinctive Ghassānid name Nufayla/Buqayla in the royal onomasticon. One must agree with the editor on this point.[13] There are three toponyms: al-Dār; Al-Mawt, which the author glosses as the cemetery of the kings of Jurhum; and the mountain of Abū Qubays. All are associated with the Jurhumites of Mecca.[14] Places with distinctly Christian association, such as Maqbarat al-Naṣāra, the cemetery of the Christians, are attested in Mecca in later Islamic sources and these could not possibly have been fabricated.[15] One is inclined to identify Maqbarat al-Naṣāra with al-Mawt, mentioned in Ibn Saʿīd as the cemetery of the kings of Jurhum.[16]

The identification is of course purely speculative, and Maqbarat al-Naṣāra may have appeared in Mecca later than the period of Jurhum, but reference in two different sources to a Christian cemetery in Mecca remains striking; there could not have been many Christian cemeteries in Mecca, and so the possibility of identification is not altogether ruled out. What this shows is that Jurhum may have been involved in

---

Kitab al-Tījān of Wahb ibn Munabbih, has been recently republished by the Center for Yamani studies (no date or place of publication) in Sanʿāʾ. There are two chapters in it on Jurhum, and a chapter on the accounts of al-Yaman by a Jurhumi historian, the Yamanite ʿAbīd ibn Sharya, (pp. 325 ff).

[12] Kropp, "Geschichte," I, 120–29. Some of these kings were mentioned by the later historians who depended on Ibn Saʿīd, such as Ibn Khaldūn, but now the fuller account is available.

[13] See the commentary of the editor on the chapter on Jurhum, ibid., II, 496–500. It is surprising, however, that a Muslim author of the 13th century and a pious Muslim such as Ibn Saʿīd, who, moveover, performed the pilgrimage twice to the Holy City, would have given Mecca these Christian rulers. This then must be an interpolation which found its way into the text in the process of its transmission. It is noteworthy that a historian of Mecca in the late Middle Ages does mention a ʿAbd al-Masīḥ among the kings of Mecca and gives him the patronymic "son of MQBLT," which can be variously vocalized. The patronymic, however, could easily be a corruption of Buqayla/Nufayla and this brings it back to the Ghassānid with that name, as M. Kropp has suggested. See M. al-Fāsī, *Shifāʾ al-Gharām bi Akhbār al-Balad al-Ḥarām* (Mecca, 1956), I, 366. It is noteworthy that his source is another Andalusian, Fatḥ ibn Mūsa ibn Ḥammad, who lived in Egypt; ibid., 365. Al-Fāsi has perhaps the longest chapter of any author on Jurhum in Mecca, in which he depends on accounts of authors now lost; ibid., 357. Although it is full of legendary accounts it cannot be entirely ignored. Al-Fāsī does not appear in the bibliography of M. Kropp's work in the chapter on Jurhum in Ibn Saʿīd.

[14] For these see M. Kropp, "Geschichite," 127–29.

[15] For this cemetery outside Mecca, see al-Azraqī, *Akhbār Makka,* II, 298. Related to this cemetery are references to al-Maqlaʿ (ibid.) and Biʾr ʿAnbasa (ibid., I, 223 note 1 and II, 227, note [in Arabic alphabet]).

[16] Note that two place names in Ibn Saʿīd are associated with a king of Jurhum who does not belong to the Ghassānids of Ḥīra. He is Muḍāḍ ibn ʿAmr ibn Muḍāḍ, with whom are associated the toponyms al-Dār and al-Mawt; see ibid., 27–128.

Christianity and that some of the place names in Mecca with Christian association may even go back to a period of Jurhumite supremacy there.[17]

4. Although the Arabic prose sources have little or no value for the history of Jurhum in pre-Islamic times, they do refer incidentally to a Jurhumite figure who must be considered a historical personage. In the chapters on *ḥukkām al-ʿArab*, that is, the arbiters or judges of the Arabs in pre-Islamic times, the sources refer to a certain Jurhumite who is called al-Afʿā, and who was considered the arbiter of the Arabs; his seat was none other than Najrān.[18] This reference must be singled out, since it does not come in the legendary accounts of Jurhum in the distant biblical past or in accounts whose religious tendentiousness is patent.

The reliability of the account that speaks of this Jurhumite *ḥakam* (arbiter, judge) is confirmed by the name al-Afʿā, which means "the serpent." Moreover it is confirmed in that primary source for the history of Najrān, the *Book of the Ḥimyarites* of the sixth century, where it appears as the name of an important personage who was employed by the Najrānite as an ambassador for the transaction of important international assignments.[19] His tribal affiliation is not given in the *Book*, but he could well have been a descendant of al-Afʿā or even the Jurhumite himself, since his date is unknown and all that is said about him is that he belonged to the world of pre-Islamic Arabia.[20] Thus only two members of Jurhum in pre-Islamic times can be considered historical personages; al-Afʿā, the *ḥakam* of Najrān, and al-Muḍāḍ, the restorer of the Kaʿba according to Aʿsha. Of the two, the former should be accorded the firmer historicity.

5. The reference in the sources to al-Afʿā involves Jurhum in that important Arab center in South Arabia, Najrān,[21] and raises the question whether Jurhum had occupied Najrān at some point in the distant past or whether it moved to Najrān and its vicinity after its expulsion from Mecca by Khuzāʿa.[22] Without more inscriptions

[17] For some correction of L. Cheikho's views on Christianity in Mecca, see below, App. 4.

[18] See, for instance, Ibn Ḥabīb, *Al-Muḥabbar,* 135. Some confused and legendary material on al-Afʿā may also be found in Ibn Saʿīd, *Nashwat,* ed. M. Kropp, I, 58–59. On the Ḥukkām, arbiters of the Arabs in pre-Islamic times, see E. Tyan, *Histoire de l'organisation judiciaire,* 33–61. Other authors, such as Ibn Durayd, give al-Afʿā a different tribal affiliation; see his *Ishtiqāq,* 362. But the most authoritative historian, Ṭabarī, knows al-Afʿā as a Jurhumite; see the many references to him in *Tārīkh,* II, 268–69.

[19] See *The Book of the Ḥimyarites,* p. lxxxvi, s.v. Afʿu in Syriac. The entry is valuable, since it refers to the epigraphic attestation of the name in Liḥyānic. On his ambassadorial functions, see *Book* p. cxv. It is not impossible that al-Afʿā was the title of these arbiters rather than their name.

[20] The account that makes al-Afʿā the arbiter between the sons of Nizār is likely to be pure legend. Besides it gives no chronological indication about his *floruit*; see Balāḏurī, *Ansab al-Ashrāf,* I, 29–30.

[21] On this important Arab city of South Arabia, see Shahîd, *Martyrs.*

[22] This city is principally associated with the tribal group Banū al-Ḥārith ibn Kaʿb, known also as Balḥārith, which occupied the city at least as early as the 5th century and which attained great prominence because of the well-known events of the 6th century involving the Ḥimaryite persecution and the martyrdoms of many Najrānites during the reign of the Ḥimyarite king Yusuf, but the history of the tribal group that possessed it in earlier times is not clear.

from South Arabia it is impossible to follow the fortunes of Jurhum. The movement of tribes in western Arabia, such as *tafarruq al-Azd*, "the dispersion of the Azd," may have contributed to its disintegration. Apparently it ceased to exist as a separate independent tribe and affiliated itself (*dakhalat*) with another. This might explain the relationship of Jurhum to Liḥyān, since the latter was considered to have been originally Jurhum and was important in the history of Ḥijāz, if only because of its proximity to Mecca and the possibility of influences emanating from there.[23]

In spite of the precious little certainty that has resulted from this discussion of Jurhum in the early history of Mecca, it is possible to think that Christianity was introduced there through the Jurhumites and that it persisted till the rise of Islam in the midst of a world of eclecticism that was tolerant to religious pluralism. The Christian poet of al-Ḥīra, ʿAdī ibn-Zayd of the sixth century, swears by the Cross and also, in the same verse, by the "Lord of Mecca," which could only have been the first person of the Christian Trinity.[24] Such a Christian presence in Mecca can possibly be ascribed to the period of Jurhumite supremacy there. At least this supremacy may have coincided with the first phase of that presence, to be followed later by a stronger representation of the Christian mission in western Arabia, possibly brought in by ʿUḏra, which accentuated that first faint presence established by Jurhum.

The Arabic sources of later times do not limit themselves to Jurhum and Khuzāʿa in telling the story of Mecca and the Kaʿba before Quraysh established itself through Quṣayy as the lords and the custodians of the Mecca and the Kaʿba. They refer to various other tribes and tribal groups, such as Banū al-Mahd ibn Jandal, the ʿAmāliq, Ṭaṣm, and Iyād. Al-Fāsī has conveniently collected their accounts, and is fully aware of the legendary nature of most of them.[25] Nevertheless, these accounts are important, since they reflect later Muslim attitudes and perceptions of the Holy City and the Holy Temple in trying to endow both with a remote antiquity in the consciousness of the Arabs. Of all these accounts two are especially interesting.

1. The first,[26] going back to al-Masʿūdī, makes a member of Banū al-Mahd

---

On Khuzāʿa, see M. J. Kister in *EI,*[2] s.v. According to Ibn Khaldūn (*Tārīkh,* II, 532–33), Jurhum occupied Najrān before Balḥārith and al-Afʿā was a Jurhumite.

[23] See Fahd, "Gerrhéens," 76. Tribal Jurhum has been epigraphically attested; above, note 6. Jurhum as the name of an individual is attested in a Safaitic inscription emanating from southern Syria and northern Jordan; see *Corpus Inscirptionum Semiticarum,* pars quinta inscriptiones Saracenicas continens (Paris, 1950), no. 1712. It would be difficult to draw conclusions from one epigraphic attestation of the name of an individual, but the Safaitic inscription could at least raise the question whether Jurhum was a north Ḥijāzi tribe. Its affiliation with Liḥyān may point in this direction. Jurhum is considered one of those tribes which changed their tribal affiliations, the *Nawāqil,* for which see *Fihrist,* 96.

[24] For this verse, see the *Dīwān,* p. 38. The last verse in the fragment refers also to the same "Lord" he had mentioned in the verse involving Mecca.

[25] The late medieval historian of Mecca M. al-Fāsī (1373–1429) is one of the most important sources, since he gathered together accounts from his predecessors al-Azraqī and al-Fākihī and other historians on Mecca. He devoted one long chapter to these tribal groups; see *Shifāʾ*, I, 352–78. This edition of *Shifaʾ* has superseded the old one, edited in part by F. Wüstenfeld. For al-Fāsī, see F. Rosenthal, *HMH,* and his article in the *EI*[2] (II, 828–29).

[26] *Shifāʾ*, 352.

the king of Mecca and relates him and his tribe to the people of Shuʿayb, that extra-biblical prophet who appears in the Koran as an Arabian prophet sent to Madyan/Midyan, and whom later Islamic exegetes and historians related to the biblical priest of Midian, Jethro/Reuel, the father-in-law of Moses. Thus as other accounts spoke of Mecca and the Kaʿba in Abrahmaic times, this one related them to the period of Moses.

2. More important is the account that associates Iyād with Mecca and the Kaʿba. Unlike Banū al-Mahd, the ʿAmāliq, and Ṭaṣm, this is a well-known Arab tribe that played an important role in the history of the Arabs before Islam. Its history is associated with the Sasanids and the Byzantines, with the rise of the Arabic script and poetry, and above all with Christianity. Its history is elusive when it makes its appearance in the Fertile Crescent, and the accounts which associate it with Mecca and the custodianship of the Kaʿaba make the tracing of its history in the Peninsular stage even more so.[27]

Without epigraphic confirmation it is difficult to draw any conclusions on the relationship of these tribes to Mecca and the Kaʿba. Of all the tribes mentioned in the sources before Quraysh and Khuzāʿa, it is only Jurhum that can be taken seriously, since documentation of its historicity and association with the Kaʿba and Mecca is strong and is on an entirely different level from later secondary literary sources.

The prophet Muḥammad threw a challenge to Byzantium in the seventh century and his successors, the caliphs, changed the course of Byzantine and world history. Any data that shed light on the history of the city that produced Muḥammad is consequently important. Especially so is the history of the tribes such as Jurhum and ʿUḏra associated with Christianity in Mecca. Their Christianity can easily be traced to the Christian mission of the Byzantine *ecclesia* in western Arabia; hence their history as it reflects the Byzantine connection is part of the theme "Byzantium and Western Arabia."

Appendix IV

Traces of Christianity in Mecca

Something has been said on Christian places in and around Mecca (above, Appendix 3), especially Maqbarat al-Naṣāra, the cemetery of the Christians. It remains to discuss a few others.

1. The enthusiastic and indefatigable L. Cheikho has a startling statement on a Christian bishop of Mecca in the period of Jurhum's supremacy.[1] However, a close examination of the source he cites, *al-Aghāni*, reveals that Cheikho misread the statement. He read and vocalized the consonantal skeleton of the phrase in question,

[27] Unlike the crucial verses of Zuhayr and al-Aʿshā (analyzed below in Appendices 5 and 6), verses on Iyād's custodianship of the Kaʿba are suspect, since they are ascribed to one of the Iyādīs, a certain Bashīr, and thus could have been a later fabrication composed for the greater glory of Iyād; for these verses, see R. Dagorn, *La geste*, 305. On Iyād, see Kister in *EI*[2], s.v. In this article, Kister draws attention to Iyād's custodianship of the Kaʿba.

[1] See L. Cheikho, *Al-Naṣrāniyya,* I, 117.

LSQF, *li usqufin*, "to a bishop," while the phrase should read *lā saqfa*, "with no roof or ceiling." This is surely the correct reading as is clear in the new edition of *al-Aghānī*;[2] the sentence makes much better sense when interpreted this way; besides, the preposition *li* is not the normal way of describing the jurisdiction of a bishop. The rejection of Cheikho's reading of the text is important: the Christian mission in western Arabia apparently never succeeded in establishing a strong Christian presence in Mecca, organized and controlled by an episcopal see.

2. Cheikho also refers to a place in Mecca which he calls Mawqif al-Naṣrānī, the stopping or halting place of the Christian, giving the lexicon *Tāj al-ʿArūs* of al-Zabīdī as his source.[3] But there is nothing in that lexicon under the root WQF or NṢR. Unlike "the bishop of Mecca," this must be a real toponym which he found in one of the Arabic sources, since the phrase is clear in what it says and there is no possibility of another interpretation or reading. It either appears in *Tāj* elsewhere than in the entry WQF or NṢR or in some other source. The term is important, since it might imply some ceremonial station for the Christians of Mecca.

3. In the *Geography* of al-Muqaddasi (al-Maqdisi) there is also a startling reference to Masājid Maryam, "the mosques or praying places of Maryam," located outside Mecca on the way to Medina.[4] The natural presumption is that Maryam is the Virgin Mary, to whom a church or complex of churches was dedicated, and this can be supported as follows. Christianity did spread in western Arabia to Mecca itself, and to its north and south; the verse quoted earlier in this chapter[5] speaks of monasteries in Wādī al-Qurā not far from Medina as late as the Umayyad period; in Mecca and in the Kaʿba itself there was a picture of the Virgin Mary in 630, when Muḥammad conquered the city.[6] The chances are, then, that there was a church or a complex of churches dedicated to the Virgin Mary near Mecca in the pre-Islamic period. Masājid Maryam in al-Muqaddasi are then "a church turned mosque,"[7] made possible by the fact that the Koran accepts the Virgin Mary; indeed, there is a *sūra* in the Koran devoted to her.

4. Finally, a most important evidence for Christianity in Mecca is the existence of the picture of the Virgin Mary and also one of Jesus in the Kaʿba itself.[8] The history of this important Christian evidence in Azraqī belongs to a later pre-Islamic period;[9] nevertheless, it has much relevance to earlier times.

[2] See A. Iṣbahānī, *Al-Aghānī,* XV, 14; also al-Fāsī, *Shifāʾ*, I, 361.

[3] L. Cheikho, *Al-Naṣrāniyya*, 118; but he does not say exactly where in the lexicon this reference is.

[4] For this, see al-Muqaddasi, *Aḥsan al-Taqāsim fi Maʿrifat al-Aqālīm,* BCA (Leiden, 1877), III, 77. "Masājid Maryam" appears in the apparatus criticus as the reading of manuscript C. This is not a statement which a Muslim historian would have fabricated, and so the chances are good that this is the correct reading.

[5] See above, 359.

[6] See al-Azraqī, *Akhbār Makka,* I, 165.

[7] There are parallels to this, notably Masjid Jarjīs, "The Mosque of Sergius," in South Arabia, for which see Shahîd, "Byzantium in South Arabia," 85–87.

[8] See above, note 6.

[9] See the article on the Kaʿba in *EI*[2], 319, where its rebuilding is associated with the name of Bāqūm, said to have been a Christian Copt. This will be discussed in *BASIC*.

5. A striking short *ekphrasis* of the mural paintings of the Kaʿba is preserved in Masʿūdī,[10] which dates to the pre-prophetic phase in Muḥammad's life. It falls into two parts.

a. The biblical part speaks of the picture of Abraham painted on the wall of the Kaʿba and opposite him that of his son Ishmael, mounted on a horse, allowing the pilgrims to pass, while the Fārūq is standing among the people.

b. The non-biblical material pertaining to the history of Quraysh consists of some sixty pictures of prominent members of the tribe, down to Quṣayy. Each picture also had the god whom the prominent Qurayshi worshipped, together with the manner of his worship and his exploits.

There is much to be said for the authenticity of this *ekphrasis*, since the authentic passage in Azraqī belongs roughly to the same period. Furthermore, the evidence presented in an earlier chapter of the present volume[11] for the appearance of some form of representational art in western Arabia in this period fortifies the case for its authenticity. The *ekphrasis* is full of interest, but since it belongs to a later period only a few observations will be made on its contents here.

a. The biblical material confirms what has been said in the course of this book on the reality of Ishmaelism among the pre-Islamic Arabs in western Arabia. The passage associated both Abraham and Ishmael with the Kaʿba, and depicts the latter as already involved in the rite of pilgrimage and in horsemanship, as the accounts of the later historians picture him.

The figure referred to as al-Fārūq could only be Jesus, whose picture in the Kaʿba is vouched for by the passage in Azraqī. What is striking here is the name given to him; it can only be Syriac Pārūqā, the term used in the Syriac Church for the Savior. The term is assimilated to the morphology and lexicology of the Arabic language, and it appears as a perfectly good Arabic word.[12]

b. The non-biblical material is the history of the important personages among the Quraysh; it is significant that the pictures stop with Quṣayy, who appears in the *ekphrasis* as a pagan worshipping one of the many gods that were painted on the walls of the Kaʿba. This is the natural interpretation of the passage and is consonant with what is known about the names of his sons, all pagan theophoric names. On the other hand, Quṣayy could also have believed in the biblical figures, for what is most striking about this *ekphrasis* is the strong eclecticism which characterized Kaʿba worship and enabled biblical and non-biblical figures to be gathered together and worshiped in one place.

The *ekphrasis* is a unique document, which corroborates in a striking fashion what has been established from other pre-Islamic sources—that "Ishmaelism" and Christianity both found their way into Mecca in pre-Islamic times.

[10] See Masʿūdī, *Murūj,* III, 10.

[11] See above, 81 note 76.

[12] For the related problem of the Koranic term *furqān* and the possibility of a Syriac origin, see A. Jeffery, *The Foreign Vocabulary of the Qurʾan,* 225–29.

Appendix V

Two Pre-Islamic Verses

The most precious documents for the involvement of the tribal groups Quraysh and Jurhum in the Kaʿba and also of the members of these tribes, Quṣayy and al-Muḍāḍ, are two verses by the pre-Islamic poets Zuhayr and al-Aʿshā. Both were considered poets of the Seven Suspended Odes,[1] and Zuhayr's verse appears in fact in one of them, in his own *muʿallaqa*, his Suspended Ode. Zuhayr speaks of Quraysh and Jurhum as having been engaged in the building of the Kaʿba, while al-Aʿshā is more specific, and actually names the two members of the Quraysh and Jurhum whose names are associated with the building or restoration. Thus the two verses complement each other and document the two phases of the custodianship and restoration of the Kaʿba, those of Jurhum and of Quraysh.

Those who have written on the Kaʿba and Quṣayy have not seriously examined these two precious verses.[2] There is no question of their authenticity and the soundness of their textual tradition. In view of the unreliability of much of the prose sources of later Islamic times about both Quraysh in the times of Quṣayy and the more remote Jurhum, it is necessary to subject these pre-Islamic documents to an intensive examination, all the more so because they have recently been examined intensively in regard to the enigmatic tribe of Jurhum.[3]

Zuhayr

One of the verses of his Suspended Ode makes a reference to the building of the Kaʿba by Quraysh and Jurhum:[4] *Fa aqsamtu bilbayti iladẖī ṭāfa ḥawlahū rijālun banawhu min Qurayshin wa Jurhumi* ("I have sworn by the House (Kaʿba) around which circumambulated men who had built it, belonging to Quraysh and Jurhum").

In defense of the authenticity and the soundness of the text of this verse the following may be adduced.

1. The verse comes in the most celebrated of the poems of a celebrated pre-Islamic poet—one of the three foremost, according to some critics.[5] Thus it does not belong to that corpus of pre-Islamic poetry which has been haunted by the ghosts of authenticity and attribution. Besides, Zuhayr was a very late pre-Islamic poet, a younger contemporary of the Prophet himself and not one who belonged to the much earlier period or to a group of minor poets about whom little or nothing is known except their names and a few solitary verses.

[1] On these, see A. J. Arberry, *The Seven Odes* (London, 1957) and Sezgin, *GAS,* II, 46–53, 109–32. On the question of the authenticity of pre-Islamic poetry, see Arberry, ibid., 228–45.

[2] Only touched upon by G. Levi Della Vida in his article on Quṣayy and not at all in Wensinck's article on the Kaʿba; see both in *EI*², s.vv. Ḳuṣayy and Kaʿba.

[3] See above, App. 4.

[4] For the verse, see Ahlwardt, *Divans*, 64, line 16.

[5] On Zuhayr, his Suspended Ode, and the occasion of the poem, see Arberry, *Seven Odes,* 90–118 and Sezgin, *GAS,* II, 118–20.

2. What is equally important is the place of the verse in the structure of this polythematic ode of Zuhayr. It does not come in that part which some hypercritical scholars have suspected of being an Islamic forgery, including two or three verses which betray a striking similarity to Koranic sentiments and lexicology.[6] These verses, however, come in the gnomic part of the poem, while the verse in question comes in the central part which is the main theme of the poem, expressing the occasion on which it was composed, namely, the resolution of the differences between the two tribes of ʿAbs and D̲ubyān, which had fought long. The two *sayyids* (chiefs) who effected the reconciliation and brought about the termination of the war are called Harim and Ḥārith, and the poem is a panegyric in their honor.

3. The syntax of the verse proves the point incontrovertibly. The line by itself is not complete, so, it cannot have been one of these "wandering verses" in the old Arabic pre-Islamic poetry which could migrate from one portion of the Qasida to another because of the atomic structure of classical Arabic verse, in which each line is a self-contained unit semantically and syntactically. This verse is semantically and syntactically incomplete, since the initial verb in the line, *fa-aqsamtu*, is a transitive verb which has for its object the first word in the following line which reads:[7] *Yaminan laniʿma assayidāni wujidtumā ʿAlā kulli hālin min saḥīlin wamubrami* ("a solemn oath I swear—you have proved yourselves fine masters in all matters, be the thread single or twisted double"). The object of the verb *aqsamtu* is *yaminan* in this line which praises and glorifies the two *sayyids* who brought about the peace between their tribes.

Thus the verse is firmly established in authenticity and in textual soundness, and no critic or editor of the *Muʿallaqat* has ever assailed the line on either of these two grounds.

Al-Aʿshā

Unlike Zuhayr's verse, al-Aʿshā's does not come in his *Muʿallaqa*. But no critic has ever doubted its attribution to this pre-Islamic poet, although doubts have been expressed on the textual soundness of the verse, as will be discussed presently. The text reads: *Wa inni wathawbay rāhibi al-Lujji wallatī banāhā Qusayyun wa al-Muḍāḍu bnu Jurhumi* ("I swear by the two robes of the monk of the monastery of al-Lujj and by that [the Kaʿba] which Quṣayy and al-Muḍāḍ, son of Jurhum, have built").[8] In view of the crucial relevance and importance of this verse to the religious history of Mecca in pre-Islamic times, the following observations may be made.

[6] Such as verses 26, 27 on p. 65 and v. 54 on p. 66 of Ahlwardt's edition of Zuhayr. It is also far from certain that the suspicion with which these verses have been viewed is justified, since both the Koran and pre-Islamic poetry draw on the same conceptual world of pre-Islamic Arabia; but at least it should be mentioned that these verses are suspect; see R. Blachére, *Histoire de la littérature arabe* (Paris, 1952), I, 176 and F. Gabrieli, *Storia della letteratura araba* (Milan, 1962), 49.

[7] For this line, see Ahlwardt, *Divans,* 65, line 1. The English version of the line is that of Arberry, *Seven Odes,* 115.

[8] For the verse, see *Dīwān al-Aʿshā al-Kabīr,* ed. M. Ḥusayn (Cairo, 1950), 125, line 6. See also the older edition of the *Dīwān* by R. Geyer, *Gedichte von al-Aʿsha,* E. J. W. Gibb Memorial Series, n.s. 4 (London, 1928), 95, line 7.

1. There is no need at all to doubt its authenticity, since its historical content is in harmony with what is known about this major pre-Islamic poet, who shares with Zuhayr a *floruit* in late pre-Islamic times, and who died in the first quarter of the seventh century. Al-Aʿshā was an "historian-poet." He had traveled extensively in the Arabian Peninsula and neighboring states of the Near East and eulogized many of the powerful rulers of Arabia, including Hawḏa ibn ʿAlī, the lord of Yamāma, and the lords of Najrān and Ḥaḍramawt. The religious currents of the period found expression in his poetry, and his *dīwān* is a mine of information for the cultural history of Arabia in the sixth century.[9]

2. Set against this background, the verse in question is a perfectly authentic one, coming from this widely traveled poet who had a special interest in the structures and buildings of the Peninsula in the sixth century and who wrote on the fairly recent past. The Kaʿba of Mecca must have attracted his attention, especially as he had mentioned the Kaʿba of Najrān, to the south of Mecca, in his poetry and given a few details about its structure.[10] These two Kaʿbas must have been rivals of some sort in the Arabia of the sixth century, the first a shrine for Christianity, the other a shrine of Arabian paganism, and both were places of pilgrimage for the Arabs.

3. In his description of the Kaʿba of Najrān he mentions its lords, Yazīd, ʿAbd al-Madān, and Qays, possibly also its builders or restorers in the sixth century.[11] It is only natural to expect him to accord the rival Kaʿba to the north some attention, the result of which was this extant verse and possibly others which have not survived. In this verse, he mentions the shrine and those responsible for its construction or restoration with the same specificity that characterized his reference to the Kaʿba of Najrān.

4. The verse comes in one of his best and longest poems, and no one has ever doubted its authenticity.[12] Furthermore, it comes in a part of the poem in which al-Aʿshā expresses special interest in Mecca and its Holy Places, such as al-Ḥajūn, al-Ṣafā, and Zamzam. Thus al-Aʿshā is well informed about the Meccan scene, and the verse also reflects what he had heard about the builders of its Kaʿba, Quṣayy and al-Muḍāḍ.

5. The verse could not have been concocted by a poet of the *Muslim* period in view of the asseverative formula that the poet employs in it. The oath is a composite one, consisting of a reference to the two robes of the monastery monk and another to the Kaʿba; thus it is an oath in which Christian and pagan objects are sworn by. This oath has the ring of pre-Islam about it, echoing the eclecticism of the Arab poets of the sixth century, who could swear by both Christian and pagan holy objects and places. Such was al-Nābigha, the celebrated court-poet of the Ghassānids and the Lakhmids.[13]

[9] For al-Aʿshā, see Sezgin, *GAS,* II, 130–32.

[10] On this, see Shahîd, "Byzantium in South Arabia," 70–74, especially 71, and 74. In this as well as in other aspects, the verse is on the same level of authenticity as that of Zuhayr.

[11] Ibid., 74.

[12] See the *Dīwān,* ed. Husayn, 123, line 11. He had also mentioned the holy place Minā five verses before and other holy places in the following line. For the verse in Geyer's edition of the *Dīwān,* see 94, line 10.

[13] On al-Nābigha, see Sezgin, *GAS,* II, 110–113. For two of the poet's verses which

6. Finally, the text of this verse has survived in two versions. The second version reads: *Fa innī wathawbay rāhibi al-Lujji wallatī banāhā Qusayyun waḥdahū wa bnu Jurhumi* ("I have sworn by the two robes of the monk of al-Lujj [the name of a monastery] and by that which Quṣayy alone and the son of Jurhum have built").[14] In the first version, the two builders are Quṣayy and al-Muḍāḍ ibn Jurhum, while in the second they are Quṣayy and ibn Jurhum. The first version must be the sound one, and in defense of its soundness the following observations may be made.

The poet has just mentioned the name of the first builder, Quṣayy. It is natural to expect the name of the second one, which he does give, adding his patronymic. Thus in the first version the two names balance each other; in the second version, the name of the second builder disappears and instead the words *waḥdahu* ("alone") appears, followed by the patronymic of the second builder only. This represents a retreat in the elegance and the order or words in the verse of a great poet. Besides, *waḥdahu* is suspect. It does not seem to serve a purpose, is too emphatic, and may be misleading. Furthermore, it raises the question of what it is supposed to imply, and why the poet should have said "Quṣayy alone." Finally, the strongest argument against this version is that *waḥdahu* rules out reference to a second builder. The point was appreciated by the medieval philologist Abū Ḥatim, who threw this second version out of court on this very ground and made an amusing analogy to demonstrate the utter worthlessness of this version through a *reductio ad absurdum*.[15]

It remains to discuss how the two versions fared with the editors of the *Dīwān* of al-Aʿshā, Rudolph Geyer and Muḥammad Ḥusayn. Geyer based his 1928 edition mainly on the Escorial manuscript,[16] which has this inferior reading *waḥdahu*, but he included in the apparatus criticus and in the notes the reading of the first version.[17] As is well known, the competent Viennese scholar was struck with paralysis in his right side while editing the *Dīwān* and completed it under extremely difficult circumstances. It was, therefore, left to Muḥammad Ḥusayn more than twenty years later to

---

reflect his religious eclecticism, see Ahlwardt, *Divans,* 7, line 19 and 8, line 1. For the commentaries of the ancient philologists on the eclecticism of al-Nābigha and his two verses, see *Dīwān al-Nābigha al-Ḏubyāni,* ed. Sh. Fayṣal (Beirut, 1968) 19–20, and *Dīwān al-Nābigha al-Ḏubyāni,* ed. M. Ibrahim (Cairo, 1977), 25. See also R. Dagorn, *La geste d'Ismaël,* 148, where the two verses are quoted.

[14] For this version, see ibid., 309. The French translation of the verse begins with *car moi* (*fa innī*), which I have omitted in order to make the English translation a complete sentence. But the verse in Arabic is incomplete, since the predicate or complement of *fa innī* is in the following verse: *la in jadda asbābu,* . . . in which the poet sounds a thundering comminatory note against his adversary, but which is irrelevant to the argument of this section. However, the incompleteness of the line fortifies the argument for its soundness and its position in the poem: it is not a "wandering line" which could have come from some other poem. In this it is like the verse of Zuhayr, which is also incomplete without the following line, and comes in a part of the poem that cannot be viewed with suspicion on the ground of authenticity.

[15] For Abu Ḥatim's commentary on this verse (44), see the notes in Geyer's edition, p. 88.

[16] *Dīwān,* ed. Geyer, xiv-xx; for the other three manuscripts, Cairo, Leiden, Paris, see ibid., xx.

[17] Ibid., 95 (Arabic numerals) and 88.

refine on the work of his distinguished predecessor and correct some of the inaccuracies[18] after a thorough rereading of all the manuscripts of the *Dīwān*. One of the results of this was the acceptance of the first version of the verse.[19] This was the version which also appears in *Shifā᾽ al-Gharām bi Akhbār al-Balad al-Ḥarām*, by a scholar who wrote some centuries before both Geyer and Ḥusayn.[20]

Al-Muḍāḍ has already been discussed in this book in relation to the biblical al-Modad, and it has been suggested that he might well have been a historical figure. Al-Aʿshā has increased our knowledge of the history of the Kaʿba and its association with Jurhum, informing that one of the members of that tribal group did build or restore the Temple. It does not necessarily follow that al-Muḍāḍ actually took part in such an endeavor. What does follow is that in pre-Islamic times such a tradition did exist, that it reached al-Aʿshā, and that he recorded it in his poetry. This verse, like that of Zuhayr, turns out to be an important source for the Kaʿba, Jurhum, Mecca, and in general for Ishmael-related accounts circulating in *pre-Islamic* Arabia.

Appendix VI

The Two Verses in *La geste d'Ismaël*

In the course of his discussion of the enigmatic tribe of Jurhum, Father Dagorn had occasion to examine the two verses of Zuhayr and Aʿshā treated in the preceding appendix. To him belongs the distinction of being the first scholar to do so. It is, therefore, important to submit his treatment to an examination and record the reservations which this examination gives rise to.

Zuhayr

Father Dagorn devoted some three pages[1] to the examination of Zuhayr's verse, in which he argued, among other things, that when Zuhayr speaks of one of the builders of the Kaʿba as Jurhum, it is quite possible that what is involved is not the tribe but an individual—that Jurhum is either his proper name or a common name for the builder. According to him, "Jurhumi̲" in the verse should read Jurhumu̲, but the poet applied the *kasra* as the last vowel because this is the terminal vowel of the monorhymed poem. Two different French versions are given in conformity with this

[18] See *Dīwān*, ed. Ḥusayn, pp. b-d (Arabic alphabet).

[19] Ibid., 125, line 6.

[20] See M. al-Fāsī, *Shifā᾽ al-Gharām*, I, 94. In this connection it should be mentioned that Geyer suspected what he called *quraišitische Zugehörigkeit* in verses 34–39 of the poem, but not in the verse in question (verse 44, p. 95 [Arabic numerals] in his edition of the *Dīwān*). He accepted it as an old authentic poem; see ibid., xxi.

However, verses 34–39 sound very much like "the cymbal of the Arabs," Aʿshā's soubriquet. But the concept is useful, and could be the perfect explanation for the appearance of *waḥdahu* in the text of the verse. The presumption is that some member of the Quraysh, or an enthusiast in Islamic times when the prestige of Quraysh stood high, resented the inclusion and intrusion of a Jurhumī in the building of the Holy Temple, and so he deleted the name of al-Muḍāḍ and substituted *waḥdau* after Quṣayy in order to reserve the full mead of honor to the ancestor of the Prophet in the fifth generation.

[1] Dagorn, *La geste*, 306–9.

view. These views encounter many serious difficulties, which may be summarized as follows:

1. It is impossible to believe that a prominent pre-Islamic poet such as Zuhayr would have changed the terminal vowel from u̲ to i̲ in obedience to an exigency imposed on him by the monorhyme. This never happens in this long Suspended Ode of his, except in the prosodically permissible *sukūn* of the imperfect when it is in the jussive mood. This is especially inconceivable in view of the fact that this would have changed the meaning of the verse. The distinctive *iʿrāb* in Arabic, the use of the desinential inflections, was designed to guard the meaning of the Arabic verse when the poet indulged in *taqdīm* and *taʾkhīr*, the transposition of words in the sentence in response to a metrical necessity.[2] Zuhayr in particular would have been immune to such prosodical malpractice, since he was considered one of ʿAbīd al-Shiʿr ("the slaves of poetry"), poets who spent a long time polishing and chiseling their poems.

2. To suggest that Jurhum in Zuhayr's line is an individual with that name is preposterous. The poet was describing the Kaʿba of Mecca, at the time governed by Quraysh, and it is inconceivable that he would have treated the contribution of Quraysh so unceremoniously as to mention in general certain men from Quraysh who built it (without naming them), aided by a figure by the name of Jurhum. This would have given prominence to a figure who did not belong to Quraysh, and thus would have honored him, while Quraysh was obscured by a general reference to men from Quraysh.[3] This would also contradict the verse of Aʿshā which credits one from Quraysh, Quṣayy, with building the Kaʿba together with al-Muḍāḍ from Jurhum.

3. The further suggestion that Jurhum in the verse may be a common noun meaning *miqdām*, a courageous man, cannot be accepted. In addition to the serious difficulties discussed above, there is in this case the difficulty of accepting the derivation and the etymology of this word as given by the medieval Arabic lexicographers. The problem is that of non-synonymous homophonous roots in Arabic. The medieval lexicographers made important contributions in this area of Arabic philology, but when it came to etymologizing an archaic word or name in Arabic they were out of their depth, especially when a knowledge of comparative Semitics would have been necessary. Even if their etymology is correct, the verse of Zuhayr would be childish, vapid, and unworthy of a great poet.

4. The author seems to think that the traditional manner of interpreting the verse (that the Kaʿba was built by men from the tribes Quraysh and Jurhum) implies that their work of restoration was simultaneous, whereas the two tribes occupied Mecca in two different periods; the Arabic sources, in fact, date Jurhum al-Ūlā ("the first Jurhum") to many centuries before Christ, going back to the days of Ishmael himself.

Surely, this is *not* what the poet meant to say and it is not what the readers and the commentators of the verse have understood Zuhayr to mean.

[2] On this point, see my review of Michael Zwettler's *The Oral Tradition of Classical Arabic Poetry*, in *JAOS* 100 (1980), 32.

[3] Especially inconceivable in the 6th century, when Quraysh were the sole lords of Mecca and the custodians of the Kaʿba.

5. Finally, in the last paragraph dealing with this verse, Father Dagorn speaks of the modest structure that the Kaʿba was and the difficulty of imagining that two different tribes were occupied in building such a modest structure. But this is not the impression that one gets from reading Zuhayr's verse, and one must remember that this is not the report of an architect but that of a *poet*. The monumental character or magnificence of the Kaʿba is not the issue; its holiness is, and the honor that redounds to those who participate in the erection or restoration of a holy place.

Al-Aʿshā

Father Dagorn sees in the verse of Aʿshā further confirmation of his view that what is involved is not the tribe of Jurhum but an individual who carried that name.[4] He accepts the second version of the verse, the second hemistich of which reads: *banāha Quṣayyun waḥdahū wabnu Gurhumi*, ("which Quṣayy alone and Ibn Jurhum built"). The following may be presented in defense of the view that the verse refers to the tribe of Jurhum and not an individual.

1. The first version of the verse, the standard one, was defended above (App. 5). But one might also say that even if the reading *waḥdahu* is retained, "ibn Jurhumi" is not a real patronymic indicating a person but rather one that draws attention to the tribal affiliation of the other builder. His father may or may not have been called Jurhum, but what is important here is his tribal affiliation, predicated through the patronymic; so "ibn" ("son") here is like "akh" ("brother") which sometimes precedes the name of a tribe to indicate affiliation with it. As said earlier, *al-Muḍāḍ* is a better reading than *waḥdahu* as it balances Quṣayy, and does not encounter all the difficulties that the latter presents.

2. The commentator of *al-Mufaḍḍaliyyāt*, al-Anbāri (Abū Muḥammad) (d. 916/917) says al-Aʿshā did not know what he was talking about when he composed his verse on the Kaʿba and its builders, since he neither knew who built it nor how it was constructed. He further adds that Quṣayy was not its restorer.[5] Surely, the itinerant and ubiquitous al-Aʿshā knew more about pre-Islamic Arabia than the armchair philologist of later Islamic times since, unlike the latter, he lived in the Peninsula, traveled extensively in and around it, and, what is more, saw for himself.[6]

Father Dagorn's conclusion from his study of the two verses of Zuhayr and Aʿshā is that one can accept Quṣayy's association with the Kaʿba, not Jurhum's. But as this intensive examination of the two verses has shown, Jurhum's association with the Kaʿba and Mecca must stand, in spite of the many obscurities that surround the Jurhumite presence in Mecca (discussed above, Appendix 3).

[4] Dagorn, *La geste,* 309–10.

[5] In all fairness to Father Dagorn (ibid., 310) it should be mentioned that he quotes al-Anbāri disapprovingly.

[6] He is known to posterity through his commentary on the anthology *al-Mufaḍḍaliyyāt,* in which al-Aʿshā does not figure. The chances then are that Al-Anbāri (Abū Muḥammad) did not know much of anything about al-Aʿshā, or at least not enough to make his ascription of ignorance to Aʿshā justifiable. His son, however, Ibn al-Anbāri (Abū Bakr) did, and Ibn al-Nadīm credits him with having collected the poems of al-Aʿshā (*Fihrist,* 75). Ibn al-Nadīm draws a comparison between father and son which shows the latter to advantage, and it may be

Appendix VII

The Tribal Affiliation of Banū al-Ḥārith ibn Kaʿb

The dominant tribe in Najrān in the fifth, sixth, and seventh centuries was Banū al-Ḥārith ibn Kaʿb, known also in the abbreviated form of Balḥārith.[1] This is the tribe that had been powerful politically and militarily in Najrān before it became so also ecclesiastically—after the martyrdoms in the sixth century, since the martyr St. Arethas was its chief (*sayyid*) and the ruler of Najrān.[2] It is therefore important to determine its correct tribal affiliation for a better understanding of the complexities of political life in western Arabia.

The Arab genealogists of later Islamic times affiliate Balḥārith with the large South Arabian tribal group Madḥij.[3] But others state that Balḥārith really belonged to the other large South Arabian tribal group al-Azd[4] and that it only later affiliated itself with Madḥij, as was the wont of Arab tribes in pre-Islamic and early Islamic times.[5] This is more likely to be the truth, and a confirmation of an Azdite tribal affiliation is provided by the most solid of all evidence, epigraphy.

An inscription published in 1968 speaks of al-Ḥārith ibn Kaʿb as the king of al-Asd[6] (al-Azd). Thus Sabaic epigraphy has preserved an echo from the distant past of the association between an individual called al-Ḥārith ibn Kaʿb and the Azd group. It is true that it is an individual, the king of the Azd, who is called al-Ḥārith ibn Kaʿb. But as often happens in the tribal onomasticon, a distinguished individual gives his name to a family, then to a clan, and then to a tribe.[7] The natural presumption is that al-Ḥārith ibn Kaʿb of the inscription gave his name to his family, which multiplied into a clan and then into a tribe within the group of al-Azd. Later, when they migrated as part of the great tribal movement in pre-Islamic Arabia known as "Tafarruq al-Azd" ("the Dispersion of al-Azd"), they settled in Najrān in the area of

inferred from this comparison that the former was not possessed of an inordinate measure of intelligence. It is interesting to note that the son accepted the first version of this verse of al-Aʿshā (which has *al-Muḍāḍ* instead of *waḥdahu*); see Geyer's edition, p. 95 (Arabic numerals) line 4 of the aparatus criticus, where Ibn al-Anbāri is referred to by his tecnonymic, Abū Bakr. Thus the confusion generated by the father has been neutralized by the more informed son. On the two Anbāri's see *EI*[2], s.vv. al-Anbāri, Abū Bakr and al-Anbāri, Abū Muḥammad.

[1] For Balḥārith, see *EI*[2] s.v.

[2] For these martyrdoms and for St. Arethas, see Shahîd, *Martyrs.*

[3] See, for example, Ibn Ḥazm, *Jamharat,* 416–17.

[4] See Ibn Saʿīd, *Nashwat At-Tarab,* I, 94; Ibn Khaldūn, quoting a different account of Ibn Saʿīd on Balḥārith, in *Tārīkh,* II, 515; and finally Masʿūdī, *Murūj al-Ḏahab,* II, 330.

[5] Tribes that changed their affiliations were called *al-Nawāqil,* and often the term "dakhalat" spoken of a tribe expresses the notion of change of tribal affiliation from one tribe to another; for the *Nawāqil,* see Caskel, *GN,* 52–62.

[6] For this inscription, see D. B. Doe and A. Jamme, "New Sabaean Inscriptions from South Arabia," *Journal of the Royal Asiatic Society* (1968), 15–16. The original form of Azd was Asd, for which see *BAFOC,* 37 note 26.

[7] "Quraysh," according to some genealogists, was originally the *laqab* of one of the members of the Kinana group before it became the name of the famous tribe of Mecca, that of the Prophet Muḥammad.

the powerful Madḥij group, while the other tribes of the Azd left South Arabia and wandered into western, eastern, and northern Arabia.[8]

The primary Syriac documents of the sixth century which recorded the history of the martyrdoms at Najrān have preserved the name of the *sayyid* of Najrān and Balḥārith, and he is none other than al-Ḥārith ibn Kaʿb, who became known in ecclesiastical history as St. Arethas.[9] This is strong confirmation of what was said in the preceding paragraph: in the sixth century, al-Ḥārith ibn Kaʿb is the *sayyid* of the tribe of al-Ḥārith ibn Kaʿb, and the namesake both in name and patronymic of the king of the Azd mentioned in the Sabaic inscription. Apparently the name was assumed by the kings or *sayyids* of the Azd, and it is just possible that the one mentioned in the inscription is none other than the ancestor of the sixth century *sayyid*.

Thus the chances that Balḥārith belonged to the Azd group are good. This has important implications to their inter-tribal relations in pre-Islamic Arabia, and would explain the close relationship between the Ghassānids, who belonged to the Azd group, and the Balḥāriths of Najrān.[10] The *anṣār* of Medina during Muḥammadan times also belonged to the Azd tribal group, into which the great-grandfather of the Prophet Muḥammad married.[11] Thus the Azdite affiliation of Balḥārith is also important in the history of early Islam.

Appendix VIII

John Diacrinomenus and the Ḥimyarites

The author[1] who has provided the student of Christianity in South Arabia with the name of Bishop Silvanus is a historian of the sixth century whose name reflects his Monophysite doctrinal persuasion.[2] And it is to the Monophysitism of John Diacrinomenus that knowledge about Silvanus is owed just as it is to the Arianism of

[8] Thus it was left isolated in South Arabia, and this may have induced it to change its affiliation to Madḥij, the powerful tribal group around Najrān. For the Azd, see EI^2, s.v. Azd. That Banū al-Ḥārith ibn Kaʿab were originally Azdites before they became Madḥijites may also be reflected in the fact that an Azdite clan with the name al-Ḥārith ibn Kaʿb also appears in South Arabia, for which see Ibn Ḥazm, *Jamharat,* 376–77. It is unlikely that there were two different tribes in South Arabia living so close to each other and carrying the same name, Balḥārith or Banū al-Ḥārith ibn Kaʿb. The chances are that there was only one tribe originally, the Azdite one, which later affiliated itself with Madḥij, as has been suspected by some historians.

[9] See above, note 2.

[10] Already touched upon in the preceding chapter on the mission of the Ghassānids to Najrān carrying the Monophysite version of Christianity. It will be treated in greater detail in *BASIC*.

[11] For the marriage of Hāshim to Salmā of the Khazraj tribe in Medina, see Tabarī, *Tārīkh,* II, 247.

[1] The few extant fragments are included in the volume that contains the *HE* of Theodore Anagnostes/Lector; see above. Hence quotations and reference to passages in his work cite the GCS edition.

[2] The Diacrinomenoi were the "hesitants" who had "reservations" about the definition of faith at Chalcedon. On them, see *Dictionnaire de théologie catholique* (Paris, 1939), IV.1, s.v. "Diacrinomènes."

Philostorgius that much is known about Theophilus, Constantius' Christian emissary to South Arabia in the fourth century.

Reference to Silvanus in his extant fragments is to be found in two places. In the first, the reference is autobiographical in tone, informing the reader that Silvanus, the bishop of the Ḥimyarites, was his maternal uncle.[3] This makes it certain that the datum about Silvanus is true beyond any shred of doubt. It is, however, the second reference that is more informative and fruitful to analyze.[4] The historian says that the Ḥimyarites had been Jews, but having become Christian in the reign of Anastasius they asked for a bishop and received one. The analysis of this passage elaborates on one or two points that were treated in the preceding chapter.

It was suggested that the dispatch of Silvanus to Ḥimyar was a response to a request made by the Ethiopian Negus after his victory over the Ḥimyarites during the first Ethiopian expedition.[5] Arguments from analogy were advanced, drawn from the history of Ethiopian intervention in South Arabia in the fourth and sixth centuries. This may now be fortified by a closer examination of the passage in Diacrinomenus which opens with the startling statement that "the Ḥimyarites, a people subject to the Persians who live in the farthest parts of the south. . . ."[6] The historian was very well informed about the Ḥimyarites, since his own uncle was dispatched to them as their bishop, and the question thus arises what to make of this statement, since it is plainly erroneous. The only way to make sense of it is to conclude that a mistake was either incorporated in the process of the transmission of the text or made initially by the author as a *lapsus calami*. The sentence is clear on the subjection of the Ḥimyarites to another people, and since they were not subject to the Persians[7] they must have been subject to another people. The only alternative to the Persians is the Ethiopians, to whom they were subject for short periods in the fourth and sixth centuries. The value of the *Book of the Ḥimyarites* becomes evident in this context, since its extant table of contents speaks of the occupation of South Arabia by the Ethiopians after the first Ethiopian expedition (chapters 4–7) and, what is more, indicates that this must have happened in the reign of Anastasius, since the date of this expedition has been inferred to have been only a few years before the date of the great persecution around 520. Here then is testimonial evidence of the subjection of Ḥimyar to a foreign power in the reign of Anastasius, exactly as the fragment from Diacrinomenus asserts. The conclusion then is irresistible that "Persians" in this passage or sentence has to be changed to "Axumites" or "Ethiopians."[8] This conclusion also derives some support

[3] *HE,* 152, lines 17–18.

[4] Ibid., 157, lines 13–16.

[5] See above.

[6] Ἰμμερινοὶ ἔθνος δὲ τοῦτο τελοῦν ὑπὸ Πέρσας, οἰκοῦν ἐν ταῖς ἐσχατιαῖς τοῦ νότου; *Historia Ecclesiastica,* 157, lines 13–14.

[7] They became so much later, in the 570s. For a different interpretation of their "subjection," see Fiaccadori, "Yemen Nestoriano," 196. This is not the natural meaning of "subjection." Besides, the interpretation rests on the doubtful assumption that the Moses whom the author has referred to was the bishop of Ḥimyar.

[8] This could derive some support from the fact that the Greek form of the term "Ḥimyarites" in this passage, Ἰμμερινοί, is strange and diverges from the form that the author used

from the realization that the Persians were Zoroastrians, who were opposed to Christianity—a missionary religion with universalistic claims. It does not, therefore, make sense to say that the Ḥimyarites under Persian rule asked for a Christian bishop and, what is more, from the arch-enemy, Byzantium. And this is especially true of the sixth century, after Nestorianism had established itself in Persia and was accepted as the tolerable form of Christianity in the realm of the Great King. Thus it is difficult to believe that the Persians would have tolerated the arrival of a Christian Monophysite bishop from Byzantium during the reign of Monophysite Anastasius, the very same emperor during whose reign hostilities with Persia were resumed after a long lull in the fifth century.[9] Thus even the request addressed to Monophysite Byzantium suggests that the overlords of the Ḥimyarites at this time could not have been the Persians. On the other hand, such a request during the period of Ethiopian domination in Ḥimyar is perfectly natural, and the events of a few years later (after the second Ethiopian invasion) afford a parallel.

Finally, some support for this conclusion could be derived from the *Kebra Negast*, especially as it comes from the last chapters of that work, which rest on a level of historicity different from the preceding ones that tell of a legendary past.[10] In chapters 116 and 117 there are relevant references to the wars in South Arabia and Najrān in this period, and it is just possible that the *Kebra Negast* may have preserved authentic echoes of the course of events and the personalities involved. The following passage tells of Najrān's (and thus South Arabia's) subjection to Ethiopia:[11] "A few Jews shall lift up their heads against our faith in Nāgrān and in Armenia in the days after this, and this God will do by His Will so that He may destroy them, for Armenia is a territory of Rome and Nāgrān is a territory of Ethiopia." Another passage in chapter 117 may also be quoted:[12] "And the king of Rome, and the king of Ethiopia, and the Archbishop of Alexandria—now the men of Rome were orthodox—were informed that they were to destroy them. And they were to rise up to fight, to make war upon the enemies of God, the Jews, and to destroy them, the King of Rome 'Ēnyā and the King of Ethiopia Pinḥas (Phinehas)."

The sentence "now the men of Rome were orthodox"—i.e., Monophysite, as the Ethiopians were—indicates a date before 518, when the Chalcedonian house of Justin came to power, and thus points to the earlier reign of Monophysite Anastasius. This

earlier when writing of Silvanus' being his uncle, which is the more natural form of the term "Ḥimyarites" in Greek. This raises the suspicion that the name of the other people mentioned in the passages, "Persians," may have experienced some drastic mutilation. Thus a scribal error cannot be ruled out. The more natural form of the term "Ḥimyarites" appears in John Diacrinomenus; cf. 152, line 17: Σιλουανὸς ἐπίσκοπος τῶν Ὁμηρηνῶν.

[9] John Diacrinomenus had written about the Persian War of the reign of Anastasius and the hostilities between the two contemporary monarchs, Anastasius and Kawad; see 156, lines 11–14.

[10] See I. Shahîd, "The *Kebra Negast* in the light of Recent Research," *Le Muséon* 89 (1976), 133–78.

[11] For the English version of the Ethiopic *Kebra Negast,* see E. A. Wallis Budge, *The Queen of Sheba and Her Only Son Menyelek* (London, 1922), 225.

[12] Ibid.

is confirmed by the name given to the Roman king, ʾĒnyā, which can only be a mutilated form of "Anastasius."

The cumulative effect of the foregoing arguments suggests that "Persians" in the passage cannot be the right word and that it must have crept into the text either as a scribal error or as a *lapsus calami* on the part of the author himself, who had written about the Persians in the earlier books of his *Historia Ecclesiastica* and thus inadvertently wrote "Persians" instead of "Axumites" or "Ethiopians."

XIV

Cultural History

I. Monasticism and the Arabs

The interaction between Arabness and Christianity in its various aspects was discussed in the preceding volume in this series, which dealt with the fourth century.[1] This interaction continued in the fifth century, during which Arab Christianity grew and matured, as will have been made clear in various chapters of this volume, especially the one on ecclesiastical history. This section will address a facet of this interaction which became especially important in the fifth century, monasticism. The Arabs had been affected by this new expression of Christianity prior to the fifth century and one of them, Moses, became a saint of the universal Church in the fourth century; but the fifth century witnessed the flowering of monasticism in Oriens and it exercised a powerful influence on the Arabs. It is therefore necessary to assemble the relevant data relating to this influence and examine its various facets.

I

1. The Arabs took kindly to monasticism and its representatives who penetrated their deserts. And it was natural that they should have done so, since monks chose to live in the Arab homeland—the desert—and sang its praises: ἡ ἔρημος ἐπολίσθη ὑπὸ μοναχῶν ἐξελθόντων ἀπὸ τῶν ἰδίων καὶ ἀπογραψαμένων τὴν ἐν τοῖς οὐρανοῖς πολιτείαν, wrote the biographer of St. Anthony.[2] St. Euthymius was described by his biographer[3] as ὁ φιλέρημος Εὐθύμιος; and St. Sabas, quoting the Psalms, exclaims of the desert of Rouba,[4] ἰδοὺ ἐμάκρυνα φυγαδεύων καὶ ηὐλίσθην ἐν τῇ ἐρήμῳ. The Arab deserts must have had a special attraction to the early hermits of this proto-Byzantine period and the fifth century, in particular, because unlike the Egyptian deserts and those of northern Oriens, these had strong biblical

[1] See *BAFOC,* 558–560.

[2] Quoted by D. Chitty, *The Desert a City* (Oxford, 1966), title page.

[3] See *Kyrillos,* p. 24, line 22.

[4] Ibid., p. 95, lines 13–14. Peter Brown has suggested that the holy men of Theodoret's *Historia Religiosa* lived on the fringe of inhabited areas rather than in the desert; see "The Rise and Function of the Holy Man," 110–11.

associations, especially in Sinai and Midian. The Decalogue was revealed in the first, while the second was hallowed by association with Moses, Jethro (Reuel), the priest of Midian, and Zipporah, his daughter and Moses' wife. Even New Testament associations were not lacking, such as St. Paul's sojourn in Arabia (whether the Provincia or the Peninsula) for reflection.

2. One Christian monastery, Pharan, in the desert of Juda, in Palaestina Prima, raises an important question. This was the first monastery in Palestine founded by St. Chariton.[5] The name naturally recalls that of the desert to which Hagar went after her expulsion by Sarah. This is usually located in the Negev or Sinai, but in the fourth century the name appears in the desert of Juda, applied to a monastery founded in the reign of Constantine, ca. 330. The name may have nothing to do with Hagar, but it is tempting to find in the account of Hagar and Ishmael in Genesis a key to why this monastery was called Pharan. The touching story of how Hagar prayed to God and how He heard her voice and responded to her in her distress may have inspired the early anchorites, who viewed this episode in the desert as a precedent and model for their own communion with God. Thus for them the toponym may have become charged with symbolic meaning.[6]

3. A preceding section has drawn a tolerably clear picture of the spread and diffusion of monasticism in the Arab area in Oriens, Ḥijāz, and western Arabia. The question arises whether these monasteries were for monks only or whether there were also convents which housed nuns. That there were Arab nuns in the sixth century is established,[7] and the chances are that nunneries appeared earlier, most probably in the fifth century, which witnessed the flowering of monasticism in this region. In support of the existence of nuns and nunneries in the fifth century, it may be pointed out that the word for nun, *rāhiba*, is well attested in early Arabic pre-Islamic poetry.[8] The case for the existence of nunneries is also supported by the pre-Islamic Arabic word *hayjumāna*, which is difficult to explain as an Arabic word.[9] It is practically

[5] On Pharan, see Vailhé, "Repertoire alphabétique," 42.

[6] The name Ishmael also must have sounded to the anchorites as a very meaningful, theophoric one in the context of their communion with God.

[7] This will be discussed in *BASIC*.

[8] As in the poetry of Imru' al-Qays. In one of his poems he speaks of the nuns (*rawāhib*), for which see Ahlwardt, *Divans,* 118, line 12. It is difficult to assume that the Arab nuns appeared only when Imru' al-Qays wrote his poem, and so the presumption is that they had appeared earlier. He is a 5th/6th-century poet. For the possibility that the daughter of the Salīḥid king Dāwūd became a nun, see below, 446–47.

[9] On the appearance of this word in Arabic, see above, Chap. 8, app. 2, and Ḥamza al-Iṣfahānī, *Tārīkh,* 89, where it appears applied to the Lakhmids. It is unlikely that it is a military term meaning "leader," since Arabic is rich in words that express military concepts; cf. Nöldeke, *PAS,* 133 note 1.

The curious phrase *Banū al-Hayjumāna* ("the sons of the Hayjumāna") occurs in the work of Hishām al-Kalbī; see Caskel, *GN*, II, 276. As has been suggested in this volume, the term

certain that this was none other than Greek ἡγουμένη, the abbess of the convent. Its application to some Arab women in this pre-Islamic period suggests that nunneries were not unknown to the Arab monastic scene.[10] The proper noun Fartanā appears in pre-Islamic poetry as a girl's name, but it has no derivation in Arabic. Its similarity to such Greek words as παρθενεία and πάρθενος, related to virginity and nuns, is striking and also suggests that there were nuns among the Arabs.[11]

4. The Arabic monastic lexicon appears established in this period; Syriac contributed the word for monastery, *dayr*, and Greek contributed *hayjumāna*. From its own resources, Arabic coined the word *rāhib* (monk), *rāhiba* (nun). This was the term which finally became the regular one for monk in Arabic,[12] hallowed later by its use in the Koran. The term means "the one who fears," and it is not entirely clear why this was the concept that was chosen to express the essence of monachism and asceticism. In any case, it reflects the Arab conception that the essence of monasticism was the fear of the Lord, the piety of fear.

5. Finally, monasticism did not fail to establish some presence in Arabic pre-Islamic poetry. It was an attractive presence, represented by the *rāhib*, his *zabūr* (his holy book sometimes translated Psalter), and his lamp or lantern (*miṣbāḥ*, or *qindīl*, the latter being a loan from Greek.[13]

---

hayjumāna in the feminine is probably an Arabicized form of the Greek word meaning "abbess." If this is the correct derivation, the three persons enumerated as "the sons of the Hayjumāna" were born before the mother put on the monastic garb. It is noteworthy that the mother, "the Hayjumāna" belonged to Iyād, the very Christian tribe that was credited with building so many monasteries in pre-Islamic times. In opting for the monastic life, this Iyādī Arab *hayjumāna* is in company with Hind, the well-known Lakhmid princess of Ḥīra.

[10] It is relevant in this connection to refer to the letter of Pulcheria, the sister of Theodosius II and wife of Marcian, to Bassa, the *hēgoumenē* of the nunnery at Ayla; for which, see E. Honigmann, "Juvenal," 256, and K. Holum, *Theodosian Empresses*, 225. Ayla was by this time an Arab town of Palaestina Tertia. It is quite likely that many of the inmates of that nunnery were Arab. Its bishop, with whom the Prophet Muḥammad made his covenant, was an Arab by the name of Jūḥannā ibn Ru'ba. In the same century, the Umayyad Marwān bin al-Ḥakam dispatched two hundred of the inhabitants of Ayla to police Medina; the presumption is that they were Arab; see A. Iṣbahānī, *Aghānī*, V, 65. Ayla was the southernmost byzantine bishopric in Oriens, closest to Arabia and Ḥijāz, and it is natural to suppose that it played an important role in the evangelization of the region. The monasteries of Ḥijāz were probably under the ecclesiastical jurisdiction of the bishop of Ayla. It is significant that its bishop is referred to in one of the synodical *Acta* as the bishop of Ayla and the Sharāt, the range of mountains in northern Ḥijāz; Cheikho, *Shuʿarāʾ al-Nasrāniyya*, 448, but he does not give his source; this will be further discussed in *BASIC*.

[11] For Fartanā in the poetry of Imru' al-Qays, whose aunt, Hind, built the famous monastery of Hind in Ḥīra, see Ahlwardt, *Divans*, 157, line 5. The "p" does not exist in Arabic and is normally transliterated as "f."

[12] For the long list of words in pre-Islamic Arabic that rivaled *rāhib* as the Arabic term for "monk," see L. Cheikho, *Shuʿarāʾ al-Nasrāniyya*, 194–201.

[13] These are attested passim in the corpus of pre-Islamic poetry, such as the *dīwān* of

II

There were more monasteries than churches in Arabia; hence the importance of the former in the life of the Arabs in the Peninsula and elsewhere in the Fertile Cresent in both its parts—the eastern under Sasanid rule and the western under Byzantine rule. The subject of Christian monasteries in Islamic times also deserves an extensive treatment, but only the salient features relevant to this volume will be treated.[14]

The monasteries of this proto-Byzantine period survived well into the Islamic period, perhaps because of their unobtrusiveness, and they were frequented by the Muslims of later times, including some of the caliphs.[15] As wine was prohibited in the Koran, Muslims found it convenient to visit the monasteries where the monks were often engaged in viticulture and winemaking.[16] It was for this reason that the Arab perception of the monastery in Islamic times degenerated and was often conceived as a tavern! But it was owing to this very misconception that a new literary genre appeared in Arabic literature, namely, poetic compositions on the monasteries.[17] And it was owing to the rise of this genre that much that is known about pre-Islamic monasteries has been preserved.

It is practically certain that this literary genre originated with Hishām al-Kalbī, who is credited with a book titled *Kitab al-Ḥīra wa- tasmiyat al-biyaʿ wa al-diyārāt wa -nasab al-ʿIbādiyyīn*, "The book of al-Ḥīra and the naming of the churches and the monasteries and the pedigree of the ʿIbād." As was explained in the preceding volume of this series, Hishām had a great interest in Ḥīra, the Lakhmids, and their structures.[18] Thus Hishām may be

---

Imruʾ al-Qays, the foremost poet of pre-Islamic Arabia; see Ahlwardt, *Divans*, 149, line 18; 52, line 15; 160, line 11.

[14] Monasticism in Islam is an important theme, both in Muhammadan and Koranic studies, and it is due for a reexamination in the light of recent research. Of the four verses in the Koran where monks and monasticism are mentioned, two are favorable and two are unfavorable, and the saying is well known, *la rahbāniyya fī al-Islām* ("There is no monasticism in Islam"). Yet Islamic asceticism is an established fact, and some scholars have argued that "the groundwork of the asceticism of the Koran is identical with that of Eastern Christianity"; and that Islamic Sufism (mysticism) may derive ultimately from this early asceticism; see H. A. R. Gibb, *Mohammedanism* (New York, 1962) 128. Striking is the statement that the monastic way of singing, *rahbāniyya,* has influenced the cantillation of the Koran; see Ibn Qutayba, *Al-Maʿārif,* 533.

[15] One of the Umayyad caliphs, ʿUmar ibn ʿAbd al-ʿAzīz, was buried in a monastery, Dayr Samʿān; Yāqūt, *Muʿjam,* II, 517.

[16] For the many reasons which induced Muslims to frequent monasteries, see G. Troupeau, "Les couvents chrétiens dans la littérature arabe," *La nouvelle revue du Caire* (Cairo, 1975), 271–79.

[17] A list of authors and books on monasteries in Arabic literature may be found in the introduction to H. Nājī, *Al-Budūr al-Musfira fī Naʿt al-Adyira* (Baghdad, 1975), 4–5; also 3 notes 2, 3.

[18] See *BAFOC,* 353–57.

considered to be the author who initiated this new literary genre in Arabic —the literature of the monasteries.

Hishām did not write a special monograph on the monasteries; his work on them was a part of a more general work on Ḥīra and the Lakhmids. It is not possible to determine with certainty the scope and nature of this work, since it has not survived; it is only quoted by later authors. Whatever the truth may turn out to be, there is no doubt that Hishām wrote a serious work largely involving the monasteries, since he immediately sensed their historical importance and their value as a source for extracting data for his monographs on the Lakhmids. That this genre degenerated later into works that contained vulgarities and bacchic verses pertaining to the monasteries can most probably be explained by the fact that the second author after Hishām to write on the subject of the monasteries was al-Iṣfahānī, who wrote a book exclusively devoted to them, *Kitāb al-Diyārat*.[19] Iṣfahānī was also the author of the monumental work titled *Kitāb al-Aghānī*, the *Book of Songs*. The title of the book speaks for itself, and reflects the interest of its author in music, song, and poetry. It is, therefore, almost certain that this development of books on monasteries into collections of verses composed in them and on them may be safely attributed to al-Iṣfahānī. While Hishām wrote a serious work on the monasteries as a historian interested in gathering from their inscriptions true information on Ḥīra and its Lakhmids, Iṣfahānī had much less serious intentions. Instead of instructing he wanted to amuse and entertain his readers; hence the deterioration in the quality of this literary genre. The fact that Iṣfahānī was not an admirer of Hishām[20] and often went out of his way to slander him may further explain this development, which thus may be attributed to Iṣfahānī's desire to make a travesty of this new genre which Hishām presented to the reader in a serious manner.

II. The Rise of the Arabic Script

The rise and development of the Arabic script in pre-Islamic times has not been definitively elucidated.[21] In spite of a large measure of agreement about certain aspects of this problem, there are some difficulties which remain to be solved. Scholarly opinion is divided on where it first appeared, which variety of Aramaic it is derived from, which groups of Arabs developed it, and under what circumstances. It is generally accepted, however, that it was developed in the Fertile Crescent out of a variety of Aramaic,[22] either Nabataean or

[19] This too has not survived, and is known only from quotations in later Islamic writers.

[20] On this, see *BAFOC*, 365 note 56.

[21] For the Arabic script in Islamic times, when it developed into one of the fine arts of medieval Islamic civilization, see A. Schimmel, *Calligraphy and Islamic Culture* (New York, 1984). See also below, Part 4, sec. V.A.

[22] The other major script in which the Arabic language was written was the *musnad* of the

Syriac. There are those who believe that the eastern half of the Fertile Crescent, in and around the Lakhmid capital Ḥīra, witnessed the rise and development of this script, while others believe that this took place in the western half of the Crescent.[23] There is no doubt that Ḥīra was the greatest center of Arab culture in the three centuries before the rise of Islam, and its association of the rise of the Arabic script is fully justified, but a good case can also be made for the western half of the Crescent, in Byzantine Oriens; indeed, the process can be examined better in this region than in Ḥīra. Thus the possibility of simultaneous development, or at least the rise of two centers for the development of this script, has to be seriously entertained. As this volume is concerned mainly with Byzantine Oriens and the Arab-Byzantine relationship, it will concentrate on the development of the Arabic script in the western half of the Crescent.[24]

I

That there was a development of the Arabic script in Byzantine Oriens may be supported by the following.

1. Not a single pre-Islamic Arabic inscription has survived in the region of Ḥīra, although six such inscriptions have been found in Byzantine Oriens:[25] the Ramm, Namāra, Zabad, Usays, Ḥarrān, and Umm al-Jimāl inscriptions. The enumeration is striking, and while it does not suggest that Ḥīra had no inscriptions,[26] it does make the task of investigating the rise of

---

Semitic peoples of South Arabia (such as the Sabaeans) who were a cognate people but quite distinct from the Arabs. As a script for the Arabic language, the *musnad* reached Ḥijāz and penetrated Oriens, where it was used in the Safaitic and Thamūdic inscriptions well into the Christian centuries but was finally eclipsed by rival Aramaic as the parent of the Arabic script.

[23] The most comprehensive account of the various views and schools of thought on the origin, rise, and development of the Arabic script may be found in A. Grohmann, *Arabische Paläographie* (Vienna, 1971), II, 7–33. He discusses the work of scholars who have dealt with this problem since the days of Nöldeke (pp. 18–33). The most important recent researchers of this topic, however, are N. Abbott, Milik, Starcky, J. Sourdel-Thomine, and Grohmann himself. See also the long article on the Arabic script by J. Sourdel-Thomine, *EI*,[2] s.v. Khaṭṭ.

[24] See the few but insightful comments of J. Sourdel-Thomine in her article, "Les origines de l'écriture arabe à propos d'une hypothèse récente," *REI* 34 (1966), 151–57, where she has argued for a Syrian provenance of the Arabic script, as opposed to J. Starcky who favored an Iraqi one centering around Lakhmid Ḥīra. In this chapter, however, serious account is taken of the descent of the Arabic script in Oriens not only from Syriac but from both Nabataean and Syriac. This does justice to what the distinguished Arabic paleographer A. Grohmann says in his detailed account of the derivation of the Arabic script.

[25] Grohmann is the only author who has conveniently put all of them together in chronological sequence with photocopies; see Grohmann, *Arabische Paläographie,* II, 16–17.

[26] In fact it had plenty of inscriptions, two of which have survived in the work of the later Islamic literary historians and geographers who read them and copied them; see *BAFOC*, 355 note 20. But since these appear in printed works, there is no way of discussing them paleographically and discovering their filiation, as is possible in the case of these six inscriptions discovered in Byzantine Oriens.

the script in Oriens easier, and points unmistakably to the spread of the Arabic script in various parts of Oriens, in the south and in the north.

2. The Arab peoples of Oriens in Roman times—the Nabataeans, the Palmyrenes, and the Edessenes—were highly literate and left behind them (especially the first and the second) numerous inscriptions written in Aramaic, the *lingua franca* of the Semitic Near East. They had experimented with the development of the Aramaic script and worked out their own peculiar varieties. It does not make much sense that in the Byzantine period the Arabs of this region suddenly sought enlightenment in this sector of their cultural life from Ḥīra, and that such literate people would have imported the art of Arabic writing from the area of Persian influence.[27]

3. The first dated Arabic inscription is that of Namāra,[28] A.D. 328. This is an Arabic inscription written in the old Nabataean script, deriving from Aramaic. The first inscription written in the new Arabic script is that of Zabad, dated around 512. It is difficult to assume that Nabataean was discontinued immediately after Imru' al-Qays' body was buried, and so the presumption is that it continued to be used for some time in the fourth century. This leaves the fifth century as the period during which the Arabic script is likely to have been developed.[29]

4. The final consideration that points to the region of Byzantine Oriens is the internal evidence of the script itself, which betrays influences from both the Nabataean script of Namāra and Syriac. The important consideration is

[27] It should also be noted in this connection that Ḥīra was a newcomer as a center of Arab culture, having been founded around 300. The Arab communities in Oriens had been experimenting with writing for centuries before the foundation of Ḥīra. This does not preclude influences on the Arabic script which may have emanated from Ḥīra, as will be discussed later in this chapter in connection with the *foederati,* but it does emphasize and give recognition to the fact that Oriens could take precedence over Ḥīra chronologically in experimenting with scripts.

It is not irrelevant to mention that the *kuttāb,* the chancellery secretaries of the Umayyad caliphs, to whom the art of writing was essential, were often recruited from the Christian Arabs of Bilād al-Shām, the former Byzantine Oriens. The *kuttāb* in Muslim Spain hailed from Shām; for the former, see Ṣāliḥ al-ʿAlī, "Muwaẓẓafū Bilād al-Shām fī al-ʿAṣr al-ʿUmawī," *Al-Abhath* (Beirut, 1966), 44–79; for the latter, see Lisan al-Dīn ibn al-Khatīb, *al-Iḥaṭa fi Tarikh Gharnāṭa,* ed. M. ʿInān (Cairo, n.d.), I, 104. This argues for the persistence of a strong tradition of the use of the Arabic script in early Islamic times which goes back to the pre-Islamic period in Byzantine Oriens.

[28] For this inscription analyzed in detail, see *BAFOC*, 31–53.

[29] The Ramm inscription has been left out in this discussion because it is undated; hence the difficulty of discussing it in a definitive fashion. H. Grimme, and after him A. Grohmann, assign it to the period before the reign of Julian, 350–363; Grohmann, *Arabische Paläographie,* II, 14–15. If their dating turns out to be correct, this will mean that the process of differentiation from Nabataean to Arabic had already begun in the middle of the 4th century. Be that as it may, the century that must have witnessed the development of the Arabic script and its differentiation remains the 5th, since it is securely bounded by the two *dated* inscriptions of Namāra and Zabad. For the latter, see Grohmann, ibid., 14.

the Nabataean, since the Syriac was widely spread over the entire Fertile Crescent, but Nabataean belonged to the southern part of Byzantine Oriens and Ḥījaz. Thus the internal evidence argues strongly for its provenance in Byzantine Oriens.[30]

The argument of those who have championed a Syrian (Oriens) origin or provenance for an Arabic script one derived from Nabataean is supported by some hard facts: (1) inscriptions in Nabataean carved by the Arab community of the Provincia Arabia are plentiful; (2) a few inscriptions carved in the new Arabic script and in the same region by the Arabs of the Provincia are also available;[31] (3) the link between the two is also available—the important Namāra inscription which was conceived in Arabic and written in Nabataean.[32] It is difficult, perhaps impossible, to deny the filiation, especially as the internal evidence points to it. Its Syriac affinities, on the other hand, are already foreshadowed in the Namāra inscription. Although its language is classical Arabic, there is in the first line the word *bar*, Syriac for "son," and the suffix *hn* in the second word of the fourth line, which is difficult to explain within the framework of Arabic, since normally an *m* and not an *n* would be used in this context, and this suggests Syriac influence. The realization that there are syriacisms in the inscription is important, not so much for deciphering it, but for suggesting that those who were experimenting with casting the Arabic language through the medium of a new script, (Nabataean) also had another language and script in mind consciously or unconsciously —Syriac, the language of cultural dominance in the Christian Orient and, what is more, of its scriptural religion, Christianity, to which the Arabs became passionately attached.

Discussion of the rise of the Arabic script in the western half of the Crescent has so far been conducted more or less in a vacuum. This chapter will now present the historical context within which the Arabic script was born in Oriens, the Arab groups that could have developed it, and the challenges or stimuli that brought it into being in the shadow of Byzantium. In view of the paucity of the data represented by only six inscriptions, it is difficult to give an account of the precise genesis of this script. However, with the elucidation of the history of the Arabs in Oriens in this volume and the preceding one, it is possible at least to make the process intelligible. The Arabs in Oriens who

[30] For the detailed argument of the Nabataean origin, see N. Abbott, "Rise of the North Arabic Script," 1–14 and Grohmann, op. cit., 18–27. However, the views of Starcky and Sourdel-Thomine must be taken into consideration, and surely the truth must lie in the views of those who suspected that the Arabic script in Oriens partakes of elements of both Nabataean and Syriac. For the latest statement of this parenthood, see A. F. L. Beeston, "The Arabic Script," in *CHAL* I, 11.

[31] On the six inscriptions, see above, note 25.

[32] On this inscription, see above, note 28.

could have developed the Arabic script were either the Rhomaic or the federate Arabs, and the simplest way of approaching this topic is, therefore, to begin by examining the possible role of each.

II

The Rhomaic Arabs in Oriens—the Edessenes, the Palmyrenes, and the Nabataeans—all used Aramaic and the Aramaic script. The Nabataeans are especially important, since more is known about them than about the other two groups as far as the Aramaic script and its relations to the Arabic are concerned.

Like the Palmyrenes, the Nabataeans were engaged in international trade in the Near East, and the *lingua franca* of that region was Aramaic. Consequently, and naturally, they did not use their native Arabic in their public inscriptions, either in the period of their independence or after their kingdom was annexed by the Romans. Instead they used Aramaic.[33] Their neglect of Arabic is very understandable. They lost their national identity politically after A.D. 106, when they were annexed by Trajan and ceased to exist as an independent Arab kingdom. Nabataea formed a province of the Imperium Romanum in which the former Nabataean Arabs became Roman provincials. In 212 *civitas* was extended to them as it was to Roman provincials, and so very possibly their sense of identity as Arabs was further diluted. It is, therefore, natural that they should have used the language or languages of the Graeco-Roman world to which they now belonged. Some even assumed Greek names which masked their Arab identity, like the Nabataean Arab sophists of the third century Heliodorus, Callinicus, and Genethlius, the last two of whom taught rhetoric in Athens;[34] to this list may be added Malchus of Philadelphia, the fifth-century historian.

In spite of their assimilation to the Graeco-Roman culture of their overlords, the Nabataeans could not have forgotten their native Arabic, and it is possible that they occasionally expressed themselves in written Arabic.[35] If

[33] Apparently not exclusively, since a Nabataean bilingual inscription of the Roman period has recently turned up, consisting of six lines of which the fourth and the fifth were conceived in Arabic. It has not been published yet but will be by Dr. Michael Negev, and I owe my knowledge of it to Prof. G. W. Bowersock, to whom Dr. Negev gave a copy of that inscription.

[34] For these three sophists, see *RA*, xxii note 9.

[35] The inscriptions of the Rhomaic Arabs in the Byzantine period are in Greek, but it is not impossible that occasionally they expressed themselves in their native language. The Arabic inscription found at Zabad not far from Chalcis and the Euphrates may have been written by Rhomaic Arabs in the northern part of Oriens. For the Zabad inscription, see Grohmann, *Arabische Paläographie,* II, 14. More important than epigraphic expression is the fact that even in the 4th century the pagan Nabataean Arabs of Petra celebrated the festival of Venus in their native language, according to St. Epiphanius; see *BAFOC*, 437.

they did not use Arabic extensively, they made an important contribution to the development of the Arabic script, for it was partly from the Nabataean, an Aramaic script adapted by them, that the Arabic script was derived and subsequently became differentiated as an independent script. Nabataean is the matrix of the Arabic script in Oriens, or one of its two matrices.

III

Unlike the Rhomaic Arabs, the *foederati* had a strong sense of Arab identity as newcomers into Oriens, which was enhanced by the fact that their legal status was that of *foederati* and not *cives*. It is therefore natural that the development of the Arabic script should be associated with them. Their involvement in its rise and development may be presented as follows.

The first question that arises is why a new Semitic script came into existence in the fifth century,[36] superseding the Nabataean of the Namāra inscription. The key must surely be sought in the fact that the *foederati* used the Arabic language in their inscriptions, which the *Rhōmaioi* had not done. It is natural for a new language to be expressed in a new script. In the case of Arabic and the Aramaic script used by the Rhomaic Arabs, there was the phonetic problem which could not be solved except by the development of a new script, based on Aramaic: there are more sounds in Arabic than either the Aramaic or the Syriac script could express or accommodate.[37]

With the identification of the *foederati* as the Arab group who were probably responsible for the development of the Arabic script in Oriens, it remains to examine in some detail the various aspects of this process of development. It will be argued that when the *foederati* came into Oriens, they possibly brought with them a tradition of Arabic writing, however primitive, but that it was their association with Byzantium, both its *imperium* and its *ecclesia*, in the shadow of which they lived for three centuries, that was the decisive factor in the crucial development of the Arabic script in Oriens.

A

Two of the dominant groups of *foederati* in these centuries, the Tanūkhids of the fourth century and Ghassānids of the sixth, had originally hailed from South Arabia, wandered in the Arabian Peninsula, and had a Mesopotamian connection before they went over to Byzantium. South Arabia had a highly sedentarized, literate society, and there is no question but that the

[36] It is striking that most of the six Arabic inscriptions of pre-Islamic times in Oriens are associated with the *foederati*. On the Zabad inscription, see the preceding note.

[37] It is noteworthy that the Arabs who employed the *musnad* script of South Arabia in their inscriptions, such as the Arabs of Qaryat al-Fāw, were not faced with this problem since the letters of the *musnad* could reflect all the sounds of Arabic; hence they did not develop a new script. For the Arabic inscription of Qaryat al-Fāw, see the next note.

Arab tribes who moved in the cultural orbit of the Ḥimyarites were familiar with the art of writing. The excavations of Qaryat al-Fāw, an urban center for one of these tribes of the south, Kinda, has established this.[38] Even the pastoralists of the Arabian Peninsula were familiar with the art of writing, which they used in order to leave records of their existence: witness the hundreds of Thamūdic inscriptions that have been found throughout the length and breadth of the Arabian Peninsula.[39] The Umm al-Jimāl II inscription with its precious reference to a *kātib* (scribe) of the tribe,[40] has indicated that the tribes were not illiterate and that while it is extravagant to expect that every member of an Arab tribe read and wrote, it is practically certain that each tribe had one or more members who could discharge the duty of *kātib*. This is even reflected in the Arabic cultural tradition about the pastoralists, who considered possessing the art of writing as one of the ingredients in the make-up of their *kamala* ("perfect man") in pre-Islamic Arabia.

Although the life of the *foederati* was relatively simple, it had enough variety and excitement to call for the continued employment of the art of writing among them. There is mention of the odes composed on the occasion of the victories of Queen Mavia over Emperor Valens in the fourth century. Thus their exploits in war would have been deemed worthy of being recorded.[41] The account of Mavia's glorious deeds, if they were indeed recorded in writing, has not survived. But the exploits of another federate king in the fourth century, Imru' al-Qays of the famous Namāra inscription, have survived, and no doubt other federate kings in the fourth century must have had their achievements recorded in a similar fashion. The Namāra inscription not only provides confirmation that the *foederati* recorded their achievements, but throws light on the first stage in the development of the new Arabic script. The South Arabian tribes must have used a form of the *musnad*—the Sabaic script—and the pastoralists used Thamūdic, which derives from it. But when the *foederati* of the fourth century recorded the achievements of their king in Oriens they discarded whatever script they had used before and used that of the region in which they settled in order to be intelligible. The script was the Nabataean, a variety of the Aramaic used by the Rhomaic Arabs of the Provincia Arabia.

The Namāra is the only dated Arabic inscription of the fourth century, so it is difficult to go beyond what has been said here on the state of the Arabic script in that century. The situation becomes clearer with the rise of

[38] For the splendid volume on these excavations, see A. R al-Ansary, *Qaryat al-Fau: A Portrait of a Pre-Islamic Civilization in Saudi Arabia* (Riyad, 1982).

[39] On these inscriptions, see Grohmann, *Arabische Paläographie,* II, 10.

[40] Ibid., 14 no. 3.

[41] On these odes see *BAFOC*, 444–46.

the Salīḥids in the next century. The native tradition of Arabic poetry, noted with Queen Mavia of the Tanūkhids, is well established in their court.[42] And it is almost certain that writing was employed in recording the poetry associated with the Salīḥids in addition to the records of their military exploits.[43] The Salīḥids are thus the most important of the three dominant groups of *foederati* in these centuries (the Tanūkhids and the Ghassānids of the fourth and fifth centuries being the other two). As noted above, it was in the fifth century that the Arabic script is likely to have become differentiated from Nabataean, and this was the century of Salīḥid supremacy in Oriens. Besides, unlike the Tanūkhids who lived in the north of Oriens, the Salīḥids lived in the south, in the Balqā' region of the Provincia Arabia—in exactly the area where the Nabataean script dominated—and thus the derivation of the Arabic script principally from the Nabataean receives considerable confirmation.

B

Imperial-federate relations must have contributed considerably to the development of the Arabic script. In dealing with her *foederati*, Byzantium needed to correspond with them. But newcomers to Oriens could not be expected to know Latin and Greek as the Rhomaic Arabs did. Even if they did know these languages, there were certain transactions between the two parties that required the use of the Arabic language, such as the drawing up of *foedera*. An example is the *foedus* which Queen Mavia struck with Byzantium during the reign of Valens, to which there is an express reference in the sources. This is the Arab queen who inspired the composition of victory odes in the Arabic language and insisted on the consecration of an Arab bishop for her *foederati*. It is difficult to believe that there was no version of the treaty in Arabic, the language of the queen who was so conscious of her Arab identity.[44] Some fifty years before, the epitaph of the federate king Imru' al-Qays was engraved in Arabic, not Greek, and this argues for a considerable measure of Arab awareness on the part of the fourth-century *foederati*. However, the script of this text of the treaty with Mavia has not survived; as has been said, the Nabataean script may have been used, just as it was in the Namāra inscription of Imru' al-Qays. Then there was the treaty of the first Salīḥid, Zokomos, with Byzantium, ca. 400 in the reign of Arcadius, although

[42] For poetry in the court of Dāwūd, the Salīḥid king, see below, Sec. IV.A.

[43] The only hope of recovering 5th-century specimens of the Arabic script rests, of course, with the archeologists. If the tombs of the Salīḥids are discovered and excavated in the Balqā', the chances are that there will be many funerary inscriptions on them similar to that of Imru' al-Qays at Namāra.

[44] On Mavia and her *foedus*, see *BAFOC*, 152–64.

nothing is known about it. The historian, Priscus mentions a peace concluded between Ardabur and the Saracens during the reign of Marcian (450–457). These are likely to have been peninsular Saracens who attacked the provinces of Phoenicia Libanensis and Arabia, and any *foedus* with such Arabs, who knew neither Greek nor Latin, must have had an Arabic version.[45] Then there was the treaty struck between Amorkesos, the adventurous phylarch of the reign of Leo, and Byzantium. Surely there must have been an Arabic version of it.[46] Finally, the *foedera* with Ghassān toward the end of the century must have been drawn up in the two languages, one of which was Arabic.[47] Thus both parties must have felt the need for the use of Arabic in important diplomatic documents and exchanges, and this must have been an incentive for the development of the Arabic script.[48]

Something has been said about the bureau of barbarian affairs (*scrinium barbarorum*) in this volume.[49] Although not much is known about it in this period, the chances are that it was the government department in Constantinople that dealt with barbarian affairs, especially when it came to entertaining a foreign visitor such as Amorkesos, accommodating him, showing him around the capital, and arranging for his conferences with the emperor. The bureau most probably kept records and had interpreters, and the presumption is that there were Arabs or other bilingual officials who could communicate with Amorkesos in his own tongue and translate or interpret his wishes or conversation.[50] The very precise information in Theophanes on the Arabs around 500 can only have come from an official document drawing on an Arabic source for its material and information, and probably kept in some such department in Constantinople or in Oriens.[51]

[45] Just as the treaty with Persia of 561 had a Persian version as well as a Greek one. For the negotiations between Ardabur and the Saracens concerning the peace, see above, Chap. 3, app. 3.

[46] On this, see above, Chap. 4, sec. v.

[47] On this, see above, Chap. 12, sec. v.

[48] The *foedera*, which are better documented in the 6th century in the work of Nonnosus. He, his father, and grandfather went on diplomatic missions, involving the Saracens of the Arabian Peninsula. They will be treated at length in *BASIC*.

In this connection, reference would be made to the *foedus* concluded between the Arab chief Ammanes and the Arab town of Pharan in the Sinai Peninsula; also, the letter addressed by Ammanes to the Pharanites, which is referred to in the *Nili Narrationes*. Unfortunately, the hagiographer does not specify the language used by Ammanes; it could have been Arabic, since both he and the Pharanites were Arab. For this, see above, 139.

[49] On this, see above, 105–6.

[50] There were interpreters in Constantinople, and references to the ἑρμηνεύς in accounts of embassies in Constantinople from foreign rulers are attested; see, for instance, the reference to a ἑρμηνεύς translating from Persian into Greek in Menander, ed. and trans. Blockley, 108, line 90. Arab interpreters are attested in the 6th century; see J. B. Bury, "The Treatise *De Administrando Imperio*," *BZ* 15 (1906), 541. This will be discussed in detail in *BASIC*.

[51] Theophanes, *Chronographia*, I, 141.

It is known that Sasanid Persia had such a department. The Arabic sources, as is well known, are much more informative on Arab-Sasanid relations than on Arab-Byzantine relations, since many of the historians who recorded these relations were Persian Muslims, like Ṭabarī, who were naturally more interested in the relations of the Arabs to their own people than to the Byzantines. These historians document the existence in Ctesiphon of an office of Arab affairs in which there were bilingual officials who knew both Persian and Arabic and wrote documents in these two languages (and sometimes in Syriac), such as ʿAdī ibn Zayd.[52] It is difficult to believe that the more developed and literate Byzantium would have neglected to have a similar establishment in its department of foreign affairs, especially in view of the fact that the two empires had the same Arab problem on their hands and must have reacted similarly.

Thus the two empires, with their developed political institutions and important relations with the Arabs, contributed to the rise of the Arabic script, and Byzantium may have contributed even more than Sasanid Persia; it had important relations with the *foederati* in Oriens, with the Arabs of the Peninsula, and with the Arab *foederati* of Persia itself, the Lakhmids.[53]

C

The *ecclesia* provided an institutional framework for the development of the Arabic script that was perhaps even more important than the secular *imperium*.

The problem of a simple Arabic liturgy and the translation of some portions of the Bible were discussed in the preceding volume on the fourth century. The Christian faith continued to spread and develop among the *foederati* and a new federate group, the Salīḥids, in the fifth century. Whether they continued to translate more portions of the Bible remains to be seen. The natural presumption is that with the progress in the spread of Christianity in the fifth century (during which there was relative peace between the two world empires) interest in the Christian liturgy and Bible must have progressed commensurately, even if there were not extensive translations of portions of the Bible and the Christian liturgy and the Bible consisted of no more than a primitive form of the former and a lectionary representing the latter for liturgical use.[54]

This presumed interest in the liturgy and the Bible must have given a strong impetus to the development of the Arabic script and its further differentiation from Nabataean. This can be illustrated by contrasting the impetus

[52] On this, see Morony, *Iraq after the Muslim Conquest,* 64–67.

[53] For Byzantine-Lakhmid relations, see *Menander, ed. Blockley,* 106–10.

[54] On the case for this see *BAFOC*, 435–43.

given by the *imperium*. While official documents drafted between Byzantium and its Arab *foederati* were short, non-literary, and limited in lexical range, Christianity—a scriptural religion with Bible and liturgy—provided its adherents with a massive Sacred Book. The translator was dealing with a text that was long, literary, and holy, all of which presented problems that were decisive in developing the script. Because the text was holy, his duty was to be faithful and accurate in reflecting biblical thought, while the wide range of vocabulary must have forced him to invent the letters for the Arabic sounds that were missing in Nabataean and Syriac. Thus the Arab translator of the biblical material was faced with problems which the engraver of a short epitaph or inscription was not. In addition to strongly developing the script in the direction of precision, the influence of the *ecclesia* must have contributed substantially toward the hybridization of the Arabic script by adding to its Nabataean paternity that of Syriac. The Semitic Arabs, it is practically certain, had for their model the Syriac, not the Greek, Bible.

If an individual could be credited with contributing to the development of the Arabic script in Oriens, it is likely to have been Dāwūd, the Salīḥid king, because his reign represented the confluence of the three currents discussed above: he had a court poet who needed the art of writing for the recording of his odes; he was a federate king, and naturally had to transact business in writing with his Byzantine overlord; and he was a pious Christian king, who renounced the world and who may, in the monastery which carried his name, have inspired such learned endeavors as the translation of portions of the Bible, especially those that were associated with his biblical namesake, David.[55]

IV

The distinguished Austrian palaeographer A. Grohmann noted that some stylistic differences obtained between the Umm al-Jimāl II inscription and the other five that were discovered in pre-Islamic Oriens.[56] He noted the rounded character of the letters in the former as opposed to the angularity that characterized the latter, and also discussed whether this style of the Arabic script that developed in Syria could be described as the Naskhī of later Islamic times. Grohmann also thought that the gap that existed between the specimens of the pre-Islamic script and Islamic Naskhī was still wide, and so he discouraged discussions of this filiation in view of the paucity of pre-Islamic inscriptions.[57] But in view of the development of the Arabic script in the fifth

[55] Further on this, see below, 434–35, 426–27.

[56] For these six inscriptions, see above, note 25.

[57] Grohmann, *Arabische Paläographie,* II, 28–30. In spite of the salutary warning, I am inclined to think that the Naskhī of Islamic times is allied to the Arabic script developed in

century, the following observations may be helpful to palaeographers who wish to pursue this line, especially in the light of future epigraphic discoveries.

A

Since the development of the Arabic script in Oriens has been shown to be associated with the Arab *foederati*, it is desirable to probe into their history for certain facts which may be helpful in shedding light on the problem of stylistic varieties.

The *foederati* of Byzantium in the fifth century were not centralized under one command, as they were to be in the sixth under the Ghassānids. There were dominant groups among them, such as the Tanūkhids of the fourth century and the Salīḥids of the fifth, but it was only around 530 that Justinian unified federate power under the Ghassānid Arethas. The Tanūkhids lived in the north, in the vicinity of Chalcis,[58] and it is therefore possible that they developed a script of their own which may have been slightly different from the one developed in the south. It was far away from the area where Nabataean and its script were dominant, and so it is likely to have been developed more under the influence of some northern script, most likely Syriac. The Salīḥids, on the other hand, lived in the Provincia Arabia in the Balqā' region, where Nabataean was the language and script of cultural dominance. Hence it is possible that within Oriens there developed two varieties of an Arabic script, if not more. These must have been very close to one another, but they may have evinced differences such as those noted by Grohmann.

In support of this rise of stylistic varieties in the Arabic script *within* Oriens, the analogy of the two other Arab communities who lived in Oriens and in the pre-Byzantine period, the Palmyrenes and the Nabataeans, may be invoked. These two used Aramaic as the language of their public inscriptions, and yet the northern community—the Palmyrene—employed a variety of Aramaic and its script different from the Nabataeans, who lived in the south. It is, therefore, not unlikely that the Tanūkhids and the Salīḥids, in the north and south of Oriens respectively, may have developed scripts that varied slightly from each other, depending on the parent script or matrix.

B

Related to the problem of stylistic varieties is that of influences and the diffusion of the Arabic script from one Near Eastern center and region to another in pre-Islamic times. Because the script in Byzantine Oriens is most

Oriens, while the monumental Kufic was developed in Ḥīra. The term *jazm* ("cutting off") used in connection with the script developed in Ḥīra could suggest the monumental style; on *jazm*, see N. Abbott, *Rise of the North Arabic Script*, 7–8.

[58] On this see *BAFOC*, 465–76.

relevant in this chapter, this section will discuss the problem in the light of new research on the *foederati*.

1. As argued in this chapter, the six pre-Islamic inscriptions found in Oriens derive from indigenous parent scripts and not from a script developed in Ḥīra, the capital of the Lakhmid clients of the Sasanids, as has been suggested by some scholars.[59] Some influence from that region, however slight, cannot be ruled out, since the Arab *foederati* are known (or supposed) to have been in that region before they affiliated themselves with Byzantium. The Tanūkhids were one such group, but it is doubtful that they brought anything with them that could have influenced the development of the script in Oriens, especially in the fourth century, during their supremacy as the dominant group of *foederati*. This must be the case, since the most outstanding of the *foederati* of the fourth century, Imru' al-Qays, found it necessary to use the Nabataean script of the region, a fact clearly implied in the choice of that script by the engraver who carved his funerary inscription at Namāra. The Ghassānids of the sixth century could have brought with them the tradition of a script developed in Iraq and Ḥīra, but the chances are slim, since the Arabic script had been developed in Oriens before their arrival and the affinities of the script of the six inscriptions with indigenous Nabataean are striking. There remains Iyād, the important Arab tribe which was associated strongly with Christianity, poetry, and the rise of the Arabic script in the Land of the Two Rivers before a portion of it left the service of the Sasanids and allied itself with Byzantium.[60] As has been noted before, Nöldeke rejected a fourth-century dating in favor of a sixth-century one for Iyād's alliance with Byzantium. But the figure of the Iyādī poet ʿAbd al-ʿĀṣ at the court of King Dāwūd in the fifth century, revealed by one of the works of Hishām al-Kalbī, has made a dating earlier than the sixth century perfectly possible, at least for a portion of Iyād. ʿAbd al-ʿĀṣ, however, is likely to have used the script of the region for recording his poetry, as had his predecessor Imru' al-Qays, who also hailed from the Land of the Two Rivers in the fourth century.

The influence in the reverse direction, that is, from Oriens to Ḥīra, is also a controversial matter. But it might be mentioned in this respect that the return of the Lakhmids to rule in Ḥīra after the defection of Imru' al-Qays may have been related to the return of his successors from Oriens after they severed their Byzantine connection.[61] If so, it is possible that they might have carried with them to Ḥīra the tradition of a script, indigenous to Oriens,

[59] For the various views on the various regions where the script was developed and whence it spread elsewhere, see the discussion in Grohmann above, note 23.

[60] On Iyād, see above, Chap. 3, app. 2.

[61] On this see *BAFOC*, 214.

which may have exercised some influence on the development of the Arabic script in that region.

2. The type of script employed by the Arabs of Ḥijāz, especially those of Mecca, the future city of Islam, has also been controversial. The Arabic tradition suggests that Mecca derived its script from Ḥīra through Dūmat al-Jandal, and the journey of the Ḥīran script to Mecca is associated with the names of the Kindite Bishr, brother of Ukaydir, the Lord of Dūmat, and Ḥarb, the Umayyad notable of Mecca. This is possible, but even if true the account suggests that Mecca had used another script before the Ḥīran one;[62] according to a poem, this is supposed to have been the *musnad* of the Sabaic inscriptions of South Arabia. This, too, is possible, but does not preclude a script developed in Oriens—possibly mediated by Quṣayy, the Meccan chief who conquered Mecca with Byzantine assistance extended through the federate tribe ʿUḏra and its chief, Rizāḥ.[63] Quṣayy could easily have carried in his cultural baggage from Oriens the Arabic script developed there. That it was (or may have been) superseded by the Ḥīran in the sixth century does not preclude the employment of this script, hailing from Oriens, in the fifth century.

If Mecca, far in the south of Ḥijāz, was naturally close to the cultural orbit of South Arabia and its *musnad* script, the rest of Ḥijāz was not. The presumption is that most of it, especially that part which was a Byzantine sphere of influence, an extension of Palaestina Tertia, must have been influenced in its script by the new one developed in Oriens, and this must have been true of tribes that were allied to Byzantium such as ʿUḏra and Juḏām.[64] The Christian monastery, which starts to appear on the Ḥijāzi cultural landscape, most probably played a great role in the process of propagating this script.[65]

III. The Problem of an Arabic Bible and Liturgy in Pre-Islamic Times

This most important problem in the cultural history of the Arabs before the rise of Islam has been examined in the preceding volume of this series for the fourth century.[66] It is argued there that the case for an Arabic Bible or an extensive liturgy was out of the question but that a simple liturgy or a

[62] A poetic fragment has survived in which it is suggested that the script of Mecca had been the South Arabian *musnad*; for the poem, see Ḥamad al-Jāsir, *Shamāl Gharb al-Jazīra,* 140.

[63] This has been suggested by N. Abbott, in *Rise of the North Arabic Script,* 10.

[64] Cf. what has been said about the region of Midian in northern Ḥijāz in connection with the rise and diffusion of the Arabic script; ibid., 9.

[65] On monasteries in Ḥijāz, see above, 294–95.

[66] See *BAFOC*, 435–43.

prayerbook could possibly have been available in Oriens in the fourth century for the use of the Christian Arab *foederati* who had a strong sense of Arab identity, reflected in the use of the Arabic language for their long inscriptions—one of which has survived—and in the composition of epinician odes to honor the victory of their Orthodox Queen Mavia over Arian Valens.

The elucidation of the history of the Arab *foederati* in the present volume provides the background for taking up the problem in the fifth century. The approach to this problem is thus fundamentally different from that of the chief protagonist of an Arabic Bible and liturgy in this period, Anton Baumstark,[67] who argued backward from an examination of the Gospels during the Islamic period to conclusions on the Gospels in the pre-Islamic times. He was forced to do so, presumably, because these three pre-Islamic centuries had never been researched, at least in such a way as to make the discussion meaningful in any other way. In contrast, our approach addresses the problem regionally and diachronically through these three pre-Islamic centuries. And of the three regions in which such an Arabic Bible and liturgy might have appeared—the Arab area in Byzantine Oriens, Persian Mesopotamia, and Ḥimyarite South Arabia—it is the first, Byzantine Oriens, that is the main concern of these volumes.

The investigation of this important problem in Oriens in the fifth century thus builds upon what has been established for the preceding century in order to find out whether the scope of the Arabic biblical and liturgical presence in the fifth century remained the same as it had in the fourth or whether it grew wider. Unlike the fourth century, the fifth was relatively peaceful; consequently it is possible to think of the enlargement of the cultural sector of Arab federate life in Oriens. Even more important, the facts of Arab federate cultural life in the fifth century are more abundant than those for the fourth and provide the background against which this problem can be set. These facts involve the rise of the Arabic script in the fifth century; the emergence of three major Arab ecclesiastical figures; the possibility of discussing the problem within certain specific regional pockets within Oriens; and finally, an intriguing reference to a Gospel, if not in Oriens, at any rate in a Byzantine sphere of influence, the Arab area in the south of the Peninsula.

[67] For his views and those of his antagonist in this dialogue, G. Graf, see A. Baumstark, "Das Problem eines vorislamischen christlich-kirchlichen Schrifttums in arabischer Sprache," *Islamica* 4 (1931), 562–75, and *Geschichte der christlichen arabischen Literatur,* Studi e testi 118 (1944), 27–52, (hereafter GCAL). More recently, S. Brock has touched upon the problem, in "Bibelübersetzungen," *Theologische Realenzyklopädie,* VI, 1/2, 209–11, where he argues that a translation into Arabic in pre-Islamic times remains a possibility. On the most recent discussion of the subject, see below, App. 1.

Oriens

Although South Arabia is associated with a specific reference to a Gospel in the fifth century, it is in Byzantine Oriens that most of the cultural facts of federate life referred to above obtained. They may be discussed as follows:

1. It was argued earlier that this century witnessed the birth of a variety of the Arabic script in Byzantine Oriens.[68] The obscurity that surrounds this birth precludes drawing certain conclusions, but the Arabic script partakes of elements of both the Syriac and Nabataean scripts. The most important Syriac texts in fifth-century Oriens were the Bible and the liturgy, thus the Syriac element in the script was a natural influence that came in the process of translation or study of these texts. These *foederati* were zealous Christians, and the Arabic inscriptions in sixth-century Oriens were partly Christian.

2. In the chapter on the Arab federate tribes it was argued that, in all probability, the tribe of Iyād, or part of it, was already in Oriens in the fifth century.[69] This is the important pre-Islamic Arab tribe whose name is associated with both the rise of the script in the eastern half of the Fertile Crescent and with Christianity. In the period of the Conquests, Ṭabarī's account of Khālid's dealing with Anbār and ʿAyn al-Tamr in Iraq involved Iyād. The people of Anbār tell Khālid that they learned the Arabic script from Iyād, while at ʿAyn al-Tamr (which had an Iyādī element in the population) Khālid finds forty boys learning the Gospel in the church.[70] This informative account refers to conditions in the seventh century, but it nevertheless remains significant, and could suggest that the same tribe which was associated with the Arabic script and Christianity in the seventh century could have been associated with both earlier, and thus might have given an impetus to some Gospel translation in Oriens when it appeared there in the fifth century.

3. Of the many Arab pockets in Oriens where the Arabic biblical and the liturgical presence might have been either enhanced or extended, the first that comes to mind early in the century is the Parembole in Palaestina Prima.[71] As argued in the chapter on the Parembole and its bishops, it is possible that the little federate community in the desert of Juda had a primitive liturgy or a prayerbook for the performance of Christian worship. The first bishop of the Parembole was Aspebetos, the participant in the Council of Ephesus and one of the emissaries of the Orthodox party to Nestorius. This is the first of three large Arab figures in the history of the ecclesiastical life of the fifth century. He was clearly possessed of considerable administrative skills, which im-

[68] See above, Sec. II.

[69] See above, Chap. 3, app. 2.

[70] Ṭabarī, *Tārīkh,* III, 375, 376–77. Iyād, together with al-Namir and Taghlīb appear defending ʿAyn al-Tamr against Khālid; 376.

[71] See above, Chap. 10, sec. III.B.

pressed St. Euthymius and Juvenal of Jerusalem, and he established a bishopric and community which lasted long. It is, therefore, quite likely that an ecclesiastic of this description would have thought of providing his community with its own Arabic version of some portions of the Bible, possibly a lectionary in conformity with the practice of the Christian Church in this respect.[72]

4. Toward the end of the century another Arab ecclesiastical figure, Elias, became the patriarch of the Holy City.[73] He, too, was an energetic administrator engaged in giving Christianity an institutional expression in Palaestina Prima through the many monasteries he founded, among other things. Elias hailed from the Provincia Arabia, and as a *Rhōmaios* he must have been aware of the problem of *diglossia* that obtained among the Arabs of the region, who spoke Arabic at home, while some of them were familiar with Greek and Aramaic. His jurisdiction included the bishopric of the Arab Parembole and others in the three Palestines, such as that of Petrus, the bishop of Amorkesos. Again, an ecclesiastic of this description could very well have thought of ways to organize his people's allegiance to Christianity and their church services. It is, therefore, not inconceivable that he gave some thought to the most important element of Christian life—its Bible and its liturgy. Again, there is no question of a Bible translation in its entirety, but possibly of a modest liturgy with a lectionary.[74]

[72] In the 8th century at the monastery of St. Sabas in Palestine, the Arab disciple of John of Damascus, Theodore Abū Qurra, argued that the credibility of Christianity derived in part from the fact that only Christian evangelists propagated their faith and proclaimed the good tidings of Christianity to each and every people in their own language. It is tempting to think that the monk of St. Sabas, who was not far removed from pre-Islamic times, could have had in mind the Christian mission to the Arabs (among other missions), and that some pre-Islamic Arabic version of the Gospel or some other biblical book did survive at St. Sabas'. For Theodore, see S. Griffith, "The Gospel in Arabic: An Enquiry into Its Appearance in the First Abbasid Century," *OC* 69 (1985), 165. More important is the natural implication of Abū Qurra's statement, that when Christianity reached the Arabs in pre-Islamic times it did so through the medium of their own language.

[73] On Elias, see above, Chap. 10, app. 4.

[74] Baumstark thought that an Arabic Psalter could have been prepared for the Parmebole community when St. Euthymius was active in his mission of converting the Arabs in the 5th century. It is likely that if such a Psalter was prepared, it was inspired by either of the two Arabs, Bishop Aspebetos or Patriarch Elias. For Baumstark's views, see "Der älteste erhaltene griechisch-arabische Text von Psalm 110 (109)," *OC* 3rd ser. 9 (1934), 55–62.

In the preceding section of this chapter it was suggested that the Salīḥid king Dāwūd, may have been the spirit behind the endeavors to develop an Arabic script in the 5th century. Aspebetos and Elias could almost certainly be added to Dāwūd in view of their possible involvement in the translation of a prayer book into Arabic, an activity related to the rise of the Arabic script. Elias may have been more involved in this than Aspebetos, since he was the patriarch of Jerusalem, within whose jurisdiction lived many Arab Christian communities in the Three Palestines. The Armenian parallel is illuminating: the spectacle of Patriarch Sahak encouraging Mesrop to develop the Armenian script, which the latter did, consulting with a Greek calligrapher in Samosata by the name of Rufinus for the final stage of its perfection.

5. Outside Palaestina Prima there was the pocket of Saracens who were associated with Simeon the Stylite in Syria, about whom Theodoret wrote extensively. What is important in their case is a specific reference to the saint's acting as their lawgiver.[75] Now these laws, if they had any efficacy or chance of permanence at all, must have been handed to them in written form so that they might observe them scrupulously and accurately. What were these laws? It is likely that they were both Old Testament and New Testament laws that regulated their behavior and weaned the Saracens away from their old pagan practices.[76] If so, they must have been biblical texts or texts based on the Bible.

6. Favorable conditions and circumstances play an important role in cultural history. More important, however, is the decisive role played by certain individuals. Armenian Christianity was the work and achievement of one man, St. Gregory the Illuminator, and its script the work of Mesrop, who also translated the Bible. If one were to choose an individual from the Arab-Byzantine world of fifth-century Oriens and credit him with enhancing Arab biblical and liturgical presence, it would be the Salīḥid king Dāwūd.

Such an undertaking implies some form of a developed institutional framework, and such a framework has been discovered in connection with the reign of this particular king—what may be called the "David Circle," composed of himself, his poet laureate, ʿAbd al-ʿĀṣ, and his anonymous poetess/daughter. His reign and his personality represent the confluence of various cultural currents, all of which are relevant.[77]

In a previous chapter in this book it was suggested: (1) that the name of the Salīḥid king is strikingly biblical and that he and his daughter, living as they did in biblical Ammonitis and Moabitis,[78] could have been inspired by the example of some distinguished biblical predecessors; and (2) that in the Oriens of the fifth century the figure of Eudocia dominated the scene, especially in the Holy Land and the adjacent provinces. Eudocia did not translate the Bible but did turn into verse, *inter alia*, the Octateuch. This interest in the Bible, coming from a literary personality, could very well have inspired her counterpart among the Salīḥids (or "the David circle") to undertake translations of some portions of the Bible.

[75] On this, see above, 149–50.

[76] OT laws were in force in Christian Ethiopia. See also what was said on the "scribe of the tribe," above, 415.

[77] See the discussion of Dāwūd above, Chap. 12, sec. III.I.B.

[78] In addition to the Balqā, (biblical Ammonitis), the Salīḥids are said by Ibn Khaldūn to have lived in Moabitis. This is perfectly credible, since this is the general area in the Provincia Arabia where they were settled. Hence the possibility of the region's evocativeness of such biblical figures as David and Ruth for the Salīḥid king and his daughter. See Ibn Khaldūn, *Tārīkh*, II, 580.

The monastery was an institution of learning in the fifth century, and it is tempting to bring all these threads together by suggesting Dayr Dāwūd, "the Monastery of David," as the place[79] where Bible translation and with it the development of the Arabic script took place,[80] under the inspiring direction of the Salīḥid king himself or his anonymous daughter.

South Arabia

It is, however, in South Arabia that there is a specific reference to a Gospel in the fifth century and this represents the earliest reference in the sources to a Gospel in Arabic. Hishām al-Kalbī makes this reference in his account of the South Arabian poet al-Barrāq.[81] In his childhood this poet, according to Hishām, was associated with a "monk (*rāhib*) from whom he learned the recitation of the Gospel (*injīl*), and he was of the same religion as the monk." In view of the importance of this account, it will be analyzed in some detail.[82]

1. In Cheikho's account, the poet is called by his *laqab* (al-Barrāq), his patronymic (ibn al-Rawḥān), and his tecnonymic (Abū Naṣr). After a South Arabian childhood he emigrated with his tribe to northeastern Arabia, became the *sayyid* of the Rabīʿa group, and took an active part in the wars of the second half of the fifth century as a contemporary of the famous Taghlibite chief Kulayb.[83]

2. The relevant and important part of the account concerns the Gospel and the monk. According to Cheikho, al-Barrāq derived this from Hishām's

[79] Baumstark suggested Ghassānid Sergiopolis or Lakhmid Ḥīra as the location where the Arabic pre-Islamic Gospel was translated. Dayr Dāwūd could be added to the list, and it is earlier than Ghassānid Sergiopolis as a Christian Arab center. For Baumstark's view, see "Das Problem," 573–74. See also above, note 70, on how Christian Arab churches were used as educational and teaching institutions.

[80] Just as the Armenian Mesrop undertook both the invention of the script and the translation of the Bible.

[81] See L. Cheikho, *Shuʿarāʾ al-Naṣrāniyya,* 141. He alluded to this in *al-Machriq* 3 (1901), 98, but developed the account of the poet associated with the Gospel in his *Shuʿarāʾ*. Georg Graf noted the reference in *al-Machriq* but did not follow it up; see *GCAL,* I, 18, and the following note.

[82] It is regrettable that the indefatigable Cheikho did not document this important reference accurately and in detail. He asserts twice, and in unambiguous terms, that he derived his account from the *Jamharat al-Nasab* of Hishām al-Kalbī (*Shuʿarāʾ*, 141, 144). But the *Jamharat* as studied by W. Caskel has no reference in its Register to the poet al-Barrāq (nor to his patronymic or his tecnonymic). Cheikho must have derived his information from some manuscript of the *Jamharat* at his disposal or from a medieval Arabic text which quoted Hishām as the source for its account of al-Barrāq.

[83] For a full account of al-Barrāq and the extant fragments of his poetry, see Cheikho, *Shuʿarāʾ*, 141–47. The Christianity of the poet seems reflected in a verse in which he refers to *al-Ilāh* (God); ibid., 146, line 3.

Jamharat al-Nasab.[84] If so, the account is very credible; Hishām was a Muslim close to the Abbāsid caliphs,[85] and it is quite unlikely that he would have fabricated an account such as this one, which attributes Christianity to a pre-Islamic poet, with specific details about his Christian background in South Arabia, involving a monk and a Gospel.[86]

3. In addition to the inherent credibility of the account, there are external sources which support it, and so it is not an isolated Arabic source.

a. The reference to a *rāhib* (a monk) should cause no surprise at all. According to no less an authority than Jerome himself, the institution of monasticism made its appearance in South Arabia (his letter to Laeta, written in 403, refers to monks visiting the Holy Land from South Arabia).[87] Monks, then, are attested in South Arabia early in the fifth century, and it would be pleasant to think that they could be related to the mission of Theophilus Indus to South Arabia during the reign of Constantius in the fourth century. If so, the mission of Theophilus was still bearing fruits in the fifth century. However, these monks could possibly be related to some other evangelizing effort.

b. The reference to an *injīl* (Gospel) implies that Christianity was not unknown to the South Arabian region in the fifth century. The presumption has always been that the Christianity preached in South Arabia by Theophilus did not last long. Even if this turns out to be true, there was the second conversion in South Arabia, carried out by Ḥannān/Ḥayyān in the first half of the fifth century in the region of Najrān.[88] A church without a Gospel in Najrān is inconceivable, and so a reference to an *injīl* in the Arab area in South Arabia is perfectly consonant with the fact that Najrān was converted in the first half of the fifth century. Thus the two important elements in Hishām's account—a monk and a Gospel in South Arabia in this period—turn out to be perfectly fortified by good external Syriac and Latin sources, and this suggests that the account is authentic.

4. Al-Barrāq was an Arab poet, and thus before he emigrated with his tribe from the south to the northeast of the Peninsula he clearly belonged to the Arab region in the Ḥimyarite South, most probably the region around Najrān or thereabouts. This makes it practically certain that the *injīl* referred

[84] He repeats it three times; ibid., 141, 144, 147.

[85] On Hishām, see *BAFOC*, 349–66.

[86] Important to the Christianity of al-Barrāq and the authenticity of the account is a reference to a monastery by the name of Dayr Ibn Barrāq. The name is very uncommon, and so this Ibn Barrāq is most likely the son of the Christian poet. He apparently founded the monastery near Ḥīra, not far from the scene of his father's activities after he emigrated from South Arabia; for Dayr Ibn Barrāq, see Yāqūt, *Muʿjam,* II, 496.

[87] On this, see above, 296.

[88] On this, see above, Chap. 13, sec. III.

to in Hishām's account was not a Ḥimyarite *injīl* but an Arabic one. This is consonant with the fact that the Arabs of Najrān and the Arabian south did not speak Syriac as some of those in the Fertile Crescent did, such as the Arabs of Ḥīra or some of the Arabs of Oriens. A Gospel in use among the Arabs of the south could only have been an Arabic Gospel.

5. Al-Barrāq's is the first of two earliest references to a Gospel, the second being some three-quarters of a century later, around 520, when a refugee from Arab Christian Najrān showed the Negus of Ethiopia a copy of the burnt Gospel after the persecutions which took place around that date.[89] This confirms the fruitfulness of seeking the Arab Gospel in pre-Islamic times in this region, where only Arabic, and not Syriac and Arabic, was spoken and understood, and hence belies the assumption that there was no need to translate the Gospel into the language of the converted Arabs because they were bilingual and could speak and understand Syriac.[90]

These two specific references to a Gospel and *injīl* in South Arabia are striking. Although the Gospel is the fundamental text of Christianity, the reference to it exclusively, and not to other parts of the Christian Bible, may be significant. It is possibly due to the fact that South Arabia had a strong Jewish community. Since the Torah is the fundamental text of Judaism and since the two faiths were competing for the soul of South Arabia, the emphasis on the Gospel as the distinctively Christian text rather than on the Old Testament or the Pentateuch, the fundamental text of Judaism, may be a reflection of this rivalry.[91] Finally, it is not irrelevant to mention that the Arabic form of Gospel, *injīl*, may have been mediated from Ethiopic by Sabaic or the Sabaean region of South Arabia.[92]

[89] On this, *injīl,* see Shahīd, *Martyrs,* 249, where it is stated that the reference to an Arabic *injīl* in South Arabia around 520 is the earliest in the Arabic sources. This reference to the *injīl* associated with al-Barrāq is earlier.

Nöldeke was not able to comment on the *injīl* of 520 because when he published his translation of Ṭabarī in 1879 the important Syriac documents for the persecutions in South Arabia had not been published or discovered; Simeon's letter was published two years later by Guidi, and the *Book of the Ḥimyarites* was published by A. Moberg in 1924. The Sabaic inscriptions of Yūsuf and the second letter of Simeon of Bēth-Arshām were published much later. For Nöldeke's silence, see *PAS,* 188.

[90] See Shahīd, *Martyrs,* 247.

[91] In the new letter of Simeon of Bēth-Arshām, the Torah appears also in the negotiations between Jewish Yūsuf and Christian Najrān as the symbol of Judaism; see Shahīd, *Martyrs,* 45. The same distinction is observed in the Koran, which may have reflected the antithesis prevalent in neighboring South Arabia.

[92] It has been pointed out by Nöldeke that the Arabic form of Gospel, *injīl,* entered Arabic from Ethiopic and not from Syriac or directly from Greek. Grimme further suggested that it may have done so through Sabaic, but so far there has been no epigraphic confirmation of this. Nevertheless, that the form *injīl* came from Ethiopic is relevant in this discussion since it most probably came through the South Arabian region, if not through a South Arabian language (Sabaic), in view of the Ethiopian occupation of the region in the 4th century and the

IV. Arabic Literature in Oriens and Ḥijāz in the Fifth Century

Arabic literature, both prose and poetry, was represented in the fourth century by the Namāra inscription and the epinician odes composed to celebrate Queen Mavia's victory.[93] No doubt, the tradition of Arabic prose and poetry continued in the fifth century, and it is the aim of this section to examine its course and its various manifestations.

Arabic Prose

The discussion of Arabic prose in fifth-century Oriens is a subject of considerable importance to historians of Arabic literature, if only because most of their discussions have turned around the beginnings of Arabic *poetry* in pre-Islamic times.[94] Many are, no doubt, discouraged by the paucity of later Islamic literary works, but a study of the beginning of Arabic prose in Oriens in this proto-Byzantine period should be especially fruitful, since it can be based on indubitable evidence—Arabic prose inscriptions, some of which are dated. The rise of the Arabic script in the fifth century, discussed in a previous chapter, is of obvious relevance to development of contemporary Arabic prose.

1. Any treatment of Arabic prose in the fifth century must begin with the Namāra inscription of the fourth,[95] the earliest specimen of "federate prose." This is the most solid piece of evidence for the state of the Arabic language in this distant past and for its use in a long eulogy, detailing the achievements of a deceased federate king.

It is impossible to believe that this was an isolated case and that the Arab federates discontinued the use of long funerary inscriptions to celebrate the achievements of their kings after the death of Imru' al-Qays. The natural presumption is that this continued throughout the fourth century, and that the practice gathered momentum in the fifth with the rise of the Arabic script and the growth of the tradition with the passage of time.[96] This earliest solid document for the Arabic language is the splendid confirmation of the truth

---

Ethiopian presence there represented by Ḥabashat. On the derivation of Arabic *injīl* from Ethiopic, see A. Jeffery, *Foreign Vocabulary,* 71–72.

[93] For both, see *BAFOC*, 443–48, 452–55.

[94] For both, see R. Blachère, *Histoire de la littérature arabe,* vol. I. For the latest on pre-Islamic prose literature, see R. B. Serjeant, in *CHAL,* I, chap. 3, pp. 114–15, 122–27, 128–31.

[95] Especially as the exploration of this dimension of the Namāra inscription was not attended to in *BAFOC* and was postponed to this volume.

[96] See the perceptive remarks of J. Bellamy in "A New Reading of the Namārah Inscription," *JAOS* 105 (1985), 46–47. On p. 46 he writes, "I am convinced that the Namārah inscription is an example of a tradition of royal epitaphs, because ignorant and unskilled men starting from scratch could never have composed an epitaph of such rhetorical perfection."

about what the Arabic scholars have called *Dīwān al-Qabīla*, which put together the poetry composed by members of the tribe and its achievements in the *ayyām*, the battle days of the Arabs in pre-Islamic times.[97] It is, therefore, natural to assume that the various tribal groups, or at least the dominant ones among them, such as the Salīḥids, the Kalbites, and the Iyādīs of the fifth century, did keep records of their achievements in special *dīwāns*. These need not have been extensive and elaborate accounts; they were probably modest in range. What is important is the fact of their existence.[98]

The next Arabic prose inscriptions that are available in Oriens pertain to the sixth century, but they shed some light on the varieties of prose that must have been developed by the fifth-century *foederati*[99] The inscriptions of Usays and Ḥarrān are the most relevant.[100] The first tells the story of the military expedition conducted by a general of the Ghassānids around 530 and the second commemorates the erection of a *martyrion* dedicated to St. John about 568. These notables among the federates cannot have been the only ones who left such inscriptions behind them. The presumption is that such achievements were recorded and probably formed part of *Dīwān al-Qabīla*, "The *Dīwān* of the Tribe."

2. The Byzantine political, military, and social scene in Oriens can also provide the context for discovering the variety of prose forms that arose in the fifth century, as they have helped in the discussion of the rise of the script. As was argued earlier, the Arab *foederati* must have used prose to correspond with the central government and the Byzantine authorities in Oriens. But by far the most important function of Arabic prose must have been the drafting of the texts of the *foedera*, and these were of two kinds: treaties between federate groups and Byzantium and treaties between Arab tribes.

a. Queen Mavia is reported in the sources to have struck a *foedus* with Byzantium, and the Salīḥids also must have struck some. Unfortunatley, the texts have not survived, except for a resume of one which the Ghassānids concluded with Byzantium around 500. Perhaps new discoveries in the world of the Arabic manuscripts will reveal some of the texts.[101]

[97] On *Dīwān al-Qabīla* and that of Tanūkh, in particular, see *BAFOC*, 448–55.

[98] On the *kātib* of the *Qabīla*, its scribe, see the Umm al-Jimāl II inscription, discussed above, 415.

[99] It has been noted that most of these Arabic pre-Islamic inscriptions in Oriens in the 6th century are Christian, and it may be added that they are mostly federate testimony to the role of both Christianity and the *foederati* in the development of the Arabic script and its prose literature.

[100] For these two inscriptions, see above, 410.

[101] Having discovered an important Syriac text of the 6th century—a new letter of Simeon of Bēth-Arshām on the Christian martyrs of South Arabia—I am of the opinion that such hopes of future discoveries are not unrealistic; for this letter, see Shahîd, *Martyrs*. The text of the Ghassānid treaty with Byzantium is discussed above, 417.

b. The student of the problem of early Arab prose is better served in the case of inter-tribal treaties, such as must have been concluded between the Salīḥids or some of the other federate groups in Oriens with other tribes.[102] None of the texts of these has survived, but reference is made to one such treaty in a work of Hishām al-Kalbī, namely, the *foedus* between Kalb and the large and powerful tribe of Tamīm in eastern Arabia, known as "ḥilf Kalb wa Tamīm."[103] The text of a similar *ḥilf* (alliance) has survived for the tribes of Central and South Arabia.[104] Even the term related to them, *mahāriq*, has survived in one of the "suspended odes" of pre-Islamic Arabia.[105]

3. The prose form discussed above belongs to the category of non-literary Arabic prose literature. The question must inevitably arise whether there was evidence of an Arabic artistic prose in this century. If prose of this description did exist, it must have been part of *Dīwān al-Qabīla*, which might have included some speeches, harangues, and exhortations, especially as it was related to the oral tradition of Arabic literature, so strong in pre-Islamic times. In any case, it could not have been well developed and must have consisted, as possibly in the case of speeches, of small pieces. But what was most probably more extensive than this secular prose was Christian religious literature, possibly represented by a simple liturgy and some translations from the Bible for liturgical use.[106] If these existed, as is likely, they would have been the most extensive specimens of Arabic prose. Their position would also have been unique, since they are likely to have been the first specimens of translations into Arabic. Whether they inspired the artistically inclined among the *foederati* to compose original religious literature can only be a matter for speculation, as will be discussed further below.

Arabic Poetry

Unlike prose, poetry is well attested in the fifth century in Oriens. Sozomen testifies to the survival of epinician odes from the fourth century, composed to celebrate the victories of Mavia. The name of one poet has survived from the Arab Oriens of the fifth century, ʿAbd al-ʿĀṣ, the court

[102] Such as the treaty between the two allies (*al-ḥalīfān*) Kalb and al-Namir, referred to in the verse composed by the daughter of the Salīḥid king on the death of her father for which, see above, 308.

[103] *BAFOC*, 359 note 29.

[104] For the text of this *ḥilf*, see below, App. 1.

[105] R. Frye has traced the etymology of Arabic *mahāriq* to Middle Persian *muhrak-i vāvaryan*, which means "an authentic, or credible document of agreement," and found it attested in the Babylonian Talmud; see his "Problems in the Study of Iranian Religions," in *Religions in Antiquity* (E. R. Goodenough Festschrift), ed. J. Neusner (Leiden, 1968), 588 note 4.

[106] Further on this, see below, App. 1.

poet of the Salīḥid Dāwūd, and reference is made in the sources to Dāwūd's anonymous daughter, from whose poetry one single verse has survived. Some significant fragments of verses have also survived on the misfortunes of the Salīḥids. The discussion of Arabic poetry in the fourth century was restricted in range because of the nature of the Greek sources and its laconic reference to poetry,[107] but the case is different for the fifth; the Arabic sources are more informative and enable an entire range of questions to be raised and discussed, involving poetry in Oriens and also in Ḥijāz, the impetus given to poetry by the Salīḥids, especially by Dāwūd, his court poet ʿAbd al-ʿĀṣ, and his daughter, the poetry of other tribes such as Kalb, Iyād, and ʿUḏra, and finally, the influence of Christianity on Arabic poetry.

In view of the importance of the rise of an attractive and important poetic genre in northern Ḥijāz,[108] which was within the sphere of Byzantine influence but not technically part of Oriens, it is well that the discussion of poetry in the fifth century be divided into sections, one dealing with Oriens and the other with Ḥijāz.

Oriens

The Salīḥids gave strong impetus to the development of Arabic poetry in the fifth century. Since they were also the dominant federate group, the discussion will begin with them.

I

Arabic federate poetry in Oriens is attested in the fourth century for Queen Mavia, and it is natural to assume that once a tradition of Arabic poetry connected with the *foederati* had started it would continue. And in both cases it is connected with the dominant federate group, the Tanūkhids of the fourth century and the Salīḥids of the fifth.

What this poetry treated can only be guessed. Although peace prevailed between the two empires, there were two wars with Persia during the reign of Theodosius II in which the Salīḥids distinguished themselves, and these wars must have given rise to some poetry on their achievements. Then there were the *ayyām*, the battle days of the Arabs, the inter-Arab wars of the century that involved Salīḥ. These too must have been remembered by the poets, and indeed, some fragments have survived. How early in the century this poetry associated with the Salīḥids began is difficult to tell. Explicit references in the sources pertain only to the reign of King Dāwūd in the second half of the fifth century, but the tradition must have continued the fourth-century tradition of

[107] On Sozomen and Arabic poetry, see *BAFOC*, 443–48.

[108] It flourished in the first century of the Islamic period but undoubtedly it went back to pre-Islamic times, as will be argued in a subsequent section.

the Tanūkhids. However, since absolutely nothing of the earlier tradition has survived, it is to the second half of the fifth century that the student must turn.

1. Dāwūd is the only Salīḥid king about whom a few facts relevant to this discussion are known: he had a court poet whose name was ʿAbd al-ʿĀṣ; his own daughter was a poetess; and the few fragments of poetry involving Salīḥ that have survived are related to him.

a. Nothing is known about the circumstances that made ʿAbd al-ʿĀṣ the court poet of Dāwūd, only the fact of his association with the Salīḥid king. This bare fact leaves a number of questions unanswered. Did Dāwūd send for him or did he come of his own accord seeking the post? Was his tribe, Iyād, already in Oriens or did he come alone, attracted by the fame of Dāwūd? What kind of poetry he composed for Dāwūd can only be guessed; no doubt he sang the praises of the dynasty. But more important is the possibility that Dāwūd may have encouraged him to compose some religious poetry.

b. Dāwūd's daughter, unfortunately left anonymous in the sources, was also a poetess. With the exception of one verse, nothing is known about her poetry. Hence the problem she poses is the same as that of ʿAbd al-ʿĀṣ. Did the king who employed a court poet encourage his daughter to compose poetry? Was she influenced by her father's religiosity? Was she influenced by the poetry of ʿAbd al-ʿĀṣ? These and other questions are difficult to answer, and will be discussed further on in the section devoted to her. But the one verse which has survived from her poetry serves to suggest that ʿAbd al-ʿĀṣ was not the only poet in the Dāwūd circle. And the fact that the daughter composed poetry could raise the question whether her poetic talents were inherited. It would not be altogether impossible that the king himself composed poetry, as many rulers in Arab history did.

c. The fall and death of Dāwūd must have impressed his contemporaries. Otherwise it is difficult to explain the poetry that it gave rise to. The meager fragments which have survived may be summarized as follows: three verses composed by one of his murderers, Thaʿlaba; the reply of his daughter, which has survived in one verse; a couplet on the death of the Salīḥid tax gatherer Sabīṭ, who was killed by the Ghassānid Jiḏʿ just before the fall of the Salīḥids.[109] These scanty remains have survived by the merest chance, and they suggest a more extensive body of poetry composed on the fall of the Salīḥids.

The literary significance of the reign of Dāwūd emerges clearly from this analysis. Perhaps the most important gain is the fact that in Oriens, as early as the fifth century at least, court poetry was not unknown to the Arabic poetic tradition. This contradicts the traditionally held view that court poetry

[109] On these three fragments, see above, 259–60, 308 and note 370.

appeared for the first time in the sixth century, both among the Lakhmids of Ḥīra and the Ghassānids of Oriens.[110]

2. Was there a *dīwān* or *kitāb* of Salīḥ, as there was a *dīwān* for Tanūkh?[111] The important lists of tribal *dīwāns* do not contain any reference to a *dīwān* of Salīḥ.[112] This, of course, is far from decisive, since they are not exhaustive; they do not contain a reference to the *dīwān* of Tanūkh, the existence of which had to be inferred and is attested in other sources. It is possible that the dynasty that was so involved in religion did not have a *dīwān*, or that if it did, the *dīwān* belonged to the larger tribal group to which Salīḥ belonged or to which it may later have affiliated itself.

On the other hand, there is a possibility that Salīḥ did have a *dīwān* or a *kītāb* in which its *ayyām*, its Persian Wars, achievements, and panegyrics on the members of the dynasty were all collected and recorded. In support of this possibility the following may be adduced.

a. This was a dynasty and federate group that played an important role in Oriens in the fifth century. It fought in the Persian Wars and also its own *ayyām* with the Arabs of the Peninsula. It is unlikely that these achievements were left unsung and unrecorded.

b. Most significantly, Dāwūd employed the services of a professional poet, the Iyādī ʿAbd al-ʿĀṣ, and thus institutionalized the art of poetry and enlisted it in the service of the Salīḥid dynasty. Dāwūd could not have been the only Salīḥid king who did this. Others must also have had poets, and it is difficult to believe that their poetry went unrecorded and remained only "winged words."

c. That these poems and achievements were recorded receives considerable fortification from two considerations: first, the fact that the development of the Arabic script took place in the fifth century, the century of Salīḥ's supremacy in Oriens; and second, ʿAbd al-ʿĀṣ himself came from Iyād, known for its Christianity, its poetry, and its association with the Arabic script. Both he and his patron must have been literate, and the conclusion is that what the poet composed on his patron and others was committed to writing, and that what all the poets had composed on the Salīḥids in its entirety must likewise have been committed to writing.

d. That some collection or record of the Salīḥids must have existed may be faintly reflected in the few fragments which have survived on their fall, one

110 On poetry at the courts of the Ghassānids and the Lakhmids, see Blachère, *Histoire de la littérature arabe,* II, 293, 344–47. But it is practically certain that poetry appeared at the court of the Lakhmids long before the 6th century. See Shahīd, "The Composition of Arabic Poetry in the Fourth Century," 89–90.

111 On *Dīwān Tanūkh,* see *BAFOC*, 448–55.

112 For these lists, see ibid., 449.

of which was composed by Dāwūd's daughter. Moreover, their *ayyām* must have been known to later Islamic poets such as al-Kumyat ibn Zayd, a poet of the first Islamic century. One of his fragments mentions the Day of Baradān, which involved Ziyād ibn Habūla.[113]

That *Dīwān Salīḥ* or *Kitāb Salīḥ*, if it ever existed, has not survived is not surprising. Salīḥ itself practically disappeared after the eighth century, when the last Salīḥid known to the sources, Usāma, the *kātib* of the Umayyads, lived.[114] Unlike Iyād, which adopted Islam and participated actively in the making of Islamic history in the Orient and the Occident, Salīḥ remained stubbornly Christian, and this may have disinclined the later collectors of poetry and tribal *dīwāns* from taking a special interest in it and its poetry.

II

The Salīḥid princess from whose poetry one solitary verse has survived deserves special treatment. Her verse was discussed earlier in this volume as a historical source for the tribal coalition which brought about the downfall of her father. It remains to discuss her and her verse in this literary context, as representing not only federate poetry written on the Salīḥids but also poetry by one of them.

1. Of the various versions of the verse discussed earlier, it was suggested that the best version—from various viewpoints, historical and other—is the one which speaks of her father's being killed by the "wolves" of the two allies Kalb and al-Namir, with the pejorative term "*awbāsh*" used to describe the group of the latter. The pejorativeness of the verse is enhanced by the employment of the term "*d̲u'ban*" (wolves), which connoted for the Arabs treachery and vileness. Thus the verse not only states the facts but also expresses contempt for the regicides and implies the rise of an aristocratic tradition reflecting the point of view of the royal house of Salīḥ on the murder of their king.[115] It is not impossible that the verse belonged to a flyting poem, replying to the triplet of the Kalbite who killed her father. The triplet is epinician; the verse of the princess is elegiac. The rhyme is the same, preceded by the long *alif al-ta' sīs*, but the meter is different; that of the Kalbite is *kāmil*, while that of the princess is *ṭawīl*.

2. The question arises as to what poetic tradition or school the Salīḥid princess belonged and whence she derived her interest in Arabic poetry. The

[113] On al-Kumayt, see Sezgin, *GAS*, II, 347–49; for the verse, see Abū al-Baqā' al-Ḥīlli, *Al-Manāqib al-Mazyadiyya*, II, 513; it reads *wayawma ibn al-Habūlati qad aqamnā khudūda al-ṣuʿri wa al-awada al-mubīna*.

[114] On Usāma, see above, Chap. 12, sec. VII.II.

[115] His enemies jeered at Dāwūd and called him al-Lathiq, "the bedraggled." His daughter countered by calling the regicides wolves and riffraff.

first name that comes to mind as an influence is that of the court poet ʿAbd al-ʿĀṣ. It is possible that he was the first and most important influence on her, since he composed poetry extolling the dynasty of which she was a princess. If so, then her poetry would have been in the style of the Iyādī poets, since ʿAbd al-ʿĀṣ belonged to Iyād, which had lived in Mesopotamia before its emigration to Oriens. It could, on the other hand, have derived from the tradition of poetry already in vogue in Oriens, represented by the odes in honor of Queen Mavia. That they were poems on a federate queen of the fourth century would have appealed to the federate princess of the fifth. Perhaps her father, as has been suggested earlier, may also have had some poetic talent.

3. Whatever the truth about the poetic tradition to which the princess belonged, she emerges as the earliest female Arab voice in the history of Arab poetry in Oriens. The misfortunes of her dynasty and family naturally cast her in the mold of an elegiast. She thus joins the company of other female poets of pre-Islamic Arabic who also wrote elegies, such as the daughter of the redoubtable Lakhmid king Mun̲dir, who is said to have written the beautiful couplet on the fall of her father.[116] Thus in a larger context she becomes the first in the tradition of Arab women elegists which reached its culmination in al-K̲h̲ansāʾ.[117]

4. The "Dāwūd circle," composed at least of the King, the court poet, and the princess who was also a poetess, makes it possible to probe further into the obscure literary history of the dynasty, especially when set against the Christian and imperial Byzantine backdrop of Oriens in the fifth century.

The death of her father must have been a traumatic experience for the princess. One can only guess what happened after his death and the fall of the dynasty. She might have taken the monastic garb as was done by other Arab princesses in similar circumstances in the following century.[118] This, however, does not tell much about her literary activity. What may tell more is the exploration of the Christian and imperial presence in Oriens in this century. The models provided by this presence may have inspired the Salīḥid princess.

This was the century that witnessed aristocratic Roman women leaving Italy and settling in Jerusalem, Bethlehem, and the Holy Land, such as Melania the Elder in the last quarter of the fourth century and her granddaughter, Melania the Younger, in the fifth. More relevant and pertinent is

[116] For these two verses which were composed on the death of al-Mun̲dir, the Lakhmid king of Ḥīra in the 6th century, see Yāqūt, *Muʿjam,* I, 61. According to the lexicon *Lisan al-Arab,* it was the daughter of Mun̲dir who composed this couplet.

[117] On the Arab poetesses of pre-Islamic times, see Blachère, *Histoire de la littérature arabe,* II, 289–92.

[118] Such as the Lakhmid princess Hind the Younger, daughter of al-Nuʿmān, the Lakhmid king who was killed around 600. For her, see Rothstein, *Die Lahmiden,* 125.

the career of Athenaïs-Eudocia, the wife of Theodosius II, who after the apple of discord incident finally settled in Jerusalem for some twenty years (443–460?). Like the princess, she was a royal personage, and a poetess who wrote both secular and religious poetry. She composed in verse the achievements of the Byzantines in the two Persian Wars of her husband and translated parts of the Old Testament (the Octateuch) into heroic verse. She also composed the *Homerocentra*, the Homeric Centos which told episodes of the life of Jesus through Homeric verses. Finally, she encouraged the learned circle at Jerusalem, erected many buildings, and restored the city walls.[119]

The Salīḥid princess may have been Eudocia's contemporary or lived slightly after her death. The latter's imperial presence was felt in Oriens, and it is impossible to believe that the Salīḥid princess, living a few miles away from Jerusalem, across the Jordan in the Balqā' region (biblical Ammonitis), would not have heard of or even met Eudocia. As a visitor to the Holy City she would have met the empress, or heard about her if she visited Jerusalem after Eudocia's death. The empress could well have been a model, and it is not impossible that the Salīḥid princess imitated her in writing on the Persian Wars, in which the Salīḥids distinguished themselves. But more importantly, she may have written religious poetry as Eudocia had done.

It is tantalizing to think that in her poems on the Persian Wars of Theodosius II Eudocia may have remembered the contributions of the Arab *foederati*, the Salīḥids, to the Byzantine war effort, as Heraclius was to do in the victory bulletin which he dispatched to the Senate after victory at Nineveh in 628. If so, the princess, most probably, would have followed the imperial model in compositions of her own on her royal house.

III

The problem of a pre-Islamic Christian Arabic literature is an old one, and it is related to that of an Arabic Bible and liturgy in pre-Islamic times.[120] This chapter will not deal with this problem over the six centuries before the rise of Islam or in all the Arab area in the Peninsula and the Fertile Crescent, but only in Oriens and in the fifth century. Since this literature, if it existed, has left only traces and faint ones at that, the discussion may be divided into two parts; the first part will deal with the hypothetical problem of its existence and can, at best, only raise the appropriate questions and give tentative answers; the second will deal with some of the traces which Christianity has left in pre-Islamic poetry.

[119] On Athenaïs-Eudocia, see Diehl, *Byzantine Empresses* (London, 1927), 22–43; also G. Holum, *Theodosian Empresses*, especially 217–28.

[120] The discussion involved mainly A. Baumstark and G. Graf, and L. Cheikho. See *BAFOC*, 435 ff.

The fact that this presumed Christian literature has not survived except in traces should not discourage the student of this problem from raising the pertinent questions.[121] The most fruitful approach is to set the whole discussion against the strongly Christian background of Byzantine Oriens in the fifth century and against the Islamic background of Oriens/Shām in the seventh century.

1. When Islam appeared among the Arabs in the seventh century, it immediately affected the warp and woof of Arabic poetry and prose, and continued to do so throughout the centuries. Is it possible to maintain that Christianity failed to function likewise in pre-Islamic times although it was, like Islam, a scriptural religion and particularly inspiring for the development of new literary genres among those to whom it was preached, as it was for practically all the other peoples of Oriens Christianus? The question acquires even more urgency when it is considered that even after Islam thoroughly permeated Arabic literature it is possible to detect traces of the influence of Christianity and the Christian Scripture in the rise of a new genre such as the *munājayāt*, the soliloquies composed in the style of the Psalms.[122]

2. The chances are that the answer to this question should be in the affirmative, especially in view of the fact that unlike some other Near Eastern peoples to whom Christianity was preached and among whom it spread, the Arabs already had a developed form of poetry. If so, it is then justifiable to go back to the Arab *foederati* of the fifth century, a group both aware of its Arabness and staunchly Christian, and, what is more important, a group for whom Arabic poetry was composed, some specimens of which have survived.[123] The "Dāwūd circle" naturally comes to mind—a court poet, a poetess daughter, and a ruler who was intensely religious and may have composed poetry himself. The imperial model of Athenaïs-Eudocia living in nearby Jerusalem has already been referred to, and it is tempting to think that the Salīḥid circle composed with the empress (living or dead) in mind as model. It is even tempting to think that the king himself may have composed

[121] The same question may be raised in regard to the related problem of the pre-Islamic Arabic Bible and liturgy; see below, App. 1.

[122] This has been persuasively argued by the distinguished Muslim scholar ʿAbd al-Raḥmān Badawī. According to him, the Invocations of Abū Ḥayyan al-Tawḥīdī (d. 1023) in his book titled *Al-Ishārat al-Ilāhiyya* were inspired by the Arabic version of the Psalms which were translated in the Abbāsid period. One of these versions was that of the celebrated Ḥunayn ibn Isḥāq (d. 373) who translated the entire Old Testament. Badawī also draws attention to the association of al-Tawḥīdī with the well-known Christian Jacobite figure Ibn Zurʿa, in his argument for biblical influence on al-Tawḥīdī; see the introduction to his edition of *Al-Ishārat al-Ilāhiyya* (Cairo, 1950), pp. 1w–1t.

[123] This is paralleled on the Lakhmid side in Ḥīra by the poetry of ʿAdī ibn Zayd on the 5th-century Lakhmid king al-Nuʿmān who renounced the world, the very same one that came to St. Simeon; for ʿAdī on Nuʿman, see *Dīwān ʿAdī ibn Zayd,* 87–90.

in the style of his biblical namesake, living as he did in Ammonitis, which was evocative of David, Bathsheba, and Uriah the Hittite, while the Trans-Jordanian scene farther to the south in Moabitis may have inspired his daughter to compose[124] or versify the book of Ruth, as Athenaïs-Eudocia had done.

3. The versification of biblical material may have been the expression of Christianity in Arabic poetry, and this can be paralleled in Islamic times, when the Muslim Arab poets tried to turn both Koranic material and the biography of the prophet Muḥammad into verse. This is, of course, pure speculation, although it is in the realm of the possible. But the existence of another type of poetry cannot be doubted, since there is express and explicit reference to it in the contemporary historian Sozomen—the poetry composed by Queen Mavia's supporters in celebration of her victories over Emperor Valens. But these were wars of religion, in which the Arab *foederati* stood for the Orthodox faith of Nicaea against Arian Valens. It is, therefore, practically certain that in this heroic verse which sang the prowess of their queen and her armies, much religious sentiment was also expressed. This could also be paralleled in the poetry of the politico-religious parties of the early Islamic period, in which Arabic heroic poetry is permeated with Islamic religious sentiments.[125] It is, therefore, perfectly natural to assume that Arabic religious poetry on Mavia of the fourth century was the model of fifth-century Arabic religious poetry. The two Persian Wars of the reign of Theodosius II must have been remembered in Arabic poetry, and since the Salīḥids fought as Christians against the pagan Lakhmids and the fire-worshiping Persians, it is certain that religion was a motif in such compositions. The model, as has been said, must have been the odes in honor of Mavia which, according to Sozomen, were still recited in the middle of the fifth century and so could have inspired poetry on the Salīḥid wars. What other types of religious poetry came into being is difficult to tell. The two types of religious poetry just discussed are supported to some extent by the Byzantine imperial model of Eudocia's verse and the Arab royal model of the Mavian odes. But it is not altogether impossible that some religious hymns were composed related to the Christian liturgy.[126]

Although no strictly religious Arabic poetry has survived, some surviving

[124] The name of this daughter remains unknown. It is tempting to think of the name of David's daughter Tamar or that of his great-grandmother, Ruth.

[125] For the poetry of these politico-religious parties of the early Islamic period, both intensely martial and intensely religious, see R. Nicholson, *A Literary History of the Arabs*, 206–20.

[126] It is noteworthy that Byzantine hymnography flourished in the early Islamic period in Oriens/Shām, at the hands of John of Damascus, Cosmas of Maiuma, and Andrew of Crete, a native of Damascus. John, the last church father, was an Arab, as the name of his grandfather, Manṣūr (which goes back to the early 7th century and so is pre-Islamic), testifies.

fragments of pre-Islamic Arabic poetry do betray the influence of the new faith. These fragments are of sixth-century vintage (more particularly the first quarter of it), but surely the tradition and the susceptibility of Arabic poetry to Christian influences goes back to the fifth century, which witnessed the spread of monasticism in Oriens and among the Arabs, and it is in the monastic establishment that one seeks the provenance of the similes that the Arab pre-Islamic poet employed in his poetry.

The figure of the monk (the *rāhib*) in his monastery starts to appear in Arabic poetry. Two elements associated with him are especially important and recur often in this poetry, namely, the Holy Book, especially the Psalter (*zabūr*) and his lamp (*miṣbāḥ*). The first provided the poet with a simile related to the deserted encampment, the second a simile related to the stars or lightning.[127] As pointed out in an earlier chapter, the monasteries apparently were strategically located along the caravan routes of pre-Islamic Arabia. This enabled the travelers and caravaneers to find their bearings, especially at night in the Arabian desert. Hence the lamp of the hermit functioned as the stars did for guiding the wayfarer. And the poets were quick to establish the likeness between the two: the stars and the lamp of the hermit. This finds expression in one of the verses of Imru' al-Qays, the foremost poet of pre-Islamic Arabia, who came from a family associated with Christianity.[128] In the seventh century the simile involving the star and the lamp of the hermit is beautifully expressed in a Koranic Revelation, in the famous Light-verse.[129]

IV

The Salīḥids were one among many Arab federate groups in Oriens and it is unreasonable to maintain that they were the only federate group for whom and by whom poetry was composed. However, little is known about the poetry associated with other tribes, with the exception of Iyād, Kalb, and ʿUḏra.[130]

Something has been said about Iyād in the history of the Arabs before the rise of Islam, and the fact that the Salīḥid court poet ʿAbd al-ʿĀṣ belonged to this tribe.[131] It was also suggested earlier in this chapter that ʿAbd al-ʿĀṣ

[127] See Ahlwardt, *Divans,* 160, line 11 and 149, line 18.

[128] His aunt Hind was the founder of the famous monastery of Hind in Ḥīra, the long famous Christian inscription of which has survived. For the verse of her nephew, Imru' al-Qays, see ibid., 152, line 15.

[129] In which "the mystical indwelling of God in His universe is suggested"; see H. A. R. Gibb, *Mohammedanism,* 56, where the Light-verse is also translated. For the Arabic version of the verse, see Koran, XXIV.V.35. Gibb's version is used in the Synthesis in this volume.

[130] Because of the importance of ʿUḏra and of its being in Ḥijāz rather than Oriens, the entire section following this one is devoted to it.

[131] See above, 261.

may have composed some religious poetry under the influence of his pious patron, Dāwūd. If the poet outlived the king, the chances are that he composed an elegy on him in much the same way that al-Nābigha was to compose on the Ghassānid al-Nuʿmān after his death, and that he included in it some Christian religious sentiments.[132] He is the only Arab poet of the fifth century that is associated with a pious Christian king, and, therefore, if one were to look for a *dīwān* of Christian Arab poetry, one would think of this Iyādī poet. This invites comparison with another poet of pre-Islamic Arabia, who also claimed descent from Iyād, Umayya ibn Abī al-Ṣalt, Muḥammad's contemporary who lived in Ṭā'if and wrote poetry permeated with biblical references. The poetry of Umayya is under a cloud but if it turns out to be truly authentic, then the chances are good that the Iyādī poet of Oriens also wrote this type of religious poetry, especially as he was under the influence of a pious patron.[133]

The appearance of an Iyādī poet in Oriens represents the extension of that tribe's literary influence from the eastern half of the Fertile Crescent[134] to the western, and it is possible that their literary contribution in Oriens was not limited to this poet laureate of the Salīḥids.

The tribe of Kalb, which was in possession of the strategic oasis of Dūma at the southern tip of Wādī Sirḥān, played an important role in the history of the region both in pre-Islamic and Islamic times. It counted among its members many poets, including Thaʿlaba, one of the two regicides who felled Dāwūd: a triplet of his verse in which he glories in the dead has survived. But Thaʿlaba is much less important than another Kalbite poet, whose name has survived in various versions, such as Ibn Ḥiḏam, or Haḏam, or Khaḏam. He is mentioned in one of the celebrated verses of Imru' al-Qays, in which the Kindite poet invites his companion to join in crying over the deserted encampment of his beloved in the style of Ibn Ḥiḏam.[135] Since Imru' al-Qays composed around 500 and in the first quarter of the sixth century, the Kalbite poet to whom he refers must belong to the preceding generation, and so to the fifth century. Other tribes claimed Ibn Ḥiḏam, but Hishām, who was a Kalbite himself and knew the history of his tribe, asserts that the poet was a Kalbite and, what is more, recounts something about him other than his name.[136] According to him, the Kalbites recite the five opening verses of

[132] See, for instance, Ahlwardt, *Divans,* 24, line 14.

[133] For Umayya's Iyādī genealogy, see L. Cheikho, *Shuʿarā' al-Naṣrāniyya,* 219. For the poet, see Sezgin, *GAS,* II, 298–300.

[134] On their poets in this part of the Crescent, Laqīṭ and Abū Du'ād, see Sezgin, *GAS,* II, 175–76, and 167–69. As ʿAbd al-ʿAṣ was at the court of the Salīḥid client-king, so was Abū Du'ād at the court of the Lakhmid client-king Munḏir, in Ḥīra.

[135] See Ahlwardt, *Divans,* 157, line 6.

[136] For Hishām al-Kalbī on this poet, see Ibn Ḥazm, *Jamharat,* 456.

Imru' al-Qays' famous "suspended ode" as verses of their own poet, Ibn Ḥidam, and contend that Imru' al-Qays included them in his ode as the opening prelude, presumably because of his admiration for the Kalbite poet. This amatory prelude became standard in the practice of pre-Islamic Arabic poetry, and even if the first opening verses of the "suspended ode" of Imru' al-Qays are not all his, there is no doubt that Ibn Ḥidam was the innovator. He was the first to open his odes with this lament over the deserted encampment and introduce the lacrimose element in the amatory prelude of the Arabic pre-Islamic ode, a practice that dominated the composition of Arabic poetry for centuries.[137] It is even possible to detect a mild Christian tone in this prelude, since it does not reflect the attitude of a sensual poet such as Imru' al-Qays himself but that of a refined and chaste lover. Hishām asserts that all Kalb, with the exception of one of its subdivisions, was Christian.[138] It is, therefore, very probable that Ibn Ḥidam was Christian and that these sentiments in the expression of his love life may be attributed to the refining influence of the new monotheistic faith which the Kalb tribe embraced.

Ḥijāz

ʿUḏra was the most important federate tribe in Ḥijāz, but there were others, such as Juḏām and Balī. In the context of Arabic poetry in Ḥijāz, however, it is ʿUḏra that merits most attention, since it is the tribe associated with a special type of love poetry which flourished in the first Islamic century, not among the urban population of the Islamic caliphate but among the pastoralists of the Arabian Peninsula in Ḥijāz and Najd.[139] It extolled a chaste and pure love that derived its name from the tribe of ʿUḏra.[140]

I

Historians of Arabic poetry have tried to explain the rise of this unique emotional experience among the pastoralists of the Arabian Peninsula in the seventh century. Many explanations refer to the new world in which the Arabs found themselves living after the Arabian revolution of ideas and conditions brought about by Islam and the Conquests, and prominence has been given to the Islamic religion in inducing in the Arab poets new ideals and standards of

[137] Imru' al Qays' opening verse in his famous suspended ode may be considered the Arabic version of Virgil's *sunt lacrimae rerum*.

[138] On this, see above, Chap. 12, sec. VII.III.

[139] For this type of poetry, see the most recent discussion of it in the chapter on Umayyad poetry by S. Jayyūsī in *CHAL,* 421–26.

[140] For a previous discussion of the tribe of ʿUḏra in connection with Quṣayy and his occupation of Mecca, see above, Chap. 13, sec. II.II.

chastity and continence.[141] There is something to be said for this view; yet it is not altogether convincing, and recently some reservations have been made concerning the soundness of this explanation. It has been pointed out that the foremost ʿUḏrī poet, Jamīl (d. 701), "shows little interest in Islam": "One can argue that the metamorphosis of the beloved into an ideal womanhood was a rebellion against polygamous marriage, against the cult of concubinage, and against the rejection of celibacy professed by Islam. There is nothing in Islam (other than the figure of the Virgin Mary) which allows for the sanctification of woman. Yet suddenly ideals of virginity and chastity come to fill the ʿUḏri poetry of the period."[142]

Since these reservations have opened the question of the genesis of this type of poetry, it is not altogether inappropriate to entertain the possibility that Christianity may have been a factor in its rise, or at least a component along with others that have been suggested.[143] The following observations may be made in support of this view.

1. It is noteworthy that this type of poetry takes its name from the tribe of ʿUḏra. This was a Christian tribe in pre-Islamic times, and its Christianity goes back to the fifth or even the fourth century, and persisted among at least some members of the tribe until well into the Umayyad period, as has been shown by the verse analyzed earlier and addressed to Jamīl, the foremost ʿUḏrī poet.[144]

2. The ideals of celibacy and asceticism, reflected in general in monasticism are more representative of Christianity[145] than Islam, which commended

[141] See M. Ghunaymi Hilāl, *Al-Ḥayat al-ʿĀṭifiyya bayn al-ʿUḏriyya wa al-Ṣūfiyya* (Cairo, 1976), I, 17–43.

[142] See Salmā Jayyūsī, herself poetess, critic, and Muslim, ibid., 421, 426.

[143] That this type of poetry is derivative from Platonic love is a view that prevails in some circles. It is quite inconceivable that this is the case in view of the fact that it arose among the pastoralists of the Arabian desert who were not exposed to such fruits of Hellenism as an acquaintance with Platonic love; see F. Gabrieli, *Storia della letteratura araba* (Milan, 1962), 131. Besides, Greek Platonic love, in Plato's view, obtains strictly between man and man, while Arab ʿUḏrite love obtains between man and woman. Perhaps the confusion of the two types of love in the writing of Orientalists and Arabists may derive from the mystic ʿAbd al-Ghanī al-Nabulusī; see the last paragraph of Massignon's article in *EI,* s.v. *ʿUḏhri.*

[144] S. Jayyūsī has already been quoted that Jamīl "shows little interest in Islam"; he was the *rāwiya,* the reciter and rhapsode of Hudba, another well-known poet from ʿUḏra who was a Christian and whom a rival poet described as belonging to Ummat al-Masīḥ, the people of Christ. Among the ancestors of Hudba in pre-Islamic times was a certain al-Kāhin, who most probably was not the pagan soothsayer but the Christian priest. If so, he would not have been an outsider sent out by the Byzantine *ecclesia* in Oriens, but a ʿUḏrite tribesman.

The tolerant Umayyads accepted religious pluralism among the Arabs, and so many of the Christian Arabs of pre-Islamic times remained Christian in Umayyad times.

For the description of Hudba's people as "the people of Christ," see L. Cheikho quoting the commentator of the *Hamasa* in *Shuʿarāʾ al-Naṣrāniyya Baʿd al-Islam* (Beirut, 1967), 96; for al-Kāhin as the ancestor of Hudba, see ibid., quoting *Al-Aghānī.*

[145] See 1 Cor. 7:1, 34.

marriage and the married life, not celibacy, and declared that there is "no monkery in Islam."[146]

3. Finally, the ideal of virginity represented by Mary belongs much more to Christianity than to Islam, in spite of the fact that the Virgin Mary appears in Islam's Holy Scripture.[147] There was a Marian presence in Ḥijāz, reflected in such structures as Masājid Maryam,[148] and there may have been some Arab nuns in the monasteries of Ḥijāz, in Wādī al-Qurā and Madyan. But Ḥijāz was the region where the tribe of ʿUd̲ra lived, and so it is not unlikely that the rise of this type of love in Ḥijāz is a reflection of a strong Christian presence among members of this tribe. ʿUd̲ra itself is significant in this context.[149]

The involvement of ʿUd̲ra in Christianity in pre-Islamic times and the analysis of the Christian elements that may have formed a component in the makeup of ʿUd̲rī love and love poetry could yield the conclusion that Christianity was a factor—or *the* factor. If so, it would be a remarkable instance of the impact of the Christian mission in Arabia.

II

If Christianity was the factor in the rise of this type of love and poetry, the question arises as to exactly when this happened. It seems unlikely that this took place after the rise of Islam, when Christianity was losing ground to the new religion. On the other hand, social and political conditions in Ḥijāz in Umayyad times have been rejected as an explanation.[150] It is, therefore, practically certain that this type of love and poetry goes back to pre-Islamic

[146] "La rahbāniyya fi al-Islām"; see H. A. R. Gibb, *Mohammedanism,* 48.

[147] In Islam it was the wives of the Prophet, especially Khadīja and ʿĀʾisha, and ʿAli's wife, Fāṭima, the Prophet's daughter, who became the models of Muslim women rather than Mary.

[148] Above, Chap. 13, app. 4.

[149] ʿUd̲ra translates "virginity," and this raises the question of whether in the distant pre-Islamic past, the tribe dedicated itself to the Virgin Mary (al-ʿAd̲h̲rāʾ Maryam) or accepted her as its patroness. One could raise the question whether this was perhaps made possible in the 5th century, when the Orient was rocked by the theological controversy centering around the Virgin Mary as Theotokos. The Christian Arab bishop of the Palestinian Parembole, Aspebetos, took an active part in the ecumenical council which discussed Nestorius' views on the Theotokos. Thus the triumph of the Orthodox view may have brought into prominence the figure of Mary among the Christian Arabs. In addition to the possible Christian connotation of the name of the tribe, it is possible, as pointed out earlier, that the name of the subdivision of the tribe, Banū Ḥunn/Ḥann, has Christian associations related to John, possibly the Christian ecclesiastic or the bishop who spread Christianity among them or was associated with them. The Arab bishop of Ayla in the 7th century was called John, Yuḥannā ibn Ruʾba. For Banū Ḥunn/Ḥann as a Christian name, compare Banū ʿAbd Y̲asūʿ, "the sons of the servant of Jesus," a group of Arabs in Najrān mentioned by Hishām al-Kalbī in his *Jamharat al-Nasab,* in British Museum MS 23297, 203.

[150] See S. Jayyūsī, in *CHAL,* 421, 425.

times,[151] and that if it arose under the influence of religion, this must have been Christianity. In what period in pre-Islamic times it appeared among the Arabs can only be guessed. The name of the tribe that gave this love and poetry its name could easily suggest that it appeared among them before it spread to other tribes, and that this could have happened in the fifth century, which witnessed both the prominence of ʿUd̲ra in the history of Ḥijāz (as is clear from a study of the career of Rizāḥ) and the great prominence that the Virgin Mary acquired because of the theological controversies that involved her. This also coincided with the spread of asceticism in Oriens and its monastic expression in the monasteries of Ḥijāz. Thus the wave of asceticism in Oriens, its expression in monasteries in Ḥijāz, and the presence of Arab monks and nuns could all have touched the sensibilities of the Arab tribes of Ḥijāz among whom Christianity spread in pre-Islamic times, and could very understandably have given rise to this type of love and poetry. The *dīwān* of ʿUd̲ra existed in Islamic times and is referred to in one of the two lists of the tribal *dīwāns*,[152] but is lost. It is almost certain that this *dīwān* contained a large section of pre-Islamic ʿUd̲rī poetry, and it is there that this early pre-Islamic love poetry has to be sought. In view of the fact that the *dīwān* has not survived, one can only make some probings in the sources for understanding how the Christian ideal of celibacy and virginity was married to the Arab ideal of *murūʾa* in heterosexual relations to produce ʿUd̲rī love and poetry in Ḥijāz.

1. The monastic map of northwest Arabia, involving Madyan, Wādī al-Qurā, and even to the south of Wādī al-Qurā, includes the monasteries of al-Qunfud̲ in Ayla, Dayr Madyan, Dayr Ḍamḍam, Dayr Wādī al-Qurā, and Masājid Maryam.[153] No doubt there were Arab monks in these monasteries as well as non-Arab ones. The existence of nunneries can only be inferred from references to the sixth century, but they must have started in the fifth,[154] and it is clear that in many cases the inmates were Arab women. In vain does the student of this period search for the name of an Arab woman associated with Christianity or its monastic expression in the Peninsula, and so the only voice

[151] "The patterns of the ʿUd̲ri love poetry and love tale was set early in pre-Islamic times," ibid., 424. Moreover, ʿUrwa ibn Ḥizām, the ʿUd̲ri poet, flourished during the caliphate of ʿUmar and ʿUthmān, and so he must have been born slightly before the rise of Islam. It is difficult to believe that he was the first representative of this type of love and poetry, and there is no record that he was its inventor.

[152] See Sezgin, *GAS*, II, 39.

[153] This is a single enumeration of what was detailed above, 294–95.

[154] See above, Sec. I.I. In the 6th century, Arab Najrān betrays important traces of cloistered maidens, represented by the "Daughters of the Covenant," although the phrase and its meaning is controversial; see *The Book of the Ḥimyarites,* chap. 17 (not extant). For the two celebrated monasteries of pre-Islamic times in Ḥīra, founded by the Lakhmid princesses Hind the Elder and Hind the Younger, respectively, see Yāqūt, *Muʿjam,* II, 541–43.

is that of the Salīḥid princess, the daughter of Dāwūd who was discussed earlier. It is not impossible that after the violent death of her father she took on the monastic garb or vowed virginity, thus becoming a "bride of Christ," perhaps an inmate of the *dayr* (monastery) built by her father.[155]

2. Although what has been said of the Salīḥid princess as a cloistered virgin is possible, the conclusion remains speculative, and the one verse that has survived from her poetic output deals with an event in the secular world and does not breathe the Christian spirit. Thus not a single verse composed by an Arab religious has survived from the pre-Islamic period, although some important Christian sentiments composed by Arab women have survived, and are datable to the sixth century.[156] But the Islamic period has preserved a precious poetic fragment—the voice of an Arab religious who spoke from inside the monastery. In view of its uniqueness and because it returns the discussion to ʿUḏra and ʿUḏrite love, it deserves a detailed analysis.

3. In one of his entries, the judicious and reliable Yāqūt, the author of the invaluable geographical dictionary *Muʿjam al-Buldān*, speaks of Dayr Buṣrā, the monastery of Bostra, the former capital of the Provincia Arabia. Yāqūt recounts that in Islamic times al-Māzinī entered Dayr Buṣrā, and was impressed by the eloquence of its monks, who were Arabs from the group Banū al-Ṣādir. Al-Māzinī expressed his surprise that they did not compose Arabic poetry in spite of their eloquence in Arabic. They replied that the only one who composed Arabic poetry was an old *amat*, servant or nun. When they brought her to al-Māzinī, he asked her to recite some poetry, and she recited a love lyric of her own composition.[157] Yāqūt's account may be analyzed as follows:

a. The Arab monks are described as being from Banū al-Ṣādir. Al-Ṣādir, is a well-known toponym in Ḥijāz in the country of ʿUḏra. Burqat Ṣādir is a toponym referred to by al-Nābigha, the court poet of the Ghassānid *foederati* in the sixth century, who mentions it in one of his poems describing the campaign of the Ghassānid king al-Nuʿmān against Banū Ḥunn/Ḥann of the ʿUḏra tribe.[158] Modern topographical and toponymical studies in Ḥijāz have confirmed the existence of Ṣādir until the present day, a mountain on the road to Medina, exactly where the Nābigha's poem suggests it was.[159] Thus Banū

[155] Cf. Hind the Younger, the Lakhmid princess, who after a vow that involved her father, al-Nuʿmān, dedicated herself to a monastic life in the monastery which she built; ibid., 541.

[156] See the speech of the Najrānite noblewoman, Ruhayma, in Shahîd, *Martyrs,* 57–59.

[157] For this account, see Yāqūt, *Muʿjam,* II, 500–1. Yāqūt adds that this is the monastery in which Baḥīra was an inmate, the monk who had an encounter with the Prophet Muḥammad before the latter's prophetic call.

[158] For this toponym, see Ahlwardt, *Divans,* 15, line 12.

[159] M. Bulayhid, *Ṣaḥīḥ al-Akhbār* (Riyad, 1972), vol. II, p. 33.

al-Ṣādir, in the account of Yāqūt, is a group that belonged to ʿUḏra, and so, in later Islamic times, the ʿUḏra had among its members Arab monks.[160] This could not have happened only in Islamic times, and it is, therefore, certain that some members of the tribe became monks in pre-Islamic times. How they appear in Bostra in the Islamic period is clear, since Ḥijāz became the Muslim Holy Land after the rise of Islam and, naturally, Christian Arabs who wanted to practice their asceticism found it convenient to emigrate to Bilād al-Shām. Thus Yāqūt's account of Dayr Buṣrā establishes the important link between ʿUḏra and the Christian ideal of asceticism, and considerably fortifies the conclusion reached in the preceding discussion on the Christian origin of ʿUḏrite love and poetry.

b. These particular monks whom al-Māzinī found at Dayr Buṣrā apparently did not compose poetry, in spite of their literary talents. But the *amat* in the *dayr* did and recited a lyric of five verses in the *ṭawīl* meter. The lyric is an attractive one, in which she bids farewell to a party departing from the *dayr* to Najd. She implores the party to transmit her longing to Najd and assures either them or someone in Najd of her love, finally expressing a desire to be in that Arcadia of Arabic poetry—Najd[161]—to see its vegetation and breathe its salubrious wind.

Both the account and the short lyric present some ambiguities. It is not clear whether the *amat* was a servant or a nun. As an Arabic term it means servant or servitor, but it also had a religious connotation, the "maid-servant of Christ," and so it is used by the Lakhmid Queen Hind in her famous inscription at Ḥīra—*amat al-Masīḥ*.[162] The use of the prepositional phrase *lanā* after *amat* in the Arabic text could suggest that she was a servitor, most probably an Arab woman who, as an act of piety, wanted to serve and minister to the needs of the monks in the monastery. She could also have been from the tribe of ʿUḏra or from some other tribe.

This short love lyric is important as the sole surviving document of what might be termed Arabic conventual poetry, that is, poetry written by members of the Arabic monastic establishment in classical Arabic times. When the *amat*-poetess recited these verses she was, according to Yāqūt, very old, and the presumption is that she had written poetry before she reached that ripe old age. What is relevant in this context is the tone and quality of this love poetry—chaste, disconsolate, and pure—the stuff of which ʿUḏrite poetry is made.[163] This anonymous *amat* of Dayr Buṣrā thus emerges in Islamic times

[160] Confirmed by the verse addressed to the ʿUḏrite poet Jamīl about monks in Wādī al-Qurā in Islamic times, analyzed above, 359.

[161] Najd is most probably used conventionally and traditionally in this verse.

[162] See Yāqūt, *Muʿjam,* II, 542.

[163] The composer is the nearest approximation in Arab monastic life to the Abbess of the Paraclete. But while Heloise' lover is known, that of the *amat* of Dayr Buṣrā remains anonymous.

as the sole female voice of the Arab monastic establishment who gave a poetic expression to the union of the Christian and the Arab ideals, just as another anonymous Arab woman, the Salīḥid princess of the fifth century, was the only female Arab poetic voice associated with Christianity in pre-Islamic times.

Appendix I

Recent Research on the Problem of a Pre-Islamic Arabic Bible

Just before the completion of the manuscript of this volume, an important article on the problem of an Arabic pre-Islamic Gospel appeared,[1] written by Sidney Griffith. As its title indicates, its main concern is the appearance of the Arabic Gospel in the first Abbāsid century, but it has material on the problem in pre-Islamic times, and consequently it is necessary to notice it briefly here.

1. The article represents an advance on the traditional treatment of the problem. As it appeared after the publication of *The Martyrs of Najrān,* it gives attention to the examination of the problem in Najrān, the third center of Arab Christianity to which *Martyrs* has drawn attention as an important center,[2] possibly more important than the others because the Arabs of that region spoke no Syriac or Greek; according to some, knowledge of these languages would have made a translation of biblical and liturgical works into Arabic unnecessary.

2. The article also appeared before my *Rome and the Arabs* and *Byzantium and the Arabs in the Fourth Century.* Hence the new material on the problem, especially in the second volume, was not utilized in the article. In spite of this, the author's conclusions are well worded, keeping the problem *sub judice* until the completion of the three volumes in this series.[3]

3. Although the article mainly addresses the Gospel in Abbāsid times, it also treats it in the pre-Islamic period, but in areas that are not the concern of this book: references in the *Sīra* (Biography of Muḥammad) to the Gospel and to Waraqa ibn Nawfal, the relative of Khadija, Muḥammad's wife.[4] The treatment is competent, but it falls outside the purview of this volume. It will be dealt with either in *BASIC* or in the first volume of the third part of this trilogy, "Byzantium and Islam."

4. More relevant to the concern of this volume is his reply to Baumstark's views on the Gospel in pre-Islamic times. Baumstark had argued that the Arabic versions of the Gospel, in two manuscripts—Vatican Borgia Arabic MS 95 and Berlin Or., Oct. MS 1108—probably go back to pre-Islamic times: more specifically, they were prepared in the sixth century in the environs of Ḥīra. Griffiths has now argued that this is not the case, and that these versions were made in Islamic times.[5]

As has been mentioned earlier in this chapter, Baumstark's approach[6] is different

[1] See S. Griffith, "The Gospel in Arabic: An Enquiry into Its Appearance in the First Abbasid Century," *OC* 69 (1985), 126–67.

[2] Ibid., 157–58.

[3] Ibid., 159. The author is aware of the imminent publication of the three volumes.

[4] Ibid., 137–49.

[5] Ibid., 153–57.

[6] Trimingham's views on the problem of a pre-Islamic Arabic Bible and liturgy appear in

from that of the present writer. Not that the quest for a lost Arabic pre-Islamic Gospel in versions of the Islamic period is illegitimate; it is indeed not and should receive attention, as it has in Father Griffith's work. The alternative approach, complementary to Baumstark's, is more profitable. It extends the search for the Arabic Gospel from two to three centers of Arab Christianity by the inclusion of the Najrān area in South Arabia, which may turn out to be the crucial one, and has chosen to treat the problem regionally and diachronically in each of the three regions of Arab Christianity—Byzantine Oriens, Persian Mesopotamia, and Ḥimyarite South Arabia. When Baumstark wrote, it was not possible to adopt this approach since these three centuries in the history of the Arabs and Arab Christianity were little known and researched. The three volumes in this series are intended to illuminate this period and thus enable the problem to be discussed along new lines.

Appendix II

Two Pre-Islamic Arabic Covenants

Reference has been made in this chapter to the texts of treaties between Arab tribes which go back to the fifth century, and it is proposed in this appendix to discuss them. They are the covenant between the Meccan ʿAbd al-Muṭṭalib and the tribe of Khuzāʿa and the covenant struck between the South Arabian tribe of Qaḥṭān and the central and northeastern Arabian tribal group of Rabīʿa.

A

Around 500 or shortly after, the grandfather of the Prophet Muḥammad, ʿAbd al-Muṭṭalib, concluded an alliance with Kuzāʿa and some other tribes, and the text of this alliance has survived. It is a good example of the inter-Arab *foedera* which must have been concluded among the federate tribes in Oriens, but which have not survived. The Meccan covenant gives an idea of the language, the style, and the oaths employed in such treaties. It has been recently examined by R. B. Serjeant, who rightly concluded that "its general tenor, language and circumstances furnish no cause to believe that it is not basically authentic." Serjeant's English version follows as an example of the language and the style of these treaties:

> In your name, o God. This is that upon which ʿAbd al-Muṭṭalib and the chiefs of Banū ʿAmr of Khuzāʿah, along with those of them of Aslam and Mālik, contracted a mutual alliance. They contracted an alliance for mutual support and partnership—a pact that unites, not one which dissolves [*ḥilf jāmiʿ ghayr mufarriq*, an alliance]. The shaykhs [chiefs] are responsible for the shaykhs, and

a very general book on Arab Christianity in the first six Christian centuries and on the Arab area in its entirety. Hence it is a useful but popular book, addressed to the general public, and cannot be cited in the same manner as the work of Baumstark, who addressed himself to this problem seriously and wrote important articles on it based on detailed and basic research. However, it deserves to be noticed in this connection, and Griffith has done so (ibid., 159). For a review of Trimingham's book, *Christianity among the Arabs in Pre-Islamic Times,* see I. Shahîd in *JSS* 26 (1981), 150–53.

the lesser men for the lesser. He who is present stands responsible for him who is absent. They contracted and covenanted together for as long as the sun rises over (Mount) Thabīr, as long as camels cry yearning in a desert, as long as the two Akhshabān (mountains) stand, and as long as a man performs the lesser pilgrimage to Mecca, an alliance for time without end, for all time, which sunrise will further confirm, and night-darkness add to its terms. ʿAbd al-Muṭṭalib b. Hāshim and the men of Banūʿ Amr have ratified it and become a single hand, as apart from Banū'l-Naḍr [all Quaraysh are Banū'l-Naḍr] against any pursuer of vengeance by land or sea, mountain or plain. Banū ʿAmr owe support to ʿAbd al-Muṭṭalib and his sons against all the Arabs of east or west, rugged highland or smooth flat plain. They make God guarantor for this, and God suffices as surety.[1]

B

The treaty between Qaḥṭān and Rabīʿa is more important and relevant, because it purports to have been concluded in the fifth century.[2] The discussion of Arabic prose in Oriens in that century and especially the *foedera,* both Arab-Byzantine and inter-Arab, provides a suitable context for the examination of the authenticity of this important treaty. Its text is the only one of its kind that has survived from the fifth century, although emanating from a region other than Oriens.

The text of this treaty has been under a cloud, mainly for two reasons. (1) Early in this century, the prevailing view was that Arabia, with the exception of Yaman, was mainly illiterate and so were the pastoralists who roamed it, such as Qaḥṭān and Rabīʿa. Thus these two tribal groups could not have been involved in a treaty that resulted in a written text such as the one preserved in Dīnawarī. (2) The status of the *fuṣḥa,* the standard literary classical Arabic in pre-Islamic times, has been controversial, involving such problems as the relation of the tribal dialects to the literary *koinē* and the time this literary *koinē* appeared as the linguistic medium of pre-Islamic poetry. Thus it was not clear at all whether the language of this covenant could have been the standard literary language of fifth-century Arabic.

Epigraphic discoveries in Arabia and in Oriens have provided answers to both questions. The South Arabian tribes were not illiterate. The exciting discoveries at al-Fāw[3] have proved beyond any shred of doubt that the South Arabian tribe of Kinda did employ the art of writing long before the rise of Islam and, what is more, that it employed not the Sabaic or the Ḥimyaritic language of the South but Arabic. It used the Sabaic *musnad* as its script.[4] Thus the survival of a text from the fifth century

[1] For the text of the treaty, see Ibn Ḥabīb, *Al-Munammaq,* 90–91. For Serjeant's view and the English version of the text, see his section entitled "Pacts and Treaties in pre-Islamic Arabia," in *CHAL,* I, 129–30.

[2] For the text of this treaty, see Abū Ḥanīfa al-Dīnawarī, *Al-Akhbār al-Ṭiwāl,* 353–54.

[3] For an example of an Arabic inscription found at al-Fāw, see A. F. L. Beeston, "Namāra and Faw," *BSOAS,* 42 (1979), 1–3. These discoveries were made by Dr. ʿAbd al-Rahmān al-Anṣāri of the King Saud University in Riyad. Beeston's text is more available and accessible to the European and American reader.

[4] This is also clear from the letter which the Najrānites, around 520, addressed to their

should not be greeted with incredulity,[5] since the tribes of that region had actually been using written Arabic for a considerable time before the fifth century. As to the language of the text, the Namāra inscription offers the answer, perhaps more clearly and decisively than the Fāw inscriptions. This is a long inscription conceived in Arabic, and its language is recognizably and resoundingly classical Arabic. This is an inscription of the early first half of the fourth century. If it had belonged to the sixth or the seventh, it would have been difficult to argue from it to that of the text of Qaḥṭān and Rabīʿa, because it would not have been evidence for ascertaining what written Arabic, the standard *fuṣḥa,* sounded like before the fifth century. But since the Namāra inscription *antedates* the text of the Qaḥṭān/Rabīʿa text, there should be no difficulty at all about accepting the authenticity of this text, at least as far as its language is concerned; if its authenticity is to be rejected, it will have to be on grounds other than language. Thus the Arabs of those regions did use written documents for the expression of their covenants, and did conceive these texts in Arabic, and this Arabic was the same *fuṣḥa* that had been in use at least since the fourth century. The facts do not necessarily make the text authentic, but they do make it highly probable that it is so. However, the internal evidence of the text, such as the employment of certain rites to solemnize the transaction and the precious reference to the Ḥimyarite king Malkīkarib,[6] all give the text the stamp of authenticity. Furthermore, it derives added support from the covenant discussed above, between ʿAbd al-Muṭṭalib and Khuzāʿa, which has been declared authentic by R. B. Serjeant; this one was written not long after the Qaḥṭān/Rabīʿa covenant, and so does not stand entirely isolated.

The juxtaposition of the texts of the three documents—Namāra, ʿAbd al-Muṭṭalib/Khuzāʿa, and Qaḥṭān/Rabīʿa—is eloquent testimony to the linguistic uniformity of the Arabic literary *koinē* in pre-Islamic times, the three texts lying as they do so far from one another in the Arab area.[7] This uniformity is rather surprising and may be added to other surprises, such as Nöldeke expressed concerning the cultural life of the Arabs in pre-Islamic times, especially in view of the vast area they inhabited and the distances that separated various tribal groups from one another.[8]

Appendix III

Iyād and ʿUḏra in Europe

For students of European literature, the subsequent fortunes of one of these Arab federate tribes in Byzantine Oriens—Iyād—and the achievement of another—ʿUḏrite love—are not without interest.

---

co-religionists in Oriens; see Shahîd, *Martyrs,* 40, 242–50. The arguments presented there on the employment of Arabic expressed through the Sabaic script have been confirmed by the epigraphic discoveries at al-Fāw.

[5] See D. S. Margoliouth, *Lectures on Arabic Historians* (New York, 1930; rpr. 1962), 23–24.

[6] This is definitely a Ḥimyarite king of the 5th century, although his exact dates are disputed.

[7] On the language of the Namāra inscription as *fuṣḥa,* classical Arabic, see Shahîd, "Composition of Arabic Poetry," 88–89.

[8] See Nöldeke's article "Arabs," *Encyclopaedia of Religion and Ethics,* ed. J. Hastings (New

Iyād

Some of the "relatives" of ʿAbd al-ʿĀṣ, the poet laureate of the Salīḥid king Dāwūd, came to Spain after the Arab Conquest of the Iberian Peninsula, and settled in Játiva in eastern Spain in the tenth century. Represented by a subdivision within Iyād, the Zuhrids,[1] they distinguished themselves in the private and public life of Muslim Spain. Through these Zuhrids, the Iyād became known to the European medieval Occident.

The Zuhrids (Banū Zuhr) were a remarkable family of four generations of scholars, physicians, and viziers. Medieval Europe knew them mainly as physicians and by their Latin names. Thus Abū al-ʿAlāʾ Zuhr appears as Aboali or Abulelizor; Abū Marwān ibn Zuhr appears as Abhomeron Avenzoar.

One of them, Abū Bakr (d. 1198–99), the son of the famous physician Avenzoar, was possessed of an astounding versatility, which ranged over medicine, Koranic and legal studies, archery, and chess. Most relevantly, he was an outstanding poet of the new style which was in vogue in Andalusia, the strophic, and composed one of the most inspired of these *muwashshaḥāt* in the entire history of Arabic Andalusian poetry. This is especially important in view of the lively interest that Romance philologists have taken in the question of the possible influence of this Arabic Andalusian on Romance literature. Such scholars as J. Ribera y Tarragó and R. Menéndez Pidal have advanced what is called the "Arab thesis," arguing for the reality of this influence.[2]

ʿUḏra

ʿUḏrite love poetry naturally became known in Arab Muslim Andalusia, and is supposed to have inspired the *amour courtois* of the Christian Middle Ages. This Appendix, however, is restricted to the specific references to ʿUḏra in French and German literature.

1. One of the poets of ʿUḏra was the famous ʿUrwa ibn Ḥizām, who lived in the first half of the seventh century. His love for his cousin ʿAfrāʾ became one of the famous legends of medieval Arabic literature and made him one of the love martyrs of that literature. The Old French *Roman de Floire et Blanchflor* is based on an episode of the legend that grew about ʿUrwa and ʿAfrāʾ[3]

York, 1928), I, 668. On that page he discusses the institution of the Sacred Months, the establishment of which in pre-Islamic Arabia he considers a "profound mystery," especially as it prevailed among pastoralists who were "widely dispersed."

[1] A good, succinct account of the Zuhrids may be found in R. Arnaldez' article in *EI²*, s.v. Ibn Zuhr.

[2] For this discussion on influences and for the counter-thesis of S. M. Stern and others, see F. Gabrieli, "Islam in the Mediterranean World," in *The Legacy of Islam,* ed. J. Schacht and C. E. Bosworth, 2nd ed. (Oxford, 1974), 94–96; and F. Rosenthal, "Literature," ibid., 340–41.

[3] R. Blachère, *Histoire de la littérature arabe,* II, 303. Its relation to another Old French work was noted by H. A. R. Gibb who wrote, "the Arabic inspiration demonstrated for the Old French romance of *Floire et Blanchefleur* is the more significant because of its relationship with the lovely *Aucassin et Nicolette,* which itself bears unmistakable witness to its Spanish-Arabic provenance in the Arabic name of the hero (al-Qāsim) and in several details of the setting." See his article "Literature," in *The Legacy of Islam,* ed. T. Arnold and A. Guillaume (London, 1931), 193.

2. Stendhal devoted chapter 53 of his *De l'amour* to Arabia and discusses ʿUḏrite love, which seems to have fascinated him.[4]

> Ce Djamil et Bothaina, sa maîtresse, appartenaient tous les deux aux Benou-Azra, qui sont une tribu célèbre en amour parmi toutes les tribus des Arabes. —Aussi, leur manière d'aimer a-t-elle passé en proverbe; et Dieu n'a point fait de créatures aussi tendres qu'eux en amour.
>
> Sahid, fils d'Agba, demanda un jour à un Arabe: De quel peuple es-tu?—Je suis du peuple chez lequel on meurt quand on aime, répondit l'Arabe.—Tu es donc de la tribu de Azra, ajouta Sahid? Oui, par le maître de la Caaba, répliqua l'Arabe.—D'où vient donc que vous aimez de la sorte? demanda ensuite Sahid.—Nos femmes sont belles et nos jeunes gens sont chastes, répondit l'Arabe.
>
> Quelqu'un demanda un jour à Arouâ-Ben-Hezam: Est-il donc bien vrai, comme on le dit de vous, que vous êtes de tous les hommes ceux qui avez le coeur le plus tendre en amour?—Oui, par Dieu, cela est vrai, répondit Arouâ, et j'ai connu dans ma tribu trente jeunes gens que la mort a enlevés, et qui n'avaient d'autre maladie que l'amour.
>
> Un Arabe des Benou-Fazârat dit un jour à un autre Arabe des Benou-Azra: Vous autres, Benou-Azra, vous pensez que mourir d'amour est une douce et noble mort; mais c'est là une faiblesse manifeste et une stupidité; et ceux que vous prenez pour des hommes de grand coeur ne sont que des insensés et de molles créatures. Tu ne parlerais pas ainsi, lui répondit l'Arabe de la tribu de Azra, si tu avais vu les grands yeux noirs de nos femmes voilés par-dessus de leurs longs sourcils, et décochant des flèches par-dessous; si tu les avais vues sourire, et leurs dents briller entre leur lèvres brunes.

3. In Heine's *Romanzero* (1851) appeared his famous lyric "Der Asra," clearly based on what Stendhal had said on ʿUḏra and its poet-lovers in *De l'amour*. Probably most European readers know ʿUḏra and its ʿUḏrite love from Heine's lyric, with its famous final verse describing these lovers.[5]

Der Asra

Täglich ging die wunderschöne
Sultanstochter auf und nieder
Um die Abendzeit am Springbrunn,
Wo die weißen Wasser plätschern.

Täglich stand der junge Sklave
Um die Abendzeit am Springbrunn,

[4] See *De l'Amour,* ed. H. Marineau (Paris, 1959), 195–96.

[5] This verse is a translation from the Arabic. I am grateful to my colleague, Prof. Richard Rogan for bibliographical orientation on Heine while I was examining his "Der Asra" and its inspiration.

Wo die weißen Wasser plätschern;
Täglich ward er bleich und bleicher.

Eines Abends trat die Fürstin
Auf ihn zu mit raschen Worten:
"Deinen Namen will ich wissen,
Deine Heimat, deine Sippschaft!"

Und der Sklave sprach: Ich heiße
Mohamet, ich bin aus Yemmen,
Und mein Stamm sind jene Asra,
Welche sterben, wenn sie lieben.

4. Those who are guiltless of Arabic and care to read specimens of this ʿUḏrite poetry in a European language will find the following fragments felicitously turned into Italian by Francesco Gabrieli.[6] They are taken from the *dīwān* of Jamīl, the principal ʿUḏrite poet of the seventh century.

Lo spirito mio si è avvinto al suo prima che fossimo creati, e dopo
che fummo gocce maturanti alla vita, e nella culla.
Crebbe come noi crescemmo, e vigoreggiò gagliardo, né, quando
morremo, romperà fede al patto giurato,
ma sopravviverà in ogni ulteriore stato, e ci visiterà nella tenebra
della tomba el del sepolcro.

Vento del settentrione, non mi vedi tu vaneggiante d'amore e visibilmente stremato?
Donami un soffio dell'aura di Bathna, e fai grazia di spirare sopra
Giamìl;
e di' a lei: "Piccola Bathna, basta all'anima mia poco di te, o piú
ancora del poco."

Giuro che non ti scorderò sinché brillerà un raggio di sole ad oriente,
sinché un miraggio ingannerà nello sconfinato deserto.
Sino a che rilucerà una stella sospesa nel cielo, e foglieranno i rami
degli arbusti del loto. . .

S'è levato il ferale nunzio, e chiaro ha proclamato il nome di Giamìl,
che è rimasto in Egitto, d'una permanenza senza ritorno. . .
Ci fu un giorno che io traevo il mantello in Wadi l-Qura, ebbro,
tra seminati e palmeti.
Sorgi Buthaina, e leva ululando un grido, e piangi l'amico tuo piú
d'ogni altro amico!

[6] See his *Storia della letteratura araba,* 132–33.

Appendix IV

Christianity and Pre-Islamic Arabic Literature: Further Reflections

The question was raised in the section on religious poetry[1] of whether it was possible for Christianity to have been widely spread among the pre-Islamic Arabs, especially those in the shadow of Byzantium, without its leaving some important traces on Arabic literature or even giving rise to a modest corpus of what is generally understood by Christian literature.

1. As observed earlier, the Bible apparently did influence authors in the medieval Muslim period, and indeed gave rise to a new genre, that of soliloquies and religious invocations in the style of the Psalms.[2]

2. Christianity has had a more palpable effect on the course of modern Arabic literature. The Arabo-American school of writers in the first half of this century exercised an immense influence on Arabic literature in the homeland and, as has been noted by the critic-poetess S. Jayyūsī, "this must be seen as a major contribution of the Christian literary tradition in Arabic literature."[3]

3. Is it possible then that of the three periods in the history of the Arabs—the pre-Islamic, the medieval Islamic, and the modern—it was only during the first that Christianity failed to produce a Christian literature? This is difficult to believe, especially as Christianity was widely spread among the pre-Islamic Arabs, and so was not an alien religion.[4] If Christianity possessed their soul, it is quite likely that it also touched their literary sensibilities. The fact that this presumed Christian literature has not survived is not a cogent argument against its existence in pre-Islamic times, since conditions for its preservation were not favorable. The martyrdoms of Najrān around 520 are illuminating in this context. Many Arabs in the South died for their faith, and their martyrdoms convulsed the Arab area in the Peninsula and the Fertile Crescent. This must have had a literary expression among the people who were then composing poetry in such abundance and to whom the genre of elegy and threnody was well known.[5] Yet hardly anything has survived to suggest that Arabic literary expression; thus non-survival cannot argue for previous non-existence.

It is not suggested here that there was a vast corpus of Christian Arabic literature

[1] See above, Sec. III.

[2] This development was also discussed in Sec. III.

[3] S. K. Jayyūsī, *Trends and Movements in Modern Arabic Poetry* (Leiden, 1977), I, 92.

[4] Even an alien religion exercises an immense influence on literatures nursed in other religious traditions. Islamic literature, translated in medieval Spain under the guidance of Alfonso el Sabio (1252–1284), exercised great influence on Spanish and other Romance literatures; see F. Gabrieli, in "Islam in the Mediterranean World," 93–94. See also the imaginative article in which the movement of translations from Arabic Islamic literature in Spain contributed, in the opinion of some, to a 12th-century renaissance; see H. and R. Kahane in "Humanistic Linguistics," *Journal of Aesthetic Education* 17 (1983), 67. This, of course, involved a translation movement, not just religious influence. But it raises the question of an Arabic Bible and liturgy in pre-Islamic times, which, if they existed, would have had great influence on Arabic literature. For this related problem, see above, Chap. 14, sec. III.

[5] Especially as some literary documents from the pen of non-Arabs have survived on these martyrs. If these Arab martyrdoms touched non-Arabs and caused them to compose, is it possible that the Arabs themselves did not do the same? See Shahîd, *Martyrs*.

in pre-Islamic times,[6] but it is inconceivable that the people who were so passionately devoted to the new faith, at least in certain parts of the Arab area such as Oriens, Ḥīra, and Najrān, would not have indulged in some literary expression reflective of their attachment. This is especially inconceivable because the Arabs perfected the art of the spoken word, their *forte* in pre-Islamic times. For obvious anthropological reasons, the pastoralists among them expressed their talents almost exclusively in the linguistic medium.

The literatures of the various peoples in Oriens Christianus came into existence in the wake of a Bible translation. In the case of the Arab sector, the problem of an Arabic Bible in pre-Islamic times is still *sub judice*; hence the discussion of a Christian Arabic literature related to a Bible translation has to be postponed until that problem is solved.[7] But the Christian faith in its various manifestations, not only its Scripture, can inspire literary artists. In the case of the Arabs, this has been suggested in connection with events of great magnitude inspired by devotion to Christianity, namely, the martyrdoms at Najrān around 520.

Appendix V
Al-Māzinī

The uniqueness of the poetic fragment associated with Dayr Buṣrā, analyzed in the preceding section on Arabic literature, makes it necessary to examine the identity of the one who was responsible for its preservation in Yāqūt's *Muʿjam,* namely, al-Māzinī, and also the circumstances that attended his visit to Dayr Buṣrā.

Of the various personalities in Islamic times who carried the name al-Māzinī, only two can be entertained in this context, the Basran philologist of the ninth century (d. 863), Bakr ibn Muḥammad, and the twelfth-century Andalusian geographer from Granada, Muḥammad ibn ʿAbd al-Rahīm,[1] who traveled to the East, resided in Baghdad, and died in Damascus in 1170.

There is no indication that the Andalusian was known to Yāqūt, since he does not figure in such works as *Irshād al-Arīb*; moreover, he wrote mostly on the marvels of the Maghrib, the Islamic Occident whence he came.[2] The ninth-century philologist, on the other hand, was well known to Yāqūt, who devoted a long chapter to him in his *Irshād.*[3] Moreover, in his introduction to his geographical dictionary, *Muʿjam al-Buldān,* Yāqūt specifies that his sources for the Arabic toponyms were *ahl*

[6] The proponent of this thesis in its extreme form was the indefatigable L. Cheikho. For his work and a position critical of it, see C. Hechaïmé, *Louis Cheikho et son livre "Le christianisme et la littérature chrétienne en Arabie avant l'Islam"* (Beirut, 1967).

[7] Perhaps the publication of *BASIC*, or possibly the first volume of *Byzantium and Islam,* will see my final statement on this problem.

[1] See S. al-Ṣafadi, *Al-Wāfī bi al-Wafayāt,* ed. S. Dedering (Wiesbaden, 1974), III, 245–46.

[2] See his *Tuḥfat al-Albāb* published by G. Ferrand in *Journal Asiatique* 207 (1925), 1–148, 193–304. He has a few entries on some localities in Bilād al-Shām, such as Baalbak, Tadmur, Ḥims, and al-Lajā, but nothing on Buṣrā; ibid., 78–79.

[3] See *Irshad al-Arīb* (Beirut, 1980), VII, 107–28.

al-adab (philologists and literati), and lists about thirteen of them.[4] Finally, from the internal evidence of the passage in Yāqūt which describes Dayr Buṣra and al-Māzinī's visit, it is clear that the questions addressed by al-Māzini to the monks of the monastery were not those of a geographer, but those of a philologist such as the ninth-century al-Māzinī, who is also known to have composed books on poetry such as *al-ʿArūḍ* and *al-Qawāfi*.[5]

It is not entirely clear what brought al-Māzinī from Iraq to Bilād al-Shām and specifically to Dayr Buṣra. Yāqūt in his *Irshād* says nothing about his wanderings to Bilād al-Shām, but does mention that he moved in the circle of the Abbāsid caliph Al-Mutawakkil.[6] Now this Abbāsid caliph is known to have moved his residence to Damascus for two months,[7] May-June in 858, and so it is possible that al-Māzinī followed him thither. If this was the occasion of his journey to Syria, then his visit to Dayr Buṣra may be pinpointed as having taken place in the year 858.

A last question arises in this connection: what induced a Muslim scholar from Basra to visit a Christian establishment, such as the monastery of Bostra? The question admits of the following interpretations. (*a*) The intelligence and originality[8] of al-Māzinī as a philologist appear clearly in Yāqūt's chapter on him, and it is just possible that he may have wanted to examine the *ʿarabiyya,* the Arabic language, as spoken and used by an Arab but non-Muslim community in Bilād al-Shām.[9] (*b*) Al-Māzinī belonged to the tribe of Bakr, a well-known Christian tribe in pre-Islamic times. Although it converted to Islam early, unlike the sister tribe Taghlīb, some of its members remained Christian. It is therefore possible that the Bakrite al-Māzinī was curious about the Arabic spoken by those who shared the religious persuasion of his tribe, Bakr, in Islamic times. (*c*) The most convincing explanation, however, must be that Dayr Buṣrā was the very same *dayr* at which, according to Muslim authors, the Prophet Muḥammad is said to have met the Christian monk Baḥīra before his prophetic call. As al-Māzinī found himself not far from Buṣrā, he could very well have developed a desire to visit the famous *dayr,* hallowed in the Muslim mind by association with the Prophet Muḥammad.

The precious poetic fragment preserved by Yāqūt and made possible by al-Māzinī's visit to Dayr Buṣra thus goes back to the middle of the ninth century. This raises the question of whether or not the inmates of the monastery had always been Arabs from the tribe of ʿUḏra and, what is more important, the tantalizing question about the ethnic identity of Baḥīra, the mysterious monk whom Muḥammad met at the *dayr.*[10]

[4] See the introduction to the *Muʿjam,* I, 11.

[5] See *Irshad,* 122.

[6] Ibid., 119.

[7] See Ṭabarī, *Tārīkh,* IX, 210.

[8] See also the first footnote in the chapter on al-Māzinī in *Irshad* (p. 107).

[9] He must also have been familiar with Arabic poetry on monasteries, which is almost a genre in medieval Arabic poetry, and this may also have led him to enter one of these religious establishments. The account which tells of his reaction to teaching a non-Muslim *dhimmi* (presumably a Christian Arab) the *Book of Sībawayh, al-Kitāb,* is relevant material in this connection; see ibid.

[10] But the Arabic sources associate Baḥīra with two other *dayrs,* Dayr al-Bāʿiqī and Dayr Najrān.

PART THREE
FRONTIER AND FEDERATE STUDIES

One of the main concerns of this series on Byzantium and the Arabs before the rise of Islam is the study of the Arab federate presence along the *limes orientalis*, both for its own sake and as a contribution to Roman frontier studies. The sections on the Arab *foederati* in this volume may then be described as a study of the Arab component in the making of the *limes orientalis*. The facts of this component are not to be found in the Greek and Latin sources for the *limes* but in the Arabic, and they are an indispensable complement to what such documents as the *Notitia Dignitatum* provide. The significance of this Arab component in frontier studies is not entirely unclear to students of the sixth century, when the Ghassānid *foederati* took over the defense of a large portion of the *limes orientalis* around 530. But its significance to students of the fifth century is obscure; hence the relevant chapters in this volume which elucidate this component.

It is proposed in this part of the present volume to examine roughly the same problems as were treated in the corresponding part in *BAFOC*[1] as they developed in the fifth century, which witnessed the rise of a new dominant Arab federate group, the Salīḥids.

I. *NOTITIA DIGNITATUM*

The most important document is the *Notitia Dignitatum*.[2] The Arab units in this document were studied in *Rome and the Arabs*, since it is agreed that the

[1] See *BAFOC*, 465–98.

[2] On the *ND*, see G. Clemente, *La "Notitia Dignitatum,"* Saggi di storia e letteratura 4 (Cagliari, 1968). See also the discussion of the *ND* in A. H. M. Jones, *LRE*, II, 1417–50, *"Notitia Dignitatum,"* *RE* 17 (1939), cols. 1077–1116. For further bibliography, see Clemente, op. cit., 385–97; also *RA*, 27 note 24.

On the army of the later Roman Empire, the standard work is still R. Grosse, *Römische Militärgeschichte von Gallienus biz zum Beginn der byzantinischen Themenverfassung* (Berlin, 1920) (hereafter, *RM*); for a more recent treatment of the same topic, see *LRE*, I, pp. 607–86; for the army in the 4th century, see D. Hoffmann, *Das spätrömische Bewegungsheer und die* Notitia Dignitatum, Epigraphische Studien 7 (Düsseldorf, 1969–70), 2 vols., with bibliography in vol. II, 227–38; for the 4th and 5th centuries, see *RM*, 221–58, 259–71, and *LRE*, 97–101, 199–204.

general picture it draws of the military dispositions in the Orient goes back to Roman times. But the *ND* belongs to the early part of the *fifth* century. It is therefore imperative for a better understanding of the role of the Arab *foederati* in the history of this century—and the proto-Byzantine period in its entirety—to open this section by reproducing the few pages devoted to this document in *RA*.[3] This will make it possible to note new developments and make further reflections on the Arab federate presence, not only in the fifth century but also in the sixth, which will be discussed in the next volume in this series.

A

The Arab units in the Byzantine frontier army (the *limitanei*) are understandably concentrated not far from the Arabian Peninsula in the Diocese of the Orient and in Egypt.[4] They are not always explicitly referred to as such, and this is one of the problems that the *Notitia* presents. The references to the Arabs fall into the following categories:

1. Some units are clearly referred to by the term *Arab*:
   (*a*) Ala tertia Arabum in *limes Aegypti* (Or. XXVIII.24)
   (*b*) Cohors quinquagenaria Arabum in Mesopotamia (Or. XXXVI.35)
   (*c*) Cohors tertia felix Arabum in Arabia (Or. XXXVII.34)
2. Other units are referred to by the term *Saracen*:
   (*a*) Equites Saraceni indigenae in Phoenicia (Or. XXXII.27)
   (*b*) Equites Saraceni in Phoenicia (Or. XXXII.28)
3. Some units are referred to by their tribal affiliations:
   (*a*) Equites Saraceni Thamudeni[5] in *limes Aegypti* (Or. XXVIII.17)
   (*b*) Cohors secunda Ituraeorum in *limes Aegypti* (Or. XXVIII.44)
   (*c*) Equites Thamudeni Illyriciani in Palestine (Or. XXXIV.22)
4. Some units are related to their city:
   (*a*) Cuneus equitum secundorum clibanariorum Palmirenorum, under the command of the *magister militum per Orientem* (Or. VII.34)
   (*b*) Ala octava Palmyrenorum in the Thebaid (Or. XXXI.49)

The Arab character of other units in the *Notitia* is inferential and ranges from the possible to the probable to the almost certain:

[3] See *RA*, 51–63. The opening paragraph in the chapter on the *ND* has been left out and a few modifications have been made in the footnotes.

[4] About 380–382, Egypt was detached from the Diocese of the Orient and became a separate diocese, its *praefectus* receiving the title *augustalis*.

[5] The most specific reference to an Arab unit in the *ND*, since it mentions both the generic name, *Saraceni*, and the specific tribal one, Thamūdeni.

1. Arab are certain units that are described as *indigenae* ("native"), e.g., those in the province of Arabia (Or. XXXVII.18–20). These can be only Arab, unlike certain units also described as *indigenae*, which are not necessarily Arab.[6]

2. Description of units by function, as (*a*) *Equites* and (*b*) *Sagittarii*, often combined with each other[7] and sometimes with *indigenae*,[8] makes probable the Arab character of some of these units. This probability is based on the association of the horse with Arabia and the Arabs in regions contiguous to the Arabian Peninsula and in areas, *intra limitem*, whose ethnic complexion was Arab. The association can also be extended to the bow, for the use of which the mounted archers of Palmyra were well known.[9] Finally, units described as (*c*) *Dromedarii* may be Arab, since the camel is a distinctly Arabian animal.[10] The unit in Palestine (Or. XXXIV.33) is likely to be Arab, and possibly so those in the Thebaid (Or. XXXI.48, 54, 57).

B

Tactically or functionally, the Arab units in the *Notitia* may be classified as follows:

1. The *Equites*:[11] so are styled in the *Notitia* the *vexillationes*, the higher grade cavalry, e.g., *Equites Saraceni* (Or. XXXII.28). Many of the *Equites* are *promoti*.[12]

2. The units of Equites are quite often also *sagittarii*: they are the mounted archers, e.g., the *Equites sagittarii* (Or. XXXII.24).

3. More complex is the *Cuneus equitum secundorum clibanariorum Palmi-*

[6] For example, those under the command of the *dux* of the Thebaid (Or. XXXI.25–29).

[7] E.g., *Equites sagittarii*, as in Syria (Or. XXXIII.21–22).

[8] E.g., *Equites sagitarii indigenae*, as in Syria (Or. XXXIII.18–20).

[9] For the archers of Palmyra in the service of Rome on the Danube and in the Sahara, see J. Starcky, *Palmyre* (Paris, 1952), 36, 43–52; and Altheim and Stiehl, *Die Araber in der alten Welt* (Berlin, 1964–68), vol. 1, pp. 661–77; the latter includes references to another Arab group as archers, namely, the Ituraeans.

[10] Arab camels and *dromedarii* in the service of Rome are attested. (*a*) A large train of camels loaded with corn accompanied the army of Corbulo from the Euphrates to Armenia (Tacitus, *Annals*, XV.xii); these could only have been Arab camels. (*b*) An *ala* of Palmyrene *dromedarii* are attested in the 2nd century; see Starcky, *Palmyre*, 43, or Starcky, ed., *Inventaire des inscriptions de Palmyre* (Damascus, 1949), X.128. (*c*) The best documentation for Arab *dromedarii* in the service of Rome comes from the papyri for Cohors XX Palmyrenorum (3rd century); see R. O. Fink, *Roman Military Records on Papyrus, Philological Monographs of the American Philological Association* 26 (Cleveland, 1971); see the index, p. 512, under *dromedarii*, the overwhelming majority of whom belonged to Cohors XX Palmyrenorum. Many of the names are recognizably Arab, while the Latin *gentilicia* must have been assumed by these Arab *dromedarii*.

[11] For these, see *RM*, 53–54.

[12] For these, see ibid., 49–50, and H. M. D. Parker, "The Legions of Diocletian and Constantine," *JRS* 23 (1933), 188.

renorum (Or. VII.34). The *cuneus*[13] is the new formation, the wedge, and its members are *clibanarii*,[14] the mailed cavalry, specifically the scale or chain armor cavalry, characteristic of the armies of Zenobia.

4. The lower grade *Alae*[15] of cavalry; they are only a few: two in *limes Aegypti* and the Thebaid (Or. XXVIII.24; XXI.49) and one in Phoenicia, which may have been Arab (Or. XXXII.38).

5. The *Cohortes*[16] of infantry: there are three of them that are definitely Arab: one in *limes Aegypti* (Or. XXVII.44), another in Mesopotamia (Or. XXXVI.35), and yet another in Arabia Or. XXXVII.34).

6. Finally, there is the camel corps, the *Ala dromedariorum*; the one stationed in Palestine is likely to be Arab (Or. XXXIV).

It is clear from an examination of the Arab contingents in the *Notitia* that the overwhelming majority of the Arab tactical units were high-grade cavalry—*Equites*, sometimes *Equites sagittarii*.

C

The extension of *civitas* to provincials by Caracalla in A.D. 212 made of the many Arabs in the Orient Roman citizens, and when these served in the Roman army, they did so as *cives*. The Arab units of the Roman frontier army in the *Notitia* discussed above fall within this category.[17] Whether *cives* of Arab origin were likewise enrolled in the *legiones* stationed in the Diocese of the Orient is not entirely clear.[18]

The employment of the term *Saraceni* to describe some Arab units in the *Notitia* raises a problem. *Saraceni* had become the technical term for the Arab allies of Byzantium in the fourth century, best represented in this century by the auxiliary troops of Queen Mavia.[19] The frequent use of the term *Saraceni*

[13] See *RM*, 51–53.

[14] On these, see J. W. Eadie, "The Development of Roman Mailed Cavalry," *JRS* 57 (1967), 169–73; A. D. H. Bivar, "Cavalry Equipment and Tactics on the Euphrates Frontier," *DOP* 26 (1972), 273–91.

[15] See *RM*, 45–47.

[16] Ibid., 42–45.

[17] On the Arab origin of the *limitanei* in these regions, see R. Dussaud, *La pénétration des Arabes en Syrie avant l'Islam* (Paris, 1907), 157; the whole chapter entitled "Rome et les Arabes," (pp. 147–58) is relevant.

[18] The description of "Legio Tertia Cyrenaica" in *Historia Augusta* ("Severus," 12.6) as *Arabica* must refer to its being stationed in the *Provincia* Arabia and not to its ethnic constitution.

[19] For these see the chapter, "The Reign of Valens," in *BAFOC*, 138–202. *Saraceni* in the 4th century also designated the *Scenitae Arabes* whether or not they were allies of Byzantium with federate status (Ammianus Marcellinus, *RG*, XXII.15.2; XXIII.6.13), thus designating Arabs who were not *cives*. The term *Arabes* then tended to designate those who were not *scenitae* (nomads), whether in the Peninsula, such as the inhabitants of Arabia Felix, or those within the *limes*, the inhabitants of the province of Arabia.

in the fourth century in the works of the ecclesiastical historians[20] coincides with the establishment of a new Arab-Byzantine relationship, reflected in the Namāra inscription of Imru'al-Qays, especially in the part that speaks of the Arab tribes as cavalry in the service of Rome.[21] These were certainly *foederati*. But whether the Saracen units in the *Notitia* were *cives* or *foederati* is difficult to tell. The term was probably used in a purely ethnic sense, following fourth-century usage in referring to the Arabs as *Saraceni*, perhaps indicating that these units had been enrolled more recently[22] than those designated Arab, who had been in the service of Rome before the fourth century.[23]

The extent of the Arab contribution to the Roman army of the fourth and fifth centuries as reflected in the *ND* can be correctly measured only by a study of the Arab units in each province where their presence is attested or presumed or suspected.[24] The major problem is to determine the ethnic

[20] The term *Saraceni* is attested before the 4th century, for which see B. Moritz's article, "Saraka," *RE*, zweite Reihe, I.A., cols. 2387–90. No entirely satisfactory explanation has been given for the etymology of this term. Its vogue in the 4th century, however, may be related to its popularity among the ecclesiastical historians, who conceived of the Arabs as a biblical people descended from Hagar and who, consequently, often referred to them by the newly coined term *Hagarenoi*, descendants of Hagar. It is possible that they conceived of *Saracenoi* as the negative biblical equivalent of *Hagarenoi*, i.e., not descended from Sarah. But as *Saracenoi* had already been established as a term for the Arabs, the ecclesiastical historians found it convenient to use, thus popularizing it in spite of false etymology. For a detailed discussion of the term *Saracenoi*, see *RA*, 123–41.

[21] On this inscription, see Shahîd, "Philological Observations on the Namāra Inscription," *JSS* 24 (1979), 33–42.

[22] "Saracen" as an epithet for a military unit in the Roman army is used in the part on Aurelian in the *Historia Augusta* which speaks of the *Alae Saracenae* (*HA*, "Aurelian," 28.2); Aurelian's *cognomen*, commemorating a victory over the Arabs, was not *Saracenicus* but *Arabicus*, for which, see H. Dessau, *Inscriptiones Latinae Selectae*, 3 vols. (Berlin, 1892–1916), no. 576.

As *foederati*, the Saracens were subordinate to their Arab *phylarchi*, rather than to the Roman *duces*. But these two units appear in *ND* under the command of the *dux* of Phoenicia, and this could imply that they were considered regular units in the Roman army and hence *cives*. On the other hand, they could have been under their own *phylarch*, unmentioned in *ND*, and only *ultimately* subordinate to the *dux* of Phoenicia.

[23] That *Saraceni* is used in an ethnic rather than a federate sense in the *ND* may be supported by the fact that the *Notitia* is a list of units whose members were *cives*, and thus the Arab *foederati* of Byzantium in the 4th and 5th centuries, who are attested elsewhere in the sources, are not likely to have appeared in this document. This dovetails with the fact that the Provincia Arabia was a major center of the *foederati*, and consequently Saracen units with federate status should have been listed for Arabia and not only for Phoenicia in the *ND*. This reasoning is confirmed by the following observation: Namāra had been an important Roman military post in the Provincia Arabia in imperial times, but it is not even listed in the *ND*; it is conspicuous by its absence, as are other posts for this region and for Trachonitis. The most natural explanation is that these inaccessible regions were left to the custody of the Arab *foederati*, who are known to have been established there since the time of Imru'al-Qays (d. 328); see R. Dussaud, *Topographie*, 269, and A. Poidebard, *La trace de Rome dans le désert de Syrie* (Paris 1934), 61–62.

[24] This is especially important because the 5th-century sources on the Arab *foederati* are

character of those units in the Diocese of the Orient described in the *Notitia* as *indigenae* and what possibility there is that they were Arab.

The Arab penetration of the Fertile Crescent in ancient times is a well-known fact.[25] With this as a general background, it is proposed here to discuss the ethnic complexion of the *indigenae* of each province by interlocking it with whatever ethnographic discussions there are in the sources on these provinces. Absolute certainty cannot be predicated of these conclusions, and some of these must remain conjectural. The uncertainty derives from the fact that some of the military stations of these units in some provinces have not been definitely identified; this leaves uncertain whether a particular station was situated in the Arab or non-Arab sector of a particular province, a consideration especially important in provinces with a multiracial complexion, such as Mesopotamia, but not so important in others, such as the province of Arabia.[26] Consequently, there is likely to be a margin of error in the identification of the oriental *indigenae* as Arab; some may turn out to be non-Arab while other units not included as Arab may turn out to be such. For this reason care has been taken to indicate the degree of certainty or uncertainty that attaches to these identifications in order to keep the margin of error very slim or as slim as possible and thus to enable the generalized result on the Arab military presence to be valid.

Magister Militum per Orientem: Or. VII

Under the command of the *magister militum*, there was a Palmyrene cavalry *cuneus*[27] entitled:

Cuneus equitum secundorum clibanariorum Palmirenorum (34)

Limes Aegypti: Or. XXVIII

Under the command of the *comes rei militaris*, three recognizably Arab units are attested:

---

exiguous. The *ND* preserves the contribution of those who were *cives*, the provincial Arabs in the Orient.

[25] For the western half of the Crescent, Syria, see Dussaud, *Pénétration*, and for both halves, see the more recent researches in Altheim and Stieh, *Die Araber in der alten Welt*, I, 139–80, 268–372.

[26] There is no up-to-date commentary on the *ND* with detailed maps for the stations of all the units; Hoffmann's work, *Das spätrömische Bewegungsheer*, has useful maps which show the stations of the legions only. The old edition of Böcking has not entirely outlived its usefulness as a commentary; see E. Böcking, *Notitia Dignitatum*, 3 vols. (Bonn 1839–53). But the student of the *ND* has at his disposal a number of excellent studies on the various provinces and regions of the Orient and these will be laid under contribution.

[27] See *RA*, 54 and note 14: on the *cuneus* in the *ND*, see E. Nischer, "The Army Reforms of Diocletian and Constantine," *JRS* 13 (1923), 29, and also p. 17, where the author infers the existence of another *cuneus* of Palmyrene *clibanarii*, the *cuneus equitum primorum clibanariorum Palmyrenorum*.

1. Equites Saraceni Thamudeni,[28] Scenas Veteranorum (17)
2. Ala tertia Arabum,[29] Thenemuthi (24)
3. Cohors secunda Ituraeorum,[30] Aiy (44)

Thebaid: Or. XXXI

One definitely Arab unit is attested, entitled:

Ala octava Palmyrenorum,[31] Foinicionis (49)

Other units that may have been Arab:[32]

1. Equites sagittarii indigenae, Tentira (25)
2. Equites sagittarii indigenae, Copto (26)
3. Equites sagittarii indigenae, Diospoli (27)
4. Equites sagittarii indigenae, Lato (28)
5. Equites sagittarii indigenae, Maximianopoli (29)
6. Equites promoti indigenae (30)
7. Ala Tertia dromedariorum, Maximianopoli (48)
8. Ala secunda Herculia dromedariorum, Psinaula (54)
9. Ala prima Valeria dromedariorum, Precteos (57)

[28] For this important tribal group, see A. van den Branden, *Histoire de Thamoud* (Beirut, 1966); and Böcking, *ND*, I, 295. The Thamūdeni appear elsewhere in the *ND* assigned to Palestine, but there they are not referred to as *Saraceni* (Or. XXXIV.22). The application of *Saraceni* to the Thamūdeni of Egypt could suggest that they entered the service of Rome more recently than those in Palestine, not described as such. Attractive is the identification of *Tendunias* in John of Nikiou with Thamudenas, suggested in Altheim and Stiehl, *Christentum am Roten Meer* (Berlin, 1971), I, 360 note 28; cf. the Coptic etymology suggested by A. J. Butler, The *Arab Conquest of Egypt* (Oxford, 1920), 217 note 1. See also Altheim and Stiehl, *Christentum*, 368 note 82, on the association of the Arabs and their tent camps with the names of localities and garrison towns in the *ND* that begin with *scenas*, such as Scenas Mandrorum, Scenas extra Gerasa, Scenas Veteranorum. This unit and the other two in the *limes Aegypti* were under the command of the *comes rei militaris*. All the Arab units in the other provinces of the Orient—the Thebaid, Palestine, Arabia, Phoenicia, Syria, Euphratensis, Osroene, and Mesopotamia—were under the command of *duces*.

[29] The use of the term *Arab* rather than *Saracen* could imply that this unit was an old one in the service of Rome. On the unit and its station, see Böcking, *ND*, I, 297–98.

[30] The Ituraeans are a well-known Arab group who served in the Roman army; see note 9, above. Another cohort of Ituraeans is attested in the *ND* for the Occident, under the command of the *comes Tingitanae* (Or. XXVI.16). Both are infantry units. On Ituraea and the Ituraeans, see Böcking, *ND*, I, 309, and II (pars posterior), pp. 540–41; *RE*, 9, cols. 2377–80; Dussaud, *Pénétration*, 176–78; A. H. M. Jones, "The Urbanization of the Ituraean Principality," *JRS* 21 (1931), 265–75.

[31] The presence of this unit in Egypt may go back to the time of Zenobia or to that of Diocletian, who may have transferred it there for his Egyptian campaign.

[32] Arabs lived in Egypt in pre-Islamic times and so these six units of *Equites* could have been Arab, but they could also have been non-Arab, belonging to one or more of the peoples of Upper Egypt and Nubia. The Arabs in Egypt lived in the well-known Arabian nome, halfway between Pelusium and Memphis, across the Nile in Arsinoites (Fayyūm), and in the Thebaid with the Blemmyes between the Nile and the Red Sea. In the 2nd century Marcian of Heraclea speaks of the Arabs between the Nile and the Red Sea and refers to them as Ἀραβαιγύπτιοι; see *Périple de Marcien d'Héraclée* (Paris, 1839), 18. In the 3rd century Dionysius of Alexandria

Phoenicia: Or. XXXII

Two definitely Arab units[33] are:

1. Equites Saraceni indigenae, Betroclus (27)
2. Equites Saraceni, Thelsee (28)

Units that are possibly[34] or likely to have been Arab:

1. Equites promoti indigenae, Saltatha (20)
2. Equites promoti indigenae, Auatha (22)
3. Equites promoti indigenae, Nazala (23)
4. Equites sagittarii indigenae, Abina (24)
5. Equites sagittarii indigenae, Casama (25)
6. Equites sagittarii indigenae, Calamona (26)
7. Equites sagittarii indigenae, Adatha (29)

Syria: Or. XXXIII

Units that are likely to have been Arab:[35]

---

refers to them as Saracens and mentions the Arabian Mountain in his letter to Fabian, Bishop of Antioch, PG 10, col. 1305. For a succinct account of the Arab presence in pre-Islamic Egypt, see Altheim and Stiehl, "Araber in Ägypten," *Lexicon der Ägyptologie*, I, 3, 360–61.

As for the three *alae* of *dromedarii*, these are not described as *indigenae*, and so they must have been brought from elsewhere; in view of the association of the Arabs with camels, the proximity of Arabia, and the presence of Arab troops in Egypt, it is likely that they were Arab. It is of interest to note that as early as A.D. 156 *dromedarii* are attested in the Thebaid; a small detachment of them formed part of Cohors I Augusta praetoria Lusitanorum; for the 19 *dromedarii* in this cohort, one of whom carried the Semitic-sounding name of Barbasatis, see Fink, "Roman Military Records on Papyrus," 232. Mommsen assigns the formation of these three *alae* to the time of Diocletian; see Mommsen, *Gesammelte Schriften* (Berlin, 1913), VIII, 561. Camel breeding by the Arabs of the Arabian nome was famous; see Altheim and Stiehl, "Araber in Ägypten," ibid. See also the entry Ἀραβικός for a reference to the Ἀραβικὸν χάραγμα in F. Preisigke, *Wörterbuch der griechischen Papyrusurkunden* (Berlin, 1931), 269.

[33] These two units of *Equites* are described as *Saraceni*. The first is described as *indigenae*, while the second is not. The difference in description may not have any significance, but it could imply that the second unit was moved to Phoenicia from some other province. Since these units were stationed in Phoenicia, they could have been Palmyrene Arabs who entered the service of Rome after the fall of Palmyra. For the two stations, see A. Musil, *Palmyrena*, 252–53; and Dussaud, *Topographie*, 270.

[34] The seven units of *Equites* described as *indigenae* are likely to be Arab, since the ethnic complexion of this region is Arab; it was in this region that the Arab principalities of Palmyra, Emesa, and Ituraea had flourished, all of which had lent their military service to the Romans. Four of these units were *sagittarii*, and as mounted archers they suggest a former Palmyrene or Ituraean connection. Whether or not the eighth unit, the Ala Prima Foenicum, is Arab is not clear. Its members may have been Aramaicized Arabs who thus were described territorially rather than ethnically, but they could have been non-Arab inhabitants of Phoenicia. On the stations of these units, see Böcking, *ND*, I, 376–84, but more authoritatively, Musil, *Palmyrena*, 252–53, and Dussaud, *Topographie*, 268–71.

[35] What has been said of the Arab complexion of Phoenicia may with equal truth be said of Syria extending to the Euphrates; this Arab complexion would have been enhanced and militarized by the rise of Palmyra in the 3rd century to a position of dominance in the whole region. Classical authors attest to the strong Arab element in the Syrian region, and of these

1. Equites sagittarii indigenae, Matthana (18)
2. Equites promoti indigenae, Adada (19)
3. Equites sagittarii indigenae, Anatha (20)
4. Equites sagittarii, Acadama (21)
5. Equites sagittarii, Acauatha (22)

Euphratensis: Or. XXXIII

Troops in Euphratensis were also under the command of the *dux* of Syria, and one unit in Euphratensis may have been Arab,[36] namely, the one stationed at Ruṣāfa:

Equites promoti indigenae, Ruṣāfa (27)

Palestine: Or. XXXIV

One unit is definitely Arab:

Equites Thamudeni Illyriciani,[37] Birsama (22)

Units that are possibly or likely to have been Arab are:[38]

Strabo may be singled out; he places the Arabs of Syria to the south of the Apameians and to the east—across the Orontes, in Parapotamia, and also in Chalcidice; see Strabo *Geography*, XVI.ii.11. For the stations of these units, see Musil, *Palmyrena*, 253–55; Böcking, *ND*, I, 387–88; and Dussaud, *Topographie*, 274–75.

[36] On the Arab tribes along the Euphrates, see Strabo, *Geography*, XVI.i.27–28; XVI.ii.1; XVI.iii.1; Pliny, *Natural History*, V.xxi.87. For Rusāfa, see Musil, *Palmyrena*, 260–72, and Dussaud, *Topographie*, 253–55, 275, and the map in V. Chapot, *La frontière de l'Euphrate* (Paris, 1907), opposite p. 408.

[37] On the Thamūdeni, see note 28, above. The Thamūdeni are enrolled in the unit of the Illyriciani just as the Mauri of unit No. 21 in Palestine. In this connection, Parker's views on the Illyriciani may be quoted: "Again, in Aurelian's army against Palmyra, Dalmatian and Moorish horsemen are found side by side with German legionaries, and it is not improbable that the cavalry contingents, called 'Illyriciani' which in the *Notitia* are found in the provinces of Phoenicia, Syria, Palestina, Osroene, Mesopotamia, and Arabia, date back originally to Aurelian's resettlement of the eastern provinces"; see Parker, "Legions," 187–88. It is interesting that Illyriciani units or troops remained in Palestine until the reign of Heraclius in the 7th century; see *Acta M. Anastasii Persae*, ed. H. Usener (Bonn, 1894), p. 26, lines 12–13, and W. Kaegi, "Notes on Hagiographic Sources for Some Institutional Changes and Continuities in the Early Seventh Century," *Byzantina* 7 (1975), 65–67.

[38] What has been said in notes 34–35 on the Arab ethnic constitution of certain parts of Syria and Phoenicia is likewise true of the southern desert of Palestine inhabited, before the region was incorporated into the empire, by the Idumaean and Nabataean Arabs; it is therefore, quite likely that these units described as *indigenae* were Arab. What has been said of the territorial term *Foenices* above in note 34 may be said of the Palestinian unit No. 34. As for the *Ala Dromedariorum*, this too is likely to have been Arab for the same reasons advanced in connection with the three *alae* in the Thebaid in note 32 above. In the *apparatus criticus* of the *ND*, the description of the *Ala* as *Antana* is questioned and *Antoniniana* is suggested instead.

The Arab character of these units is corroborated by the Arab military presence represented by the phylarchs. These were enlisted in the service of Byzantium in southern Palestine and are attested in the Nessana Papyri and in the Edict of Beersheba. See above, Secs. II–III. For the stations of the units of *Equites* and *Ala Dromedariorum*, see Böcking, *ND*, 345–48, 351–52.

1. Equites promoti indigenae, Sabaiae (23)
2. Equites promoti indigenae, Zodocathae (24)
3. Equites sagittarii indigenae, Hauanae (25)
4. Equites sagittarii indigenae, Zoarae (26)
5. Equites sagittarii indigenae, Robatha (27)
6. Equites primi felices sagittarii indigenae Palaestini, Sabure sive Veterocariae (28)
7. Equites sagittarii indigenae, Moahile (29)
8. Ala Antana dromedariorum, Admatha (33)

Osroene: Or. XXXV

Units that are possibly or likely to have been Arab are:[39]

1. Equites promoti indigenae, Banasam (18)
2. Equites promoti indigenae, Sina Iudaeorum (19)
3. Equites sagittarii indigenae, Oraba (20)
4. Equites sagittarii indigenae, Thillazamana (21)
5. Equites sagittarii indigenae, primi Osroeni, Rasin (23)

Mesopotamia: Or. XXXVI

Units that are definitely Arab:

Cohors quinquagenaria Arabum, Bethallaḥa (35)

Units that are possibly Arab[40] are:

Abel's discussion of *all* the units of the *Notitia* in Palestine is valuable and so is his map; see F. M. Abel, *Géograpie de la Palestine*, II, 178–84, and map 10.

[39] The Arab complexion of the Trans-Euphratesian provinces—Osroene and Mesopotamia—was as strong as that of the Cis-Euphratesian ones, Syria and Phoenicia. The western part of the region was even referred to as "Arabia" in the classical sources (Pliny, *Natural History*, V.xx.85), while the eastern part was called Bēth-ʿArabāyē in the Syriac sources; in Islamic times these regions were called Diyār Muḍar and Diyār Rabīʿa, for which see *EI*, s.v. In addition to these significant designations in the classical and the Syriac sources for the region in pre-Islam, both these sources testify to the strong element in the northern half of the Land of the Two Rivers; for the classical sources, see Strabo, *Geography*, XVI.i.26; and Pliny, *Natural History*, V.xx–xxi; the latter is more specific as he identifies Osroene with "Arabia" and speaks of the Arab tribe of Praetavi in Mesopotamia, whose capital was Singara. For the Syriac sources on the Arabs in this region, see J. B. Segal, "Mesopotamian Communities from Julian to the Rise of Islam," *Proceedings of the British Academy* 41 (1955), 119–20. The distinction between the ʿArab and the Ṭayāyē in Segal's article must be only social not ethnic and corresponds to the distinction sometimes made in classical writers between Arabs and Scenitae; the former were considered more sedentary and developed than the latter but both were considered Arab. The two most important Arab kingdoms of the Trans-Euphratesian region were Edessa and Hatra. The first, the kingdom of the Abgarids, became the Roman province of Osroene. Pliny (*Natural History*, VI.117) and Tacitus (*Annales*, XII.12) refer to the Edessenes simply as *Arabes*.

On the stations of these five units of *Equites* in Osroene see Böcking, *ND*, I, 398–400, and Chapot, *Frontière*, 275, 320. See also the map in Chapot opposite p. 408.

[40] On the Arab element in Mesopotamia, see note 39, above. This region was known in

1. Equites promoti indigenae, Constantina (24)
2. Equites sagittarii indigenae Arabanensis, Mefana Cartha (25)
3. Equites sagittarii indigenae Thibithenses, Thilbisme (27)
4. Equites sagittarii indigenae, Thannuri (28)

Arabia: Or. XXXVII

Units that are definitely Arab:

Cohors tertia felix[41] Arabum, in ripa Vade Afaris fluvii in castris Arnonensibus (34)

Units that are most likely to have been Arab[42] are:

1. Equites promoti indigenae, Speluncis (18)
2. Equites promoti indigenae, Mefa (19)
3. Equites Sagittarii indigenae, Gadda (20)
4. Equites sagittarii indigenae, Dia-Fenis (23)

II. Further Observations on the *Notitia Dignitatum*

The enumeration of the Arab units in the *ND* undertaken above reflects the extent of Arab participation in the defense of Oriens. This was the picture in

---

Islamic times as Diyār Rabīʿa, and it is almost certain that the Rabīʿa group was represented in the Trans-Euphratesian regions in pre-Islamic times. On the stations of these four units, see Böcking, *ND*, I, 411–12, 414; and Chapot, *Frontière*, 303, 310. On the second unit, described as *Arabanenses*, and its two stations, see ibid., 299, and Dussaud, *Topographie*, 483–85, 489, 491–92, 521; see also the map in Chapot, *Frontière*, opposite p. 408, and the map in Poidebard, *La trace de Rome*, atlas volume.

It is relevant to mention that even in Islamic times, the large Arab tribal group Rabīʿa, which lived along the Khabūr/Aborras in Mesopotamia was mostly Christian. They could have been converted to Christianity only in pre-Islamic times. On their Christianity in medieval Islamic times, see Ibn ʿAbd Rabbihi, *Al-ʿIqd al-Farīd*, ed. A. Amin, I. al-Abyārī, and ʿA. Hārūn (Beirut, 1982), VIv, 252.

[41] "Felix" is attested for another Arab unit in Palestine, the Equites felices primi sagittarii indigenae Palestini (Or. XXXIV.28).

[42] The basic work on the province of Arabia is still the monumental work by R. E. Brünnow and A. von Domaszewski, *Die Provincia Arabia*, 3 vols. (Strasbourg, 1904–9); for the *castella* of the *limes Arabicus*, see R. E. Brünnow, "Die Kastelle des arabischen Limes," *Florilegium ou recueil de travaux d'érudition dédiés à Monsieur le marquis Melchior de Vogüé* (Paris, 1909), 65–77. For the employment of native troops, see Brünnow, "Die Kastelle," 76. More accessible and recent is Abel's *Géographie*, vol. 2; for the stations of the four units of *Equites* and that of the *Cohors*, see 187–91 and map 10. But these works on the Provincia Arabia have been overtaken by recent researches; see H. I. MacAdam, *Studies in the History of the Roman Province of Arabia* (University of Manchester Doctoral Dissertation, 1979); D. L. Kennedy, "Archaeological Explorations on the Roman Frontier in North-East Jordan"; Bowersock, *Roman Arabia*; Sartre, *TE* I; idem, "Bostra: des orgines à l'Islam," Institut français d'archéologie du proche-orient (Paris, 1985), vol. cxvii; S. T. Parker, *Romans and Saracens*, ASOR (Winona Lake, Ind., 1986); and articles of M. Speidel, especially "The Roman Army in Arabia," in *Aufstieg und Niedergang der römischen Welt*, II, 8 (1977), 687–730.

fourth century and also in the fifth, but certain changes and modifications should be noted.

1. About the middle of the fourth century, the size of the Provincia Arabia was considerably reduced and out of it was carved the new province of Palaestina Tertia or Salutaris, the capital of which was Petra, and which included Sinai, the Negev, and Trans-ʿAraba.[43] Thus throughout the fifth and sixth centuries, the Byzantine sphere of influence in Ḥijāz was an extension not of the Provincia Arabia but of Palaestina Tertia, and so Ḥijāz' history as far as federate relations are concerned is now part of the provincial history of a new province.[44]

Egypt is no longer a part of the Diocese of Oriens. Early in the reign of Theodosius II (380–382), it was separated from Oriens and its *praefectus* had now the title of Augustalis. The number of Arab units in the *limes Aegypti* and the Thebaid, specifically referred to by names that clearly disclose their ethnic origin, is striking.[45] Three of them must have been withdrawn from Oriens, since their names relate them to Ituraea, Palmyra, and Thamūd. When they were stationed in Egypt is not clear, but if this took place early in the fifth century the fact may be related to the peace that obtained between Persia and Byzantium following the settlement of Theodosius I with Persia. Some light was shed on the history of these Arab units in Egypt by one of the letters of Synesius written in 404, in which he speaks of a *turma* of Arab soldiers aboard a ship that was carrying them to Cyrene or Pentapolis.[46]

The existence of a pocket of Arabs in Egypt not included or mentioned in the *ND* could possibly be inferred from the data of ecclesiastical history. A few years after the Council of Chalcedon in 451, a bishop by the name of Petrus signs with Nestorius, the bishop of Phagroriopolis in Augustamnica II, a letter addressed to Anatolius, the patriarch of Constantinople, and another letter to Emperor Leo I.[47] This bishop is described as Episcopus Scenarum Mandrarum. In view of the description of his episcopate and its geographical location, he could have been the bishop of a group of Arabs in Arabia, the Egyptian nome.[48]

[43] On the boundaries of the Provincia Arabia, see Bowersock, *Roman Arabia*, 90–122; and Sartre, *TE*, 17–75.

[44] On this new province, see K. C. Gutwein, *Third Palestine*.

[45] See above, 464–65.

[46] See above, 9–12.

[47] Schwartz, *Acta conciliorum* II, vol. V, pp. 11–21. His signature appears on p. 17 as Episcopus Cynorum mandrarum and in the index volume of the *Acta* (p. 406) as Episcopus Scenarum Mandrarum.

[48] The term Scenas Mandrarum in the *ND* (p. 59), however, appears as the quarters of Ala Septima Sarmatarum. This could weaken the argument. But the names of these units do not necessarily always reflect ethnic origin and often they were recruited locally while retaining their old names. The bishop, however, would not have represented the Ala of the *Notitia*, but

2. The *ND* has two Saracen units stationed in Phoenicia Libanensis, at Betroclus and Thelsee. The many problems posed by these two units have been discussed in various contexts in both *RA* and *BAFOC*.[49] With the elucidation of the history of Arab-Byzantine relations in the fifth century to which the *ND* belongs, it is appropriate to make further observations on these two units.

Phoenicia is not far from where the Tanūkhids were settled—Chalcidice. It is possible that these two units were Tanūkhid *foederati* who were stationed in Phoenicia after the events of the early reign of Theodosius I, during which they revolted and were crushed by Richomer. Their stationing in Phoenicia could have been an accommodation with Byzantium after they ceased to be the dominant federate group in Oriens, and their status as *foederati* may even have changed, which would explain their inclusion in the *official* document (the *ND*) which lists regular Roman units.

Alternatively, they could have been Salīḥids, the new dominant group in Oriens in the fifth century. The whereabouts of the Salīḥids in Oriens does not help in explaining why they should have been stationed in Phoenicia Libanensis. The Salīḥids might have been called upon to furnish troops in Phoenicia as the new dominant group against some threat in that sector of the *limes orientalis*.

The conversion of thirty thousand Saracens mentioned in the *Vita S. Pelagiae* cannot be left out of this discussion. They were converted in Phoenicia Libanensis itself and also in the fifth century, and thus are of obvious relevance to the history of the two units. As explained earlier,[50] the episode is haunted by a number of ghosts; nevertheless, it is important and its thirty thousand Saracens must be taken into account in any discussion of the two Saracen units of the *ND*.

Finally, something has been said on the tribal structure of the federates in Oriens in the fifth century, which involved the three tribes, Iyād, Namir, and Kalb. It is not unlikely that the two Saracen units belonged to one or two of these tribes, but there is no way of stating their tribal identity with certainty. Only future discoveries can decide in favor of one tribal group or another.[51]

---

more likely the community in or around the locality, which had an Arab ethnic complexion. Phagroriopolis may have been the Ptolemaic metropolis of Arabia; see Jones, *Cities*, 299.

[49] See *RA*, 23 note 14, 22, 29, 52, 59 note 33; and *BAFOC*, 393, 398–99.

[50] See above, Chap. 1, app. 1.

[51] Dayr Dāwūd built by the Salīḥid king between Isriye and Ruṣāfa/Sergiopolis is not far from where the two units were stationed, but this is a Salīḥid foundation late in the 5th century, while the *ND* goes back to around 400. Otherwise it would be possible to relate the Salīḥid establishment in the north to the stationing of Salīḥid troops in Phoenicia.

III. Federate Toponymy and Tribal Structure

The examination of the tribal structure of the federate shield in Oriens in the fourth century and the history of Arab-Byzantine relations in the fifth century shed some light on the tribes, both old and new, and also on federate toponymy.

1. The first and most important of the new tribes is Salīḥ itself, the dominant federate tribal group of the fifth century. It has been argued that it had wandered into Oriens from the area of Wādī Sirḥān and was settled in the Balqā' and the Maw'āb regions, the biblical Ammonitis and Moabitis, which in the fifth century formed parts of the Provincia Arabia and Palaestina Tertia respectively.[52] And it is practically certain that it had settlements extending both to the north in Arabia and Phoenicia Libanensis and to the south in Palaestina Tertia.

2. The tribe of Iyād was represented by ʿAbd al-ʿĀṣ, Dāwūd's court poet, and it has been argued that this, in all probability, has to be construed as a signal that the important Mesopotamian tribe had emigrated at least in part to Oriens and had allied itself with Byzantium in the fifth century.[53] Where in Oriens it was settled in the fifth century, it is difficult to tell.

3. The two sister tribes al-Namir and Kalb, old tribes settled in the region from olden times, start to be mentioned in the sources related to the Salīḥids and present the spectacle of two related tribes with a *ḥilf*, a confederation. They appear united against the power of the dominant federate group, Salīḥ, and actually succeed in bringing about the downfall of the Salīḥid king Dāwūd in a battle in Bāshān or the Gaulanitis.[54] The chances are that they were settled *extra limitem* but must have had access to Oriens through their federate status, since they appear fighting Dāwūd *intra limitem*.

4. The role of two Ḥijāzi tribes Balī and ʿUḏra as *foederati* of Byzantium also becomes clear. The first lived not far from Ayla and the second to the south of it, deep in Ḥijāz as far as Wādī al-Qurā near Medina. ʿUḏra is the much more important tribe in the history of Byzantium and its indirect influence in Ḥijāz.[55]

5. Finally, the Ghassānids appear late in the fifth century in Oriens, most probably for the first time as the group of Amorkesos, the adventurous phylarch of the reign of Leo I, and then under the leadership of Thaʿlaba. They are settled in Palaestina Tertia and in Arabia, and after a period of cohabitation with the Salīḥids, they overturn and replace them as the dominant federate group in Oriens in the sixth century.[56]

[52] See above, 245–48.

[53] See above, Chap. 2, app. 2.

[54] See above, 260–61.

[55] On these two tribes, see Chap. 12, sec. VIII.III.

[56] See above, Chap. 12, sec. V.

The paucity of the sources on the *foederati* of the fifth century is not helpful in compiling a list of toponyms for them. They are not uninformative on the Salīḥids, but unfortunately and curiously, primarily so for the period *before* the fifth century and *after* it, when they ceased to be the dominant federate group.

1. It is clear from the various sources that the Salīḥids were settled in the districts of Balqā' and Maw'āb, that is, in the Byzantine provinces of Arabia and Palaestina Tertia. This is confirmed by the survival of the modern toponyms in presentday Jordan, the village of al-Salīḥī and the Valley of al-Salīḥī near Amman. Dayr Dāwūd is the most solid toponym in the history of the Salīḥids, since it can be pinpointed to a location between Isriye and Ruṣāfa/Sergiopolis. The Salīḥid who built Dayr Dāwūd was killed in a battle that raged in Bāshān or Gaulanitis, between Ḥārib and al-Qurnatayn.

Before the fifth century, the Arabic sources place them in a long stretch of land in Oriens between Qinnasrīn, Chalcis, and Filasṭīn (Palestine). What is important in this account is that in the third century they were deployed along Manāẓir al-Shām, the watchtowers of Syria in Oriens, thus suggesting a military role related to the defense of the *limes orientalis*. In the times of the Muslim Conquest they are also associated with the southern sector of Oriens in Zīza and in Dūmat al-Jandal. Al-Hamdānī of later Islamic times places them in al-Balqā', Salamiyya, Ḥuwwārin, and al-Zaytūn.

What is important is their whereabouts in the fifth century, and this is fairly established with certainty; it was in the southern sector of Oriens, in Arabia and Palaestina Tertia. This is also consonant with the toponym Zagmais in Ptolemy which, as has been argued, is none other than Dajʿam, the eponym of the Salīḥids, and this brings Wādī Sirḥān within the range of Salīḥid toponymy.[57]

2. Ḥijāz, the region of indirect Byzantine influence through the Arab federates settled there, supplies some toponyms which are important. Ayla, Midian, Kilwa, and Wādī al-Qurā were among the locations at which Byzantine monasteries were built.[58] It is practically certain that these, although not military posts, were centers of Byzantine influence for the *imperium* as well as for the *ecclesia*. They were almost certainly guarded by the Christianized tribes settled around them, in much the same way that the present-day monastery of St. Catherine on Mount Sinai is protected by the surrounding Arabs.

In addition to these toponyms and those associated with the tribe of ʿUḏra in Ḥijāz, Yāqūt mentions a place called Thamad al-Rūm, Thamad of the Romans, somewhere between Oriens (Shām) and Medina.[59] The account

[57] For Salīḥid toponymy before, during, and after their period of dominance, see Chap. 12, sec. II.B.

[58] For monasteries in Ḥijāz, see above, Chap. 12, sec. VI.

[59] See Yāqūt, *Muʿjam*, II, 84.

which tells why it was called Thamad—involving the pursuit of Jews from Palestine by the Romans, who died at that spot—may be dismissed as fictitious. What matters is the toponym, which must have witnessed a Roman presence, possibly a military post. After the fall of Nabataea, Rome annexed almost the whole of Nabataea in Ḥijāz which, later and gradually, it evacuated, keeping indirect control over the region through the Arab *foederati*. A reliable modern Saudi scholar and traveler in Ḥijāz places Thamad al-Rūm about twenty-two kilometers south of Khaybar.[60] When exactly this post was occupied and abandoned it is difficult to tell.

IV. Archeology and the *Foederati*

Both sets of sources for frontier studies—the Greek and Latin on the one hand and the Arabic on the other—are limited. Consequently, the only advances that can be made are through archeology, which has added more to the data supplied by the Greek and Latin sources than to that supplied by the Arabic sources. But the two sets of sources are complementary, although they deal with different components of the *limes*. Hence the Arabic sources and their data are naturally responsive to archeological research. It is therefore proposed in this chapter to discuss the facts of the Arab component of the *limes orientalis* in relation to recent archeology.

Romans and Saracens: A History of the Arabian Frontier[61] is the most recent work on the *limes Arabicus* and makes use of other works[62] that have recently appeared. As it deals with the Arabian frontier till the seventh century, based on archeological research, and especially as its author is aware of the role of the Arab *foederati* in frontier defense, this work deserves special notice.

1. The author, S. Thomas Parker, divides the *limes Arabicus* into three sectors: the northern sector, which extended from Bostra to Philadelphia; the central, from Philadelphia to Wādī al-Ḥasā; and the southern, from Wādī al-Ḥasā southward to ʿAqaba.

In his chapter on the northern sector, he discusses the place of Wādī Sirḥān in the defense system,[63] about which G. W. Bowersock had written that it "played a vital role in the prosperity and the defenses of Roman Arabia."[64] An inscription found at Jawf/Dūmat at the southern outlet of Wādī

[60] See H. al-Jāsir, *Shamāl Gharb al-Jazīra*, 312, 493. Thamad is about 125 kilometers to the north of Medina, thus answering to Yāqūt's description of it as lying between Medina and al-Shām. According to al-Jāsir (ibid., 493) it is a station where Saudi pastoralists were settled in a *hujrat*, and so it appears as Hujrat Thamad in Philby's map; see H. St. John Philby, *The Land of Midian* (London, 1957), opp. p. 262.

[61] See Parker, *Romans and Saracens*.

[62] For these, see above, 469 note 42.

[63] *Romans and Saracens*, 15–16.

[64] See his *Roman Arabia*, 159.

Sirḥān suggests that detachments from III Cyrenaica patrolled the *wadī* at some time. Whether this became a regular duty for III Cyrenaica is not clear, and Parker doubts it. The elucidation of the history of Salīḥ in the region of Arabia and Palaestina Tertia not far from Wādī Sirḥān, whence they had entered Oriens, could offer a satisfactory answer to this question. They are the more likely group to have patrolled the *wadī* so familiar to them, and this is the sort of activity that they could perform better than the regular Roman soldiers, especially as this region had been their original abode before they became the *foederati* of Byzantium.

2. In the historical conclusions of his chapter on the central sector of the *limes Arabicus*, the author notes a dramatic happening, namely "the abandonment of virtually all these Roman forts during the 5th and 6th centuries. The watchtowers, which functioned as the eyes and the ears of the *limes*, apparently were all evacuated by the beginning of the 6th century. . . . Most of the castella shared a similar fate. Qastal Thurayya, Bshir, and Fityan were abandoned by the end of the 5th century as were the forts of the caravanserais of Khan ez-Zebib and Umm el-Walid."[65]

The evidence from archeology admits of one of two explanations. These watchtowers and forts may have been denuded because many of the military units that manned them were transferred to the West by Emperor Leo for his expedition against the Vandals, a transfer made possible by the peace that prevailed between Persia and Byzantium.[66] Alternatively, the rise of a strong federate power in exactly this region, namely, the Salīḥids, could explain the observation of the archeologist. In the fourth century, the dominant federate group, the Tanūkhids, were deployed in the north in Chalcidice. In the fifth, the dominant federate group, the Salīḥids, were deployed in the south in Arabia and Palaestina Tertia, partly because they entered Oriens from Wādī Sirḥān and partly because of the peace between Persia and Byzantium, which made it possible to keep the powerful new group away from the Persian front and in the south. This was justified in the event, because in the fifth century the serious thrusts from Arabia did come from this sector, as the chapters in this volume on Amorkesos and the fall of Salīḥ have made clear.

3. In his chapter on the southern sector of the *limes Arabicus*, Parker notes that "the Romans probably policed the caravan route through the southern Ḥismā and northern Ḥijāz, but there is no evidence of a defensive system

[65] *Romans and Saracens*, 84–85.

[66] On this, see above, Chap. 4, sec. vi. A parallel to this in a small way is the transfer of the Equites Nona Dalmatae from Umm al-Jimāl in the Provincia Arabia to the environs of Constantinople after the defeat of Adrianople, as noted by the author; see Parker, *Romans and Saracens*, 146.

beyond the line of forts along the *via nova*. This area probably was controlled by allied Thamudic tribes, serving as *foederati* in the second century."[67]

It is practically certain that when Trajan annexed Nabataea he also annexed its Ḥijāzi territories down to ʿUlā and Madā' in Ṣāliḥ.[68] But gradually the Romans started to withdraw from active and direct control of the Ḥijāz region, or most of it. In the second century this is clearly illustrated by bilingual inscriptions of the tribal group Thamūd, who lived in Ruwwāfa. This was close to Ayla and the *limes*, and Ruwwāfa was within the area of direct Roman rule. But there is no evidence in later times of direct rule to the south of Ruwwāfa. There is evidence for what most probably was police patrol activity.[69] Thus Ḥijāz, a vast area extending as far in the south as Mecca and Ṭā'if, must be seen as a sphere of Roman influence, of indirect control through the convenient device of the Arab *foederati* in this region. The precious inscriptions at Ruwwāfa cannot have been an isolated case. When northwest Arabia is opened for archeological research,[70] the names and affiliations of all the federate tribes in the northern half of Ḥijāz, from Ḥismā to as far south as Wādī al-Qurā near Medina, will become known just as Thamūd is.

4. In his section on the Arabian frontier in the fourth and fifth centuries, Parker suggests various reasons for the prosperity of Palestine in this period, and relates this to the fact that the *limes Arabicus* was heavily fortified.[71]

Surely the strong federate presence which Byzantium wanted to obtain in Arabia and Palaestina Tertia, represented by the Salīḥids, can be mentioned in this connection. The Salīḥids and other federates must have taken an active part in the protection of the region in the areas for which it became important: (*a*) the defense of the Holy Land against Saracen incursions;[72] (*b*) the protection of the caravans of international commerce that came from Ḥijāz and Arabia and passed through the region north of Bostra and Damascus and west to Gaza; and finally (*c*) the protection of the provinces and the provincials from the nomads and raids that emanated from the Peninsula. The Salīḥids, having been originally Arabians themselves, were thoroughly familiar with these raiders and all the dangers they posed; hence they were invaluable for dealing with these threats.[73]

67 Ibid., 112.

68 See Bowersock, *Roman Arabia*, 95–96.

69 As the stele from Madā'in Ṣāliḥ reveals that a detachment from the III Cyrenaica reached that locality; ibid., 96.

70 Of all the regions, those of Dūmat al-Jandal and Wādī al-Qurā should prove the most rewarding.

71 See *Romans and Saracens*, 143–44.

72 In the 5th century a new dimension was added to the holiness of Palestine by the rise of the monastic establishment in that province. This, too, needed protection.

73 Archeological evidence from Umm al-Jimāl and Qasr al-Bāʿiq early in the 5th century could support the view that the region was open to Saracen raids. This was suggested by Bowersock and accepted by the author as likely; Parker, *Romans and Saracens*, 146.

5. Within this archeological context, it is of interest to note that the names of many elements of this Roman military establishment entered the Arabic language in pre-Islamic times. Such are: Arabic *qaṣr*, a castle or palace, from Latin *castrum* through Greek *kastron* and Aramaic; *ṣiraṭ*, Arabic "way," "path," from Latin *strata*, through Greek and Aramaic; *zukhruf*, Arabic for ornamentation from Greek *zōgraphia*; and *mīl*, Arabic for mile and milestone, from Latin *milliarium*. The first three made their way into the lexicology of the Koran.[74]

V. The Two Federate Shields

The two federate shields, the Inner and the Outer, were touched upon in *BAFOC*,[75] but the facts of federate history did not permit a detailed discussion. However, these facts are more abundant for the fifth century and thus it is possible to refine on what was said there and present it more clearly and with more detail.

The Arab federate tribal groups associated with the *limes orientalis* were many, but their variety and number may be divided into two principal groups; those who lived *intra limitem* and those who lived *extra limitem*, and who may be called the Inner or Interior Shield and the Outer or Exterior Shield respectively.

The Inner Shield

There is no doubt about the reality of Arab tribal settlement *intra limitem*, which is supported by knowledge of well-known toponyms associated with the tribes and definitely within the boundaries of the limitrophe provinces of Oriens. The clearest examples are the Ghassānids of the sixth century and the Tanūkhids of the fourth settled in Chalcidice. That the Salīḥids enjoyed the privilege of living *intra limitem* in the fifth century is clear from a discussion of their toponyms. The other tribe of the fifth century that

[74] For these three terms, see A. Jeffery, *The Foreign Vocabulary of the Qur'an*, 150, 194, 240. The exciting discovery of a stele, at Ḥijr/Madā' in Ṣāliḥ with the inscription in which the word, ζωγράφος (painter) appears, makes certain that the etymology of *zukhruf*, (ornamentation) deriving from Syriac or Persian as given in Jeffery (p. 150) is erroneous. The derivation from the Greek is convincing on phonological grounds alone, and the discovery of the stele which attests the word geographically not far from where the Koranic revelation took place in Mecca, Ḥijāz, clinches the point. For the stele and the inscription, see G. W. Bowersock, "A Report on Arabia Provincia," *JRS* 61 (1971), 230. For what these military painters could do on shields as parade armor (designs of an Amazonomachy, the Trojan Horse and the capture of Troy), see G. M. A. Hanfmann, "A Painter in the Imperial Arms Factory at Sardis," *American Journal of Archaeology* 85 (1981), 87–88.

Arabic *ʿaskar* most probably derives from Persian *lashkar*, but its derivation from Latin *exercitus* remains a remote possibility.

[75] See *BAFOC*, 477–79.

possibly was similarly privileged was Iyād.[76] The history of these tribes within the *limes* calls for the following observations.

1. That some tribes, such as Ghassān and Tanūkh, were settled within the *limes* becomes explicable when it is realized that these were newcomers to northern Arabia, having emigrated from the Arabian south and from Mesopotamia respectively. So they had no place in the tribal world of North Arabia, where each tribe had its own jealously guarded territory. Besides, these were militarily powerful tribal groups, which were able to hew their way through the Peninsula and the *limes* and thus confronted the empire with a *fait accompli*.[77]

2. These federate troops had close relations with Byzantium and were integrated in its military system and cultural life. They are the tribes which appear in official documents, and whose chiefs were called phylarchs, who were endowed with the titles and ranks of the Byzantine hierarchy[78] and with whom *foedera* were struck.

3. The duties that were laid upon them fully explain why Byzantium tolerated and accepted their presence within the *limes*. (*a*) They were indispensable for internal security within the *limes orientalis*, especially the outlying provinces, mostly arid zones in which the problem of security was important. (*b*) The permanent geopolitical factors that shaped the history of the Arab tribes who lived in North Arabia gave these federate groups a regular function in defending the *limes* against incursions from the Arabian Peninsula. (*c*) The protection of the caravans that traveled along the important international commercial routes of the region was another important function. (*d*) Finally, they participated in the regular campaigns of the army of the Orient against the Persians and, occasionally, outside Oriens—as when the Tanūkhids participated in the Gothic War of the reign of Valens in the fourth century or when the Salīḥids (most probably) participated in Leo's expedition against the Vandals in the fifth.

The Outer Shield

It was not possible in *BAFOC* to discuss the Outer Shield in detail in view of the paucity of data about the area east of the *limes orientalis* in the fourth century, but the details are more plentiful for the fifth. The region where Salīḥ was settled was in the south, in Arabia and Palaestina Tertia, not

[76] The case of the Cantabrians of Spain and the Isaurians of Asia Minor, both of whom lived within the confines of the empire, may be cited as parallels.

[77] See Jones, *LRE*, 199 where he explains how the empire sometimes had no choice but to accept military barbarian groups within its boundaries, since the alternative of crushing them or warring them was very hazardous and costly.

[78] For a detailed account of this, see Shahîd, "The Patriciate of Arethas," 321–43.

far from Ḥijāz, the vast area of indirect Byzantine control which (or at least a large part of it) had formerly formed part of the Provincia Arabia after Trajan annexed the Nabataean kingdom. Thus Ḥijāz provides the most fruitful discussion of the Outer Shield.

1. Of the three tribes that lived in this region, Judām, Balī, and ʿUdra, it is the last that emerges as the most important federate tribe of the Outer Shield. Its history and the Byzantine profile of that history were elucidated in a previous chapter. It was settled deep in the heart of Ḥijāz, in Wādī al-Qurā, not far from Medina, and thus represents the southernmost point of Byzantine influence in Ḥijāz. That influence was also extended as far as Mecca when the ʿUdrite chief Rizāḥ helped Quṣayy in his conquest of Mecca.[79]

2. The most important duty of these federate tribes of the Outer Shield was undoubtedly the protection of the caravans that passed through Ḥijāz, the bridge between the world of South Arabia and the Indian Ocean on the one hand and that of the Mediterranean on the other. Thus they performed an important function in the internal commerce of the fifth century, when the West Arabian route assumed great importance. That they participated in the spreading of Byzantine culture through their adoption and propagation of Christianity has also been pointed out. Thus they must also have protected those outposts of Byzantine Christianity—the monasteries of northwestern Arabia.

In addition to Ḥijāz and the toponyms that have been identified in the preceding chapters, there was the area to the northeast, which also must have been the region of other federate tribes of the Outer Shield—Kalb, Namir, and possibly Ṭayy. The toponyms Dūmat al-Jandal, Ilāha, and Malikān[80] are associated with them. And of these the most important is undoubtedly Dūmat which, like Wādī al-Qurā, must be an archeologist's paradise.

It has been noted by students of the Roman frontier that the legionaries in this period became *limitanei* and that many of the units which are listed in the *ND* were locally recruited; a former chapter has analyzed the Arab units in the *ND* for the limitrophe provinces and found them to be many. This fact may now be brought to bear on federate-imperial relations. Unlike the German *foederati* in the West, the Arab ones in the East were settled and quartered among regular *Rhōmaioi* who were ethnically Arab like themselves. This important fact explains the responsiveness and the degree of symbiosis between the two groups, which no doubt contributed to habits of cooperation.

[79] For this, see above, Chap. 12, sec. II.II.

[80] On these two toponyms, see *BAFOC*, 416–17.

VI. Miscellaneous Observations

What was said in *BAFOC*[81] regarding the federate status of the Arabs in the fourth century and related problems is largely true of the Arab *foederati* in the fifth century, and need not be repeated here. Instead, this section will deal with some aspects of this theme which bear further treatment and development.[82]

1. One question arises concerning the crucial term *foederati*, which is the technically accurate term for the Arab allies of Byzantium. It is virtually certain that it was used in the same sense as it was for the Germanic tribes of the West, such as the Goths and the Vandals.[83] The Arabs in the sources for the fifth and also the fourth century are mostly described by the Greek terms ἔνσπονδοι or ὑπόσπονδοι, which corresponds exactly to the Latin *foederati*, and there is an explicit statement in Malchus on the equivalence of these terms.[84] It is quite unlikely, perhaps inconceivable, that the Romans would have used in official documents one and the same term to express two different meanings. Surely the clauses of the *foedus* with the Arabs may not have been identical with those with the Germanic peoples, but this does not invalidate the identity of the two terms in their application to the two peoples. There must have been regional variations and, of course, the Germanic *regna* of the *foederati* of the Occident were much larger and more powerful than those of the Arabs in the Orient.

2. The key to understanding much about the status and conditions of the settlements for the Arab *foederati* is, of course, the text of the *foedus*. Unfortunately, not a single text for the fifth century has survived which would enable the student of this aspect of federate history to draw the right conclusion. The only semblance of a text that has survived goes back to ca. 502, the *foedus* with the new dominant group in the sixth century, the Ghassānids.[85] It is an Arabic document which speaks of mutual military assistance in time of war, and it is impossible to extract from it any informative data on the conditions of the settlement of the *foederati*. Thus most of these conditions have to be inferred from hints here and there in the sources that sporadically remember the *foederati*.

3. The most important question that arises is whether these *foederati* were

[81] See *BAFOC*, 498–521.

[82] It is noteworthy that evidence for federate history in the 5th century mainly concerns the two provinces in the south, Palaestina Prima and Tertia, while for the 4th century it relates to the north, in Chalcidice where Tanūkhid power was centered.

[83] The question has been posed to me by E. Chrysos.

[84] For this equivalence, see the opening sentence in fragment 15 in Malchus, in Blockeley, *CH*, II, 408.

[85] For this *foedus*, see above, Chap. 12, sec. v note 260.

provided for by the *annona foederatica* or by the system of *hospitalitas*. Were they billeted on Roman estates and did they have a *sors*, a share or part of an estate on which they were quartered? If they were so treated there are no sources available to confirm it.[86] The Salīḥids lived within the *limes* on Roman territory, but there is not a single source that sheds light on any of these questions.

On the other hand, there are hints and echoes in the sources, sporadic as they are, that food and shelter were provided by the system of the *annona*. Reference to this is made in the *Codex Theodosianus* concerning the Arab *foederati* in Palestine.[87] *Munera* and *salaria* are mentioned in the sources for the *foederati* of the fourth century.[88]

4. The state of the extant sources for the fifth century is such that most of the documentation for the federates is for the Palestines, Prima and Tertia. The other provinces of the limitrophe are left without documentation for federate history. Hence, with the exception of the one reference to Zokomos, the eponym of the Salīḥids, there is no explicit and direct evidence for the history of the dominant federate group in the Byzantine sources to guide the student regarding such a problem as whether it was the system of *hospitalitas* or *annona* that provided for the Salīḥids. They were certainly settled within the *limes*, where they were the dominant federate group for a century and remained for more than a century after their fall ca. 500. What arrangement was worked out for them by Byzantium must remain in the realm of guesswork.[89] The problem is easier to examine in the case of the Ghassānids of the sixth century, for whom the sources are slightly informative on this point.

The cases of the island of Iotabe and its occupation by Amorkesos during the reign of Leo is the only piece of solid evidence in the primary Greek sources for examining the problem. Malchus could give the impression that the Arab chief presented the Romans with a *fait accompli* and became the

[86] How fortunate by contrast is the historian of the Germanic *foederati*, who has at his disposal many of the *leges* drawn up under barbarian rule. On *hospitalitas*, see the recent treatment in W. Goffart, *Barbarians and Romans*, A.D. *418–584* (Princeton, 1980), 162–75.

[87] On this, see Chap. 2, sec. V, above.

[88] See *BAFOC*, 112. Goffart's conclusions in his above-mentioned book would bring the Arabs even closer to the Germans as *foederati*, since he argued that the process of accommodating the Germans was based on the system of taxation rather than on *hospitalitas*.

[89] There is, however, that statement in *al-Kāmil* of Ibn al-Athīr, the late Muslim historian, that neither Salīḥ nor Ghassān owned a *shibr* ("a span") of the territory in which they were settled in Oriens. The Muslim historian was not speaking the language of Roman jurists on the system of *hospitalitas*, of which he had no knowledge. He was simply asserting that the Salīḥids and the Ghassānids were settled on Byzantine territory not as owners of the land but as clients of the Byzantines. The statement in Ibn al-Athīr is, of course, an over-simplification, at least as far as the Ghassānids are concerned, since much more is known about them than about the Salīḥids; they will be discussed in detail in *BASIC*. See Ibn al-Athīr, *Al-Kāmil*, I, 510.

master of this bit of imperial territory by force, which he and his successors occupied until they were dislodged some twenty-five years later by Romanus, the *dux* of Palestine. Yet it is impossible to believe that Rome would have indulged in a *cessio*, even though it related to so diminutive a portion of the imperial soil as the island of Iotabe. This was so much against the imperial grain that it was, perhaps, only indulged in once, by Emperor Jovian after the disastrous campaign of Julian against the Persians. The *fait accompli* must have been recognized, but only after Amorkesos pleaded for an audience with Leo in Constantinople and after a *foedus* was struck between the two parties, thus making the Arab chief a servant of Rome and a recipient of its *annona*.

5. The question of the two concepts of the *basileia* and *phylarchia* was raised in connection with the *foederati* of the fourth century in the preceding volume.[90] The data concerning these two concepts for the fifth century may be presented as follows.

While the Arabic sources consistently refer to the chiefs of the Salīḥids as kings, the Byzantine sources equally consistently refer to the Arab *foederati* of this century as phylarchs. Sozomen, who is the chief Byzantine source on the Salīḥids, refers to their eponym, Zokomos, as phylarch and not as king. This is significant, coming as it does from the same historian who in speaking of the earlier *foederati* of Queen Mavia in the reign of Valens, referred to Mavia's husband as a king.[91] This shift in usage is striking and calls for an explanation. As applied to the Salīḥid eponym by Sozomen, the term is probably used in the first of three senses that it bears,[92] namely, a tribal chief, but Sozomen could also have been implying that he was also a phylarch, in the technical sense of an Arab chief in a treaty relationship to Byzantium. What is important is that the term "king" is not applied to him, and this probably derives from the fact that while the Tanūkhids and the Lakhmids had come from Persian territory where they had been kings and thus continued to use that title, the Salīḥids had a different provenance and had not had a royal tradition among them. The Byzantines, however, could have applied the title "king" to them later, which found an echo in the Arabic sources.

Thus it is possible that the inception of the supremacy of the new federate group witnessed the resuscitation of an old term, phylarch, which had not been used in the extant sources for the rulers of the dominant federate group in the fourth century. Throughout the fifth, it is this term that describes the Arab chief in federate relationship with Byzantium: (*a*) in the third decade of the century, for Aspebetos, the phylarch of the Palestinian Parembole; (*b*)

[90] See *BAFOC*, 510–21.

[91] Ibid., 140.

[92] On these three senses, see ibid., 516.

around 460, regarding the strife between the phylarchs of the Parembole and Arabia; and (*c*) around 473, to describe Amorkesos. In all three instances the term is used with technical accuracy. And of course it continued to be so used through the sixth century, during which the titles of the Arab *foederati*, the Ghassānids, became very complex, comprising as they did, *inter alia*, both *basileus* and *phylarchos*.[93]

6. In the few Arabic sources on the Salīḥids the Salīḥid fighting force is not described by the general term for the tribes of pre-Islamic Arabia but by the technical term *jaysh, stratos*.[94] This is reminiscent of the term used by the ecclesiastical historian[95] for the forces of Queen Mavia that helped in the defense of Constantinople after Adrianople in 378. It also brings to mind the one used by the contemporary Arab poets to describe the fighting forces of the more powerful Ghassānids in the sixth century. This is noteworthy in view of the peace that obtained between Persia and Byzantium, which might have inclined the historian to think that, unlike the Tanūkhids and the Ghassānids, the Salīḥids did not employ their military talents very frequently. But there were the two wars of the reign of Theodosius II and also the *ayyām* involving the Arab tribes. And it is not impossible that the Salīḥids inherited the military techniques of their predecessors in the service of Byzantium, namely, the Tanūkhids of the fourth century, who had employed the tactic of the *cuneus*.[96]

7. One of the military terms of pre-Islamic Arabia is *jarrār*, the commander of a thousand. Although it is applied to military chiefs sometimes far from the Byzantine border in Yaman, some who held this title came from tribes that were in federate relationship to Byzantium: Kinda, Kalb, ʿUd̲ra and Salīḥ.[97] The question arises whether or not this too was the translation of the term chiliarch, *millenarius*. Chiliarch is the equivalent of *millenarius* and also of the Latin term *tribunus*. But *tribunus* also translates "phylarch,"[98] and this raises the tantalizing question whether the term *jarrār*, assumed by or applied to these Arab chiefs who were federates, also implies that they were phylarchs for the Romans. If so, the *jarrār* could have been the Arabic equivalent of phylarch in the technical military sense.

In the study of federate-imperial relations, especially as pertains to the

[93] See Shahîd, "The Patriciate of Arethas," 321–43. The titulature of his son Mund̲ir becomes even more complex.

[94] For some preliminary observations on the term *jaysh*, see above, 280. On the use of the terms *jaysh* in relation to the Salīḥids/Zokomids, see Ibn Ḥabīb, *Al-Munammaq*, 454.

[95] See *BAFOC*, 177 note 142.

[96] On this, see *BAFOC*, 177–78, 256–57.

[97] On these *jarrārs*, see Ibn Ḥabīb *al-Muḥabbar*, 250–51. Three of them have been discussed in this volume: Dāwūd and Ziyād, the two Salīḥids, and Rizāḥ from ʿUd̲ra.

[98] See *BAFOC*, 516.

The Greek-Nabataean Bilingual Inscription of Ruwwāfa

Only a portion of the inscription is reproduced here (after Altheim and Stiehl, *Die Araber in den alten Welt*, V/2, p. 549). The enlargement shows the crucial word *šrbt*, which is relevant to the etymology of "Saraceni" (see *Rome and the Arabs*, 123–41, and below, p. 543).

question of the settlement of the *foederati* within the *limes*, a most important fact should be borne in mind, which distinguishes Arab-imperial relations from German-imperial relations in the West.[99] While the Germans were settled on soil inhabited by non-Germans, the Arab *foederati* were settled on soil that had long been Arab, even before Rome appeared on the stage of Near East history. This was especially true of the limitrophe provinces, which had previously been the kingdoms of the Nabataean, Palmyrene, and Edessene Arabs. Thus the Rhomaic provincials among whom the *foederati* moved and settled were Arab like themselves. And so were many of the regular units in the Roman army that manned the *limes orientalis*. This basic fact explains the ease and the smoothness with which the process of accommodation took place. The system or pattern of land tenure under which the *foederati* were settled on Roman soil, whatever it was, enabled Arab-Roman relations to be symbiotically fruitful and to be attended by a minimum of friction.[100]

This aspect of federate-imperial relations, this harmonious symbiosis, can be related to what may be termed "War and Society." The performance of an army on the battlefield depends to a great extent on the sound relationship that obtains between it and the society within which it lives in peacetime.[101]

[99] For a preliminary remark on this point, see above, 479.

[100] Contrast the friction between the Alans and the Gallo-Romans of the Loire Valley in France during the reign of King Goar in the 5th century; see L. Musset, *The Germanic Invasions*, trans. E. and C. James (University Park, Penn., 1975), 217.

[101] For an important recent work that addresses the various problems related to the sociology of war, see R. Holmes, *Acts of War* (New York, 1986).

PART FOUR
SYNTHESIS AND EXPOSITION

The sections of this Synthesis are based on various chapters in this volume according to the following scheme:

I. "Federate-Imperial Relations": Part One, Chapters 1–6
II. "The Foederati: *Foedus, Phylarchia*, and *Basileia*": and Part Three, Sec. VI
III. "The Frontier: *Limes Orientalis*": Part One, Chapter 7 and Part Three, Secs. I–V
IV. "The Arab Church": Part I, Chapters 8–11; Part Two, Chapter 12, Sec. VI and Chapter 14, Sec. I
V. "Federate Cultural Life": Part Two, Chapter 14, Secs. I–IV
VI. "The Arab Church": Part I, Chapters 8–11; Part Two, Chapter 12, Sec. VI and Chapter 14, Sec. I
VII. "Byzantinism and Arabism: Interaction": Part One, Chapters 8–11; Part Two, Chapter 13, Sec. I, and Chapter 14, Secs. I, IV
VIII. "Arabs in Service of Byzantium": the relevant chapters in Parts One and Two that deal with the four personages
IX. "The Image": Part One, Chapters 1, 4, and 7

I. Federate-Imperial Relations

The Arab *foederati* of the fifth century served six emperors: Arcadius, Theodosius II, Marcian, Leo, Zeno, and Anastasius. In addition to fighting in the familiar terrain of the Syro-Mesopotamian frontier and the *limes orientalis* through participation in the Persian Wars of the reign of Theodosius, the Arabs saw service in faraway Pentapolis under Arcadius and most probably in Africa as a contingent in Leo's expeditionary force against the Vandals. Unlike federate-imperial relations in the fourth century, these relations remained harmonious throughout the fifth. The *foederati* shared the doctrinal orthodoxy of the Theodosian dynasty, while the Monophysitism of two members of the Leonine, Zeno and Anastasius, does not seem to have ruffled them except towards the very end. The reign of Leo is the watershed in the history of federate-imperial relations—the beginning of the end for the supremacy of Salīḥ as the dominant federate group of the fifth century. It is almost certain that in this reign the Salīḥids were drafted to fight in Leo's expedition against the Vandals and their federate units must have been decimated in the battle of Cape Bon. The same reign witnessed the unfolding of the extraordinary career of Amorkesos, the adventurous phylarch who dominated the scene of Arab-Byzantine relations in Palaestina Tertia, the Red Sea, and Ḥijāz. He was most likely a Ghassānid, and thus his phylarchate may be considered the first phase of the Ghassānid penetration of the *limes Arabicus*. Of the Arab chiefs in the service of Byzantium in the fifth century, Amorkesos and Dāwūd are the best representatives of the two contending federate groups. The first belongs to the new Ghassānid dynasty, which carved its federate status with its swords and became the efficacious shield of Byzantium against the Arabian Peninsula in the sixth century. The second belongs to the old Salīḥid dynasty which, after association with the Christian Roman Empire for a century, was touched by the spirituality of its new ambience and produced a phylarch who finally renounced the world and built the monastery that bore his name. The history of federate-imperial relations in this century together with that of the rise, decline, and fall of the dominant group, the Salīḥids, may be presented as follows.

The Theodosian Dynasty

It was most probably during the reign of Arcadius that Zokomos, the eponym of the Zokomids/Salīḥids, acquired phylarchal and federate status. The Salīḥids continued to prosper during the two subsequent reigns of the dynasty, those of Theodosius II and Marcian.

Arcadius

The reign of Arcadius (395–408) was propitious for the rise of a new Arab federate supremacy in Oriens. The previous reign had witnessed pro-German and anti-Arab policies which were dramatically reversed under Arcadius. The anti-German sentiment in Constantinople (reflected by Synesius in his Περὶ Βασιλείας) resulted in an operation that rid the capital of the German influence and presence. This is the historical background that may explain the rise to power of a new group of barbarians in Oriens—the Salīḥids. The victory of the Gothic horse at Adrianople had established cavalry as the important arm in warfare; but the loss of the German Gothic horse could be compensated by the Arabian which, moreover, had beaten the Gothic outside the walls of Constantinople itself as recently as 378. Moreover, these Arabs *foederati*, unlike the Germans, were not heretical Arians. Thus they were wanted and needed both by *imperium* and *ecclesia*. The Arab horse was mettlesome and its rider was orthodox.

Arcadius inherited from his father a stable front with Persia, and peace prevailed throughout his reign. Hence the sources are silent on wars on the Persian front and, consequently, on any Arab participation in them. The silence is broken, however, by an extraordinary reference in an unlikely author, the baptized Neo-Platonist of Cyrene, Synesius. In one of his letters, written in 404 to his brother Euoptius while on his way back by sea to Cyrene, he discusses a *turma* of Arab horsemen who boarded the ship with him. These were not Arab *foederati* but regular soldiers in the Roman army, *stratiōtai*, detached most probably from the Ala Tertia Arabum stationed at Thenemuthi in Egypt. This took place during the governorship of the incompetent Cerialis over Cyrene and these and other troops were needed to restore order in Pentapolis and protect it against the Ausurians. The movement of troops from Egypt to faraway Pentapolis suggests that this *turma* formed part of the *exercitus comitatensis* of Egypt. The distance is striking and speaks for the usefulness of the concept of the *exercitus comitatensis* and the mobility of the Arab horse. How often it was called upon to perform in various parts of the empire is not recorded, but this unexpected reference in Synesius suggests that it was not an isolated case.

Two Latin sources mention two episodes related to the Arabs, not of Egypt but of Oriens. John Cassian records the massacre of some solitaries in the region of Tekoa in Palaestina Prima by a band of raiding Saracens, while the *Vita S. Pelagiae* records the conversion of a large number of Saracens in Phoenicia Libanensis. The first indicates that Palaestina Prima, the Holy Land itself, was still not safe from marauding Saracens who were not yet converted to Christianity; hence the importance of the system of *phylarchi* and *foederati* for internal security. The second suggests that there were still large pockets of paganism in Oriens, although these Saracens may have been transhumant Arabs who had crossed the *limes*, driven by some climatic or other exigency.

Theodosius II

The emperor whose reign witnessed such cultural achievements as the foundation of the University of Constantinople and the promulgation of the *Codex Theodosianus*, also witnessed the outbreak of two wars with Persia, a departure from the good neighbor policy of Theodosius I. The reign is rather well documented for Arab-Byzantine relations, for which it was a happy period; the Arabs performed well for the *imperium* in the Persian Wars and for the *ecclesia* in the ecumenical councils.

Although peace between the two world powers was not broken until 421, the Arabian front was operational early in the reign. Even as Alaric was sacking Rome in 410, the Saracens launched a major offensive against Oriens from the Euphrates to the Nile, involving the limitrophe provinces, and the reverberation of the offensive was felt as deeply as Bethlehem in Palaestina Prima. It is impossible to determine the identity of the Arab group that mounted this offensive or the force that impelled it. It could have been a drought or the offensive of some powerful tribal group that was seeking political and military expression in northern Arabia—a chapter in what might be termed the anonymous war of Byzantium in this region, waged as it was, against tribes whose identity has been left unspecified in the sources. These could have belonged to the tribe of Kalb or Kinda or Lakhm. Just as the identity of this group is unknown, so also is the role of the Salīḥids in its repulse.

The role of the Arabs must be sought in the two Persian Wars of the reign. (1) The first war (aptly termed Pulcheria's Crusade), 421–422, was occasioned by the flight of some Persian Christians to Roman territory and the refusal of the empire to hand them back. Who these were is not clear, but they may have been the Iyād group. The war is not well documented but the sources refer with some specificity to the Lakhmid Arabs, the clients of Persia, rather than to the Roman Arabs, the Salīḥids. Mundir, the Lakhmid king, emerges as the warmonger, recommending a campaign the objective of which was Antioch itself. The campaign ends in disaster and the drowning of many in the Lakhmid contingent in the Euphrates. The Roman commander, Vitianus, gives short shrift to those who survived the river. The Salīḥids are not mentioned by name, but it is clear that they took an active part and performed creditably, as is recorded by the ecclesiastical historian. The Arabs on both sides who took an active part in the war are mentioned in the peace treaty that concluded it. It was stipulated that neither party should receive the Arab allies of the other when they defected, a clause that seems to have been honored more in the breach than in the observance. (2) The second Persian War, 440–442, was less important than the first. In spite of the anonymity of the participants in this war, it is practically certain that the Arabs took an active part in it; the Lakhmid king Mundir may even have instigated it in order to regain his reputation, tarnished in the first Persian War. It is also certain that the clause pertaining to the Arabs in the treaty that was concluded after the first Persian War was renewed at the end of this second war.

To the reign of Theodosius belongs one of the most remarkable episodes in the history of Arab-Byzantine relations, the rise of the phylarchs of the Palestinian Parembole in the desert of Juda. A Persian Arab, Aspebetos, outraged by the persecutions of the Christians there, flees Persia and seeks refuge in

Byzantium. He is received by Anatolius, the *magister militum per Orientem*, and is made the phylarch of the Provincia Arabia. After St. Euthymius cures his son Terebon, he moves to Palaestina Prima with his Saracens and becomes the first phylarch of the Palestinian Parembole. His subsequent career, during which he became a bishop and a delegate to the Council of Ephesus, belongs to ecclesiastical history. He must have been an impressive figure, since he won the approval and admiration of such widely different people as Anatolius, Euthymius, the Saint of the desert of Juda, and Juvenal, the bishop of Jerusalem. Aspebetos assumed the name Petrus on his conversion and most probably continued in the phylarchate of Palaestina Prima until such time as his son Terebon was old enough to assume it. What Arab tribal group he belonged to remains unknown. If his surname Aspebetos is an indication, it is possible that he belonged to the Tamīm group, since the surname appears among them. If so, then the Tamīm may be added as a component in the tribal structure of the Arab *foederati* in Oriens in the fifth century.

The best and most eloquent commentary on the performance of the Arab *foederati* and the success of the federate experiment is a *novella* issued in 443. The ecclesiastical historian of the reign had already spoken in laudatory terms of the Salīḥids when he said that they became formidable to the Persians, and the *novella* confirms this by implication, reflecting the importance of the various *limites* that protected the Empire amidst the dark clouds of international relations, with the Germans and the Huns hammering at the Empire's frontiers. It singles out the Arabs by name as it enjoins fairness on the limital *duces* in matters pertaining to the *annona foederatica*, which the *foederati* must receive without diminution. The watch over the Arabian and Persian frontiers was important to keep and it was performed partly by the Arabs. Hence it was necessary to keep them satisfied by the application of one of the most important clauses of the *foedus* with them, namely, the regular extension of the *annona*.

The sources record another Arab offensive in 447. However, it is described in such general terms that it is difficult to tell who mounted it or the reasons behind it.

Marcian

This was the last member of the House of Theodosius, and quite early in his reign, in 451, two important events took place—the victory of Aetius over Attila and the convocation of the Council of Chalcedon. The second event proved to be of far-reaching effect on the course of Arab-Byzantine relations, especially in the sixth century, but even as early as the reign of Marcian it was related to an event involving the Arabs.

Two military operations took place in this reign, and unlike those recorded for the reign of Theodosius, these are attended by some specificity pertaining to their geographical location. The first took place in Phoenicia Libanensis in the region of Damascus and engaged the *magister militum* himself, Ardabur, the son of Aspar. The historian Priscus, who recorded it, was also present while the *magister* was conducting negotiations with the ambassadors of the Saracens. This must have been a major Saracen thrust into Phoenicia; otherwise it would not have called for the conduct of military operations and negotiations by the *magister militum per Orientem* but would have been left to the *dux* of Phoenicia and his *foederati*. Who these Arabs were, is difficult to tell—possibly one of two groups of Arabs in northern Arabia who were restless in this period, the Kindites or the Ghassānids, with both of whom Byzantium was to strike *foedera* later in the century.

The second operation took place in the same year 453. It was conducted by Dorotheus, *comes (et dux Palaestinae)* against an Arab force in Moabitis in Palaestina Tertia, southeast of the Dead Sea. But even as Dorotheus was battling the Arabs in Moabitis disturbances broke out in Palaestina Prima in the wake of the Council of Chalcedon. The Monophysite party chased out of Jerusalem its patriarch, Juvenal, who had just returned from Chalcedon, having subscribed to the diophysite definition of faith and won independence for his see from the patriarch of Antioch.

In the short accounts of both operations there is no mention of the Arabs. But this does not amount to saying they did not participate. Two Saracen units of *equites* listed in the *Notitia Dignitatum*, were stationed in Phoenicia Libanensis and these must have participated in repelling the invaders in the first operation. The Salīḥids must have participated in at least the second since they were stationed in the Provincia Arabia and possibly in the region of Palaestina Tertia. It is noteworthy that the two operations took place simultaneously, or at least in the same year. This might suggest that they were synchronized, and if so they point to habits of co-operation among the barbarians which Byzantium dreaded. If the two operations were indeed synchronized, they foreshadowed the much more important and dangerous operations of 500 during the reign of Anastasius, when the powerful Kindite and Ghassānid tribal groups succeeded in forcing the hand of the Romans and extracting from them favorable *foedera* in 502.

The Leonine Dynasty

If the period of the Theodosian dynasty witnessed the rise and growth of the Salīḥids, that of the Leonine dynasty witnessed its decline, which began during the reign of Leo and continued during the two subsequent reigns of Zeno and Anastasius.

Leo

Arab-Byzantine relations are exceptionally well documented for the reign of Leo through that most informative long fragment which has survived from the *History* of Malchus. The fragment tells the history of one of the most enterprising of Arab chiefs who ever crossed the path of Byzantium, Amorkesos, who had been in the service of the Great King when for some unknown reason he decided to sever his relations with Persia and seek a Roman connection. After an adventurous military career in North Arabia, he approached the Byzantine frontier in Palaestina Tertia, penetrated it, and finally crowned his victorious career with the occupation of the strategic island of Iotabe, whence he drove the Roman customs officers. After this display of military strength, he made overtures of peace and, what is more, expressed his desire to become a phylarch of Byzantium. To the achievement of that end, he sent the bishop of his tribe, Petrus, to Constantinople, where the latter succeeded in convincing Leo of the desirability of inviting Amorkesos to Constantinople. Amorkesos made the journey to the capital, where he was royally entertained by the emperor, who had him eat at his table and sit in the Senate among the first patricians. After an exchange of gifts, Leo struck a *foedus* with Amorkesos, which confirmed his possession of the island of Iotabe and endowed him with the phylarchate of Palaestina Tertia. The *foedus* was struck in 473, one year before Leo's death.

Leo may have deserved the surname "butcher" applied to him by Malchus, but the butcher was no fool. Crucial imperial interests, both military and commercial, were at stake, involving the Red Sea and western Arabia and possibly the Indian Ocean. The energetic and warlike Amorkesos was clearly deemed the ideal phylarch for guarding imperial interests in that strategic area, especially after the extension of Byzantine influence in western Arabia, both in Mecca and Najrān, in the first half of the fifth century. This must be the explanation for the otherwise unintelligible royal treatment which Leo accorded an adventurer who, after all, had administered a blow to the *maiestas* of the *imperium* with the occupation of Iotabe. The conferment of the phylarchate relieved him of the status of conqueror of Iotabe and made him an officer in the Byzantine army, serving imperial interests on that island. Thus by his employment of this capable chief, Leo may be said to have strengthened considerably the Byzantine presence in northwestern Arabia. Furthermore, he started the involvement of the empire with the powerful military group that was searching for a place and role in the political and military history of northwestern Arabia and the Roman frontier, the Ghassānids. For it is practically certain that the tribal affiliation of Amorkesos was Ghassānid, and thus he represents the first phase of the assimilation of the Ghassānids into the Byzantine system as phylarchs and federates.

Leo's receptivity to Amorkesos' overtures has been explained as related to imperial interests which Amorkesos could serve. It remains to explain Amorkesos' military successes in Palaestina Tertia and Arabia, through which the *limes Arabicus* passed and where the Salīḥids, the dominant group of Arab *foederati* of Byzantium in the fifth century, were stationed. These successes are most probably related to Leo's expedition against the Vandals in Africa. Regular Roman troops and Salīḥid *foederati* must have been withdrawn from their stations in these provinces to take part in the great armament that sailed against the Vandals in 468, where they were most probably decimated in the battle of Cape Bon. This has precedents in the withdrawal of the Arab federates of Queen Mavia during the reign of Valens in the fourth century to fight the Goths in Thrace outside the walls of Constantinople in 378; earlier in the fifth century (in 404) a *turma* of Rhomaic Arabs was moved from Egypt to fight in Pentapolis. Thus Arab troops from Oriens fought in the West in the fifth century. Whether they did also in the reign of Theodosius II, who, like Leo and unlike Marcian and Zeno, intervened in the West, is not clear. In any case, participation in Leo's Vandal expedition had denuded the Provincia Arabia and Palaestina Tertia of federate and regular Roman troops who could have repelled the attacks of Amorkesos. The battle of Cape Bon represented the beginning of the end for the Salīḥids, as participation in the battle of Adrianople in 378 had spelled ruin for the Tanūkhids.

Just as Amorkesos' successes were related to Leo's expedition against the Vandals, so was Leo's interest in the Red Sea and the Indian Ocean, and with this his receptivity to Amorkesos' overtures. Leo had hoped to wrest Africa from the Vandals and restore order and some unity in the Mediterranean by his victory over the barbarians who, according to one view, had split that unity. With the disastrous failure of his expedition against the Vandals and the collapse of his hopes for the Mediterranean, it is natural to suppose that he would have looked to the Red Sea and the Indian Ocean as new fields for Byzantine commerce and influence, especially as a Byzantine presence had been established in western Arabia in the first half of the century by his imperial predecessors. Hence his interest in a strong and reliable ally such as Amorkesos, who could contribute substantially towards this goal in that strategic area. Perhaps something else commended the Arab to his attention. Leo had just disposed of the Alan Ardabur and his son Aspar, and wiped out German influence in the East; so he could have considered the new ethnic group, the Arabs, safe and reliable allies as the Isaurians he had welcomed. Thus there were substantial reasons for Leo's interest in Amorkesos and the Arabs. This could suggest that Leo did have a clear policy toward the Arabs and justify the phrase "Leo's Arab policy." In courting the Arab, Leo pursued a diplomatic course which was started in this proto-Byzantine period by Constantine but neglected after the death of Constantius. He may thus have laid the foundation for an Arab and eastern policy which reached its climax in the reign of Justinian.

Zeno

Arab-Byzantine relations were ruffled twice in the reign of Zeno, first in 474, the first year of the reign, and then late in 485.

The first Arab-Byzantine encounter apparently took place in the region of Mesopotamia and was possibly inspired by the Persians, who may have been unappreciative of the reception accorded by the Romans to one of their allies, Amorkesos. This reception violated the terms of the peace treaty concluded in the reign of Theodosius II which forbade such treatment of rebellious allies. Not much is known about this encounter, but a little more is known about the second, in 485. This too may have been inspired by Persia after Zeno stopped paying the annual subsidies for the upkeep of the Caspian Gates, or it may have been caused by the drought which had plagued the region. The military authorities on both sides intervened and brought the conflict to an amicable conclusion. Some significant details emerge from the accounts of this encounter: the Persian Arabs of only one tribal group could muster as many as four hundred horses for their assault against Roman territory; the Lakhmid king of Ḥīra is ordered by the Persian king to hurry to the north to keep the unruliness of the Persian Arabs under control; and the Byzantine *dux* of Mesopotamia brings the Arab *foederati* of Byzantium into action in that province. The third item is a welcome datum for the history of the Arab *foederati* in Oriens as it documents federate presence in that northerly province in Oriens, so badly documented in the sources.

In the cultural history of Byzantium, the reign of Zeno is known for the *Henotikon*, issued in 482, designed to reconcile conflicting parties which sprang up after Chalcedon. A letter addressed to the Church of Egypt, the *Henotikon* reflected the emperor's Monophysite tendencies, which finally led to that fatal turbulence in imperial-federate relations in the sixth century. How the *foederati* of the fifth reacted to this document is not recorded in the sources, but it is almost certain that the Salīḥids ignored it and remained Orthodox.

Anastasius

Anastasius was the last member of the house of Leo. His reign closes the fifth century and opens the sixth including almost one decade in the former and two in the latter. The reign is a watershed in the history of Persian-Byzantine relations, since it witnessed the outbreak of the Persian War of 502–506, in which the Arabs were involved. The war broke the long peace of the fifth century and preluded the series of wars that broke out continually in the reign of each emperor from Anastasius to Heraclius. It is, however, the first decade of his reign that is the concern of this volume on the fifth century.

After a Saracen invasion of Phoenicia Libanensis which reached the region of Emesa in 491–492, the sources are silent until the year 498, when three powerful Arab groups suddenly converged on the *limes orientalis* in the north and the south. It was the most serious Arab assault of the century; the Greek source is unusually informative and it is strikingly specific as it details the names of the Arab commanders, the Byzantine commanders, the geographical location of the military operation, and the date.

The first offensive was mounted by the Lakhmid king Nuʿmān against Sergiopolis, either as an expression of anti-Christian sentiment against the holy shrine of the Christians, or inspired by greed and the prospect of spoils from the rich shrine. It is quite likely that it was also Persian inspired and, if so, it preludes the aggressive policy of the Persian king Kawad, which found more violent expression after the turn of the century. Success, however, did not attend Lakhmid arms and Eugenius the *dux* of Syria and Euphratensis defeated the Lakhmid king.

The second offensive was mounted by Jabala, the Ghassānid chief, in Palestine. This was most probably a revolt, and a reaction to the stringent measures taken by Anastasius to restore the economic situation and stop the drain on the treasury. One of these was the return of the island of Iotabe to direct Roman rule, after its occupation by the Arabs since 473. Romanus, the energetic *dux* of Palestine, beat Jabala and after hard-fought battle dislodged him from the island. The events of this operation suggest that the Romans were not genuinely reconciled to the Arab occupation of the island, in spite of the fact that its master had been a phylarch in the employ of Byzantium since Leo confirmed Amorkesos in his possession of Iotabe. That this took place as late in the decade as 498 was perhaps due to the fact that it was only then that Anastasius had rid himself of the Isaurians, and this may also explain his tough attitude toward the Arabs, the other ethnic group which had won favor in Leo's eyes. But only some four years later, the emperor had to come back to the position of Leo and compound with the Arabs.

The third offensive was mounted by Kinda, the powerful Arabian power that was restlessly moving in all directions in the fifth century. Relations between Kinda and Ghassān were friendly, and it is quite likely that this third offensive was mounted by Kinda in response to an appeal for assistance sent by their friends the Ghassānids, who had been worsted by Romanus. The same fate awaited the Kindites, whose commander, Ḥujr, son of Arethas, was worsted by the capable *dux* of Palestine.

This was a veritable crisis just before the turn of the century but it was weathered by the two Roman commanders, Eugenius and Romanus. What Rome always feared might happen—co-operation in the camp of the barbarian enemy—did happen in 498. Although the Lakhmid thrust in the north cannot be related to the two other thrusts in the south, it is practically certain that Kinda and Ghassān acted in unison. Luckily for Byzantium, they did not act simultaneously and did not synchronize their efforts. The third offensive was posterior to the second; hence Romanus could deal with them separately. It was not long, however, before Anastasius had to bow to political and military exigencies, which forced him to compound with both Kinda and Ghassān. In 502 he had to conclude *foedera* with both of the two Arab tribal groups, alarmed by the prospect of having to fight on two fronts, the Persian and the Arab. In so doing, he initiated a new federate supremacy, that of the Ghassānids, who emerged as the dominant federate group of Byzantium in the sixth century.

II. The *Foederati*: *Foedus*, *Phylarchia*, and *Basileia*

More is known about the structure and organization of federate life in the fifth than in the fourth century, but the data gathered for the latter are invaluable as a foundation for the discussion of this theme in the former and for noting new developments. Scanty and arid as the sources are for Byzantino-arabica in the fifth century, some of them fortunately contain some significant details which throw light on aspects of federate life.

1. The dominant group of *foederati* in the fifth century were the Salīḥids, but it is practically certain that federate power was not centralized as it was to be in the sixth century, when, around 530, Justinian made Ghassānid Arethas supreme phylarch and king over all or most of the Arab federates in Oriens. Thus the Salīḥids exercised no power or authority over other federate tribal groups. Among these the most important were the Tanūkhids, who had been the dominant federates in the fourth century and who persisted in Oriens, settled in Chalcidice in the north, thus balancing the Salīḥids, who were settled in the south in the Provincia Arabia, in biblical Ammonitis and Moabitis. The Salīḥids, nevertheless, were the most prestigious of all the federate groups in the fifth century and the fact is reflected in the Greek as well as the Arabic sources.

2. The instrument that converted the Arab groups who breached the *limes orientalis* into the limitrophe and became allies of the empire was the *foedus*, the treaty which regulated and governed their relations with Byzantium and the conditions of their settlement.

a. The *foedus* made of the Arab groups *foederati*, allies of the empire, and both this Latin term and the Greek equivalents, ὑπόσπονδοι and ἔνσπονδοι, were consistently applied to these Arab groups throughout the fifth century. These same terms were applied to the Germanic tribes in the West who were in a similar relationship to the empire, and the terminological identity enables the two federate groups, the Germans and the Arabs, to be studied within the comparative context. The study should prove mutually illuminating.

b. The question has been raised whether such *foedera* with prospective allies were made in Constantinople or in one of the provinces with the *dux* or the *magister militum* in Oriens. It is almost certain that while *foedera* with relatively unimportant groups were entered into locally, the more important ones entailed a journey to Constantinople and an audience with the emperor. This is illustrated by Amorkesos, who came to Constantinople and was royally entertained by Emperor Leo before the *foedus* was agreed upon. Another Arab is reported to have appeared in Constantinople, Ḥannān/Ḥayyan from Najrān, although what exactly happened to him in the capital remains obscure. At any rate, the careers of these two Arabs suggest that the journey to Constantinople was not unusual, and so both Imru' al-Qays and Mavia of the fourth century may have made the journey at some point in their careers.

c. An exceptional *foedus* was struck in the Sinai Peninsula sometime in this century. The account of the hagiographer suggests that it was made between the Arab chief, Ammanes, who lived in the north of the Sinai Peninsula, and the Arab city of Pharan in the south, thus leaving the provincial *dux* and the authorities in Oriens out of this transaction. If the hagiographer reported accurately and was not elliptical in his account, this must have been an exceptional case, made possible by the vastness and inhospitableness of the Sinai Peninsula. These geographical facts perhaps inclined the provincial authorities to allow the powerful chief to have his *foedus* with Pharan, but it is inconceivable that this implied absolute independence or sovereignty for the Parembole of the Arab chief within Sinai. This was Roman territory, and whatever autonomy may have been allowed this chief must be understood as imperial tolerance of a local arrangement on the grounds of convenience, but ultimately he was under the jurisdiction of the provincial *dux* of the three Palestines, of which Sinai was an integral part. This is made clear by the account which describes the first *foedus* that the Ghassānids made with the Salīḥids later in the century, when they first penetrated the *limes* and asked to settle within it during the reign of Anastasius. The negotiations were conducted between the two Arab groups, but before the treaty was concluded the Salīḥids had to write to the authorities in Antioch.

Were these *foedera* written documents and, if so, in what language were they written? The texts have not survived in any source that can be described as a document; there are only references to them in the literary sources. Surely there were Latin and Greek versions, but was there an Arabic version? Unfortunately, the only Greek source that speaks of a correspondence concerning a *foedus* between an Arab party and a Byzantine establishment is a literary one: the author of the *Nili Narrationes* only says that Ammanes actually *wrote* to the people of Pharan. So the Arab parties in these treaties were not illiterate, and the chances are that there were Arabic versions of these *foedera*.

d. Different *foedera* had different terms, depending on the circumstances that led to the conclusion of the *foedus* and the identity of the non-Roman party. Although the sources are not very informative on these terms, references to two *foedera* in this century provide material for discussing them. The first is the *foedus* between Ammanes and the town of Pharan. Most of the terms are inferable from what the chief was willing to do in case the *foedus* was violated as in fact it was. Clearly the principal obligation which lay upon the chief was to insure security in the region, especially for those who traversed the Sinai Peninsula or who ventured to travel within its confines. Apparently, there was a clause that insured compensation on the part of the chief in case he failed in his duties as guardsman of the desert, and what this compensation consisted of is enumerated. It is clear that in return the chief received from the town of Pharan material benefits, to which he refers and which he was loath to forfeit. The second *foedus* is that concluded between Salīḥ and Ghassān early in the reign of Anastasius. The Arabic source is informative on one of the clauses in the treaty pertaining to the conditions of settling Ghassān on Roman soil, namely, that each male should pay one or two *dīnār*, according to his station and wealth. Such terms as are included in these two *foedera* are specific and remain matters of detail. What emerges from a study of federate-imperial relations is the fact that *foedus* extended privileges to the new federate group and also imposed duties on them. The latter are not difficult to enumerate for the powerful federate groups: participation in the Persian Wars, fighting against the Arabs of the Peninsula when these conducted raids against Roman territory, protection of the region in which they were settled, and guarding the caravan routes which passed through their territory.

e. Less clear are the privileges which the Romans granted. For those who were settled outside the *limes*, the federates of the Outer Shield, the privileges most probably consisted in payment of money, which insured their loyalty and the performance of their duty. For those within the *limes*, those of the Inner Shield, the privileges were many and more complex. They were allowed to settle on Roman territory within the *limes*, were integrated within the Roman military and administrative system, and most probably received the *insignia* which the Greek sources for the sixth centuries have described for the chiefs of the Mauri and the Armenians, who also were allies of the Romans. Whether they were provided for by *hospitalitas* or the *annona foederatica* cannot be resolved by an appeal to the fifth-century sources. Hints and occasional references to the *foederati* of the fourth century speak of *munera* and *salaria*, and this suggests that the *foederati* of the fifth also received the *annona foederatica*. The *annona* is referred to in one of the novellae of Theodosius II but whether it was delivered in money or in kind is not clear. As to their legal status, the literary sources of the fifth century (conciliar lists, and imperial novellae) speak of the Arabs as a *gens* or *ethnos* and this confirms what has been suspected for the *foederati* of the fourth century—that they remained non-citizens and were not considered *Rhōmaioi*. The occupation of the island of Iotabe by Amorkesos presents a curious spectacle in the history of the federates of the Inner Shield: he first seized Iotabe from the Romans by force and then, after his *foedus* with the emperor Leo, administered it for the Romans. It is practically certain that it was not an instance of *cessio*. Faced with the *fait accompli* of its occupation by a powerful Arab chief who, furthermore, had demonstrated his value to crucial imperial interests in western Arabia and the Red Sea area, the imperial government through the convenient *foedus* simply confirmed him in the occupation of the island in order that he might serve Byzantine interests in those regions.

3. While the sources for the fourth century generally refer to the Arab federate chiefs as kings (*basileis, reges*, and *reguli*), those for the fifth generally refer to them as phylarchs. This is the term applied to Zokomos, the eponym of the Zokomids/Salīḥids, Aspebetos, the first phylarch of the Palestinian Parembole, and to Amorkesos. The term *basileus* appears only in the sources for the fifth century, applied to an Arab Sinaitic chief in a literary source that is not of the same order of accuracy as those that speak of the federate chiefs as phylarchs. References to a *basilis* or *basileus* in Theodoret are to Arabs who did not have federate status. The application of *phylarchos* rather than *basileus* to these federate Arab chiefs may or may not be significant. The Arab chiefs of the fourth century most probably had been kings and belonged to Arab royal houses before they crossed the paths of the Romans, and so the Romans continued to apply to them titles they already had. This may not have been true of the Arab federate chiefs of the fifth century. The Arabic sources, on the other hand, regularly refer to the chiefs of Salīḥ as kings (*mulūk,* plural of *malik*), possibly because of the application of the term to the Tanūkhid chiefs of the fourth century and the Ghassānid chiefs of the sixth, extending the same term to those of the fifth. Thus the Greek sources must remain the guide in this terminological problem, and it can be safely concluded that the term "phylarch" emerged clearly in the fifth century as the technical term that designated the Arab chief who was a federate of Byzantium. It was only in the sixth century that Procopius clearly defined it in a well-known passage in the *History*. The term thus emerges as an important official Byzantine title in the fifth century. It is not inconceivable that the phylarchs of the fifth century

were also kings to their people but there is no echo in the Greek and Latin sources to this effect. Also, the Romans do not seem to have applied the native title *malik* in a significant way to these federate chiefs, as Justinian was to do around 530 when he applied it to Arethas in order to centralize the Arab phylarchate of the Orient.

4. The phylarchate as a new element in the Byzantine administrative system receives much illumination from the sources on the sixth century. Various aspects of it are extremely clear, such as the application of the sequence of honorific titles *clarissimus–spectabilis–illustris*, and even *patricius*, to the distinguished phylarchs. None of this is clear from the extant sources on the fifth century and so the question of whether or not the Arab phylarchs of this century were endowed with such titles must remain open. However, the sources have sporadic hints related to the phylarchate which may be brought together in this context.

a. In this century the phylarchate became an office in the Byzantine administrative system in the Orient, and when the title phylarch is used in texts that document Arab-Byzantine relations it almost certainly means an Arab official in the service of Byzantium, a *foederatus*, not a tribal chief, a *sayyid* or *shaykh*. This is reflected in the use of the term νέος in one of the Nessana Papyri to describe a phylarch where the meaning is clearly "the newly appointed"; thus the phylarch moved in the Byzantine administrative orbit and was appointed by the authorities.

b. There is no doubt that each province of the limitrophe had its own phylarch or group of phylarchs who were subordinate to the *dux* of the province. Whether the phylarchs of each province were also under a chief phylarch is not clear. The Edict of Beersheba speaks of a *koinon* of *archiphyloi* in Palaestina Prima. The *koinon* is clearly a tax unit, possibly involving Arabs who were not federates. But it must remain a possibility that if these non-federate chiefs were organized in *koina* the federate chiefs were similarly organized, especially in large provinces such as Palaestina Tertia, which extended far and wide and must have had more than one phylarch and possibly a *koinon* of them.

c. The Arab *foederati* were commanded by their own phylarchs, but it is possible that occasionally they were also commanded by imperial officers, just as the German units were after the elimination of German influence under Arcadius. In 421 *foederati* appear fighting on the Persian front under the *magister militum*, the Goth Areobindus. It has been argued that the *foederati* concerned could only have been Arab and that they could have been commanded by the non-Arab Areobindus, who is described as *comes foederatorum*, in much the same way that they were commanded in 503 by his grandson and namesake. The account of the latter operation is more specific, and suggests that when this happened the *foederati* were led by their own phylarchs but were ultimately responsible to the *comes foederatorum*.

d. Byzantine offices were non-hereditary. But the newly created phylarchate partook of both the non-hereditary Byzantine and the hereditary Arab traditions, since its phylarchs were related to both. As its incumbents were Arab, they naturally brought with them to the new office the Arab hereditary principle: the son of the *sayyid*, the chief of the tribe, could succeed him, and this was especially true of the royal houses. But as an incumbent of a Byzantine office, the phylarch had to be appointed by the authorities. Hereditary succession may not have been the case with the minor phylarchs but apparently was with the dominant group, where there was possibly a royal tradition which made dynastic succession even more natural. This was the case with the Salīḥids, who appear as a dynasty, although each ruling member had to be appointed by the emperor.

III. The Frontier: *Limes Orientalis*

The various elements in the discussion of the *limes orientalis* have been identified and discussed for the fourth century. These elements persist in the fifth century, so that only changes and developments will be noted here.

1. Towards the beginning of the reign of Theodosius I, Egypt was separated from the Diocese of Oriens, and thus the *limes orientalis* in the fifth century consists in only that segment of the *limes Diocletianus* that extended from Mesopotamia in the north to Palaestina Tertia near the Red Sea in the south. It will also be remembered that in the reign of Constantius, Palaestina Tertia was carved out of the Provincia Arabia and was attached to Palestine. Thus Ḥijāz, or rather the northern half of it, that sphere of Byzantine influence, became throughout this century, an extension not of the Provincia Arabia but of Palaestina Tertia.

2. The most important document for the study of the *limes orientalis* in the fifth century is undoubtedly the *Notitia Dignitatum*. This has been analyzed in detail and it has been concluded that many of the units listed were ethnically Arab, especially in the limitrophe provinces. Egypt, which was then a separate diocese, had units the names of which were explicitly Arab—such as Thamūdi, Arab, and Ituraean in the *limes Aegypti*, and Palmyrene in the Thebaid. These were regular units in the army and their members were Roman citizens. Other units, described as *Equites sagittarii indigenae*, were most probably Arab, and these were also *Rhōmaioi*. There were probably other Arabs who were not *Rhōmaioi* in the service of Byzantium in Egypt. This was probably the case for those in Augustamnica II, since the bishop of Phagroriopolis, in a document dated shortly after Chalcedon in 451, signs *Episcopus Scenarum Mandrarum*. The Arab element in the units listed in the *Notitia Dignitatum* can be illustrated for other provinces of the limitrophe.

Especially noteworthy in this document are two units referred to as *Equites Saraceni indigenae* and *Equites Saraceni* assigned to Phoenicia Libanensis. These two mysterious units were noted in the course of the discussion of the fourth century. Their legal status in the fifth century remains obscure, but their identity could be related to one of the four following groups: (*a*) the Tanūkhids, who after their fall as the dominant federate group late in the fourth century, were enrolled in the army of the Orient and thus become regular units in that army; (*b*) the new dominant group in the fifth century, the Salīḥids; (*c*) the large pockets of Saracens attested in Phoenicia in this century in the *Vita S. Pelagiae*; (*d*) one of the tribal groups Kalb, Namir, and Iyād, who lived not far from Betroclus and Thelsee, where these two units were stationed.

3. As it was throughout the entire proto-Byzantine period, the *limes orientalis* in the fifth century was the most important fact of Arab-Byzantine coexistence, warding off raids and thrusts from Arabia as well as from Sasanid Persia. Yet the *limes* could not entirely prevent powerful Arab military groups from effecting dents and sometimes breaches in the *limes* which extended over a vast area. Important breaches took place, possibly toward the beginning of the century, when the Salīḥids wandered through Wādī Sirḥān and established themselves as a federate group *intra limitem* and finally emerged as the dominant federate group in the fifth century. Toward the end of the century, other powerful groups, the Ghassānids and the Kindites, effected deep penetrations in the limitrophe, finally forcing Byzantium to make *foedera* with them. One of the two *foedera* made the Ghassānids the new federate supremacy in Oriens, replacing the Salīḥids. Other tribal groups could also penetrate the limitrophe, such as Kalb and Namir, who appear fighting the Salīḥids in either the Gaulanitis or Bathaniyya in Palaestina Secunda and Arabia, respectively.

Archeologists have accorded the *limes orientalis* much attention, especially that part of it which runs from Bostra to Ayla, the *limes Arabicus*. This is usually divisible into three sectors, the northern, the central, and the southern. The data gathered together on the Arab-Byzantine relationship in the fifth century may now be brought to bear on what the archeologists have discussed. (*a*) Wādī Sirḥān was one of the major routes that led from northern Arabia into Oriens and ran into the southern sector of the *limes Arabicus*, which extended from Wādī Ḥasā into Ayla. This was the historic route of the pastoralists since the days of Gideon and the Midianites. A Latin inscription was found at Dūma, the southern terminus of this *wādī*, left there by a detachment of the III Cyrenaica, the legion of Arabia. The inscription has raised the question of who patrolled this Wādī for the Romans and whether the Romans patrolled it regularly; critical opinion is divided on this issue. In light of the role of the Arab *foederati* in the Roman defense system in this proto-Byzantine period, it is quite likely that patrol duties in this *wādī* were performed by them in the fourth and fifth centuries. This task was congenial to the *foederati*, as it sent them to terrain and climate they were familiar with and which they could endure better than the regular Roman soldiers. In the fifth century, this likelihood is enhanced by the fact that the new dominant federate group, the Salīḥids were stationed not far from the northern terminus of the *wādī* and had hailed from the *wādī* before they entered Oriens and acquired federate status. (*b*) Questions have also been raised about the central sector of the *limes Arabicus*, which extended from Philadelphia to Wādī Ḥasā in the south. It has been noted that the Roman forts of this sector were abandoned in the fifth century. If the reading of the archeological evidence is correct then two explanations may be offered, one of which is drawn from the history of Arab-Byzantine relations. Late in his reign, Emperor Leo sent two expeditions against the Vandals in Africa. In view of the peace that obtained with Persia, it is practically certain that he drew away many of the units that manned military posts along the *limes orientalis* for the great but disastrous military adventure. Most of these troops did not return, and this could explain the non-occupation of the forts of the central section of the *limes Arabicus*. Alternatively, the defense of this sector may have devolved to a large extent on the Salīḥids, the new dominant federate group who were stationed in this very region.

Many toponyms were associated with the Tanūkhids, the dominant federate group of the fourth century. This is not the case for the Salīḥids. Most of the toponyms that the sources associate with them belong to either the period *before* or *after* they became the new federate supremacy in the fifth century. Only two explicitly Salīḥid toponyms are recoverable from the sources, both near Philadelphia, presentday Amman in Jordan. One is Wādī al-Salīḥī and the other is a village called al-Salīḥī. Another toponym in the northern part of Ḥijāz must have been a Roman military post or an establishment associated with the Romans, since it is called Thamad al-Rūm (Thamad of the Romans). It is located between Medina and Oriens (Shām) near Khaybar, but almost nothing else is known about it.

4. The protective function that the *limes orientalis* performed for Byzantium was complemented by what may be termed the Arab component in the makeup of the defense system in Oriens, namely, Arab federate power, which consisted in the system of *phylarchi* and *foederati* of the proto-Byzantine period. For a correct appreciation of the working of this defense system in its entirety, it is imperative to discuss briefly the role of the Arab *foederati*.

The obsolescence of the concept of the *limes exterior* and *limes interior* in the terminology of frontier studies calls for a new set of conjugates related to the *foederati*, who were deployed partly within the *limes* and partly without. Thus it is possible to speak of two federate shields in this proto-Byzantine period—the inner and the outer federate shields. The Greek and Latin sources have referred vaguely and in general terms to these *foederati* who are known to them as Saracens, but this anonymity has been terminated by the Arabic sources. It is therefore possible to write the history of this Arab component in the *limes orientalis* with some specificity and, what is more, with reference to whether these tribes were settled within or without the *limes*.

a. *The inner shield.* Within the *limes orientalis* the various Arab federate tribes were deployed in the limitrophe provinces, from Mesopotamia to Palaestina Tertia. The dominant group among them in the fifth century were the Salīḥids who were settled roughly in the Provincia Arabia and Palaestina Tertia. The Tanūkhids of the fourth century persisted in Oriens after their fall as the dominant group, and were settled in the north in Chalcidice. In addition to the other tribal federate groups enumerated for the fourth century, there were some newcomers to Oriens in the fifth, or some tribes to whom the sources give prominence as active in this century. Such is the Iyād, which had migrated from the Land of the Two Rivers, and the two sister tribes Kalb and Namir, which seem to have penetrated the *limes* on one occasion when they fought the Salīḥid king Dāwūd and brought about his downfall. It is possible that they were partly within and partly without the *limes*. Toward the end of the century, the Ghassānids also made their appearance within the *limes* when one of their chiefs, Amorkesos, established a federate presence in Palaestina Tertia.

A good deal of precision is provided by the account of the federates of the Parembole. In an unusual mood, the Greek source gives valuable information on the phylarchs of the Desert of Juda in Palaestina Prima, including their names—Petrus I, Terebon I, Petrus II, and Terebon II. As far as frontier studies are concerned, the data on the phylarchs of the Palestinian Parembole support the view that Oriens did have phylarchal and federate pockets within the *limes*; that they were far from the *limes orientalis*, as in the case of this one in Palaestina Prima; and that they were important for internal security reasons. The exposure of the monastic establishment of the Desert of Juda to some Saracen invasions, especially the violent and ravaging one during the reign of Anastasius, evidences the danger posed to the monasteries and justifies the rise of these internal pockets of federates. Of the same order is that pocket in Sinai, in Palaestina Tertia not far from the transverse *limes Palaestina*, which the *Nili Narrationes* have revealed. The account involves the phylarch Ammanes, who had a parembole in the north of Sinai and who clearly was charged with keeping law and order in the region and preventing acts of violence against the inhabitants of Pharan in the south of the Sinai Peninsula. The case of the Sinaitic Parembole is perhaps more illustrative of the value of the phylarchal and federate system than the Palestinian Parembole. Here was a vast area (according to the hagiographer, it was a twelve days' journey from

Pharan to the Parembole) in difficult desert terrain, which could be controlled most efficiently by an Arab federate phylarch.

The federates of the inner shield were integrated in the Byzantine system in a way that those of the outer shield probably were not. It is practically certain that the phylarchal and federate system obtained in each of the limitrophe provinces, from Mesopotamia in the north to Palaestina Tertia in the south. Each province had its own phylarch (and most probably phylarchs), especially such vast provinces as Palaestina Tertia, which, moreover, was so curiously shaped as to make it necessary to have in it more than one phylarch. The tribal chiefs of Saracens in Palaestina Prima who were not federates formed a *koinon*. This suggests that there may also have been federate *koina* in the large provinces. The phylarch of the province was, of course, subordinate to the provincial *dux*, and the entire phylarchate of Oriens was no doubt subordinate to the *magister militum* of Oriens.

Although the duties of the Arab federates were normally performed in Oriens itself and its neighboring regions such as Arabia and Persia, there is reference in one Greek source to the employment of Arab troops away from their stations in Egypt to serve in Pentapolis during the reign of Arcadius. And it has been argued that Leo must have drafted the Salīḥids and possibly other *foederati* in his expedition against the Vandals, especially in view of the peace that prevailed with Sasanid Persia. If so, the Salīḥids would have fought at the battle of Cape Bon. The Arabic sources speak of their *jaysh*, their "army," and this suggests that they were powerful and that they reached a high degree of military efficiency. They could therefore have formed part of the *exercitus comitatensis* of Oriens and could well have been dispatched to Africa to fight against the Vandals.

b. *The outer shield*. This consisted of the tribes who lived without the *limes orientalis* and were related to Rome as allies, but in a less intimate way than those of the inner shield. It has been suggested that such were Kalb and Namir, who may have been deployed partly within and partly without the *limes*. The same may hold true of such tribes in northern Ḥijāz such as Balī and Juḏām, which lived in Palaestina Tertia but possibly also outside it in that part of northern Ḥijāz which was a Byzantine sphere of influence. The status of these tribes is not certain, but ʿUḏra, which lived farther to the south (as far as Wādī al-Qurā near Medina) may definitely be taken as an example of a federate tribe that belonged to the outer shield in Ḥijāz. It was less intimately related and integrated in the Byzantine system than Salīḥ, and its chief was probably called *sayyid* or *shaykh* rather than phylarch, which was an official Byzantine title applied to the Arab chiefs of the inner shield. The title of the Arab chief of the outer shield was possibly the Arabic word *jarrār*, which seems to be a translation of "chiliarch." It was this powerful tribe of

ʿUḏra that extended the Byzantine sphere of influence deeper in Ḥijāz through assistance rendered by Rizāḥ, its energetic chief, to Quṣayy, who thus captured Mecca and opened a new chapter in the history of the future city of Islam. The historian of the Roman frontier in Ḥijāz operates with the bilinguis of Ruwwāfa, but other and perhaps more important inscriptions are buried farther to the south in Ḥijāz, waiting to be disinterred. Once they are, the full extent of the Roman presence in Ḥijāz will be revealed. And it should not come as a surprise if inscriptions involving ʿUḏra turn up in what was, after all, Byzantium's sphere of influence.

5. The *castra, castella, strata*, and *milliaria* of the Roman military establishment in Oriens have either disappeared or left faint traces in the desert scene of the present-day Near East. Not so the lexemes that stood for them and which have entered the lexicology of the Arabic language: *castra* appears as *qaṣr, strata* as *ṣirāṭ, milliarium* as *mīl*, and *veredi* as *barīd*. Additionally, the Roman military painter of legionary shields (ζωγράφος) and the concept related to it (ζωγραφία) have become naturalized in Arabic as *zukhruf*, which appears in the Koran, along with *qaṣr* and *ṣirāṭ*, a reminder of the strong military presence that Rome established in Oriens in the first centuries of the Christian Era.

IV. The *Foederati* in the Arabic Sources

The value of the Arabic sources derives mainly from their specificity, the intimate details they provide on the *foederati* which are not to be found in the Byzantine sources and are crucial for writing their history, especially their cultural history. The data scattered in these sources come ultimately from Hishām, the reliable historian of pre-Islamic Arabia and the *foederati*. Apparently he did not write a special monograph on the Salīḥids, as he did on the Tanūḵhids, but he did write an authoritative one on an important federate tribe that appears in Oriens in the fifth century, Iyād. The data provided by the Arabic sources throw light not only on internal federate history in Oriens but also in western Arabia.

Oriens

Although the federates were not centralized, there was a dominant group, the Salīḥids, who shared the defense of Oriens with the other federate tribes of the inner and the outer shields.

The Salīḥids

The history of the Salīḥids in the Peninsular stage is shrouded in obscurity, but they almost certainly made their way into Oriens from that north Arabian gateway, Wādī Sirḥān. They were settled roughly in the Provincia

Arabia and the northern part of Palaestina Tertia, the biblical Ammonitis and Moabitis, a fact confirmed by the survival of two toponyms, namely, the village of al-Salīḥī and the valley, Wādī al-Salīḥī, both near present day Amman in Jordan.

The names of the Salīḥid kings of the fourth and fifth centuries, unlike those of the Tanūkhid and the Ghassānid kings, have not survived in a list, but what may be termed the ruling clan among them was the Zokomids, named after the eponym Zokomos, also attested in the Greek sources. Several members of this clan deserve special notice.

1. The most celebrated of all the Salīḥid kings is undoubtedly the one who had the biblical name Dāwūd/David, evidence of the attachment of the dynasty to Christianity and the biblical tradition. Towards the end of his career, he became very religious and performed acts of humility such as carrying water and mortar for building the monastery that bore his name, the ruins of which still stand midway between Ruṣāfa and Isriye in the north of Oriens. For doing this he was nicknamed al-Lathiq, the bedraggled. His reign is remarkable culturally, for he had in his court or retinue a poet laureate from the tribe of Iyād by the name of ʿAbd al-ʿĀṣ. Dāwūd died in battle, felled by Thaʿlaba and Muʿāwiya, tribesmen of Kalb and Namir, respectively. The battle took place somewhere between the Gaulanitis and Bathaniyya. He was survived by a daughter who wrote an elegy on his death of which one verse has survived, as also survived a triplet composed by one of the regicides, glorying in his victory over the Salīḥid king.

2. Four other members of the clan deserve some notice, although not much is known about them: (*a*) Ziyād who most probably acted as general for Dāwūd. He was one of the *jarrārūn* (chiliarchs) of pre-Islamic Arabia. The sources mainly remember him in connection with the famous *yawm* (a battle day of the pre-Islamic Arabs) of al-Baradān, in the Samāwa not far from the Euphrates, in which he was defeated as he faced the powerful Kinda and its king, Ḥujr. (*b*) Al-Habūla, sometimes mentioned as the father of both Ziyād and Dāwūd; his name is striking and suggests attachment to Christianity if its etymology is related to the Christian concept of *salos*, the fool. (*c*) Ibn Mandala, one of the last Salīḥids, who apparently was a warrior. His name, too, could suggest some attachment to Christianity if it can be related to a censer which he may have donated to a church. (*d*) Finally, Sabīṭ, the *jābī* (tax collector) who, toward the end of the century, was involved in a dispute with a Ghassānid chief and was killed by him. His death signals the beginning of the end for Salīḥid supremacy in Oriens.

After a century of federate supremacy, the Salīḥids fell and gave way to another Arab federate group. Various factors contributed to this fall. It is possible that what is said about Dāwūd in the Arabic sources may have been true of the Salīḥids in general, namely, that their strong attachment to Christianity to some degree eroded their martial spirit. But surely the more plausible explanation must be related to the fact that they had to face an alliance composed of the two most powerful groups that were seeking to penetrate the *limes orientalis*, Kinda and Ghassān. The former had beaten them on the battlefield of al-Baradān and the latter, after a period of coexistence with them, finally won the upper hand and forced Byzantium to accept the fait accompli of their victory by concluding a *foedus*. The Salīḥids had no control over the new forces that had been unleashed in Arabia and which had been seeking political and military expression along the *limes orientalis*. *Tafarruq al-Azd*, "the Dispersion of the Azd," is the Arabian equivalent of the German *Völkerwanderungen* in the history of pre-Islamic Arabia. This historic wave, represented by the Ghassānids, reached the Roman frontier and swept away the Salīḥids from their federate supremacy in Oriens. Traces of interfederate strife are also discernible in the Arabic sources and these give some conception of the political alignments involving the federates. Two clans from Kalb and Namir appear aligned in the fatal battle that brought about the downfall of Dāwūd. And there is reference to a clan from Namir, Labwān, aligned with Salīḥ. The cause of this discontent in the federate camp is not clear, but it did contribute towards the destabilization of Salīḥ. It is also just possible that before the Salīḥids had to face the combined power of Kinda and Ghassān, they had taken part in Leo's disastrous expedition against the Vandals. If so, the Salīḥid ranks must have been considerably thinned, if not decimated, at the battle of Cape Bon.

The Two Shields

The Arabic sources also provide specific information about other tribes of the federate shield, some of which has already been discussed as part of the history of Arab-Byzantine relations in the fourth century. Some of this information, especially on ʿUḏra, is of considerable historical significance.

1. The tribe of Balī, which was settled not far from Ayla in Palaestina Tertia, appears as a Christian tribe which built a monastery, Dayr al-Qunfuḏ, in Ayla itself, since this most unusual name for a monastery is also the name of one of its clans. The mine of Fārān in Ḥijāz belonged to them and Balawī tribesmen worked as smiths. Kalb and Namir appear allied against the Salīḥid king Dāwūd. The sources give important genealogical data on the two regicides from these two tribes, and thus give a glimpse of the inter-Arab history of the federate shield, which contributed to the eventual downfall of the dominant federate group. Iyād was a newcomer to Oriens in the fifth century and Dāwūd's court poet belonged to this important tribal group, which had contributed much to Arab culture before it emigrated to Byzantine territory.

2. Important as all these tribes were, however, it is ʿUḏra that emerges as the most important tribe in Ḥijāz, belonging probably to the outer shield. In the fifth century it is under a powerful and energetic chief, Rizāḥ, who appears as the master of Ḥijāz and a factor in the history of the West Arabian region, all of which redounded to the benefit of Byzantium. The role he played in the history of this region may be summarized as follows. (*a*) He changed the ethnographic map of Ḥijāz by changing the affiliations of four of its tribes and sending one to the south as far as Tathlīth. What was behind these measures is not entirely clear, but a Byzantine profile to them is not entirely ruled out. (*b*) Much more important was the role he played in extending assistance to Quṣayy for the occupation of Mecca. In strictly Byzantine terms this meant the extension of Byzantine indirect influence deep in the heart of Ḥijāz. The ʿUḏrite chief could not have foreseen at the time that he was contributing the most important element to the making of Mecca, the future city of Islam which in the seventh century produced the Prophet Muḥammad, a lineal descendant to Quṣayy, whose successors broke the two federate shields and wrested Oriens itself from Byzantium.

Western Arabia

The fifth century witnessed a revival of Byzantine interest in western Arabia reminiscent of that evinced by Constantius in the preceding century. And it involved Mecca, the future city of Islam; Najrān, the great Arab urban center in the Ḥimyarite South; and Ḥimyar itself.

1. *Mecca*. The future city of Islam owes so much to Quṣayy that it is possible to say that he was the organizer of its social, political, and religious life, who thus laid the foundation for its emergence as the great caravan city of Arabia in the sixth century and the birthplace of the Prophet Muḥammad. According to the Arabic sources, Quṣayy established the institutional framework within which the various facets of Mecca's life evolved, and this involved his tribe Quraysh and the Kaʿba, to which, according to the sources, he reintroduced Ishmaelism. But it was a federate of Byzantium, none other than Rizāḥ, the powerful chief of ʿUḏra and half-brother to Quṣayy, who extended assistance to the latter in the occupation of Mecca, and in so doing worked, consciously or unconsciously, directly or indirectly, toward extending the Byzantine sphere of influence in Ḥijāz, both that of the *imperium* and of the *ecclesia*. Not much is known about a Byzantine imperial presence in Mecca other than that ʿUḏrite federate troops fought with Quṣayy in the battle against Khuzāʿa for the occupation of Mecca, but something is known about the presence of the Byzantine *ecclesia* in Mecca. References to a few toponyms with a distinct Christian ring have survived in the Arabic sources: Maqbarat al-Naṣāra, the cemetery of the Christians; Mawqif al-Naṣrāni, the station of

the Christian; and Masājid Maryam, the praying places or mosques of Mary, located outside Mecca on the way to Medina. In view of the fact that Byzantium's first contact with Mecca took place in this century through ʿUḏra, the strongly Christian tribe, the chances are that these toponyms also go back to the fifth century, supplying evidence for the extension of the Christian mission to Mecca.

2. *Najrān*. The Byzantine involvement in Najrān turns largely round the figure of Ḥannān/Ḥayyān, the Najrānite merchant who visited Constantinople sometime in the first two decades of the fifth century. The visit is shrouded in obscurity as to its background, but there is no doubt that the future convert to Christianity must have been impressed by the Christian monuments and other expressions of Christianity in Constantinople. Later on, after his conversion in Ḥīra, he embarked on an evangelizing effort to convert Najrān and Ḥimyar. Byzantium, it has been argued, may have helped Ḥannān in his efforts to evangelize part of Ḥimyar. The doctrinal complexion of the Christianity that was introduced to Najrān by Ḥannān/Ḥayyān was neither Nestorian nor Monophysite, since its introduction antedated the theological controversies involving these two doctrinal positions. But later in the fifth century and in the sixth, Najrān appears as a center of Monophysitism, and Byzantium was most probably also involved in connection with this development. The Arabic sources speak about the introduction of Christianity to Najrān by the Ghassānids of the north. The statement can only mean the introduction of the Monophysite version of Christianity to which the Ghassānids—the *foederati* of Byzantium under Anastasius—belonged. Ghassān may have acted as the link between Philoxenus, the energetic bishop of Mabboug, and Najrān, since the first bishop of Najrān, Paul I, was consecrated by Philoxenus, possibly around 500. Thus, unlike the mission to Mecca, that to Najrān was crowned by the creation of an episcopal see. It is to the energy of this first bishop, who was an Arab, that the spread of Christianity in Najrān and its region must be ascribed and together with it the rise of a Christian hierarchy, which is attested in the primary documents that are extant on the religious wars of the region some two decades later.

3. *Ḥimyar*. The Byzantine-Ḥimyarite relationship is represented in the sources by the dispatch of a bishop for Ḥimyar, namely, Silvanus, during the reign of Anastasius. It has been argued that this must have happened at a propitious moment, when Ḥimyar was in a receptive mood to accept from its traditional enemy a bishop of a religion that had been viewed with suspicion by Ḥimyar as involving Byzantine influence. This moment came most probably during the first Ethiopian expedition against Ḥimyar under Negus Kaleb, which was successful; it must have been in its wake that the Negus asked for a bishop for Ḥimyar. Where his episcopal see was located is not clear. It could

have been Mukha or Ẓafār, or Najrān itself, whose bishop had been martyred and whose vacant episcopate thus could accommodate a new bishop. This may have been the one that appears with the name Paul II as bishop of Najrān during the events of the celebrated persecutions. This must have happened slightly after the turn of the century. The dispatch evokes the mission of Theophilus Indus in the reign of Constantius in the fourth century, and preludes the more active Arabian policy of Justin and Justinian in the sixth.

V. Federate Cultural Life

Before they fell, the Salīḥids contributed to the cultural history of the Arabs in Oriens. Theirs is the first and the earliest attested court poet of Arabic in that region, although the chances are that he was not the only one. The rise of the Arabic script could possibly be attributed at least in part to the initiative of this dynasty of the fifth century, as that script emerges from the Nabataean script of the fourth century to the Arabic of the early sixth. And the possibility must be entertained that in the Oriens of the fifth century there was a simple form of an Arabic liturgy and some translations of biblical texts relevant to liturgical use, possibly a lectionary. The monastery built by the Salīḥid king Dāwūd may have become an Arab cultural center.

The Salīḥids were not the only federates who contributed to Arab cultural life in Oriens in the fifth century. The other federates also did, especially the three tribes, Kalb, Iyād, and ʿUdra, about whom some significant data have survived. Because they were not *Rhōmaioi*, they maintained a stronger sense of Arab identity and, therefore, it is among the federate rather than the Rhomaic Arabs that the roots of Arab culture in pre-Islamic Oriens are to be sought. But the latter were not entirely indifferent or passive toward the culture of their congeners in Oriens, and they may have given an impetus to the rise of a simple Arabic liturgy and lectionary in the fifth century. The contribution of the Arabs, Rhomaic as well as federate, in Oriens in the fifth century may be briefly summarized as follows.

The Arabic Script

Oriens was one of the centers for the rise of the Arabic script in pre-Islamic times. All the extant Arabic inscriptions of that period in the Fertile Crescent were found in Syria. One of them, the longest, the Namāra inscription, written in Nabataean characters, belongs to the fourth century, while the others, written in a script differentiated from Nabataean and recognizably Arabic, belong to the sixth. Thus the process of differentiation through which the Arabic script emerged must be assigned to the fifth century. The earliest of the inscriptions written in this new script goes back to the early sixth century (512) and was found at Zabad in the north of Oriens. Thus "From Namāra to Zabad" would be a convenient rubric to describe the progress in the development of this script.

The internal evidence from the shape of its letters points to the fact that the new script emerged with elements of both the Nabataean and Syriac scripts. The phonology of the Arabic language called for a new Semitic script, since neither the Nabataean nor the Syriac was capable of accommodating all of its sounds. Historical circumstances in Oriens were favorable to the rise and development of the new Arab groups that appeared there in this proto-Byzantine period—the *foederati*. Unlike the Rhomaic Arabs, these were possessed of a strong sense of Arab identity and their life and external relations with the central government called for the use of an Arabic script, all of which led to its appearance in Oriens in the fifth century. As the Namāra inscription testifies, the *foederati* wanted and did express the achievements of their kings in writing, and this precious inscription may be considered an epigraphic microcosm of *Kitāb al-Qabīla* (the Book of the Tribe) of pre-Islamic Arabia. This *kitāb* also included the poetry composed by the tribal group and composed for it. The Salīḥid Dāwūd had as his court poet ʿAbd al-ʿĀṣ, who is especially important in this connection. He belonged to the tribe of Iyād, which was known in pre-Islamic times for having developed the Arabic script in the Land of the Two Rivers. The emigration of this literate tribal group to Oriens must have given an impetus to the development of the Arabic script. Imperial-federate relations also contributed toward this development. *Foedera* between the two parties were struck, and the presumption is that there were Arabic versions of these *foedera*, especially when they were concluded with groups who had just entered Roman territory and thus were not familiar with Latin or Greek. The *scrinium barbarorum* in Constantinople had interpreters and translators, and must have had Arabs who also performed this function. The Sasanid state had an "office of Arab affairs" with Arab translators and secretaries, and the presumption is that Byzantium at least was not behind its rival in the creation of such an administrative unit for the transaction of its foreign policy with the Arabs. A powerful impetus for the development of the Arabic script must also have come from the Byzantine *ecclesia*: the rise of a simple Arabic liturgy and a biblical lectionary in this proto-Byzantine period must have contributed to the parallel development of the script. Unlike short inscriptions and *foedera*, these were long texts which required precision for the expression of the liturgical and the biblical language. The same process was operative later in Islamic times, when the need for expressing with precision the word of God in the Koran resulted in the further perfection of the Arabic script with the invention of the vowels and diacritical marks. The rise of the

Arabic script in Oriens is plagued with anonymity, but the name of a figure who may have been instrumental in this process may be suggested. Hints and data that have survived in the sources point to Dāwūd as the focus of a little cultural circle, consisting of his poet laureate, a daughter who composed verse, and a monastery which he built as a pious Christian. It is therefore not unreasonable to suggest him as the figure possibly associated with the rise of the script. This variety of the Arabic script, developed in Oriens, is likely to be the one that spread in northern Ḥijāz, since this was a Byzantine sphere of influence, inhabited by federate tribes of the outer shield. Its spread must have been facilitated by the Christian monasteries which dotted that region, since it is fairly safe to assume that these were inhabited by literate monks and since the monasteries became, even in this early period, centers of learning. Literacy in the monasteries was noted by the Arab poets of pre-Islamic Arabia, who often refer to books and writing which they associate with monks and Christian establishments.

The rise of Islam and the Arab Conquests opened a new chapter in the history of this Arabic script developed in pre-Islamic times. The Koran made Arabic a holy language, while the Conquests made it a world language. The former led to the creation of Arabic calligraphy, making it one of the arts of medieval Islamic civilization, while the second spread this script over vast tracts of the globe. The praises of the Arabic Islamic script and its relation to the religion that made it an art are well expressed by one of the keenest observers of the Muslim scene and one of its most eloquent interpreters:

> The divine in the didactic is the meaning of calligraphy. Islam, we might say, marries with the cursive flow of the Arabic hand, and the authority of that ever-running script, with its endless occasions of artistic freedom within the rigorous constraints of its curving shapes and lines and parallels, occupies Islamic art hardly less thoroughly than the scripture determines its religion. The believer must be reader, not spectator: he will not be educated by imagery, only the text. It is the pen, celebrated in the Qur'an, which merits the perpetual pride of hand and eye.

Thus the major phases in the history of this Islamic art are three. Developed as a functional script by the Arabs of pre-Islamic times in Oriens and in Ḥīra, it was brought to perfection by the Muslims and Muslim Arabs, and finally converted into an art—that of calligraphy, the most Arabic of all medieval Islamic arts. The Arabic script of the fifth century emerges as an important component of the Arab cultural patrimony of pre-Islamic times.

The Arabic Bible and Liturgy

The case for an Arabic liturgy and biblical lectionary is stronger for the fifth century than it is for the fourth. This is possible to maintain in view of the progress which Christianity made among the Arabs in the course of a century, the arrival of a new group of *foederati* from the Land of the Two Rivers who had been associated with the Arabic script and with Christianity in that region, and the emergence of three Arab personalities in Oriens who might have encouraged the appearance of an Arabic liturgy and Bible in the fifth century. Furthermore, the earliest reference to a Gospel in South Arabia goes back to this century.

Oriens

The various elements connected with an Arabic liturgy and Bible in Oriens may be presented as follows.

1. It has been noted that there is a Syriac matrix in addition to the Nabataean in the Arabic script that developed in Oriens in this century. The most important works written in Syriac, the holy language of the Christian Orient, were naturally the liturgy and the Bible. These were most probably the models for those who were developing the Arabic script, and it is natural to suppose that this development took place during the process of translating the liturgy and the biblical lectionary from Syriac.

2. The appearance of the tribe of Iyād in Oriens in this century must also have been a factor. This is a most important tribe in the cultural history of the Arabs before the rise of Islam, since it is associated with Christianity, the construction of many monasteries, and with the employment of the Arabic script. Some significant data have been preserved in the Arabic sources on Iyād during the Muslim Conquest of Iraq. These are posterior to the fifth century, but there are others that associate Christianity and the script with Iyād much earlier, and so the chances are good that the advent of Iyād in Oriens was a contributing factor in the development of the Arabic script, and with it the appearance of an Arabic liturgy and lectionary.

3. The relevant data for the fifth century are not abundant, but they are sufficient to point to specific personalities and Christian Arab pockets in Oriens where such religious texts may have come into existence.

a. There is first the episcopate of the Parembole in Palaestina Prima, where it is conceivable that such Arabic texts may have appeared for the benefit of the small Arab community which had emigrated from Persian territory. Aspebetos, its first bishop, and his brother-in-law Maris, who became a monk and the *hēgoumenos* of a monastery in the desert of Juda, were dedicated Christians and energetic ecclesiastics working for the welfare of the small Arab community in the Jordan Valley. It is perfectly possible that they also worked for the appearance of these religious texts, indispensable in church service for the benefit of the Arab parishioners.

b. Around 500 the patriarch of Jerusalem was an Arab by the name of Elias. He was an exceptionally energetic ecclesiastic and his patriarchate was notable, among other things, for his careful administration of the three Palestines under his jurisdiction. Elias had under him various Arab federate bishops in Sinai, in the Negev, and in Palaestina Prima. Two of them are known by name—Petrus II of the Parembole and Petrus, the bishop of the group of Amorkesos of the reign of Leo—and it is certain there were others. It is perfectly possible that the thought occurred to the Arab patriarch to organize Christian worship for the various Arab federate communities scattered in his patriarchate, and so he may have inspired the preparation of these religious texts.

c. In the north of Oriens there was also Simeon Stylite, who from his pillar was a potent factor in the spread of Christianity among the Arabs of that region. His biographer records that he gave laws to the Arabs. No doubt these must have been ecclesiastical laws, most probably taken out of both the Old and the New Testaments. The presumption is that laws would have been written, if they were to be effective, and it is natural to suppose that they would have been written in the language of their beneficiaries, Arabic.

d. Finally, the most notable figure of this century among the Christian federate Arabs was undoubtedly Dāwūd, the Salīḥid king. The cultural circle around him—composed of his court poet ʿAbd al-ʿĀṣ and his daughter the poetess—and his building the monastery of David suggest that he could have been the spirit behind translating some of these religious texts. The example of Empress Eudocia across the Jordan in the Holy Land may also have inspired Dāwūd or his daughter to engage in such an activity, since the empress engaged herself in a related if not identical activity, the turning into verse of the Octateuch.

South Arabia

The most tantalizing data concerning Arabic religious texts in the fifth century refer to the South Arabian region, and specifically to a Gospel. In a text that purports to go back to Hishām, an Arab poet and leader by the name of Barrāq is said to have learned from a *rāhib* (a monk) in South Arabia the recitation of the *Injīl*, the Gospel. The poet later emigrated to northeastern Arabia and took part in its tribal wars.

The difficulty of tracing these data to their original sources dilutes their crucial importance. But something could be said for their reliability, because Christianity and monasticism are attested in the South Arabian region since the mission of Theophilus Indus in the fourth century and the conversion of Najrān early in the fifth. Furthermore, there is unquestionably a monastery by the name of Dayr Ibn Barrāq near Ḥīra, which gives strong support to the reliability of these data concerning Barrāq, the monk, and the Gospel in the South Arabia of the fifth century.

It is noteworthy that the fifth century witnessed the translation of the Bible into two of the languages of the Near East, Armenian and Georgian; and Jerome's Latin version, too, was completed in Bethlehem earlier in the century.

Arabic Literature

Literature is the third component in the Arab cultural frontier in Oriens and also in the area of indirect Byzantine influence in Ḥijāz. It is possible to detect echoes of three or four types of poetic genres; religious, amatory, elegiac and court poetry, and also verses that remember the *ayyām* and the last days of Salīḥ. Only fragments of the last have survived as specimens of what may be termed federate poetry; no prose texts have survived.

Federate life within the imperial and ecclesiastical structure of Oriens provided the outer framework for the development of both Arabic prose and poetry in the fifth century.

Prose

The Arab federates of the fourth century who composed the long epitaph on their deceased king in 328 gave expression to what may be described as the epigraphic confirmation of the Book of the Tribe (*Kitāb al-Qabīla*) of pre-Islamic Arabia. The presumption is that the federates continued to record the achievements of their kings and the tribes throughout the fourth and the fifth centuries and it is practically certain that the Salīḥids and other federate tribes each had its *kitāb*. The prose part of this *kitāb* most probably should be classed as non-literary or non-artistic prose. Other expressions of it must have been the texts of the *foedera* concluded between these tribal groups and Byzantium. Whatever artistic prose existed must have consisted of harangues, speeches, and testaments which may have been included in the *kitāb* of the tribe. Whether the artistic prose of the Bible found expression in an Arabic translation is not clear, but if it did, it is likely to have inspired Arabic religious prose possessed of some literary quality.

Poetry

The epinician odes celebrating the victories of Queen Mavia over Emperor Valens in the fourth century survived well into the fifth. The chances are that the Salīḥids, like their predecessors, the Tanūkhids, had their achievements, both in the *ayyām* (the battle days of the Arabs) and in the Persian Wars sung by poets. Poetry on the Salīḥid royal house is associated only with the name of Dāwūd, one of the last of the Salīḥid kings, but federate poetry in Oriens in the fifth century is a continuation of the unbroken tradition from the fourth century.

The few data that have survived on Dāwūd suggest that there was a little literary circle, composed of his court poet ʿAbd al-ʿĀṣ and his daughter, who is left anonymous in the sources. The fragments that have survived on the Salīḥids turn largely around Dāwūd and his reign. He was also the builder of Dayr Dāwūd, which may have been a literary as well as a religious center, as was sometimes the case in those days.

A tantalizing figure in this circle is the daughter, although her anonymity raises a number of questions for which there are no answers. It is not clear whether her father was the literary influence on her or whether it was ʿAbd al-ʿĀṣ the court poet, or perhaps the empress Eudocia, whose literary talents found expression in biblical translations and poetry on the Persian Wars of her husband Theodosius.

As already indicated, the anonymous princess was not the only sparrow in the Salīḥid poetic spring. There was ʿAbd al-ʿĀṣ, who represented the Iyādī tradition in poetic composition, which he brought with him from the Land of the Two Rivers. As a court poet he certainly composed panegyrics on his patron and the dynasty, but in view of the religiosity of Dāwūd it is quite likely that he composed some religious poetry or imparted to his poetry some religious sentiments.

The last days of Salīḥ did not pass unsung. Of the few fragments that have survived, those of the anonymous princess and of the regicides are the most attractive. Dāwūd's daughter must have written an elegy on the fall of her father, of which only one solitary verse has survived. The verse breathes the spirit of contempt towards the scoundrels who felled her father. The daughter's lament was answered by one of the victors (in their self-image not regicides but tyrannicides) in a triplet that has resounded throughout the centuries, exulting in his victory and thus drowning the daughter's sorrowful lament.

The Salīḥids are not the only federate group with whom Arabic poetry is associated in Oriens. Mention has already made of the Iyād, to whom the court poet of Dāwūd belonged, but otherwise little or nothing is known about Iyād's poetry in Oriens. Something, however, is known about Kalb, the large tribal group of the outer shield which produced a poet whose name is variously spelled; one of these variations is Ibn Ḥizām. This fifth-century Kalbite poet was apparently the first to open his odes with an Arabic *sunt lacrimae rerum*, a lament over the deserted encampment of his beloved and an invitation to his fellow riders to halt and shed tears over it. The practice became standard in the composition of the Arabic ode for centuries before and after the rise of Islam. The refined sentiments in such preludes and the lacrimose element are in all probability inspirations from Christianity, to which the poet almost certainly belonged—more specifically, to monastic Christianity, which spread in the Ḥijāz and northern Arabia in the shadow of the imperial Roman *limes*.

Although ʿUd̲ra wrote an important chapter in the political and military history of Ḥijāz in the fifth and sixth centuries, it was a special type of poetry, to which it gave its own name, that has assured it of a certain immortality in the literary consciousness of the Arabs. Among the pastoralists of Ḥijāz in Arabia there appeared a new type of Arabic poetry, which was chaste and pure. Its genesis is not entirely clear. The influence of Islam on the pastoralists has been suspected as a factor in its rise but it cannot have been the only one, and if its origins go back to pre-Islamic times, as is practically certain, the formative influence of another religion, Christianity, has to be considered. Certain features of Christianity seem to commend this view, especially the ideals of asceticism, celibacy, and virginity. The name of the tribe itself, which lent its name to this type of poetry—called ʿUd̲rī or ʿUd̲rite—means virginity. This may or may not be related to the Christian concept, but the Virgin Mary as Theotokos in the fifth century was the subject of intense theological discussions, and she apparently was venerated in Ḥijāz since there is a toponym called Masājid Maryam (the Mosques of Mary) not far from Mecca. These facts suggest some genetic relationship between these Christian associations and the rise of ʿUd̲rite poetry under their inspiration. Nothing of this pre-Islamic poetry has survived, but a love poem composed in later Islamic times by a nun or inmate in the monastery of Buṣrā/Bostra seems to be a specimen of this poetry. It is noteworthy that the monks of that monastery were from the tribe of ʿUd̲ra, which apparently remained Christian well into Islamic times. This is the sole female Arab voice on record that is known to have composed from inside a monastery, and it brings to mind the anonymous Salīḥid princess and the question whether in addition to the elegy she wrote on the death of her father, she might also have composed some ʿUd̲rite poetry. ʿUd̲rite love poetry did not last long after the eighth century, except fitfully, but it was assured of a longer life by the Arab Conquest of Spain, where it inspired the rise of courtly love in the medieval society of Western Europe. Since then it has been noted occasionally in European literature, as in Stendhal's *De l'Amour* and in Heine's "Asra."

Christianity must have received an artistic expression among the Arabs as it did among all the other peoples of the Christian Orient, and this expression is likely to have been through the medium that the Arabs considered their forte, namely, the spoken word of literature. This Christian Arabic literature, if it existed, has not survived. Only faint traces or echoes of it in poetry are extant, mainly in similes and metaphors that suggest a strong Christian presence among the Arabs. And of this Christian presence the monastic scene takes precedence over others, reflected in such figures as the hermit, his hermitage, and his holy book, especially the Psalter (*Zabūr*). It is, however, the lamp of the hermit that riveted the attention of the Arab poet, who employed it in his similes, since it stood for light in the desert darkness, warmth in its cold, and hospitality in the midst of its aridity. The Arabs were guided by the stars in their journeys in Arabia, and the lamps of the monasteries—the lamps of Christianity in Arabia—functioned similarly. The foremost poet of pre-Islamic Arabia brought the two together and presented these lamps as stars that guided the caravaneers on their way back home. The most celebrated expression of this union of heavenly and earthly lamps, however, comes in the Light-verse of *Surat al-Nūr*, the twenty-fourth chapter of the Koran:

> God is Light of the Heavens and of the Earth. The similitude of His Light is as it were a niche wherein is a lamp, the lamp within a glass, the glass as though it were a pearly star. It is lit from a blessed Tree, an olive-tree neither of the East nor of the West, the oil whereof were like to shine even though no fire were applied to it; Light upon Light; God guideth to His Light whom He will.

VI. The Arab Church

A careful examination of the ecclesiastical sources of the fourth century has revealed the existence of an Arab church as a component in the patriarchate of Antioch. This church grew naturally, stimulated by the rise of a new federate supremacy in Oriens in the fifth century, that of the Salīḥids, and by the arrival of new groups who become *foederati*. These were either already Christian or became Christianized after they acquired federate status, and this entailed the assignment of priests and bishops to serve their spiritual needs. This growth is reflected in the sources, which yield only three bishops of the Arabs for the fourth century in its entirety but significantly more for the fifth, both Rhomaic and federate; and this is consonant with a statement in the ecclesiastical historian Sozomen, who comments on the large number of Arab bishops in the fifth century. The same phenomenon of growth is also noticeable in the sources for Arab monasticism in the fifth century, and Sozomen also speaks of the importance of monasticism in the life of the Arabs and as the instrument of their conversion. In fact, the Christianity of the dominant Arab group, the Salīḥids, began with the conversion of Zokomos by a monk.

The Episcopate

The discovery of two types of Arab bishops for the fourth century—federate and Rhomaic—is important, and the following discussion observes this distinction.

1. *The federate bishops*. The conciliar lists are the best sources for recovering the names of these bishops. The fact that there were three councils in the fifth century, compared to two in the fourth, explains the longer list of federate bishops for that century.

a. The Council of Ephesus in 431 was attended by Aspebetos/Petrus, the first bishop of the Palestinian Parembole. This is a unique council in the ecclesiastical annals of the Arab federates, since their representative appears not only as a name among the subscriptions but also as a personality who played an important part in the proceedings and in the negotiations with Nestorius and John of Antioch. The second Council of Ephesus, the Latrocinium of 449, was attended by another bishop of the Palestinian Parembole, Auxolaus, the successor of Petrus. The Council of Chalcedon in 451 was attended by two, possibly three, Arab bishops. John, successor of Auxolaus, was the bishop of the Parembole. Eustathius appears as a bishop of the Saracens of Phoenicia Libanensis, but the identity of the Saracens over whom he was bishop is not entirely clear; they could have been the two Saracen units listed in the *Notitia Dignitatum* or they could have been the Salīḥids. Eustathius appears again some six years after Chalcedon, as subscriber to a letter sent by the bishops of Phoenicia Libanensis to the emperor Leo in defense of Chalcedon. His episcopal see is unknown, but it could have been Thelsee in Phoenicia Libanensis. A third bishop, also called John of the Saracens, signed with the bishops of Osroene and may have been identical with the bishop of the Parembole. There is, however, a slight chance that he was the bishop of a federate Arab group in Osroene.

b. The conciliar lists may have reflected only a small fraction of the entire federate episcopate within the Patriarchate of Antioch, which contained many more federate Arab bishops than were represented at the ecumenical councils. Sozomen explicitly testifies to the large number of Arab bishops, and his testimony can be supported by the very structure of Arab federate presence in Oriens. This was extensive, especially in the limitrophe provinces of Palaestina Tertia, Arabia, Phoenicia Libanensis, Syria Salutaris, Osroene, and Mesopotamia. In addition to the Salīḥids, there were other federate tribal groups, such as the Tanūkhids and the Iyād. The strong feeling of tribal identity makes it practically certain that each tribe had its own bishop. If it was a large tribal group deployed in more than one province, chances are that it had more than one bishop. The episode of Amorkesos illustrates the federate episcopal presence within tribal groups other than the dominant one and the assignment of bishops along tribal lines. The same episode illustrates the pivotal importance of the bishop in Arab federate life. Bishop Petrus acts as spokesman for Amorkesos with Leo and prepares the ground for the *foedus* between the two. The case of Leo could not have been an isolated one, and thus these various Arab tribal groups who were federates of Byzantium in the fifth century may each have had its own bishop. Their non-attestation in the sources is no argument for their non-existence. No ecumenical councils were convened in that century after Chalcedon, and so the valuable conciliar lists which reflected federate episcopal presence in the first half of the century do not exist, while the survival of a fragment such as the one on Amorkesos implies the existence of federate bishops whose names were either unrecorded or, if they were, are not extant. The conciliar lists of the three councils illustrate this well. The Palestinian Parembole was a diminutive bishopric, corresponding to an equally diminutive federate phylarchate. And yet it is disproportionately projected in the lists, with three bishops. This is certainly owing to two circumstances. First, the energetic Juvenal of Jerusalem insured this Parembole representation in order to have its support at the three councils, and the work that recorded this representation, that of Cyril of Scythopolis, has survived. Second, the large number of Arab bishops in the other parts of Oriens and the Patriarchate of Antioch were not so fortunate. "Vixere fortes ante Agamemnona multi," but they had neither a Juvenal nor a Cyril to remember them and give them visibility.

c. Diminutive as the episcopate of the Parembole was, nevertheless it is the best documented of all the Arab churches of the Patriarchate of Antioch in the fifth century, and therefore presents the best opportunity for examining the ecclesiastical history of an Arab federate community living in the protective shadow of the Christian Roman Empire. The community started as a federate one, a phylarchate controlled by the chief of the community, Aspebetos, a defector from Persian territory for reasons of conscience. He was converted by the Saint of the desert of Juda, Euthymius, and became the first bishop of his community under the baptismal name of Petrus. In addition to establishing the bishopric of the Parembole and the line of its bishops, Petrus attended the Council of Ephesus in 431 and played an important role in the negotiations with both Nestorius and John of Antioch. He was the voice of Arab Orthodoxy at the Council. His brother-in-law Maris represented the Arabs of the Parembole in the other form of institutional Christianity that spread in Oriens in the fifth century, monasticism. He donated all his wealth to the monastery of St. Euthymius and in 466, after the death of its *hēgoumenos* Theoctistus, he was appointed to the hegoumenate of the monastery by Euthymius himself. Thus these figures represent the high degree of Arab integration in the Byzantine *ecclesia*, as the phylarchs of the Parembole represent Arab integration in the Byzantine *imperium*. In the annals of the Arab episcopate in Oriens, the Parembole presents the longest line of Arab bishops whose names are attested, extending to the middle of the sixth century: Petrus, who died sometime in the forties; Auxolaus, who participated in the Latrocinium of Ephesus in 449; John, who attended the Council of Chalcedon in 451; Valens, who participated in the Council of Jerusalem in 518; and Petrus II, who attended the Council of Jerusalem in 536.

2. *The Rhomaic bishops*. Just as the *imperium* recruited many of its military units locally in Oriens, so did the *ecclesia*. The Arab ethnic complexion of the limitrophe provinces make it practically certain that at least some of the bishops who appear in conciliar lists are ethnically Arab. The assumption of Graeco-Roman names by some of the Arab bishops on their consecration make it hard to discern their Arab identity, but it is easy to do so when clearly Arab names have been retained. The following may be mentioned, and the list is probably not exhaustive, since there may be a few others whose Arab names have been Hellenized beyond recognition.

a. Ephesus (431). Three bishops took part in this council: Abdelas, the bishop of Elusa, and Saidas, the bishop of Phaeno, both of Palaestina Tertia; and Natiras, the bishop of Gaza. The name of the first presents the spectacle of complete Hellenization, as his Arabic name, Abdallah, is translated into Θεόδουλος metamorphosed into Greek 'Απέλλας.

b. Latrocinium (449). An Arab bishop of Phaeno by the name of Caioumas (Qā'im or Qayyūm) took part in this Council.

c. Chalcedon (451). Four Arab bishops attended this council: Aretas, the bishop of Elusa in Palaestina Tertia; Natiras, the bishop of Gaza; Caioumas, the bishop of Marciopolis in Osroene; and Gautus, the bishop of Neila in the Provincia Arabia. It is noteworthy that one of these bishops, Natiras, attended two Councils, since he had attended the Council of Ephesus twenty years before. Like the bishopric of the Parembole, the bishopric of Elusa presents a long line of Rhomaic Arab bishops well into the sixth century.

The Rhomaic Arab bishops were not an *ecclesia in ecclesia* as far as the Patriarchate of Antioch was concerned. But the fact of their Arabness has important implications for Arab federate life in Oriens in this proto-Byzantine period, and in the seventh century it went beyond the boundaries of Arab federate life or federate-imperial relations. Around 630 a peace treaty was struck between Muḥammad and Byzantine Ayla on the Gulf of Eilat. It is significant that it was the Rhomaic Arab bishop Juḥannā ibn Ru'ba who represented Byzantium; the resoundingly Arab patronymic Ibn Ru'ba of the Rhomaic bishop must have induced Muḥammad to make the significant gesture of endowing the bishop with his own mantle.

Monasticism

The spread of monasticism from Egypt to Oriens was of considerable importance to the relationship of the Arabs to Christianity. As Sozomen testifies, it was a potent instrument of conversion among them. This was especially true among the Arab pastoralists and semi-pastoralists, and the Christianity of the Salīḥids goes back to the conversion of the eponym Zokomos by a monk. That monasticism should have acted so powerfully among the Arabs was only natural. The retreat of the anchorites and eremites to the deserts of Oriens was a spectacle that must have appealed to the Arabs, for whom the desert was the homeland. The Arab pastoralist had a natural affinity with those who chose the desert—their own inhospitable homeland—as their haunts, enduring the rigors of its inclement terrain and climate even as the Arab pastoralist did.

The two principal figures who exercised the greatest influence on the Arabs of Oriens were St. Simeon in Syria and St. Euthymius in Palestine. Both endured long in their ministries and as influences on the Arabs until their deaths in 457 and 473, respectively. The attachment of the Arabs to both was profound: in the case of Simeon it was reflected in the fact that on his death the Arabs wanted to possess his corpse and keep it, and it was only the presence of the *magister militum*, Ardabur, that prevented them from doing so. From his famous pillar, St. Simeon converted many Arabs and also acted as lawgiver to them, but the Arabs he converted and associated with are largely anonymous. In contrast, St. Euthymius was closely connected with the phylarchs and bishops of the Parembole in Palestine, and it was this association that gave rise to this Arab episcopate in Palaestina Prima. The influence of these two principal saints spread far and wide among the Arabs of Oriens—beyond the immediate boundaries of the provinces in which they lived in Syria Prima and Palaestina Prima, into the various desert regions in which the Arabs lived, such as Sinai, Midian, and the Negev in the south and in Chalcidice and in Euphratensis in the north, where the bones of another saint dear to the Arabs, Sergius, rested in Ruṣāfa. By far the holiest of all these regions where monasticism spread was the desert of Juda, where the bishopric of the Arab Parembole was located. It was in the Holy Land, lying between the Holy City and the Holy River.

Many who took on the monastic garb must have been Arabs, and yet the sources have preserved the names of only a few. Such are the monks who appear in Sozomen as Abdaleos, Abbas, Gaddanes, and Azizos. More important in ecclesiastical history are those Arabs who became *hēgoumenoi* of monasteries in Oriens, such as Abbas, who became the *hēgoumenos* of the monastery of Teleda, which lay to the east of Antioch and to the west of Beroea. In the south of Oriens there was of course the important Arab monastic center of

Rhaithou in the Sinai Peninsula, famed for its Arab holy man of the fourth century, Moses. Closer to the range of Euthymius' influence were the monasteries of the desert of Juda in Palaestina Prima. Two Arabs became *hēgoumenoi* of monasteries in this region: Maris, the brother-in-law of Aspebetos, who became the *hēgoumenos* of the monastery of Theoctistus for two years (466–468), and Stephanus who became the *hēgoumenos* of the monastery of St. Euthymius early in the sixth century (514–535). Undoubtedly the most famous and influential Arab monk of the century was Elias, one of the disciples of St. Euthymius, who was later elevated to the priesthood of the Church of the Anastasis in Jerusalem and then became the Patriarch of Jerusalem in 494. Among the more important of his foundations were the monastery he built in Jerusalem near the episcopal mansion and the Church of Theotokos, which he started in Jerusalem but which was completed later in the reign of Justinian and dedicated in 543.

In addition to monasteries associated with Arab *hēgoumenoi* in the Greek sources, there are a few references in the Arabic sources to others, both in Oriens and in Ḥijāz.

a. Of monasteries founded by federate groups such as the Tanūkhids and the Iyādīs in Oriens, hardly anything is recorded in these Arabic sources, although they are more informative on the monastic foundations of these groups in and around Ḥīra on the lower Euphrates. Yet the federates of Oriens must have founded many monasteries, as they had before they came over to the Romans, possibly in the north in Chalcidice and the region of Ruṣāfa. The only monastery that can be unequivocally attributed to a federate in this century is that of Dayr Dāwūd, the monastery of the Salīḥid king, which is located in presentday al-Turkumāniyya, between Isriye and Ruṣāfa. Another one is the "Monastery of the Hedgehog" (Dayr al-Qunfuḏ) in Ayla, and it is practically certain that it was founded by a clan of the tribe of Balī which lived in the neighborhood and which had that name. Finally, Dayr Kaʿb is mentioned in the sources as being in Oriens, but where it was or who built it is not recorded.

b. Especially important are the monasteries which were founded not within Oriens but in that sphere of Byzantine influence in northwestern Arabia in Ḥijāz, through which passed the trade routes and caravans from South Arabia to the Mediterranean. The few references to the monasteries that have survived could suggest that they were founded at strategic locations on the caravan routes. The monastery, with its ideal of hospitality and *philanthropia*, must have functioned in the eyes of the Arab traders as a caravanserai. The implication of all this for the Christian mission in Arabia, the circulation and dissemination of Christian ideas, is clear. Where the church could not reach and penetrate the monastery did, and where the monks could not further reach, the caravaneers could and did, influenced by Christian ideas which they acquired during their sojourns in these monasteries, where they stayed in order to break their long journeys. Although Ḥijāz was outside the boundaries of Byzantine Oriens, it was Bibleland, especially the region of Midian/Madyan associated with Moses, Jethro, and Sepporah, and the sources speak of a monastery there by the name of Dayr Madyan. To the south of Madyan and the north of Medina was the Wādī al-Qurā region where the Christian federate tribe of ʿUḏra lived, and monks are attested in this region. In the northeastern part of Ḥijāz, at Kilwa, traces of a Christian structure, probably a monastery, were found. The names of three monasteries in Ḥijāz are attested in the sources but not much is known about them; Dayr Ḥismā, probably belonging to the Christian tribe of Juḏām, which lived in the Ḥismā region in Northern Ḥijāz; Dayr Ḍamḍam; and Dayr Saʿd, in the territory of the tribe of G̱haṭafān. Three other monasteries are mentioned in the sources with distinctly Arab names: Dayr Ibn ʿĀmir, Dayr Arwā, and Dayr Ḥabīb but the sources are silent on their exact locations and on their builders.

Arab Orthodoxy

The Arab federates of the fifth century were Orthodox in the midst of the christological controversies that gave birth to two heresies, Nestorianism and Monophysitism. The Arab tribal groups who struck *foedera* with Byzantium before Chalcedon did so with an Orthodox Byzantine state, and it is almost certain that they continued to be so after Chalcedon. The Orthodoxy of the Arab federates is reflected in the conciliar lists, with the exception of that of the Latrocinium of 449, when Auxolaus strayed from the path of Orthodoxy in response to Juvenal's position. Two years later Juvenal and the Parembole returned to the Orthodox fold. The doctrinal persuasion of the Arab federates almost certainly remained Orthodox during the reigns of Marcian and Leo, two Orthodox emperors. The last quarter of the century, after the accession of Zeno in 474, presents a problem, since Zeno and Anastasius were inclined toward Monophysitism, and the question arises whether or not the Arab federates were affected by this change in doctrinal color. Nothing is noted in the sources about a change in federate doctrinal persuasion or of any friction in imperial-federate relations. The Arab federates probably remained loyal to their Orthodox faith in much the same way that their predecessors had, the Tanūkhids of the fourth century, who, moreover, fought wars of religion with the Arian emperor Valens in defense of Orthodoxy. The Ghassānids of the sixth century are the Arab federates associated with Monophysitism, and the fact is reflected in the sources. But one of them, it has been argued, acquired federate status in the second half of the fifth century—Amorkesos in the reign of Leo—and the question naturally arises whether or not he was a Monophysite.

This could not have been the case, since Amorkesos became *foederatus* in the last years of Leo's reign and this emperor was Orthodox. An Arab chief who struck a *foedus* with an Orthodox emperor and became a Christian during his reign could only have been Orthodox. The presumption is that he continued to be so till the end of his life unaffected by the *Henotikon* of Zeno. It was only with the arrival of a new wave of Ghassānids toward the end of the century, around 500, and possibly belonging to a different clan, that the Ghassānids adopted a Monophysite form of Christianity, most probably because the emperor during whose reign they penetrated the *limes* and struck the *foedus* was a Monophysite. Hence the Monophysitism of the new dominant federate group in the sixth century, the Ghassānids. It was during the sixth century that the full consequences of Chalcedon began to tell on the Arab *foederati*; throughout the fifth century the *foederati* remained Orthodox, and thus federate-imperial relations, unlike those in the sixth century, remained unruffled. The further and related question of federate separatism in the proto-Byzantine period does not even arise. The strong voice of Arab Orthodoxy in the fifth century was expressed in the conciliar subscriptions of Ephesus and Chalcedon. Of the Arab ecclesiastics who voiced this Orthodoxy in this century, two stand out: Aspebetos, the bishop of the Parembole who played an active part in the defense of Cyrillian Orthodoxy against Nestorius at Ephesus; and Elias, the patriarch of Jerusalem who stood for Orthodoxy against imperial Monophysitism. When faced with the choice of deposition or recantation, Elias chose the former and was exiled to Ayla, where he died after prophesying the death of his heretical adversary, the emperor Anastasius. Both figures foreshadow a third Arab ecclesiastic who was to appear in the same region—in the desert of Juda which produced both Aspebetos and Elias. At the monastery of St. Sabas in the eight century and in the shadow of the Islamic New Oriens, John of Damascus wrote the final defense of Orthodoxy, *De Fide Orthodoxa*, and in so doing became the last of the church fathers.

Ecclesiastical Organization

Little is known about the ecclesiastical organization of the Arab federate church in the fifth century. But a few data have survived, related to the Arab federate bishops who moved in the orbit of Juvenal of Jerusalem and to Eustathius, the bishop of the Saracens who was associated with the episcopal see of Damascus.

Federate ecclesiastical organization followed imperial provincial organization in Oriens. The Arab bishops of a particular province were subordinate to the metropolitan bishop of the province; they were his suffragans. Thus the Arab bishops of Phoenicia Libanensis, of whom Eustathius was one, were subordinate to the metropolitan bishop of Damascus. This is clearly reflected at the Council of Chalcedon, at which Eustathius signs with the bishops of Phoenicia, or when he subscribes to the letter addressed by his metropolitan, John of Damascus, to Emperor Leo. The relations of the suffragan Arab bishop to his metropolitan was parallel to that of the Arab phylarch to the provincial *dux*. Whether the bishop of the dominant Arab federate group, the Salīḥids, was superior to or more influential than those of the other federate groups is not clear. Perhaps he was not, since the Arab phylarchate of Oriens was not centralized in the fifth century and it was only around 530 that it became so. All the federate Arab bishops in Oriens were ultimately subordinate to the Patriarch of Antioch, in much the same way that the Arab phylarchs were ultimately responsible and subordinate to the *magister militum per Orientem*.

The year of Chalcedon, 451, was fateful not only for ecclesiastical unity but also for the Arab church in Oriens. At that council the three Palestines were separated from the jurisdiction of the Patriarchate of Antioch, and consequently the Arab church in the imperial Diocese of Oriens was divided between the patriarchates of Antioch and Jerusalem. Thus Petrus, the bishop of the tribal group of Amorkesos of the reign of Leo, whose bishopric was in Palaestina Tertia, was ultimately responsible to the Patriarch of Jerusalem, which had not been the case before 451, when the bishops of Palaestina Tertia were ultimately responsible to the Patriarch of Antioch. The separation of the three Palestines did not have an immediate effect on the Arab church of the federates, who remained staunchly Orthodox. With the growth of Monophysitism in Oriens in the sixth century, especially after the impetus given to it by Emperor Anastasius, the Patriarchate of Palestine remained the stronghold of Orthodoxy in Oriens, and this affected the history of the Arab church. The Arab federates of the three Palestines, at least Prima and Secunda, remained staunchly Orthodox, while those outside the jurisdiction of the Patriarchate of Jerusalem were mostly Monophysites, especially the dominant group, the Ghassānids. Thus the federate church in the sixth century was divided, as the federates were in doctrinal and other matters, and this seriously ruffled federate-imperial relations and finally broke the federate protective shield late in the century. This division within the Arab church is reflected in Palestinian hagiography, where the image of the Orthodox phylarchs of the Parembole in Palaestina Prima is bright and that of the Ghassānids of Arabia is dim.

VII. Byzantinism and Arabism: Interaction

Of the three constituents of Byzantinism—the Roman, the Greek, and the Christian—it was the last that affected, influenced, and sometimes even controlled the lives of those Arabs who moved in the Byzantine orbit. Something has been said on this influence in the fourth century, and these conclusions may be refined and enlarged with new data for the fifth.

1. Christianity presented the Arabs with new human types unknown to them from their pagan and Peninsular life—the priest, the bishop, the martyr, the saint, and the monk—and the Arab community in Oriens, both Rhomaic and federate, counted all of them among its members. In the fourth century, it contributed one saint to the universal Church—Moses, whose feast falls on the seventh of February—and in the Roman period it had contributed Cosmas and Damian. In the fifth century the Arab episcopate grew in number, both Rhomaic and federate, as is clear from conciliar lists and from the number of Arab bishops compared to those of the fourth century. As a result, the Arab ecclesiastical voice was audible in church councils, and was at its most articulate at Ephesus in defense of Cyrillian Orthodoxy.

2. The priesthood and the episcopate subjected the Arabs to a new form of authority and discipline to which they had not been accustomed. It was a spiritual form of authority, to which even the powerful federate phylarchs and kings were subject, and it thus induced in the Christian Arabs a new sense of loyalty which was supra-tribal, related not to tribal chauvinism but to the Christian *ecclesia*. This new loyalty was to find expression on the battlefield. The federate troops under their believing phylarchs fought the fire-worshiping Persians and the pagan Lakhmids with a crusading zeal, and they probably considered those who fell in such battles martyrs of the Christian faith.

3. Christianity influenced the literary life of the Arabs in the fifth century as it had done in the fourth. The conclusions on this are mainly inferential, but less so for poetry than for prose. If there was an Arabic liturgy and a biblical lectionary in the fifth century, the chances are that this would have influenced the development of Arabic literary life, as it invariably influenced that of the other peoples of the Christian Orient. It is possible to detect such influences in the scanty fragments of Arabic poetry and trace the refining influence of the new faith on sentiments. Loanwords from Christianity in Arabic are easier to document, and they are eloquent testimony to the permanence of that influence in much the same way that other loanwords testify to the influence of the Roman *imperium*.

4. By far the most potent influence of Christianity on the Arabs was that of monasticism. The new type of Christian hero after the saint and the martyr, the monk who renounced the world and came to live in what the Arabs considered their natural homeland, the desert, especially appealed to the Arabs and was the object of much veneration. The monasteries penetrated deep in the heart of Arabia, into regions to which the church could not penetrate. Thus the monastery (the *dayr*) turned out to be more influential than the church (the *bīʿa*) in the spiritual life of the Arabs, especially in the sphere of indirect Byzantine influence in the Peninsula. The monastery was also the meeting place of two ideals—Christian *philanthropia* and Arab hos-

pitality. According to Muslim tradition, the Prophet Muḥammad met the mysterious monk Baḥīra in one of these Byzantine monasteries.

5. The Christian mission to the Arabs, especially if it entailed the translation of some books of the Bible such as the Pentateuch, must have acquainted the Arabs with the biblical concept of their descent from Ishmael. This marked them as a biblical people, gave them a new identity, and, what is more, affiliated them with the first patriarch himself, Abraham. This was not an unmixed blessing to the Christian Arabs, since it carried with it the implication that they were "outside the promise." However, their allegiance to Christianity rid them of this opprobrium, since it affiliated them spiritually with the new people of God. There was, however, a pocket in Arabia where the seed of Ishmaelism was sown, and where it had a different meaning to its Arabs, who apparently harbored no regrets whatsoever that they were descended from Hagar. In the following century the Prophet Muḥammad appeared in their midst, and forty years after his birth proclaimed Islam as the true religion of the straight path. In the Koran the first patriarch appears as the founder of pure monotheism, and his son Ishmael appears not as a biblical outcast but as a prophet.

6. One of the most fruitful encounters of Christianity with Arabism took place in northwestern Arabia, in Ḥijāz, the sphere of indirect Byzantine influence. The federate tribe of ʿUḏra lived in this region and adopted Christianity quite early in the Byzantine period. Among its many achievements was a special type of poetry, known as ʿUḏrī or ʿUḏrite, which was inspired by a special type of love, also called ʿUḏrī. It is practically certain that this type of love and poetry appeared under the influence of Christianity in pre-Islamic times, although it may later have had an Islamic component. It represents the fruitful encounter of the chivalrous attitude toward women in pre-Islamic Arabia and the spiritualization of this attitude through the refining influence of Christianity. Through the Arab Conquests it appeared as *amour courtois* in western Christendom, whose religion had inspired it in the first instance.

VIII. Arabs in the Service of Byzantium

The sources on the Arabs who were important for the Arab-Byzantine relationship in this pre-Islamic period are neither abundant nor detailed enough to make it possible to draw sketches of the more outstanding among them. For the fourth century, it was not possible to recover the features of more than three figures: Imru' al-Qays, the federate king of the Namāra inscription; Mavia, the warrior queen of the reign of Valens; and Moses, the eremite who became the bishop of the federates. For the fifth century it is possible to discuss only four of the figures who served both the Byzantine *imperium* and *ecclesia*.

1. *Aspebetos/Petrus*. The career of this Arab chief was truly remarkable, as he moved through one phase to another. He started as a military commander in the service of the Great King, then became the Byzantine phylarch of the Provincia Arabia, then that of Palaestina Prima, then the bishop of the Palestinian Parembole. The climax of his career was his participation at the Council of Ephesus, where he appears not merely as a subscription in the conciliar list but as an active participant in the debates and a delegate of the Council to Nestorius.

2. *Amorkesos*. His is an equally remarkable career, and reminiscent of Aspebetos' in that he too had been in the service of the Great King before he defected to Byzantium. But unlike Aspebetos he remained a servant of the *imperium*, not the *ecclesia*, although he used the latter in his diplomatic offensive. The former chief in the service of Persia entered a second phase of his life when he became a military power in North Arabia, and a third when he mounted an offensive against the Roman frontier which culminated in his occupation of the island of Iotabe in the Gulf of Eilat. Ecclesiastical diplomacy followed his military achievements and resulted in a visit to Constantinople and royal treatment by Leo. He returned, having concluded a *foedus* with the emperor, which endowed him with the phylarchate of Palaestina Tertia. What is striking in the success story of this Arab chief is his desire to become a phylarch of the Romans in spite of the power base he had established for himself in the Arabian Peninsula. The lure of the Byzantine connection is nowhere better illustrated than in the career of this chief, who preferred to serve in the Byzantine army than to be an independent king or chief in the Arabian Peninsula. This conclusion, which may be safely drawn from an examination of his career, is relevant to the discussion of the *prodosia* charge trumped up against the Ghassānid phylarchs of the sixth century. All these Arab chiefs gloried in the Byzantine connection and preferred it to their former Arabian existence.

3. *Dāwūd/David*. The Salīḥids were fanatic Christians, and they owe this to the fact that their very existence as federates and dominant federates was related to Christianity—when a monk cured the wife of their eponym, Zokomos, of her sterility and effected the conversion of the chief. His descendants remained loyal to the faith which their ancestor fully embraced, but of all these Dāwūd is unique in that toward the end of his life his religiosity increased to the point which possibly made him a monk or an ascetic. He built the monastery which carried his name, Dayr Dāwūd, and he had a court poet from Iyād and a daughter who also was a poetess. The gentleness induced in him by Christianity apparently was taken advantage of by a coalition of two of the federate tribes, who finally brought about his downfall. His career presents the spectacle of an Arab federate king who loyally served both the *imperium* and the *ecclesia* and payed for this service with his life.

4. *Elias*. Entirely different in background from all the preceding figures is Elias, the Arab Patriarch of Jerusalem towards the end of the century. While the other three were federate Arabs, Elias was Rhomaic, born in Arabia, either the Provincia in Oriens or the Ptolemaic nome in the *limes Aegypti*, one of the many Rhomaic Arabs in the service of the *imperium* or the *ecclesia* whose Arab identity has been masked by their assumption of either biblical or Graeco-Roman names. His, too, was a remarkable career in the ecclesiastical *cursus*. He started as a monk in the desert of Juda, associated with St. Euthymius, then drew the attention of Patriarch Anastasius, who ordained him priest of the Church of Anastasia in Jerusalem; finally he became the Patriarch of the Holy City, and engaged in a vigorous administration of his patriarchate. He paid attention to both churches and monasteries and laid the foundation of the Church of the Theotokos in Jerusalem, the splendid church completed in the reign of Justinian and dedicated in 543. He was a strong and stern ecclesiastic who was unwavering in his Orthodoxy, to the point of taking on the emperor Anastasius himself. He paid for this by being exiled to Ayla in 516, where he died. It is possible that he was associated with the translation of a simple liturgy and biblical lectionary into Arabic for the benefit of the various Christian Arab communities scattered in the three Palestines which constituted his ecclesiastical jurisdiction.

These are the four large historical figures in the history of Arab-Byzantine relations in the fifth century. Their careers call for two observations. (1) They were very different from one another: bishop, phylarch, federate king, and patriarch, but all four were involved in both the *imperium* and the *ecclesia*, a reflection of the intimate and inseparable relationship that obtained between the two in the Christian Roman Empire. Three of them were federate Arabs and one was Rhomaic. The four different careers are also a reflection of the wide range of Arab involvement in the life of the empire and of the new opportunities open to them. (2) Their careers reflect the profound metamorphosis that each of them experienced as a result of the Byzantine connection. Perhaps that of Aspebetos is the most remarkable: from a pagan chief to a Byzantine phylarch, to a baptized one, to a bishop of the Parembole, to a participant at the Council of Ephesus and a delegate to Nestorius expressing the strong voice of Arab Orthodoxy. Thus his career represents the highest degree of assimilation that a federate Arab could experience.

IX. The Image

Both streams of Byzantine historiography, secular and ecclesiastical, continue to transmit images of the Arabs in the fifth century. Although the negative image of the fourth century is not dead, there is a marked improvement in that image in both streams of fifth-century historiography.

Ecclesiastical

A new generation of ecclesiastical historians appear in the fifth century, emancipated from the bondage of the Eusebian image of the Arabs as uncovenanted Ishmaelites, outside the promise. These ecclesiastical historians expressed the true spirit of the Christian *ecclesia* in their vision of the peoples of the limitrophe, including the Arabs. Socrates, Sozomen, and Theodoret remembered the exploits of Queen Mavia on behalf of Orthodoxy and described the progress of Christianity among the Arabs. It is, however, Theodoret who has the most informative passages on the Arabs.

1. *Historia Religiosa*. The passage on the Arab Abbas, who became the *hēgoumenos* of the monastery of Teleda, occurs in this work. The importance of this passage is that it enables Theodoret to reflect theologically on the Arabs as a biblical people, the descendants of Ishmael and ultimately of Abraham, and provides him with occasion to describe the spiritual metamorphosis of Abbas from an unredeemed Ishmaelite outside the promise, to participation in the patrimony of Abraham, to membership in the New Israel, the gateway to the Kingdom of Heaven. The spiritual path of Abbas is that traversed by all the Christianized Ishmaelites.

2. *Curatio*. In this work, "The Cure of Pagan Maladies," Theodoret projects an image of the Arabs in the context of a pagan world peopled by Greeks and barbarians, and tries to argue for the unity of the human species affirmed by Scripture. He reviews the various peoples and tries to discover their respective virtues. When he comes to the Arabs, he grants them "an intelligence, lively and penetrating . . . and a judgment capable of discerning truth and refuting falsehood."

The strong affirmative note sounded by Theodoret is supported and fortified by the ecclesiastical documents of the century, especially those of the two ecumenical councils of Ephesus and Chalcedon, in 431 and 451 respectively. The number of Arab bishops, both Rhomaic and federate who participated is remarkable, and they expressed the strong voice of Arab Orthodoxy, first Cyrillian Orthodoxy at Ephesus and then Leonine at Chalcedon. Especially prominent in this expression was Petrus I, the bishop of the Palestinian Parembole, who participated actively at Ephesus and was one of the delegates whom the Council sent to negotiate with Nestorius.

The two evaluations of the Arabs in Theodoret are striking, coming as they do from a distinguished theologian and church historian, and so is the evidence from the *Acta* of the two ecumenical councils. But even as the image of the Arabs was being improved by the Greek ecclesiastical writers, it continued to suffer at the hands of a Latin church father.

1. Jerome, who inherited his image of the Arabs from Eusebius, continued to write about them as unredeemed Ishmaelites, a concept from which,

as a biblical scholar and exegete, he could not liberate himself. There was another reason behind Jerome's fulminations against the Arabs. He had lived in the monastic community of the desert of Chalcis and later at Bethlehem. Both were subject to Saracen raids that spelt ruin to monasteries, especially at Bethlehem which was actually occupied by the Saracens. Consequently, he fell back on biblical texts which enabled him to refer to these Saracens as *servorum et ancillarum numerus*. His older contemporary, St. Augustine, followed in the steps of those who had written on heresies in the East, and naturally the Arabs appear in his *De Haeresibus* (sec. 83).

2. On the other hand, another Latin author, Rufinus, spoke in complimentary terms of the Arabs in his *Ecclesiastical History*, as upholders of Orthodoxy. Indeed, he heralded the new generation of ecclesiastical historians in the East—Socrates, Sozomen and Theodoret—who were sympathetic to the world of the barbarians, including the Arabs. But the voice of Rufinus was drowned out by those of the two immensely influential ecclesiastics of the West, Jerome and Augustine, and consequently the image of the Arabs remained dim in the West even before they reached it in the seventh century as conquerors of North Africa and Spain.

Secular

As Rufinus opened a new chapter in the history of the image of the Arabs in ecclesiastical historiography, so did Synesius in secular historiography:

1. In one of his letters, written in 404, Synesius praises the courage of the Arabs, soldiers who had been withdrawn most probably from the Ala Tertia Arabum in the *limes Aegypti* to fight in Pentapolis. In another passage in the same letter he describes the despair of the passengers on the storm-tossed ship that was sailing to Pentapolis and lauds the attitude of the Arab soldiers who were prepared to fall on their swords rather than die by drowning. He even grows lyrical and refers to them as "by nature true descendants of Homer."

That a Greek who was nursed in a tradition that viewed mankind in terms of Greek and barbarian should be so emancipated and, what is more, refer to the Arabs as descendants in spirit of the Homeric heroes is surely extraordinary and calls for an explanation. His city, Cyrene, had no Arabs in it and so there was no friction between his community and the Arabs; as a Neo-Platonist he may have remembered that some important Neo-Platonic figures, such as Iamblichus, were Arab; his anti-German sentiments, which he expressed while he was at Constantinople around 400, may have inclined him toward the Arabs, who had saved Constantinople from the German Goths in 378 after Adrianople; and finally, his literary models on the Arabs, most probably, were authors such as Diodorus Siculus, who spoke well of the Arabs, rather than Ammianus, of whom he was probably unaware.

2. Not only in the works of a Neo-Platonist but also in official imperial documents, the image of the Arabs appears reasonably bright and no longer that of raiders of the frontier or traitors to the Roman cause, undesirable as allies or as enemies. In one of the *novellae* of 443, Theodosius and Valentinian instruct that the limital *duces* should not abstract anything from the *annona* of the *foederati*, especially the Saracen ones. This could only imply that the central government was happy with their performance and loyalty to the state. The date of the *novella*, coming so close after the end of the Second Persian War of the reign of Theodosius II, suggests that the Arab *foederati* had performed creditably in that conflict. Their performance was consistently satisfactory on the battlefield. The *prodosia* theme elaborated by Procopius in the sixth century was without any foundation and the satisfaction of the *imperium* was to find expression in the seventh, in the victory bulletin which Heraclius addressed to the Senate after his victory at Nineveh.

3. This bright image in the secular sources was somewhat dimmed later in the century when Malchus of Philadelphia, himself most probably a Rhomaic Arab, wrote and almost neutralized what Synesius had said about the Arabs. In a long and detailed fragment on the emperor Leo in the penultimate year of his reign, Malchus relentlessly criticized the emperor for his relations with the Arab chief Amorkesos, and by implication gave an uncomplimentary picture of the Arabs even though they became *foederati* of the empire.

The background of this attack on the Arabs, especially as it was voiced by one of them, is as complex as that which inspired Synesius to draw his picture of the Arabs in bright colors. Four main reasons may be detected behind Malchus' hostile attitude. First and foremost comes *Kaiserkritik*. The historian was not an admirer of the emperor, and expressed his disapproval of Leo's administration by criticizing his Arab policy. Malchus also wrote as a concerned *Rhōmaios* and an analyst of Roman decline. For him, the barbarians had brought about the downfall of the empire in the West in 476. Leo had depended on another group of barbarians, the Isaurians, and now he was also employing the services of the Arabs, represented by Amorkesos. Malchus wrote not in his native Provincia Arabia, but in Constantinople and under Anastasius. He was an assimilated *Rhōmaios*, like others who came from the Provincia and are hardly recognizable as Arabs. Hence he acquired the ethnocentricity of those who belonged by birth to the Graeco-Roman establishment and voiced their racism with a vengeance. Finally, it is possible, judging from his phraseology, that he was writing with a literary model in mind—Ammianus, whose anti-Arab outbursts, expressed in vivid and graphic phrases, have riveted the attention of posterity, endured throughout the ages, and with staggering tenacity retained their hold on those who have dealt with the image.

In spite of the negative image that secular and ecclesiastical historiography, represented by Malchus and Jerome projected, the image of the Arabs experienced a marked improvement. Toward the end of the century, in the reign of Anastasius, there arose another group of *foederati*, who possibly became involved from the beginning in Monophysitism. This completely blackened the image of the Arabs in the sixth century during which both secular and ecclesiastical historiography combined to project a most uncomplimentary image which damned them as traitors to the *imperium* and heretics to the *ecclesia*. Thus the fifth century is the golden period in the history of the Arab image, unlike the fourth and the sixth, during which it was tarnished mainly by sharp friction with the central government on doctrinal grounds. The coin of Arab identity looked good on both of its sides. To the *imperium* the Arabs appeared as faithful guardians of the Roman frontier; to the *ecclesia* they appeared as conforming Orthodox believers.

The Arab Self-Image

The significance of two ecclesiastical historians, Sozomen and Theodoret, is immense for the Byzantine perception of the Arabs in the fifth century. In addition to the improved image that their works provide, they also, especially Theodoret, have preserved data on the Arabs which strongly suggest that the Arabs of this period perceived themselves as descendants of Ishmael. Whether this perception was indigenous among the Arabs or adventitious, having reached them from the Pentateuch either directly through the spread of Judaism in Arabia or mediated through the Christian mission, is not entirely clear. Its reality, however, is clear and certain, and the idiom of Theodoret even suggests that their perception was mixed with pride in the fact of their descent from Ishmael.

This is the important new element that appears in the fifth century and adds a second mirror to the one that reflects the Byzantine perception of the Arabs. In this new mirror, Ishmael is rehabilitated. He is no longer a figure that embarrasses the Arabs through certain biblical associations but a revered ancestor of whom they are proud. This image became a most important element in Arab religious life in the seventh century, which witnessed an even more complete rehabilitation of Ishmael. In the Koran, Ishmael appears not as the pater eponymous of the Arabs but as the son of the First Patriarch, Abraham, and a prophet. The precious passage in the *Historia Religiosa* of Theodoret proves beyond doubt that the eponymate of Ishmael is rooted in the pre-Islamic Arab past and that it goes back to at least the fifth century.

Epilogue

I

The Salīḥids endured for almost a century in the service of Byzantium. They represent the golden period in the history of federate-imperial relations. Unlike the Tanūkhids and the Ghassānids, the Salīḥid doctrinal persuasion was that of the imperial government in Constantinople. Consequently federate-imperial relations were not marred by violent and repeated friction such as vitiated these relations in the fourth and sixth centuries.

The Salīḥids fought for Byzantium on the Persian front and distinguished themselves in the two Persian Wars of the reign of Theodosius II. It is also practically certain that they participated in Leo's Vandal Expedition, taking part in the battle of Cape Bon, during which their numbers must have been thinned. This is the most plausible explanation for their ineffectiveness in the defense of the *limes Arabicus* around A.D. 470. Finally, the law of generation and decay which governed the rise and fall of Arab polities before the rise of Islam caught up with them. Powerful Peninsular groups such as the Ghassānids and the Kindites had hewn their way through the Arabian Peninsula and had reached the Roman frontier. The Salīḥids, already weakened considerably by their participation in the Vandal War, could not withstand the impact of the combined force of the two new powerful tribal groups. They succumbed in the contest for power and the Ghassānids emerged as the dominant federate group in the sixth century.

Although no longer supreme in federate history in Oriens, the Salīḥids remained an important political and military fact in the structure of the federate shield. Their history is divisible into the following phases: (1) 502 to 529, when they constitute one of the federate groups in Oriens, who obeyed their own phylarchs and the *dux* of the province to whom they were ultimately subordinate; (2) 529–580, when they were most probably subordinate to the Ghassānid supreme phylarch, who was installed in that position by Emperor Justinian around 529, and must have continued in that subordinate relationship until ca. 580, when Ghassānid-Byzantine relations soured considerably and the Arab phylarchate of Oriens was decentralized; (3) 580 to 610, during the period of much eclipse for the Ghassānids, when the power of the Salīḥids may have been revived or at least made independent of the former, since one of their phylarchs appears fighting with the Byzantines in 586 during the siege of Mardīn. Not much is known about them after this period until they appear fighting together with the other federates against the Muslim Arabs. The last mention of them during the Muslim Conquest of Oriens occurs in connection with the capitulation of Chalcis. The Muslim commander asks them to accept Islam, but they refuse.

Unlike other federate groups such as the Iyādīs, the Salīḥids remained staunch Christians throughout the Muslim period. This explains why they attained no prominence in Islamic times. Usāma ibn Zayd was the exception: he served four Umayyad caliphs in important administrative roles, his durability in their service being testimony to his talent. After him the sources are silent on the Salīḥids, who dispersed in various parts of the Fertile Crescent and possibly affiliated themselves with other tribes. They appear in one of the verses of Islamic times as an example of dispersion and evanescence worthy of the classical lament of the Arab poet: *"ubi sunt qui ante nos in mundo fuere?"*

II

The other tribes of the federate shield took part in the defense of the *limes orientalis* and in the Persian Wars. They also protected the caravans that moved along the arteries of international trade in north and northwestern Arabia. The Salīḥids did not control these tribes as the Ghassānids were to do in the sixth century. The Arabic sources record feuds among these federate tribes. Two of them, Kalb and Namir, united against the dominant group Salīḥ, brought about the downfall of the Salīḥid king Dāwūd, and must have weakened the power of Salīḥ, thus contributing ultimately to the victory of the Ghassānids over them and the emergence of a new federate supremacy, the Ghassānid, which controlled most or all of the other tribes of the federate shield in Oriens for almost half a century.

In addition to their military role, these federate tribes made some important contributions to Arabic culture in pre-Islamic times. The names of Iyād, Kalb, and ʿUḏra stand out in connection with the rise of the Arabic script in Oriens in the fifth century and of a new type of love and love poetry, called ʿUḏrite in Arabic, which represented the confluence of the pre-Islamic chivalrous attitude with Christian ideals of chastity and continence.

All these federate tribes fought on the side of Byzantium in the period of the Arab Conquests. After the crushing defeat at Yarmūk in 636, they dispersed and their history as *foederati* came to an end. Some of them emigrated to Anatolia, some stayed on in Oriens, now Arab Bilād al-Shām, and formed part of the Umayyad *ajnād* system. While the Salīḥids remained staunchly Christian, some of the other federate tribes accepted Islam, which enabled them to participate actively in the shaping of Islamic history.

Before they made their Byzantine connection, these tribes had moved in the restricted and closed orbit of the Arabian Peninsula. In all probability they would have continued to move in that orbit, and history would not have taken notice of them and their achievements. It was the Byzantine connection that drew them into the world of the Mediterranean and gave an international dimension to their history. One of the three constituents of Byzantium, Christianity, terminated their isolation and peninsularism by making them members of the large world of Christendom and its universal *ecclesia*.

Islam was to do what Byzantium had done but in a more substantial way. It made the tribes assume a more active role in shaping the history of the Mediterranean world in both East and West. In the East they formed part of the *ajnād*, participated in the annual expeditions against the Byzantine heartland, Anatolia, and took part in many sieges of Constantinople. In the West some of them settled on European soil, but their more important role in Spain was cultural. One of these tribes, Iyād, produced the talented family of the Zuhrids, known to medieval Europe as physicians and to Arabic scholars as composers of strophic odes. The influence of another, ʿUḏra, crossed the Pyrenees, and either gave rise to, or formed one ingredient in, the rise of that attractive type of love known to medievalists as *amour courtois*. Few readers of the medieval literary works that this type of love inspired realize that they are owed to an Arabian tribe which in the fifth century defended the southern approaches to the *limes orientalis* of Byzantium as a tribe of the outer shield. And it is mainly to the well-known lyric of the German-Jewish poet with its haunting couplet that modern Europe owes its vague recollection of that Arab tribe of the fifth century which inspired the rise of this love and gifted it with its own name:

Und mein Stamm sind jene Asra,
Welche sterben, wenn sie lieben.

Addenda et Corrigenda

As *RA, BAFOC*, and *BAFIC* are related to one another, I include the following addenda et corrigenda for the three volumes.

Rome and the Arabs

Edom

Even before the rise of Islam, the Arabs inhabited a large area of the Near East, both in the Arabian Peninsula and in the Fertile Crescent. Before any meaningful history of the Arabs in this period can be written, it is necessary to define clearly the Arab area. I have done this when dealing with the Arabian Peninsula by excising the old Semites of southwestern Arabia, who in the early Christian centuries were called the Ḥimyarites, Semitic peoples often confused with the Arabs but actually only cognates and quite distinct from them.[1] I have also done the same for the Fertile Crescent in both its eastern and its western halves. More recently, for the western half, I have limited the Arab area in Oriens, Bilād al-Shām, to the limitrophe, the eastern sector bordering on the Arabian Peninsula and Arabia in Mesopotamia, where roughly the three Arab peoples, the Osroeni, the Palmyrenes, and the Nabataeans lived. In so doing I have attempted to disentangle the strictly Arab zone in Oriens from the two others, the Greek and the Semitic, wherein lived the Jews and the Aramaic-speaking peoples of the Orient. The Edomites were mentioned among the various Arab groups that Pompey found in the region when he made his famous Settlement.[2] I have not made independent researches on the Edomites. I have always assumed that they were an old Arab people, having been influenced by those who wrote on them and on Edomite-Jewish relations, such as the late Michael Avi-Yonah.[3] And this is how they appeared in *RA* as Arabs. Since the appearance of *RA*, the Arabness of the Edomites has been questioned, and indeed has been rejected by some in a recent scholarly debate concerning the appearance in a papyrus of the phrase "Nea Arabia."[4] The presumed Arabness of the Edomites has thus become a matter of

[1] See I. Shahîd, "Pre-Islamic Arabia," in *CHI* I, 3–29, esp. p. 6.

[2] See *RA*, 5.

[3] See M. Avi-Yonah: *The Holy Land*, 25–26, 61–62, 65, where their Arabness is expressed in strong and unambiguous terms. And so also in the work of S. Perowne, *The Life and Times of Herod the Great* (London, 1956).

[4] For this debate, see Mayerson's replies to T. Barnes and G. Bowersock in "P.Oxy. 3574: Eleutheropolis of the New Arabia," *ZPE* 53 (1983), 251–58 and in "Nea Arabia (P.Oxy. 3574): An Addendum to *ZPE* 53," *ZPE* 64 (1986), 139–40.

some importance in this new context of provincial Roman history, and it is therefore necessary to make some observations on this issue.

1. One ancient author, Uranius of the third/fourth century A.D., specifically refers to them as an Arab *ethnos*,[5] and he was presumably echoing earlier sources.[6] So those who were close to the Edomites in time apparently conceived of them as Arabs. Josephus, who has the right to be heard on the subject, apparently did not, but his ethnographic conceptions were biblical; he conceived of the Arabs as the sons of Ishmael, to whom the Edomites did not belong.[7]

2. In the Bible the Edomites appear more related to the Jews through their descent from Isaac who begat Esau, their eponym. But as is well known, the table of nations in the Bible is not accurate and the affiliation of the Edomites as documented there may be an instance of such inaccuracy. However, even in the Bible there is an Arab dimension to the Edomites, reflected in the marriages of Edom/Esau. According to Genesis he visited his uncle Ishmael, the eponym of the Arabs, and married his daughter Mahalath, the sister of Nabaioth; in another passage he married another daughter, Bashemath.[8] Thus in biblical terms the Edomites are the children of an Arab woman whom their eponym, Esau,[9] married. This inter-marriage involving Esau/Edom and an Ishmaelite woman, the sister of Nabaioth, could suggest that the Edomites and the Ishmaelites were two consanguineous groups, related to each other as Arabs.[10]

3. Unlike the Hurrians whom they displaced, the Edomites were a Semitic people, and it might be plausibly argued that they belonged to one of the three major waves of Semitic migrations into the Fertile Crescent, Ammorite, Canaanite, and Aramaean.[11] With the exception of the word *allufim*, nothing has survived of Edomite which might give an indication of their linguistic affiliation. But their geographical location, deep in the *south* of the Fertile Crescent, is significant and could be a strong argument for their Arab and Arabian provenance. Like the Ammonites and the Moabites in what might be called in this period Trans-Jordania Tripartita, the Edomites could be viewed as Arabians who irrupted into Trans-Jordan through the two gateways from the Arabian Peninsula, north Ḥijāz and Wādī Sirḥān. Their Arabian connection seems even stronger than the Ammonites and Moabites, since they lived even farther to the South, and this suggests a closer link with Arabia

[5] For this see Mayerson, ibid., 139 and his own observations.

[6] Possibly Strabo, who thought that the Edomites had separated themselves from their Arab brethren when they crossed from Trans-Jordan to Palestine; quoted by M. Avi-Yonah, *The Holy Land*, 62 note 66. On the Idumaeans as Nabataean Arabs, see Strabo, *Geography*, XIV.ii.34.

[7] Hence his conception of Herod as an Edomite and the pointed reference to only his mother (Cyprus, the daughter of the Nabataean Arab king) as an Arab.

[8] Gen. 28:9, 36:3.

[9] Even the name Esau sounds close to Arabic ʿĪṣ and ʿĀṣ, well known in Hijāz.

[10] It should be noted, however, that this is more true of his marriage with Mahalath than with Bashemath, who appears as one of many wives whom Esau married. These are described as Canaanite, Hittite, and Hivite, respectively.

[11] Gen. 36:3 separates them from the Canaanites and, consequently, also from the Ammorites who preceded the latter.

through north Ḥijāz. Unlike these two other peoples, the Edomites were possessed of a very strong sense of identity since they resisted absorption, and thus they present a spectacle not unlike that of such Arab tribes as Tamīm and Taghlīb of later times.

4. The most distinguished figure in Edomite history was undoubtedly Herod the Great. His father Antipater married Cyprus, the daughter of the Nabataean Arab king Arethas. This recalls the marriage of the eponym of the Edomites, Esau, to the sister of Nabaioth, the Arab son of Ishmael. So through his mother Cyprus, Herod was half Arab. His name, too, may also suggest an Arab origin. It is supposed to be Greek Ἡρῴδης, but it could also be Arabic Ḥarūd,[12] assimilated to the Greek name in much the same way that the Arab Palmyrene Queen whose real name was Bath-zabbai appeared as Greek Zenobia.

5. The reference to a newly created but short-lived province early in the fourth century by the name of Nea Arabia could give support to the Arab character of the Edomites.[13] John Rea and Philip Mayerson have argued against Timothy Barnes and Glen Bowersock that Nea Arabia was in southern Palestine and not in Egypt. Should the former turn out to be right, this will give strong support to the Arab character of the Edomites, since it would reflect the Roman perception of that region in Palestine (Idumaea) as ethnically Arab.

6. Finally, an important pointer to the possible Arabness of the Edomites comes from an examination of the Arab tribal onomasticon in this very region where the Edomites of ancient times had lived. The name of one of these tribes, Juḏām, bears a striking resemblance to Edom, even after the process of transliterating an Arab name into Hebrew had changed the original name. Juḏām is an old and "archaic" tribe which was indigenous to this area for a very long time before the rise of Islam, unlike many tribes which flocked to Oriens with the Muslim Conquest.[14] Nöldeke suspected that the biblical Kenites survived in the Arab tribe of Qayn or Banū al-Qayn, and the Amalec survived in ʿĀmila.[15] If he is right, it is not extravagant to think that Edom survived in Juḏām, that Edom was an old, "archaic" Arab tribe that had found its way into the southern corner of the Fertile Crescent through northern Ḥijāz,[16] and that it was already installed in that corner where the Israelites found them during their wanderings from Egypt to Canaan.

The foregoing have not been arguments but observations, advanced to suggest that a case can be made for the Arabness of Edom. Even if not originally Arab, the Edomites probably became Arabized[17] through long and intimate association with

---

[12] The morphological pattern ḥarīd means "a man who separates himself from others" and ḥarūd would be the intensive form; see Lane, Arabic-English Lexicon, Bk. I, pt. 1, 544. The name is not inappropriate for Herod. It is also noteworthy that in northern Palestine the name survives in a toponym, ʿAyn Ḥarūd. In support of this Semitic name for Herod, it may be pointed out that his four brothers all had Semitic names.

[13] See above, note 4.

[14] For Juḏām, see BAFOC, Index, s.v.

[15] For these see ibid., Index, s.vv. Balqayn and ʿĀmila.

[16] Whence, from this Arabophone area, they brought with them such possibly Arabic-sounding names as Esau and Bashemath.

[17] It is noteworthy that their god was the Arab Qaws.

the Arabs of the area such as the Nabataeans, the dominant Arab group in the region. These observations were in my mind when I conceived of the Edomites as Arabs and included them among the Arab groups that formed the Arab presence in the Orient in Roman times. If the Edomites turn out to be non-Arabs, they should be struck from the list of Arab groups enumerated in *RA*.

Saracenus

The term *Saraceni* formed one of the topical studies in the second part of *RA* (pp. 123–41). In his interpretation of the Ruwwāfa Bilinguis, J. T. Milik read one of the words as "šrkt," to which he gave the meaning of "federation." D. Graf and M. O'Connor have based their new etymology of the term "Saraceni" on Milik's reading and interpretation. I examined this new etymology twice in *RA*, first in the body of the chapter (pp. 128–31) and then in an appendix (pp. 138–41). It was only after extensive discussion of the new etymology that it occurred to me that the basic mistake in the argument for this new etymology was made not by Graf and O'Connor but by Milik himself, and in the last paragraph of the last note of the appendix, I ventured the rejection of the etymology on palaeographic grounds, namely, that the crucial word should be read "šrbt" and not "šrkt," which reading would also translate correctly the word *ethnos* in the Greek version of the Ruwwāfa Bilinguis and would give it its natural meaning (*RA*, p. 141 note 13).

Since the writing of that paragraph, I have tried to examine photographs of the inscription, which I have been able to do through the kindness of Prof. A. Jamme, who asked Prof. Ruth Stiehl for the photographs. The examination has confirmed my suspicion that the crucial word is indeed "šrbt" and not "šrkt." The photographs have also been seen and examined by two distinguished Semitic palaeographers, Profs. A. Jamme and Franz Rosenthal, and both have read the word as "šrbt" and not "šrkt." This rules out the new etymology of *Saraceni* based on the reading "šrkt" in the Ruwwāfa Bilinguis, and could make the argument in *RA* against the new etymology superfluous. However, the argument may not have outlived its usefulness entirely, since it constitutes a reply to those who prefer to read the "šrbt" of the inscription as "šrkt."

Byzantium and the Arabs in the Fourth Century

1. On p. 33 of *BAFOC*, while discussing the Christianity of Imru' al-Qays, I wrote of his being buried in a church. But when I was preparing the manuscript of *BAFOC* for press, I discovered that I had lost the documentation for this statement. I therefore deleted all the references to it in the manuscript, but missed this one reference, to which G. Bowersock has drawn attention (in *CR* 36, p. 115). However, the truth about the building where the tomb of Imru' al-Qays was found does not affect the argument about his Christianity, which stands firm without it. His Christianity is vouched for by the foremost historian of pre-Islamic Arabia and the house of Imru' al-Qays, Hishām al-Kalbī, and there is an entire section in *BAFOC* (pp. 32–35) which discusses this point without further reference to the place of his burial.

As to whether the building was religious or secular the question is an open one.

The famous Ghassānid structure outside Ruṣāfa/Sergiopolis has been the subject of a controversy and it is not absolutely certain whether it was a *praetorium* or an *ecclesia extra muros*.[18] And it cannot be entirely ruled out that the building at Namāra where the tomb of Imru' al-Qays was found could have been a modest structure, which was architecturally and decoratively not a church but only functionally used as such. Nothing is known about the circumstances of his death, which may have been inclement and could explain why the "king of all the Arabs" was interred in this insignificant corner.

2. In an appendix (*BAFOC*, 72–73), I tried to suggest the relevance of the bilingual Latin-Greek inscription of Barāqish in South Arabia to the campaign of Imru' al-Qays against Najrān. P. M. Costa has argued that it is a late third- or fourth-century inscription, while G. W. Bowersock has argued for a first-century B.C. dating. I suggested that the Publius Cornelius of the inscription could have been a Byzantine officer sent with the expeditionary force of Imru' al-Qays against Najrān. Since then it has occurred to me that a parallel to this joint Arab-Byzantine expedition may be provided from the pages of Procopius. During the Assyrian Campaign of Belisarius, a joint Arab-Byzantine expeditionary force was dispatched across the Tigris under the command of the Ghassānid Arethas and two Byzantine officers, Trajan and John; Procopius, *Wars*, II.xix.15–16.

In a publication that has appeared since then, P. M. Costa has had more observations to present, defending his position on the dating of the inscription; see "Further Comments on the Bilingual Inscription from Barāqish," *Proceedings of the Nineteenth Seminar for Arabian Studies* (London, 1986), 33–36. The identity of Publius Cornelius remains controversial. He may well have been what Costa thinks. If his dating turns out to be the correct one, the *eques* in question could have been a businessman and not a soldier. But this interpretation, attractive as it is, remains pure guesswork unsupported by any evidence in the sources or the history of the period, while the interpretation I offered in *BAFOC* has the advantage of being supported by an important echo in the Namāra inscription of the campaign of an Arab-Byzantine client-king against Najrān and the parallel provided by Procopius' account of Belisarius' Assyrian Campaign during the reign of Justinian.

3. Two chapters were devoted to Theophilus Indus in *BAFOC* (pp. 86–100). While the volume was being printed, an article on Theophilus Indus appeared in print by G. Fiaccadori, who was good enough to send me an offprint; see his "Teofilo Indiano," *Studi classici e oriental* 33 (Pisa, 1983), 295–331. The article is an important contribution to the literature on Theophilus Indus and has an extensive bibliography. My two chapters did not aim at bibliographical completeness, since they concentrated on presenting conclusions on Theophilus in the new context of the volume on the fourth century. Hence many bibliographical items were left out which may be retrieved in "Teofilo Indiano."

On pp. 98–99, I explored new possibilities for the site of the third church

[18] After being declared a *praetorium* by many, it has been considered a church by the latest to write on the subject, J. Wilkinson, who so argues in the manuscript of his forthcoming book, *Building God's Palace*. However, I am inclined to think it is a *praetorium*.

which Theophilus Indus founded in South Arabia. I should like to say now that Soḥār in present-day Oman may be added to the list, since it is attested as an episcopal see in the fifth century and it is just possible that it owes this status to its having had a church already in the fourth century.

4. In *BAFOC* (pp. 297–319), I discussed the martyrs of Sinai and defended the essential authenticity of the account which described their martyrdom. In the same year that *BAFOC* appeared (1984) there appeared a new contribution to the literature on these martyrs which was unknown to me when I wrote, just as my defense of the authenticity of the account was unknown to Father F. Halkin, the author of the new contribution; see his "Les moines martyres du Sinaï dans le ménologue impérial," in *Mémorial André-Jean Festugière*, Cahiers d'orientalisme 10 (Geneva, 1984), 267–73.

5. I have an appendix on Jabala b. Sālim in *BAFOC* (pp. 410–12). For Sālim, see now, D. Latham in *CHAL*, pp. 155–64. Apparently the father, Sālim, was a *mawlā* (client) (ibid., 161). And so he appears as the *mawlā* of Saʿīd b. ʿAbd al-Malik in M. al-Jahshiyāri, *al-Wuzarāʾ wa al-Kuttāb*, 68. But it is not clear whether or not he was a *mawlā ʿatāqa* as Usāma ibn Zayd al-Salīḥī was not; for whom see above, Chap. 12, sec. VII.II. If so, Sālim could have been an Arab; see *BAFOC*, 409 note 5. Sālim had another son who was also a *kātib*, Abdullah; see Latham, op. cit., 164 and al-Jahshiyāri, op. cit., 68.

6. In an appendix in *BAFOC* (416–17) I discussed two toponyms important to the Arab-Byzantine relationship, Malikān and Ilāha. One of these can now be identified, since it appears on A. Musil's map in *Arabia Deserta*, lying 120 miles to the north of Dūmat al-Jandal (Jawf).

7. Elath/Ayla is an important town in the history of Arab-Roman-Byzantine relations, for which see the index in both *RA* and *BAFOC*, s.v. Ayla. Its orthography has presented a problem which I have solved by adopting the form accepted by Harold Gliden in *EI*²—Ayla. These are my reasons for the choice of this form.

(*a*) In biblical times the correct orthography was Elath, with a consonant at the end of the word. But as M. Avi-Yonah points out in his article in *Encyclopaedia Judaica* (s.v. Elath) the town had become a Ptolemaic port in Hellenistic times and later became a Nabataean port, renamed Aila, which thus dropped the final consonant of the biblical orthography.

(*b*) But stripped of the final consonant, the orthography presented a bewildering variety of forms: It has at least five varieties in Greek (for which see *Excavations at Nessana*, III, No. 51, p. 146): Αἰλανή, τὰ Αἴλανα, 'Ελάνα, 'Αειλά, and 'Αϊλάς. In French it has at least nine forms (see S. Vailhé's article in *DHGE*, I, col. 647): Elath, Ailat, Ailath, Ailone, Elana, Ailon, Eloth, Aelath, Aela.

As I was not discussing the town in biblical times, I decided to accept the orthography of the word without the final consonant and also to write it as Ayla, reflecting the diphthong in Arabic, which thus distinguishes it from the many other forms and, what is more, from another almost homophonous term, Aelia Capitolina. "ʿAqaba" appears later and should not be used for the town or the Gulf in Byzantine and early Islamic times; the Gulf of Eilath would be the appropriate term to use in these periods.

Reviews

Of the reviews which have appeared since the publication of *RA* and *BAFOC*, that of G. W. Bowersock has been the most extensive (*Classical Review* 36.1 [1986], 111–17). I accept as valid only four of the points he has made, three of which pertain to *RA* and one to *BAFOC* (discussed as item 1 in the preceding section).

(*a*) The province of Osroene was annexed not by Gordian III (as in *RA*, 21) but by Septimius Severus. The former only terminated the rule of the Abgarids, the Arab rulers of Edessa, and made the city a Roman colony in A.D. 243.

(*b*) Bowersock is our authority on the Second Sophistic, and so his modification of what I wrote (p. 34) on Julia Domna and her commissioning Philostratus to write *The Life of Apollonius of Tyana* has to be accepted.

(*c*) The dossier on Philip the Arab is enriched by his reference to the lines in the thirteen Sibylline oracles and the coins of Philip. The latter, however, do not affect the conclusions on the Christianity of the emperor (see *RA*, 72–75). Unlike Constantine, Philip was not converted while he was in the purple and so his Christianity did not attract the attention of pagan writers; see *RA*, 71–72 and Bowersock, *Roman Arabia*, 125–26. Besides, the argument from silence is often deceptive; Aurelius Victor is silent on one of the most important episodes in the reign of Aurelian, namely, the conquest and destruction of Palmyra, but it cannot be argued from this silence that it did not happen.

In the last analysis there are two approaches to the problem of Philip's Christianity. One may start with the *logos* in Eusebius, which unequivocally vouches for it in a detailed manner, and then proceed to the data which reflect the pagan expressions of Philip's reign. Alternatively, one may start from these pagan expressions and proceed to the *logos*. The former approach must end with declaring for Philip's Christianity, because it is easy to explain away the pagan expressions as those pertaining to the duty of Philip as the *imperator* of a pagan Roman empire. The latter approach encounters the difficulty of the *logos*, which cannot be explained away as the pagan expressions can. To say that Philip attended the service on Easter Eve as a tourist or out of curiosity must be thrown out of court, since the *logos* is detailed and explicit on his Christianity. Furthermore, it was written by the father of ecclesiastical history himself, who was interested in this very point—the identity of the first Christian Roman emperor—and who was writing not about the distant Christian past but about an event which took place some fifty years before his *floruit* and, what is more, in the same region where he lived, in Oriens. Thus the *logos* cannot be explained away. Consequently, the latter approach has to be abandoned, and with it the quest for the de-Christianization of Philip.

In a private communication, S. Thomas Parker drew my attention to the following.

(*a*) On p. 20 notes 5 and 6 of *RA*, I referred to the work of D. Graf and his view that the southern boundary of the Provincia Arabia "was the southern slope of al-Sherā range" and that there was a gap in the fortification system of the southern sector of the *limes Arabicus* from ʿAqaba to Sadaqa. Thomas Parker informs me that there is really no such gap, that milestones of the Via Nova Traiana have been found all the way to ʿAqaba, and that "the single line of fortifications guarding the Via Nova sufficed in this sector."

(*b*) He also drew my attention to T. D. Barnes' suggestion that Diocletian's campaign against the Arabs took place near Emesa in central Syria. This suggestion may be found on p. 51 of Barnes' *The New Empire of Diocletian and Constantine* (Cambridge, Mass., 1982), which I was unable to consult since it became available to me after *RA* went to press. The same was true of his other book, *Constantine and Eusebius*, published by the same press a year earlier in 1981. Both are important and relevant to *RA* and *BAFOC*.

Colin M. Wells has brought to my attention an Arab unit which fought in the Roman army in Europe, namely, Cohors I Hemesanorum, stationed at Intercisa on the Danube south of Budapest from about A.D. 180 to 260. The details may be found in *Les Syriens à Intercisa*, Coll. Latomus 122 (Brussels, 1972). Of this unit Prof. Wells writes that "it continued to recruit from Syria and attracted a considerable Syrian community, which seems to have maintained its separate linguistic and cultural identity for roughly a century."

In his review of *RA* in *Historische Zeitschrift* 243 (1986), 403 f, Erich Kettenhofen has drawn attention to a misprint on p. 103; the death of Abgar the Great took place in A.D. 216, not 218.

I should like to thank the three scholars for their reviews and communications.

Byzantium and the Arabs in the Fifth Century

1. Something has been said on the high cultural level that the Nabataean Arabs reached in Roman times.[19] And it has been argued in *BAFIC* (Chap. 4, sec. VIII.D) that Malchus, the historian from Philadelphia, was ethnically an Arab from the Provincia Arabia. To Malchus and such figures from Arabia Nabataea may be added two more:[20] Dousareios, who participated in the controversies of the Neo-Platonist philosophers; and Gesios, who surfaces in the reign of Zeno as a philosophical doctor, a student of the Jew Domnos. The name Γέσιος is Semitic and is likely to be Arabic Qays, written without diphthongization and with the letter G substituted for Q, as happens when Qāsim becomes Gāsim in some Arabic dialects.

2. The Edict of Beersheba was discussed above (Chap. 7, sec. II). The view was entertained there that the Edict of Beersheba was issued by Anastasius (see also above, Chap. 6, app. 1). Philip Mayerson has now argued that the Edict of Beersheba was issued by Justinian in 536; see *ZPE* 64 (1986) 141–48.

3. In Appendix 3 of Chapter 10 I examined the Arab identity of two bishops of Jerusalem whose names sound Palmyrene, Mazabanes and Zabdas. My attention has

[19] On the three Nabataeans from Petra, sophists of the third century—Heliodorus, Callinicus, and Genethlius—see *RA*, xxii note 9.

[20] On these two Nabataean Arabs, see J. Bernays, "Ein nabatäischer Schriftsteller," *Gesammelte Abhandlungen von Jacob Bernays* (Berlin, 1885), II, 291–93. Dousareios may thus be added to Iamblichus as an Arab Neo-Platonist; see *RA*, xxii. For other attestations of Dousareios as a Nabataean Arab name which confirm Bernays's conclusion, see A. Alt, "Zwölf christliche Grabsteine," 223–24 and 224 note 1.

been drawn to a Palmyrene Arab by the name of Anʿam who was an armored cavalryman, a *clibanarius*, and who was buried in Jerusalem. Both his Arab identity and his Palmyrene provenance are attested in a funerary inscription, which according to its editor goes back to the fourth or fifth century. Anʿam may thus be added to the list of Palmyrenes associated with Jerusalem in the early Christian centuries; for the inscription, see Peter Thomsen, "Die lateinischen und griechischen Inschriften der Stadt Jerusalem," *ZDPV* 129 (1921), 92–94.

I am grateful to Frank Trombley for bringing this inscription to my attention.

4. After the typescript of *BAFIC* had gone to press, I found epigraphic confirmation of Jurhum as a South Arabian tribe in a work published in Arabic in which a number of new Sabaic inscriptions are presented: M. al-Iryānī, *Fī Tārīkh al-Yaman* (Cairo, 1974), 174.

Jurhum appears twice in inscription no. 34, once in line 2 and again in line 4; in both cases it appears with two mīms, the last letter of "Jurhum" followed by mimation. This inscription contains the first and only attestation of Jurhum in the Sabaic inscriptions. It thus confirms the historicity of this important tribe which, before this inscription was published, had only the testimony of confused and mostly legendary Arabic literary sources. It is a welcome addition to other inscriptions which have confirmed other tribes such as Asd/Azd and Ghassān, important to the Arab-Byzantine relationship. The inscription clinches the South Arabian provenance of Jurhum and presents serious objections to the views discussed above (Chap. 13, app. 3) that the tribe had emigrated from Gerrha, especially as the last letter in "Jurhum" cannot now be explained as Sabaic mimation.

The new collection of Sabaic inscriptions assembled by M. Iryānī was reviewed by J. Ryckmans; see his general evaluation in "Himyaritica 3," *Le Muséon* 87 (1974), 237–39, and his discussion of inscription no. 34 in "Himyaritica 4," ibid., 493–99. To my knowledge, no Sabaicist has commented on the historical significance of this inscription involving Jurhum; most of the comments have been philological and anthropological.

5. In a forthcoming volume of *Jerusalem Studies in Arabic and Islam* (Jerusalem), there are two articles by U. Rubin which evidently are relevant to certain chapters in *BAFIC*—possibly to "Sozomen and the Arabs," "Ishmaelism," and "Byzantium and Mecca." The two articles are: "Places of Worship in Mecca" and "Ḥanīfiyya and Kaʿba: An Enquiry into the Arabian pre-Islamic Background of Dīn Ibrahīm." They will be noticed in *BASIC*.

Stemmata of the Rulers of the Near East in the Fifth Century

The stemmata of the Byzantine, Sasanid, Lakhmid, and Kindite rulers are adapted from those in *PLRE*. The stemma of the Salīḥids derives from Hishām's *Jamharat* and has been limited to members of the family that had relations with Byzantium. For a complete tribal stemma of the Salīḥids, see Caskel, *GN*, I, 326. The stemma of the phylarchs of the Parembole derives from Cyril of Scythopolis, while the two other phylarchs are attested in Sozomen and Malchus.

THE BYZANTINE DYNASTIES

The House of Theodosius, 379–457

Theodosius I
(379–395)

Eudoxia = Arcadius (385–408)
Honorius (395–423)

Marcian (450–457) = Pulcheria (+453)
Theodosius II (408–450) = Eudocia (Athenais)

The House of Leo, 457–518

Leo I
(457–474)

Zeno (474–491) = Ariadne = Anastasius I (491–518)

Leo II
(474)

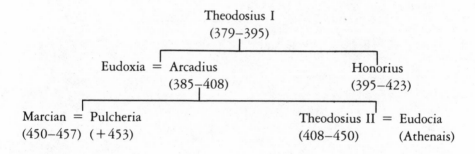

The Sasanid Kings

- Yazdgard I (399–420)
  - Bahrām Gūr (420–438)
    - Yazdgard II (438–457)
      - Hormisd (457–459)
      - Pērōz (459–484)
        - Kawād (488–496, 498–531)
        - Jāmāsp (496–498)
      - Balāsh (484–488)

The Lakhmids

- Nuʿmān (ca. 400–418)
  - Munḏir I (ca. 418–462)
    - Aswad
      - Nuʿmān (499–503)
    - Munḏir II

The Kindites

- Ḥujr
  - ʿAmr
    - Ḥārith (ca. 498–528)
      - Ḥujr
      - Maʿdī-Karib

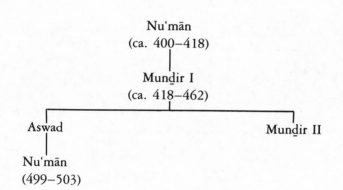

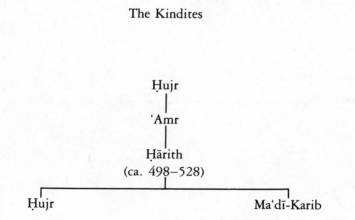

The Salīḥids

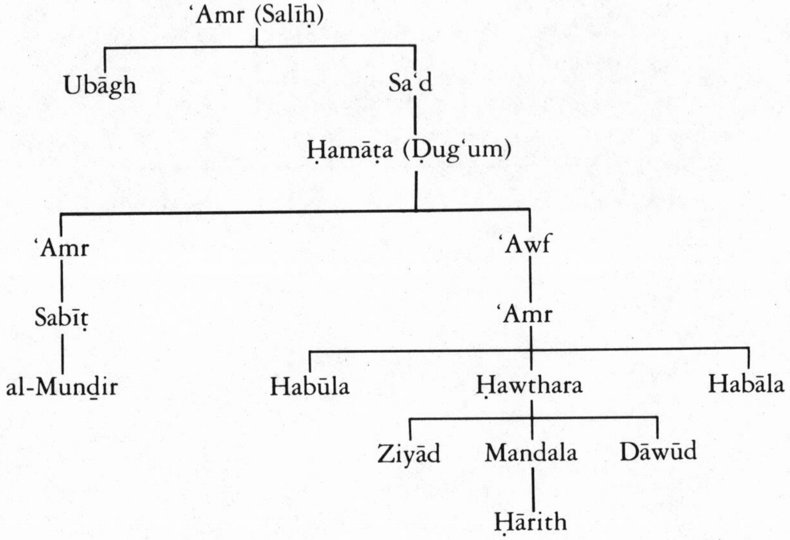

The Phylarchs of Oriens

I
The Phylarchs of the Parembole

1. Petrus (Aspebetos I), d. before 449
2. Terebon I, d. 485
3. Petrus II, possibly succeeded Terebon I
4. Terebon II, ca. 550

II
Other Phylarchs

1. Zokomos, ca. 400, the Salīḥid phylarch, possibly of the Provincia Arabia
2. Amorkesos, ca. 473, phylarch of Palaestina Tertia

Lists of Ecclesiastics in the Patriarchate of Antioch in the Fifth Century

The lists of the patriarchs of Antioch and those of Jerusalem, including its bishops before Juvenal, are those of J. B. Bury in *LRE*, but, as Bury observes, the dates are uncertain. For modifications of these lists, the reader may consult R. Devreesse, *Le patriarcat d'Antioche*, 117–18 and A.-J. Festugière, *Les moines d'Orient*, III.i.142.

The lists of Arab ecclesiastics represent the Arab component in the Patriarchate of Antioch, a fragment of what the Arab church must have been, but even this fragment conveys something of the Arab hierarchical presence in the fifth century. The episcopal presence is divisible into federate and Rhomaic: the list that attests the former derives principally from Cyril of Scythopolis, while that which attests the latter derives from the *Acta* of the Councils. The Parembole in Palaestina Prima and Elusa in Palaestina Tertia are two Arab bishoprics for which the lists are not so incomplete. For the bishops of the Parembole, see the chapter on Cyril of Scythopolis in *BAFIC*; for those of Elusa, see R. Devreesse, "Le christianisme dans le Sud palestinien," *Revue des sciences religieuses* 20 (1940), 247–48.

PATRIARCHS OF ANTIOCH

Flavian I (381–404)
Porphyry (404–413)
Alexander (413–421)
Theodotus (421–429)
John I (429–442)
Domnus II (442–449)
Maximus II (449–455)
Basil (456–458)
Acacius (458–459)
Martyrius (460–470)
Julian (471–475)
Peter the Fuller (476–477)
John II (478)
Stephen II (478–481)
Calandio (481–485)
Peter the Fuller (485–489)
Palladius (490–498)
Flavian II (498–512)

BISHOPS AND PATRIARCHS OF JERUSALEM

Johannes (388–415/6)
Praylius (415/6–421 [?425])
Juvenal (421–458)
Anastasius (458–478)
Martyrius (478–486)
Sallustius (486–494)
Elias (494–516)

The Arab Church within the Patriarchate of Antioch

Hēgoumenoi

1. Maris, the *hēgoumenos* of the monastery of St. Euthymius
2. Abbas, the *hēgoumenos* of the monastery of Teleda

Federate Bishops

A. Bishops of the Parembole
   1. Petrus I (Council of Ephesus, 431)
   2. Auxolaus (Second Council of Ephesus, 449)
   3. John (Council of Chalcedon, 451)
   4. Valens (Council of Jerusalem, 518)
   5. Petrus II (Council of Jerusalem, 536)

B. Others
   1. Eustathius, bishop of the Saracens in Phoenicia Libanensis (Chalcedon, 451) and 458
   2. Petrus, bishop of the phylarch Amorkesos in Palaestina Tertia, ca. 473

Rhomaic Bishops

A. Council of Ephesus, 431
   1. Abdelas, bishop of Elusa
   2. Saidas, bishop of Phaeno
   3. Natīras, bishop of Gaza

B. Second Council of Ephesus, 449
   Caioumas of Phaeno

C. Council of Chalcedon, 451
   1. Aretas, bishop of Elusa
   2. Natīras, bishop of Gaza
   3. Caioumas, bishop of Marciopolis in Osroene
   4. Gautus, bishop of Neila in the Provincia Arabia

D. The Bishops of Elusa
   1. Abdullah (Apellas) (Council of Ephesus)
   2. Aretas (Council of Chalcedon)
   3. Peter (Council of Jerusalem, 518)
   4. Zenobius (Council of Jerusalem, 536)

Patriarchs

Elias, patriarch of Jerusalem, 494–516

Bibliography

Only what is directly relevant to the Arab-Byzantine relationship in the fifth century is included here. Comprehensive bibliographies of the sources and the literature on this century may be found in J. B. Bury, *A History of the Later Roman Empire*, I, which deals exclusively with this period, and in E. Stein, *Histoire du bas-empire*.

I. Sources

The two principal sets of sources are the Byzantine and the Oriental. Under the former are classed the Greek and the Latin sources, and under the latter the Arabic, the Syriac, the Ethiopic, and the Sabaic. Inscriptions in five of these languages are classed together and placed at the end.

The Greek Sources

Secular

Agathias. "Agathias on the Sassanids." Ed. Averil Cameron. *DOP* 23–24 (1969–70).

Cedrenus. *Historiarum Compendium*. Ed. I. Bekker, 2 vols. Bonn: 1838–39.

Constantine Porphyrogenitus. *De Ceremoniis*. Ed. A. Vogt, 2 vols. Paris: 1935–39.

Cosmas Indicopleustes. *Topographie chrétienne*. Text, translation, and commentary by W. Wolska-Conus. SC. Paris: 1968–73.

Historici Graeci Minores. Ed. L. Dindorf. Leipzig: 1870–71.

Josephus. *Jewish Antiquities*. Loeb Classical Library. Vols. IV–IX. London: 1930–65.

Lydus. *De Magistratibus Populi Romani Libri Tres*. Ed. R. Wünsch. Bibliotheca Teubneriana. Leipzig: 1898. It appeared with the title *Ioannes Lydus: On Powers*, with introduction, translation, and commentary by A. C. Bandy. Philadelphia: 1983.

Malalas. *Chronographia*. Ed. L. Dindorf. Bonn: 1831.

Malchus. *Malco di Filadelfia: Frammenti*. Ed. L. R. Cresci. Naples: 1982.

Malchus and Priscus. *The Fragmentary Classicising Historians of the Later Roman Empire*. Ed. and trans. R. Blockley, 2 vols. Liverpool: 1981–83.

Maurice. *Stratēgikon*. Trans. G. T. Dennis. Philadelphia: 1984.

Menander Protector. *The History of Menander the Guardian*. Ed. and trans. R. Blockley. Liverpool: 1985.

Procopius Caesariensis. *De Bellis Libri I–IV*. Ed. J. Haury and G. Wirth. Bibliotheca Teubneriana. Leipzig: 1962.

Procopius of Gaza. *Panegyricus*. Bonn: 1829.

Stephanus of Byzantium. *Ethnica*. London: 1688.

Strabo. *Géographie*. Ed. and trans. G. Aujac, R. Baladie, F. Lassere. Collection des universités de France. Paris: 1966–81.

Synesius. Περὶ Βασιλείας. In A. Fitzgerald, *The Essays and Hymns of Synesius of Cyrene*. Oxford: 1930.
———. *Synesii Cyrenensis Epistolae*. Ed. A. Garzya. Scriptores Graeci et Latini Consilio Academiae Lynceorum Editi. Rome: 1979.
———. *Synesii Cyrenensis Hymni et Opuscula*. Ed. N. Terzaghi. Scriptores Graeci et Latini Consilio Academiae Lynceorum Editi. Rome: 1944.
Theophanes Confessor. *Chronographia*. Ed. C. de Boor, 2 vols. Bibliotheca Teubneriana. Leipzig: 1883–85.

Ecclesiastical

Antonius. Greek *Vita* of Simeon Stylites (see below, *Syriac Sources*).
Cyril of Scythopolis. *Kyrillos von Skythopolis*. Ed. E. Schwartz. TU 49 (1939).
Evagrius. *Historia Ecclesiastica*. Ed. J. Bidez and L. Parmentier. London: 1898.
John of Damascus. *De Haeresibus Compendium*. PG 94, cols. 764–73.
Nicephorus Callistus Xanthopulos. *Historia Ecclesiastica*. PG 146.
Philostorgius. *Historia Ecclesiastica*. Ed. J. Bidez. GCS 21. Berlin: 1913; revised by F. Winkelmann, 1972.
Socrates. *Historia Ecclesiastica*. Ed. R. Hussey. Oxford: 1853.
Sozomen. *Historia Ecclesiastica*. Ed. J. Bidez. GCS 50. Berlin: 1960.
Theodoret. *Historia Ecclesiastica*. Ed. L. Parmentier. GCS 19. Leipzig: 1911.
———. *Historia Religiosa*. Ed. P. Canivet and A. Leroy-Mollinghen. *Histoire des moines de Syrie*, 2 vols. SC. Paris: 1977–79.
———. *Graecorum Affectionum Curatio*. Ed. P. Canivet, *Théodoret de Cyr: Thérapeutique des maladies helléniques*, 2 vols. SC. Paris: 1957.
Theodorus Anagnostes. *Historia Ecclesiastica*. Ed. G. C. Hansen. *Theodoros Anagnostes: Kirchengeschichte*. GCS 54. Berlin: 1971.

Nili Narrationes. PG 79: cols. 589–694.
Martyrium Arethae. Ed. E. Carpentier. *ActaSS*, Octobris, 10 (1861), 721–59.
Leges Homeritarum. Attributed to St. Gregentius. PG 86: cols. 568–620.
Acta Conciliorum Oecumenicorum. Ed. E. Schwartz. Berlin-Leipzig: 1922–40.

The Latin Sources

Secular

Ammianus Marcellinus. *Res Gestae*. Ed. W. Seyfarth, 4 vols. Bibliotheca Teubneriana. Berlin: 1968–71.
Marcellinus Comes. MGH, *Chronica Minora*, II.
Priscian. *Panegyricus*. Bonn: 1829.

Ecclesiastical

Cassian. *Collationes*. PL 44.
———. *Iohannis Cassiani Conlationes XXIIII*. Ed. M. Petschenig. Vienna: 1886.
Jerome. *Select Letters of St. Jerome*. Ed. and trans. F. A. Wright. Loeb Classical Library. London: 1933.
———. *Sancti Eusebii Hieronymi Epistulae*. Ed. I. Hilberg. CSEL 56. Leipzig-Vienna: 1918.

Pélagie la Pénitente. Métamorphoses d'une légende. Tome I: *Les textes et leur histoire.* Ed. P. Petitmengin et al. Études augustiniennes. Paris: 1981.

Rufinus. *Historia Ecclesiastica.* Ed. Th. Mommsen. GCS 9. Leipzig: 1908.

Documents

Codex Theodosianus. Ed. Th. Mommsen and P. M. Meyer. *Theodosiani Libri XVI cum Constitutionibus Sirmondianis.* Berlin: 1905.

Notitia Dignitatum Omnium tam Civilium quam Militarium in Partibus Orientis et Occidentis. Ed. E. Böcking, 3 vols. Bonn: 1839–53; ed. O. Seeck. Berlin: 1876.

The Arabic Sources

Literary

ʿAbbāsī, A. *Maʿāhid al-Tansīs ʿala Shawāhid al-Talkhīs.* Ed. M. Abdul-Hamid, 4 vols. Beirut: 1947.

Ibn ʿAbd Rabbihi. *Al-ʿIqd al-Farīd.* Ed. A. Amin et al. Cairo: 1982.

Iṣbahānī. *Kitāb al-Aghānī,* 25 vols. Beirut: 1962.

Jāḥiẓ. *Kitāb al-Ḥayawān.* Ed. A. ʿHārūn. Cairo: 1943.

———. *Al-Bayān wa al-Tabyīn.* Ed. ʿA. Hārūn. Cairo: 1961.

al-Maʿarrī, Abū al-ʿAlā'. *Risālat al-Ghufrān.* Ed. ʿA. Abd al-Raḥmān. Cairo: 1963.

Marsafī, H. *Al-Wasīla al-Adabiyya.* Cairo: 1872–73.

Marzubānī. *Al-Muwashshaḥ.* Ed. A. M. al-Bajāwi. Cairo: 1965.

Nashwān ibn Saʿīd al-Ḥimyari. *Shams al-ʿUlūm.* Ed. ʿA. Ahmad. Gibb Memorial Series 24. Leiden: 1916.

Qāli, A. *Ḏayl al-Amālī wa al-Nawādir.* Beirut: 1926.

Yāqūt. *Irshād al-Arīb ilā Maʿrifat al-Adīb.* Ed. D. S. Margoliouth. Gibb Memorial Series 1–7. London: 1923–31.

Historical

Azraqī, M. *Akhbār Makka.* Ed. R. Malḥas. Mecca: 1965.

Balāḏurī. *Futūḥ al-Buldān.* Ed. S. Munajjid, 2 vols. Cairo: 1956.

———. *Ansāb al-Ashrāf.* I. Ed. M. Ḥamīdullah. Cairo: 1959.

Dīnawarī. *Al-Akhbār al-Ṭiwāl.* Ed. A. ʿĀmir and J. Shayyāl. Cairo: 1960.

Fāsī, M. *Shifā' al-Gharām bi Akhbār al-Balad al-Ḥarām.* Mecca: 1956.

Ḥamza al-Iṣfahānī. *Tārīkh.* Beirut: 1961.

Ḥillī, A. *Al-Manāqib al-Mazyadiyya fī Akhbār al-Mulūk al-Asadiyya.* Ed. S. Daradika and M. Khuraysāt, 2 vols. Amman, Jordan: 1984.

Ibn al-Athīr. *Al-Kāmil,* 13 vols. Beirut: 1965–67.

Ibn Ḥabīb. *Al-Muḥabbar.* Ed. I. Lichtenstädter. Heyderabad: 1942; rpr. Beirut: n.d.

———. *Al-Munammaq.* Heyderabad: 1964.

Ibn Hishām. *Sīrat al-Nabī.* Ed. M. ʿAbdulhamīd, 4 vols. Cairo: 1937.

Ibn al-ʿIbrī. *The Chronography of Abu Faraj,* I. Trans. E. A. W. Budge. London: 1932.

Ibn Khaldūn. *ʿIbar,* II. Beirut: 1956.

Ibn Khallikān. *Wafayāt al Aʿyān.* Ed. I. ʿAbbās. Beirut: 1977.

Ibn al-Nadīm. *Al-Fihrist.* Ed. G. Flügel. Rpr. Beirut: 1964.

Ibn Qutayba. *Kitāb al-Maʿārif.* Ed. Th. ʿUkāsha. Cairo: 1960.

Ibn Saʿīd al-Maghribi. *Die Geschichte der "reinen Araber" vom Stamme Qaḥṭan aus dem*

Kitāb Naśwat aṭ-Ṭarab fī Tarīḫ Ǧāhilyyat al-ʿArab des Ibn-Saʿīd al-Magribi. Ed. and trans. M. Kropp. Inaugural-Dissertation. Heidelberg: 1975.
Jahshiyārī, M. *Al-Wuzarāʾ wa al-Kuttāb*. Ed. M. Saqqā, I. Abyārī, and A. Shalabī. Cairo: 1938.
Khalīfa ibn Khayyāṭ. *Tārīkh*. Ed. A. al-ʿUmarī. Beirut: 1977.
Khazraji, A. *Kitāb al-ʿUqūd al-Luʾluʾiyya (The Pearl Strings)*. Ed. M. ʿAsal. Gibb Memorial Series III.4. Leiden: 1913.
Masʿūdī. *Al-Tanbīh wa al-Ishrāf*. Ed. M. J. de Goeje. BGA 8; and ed. ʿA. al-Ṣāwī. Cairo: 1938.
———. *Murūj al-Ḏahab wa Maʿādin al-Jawhar*. Ed. Ch. Pellat, 5 vols. Beirut: 1965–74.
Saʿīd b. al-Baṭrīq (Eutychius). "Annales." CSCO, Scriptores Arabici 50.
Shahrastāni. *Al-Milal wa al-Niḥal*. Ed. A.ʿal-ʿAbd. Cairo: 1977.
Subkī. *Ṭabaqāt al-Shāfiʿiyya al-Kubrā*. Ed. M. al-Ṭanāḥī and H. al-Ḥulw. Cairo: 1964.
Ṭabarī. *Tārīkh*. Ed. A. Ibrāhīm, 9 vols. Cairo: 1960–68.
Wahb ibn Munabbih. *Kitāb al-Tijān*. Center for Yamani Studies. N.p.: n.d.
Yaʿqūbī. *Historiae*, 2 vols. Leiden: 1883.
———. *Tārīkh*, 2 vols. Beirut: 1960.

Histoire nestorienne. Ed. A. Scher, PO 4, 5, 7.
Maris Amri et Slibae de Patriarchis Nestorianorum Commentaria. Ed. H. Gismondi. Rome: 1899.

Geographical

Abū Ḥāmid al-Andalusī. *Tuḥfat al-Albāb*. Ed. G. Ferrand. In *Journal asiatique* 207 (1925), 1–148, 193–304.
Bakrī. *Muʿjam ma Istaʿjam*. Ed. M. Saqqā, 4 vols. Cairo: 1945–51.
Hamdānī. *Ṣifat Jazīrat al-ʿArab*. Ed. M. al-Akwaʿ. Riyad: 1974.
Istakhrī. *Masālik al-Mamālik*. Ed. M. J. de Goeje. BGA 1. Leiden: 1870.
Muqaddasī. *Aḥsan al-Taqāsim fi Maʿrifat al-Aqālīm*. Leiden: 1877.
Yaʿqūbī. *Kitāb al-Buldān*. Ed. A. W. T. Juynboll. BGA 7. Rpr. Leiden: 1967.
Yāqūt. *Muʿjam al-Buldān*, 5 vols. Beirut: 1955–57.

Genealogical

Hishām al-Kalbī. *Ǧamharat an-Nasab: Das genealogische Werk des Hišām ibn Muḥammad al-Kalbī*. Ed. W. Caskel, 2 vols. Leiden: 1966.
———. *Jamharat al-Nasab*. Ed. ʿA. Farrāj. Kuwait: 1983.
———. *Jamharat al-Nasab*. Ed. M. F. al-ʿAẓm. Damascus: 1983.
———. *Al-Muqtaḍab*. A résumé of Hishām's genealogical work made by Yāqut; ibid., I, 106.
Ibn Durayd. *Al-Ishtiqāq*. Ed. ʿA. Hārūn. Cairo: 1958.
Ibn Ḥazm. *Jamharat Ansāb al-ʿArab*. Ed. ʿA. Hārūn. Cairo: 1962.
Zubayr ibn Bakkār. *Jamharat Nasab Quraysh*. Ed. M. Shākir. Cairo: 1961–62.
al-Nuwayrī. *Nihāyat al-Arab*. Cairo: 1924.

Dīwāns

ʿAdi ibn Zayd. *Dīwān*. Ed. M. Muʿaybid. Baghdad: 1965.
Afwah al-Awdi. *Dīwān*. Ed. A. Maymanī. In *Al-Tarāʾif al-Adabiyya*. Beirut: 1937.
al-Aʿshā. *Dīwān al-ʿAshā al-Kabīr*. Ed. M. Ḥusayn. Cairo: 1950.
———. *Gedichte von al-Aʿsha*. Ed. R. Geyer. Gibb Memorial Series, n.s. 4. London: 1928.
Hatim al-Ṭāʾī. *Dīwān Shiʿr Ḥātim al-Ṭāʾī*. Ed. ʿĀ. S. Jamāl. Cairo: 1975.
Imruʾ al-Qays. *Dīwān*. Ed. M. Ibrāhīm. Cairo: 1964.
Jamīl. *Dīwān Jamīl*. Ed. Ḥ. Naṣṣār. Cairo: 1967.
al-Nābigha al-Dubyāni. *Dīwān*. Ed. Sh. Fayṣal. Beirut: 1968.
———. *Dīwān*. Ed. M. Ibrāhīm. Cairo: 1977.
Nābigha al-Jaʿdi. *Dīwān*. In *Al-Maktab al-Islāmi*. Damascus: 1964.

Shantamarī. *The Divans of the Six Ancient Arabic Poets*. Ed. W. Ahlwardt. London: 1870.
Al-Mufaddaliyyāt. Ed. A. Shākir and ʿA. Hārūn. Cairo: 1941.
Al-Hamāsa al-Baṣriyya. Ed. A. J. Sulaymān. Cairo: 1978.

Manuscripts

Hishām al-Kalbī. *Kitāb Nasab Maʿadd wa al-Yaman al-Kabīr*. British Museum Add. 22376.
———. *Mukhtasar Jamharat al-Nasab*. See R. Mach, *Catalogue of Arabic Manuscripts (Yahuda Section) in the Garrett Collection, Princeton University Library* (Princeton, 1977), p. 385, no. 4487.

The Syriac Sources

Historical

Bar-Hebraeus. *The Chronography of Gregory Abūʾl Faraj*. Trans. E. A. W. Budge, 2 vols. London: 1932.
John of Ephesus. *Historia Ecclesiastica*. Ed. E. W. Brooks, CSCO, Scriptores Syri ser. 3 tom. 3.
Joshua the Stylite. *The Chronicle of Joshua the Stylite*. Ed. and trans. W. Wright. Cambridge: 1882.
Michael Syrus. *Chronique de Michel le Syrien*. Ed. and trans. J. B. Chabot, 4 vols. Paris: 1899–1924.
Simeon of Bēth-Arshām. "La lettera di Simeone vescovo di Bêth-Arśâm sopra i martiri omeriti." Ed. I. Guidi in *Atti della R. Accademia dei Lincei*, ser. 3, *Memorie della Classe di Scienze morali, storiche e filologiche* 7 (Rome, 1881), 471–515.
———. A second letter of Simeon has been discovered, edited, translated, and commented upon by I. Shahîd in *Martyrs of Najrân*, Subsidia Hagiographica 49. Brussels: 1971.
———. *The Book of the Ḥimyarites*. Ed. and trans. A. Moberg. Lund: 1924.
Vita of Simeon Stylites. Ed. H. Lietzmann, *Das Leben des heiligen Symeon Stylites*. TU 32.4. Leipzig: 1908; German translation by H. Hilgenfeld, ibid., 80–180.

Documents

Synodicon Orientale. Ed. J. B. Chabot. Paris: 1902.

Honigmann, E. "Nordsyrische Klöster in vorarabischer Zeit." *Zeitschrift für Semitistik und verwandte Gebiete* 1 (1922), 15–33.

Nöldeke, Th. "Zur Topographie und Geschichte des damascênischen Gebietes und der Haurângegend." *ZDMG* 29 (1875), 419–44.

Wright, W. *Catalogue of Syriac Manuscripts in the British Museum*, 3 vols. London: 1870–72.

The Ethiopic Sources

Acts of ʿAzqīr. In "Un documento sul cristianismo nello Iemen ai tempi del Re Šarāḥbīl Yakkuf." Ed. and trans. C. Conti Rossini. *Rendiconti della R. Accademia dei Lincei, Classe di scienze morali, storiche e filologiche* 19, ser. 5a (Rome, 1910), 705–50.

Kebra Nagast. English version by E. A. Wallis Budge, *The Queen of Sheba and Her Only Son Menyelek*. London: 1922.

Inscriptions

Greek

The Edict of Beersheba. A. Alt, *Die griechischen Inschriften der Palaestina Tertia westlich der ʿAraba* (Berlin-Leipzig, 1921), 4–13.

Tsaferis, V. "Mosaics and Inscriptions from Magen." *BASOR* 258 (1985), inscription 4, p. 28.

Al-Ḥijr inscription in Ḥijāz. G. W. Bowersock, "A Report on Arabia Provincia," *JRS* 61 (1971), 230.

The Ḍumayr inscription. W. H. Waddington, *Inscriptions grecques et latines de la Syrie* (rpr. Rome, 1968), 585, no. 2562c.

Latin

Unpublished inscription found at Dūmat al-Jandal in northern Arabia. G. W. Bowersock, "Syria under Vespasian," *JRS* 63 (1973), 139.

Dessau, H. *Inscriptiones Latinae Selectae*, 3 vols. Berlin: 1892–1916.

Arabic

The Namāra inscription. *Revue archéologique* 2 (1902), 409–21; *Répertoire chronologique d'épigraphie arabe* (Cairo, 1931), I, 1–2.

The Christian Arabic inscription of Dayr Hind in Ḥīra. Yāqūt, *Muʿjam al-Buldān*, II, 542.

The Umm al-Jimāl inscription II. E. Littmann, *PPUAES*, Division IV, Semitic Inscriptions; Arabic Inscriptions (Leiden, 1949), 1–3.

Sabaic

D. B. Doe and A. Jamme, "New Sabaean Inscriptions from South Arabia," *Journal of the Royal Asiatic Society* (1968), 2–28.

Ethiopic

Kaleb's Ethiopic inscription found at Axum. A. J. Drewes, "Kaleb and Himyar: Another Reference to HYWN'," *Raydan: Journal of Ancient Yemeni Antiquities and Epigraphy* 1 (1978), 27–32.

Multilingual Inscriptions

The Greek-Aramaic bilingual inscription of Ruwwāfa in Ḥijāz. G. W. Bowersock, in *Le monde grec (Hommages à Claire Préaux)* (Brussels, 1975), 513–16.

The Greek-Arabic-Syriac trilingual inscription of Zabad in northern Syria. *IGLSYR*, II, p. 178.

Papyri

The three Greek papyri from Nessana (21, 51, 80) and fragment (160). *Excavations at Nessana*, III, ed. C. J. Kraemer (Princeton, 1958).

II. Literature

Abbott, N. *The Rise of the North Arabic Script*. Oriental Institute Publications. Chicago: 1939.

Abel, F. M. *Géographie de la Palestine*, II. Paris: 1938.

______. "L'île de Jotabè." *RB* 47 (1938), 510–38.

______. "Jérusalem." *DACL* 7, cols. 2344–53.

______. "Mélanges." *RB* 36 (1927), 567–70.

Adontz, N. *Armenia in the Period of Justinian*. Lisbon: 1970.

Ahlwardt, W. *The Divans of the Six Ancient Arabic Poets*. London: 1870; rpr. Osnabrück: 1972.

Aigrain, R. "Arabie." *DHGE* 3, cols. 1158–1339. Paris: 1924.

ʿAlī, J. "*Jamharat al-Nasab li Ibn al-Kalbī.*" *Majallat at-Majmaʿ al-ʿIlmi al-ʿIrāqī*. Baghdad: 1950.

al-ʿAlī, S. "Muwaẓẓafū Bilad al-Shām fī al-ʿAṣr al-ʿUmawī." *Al-Abḥath* (Beirut, 1966), 44–79.

Alt, A. *Die griechischen Inschriften der Palästina Tertia westlich der ʿAraba*. Berlin-Leipzig: 1921.

______. "Limes Palaestinae." *Palästina Jahrbuch* 26 (1930), 43–82.

______. "Zwölf christliche Grabsteine aus Moab." *ZDPV* 51 (1928), 18–33.

Altaner, B. *Patrology*, trans. H. C. Graef. New York: 1960.

Altheim, F., and R. Stiehl. "Araber in Ägypten." *Lexicon der Ägyptologie* 1, 3, cols. 360–61.

______. *Die Araber in der alten Welt*, 5 vols. Berlin: 1964–68.

______. *Christentum am Roten Meer*. Berlin: 1971.

al-Alūsī, M. *Bulūgh al-ʿArab fī Maʿrifat Aḥwāl al-ʿArab*. Cairo: 1964.

al-Ansary, A. R. *Qaryat al-Fau: A Portrait of a Pre-Islamic Civilization in Saudi Arabia*. Riyad: 1982.

Arberry, A. J. *The Seven Odes*. London: 1957.

Arnaldez, R. "Ibn Zuhr." *EI²*.

al-Asad, N. *Maṣādir al-Shiʿr al-Jāhilī*. Cairo: 1982.

Avigad, N. *Discovering Jerusalem*. Nashville: 1983.

Avi-Yonah, M. "Elath." *Encyclopedia Judaica*.

———. *The Holy Land: A Historical Geography*. Grand Rapids, Mich.: 1966.

———. *The Jews of Palestine*. New York: 1976.

Baldwin, B. "Malchus of Philadelphia." *DOP* 31 (1977), 91–107.

Barnes, T. D. *Constantine and Eusebius*. Cambridge, Mass.: 1981.

———. *The New Empire of Diocletian and Constantine*. Cambridge, Mass.: 1982.

Baron, S. W. *A Social and Religious History of the Jews*, 11 vols. New York: 1952–67.

Baumstark, A. "Der älteste erhaltene griechisch-arabische Text von Psalm 110 (109)." *OC*, 3rd. ser., 9 (1934), 55–66.

———. *Geschichte der syrischen Literatur*. Bonn: 1922.

———. "Das Problem eines vorislamischen christlich-kirchlichen Schrifttums in arabischer Sprache." *Islamica* 4 (1931), 562–75.

Baynes, N. H. *Byzantine Studies and Other Essays*. London: 1960.

Beck, H. G. *Kirche und theologische Literatur im byzantinischen Reich*. Munich: 1959.

Beeston, A. F. L. *L'Arabie du Sud.*, I. Ed. J. Chelhod. Paris: 1984.

———. "The Martyrdom of Azqir." *Proceedings of the Seminar for Arabian Studies* 18 (London, 1985), 5–10.

———. "Namara and Faw." *BSOAS* 42 (1979), 1–6

———. *Sabaic Grammar*. Manchester: 1984.

Bellamy, J. "A New Reading of the Namārah Inscription." *JAOS* 105 (1985), 46–47.

Bellinger, A. "The Coins and Byzantine Imperial Policy." *Speculum* 31 (1956), 70–81.

Berchem, D. van. *L'armée de Dioclétien et la réforme constantinienne*. Paris: 1952.

Bernays, J. "Ein nabatäischer Schriftsteller." *Gesammelte Abhandlungen*, II. Berlin: 1885.

Bivar, A. D. H. "Cavalry Equipment and Tactics on the Euphrates Frontier." *DOP* 26 (1972), 273–91.

Blachère, R. *Histoire de la littérature arabe*. Paris: 1952.

Blau, O. "Arabien im sechsten Jahrhundert." *ZDMG* 23 (1869), 559–92.

———. "Die Wanderung der sabäischen Völkerstämme im 2. Jahrhundert." *ZDMG* 22 (1868), 654–73.

Böcking, E. *Notitia Dignitatum*, 3 vols. Bonn: 1839–53.

Bowersock, G. W. "A New Antonine Inscription from the Syrian Desert," *Chiron* 6 (1976), 349–55.

———. "A Report on Arabia Provincia." *JRS* 61 (1971), 219–42.

———. *Roman Arabia*. Cambridge, Mass: 1983.

Branden, A. van den. *Histoire de Thamoud*. Beirut: 1966.

Bregman, J. *Synesius of Cyrene*. Berkeley: 1982.

Bréhier, L. *Le monde byzantin*, II. Paris: 1948.

Brock, S. "Bibelübersetzungen." *Theologische Realenzyklopädie* 6, 1/2, 209–11.

Brockelmann, C. *Geschichte der arabischen Literatur*, 2 vols. and 3 suppls. Leiden: 1943–49.

Broome, E. C. "Nabaiati, Nebaioth, and Nabataeans: The 'Linguistic Problem.'" *JSS* 18 (1973), 1–16.

Brown, P. "The Rise and Function of the Holy Man in Late Antiquity." In *Society and the Holy in Late Antiquity* (London, 1982), 103–52.

Brünnow, R. E. "Die Kastelle des arabischen Limes." In *Florilegium Melchior de Vogüé* (Paris, 1909), 65–77.

Brünnow, R. E., and A. Domaszewski. *Die Provincia Arabia*, 3 vols. Strasbourg: 1904–9.
Bulayhid, M. *Ṣaḥīḥ al-Akhbār*. Riyad: 1972.
Bury, J. B. *History of the Later Roman Empire*, 2 vols. London: 1923.
______. *The Imperial Administrative System*. London: 1911.
______. "The Treatise *De Administrando Imperio*." *BZ* 15 (1906), 517–77.
Butler, A. J. *The Arab Conquest of Egypt*. Oxford: 1920.
Butler, H. C. *Early Churches in Syria: Fourth to Seventh Centuries*. Princeton: 1929.
Caetani, L. *Annali del Islam*. Rome: 1904.
Cambridge History of Arabic Literature. Cambridge: 1983.
Cambridge History of Iran. Cambridge: 1983.
Cambridge Medieval History, The Byzantine Empire, II. Cambridge: 1967.
Cameron, Alan. "Agathias on the Sassanians." *DOP* 23–24 (1969–70), 67–183.
______. "The Date of Priscian's *De laude Anastasii*." *GRBS* 15 (1974), 313–16.
Canard, M. "Sayf al Daula." *Bibliotheca Arabica* (Algiers, 1934).
Canivet, P. *Le monachisme syrien selon Théodoret de Cyr*. Théologie historique 42. Paris: 1977.
Caskel, W. *Ǧamharat an-Nasab: Das genealogische Werk des Hišām ibn Muḥammad al Kalbī*, 2 vols. Leiden: 1966.
Chapot, V. *La frontière de l'Euphrate*. Paris: 1907.
Chadwick, O. *John Cassian*. Cambridge: 1968.
Charles, H. *Le christianisme des arabes nomades sur le limes*. Paris: 1936.
Cheikho, L. *Al-Naṣrāniyya wa Ādābuhā bayn ʿArab al-Jāhiliyya*, 3 vols. Beirut: 1912–23.
______. *Shuʿaraʾ al-Naṣrāniyya baʿd al-Islam*. Beirut: 1967.
Chitty, D. *The Desert a City*. Oxford: 1966.
Christensen, A. *L'Iran sous les Sassanides*. Copenhagen: 1944.
Christides, V. "Arabs as *barbaroi* before the Rise of Islam." *Balkan Studies* 10 (1969), 315–24.
______. "Once again the 'Narrations' of Nilus Sinaiticus." *Byzantion* 43 (1973), 38–50.
______. "Pre-Islamic Arabs in Byzantine Illuminations." *Le Muséon* 83 (1970), 167–81.
Chrysos, E. "Some Aspects of Roman-Persian Legal Relations." *Kleronomia* 8 (1976), 1–60.
Clemente, G. *La "Notitia Dignitatum."* Saggi di storia e letteratura 4. Cagliari: 1968.
Corpus Inscriptionum Semiticarum. Pars quinta inscriptiones Saracenicas continens. Paris: 1950.
Costa, P. M. "Further Comments on the Bilingual Inscription from Barāqish." *Proceedings of the Seminar for Arabian Studies* 19 (London, 1986), 33–36.
Courtois, Ch. *Les Vandales et l'Afrique*. Paris: 1955.
Cragg, K. "The Art of Theology: Islamic and Christian Reflections." In *Islam, Past Influence and Present Challenge*, ed. A. Welch and P. Cachia (Edinburgh, 1979), 276–95.
Croke, B. "Dating Theodoret's Church History and Commentary on the Psalms." *Byzantion* 54 (1984), 59–74.
Crone, P. *Meccan Trade and the Rise of Islam* (forthcoming).
Dagorn, R. *La geste d'Ismaël d'après l'onomastique et la tradition arabe*. Paris: 1981.

Delehaye, H. *Les saints stylites*. Subsidia Hagiographica 14. Brussels: 1923.
Devreesse, R. "Le christianisme dans la péninsule sinäitique, des origines à l'arrivée des musulmans." *RB* 49 (1940), 205–23.
______. "Le christianisme dans le Sud palestinien." *Revue des sciences religieuses* 20 (1940), 235–51.
______. *Le patriarcat d'Antioche, depuis la paix de l'église jusqu'à la conquête arabe*. Paris: 1945.
De Vries, B. *Umm El-Jimal in the First Three Centuries A.D.* BAR Monograph 8. Oxford: 1986.
Diehl, Ch. *Byzantine Empresses*. London: 1927.
Doe, D. B., and A. Jamme. "New Sabaean Inscriptions from South Arabia." *Journal of the Royal Asiatic Society* (1968), 2–28.
Duri, A. A. *The Rise of Historical Writing among the Arabs*. Princeton: 1983.
Dussaud, R. *Les Arabes en Syrie avant l'Islam*. Paris: 1907.
______. *La pénétration des Arabes en Syrie avant l'Islam*. Paris: 1955.
______. *Topographie historique de la Syrie antique et médiévale*. Paris: 1927.
Dvornik, F. *Origins of Intelligence Services*. New Brunswick, N.J.: 1974.
Eadie, J. W. "The Development of Roman Mailed Cavalry." *JRS* 57 (1967), 161–73.
Ensslin, W. "Aus Theodorichs Kanzlei." *Würzburger Jahrbücher für die Altertumswissenschaft* 2, 1 (1947), 75–82.
Ephʿal, I. *The Ancient Arabs*. Leiden: 1982.
______. "'Ishmael' and 'Arab(s)': A Transformation of Ethnological Terms." *JNES* 35 (1976), 225–35.
Excavations at Nessana, I, ed. H. D. Colt. London: 1962; II, ed. L. Gasson and E. L. Hettich. Princeton: 1950; III, ed. C. J. Kraemer. Princeton: 1958.
Fahd, T. *La divination arabe*. Leiden: 1966.
______. "Gerrhéens et Ǧurhumites." In *Studien zur Geschichte und Kultur des Vorderen Orients: Festschrift für B. Spuler*, ed. H. R. Roemer and A. Noth. Leiden: 1981.
______. *Le panthéon de l'Arabie centrale à la veille de l'Hégire*. Paris: 1968.
Festugière, A. J. *Les moines d'Orient*, 4 vols. Paris: 1961–65.
Fiaccadori, G. "Teofilo Indiano." *Studi classici e orientali* 33 (1983), 295–331.
______. "Yemen Nestoriano." In *Studi in onore di Edda Bresciani* (Pisa, 1985), 192–212.
Fink, R. O. *Roman Military Records on Papyrus*. Philological Monographs of the American Philological Association 26. Cleveland: 1971.
Fischer, A. "Imra'alqais." *Islamica* 1, I (1924),1–9; 1, 2 (1925), 365–89.
Fitz, J. *Les syriens à Intercisa*. Collection Latomus 122. Brussels: 1972.
Fitzgerald, A. *The Letters of Synesius of Cyrene*. London: 1926.
Flusin, B. *Miracle et histoire dans l'oeuvre de Cyrille de Scythopolis*. Études augustiniennes. Paris: 1983.
Frye, R. "Problems in the Study of Iranian Religions." In *Religions in Antiquity* (E. R. Goodenough Festschrift), ed. J. Neusner (Leiden, 1968), 583–89.
Fück, J. "ʿAmr ibn Luḥayy." *EI*².
Gabrieli, F. "Islam in the Mediterranean World." In *The Legacy of Islam*, ed. J. Schact and C. E. Bosworth. 2nd ed. (Oxford, 1974), 63–104.
______. *Storia della letteratura araba*, 3rd ed. Milan: 1962.

Gascou, J. "L'institution des bucellaires." *Bulletin de l'Institut Français d'Archéologie Orientale* 76 (1976), 143–84.

Génier, R. *Vie de Saint Euthyme le Grand.* Paris: 1909.

Geyer, R. *Gedichte von al-Aʿshā.* Gibb Memorial Series, n.s. 6. London: 1928.

Gibb, H. A. R. *Mohammedanism.* New York: 1962.

Gibbon, E. *The Decline and Fall of the Roman Empire,* III. Ed. J. B. Bury. London: 1897.

Glueck, N. "Explorations in Eastern Palestine, III." *The Annual of the American Schools of Oriental Research* 18–19 (1939).

Goffart, W. *Barbarians and Romans, A.D. 418–584.* Princeton: 1980.

Gordon, C. D. *The Age of Attila.* Ann Arbor: 1960.

Goitein, S. *Jews and Arabs.* New York: 1955.

Grabar, O. *The Formation of Islamic Art.* New Haven: 1973.

Graf, G. *Geschichte der christlichen arabischen Literatur.* Studi e testi 118. Vatican City: 1944.

Gregory, T. E. *Vox Populi.* Columbus: 1979.

Griffith, S. "The Gospel in Arabic: An Enquiry into Its Appearance in the First Abbasid Century." *OC* 69 (1985), 126–67.

Grimme, H. "Der südarabische Levitismus und sein Verhältnis zum Levitismus in Israel." *Le Muséon* 37 (1924), 169–99.

Grohmann, A. *Arabische Paläographie,* 2 vols. Vienna: 1971.

Grosse, R. *Römische Militärgeschichte von Gallienus bis zum Beginn der byzantinischen Themenverfassung.* Berlin: 1920.

Gutwein, K. C. *Third Palestine.* Washington, D.C.: 1981.

Halkin, F. "Les moines martyres du Sinaï dans le ménologue impérial." *Mémorial André Jean Festugière.* Cahiers d'orientalisme 10 (Geneva, 1984), 267–73.

Hamīdullāh, M. "Die Neutralität im islamischen Völkerrecht." *ZDMG* 89 (1935), 68–88.

Hanfmann, M. A. "A Painter in the Imperial Arms Factory at Sardis." *American Journal of Archaeology* 85 (1981), 87–88.

Hechaïmé, C. *Louis Cheicko et son livre "Le christianisme et la littérature chrétienne en Arabie avant l'Islam."* Beirut: 1967.

Henninger, J. "Ist der sogenannte Nilusbericht eine brauchbare religionsgeschichtliche Quelle? *Anthropos* 50 (1955), 81–88.

Herzfeld, E. "M<u>sh</u>atta, Ḥīra und Bādiya." *Jahrbuch der Preussischen Kunstsammlungen* 42 (1921), 113–16.

Hilāl, M. G. *Al-Ḥayat al-ʿĀṭifiyya bayn al-ʿU<u>d</u>riyya wa al-Ṣūfiyya.* Cairo: 1976.

Hild, F., and M. Restle. *Kappadokien.* Vienna: 1981.

Hinds, M. "The Banners and Battlecries of the Arabs at Ṣiffīn." *Al-Abḥath* (Beirut, 1971).

Hirschberg, J. W. "Nestorian Sources of North-Arabian Traditions on the Establishment and Persecution of Christianity in Yemen." *Rocznik Orienalistyczny* 15 (1939–49), 321–38.

Hitti, P. K. *A History of Syria.* London: 1951.

———. *History of the Arabs.* London: 1937.

Hodges, R., and D. Whitehouse. *Mohammed, Charlemagne, and the Origins of Europe.* Ithaca: 1983.

Hoffmann, D. *Das spätrömische Bewegungsheer und die* Notitia Dignitatum, 2 vols. Epigraphische Studien 7. Düsseldorf: 1969–70.
Holma, H. "Que signifie, chez Diodore de Sicile, le nom propre arabe Βανιζομεν-(εῖς)?" *Orientalia,* n.s. 13 (1944), 356–61.
Holmes, R. *Acts of War*. New York: 1986.
Holum, K. G. "Caesarea and the Samaritans." *Abstracts of Papers, Byzantine Studies Conference*. Washington, D.C.: 1977.
______. "Pulcheria's Crusade, A.D. 421–22, and the Ideology of Imperial Victory." *GRBS* 18 (1977), 153–72.
______. *Theodosian Empresses*. Berkeley: 1982.
Honigmann, E. "Juvenal of Jerusalem." *DOP* 5 (1950), 209–79.
______. "The Original Lists of the Members of the Councils of Nicaea, the Robber-Synod and the Council of Chalcedon." *Byzantion* 16 (1942–43), 20–80.
______. "The Patriarchate of Antioch." *Traditio* 5 (1947), 135–61.
______. "Studien zur *Notitia Antiochena*." *BZ* 25 (1925), 60–88.
______. *Le Synecdèmos d'Hiéroclès*. Brussels: 1939.
Horsefield, A. "Journey to Kilwa." *The Geographical Journal* 102 (August, 1943), 71–77.
Hunger, H. *Die hochsprachliche profane Literatur der Byzantiner*, I. Munich: 1978.
The Interpreter's Dictionary of the Bible. New York: 1962.
Irvine, A. K. "Kaḥṭān." EI^2.
______. "Habashat." EI^2.
al-Iryānī, M. *Fī Tārīkh al-Yaman*. Cairo: 1974.
Janin, R. "Élie" (no. 22). *DHGE* 15 (1963), cols. 189–90.
al-Jasir, Ḥ. *Shamāl Gharb al-Jazīra*. Riyad: 1981.
Jayyusi, S. K. *Trends and Movements in Modern Arabic Poetry*. Leiden: 1977.
Jeffery, A. *The Foreign Vocabulary of the Qur'an*. Baroda: 1938.
Jones, A. H. M. *Cities of the Eastern Roman Provinces*. Oxford: 1971.
______. *The Later Roman Empire*, 2 vols. Norman, Okla.: 1964.
______. "The Urbanization of the Ituraean Principality." *JRS* 21 (1931), 265–75.
______. "Were the Ancient Heresies National or Social Movements in Disguise?" *Journal of Theological Studies*, n.s. 10 (1959), 280–98.
Jones, A. H. M., J. R. Martindale, and J. Morris. *The Prosopography of the Later Roman Empire*, II. Cambridge: 1980.
Jordan: Official Standard Names. U.S. Army Topographic Command. Washington, D.C.: 1971.
Kaegi, W. *Byzantium and the Decline of Rome*. Princeton: 1968.
______. "Notes on Hagiographic Sources for Some Institutional Changes and Continuities in the Early Seventh Century." *Byzantina* 7 (1975), 61–70.
Kahane, H. and R. "Humanistic Linguistics." *Journal of Aesthetic Education* 17 (1983).
Kennedy, D. L. *Archaeological Explorations on the Roman Frontier in North-Eastern Jordan*. British Archaeological Reports, International Series 134. Oxford: 1982.
Kister, M. J. "Al-Ḥīra: Some Notes on Its Relations with Arabia." *Arabica* 15 (1968).

———. "Kuḍāʿa." *EI*².
———. *Studies in Jāhiliyya and Early Islam*. London: 1980.
Knauf, A. "Bemerkungen zur frühen Geschichte der arabischen Orthographie." *Orientalia* 53 (1984), 456–58.
———. "Supplementa Ismaelitica." *BN* 30 (1985), 19–28.
———. "Umm El-Jimal: An Arab Town in Antiquity." *RB* 91 (1984), 576–86.
Kretschmar, G. "Origenes und die Araber." *Zeitschrift für Theologie und Kirche* 1 (1953), 258–79.
Krumbacher, K. *Geschichte der byzantinischen Literatur*. 2nd ed. Munich: 1897.
Labourt, J. *Le christianisme dans l'empire perse sous la dynastie sassanide*. Paris: 1904.
Lammens, H. "La Meccque à la veille de l'hégira." *Mélanges de l'Université Saint Joseph, Beyrouth* 60 (1924), fasc. 3.
Lane, E. W. *Arabic-English Lexicon*. New York: 1956.
Lassus, J. *Sanctuaires chrétiens de Syrie*. Paris: 1947.
Levi della Vida, G. "Ḳuṣayy." *EI*.
Liebeschütz, J. H. W. G. *Antioch: City and Imperial Administration in the Later Roman Empire*. Oxford: 1972.
Littmann, E. "Zur Topographie der Antiochene und Apamene." *Zeitschrift für Semitistik und verwandte Gebiete* (1922), 163–95.
MacAdam, H. I. *Studies in the History of the Roman Province of Arabia*. Ph.D. dissertation, University of Manchester: 1979.
Mackensen, M. *Resafa I. Eine befestigte Anlage vor den Stadtmauern von Resafa*. Mainz: 1984.
Magdalino, P. "Byzantine Kaiserkritik." *Speculum* 58 (1983), 326–46.
Majallat al-ʿArab. Riyad: 1975.
Mango, C. *Byzantine Architecture*. New York: 1976.
Margoliouth, D. S. *Lectures on the Arabic Historians*. New York: 1930; rpr. 1962.
Mayerson, P. "The Desert of Southern Palestine according to Byzantine Sources." *Proceedings of the American Philosophical Society* 107.2 (1963), 160–72.
———. "Eleutheropolis of the New Arabia" (P,OXY, 3574). *ZPE* 53 (1983), 251–58.
———. "Nea Arabia" (P,OXY, 3574): An Addendum to ZPE 53." *ZPE* 64 (1986), 141-48.
———. "Observations on Nilus' *Narrationes*: Evidence for an Unknown Christian Sect?" *Journal of the American Research Center in Egypt* 12 (1975), 51–58.
———. "The Saracens and the Limes." *BASOR* 262 (1986).
Mierow, C. C. *The Gothic History of Jordanes*. Rpr. Cambridge: 1960.
Milik, J. T. "La tribu des Bani ʿAmrat en Jourdanie de l'époque grecque et romaine." *ADAJ* 24 (1980), 41–54.
Moberg, M. *Über einige christliche Legenden in der islamischen Tradition*. Lund: 1930.
Momigliano, A. "Pagan and Christian Historiography in the Fourth Century A.D." In *Paganism and Christianity in the Fourth Century* (Oxford, 1963), 79–99.
Mommsen, Th. *Gesammelte Schriften*. Berlin: 1913.
Moravcsik, G. *Byzantinoturcica*, 2nd ed., 2 vols. Berlin: 1958.
Moritz, B. "Saraka." *RE*, zweite Reihe, I. A, cols. 2387–90.
Morony, M. *Iraq after the Muslim Conquest*. Princeton: 1984.
Moss, H. St. L. B. "Economic Consequences of the Barbarian Invasions." *The Economic History Review* (May 1937), 209–16.

Musil, A. *Arabia Deserta*. New York: 1927.
———. *The Middle Euphrates*. New York: 1927.
———. *The Northern Heǧāz*. New York: 1926.
———. *Palmyrena*. American Geographical Society, Oriental Explorations and Studies 4. New York: 1928.
Musset, L. *The Germanic Invasions*. Trans. E. and C. James. University Park: 1975.
Nājī, H. *Al-Budūr al-Musfira fī Naʿt al-Adyira*. Baghdad: 1975.
Negev, A. *The Greek Inscriptions from the Negev*. Jerusalem: 1981.
Nicholson, R. *A Literary History of the Arabs*. Cambridge: 1966.
Nischer, E. "The Army Reforms of Diocletian and Constantine." *JRS* 13 (1923), 1–55.
Nöldeke, Th. "Arabs." *Encyclopedia of Religion and Ethics* 1, ed. J. Hastings. New York: 1928.
———. *Geschichte der Perser und Araber zur Zeit der Sassaniden*. Leiden: 1879.
———. *Die Ghassânischen Fürsten aus dem Hause Gafna's*. Abhandlungen der königl. Akademie der Wissenschaften zu Berlin. Berlin: 1887.
Olinder, G. "Āl-al-Ǧaun of the Family of Ākil al-Murār." *Le monde oriental* 25 (1931), 208–29.
———. *The Kings of Kinda*. Lund: 1927.
Pando, J. C. *The Life and Times of Synesius of Cyrene as Revealed in His Works*. Washington, D.C.: 1940.
Paret, R. "Dār al-Nadwa." *EI*.
———. "Ismāʿil." *EI*.
Parker, H. M. D. "The Legions of Diocletian and Constantine." *JRS* 23 (1933), 174–89.
Parker, S. T. *Romans and Saracens: A History of the Arabian Frontier*. ASOR Dissertation Series 6. Winona Lake, Ind., 1986.
Payne Smith, R. *Thesaurus Syriacus*. Oxford: 1879–1901.
Peake, F. G. *History and Tribes of Jordan*. Miami: 1958.
Peeters, P. *Orient et Byzance: Le tréfonds oriental de l'hagiographie byzantine*. Subsidia Hagiographica 26. Brussels: 1950.
———. "S. Symeon Stylite et ses premiers biographes." *AB* 61 (1943), 30–42.
Perowne, S. *The Life and Times of Herod the Great*. London: 1956.
Philby, H. St. John *The Land of Midian*. London: 1957.
Piccirillo, M. *Um er-Rasas Kastron Mefaa in Giordania* (Supplemento a "La Terra Santa," Nov.–Dec. 1986). Jerusalem: 1986.
Poidebard, A. *La trace de Rome dans le désert de Syrie*. Paris: 1934.
Preisigke, F. *Wörterbuch der griechischen Papyrusurkunden*. Berlin: 1931.
Price, R. M. *A History of the Monks of Syria*. Cistercian Studies Series 88. Kalamazoo: 1985.
Puhvel, J. *Hittite Etymological Dictionary*. Berlin-New York: 1984.
Quasten, J. *Patrology*, III. Westminster, Md.: 1960.
Rosenthal, F. *A History of Muslim Historiography*. Leiden: 1968.
Rothstein, G. *Die Dynastie der Laḫmiden in al-Ḥîra*. Berlin: 1899.
Rubin, U. "Hanifiyya and Kaʿba: An Enquiry into the Arabian Pre-Islamic Background of Dīn Ibrāhīm." *Jerusalem Studies in Arabic and Islam* (forthcoming).
———. "Places of Worship in Mecca." *Jerusalem Studies in Arabic and Islam* (forthcoming).

Ryckmans, G. "Inscriptions sud-Arabes." *Le Muséon* 64 (1951), 93–126.

Ryckmans, J. "Le christianisme en Arabie du sud préislamique." In *L'Oriente cristiano nella storia della civilità,* Accademia Nazionale dei Lincei (Rome, 1964), 413–53.

———. "Himyaritica 3 and 4." *Le Muséon* 87 (1974), 237–63; 493–521.

———. *L'institution monarchique en Arabie méridionale avant l'Islam.* Louvain: 1951.

Rydén, L. "The Holy Fool." In *The Byzantine Saint* (Birmingham, 1980), 106–13.

———. "The Life of St. Basil the Younger and the Date of the Life of St. Andreas Salos." *Harvard Ukrainian Studies* 7 (1983), 568–86.

———. "The Role of the Icon in Byzantine Piety." *Scripta Instituti Donneriani Aboensis* 10 (1987), 41–52.

Saller, S. J., and B. Bagatti. *The Town of Nebo.* Publications of the Studium Biblicum Franciscanum 7. Jerusalem: 1949.

Sartre, M. *Bostra: Des origines à l'Islam.* Institut Français d'Archéologie du Proche-Orient. Paris: 1985.

———. *Trois études sur l'Arabie romaine et byzantine.* Collection Latomus 178. Brussels: 1982.

Schimmel, Annemarie. *Calligraphy and Islamic Culture.* New York: 1984.

Schmidt, L. *Geschichte der Wandalen.* Munich: 1942.

Schwartz, E. "Kyrillos von Skythopolis." TU 49 (1939).

Segal, J. B. "Mesopotamian Communities from Julian to the Rise of Islam." *Proceedings of the British Academy* 41 (1955), 109–39.

Sezgin, F. *Geschichte des arabishcen Schrifttums*, I–II. Leiden: 1967–75.

Shahîd, I. "The Arabs in the Peace Treaty of A.D. 561." *Arabica* 3 (1956), 181–213.

———. "Arethas, Son of Jabalah." *JAOS* 75 (1955), 205–16.

———. "*Byzantino-arabica*: The Conference of Ramla, A.D. 524." *JNES* 23 (1964), 115–31.

———. "Byzantium and Kinda." *BZ* 53 (1960), 57–73.

———. *Byzantium and the Arabs in the Fourth Century.* Washington, D.C.: 1984.

———. "Byzantium in South Arabia." *DOP* 33 (1979), 33–94.

———. "The Composition of Arabic Poetry in the Fourth Century." In *Studies in the History of Arabia; Pre-Islamic Arabia.* Riyad: 1984.

———. "Ghassan and Byzantium: A New *terminus a quo.*" *Der Islam* 33 (1959), 232–55.

———. "Ghassān *post* Ghassān." In *The Islamic World from Classical to Modern Times: Essays in Honor of Bernard Lewis* (forthcoming).

———. "The Iranian Factor in Byzantium during the Reign of Heraclius." *DOP* 26 (1972), 293–320.

———. "The *Kebra Negast* in the Light of Recent Research." *Le Muséon* 89 (1976), 133–78.

———. "Kinda." *EI*^{2}.

———. "The Last Days of Salīḥ." *Arabica* 5 (1958), 145–58.

———. *The Martyrs of Najrān: New Documents.* Subsidia Hagiographica 49. Brussels: 1971.

———. "The Patriciate of Arethas." *BZ* 52 (1959), 321–43.

———. "Philological Observations on the Namāra Inscription." *JSS* 24 (1979), 33–42.

———. "Πιστὸς ἐν Χριστῷ Βασιλεύς." *DOP* 34–35 (1982), 225–37.
———. "Procopius and Arethas." *BZ* 50 (1957), 39–67; 362–82.
———. *Rome and the Arabs*. Washington, D.C.: 1984.
Simeon, X. *Untersuchungen der Briefe des Bishofs Synesios von Kyrene*. Paderborn: 1933.
Sourdel-Thomine, J. "Khat." *EI*².
———. "Les origines de l'écriture arabe à propos d'une hypothèse récente." *REI* 34 (1966), 151–57.
Speidel, M. "The Roman Army in Arabia." In *Aufstieg und Niedergang der römischen Welt*, II, 8 (1977), 687–730.
Starcky, J., ed. *Inventaire des inscriptions de Palmyre*. Damascus: 1949.
Stark, J. K. *Personal Names in the Palmyrene Inscriptions*. Oxford: 1971.
Stein, E. *Histoire du bas-empire*, I. Amsterdam: 1968.
Steingass, F. *Persian-English Dictionary*. London: 1892.
Stendahl. *De l'amour*. Ed. H. Marineau. Paris: 1959.
Stern, M. *Greek and Latin Authors on Jews and Judaism: From Tacitus to Simplicius*, II. Jerusalem: 1980.
Syria: Publications of the Princeton University Archaeological Expeditions to Syria in 1904–5 and 1909. Ed. E. Littmann, D. Magie, and D. R. Stuart. Leiden: 1921.
Tāj al-ʿArūs, VIII. Beirut: 1966.
Tchalenko, G. *Villages antiques de la Syrie du Nord*, 3 vols. Paris: 1953–58.
Thelamon, F. *Païens et chrétiens au IV siècle*. Etudes augustiniennes. Paris: 1981.
Thomsen, P. "Die lateinischen und griechischen Inschriften der Stadt Jerusalem." *ZDPV* 44 (1921), 90–168.
Tinnefeld, F. H. *Kategorien der Kaiserkritik in der byzantinischen Historiographie von Prokop bis Niketas Choniates*. Munich: 1971.
Trimingham, J. S. *Christianity among the Arabs in Pre-Islamic Times*. London: 1979.
Troupeau, G. "Les couvents chrétiens dans la littérature arabe." *La nouvelle revue du Caire* (1975), 271–79.
Tsaferis, V. "Mosaics and Inscriptions from Magen." *BASOR* 258 (1985), 17–32.
Tyan, E. *Histoire de l'organisation judiciaire en pays d'Islam*. Leiden: 1960.
Vailhé, S. "Notes de géographie ecclésiastique." *EO* 4 (1900–1901), 11–17.
———. "La province ecclésiastique d'Arabie." *EO* 2 (1898–99), 166–79.
———. "Répertoire alphabétique des monastères de Palestine." *ROC* 5 (1900), 19–48.
Vasiliev, A. A. *History of the Byzantine Empire*. Madison: 1952.
———. *Justin the First*. Cambridge, Mass.: 1950.
Vincent, H., and Abel, F. M. *Jerusalem*. Paris: 1922.
Vööbus, A. "Discovery of New Manuscript Sources for the Biography of Simeon Stylite." *After Chalcedon*, Orientalia Lovaniensia Analecta 18. Louvain: 1985.
———. "Important Manuscript Discoveries for the Syro-Roman Law Book." *JNES* 32 (1973), 321–23.
Watt, W. M. *Muhammad at Mecca*. Oxford: 1953.
Wells, C. M. *Les Syriens à Intercisa*. Collection Latomus 122. Brussels: 1972.
Wensinck, A. J. "Kaʿba." *EI*.
Wetzstein, J. G. *Reisebericht über Hauran und die Trachonen*. Berlin: 1860.
Wilkinson, J. *Building God's Palace* (forthcoming).
———. *Jerusalem Pilgrims before the Crusades*. Warminster: 1977.
Wilson, R. R. *Genealogy and History in the Biblical World*. New Haven: 1977.

Winnett, F. V. *Ancient Records from North Arabia*. Toronto: 1970.

———. "The Arabian Genealogies in the Book of Genesis." In *Essays in Honor of Herbert Gordon May*, ed. H. T. Frank and W. L. Reed. New York: 1970, 171–96.

Wissman, H. von. "Makoraba." *RE*, supp. 12.

Woodward, E. L. *Christianity and Nationalism in the Later Roman Empire*. London: 1916.

Zgusta, L. *Kleinasiatische Ortsnamen*. Heidelberg: 1984.

MAPS

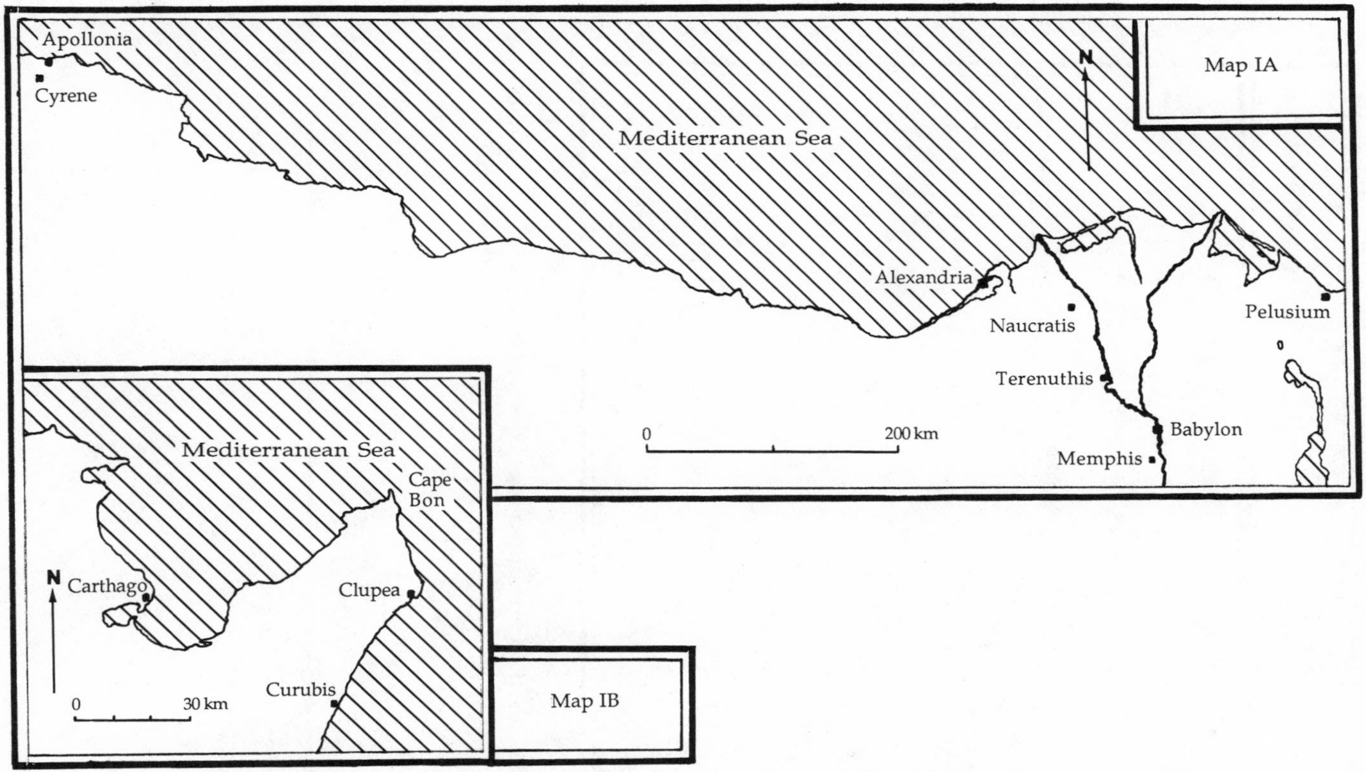

Map I illustrates the voyage of the Arab *turma* from Terenuthis in Egypt to Cyrene in Pentapolis, described by Synesius above, Chapter I. The inset relates to Chapter IV above and to possible Arab participation in the expedition against the Vandals in Africa.

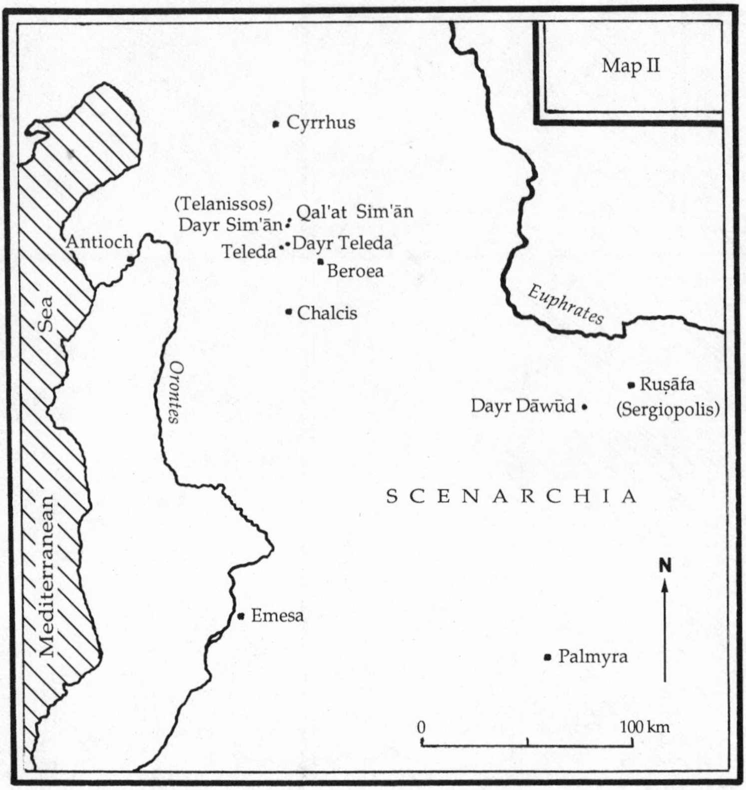

Map II indicates the Christian centers, especially monastic ones in northern Syria, with which the Arabs were associated, as discussed above, Chapter VIII.

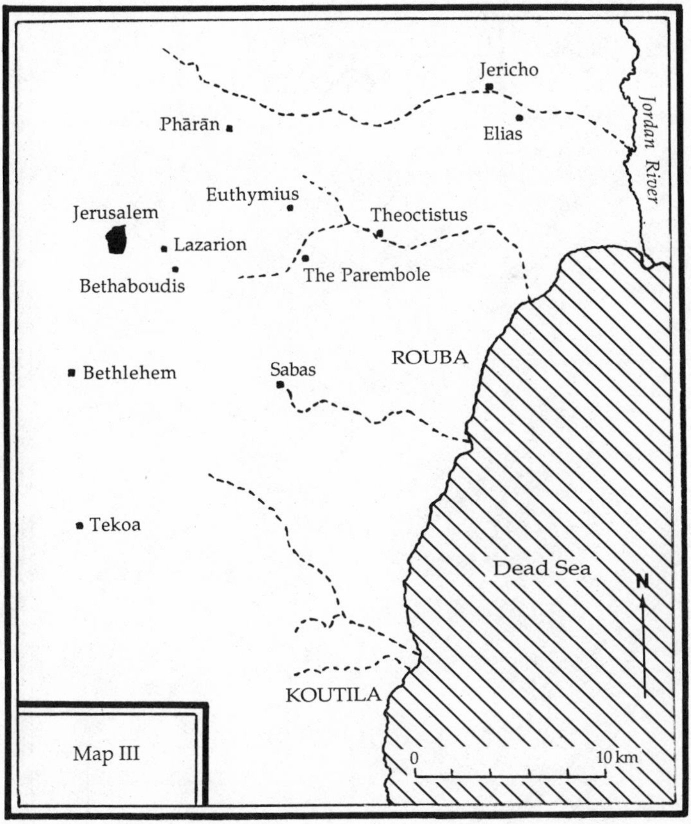

Map III indicates Christian centers in Palaestina Prima, especially in the desert of Juda. It illustrates Chapter X above.

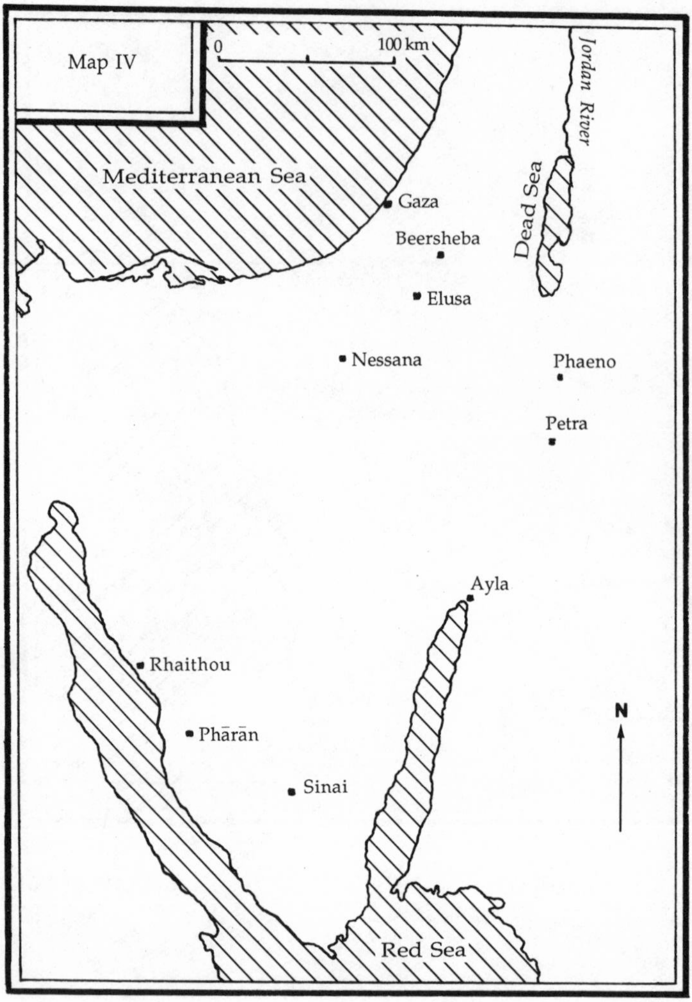

Map IV shows Christian centers in Palaestina Tertia, comprising the Negev and Sinai. It illustrates various sections above on ecclesiastical history.

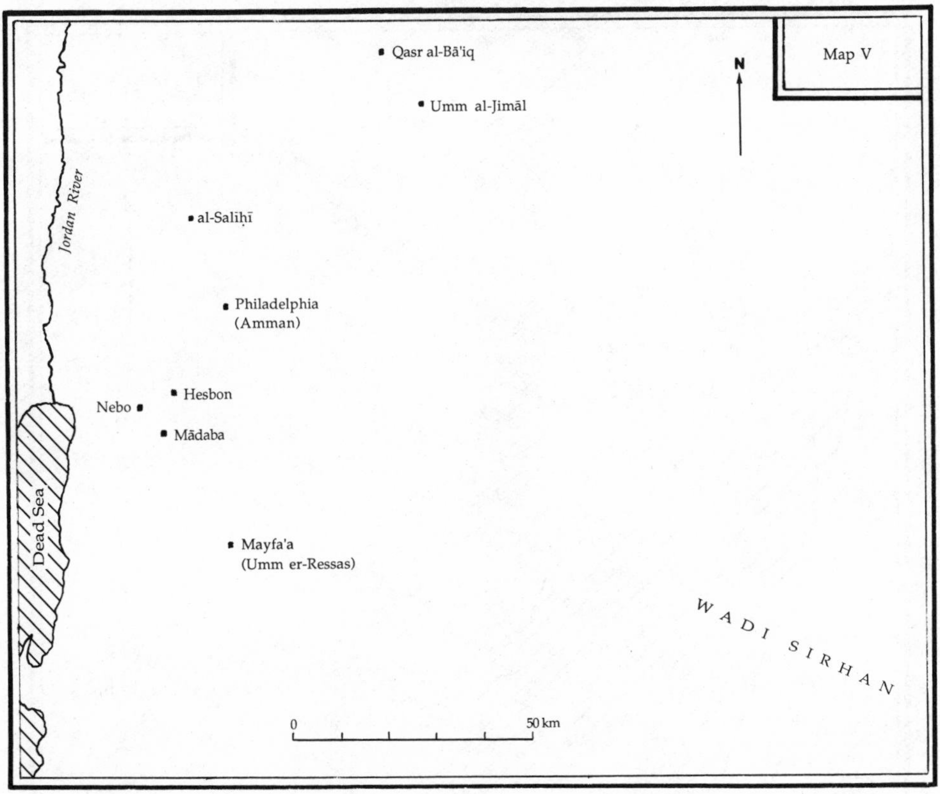

Map V indicates toponyms in Trans-Jordan, some of which are associated with the Salīḥids, discussed above, Chapter XII.

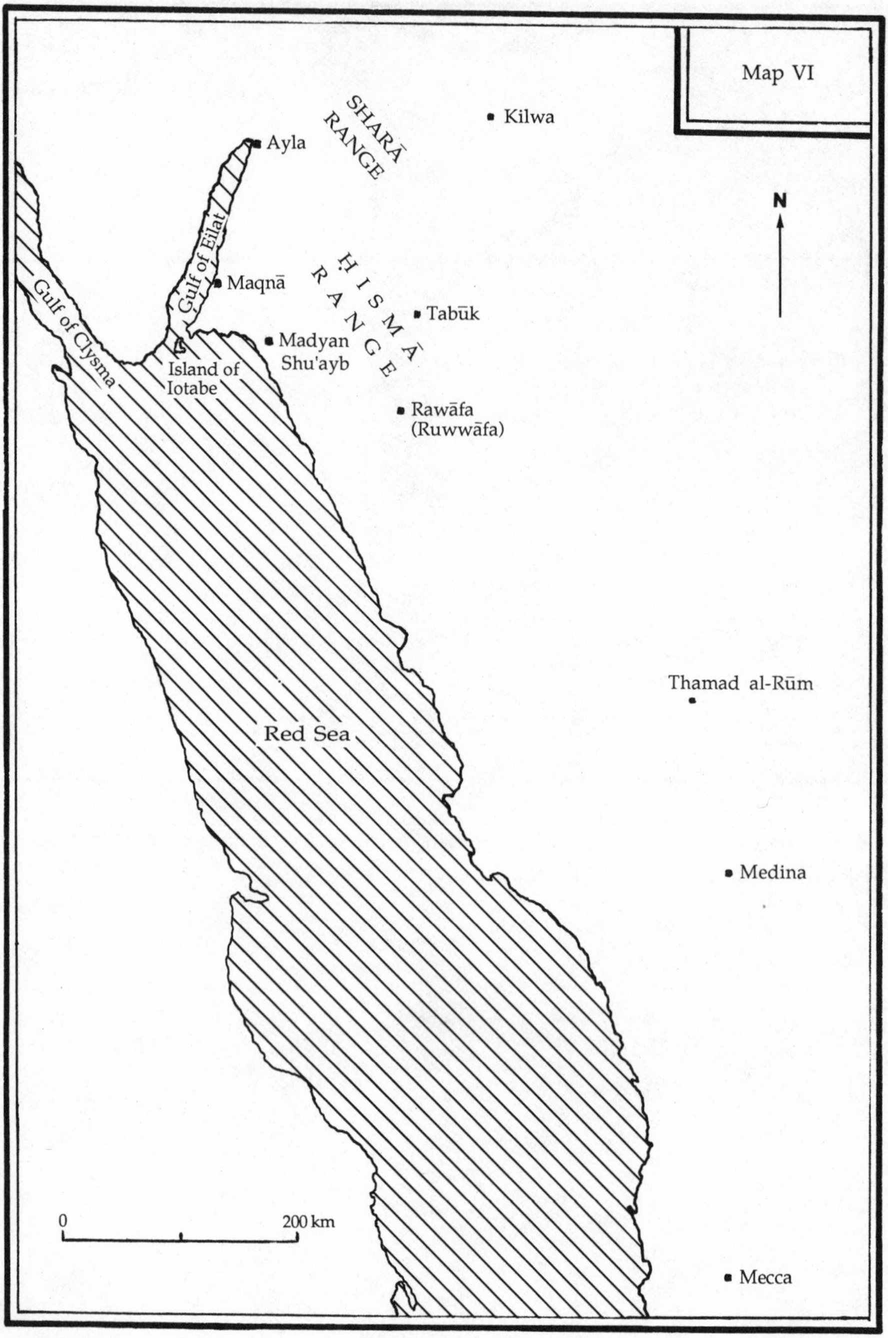

Map VI shows toponyms in northwestern Arabia, Ḥijāz, illustrating the extent of Byzantine influence, discussed above, Chapter XIII.

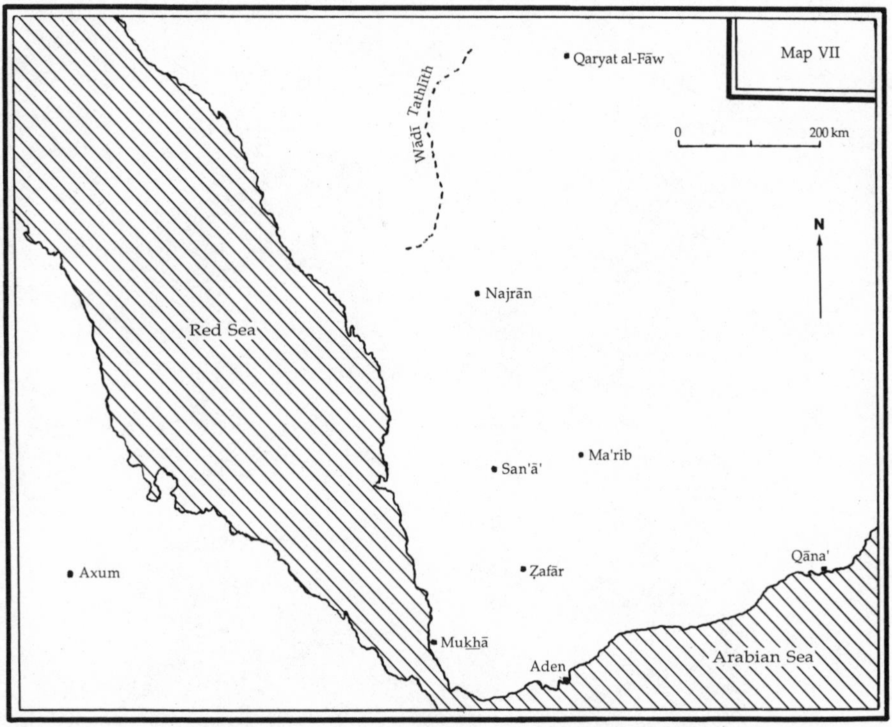

Map VII shows toponyms that illustrate the spread of Christianity and Byzantine influence in southwestern Arabia, discussed above, Chapter XIII.

Index

ʿAyn al-Salīḥī

The Spring of al-Salīḥī is one of the few traces that have survived of the Salīḥids of the fifth century in Jordan (see above, pp. 321–22).